FEMINIST INTERPRETATIONS OF MARY DALY

RE-READING THE CANON

NANCY TUANA, GENERAL EDITOR

This series consists of edited collections of essays, some original and some previously published, offering feminist reinterpretations of the writings of major figures in the Western philosophical tradition. Devoted to the work of a single philosopher, each volume contains essays covering the full range of the philosopher's thought and representing the diversity of approaches now being used by feminist critics.

Already published:

Nancy Tuana, ed., *Feminist Interpretations of Plato* (1994)

Margaret Simons, ed., *Feminist Interpretations of Simone de Beauvoir* (1995)

Bonnie Honig, ed., *Feminist Interpretations of Hannah Arendt* (1995)

Patricia Jagentowicz Mills, ed., *Feminist Interpretations of G. W. F. Hegel* (1996)

Maria J. Falco, ed., *Feminist Interpretations of Mary Wollstonecraft* (1996)

Susan J. Hekman, ed., *Feminist Interpretations of Michel Foucault* (1996)

Nancy J. Holland, ed., *Feminist Interpretations of Jacques Derrida* (1997)

Robin May Schott, ed., *Feminist Interpretations of Immanuel Kant (1997)*

Céline Léon and Sylvia Walsh, eds., *Feminist Interpretations of Søren Kierkegaard* (1997)

Cynthia Freeland, ed., *Feminist Interpretations of Aristotle* (1998)

Kelly Oliver and Marilyn Pearsall, eds., *Feminist Interpretations of Friedrich Nietzsche* (1998)

Mimi Reisel Gladstein and Chris Matthew Sciabarra, eds., *Feminist Interpretations of Ayn Rand* (1999)

Susan Bordo, ed., *Feminist Interpretations of René Descartes* (1999)

Julien S. Murphy, ed., *Feminist Interpretations of Jean-Paul Sartre* (1999)

Anne Jaap Jacobson, ed., *Feminist Interpretations of David Hume* (1999)

FEMINIST INTERPRETATIONS OF MARY DALY

EDITED BY
SARAH LUCIA HOAGLAND
AND
MARILYN FRYE

THE PENNSYLVANIA STATE UNIVERSITY PRESS
UNIVERSITY PARK, PENNSYLVANIA

Library of Congress Cataloging-in-Publication Data

Feminist interpretations of Mary Daly / edited by Sarah Lucia Hoagland and
Marilyn Frye.
p. cm. — (Rereading the canon)
Includes bibliographical references and index.
ISBN 0-271-02018-0 (cloth : acid-free paper)
ISBN 0-271-02019-9 (pbk. : acid-free paper)
1. Daly, Mary, 1928– 2. Feminist theory. 3. Feminist theology. I. Hoagland, Sarah Lucia, 1945– II. Frye, Marilyn. III. Series.

HQ1190.F453 2000
305.42′01—dc21 99-058656

Printed in the United States of America
Published by The Pennsylvania State University Press,
University Park, PA 16802–1003

It is the policy of The Pennsylvania State University Press to use acid-free paper for the first printing of all clothbound books. Publications on uncoated stock satisfy the minimum requirements of American National Standard for Information Sciences—Permanence of Paper for Printed Library Materials, ANSI Z39.48–1992.

Contents

Acknowledgments

We each wish to acknowledge that this work would have been impossible without the other's immeasurable and interestingly different contributions, skills, and resources. Putting editors' names in linear order cannot represent what goes on in such a collaboration. Such are the perils of PUD.

Sarah Lucia Hoagland wishes to thank Northeastern Illinois University for a COR Faculty grant that provided a fax machine as well as funds for faxing and xeroxing and travel for two terms.

The following works included in this volume are reprinted with permission:

Wanda Warren Berry, "Feminist Theology: The 'Verbing' of Ultimate/Intimate Reality in Mary Daly" is reprinted by permission of the University of Toronto Press from *Ultimate Reality and Meaning: Interdisciplinary Studies in the Philosophy of Understanding*, 11 (1988): 212–32.

Laurel C. Schneider, "From New Being to Meta-Being: A Critical Analysis of Paul Tillich's Influence on Mary Daly" is reprinted by permission of *Soundings: An Interdisciplinary Journal* 75 (Summer/Fall 1992): 421–39. It appears in this volume with very slight modifications under the title "The Courage to See and to Sin: Mary Daly's Elemental Transformation of Paul Tillich's Ontology."

Amber Katherine, "(Re)reading Mary Daly as a Sister Insider," is reprinted by permission of the University Press of Kansas from *On Feminist Ethics and Politics*, edited by Claudia Card (1999).

Preface

Nancy Tuana

Take into your hands any history-of-philosophy text. You will find compiled therein the "classics" of modern philosophy. Since these texts are often designed for use in undergraduate classes, the editor is likely to offer an introduction in which the reader is informed that these selections represent the perennial questions of philosophy. The student is to assume that she or he is about to explore the timeless wisdom of the greatest minds of Western philosophy. No one calls attention to the fact that the philosophers are all men.

Though women are omitted from the canons of philosophy, these texts inscribe the nature of woman. Sometimes the philosopher speaks directly about woman, delineating her proper role, her abilities and inabilities, her desires. Other times the message is indirect—a passing remark hinting at women's emotionality, irrationality, unreliability.

This process of definition occurs in far more subtle ways when the central concepts of philosophy—reason and justice, those characteristics that are taken to define us as human—are associated with traits historically identified with masculinity. If the "man" of reason must learn to control or overcome traits identified as feminine—the body, the emotions, the passions—then the realm of rationality will be one reserved primarily for men,[1] with grudging entrance to those few women who are capable of transcending their femininity.

Feminist philosophers have begun to look critically at the canonized texts of philosophy and have concluded that the discourses of philosophy are not gender-neutral. Philosophical narratives do not offer a universal perspective, but rather privilege some experiences and beliefs over others. These experiences and beliefs permeate all philosophical theories whether they be aesthetic or epistemological, moral or metaphysical. Yet this fact has often been neglected by those studying the traditions of philosophy. Given the history of canon formation in Western philosophy, the perspective most likely to be privileged is that of upper-class white males. Thus, to be fully aware of the impact of gender biases, it is imperative that we re-read the canon with attention to the ways in which philosophers' assumptions concerning gender are embedded within their theories.

The new series, Re-Reading the Canon, is designed to foster this process of reevaluation. Each volume will offer feminist analyses of the theories of a selected philosopher. Since feminist philosophy is not monolithic in method or content, the essays are also selected to illustrate the variety of perspectives within feminist criticism and highlight some of the controversies within feminist scholarship.

In this series, feminist lenses will be focused on the canonical texts of Western philosophy, both those authors who have been part of the traditional canon, as well as those philosophers whose writings have more recently gained attention within the philosophical community. A glance at the list of volumes in the series will reveal an immediate gender bias of the canon: Arendt, Aristotle, de Beauvoir, Derrida, Descartes, Foucault, Hegel, Hume, Kant, Locke, Marx, Mill, Nietzsche, Plato, Rousseau, Wittgenstein, Wollstonecraft. There are all too few women included, and those few who do appear have been added only recently. In creating this series, it is not my intention to reify the current canon of philosophical thought. What is and is not included within the canon during a particular historical period is a result of many factors. Although no canonization of texts will include all philosophers, no canonization of texts that excludes all but a few women can offer an accurate representation of the history of the discipline, as women have been philosophers since the ancient period.[2]

I share with many feminist philosophers and other philosophers writing from the margins of philosophy the concern that the current canonization of philosophy be transformed. Although I do not accept the position that the current canon has been formed exclusively by power relations, I do believe that this canon represents only a selective history of the tradition. I share the view of Michael Bérubé that "canons are at once the location, the index, and the record of the struggle for cultural representation; like any other hegemonic formation, they must be continually reproduced anew and are continually contested."[3]

The process of canon transformation will require the recovery of "lost" texts and a careful examination of the reasons such voices have been silenced. Along with the process of uncovering women's philosophical history, we must also begin to analyze the impact of gender ideologies upon the process of canonization. This process of recovery and examination must occur in conjunction with careful attention to the concept of a canon of authorized texts. Are we to dispense with the notion of a tradition of excellence embodied in a canon of authorized texts? Or, rather than abandon the whole idea of a canon, do we instead encourage a reconstruction of a canon of those texts that inform a common culture?

This series is designed to contribute to this process of canon transformation by offering a re-reading of the current philosophical canon. Such a re-reading shifts our attention to the ways in which woman and the role of the feminine is constructed within the texts of philosophy. A question we must keep in front of us during this process of re-reading is whether a philosopher's socially inherited prejudices concerning woman's nature and role are independent of her or his larger philosophical framework. In asking this question attention must be paid to the ways in which the definitions of central philosophical concepts implicitly include or exclude gendered traits.

This type of reading strategy is not limited to the canon, but can be applied to all texts. It is my desire that this series reveal the importance of this type of critical reading. Paying attention to the workings of gender within the texts of philosophy will make visible the complexities of the inscription of gender ideologies.

Notes

1. More properly, it is a realm reserved for a group of privileged males, since the texts also inscribe race and class biases that thereby omit certain males from participation.

2. Mary Ellen Waithe's multivolume series, *A History of Women Philosophers* (Boston: M. Nijhoff, 1987), attests to this presence of women.

3. Michael Bérubé, *Marginal Forces/Cultural Centers: Tolson, Pynchon, and the Politics of the Canon* (Ithaca: Cornell University Press, 1992), 4–5.

Introduction

Our volume on Mary Daly is a complex multilayered act of "re-reading the canon." We are of course re-reading the declared boundaries of the Western philosophical canon. Like the editors of the Simone de Beauvoir, Hannah Arendt, and Mary Wollstonecraft volumes in this series, we are reading women into a canon which has been crafted to exclude women. As Peg Simons writes: "The contemptuous dismissal of Beauvoir from the philosophical canon was so complete that the most radical disruption caused by feminist interpretations of Simone de Beauvoir may be in reading her work at all."[1] European and American elite intellectual canon-makers have failed to acknowledge Mary Daly without even the minimal notice implied by contempt. This volume, by publishing serious and not-uncharitable exegesis, critical interpretation and extension of Mary Daly's works, not only deauthorizes the official canon of Western philosophy, but also disrupts a related story told by some influential feminists, according to which Mary Daly's work is unworthy of re-reading because it contains errors represented as egregious, indeed fatal.

As with these other volumes about women thinkers, our project is fraught with political ambiguity analogous to women's aspiring to membership in exclusive male clubs and gays' and lesbians' ambitions to legally marry. Why would any of us want to read women into a tradition dedicated to the denial of women's subjectivity, agency, intellectual power, competence, and transcendence? One might want to challenge the idea that there are no great women thinkers, but the document record of women's thoughts is sparse and only gets more so the further back one goes, and one therefore runs the risk of succeeding mainly in giving the impression that there are only very few women thinkers. Furthermore, is the canon changeable by this willful insertion of women's work, or will reading it into the canon instead change the work and change us? Or both? And to whose benefit? Perhaps we should adopt Jeffner Allen's suggestion about Simone de Beauvoir and her relation to existentialism: it would be better to focus on her relation to the women for whom she wrote than to the "existentialism" devised by men who selectively appropriated her original insights and expressed disdain for any of her thoughts they could not understand or exploit.[2]

It might seem particularly problematic to be reading Mary Daly, a radical feminist, into the very canon which she herself has argued is a branch of patriarchal religion grounded in the dismemberment of the Goddess, and which her work is dedicated to undermining by means of animating women's possibilities. We certainly are not trying to "elevate" Mary Daly to canonical "equality" and thereby authorize her by her association with that august company. And there is no way the canon can assimilate Mary Daly. It is a kind of playful and ironic conspiracy of feminist editors and writers that places this volume in this series, twisting the series toward our goal of perverting philosophy into and within a practice of women addressing themselves primarily to and conversing primarily with women. This volume is the result of five years of those conversations and is dedicated to expanding them.

The complexities pile up: the investment by the authors here, reading and re-reading Mary Daly's works in earnest woman-to-woman conversations, also yields the understanding that Mary Daly *is* located in the Western intellectual tradition. Re-read in the history of her acknowledged feminist genealogy—her debt to Virginia Woolf and Matilda Joslyn Gage—she can be recognized as a sister-insider in relation to sister-outsiders constructed by her work and methods. As Amber Katherine writes: "The trick, I think, is to (re)read Daly's *Gyn/Ecology* in a way that reveals *both* the feminist Outsider and the Eurocentric insider."

Mary Daly does explicitly situate herself in relation to the tradition of Western philosophy and theology. She situates herself as a pirate. As Laurel Schneider argues, Mary Daly's radicalness lies not in rejecting Western epistemological and theological traditions, but in her creative and critical appropriation of themes and artifacts from these traditions—taken quite deliberately "out of context"—for the building of her own systematic philosophy. Her relation to the canon is also interestingly complicated by the fact that one of the first inklings of the women's symbolic she both seeks and constructs is gained by understanding the reversals on which the dominant spiritual and political order is constructed (e.g., substituting the mythic woman-born-of-man [Eve and

Adam] for the material man-born-of-woman). As Laurel Schneider says below in arguing against the charge that Mary Daly is a utopian, "for beneficiaries of the 'sado-state' and 'sado-spirituality' to confront Mary Daly as a true daughter of the tradition may mean to accept a threat to patriarchy that is much closer to home, and ultimately more damning."

To understand all this, we must first visit Mary Daly the theologian. We begin this collection with theologians who orient us. Much of the philosophical and political critique of Mary Daly ignores her intellectual grounding in theology and its distinctive conceptual terrain—ontology, teleology, transcendence, process subjectivity—all important to grasp in understanding what Mary Daly is and is not doing.

Wanda Warren Berry introduces Mary Daly as the inventor of feminist theology and argues that grasping the sociology of knowledge, or social constructionism, Mary Daly does not turn to epistemological relativism but takes an actively constructive ontological turn, concerning herself with a new conception of ultimate reality that can liberate women's potential. Wanda Warren Berry argues that Mary Daly, along with other feminist theologians, recognizes that theology is metaphor that, when reified, enforces and reinforces the social structures that gave rise to it. She explains the very important place of metaphor in Mary Daly's revolutionary strategy. Making and mobilizing new metaphors changes the logic, thereby changing perception and imagination and provoking new action; it is a way of changing the world. Naming is Mary Daly's root metaphor for feminist method, and the Verb is Mary Daly's root metaphor for ultimate reality (notably non-gendered).

The metaphor of the Verb gives a way of thinking about ultimate reality as a process rather than an unchanging substance. It is not "transcendent" in the old sense of "outside" or "beyond" the world of our lives, but transcendent in a new sense—a way of be-ing that we participate in and that is constantly transformative. Wanda Warren Berry argues that transformation of people, thought, and social structures is not possible without shifting the ground of ontological metaphor—using new metaphors for being, for ultimate reality.

The metaphor of Naming, for women's active processes of self- and social construction, relocates women on the map of being, from objects to living, world-making subjects transcending the dichotomous construction of "immanence/transcendence."

Laurel Schneider traces Paul Tillich's influence in Mary Daly's ontological work, her explorations of ultimate meaning. She argues that Mary

Daly, like Tillich, correlates existential questions with ontological/theological concerns. But what begins in Mary Daly's philosophy as a more or less direct critique of Tillich's more promising concepts (being/nonbeing, courage and New Being) develops into a profoundly different understanding of being and existence.

Tillich attends to *Man's* existential dread of non-being. His Man is fixated on his own finitude in the abstract possibility of there being nothing, and so needs something to provide hope and meaning. Talking about the courage needed to confront non-being, Tillich offers the consolation of a christ understood through the metaphor of New Being.

Mary Daly attends to women's oppression in patriarchy. The "shock of non-being" (Tillich's term) that Mary Daly responds to is, Laurel Schneider argues, a woman waking up to the "awful reality of her mutilated life, the depth of her non-being in patriarchy." Rejecting the idea that christ-images offer anything positive to women, Mary Daly develops Be-ing not as a matter of confronting a fear of nothingness, but as a matter of the courage to be in the face of annihilation. This courage is the courage to see and courage to sin: to see the full horror of patriarchy's structural evil and to do what is most "sinful" for women in patriarchy, namely to self-name, to be the verb, to engage in Be-ing, an ongoing process of liberation.

The Tillichean concept of New Being is transformed by Mary Daly into the rich and complex Metabeing. Laurel Schneider explains that the four etymological roots of the prefix *meta* are mixed and combined in the notion of Metabeing. Metabeing is a concept of nonlinear history, of participation in the Powers of being that are available to women after they have recognized that patriarchal blockage of their powers is insufferable, of transformation and reweaving, and of transcendence. Mary Daly's Powers of be-ing are both biophilic and immanent. Ultimate meaning is manifest in the process of be-coming, and transcendence requires immanence, resisting oppression through engaging in elemental reality.

Addressing the complex role of religious faith in Mary Daly's works, Anne-Marie Korte interprets her seemingly contradictory combination of antiessentialism and gynocentrism in terms of her ambiguous stance toward the role of religion in women's struggle for self-actualization. Exploring Simone de Beauvoir's influence on Mary Daly, Anne-Marie Korte argues that Mary Daly extended Simone de Beauvoir's negative view of the Catholic church to the conclusion that patriarchy is a planetary religion destructive of women's selves. But Simone de Beauvoir's reading of religion is ambiguous: she sees it both as promoting devastating bad faith and as providing a context or an opening for women to move by extraordinary religious experience out of subordination to and dependence on the spiritual and intellectual authority of mortal men. Agreeing with Simone de Beauvoir's claim that (in patriarchy) women have no history or symbols and thus are dependent on the authority of a male symbolic, Mary Daly went on to create (nonlinear) herstory and symbols of ultimate reality or Be-ing which might be adequate to women's passion for depth and transcendence, symbols which would support women's self-realization. Mary Daly goes beyond Simone de Beauvoir's exploration of women's victimization and bad faith to strategies of resistance and world-making.

Anne-Marie Korte argues that Mary Daly's feminist faith is about establishing a female subject position to counter the objectification of women. She reinvents this faith that can ground a moving-out of dependence by deconstructing patriarchal religion, myth, and imagery, and reclaiming/making women's lost or suppressed religious heritage in a gynocentric context. This is not a reversion to any static and "given" female essence, but an invention (which, with the metaphor of the Verb, she understands as always ongoing).

Anne-Marie Korte goes on to argue that Mary Daly conceives of a subjectivity which does not constitute itself in opposition to an *other*. Departing from fragmentation and absence of self in a patriarchal symbolic, Mary Daly draws on Thomistic, premodern notions of subjectivity and develops a subject which has varying degrees of fullness or intensity of being—a subjectivity which is never given, but must always be actualized. Borrowing from Virginia Woolf, Mary Daly argues that the fragmentation can be healed in moments of being. The main problem is not a question of unity and identity, but a lack of re-membering and an absence of focus. Like Laurel Schneider, Anne-Marie Korte establishes that the question of the subject arises not from fear of non-being but from a quest for (more) being.

Reminding us that Mary Daly is horrified that Christianity opposes the pain and suffering of murder and victimization in the center of its myth and ritual but ignores this evil systematically in the case of women, Anne-Marie Korte sees Mary Daly's response to this evil as every bit as theological as it is ethical. Documenting how Mary Daly is seen in a myriad of ways, "a polysemic ambiguity," Anne-Marie Korte argues that Mary Daly reinterprets classical theology with a distinctively postmodern signature.

Of the essays in this anthology, Marja Suhonen's most directly addresses the charge (often repeated, if not often defended in some schools of feminist theory) that Mary Daly's views are essentialist. She documents the obvious point that Mary Daly's first two books are explicitly antiessentialist about women and sex difference, indeed that antiessentialism is one of their main theses, and goes on to argue that while in her later work there are obvious changes in her thinking, there is no reversal about essentialism. She argues that for Mary Daly, acting and doing precede essence—Mary Daly is more an existentialist than an essentialist. But her later work is focused on metamorphosis and transformation, Marja Suhonen argues, and her concept of self goes beyond existentialism, in part by appropriating elements pirated from Aristotle.

Aristotle's notion of being is teleological, not causal: "what serves the purposes of a being's being seeks to be realized." But Aristotle was thinking of the realization of some fixed potential "given" by an essence. Mary Daly revises this to a constantly ontologically creative realization. She puts the soul (self, being) into ontological motion: the constant essence is replaced by an always-changing be-ing. Thus, Marja Suhonen argues, Mary Daly plucks a notion of realization from Aristotle's teleology while rejecting his essentialism.

Marja Suhonen argues that Mary Daly also rejects that aspect of Aristotelian essentialism which portrays sex-difference as accidental: for Aristotle sex doesn't delineate a(n essential) difference of species . . . women are just less human. In fact, according to Marja Suhonen, Mary Daly goes on to reject the traditional notion of species. What differentiates us into something like different species concerns our choices. Our lives are differently oriented depending on whether our lived decisions are necrophilic, committed to fixedness; or biophilic, engaged in continuous process. In this way, the concept of species involves an attitude toward life, and Marja Suhonen argues that Mary Daly's thinking resembles that of Levinas, Simone de Beauvoir, and Luce Irigaray, where ethics precedes ontology, or choice precedes value, or existence precedes essence. Thus essences depend on choices and are open to change; indeed, the future is always open.

Biophilic being is "Female," in a metapatriarchal sense, but it is not necessarily chosen and adopted by all and only females, in the scientific, anatomical sense of the word. Marja Suhonen suggests that the misreading of Mary Daly as essentialist arises from reading her through the lens of "sex/gender theory" which, updating the Aristotelian essence/accident ontology, makes sex a natural given (essence) and gender a social construction (accident). Such a reading coerces Mary Daly's thought into precisely the biological/social and essence/accident dualism which she explicitly rejects, and then attributes that dualism to her.

The theological dimension of Mary Daly's work is particularly important because many of us ignore the highly ritualized nature of much social interaction and consequently miss the possibilities of pattern-detecting that show a depth of evil in seemingly random, unrelated happenings. Sheilagh A. Mogford expounds Mary Daly's understanding of the play of myth and ritual in maintaining the social order; the myths and rituals reinforcing the suppression and control of women in male-dominant orders perform Goddess murder by murdering or dismembering women's powers of divinity in any of their manifestations. Mary Daly categorizes these myths and rituals in her exposition of the Sado-Ritual Syndrome, and Sheilagh Mogford uses this framework for reading Margaret Atwood's "futuristic" novel *The Handmaid's Tale*, while simultaneously reading that future into our present.

The Handmaid's Tale is about North America being taken over by religious fundamentalists following a military coup in the late twentieth century. Sheilagh Mogford argues that Margaret Atwood chose the late twentieth century to explore precisely because women have achieved some level of independence and those in power are reacting with fear in a backlash against the gains the feminist movement has made. As Marja Suhonen reminds us, for Mary Daly the future is open, wide open. The desire to control women and keep us in line is both overt and covert in North America. Both in spite of and because of our gains, we are under siege.

Sheilagh Mogford's reading of *The Handmaid's Tale* in terms of the Sado-Ritual Syndrome offers us an opportunity to consider how to refuse collusion. Developing our capacity for refusal is one aspect of biophilic choice that Marja Suhonen discusses: resisting killing the divine in ourselves. This is particularly important, Sheilagh Mogford argues, as U.S. cultural machinery keeps producing and marketing "new" practices, attitudes, and tastes which are designed to appeal to women and which veil and maintain the same old dominant/subordinate relationships.

Central to biophilia, to refusing rituals of Goddess murder, is separation. Linking Mary Daly's experience and her writing, Debra Campbell follows Mary Daly's own journey as a transformational practice of separation, a sequence of Be-Leavings, Great departures, Movings Out, in which she stepped across thresholds from one realm of being to another (carrying with her pirated wealth that would support her in this next realm).

Various authors in this anthology situate Mary Daly in relation to other philosophers, theologians, and theorists. Mary Daly situates herself in the tradition of Hagography. Her own Hagography, which she presents at many points as a series of Be-Leavings, and through which she explores her multiple Selves, is instructive with respect to the art of creative Self-transformation, the art of be-ing.

For there to be biophilic be-ing, there must be Be/Leaving. Debra Campbell argues that in Mary Daly's cosmology, be-ing and Be/Leaving are inseparable. Not a single event, Be/Leaving is a never ending process, and involves feminist faith, if you will, the unconditional faith in women's possibilities of transformation and self-actualization that Anne-Marie Korte refers to, a faith that lets us leap into spaces only vaguely imagined, wherein we can spin webs of meaning fast enough to sustain us as we fly into an abyss. The future is open.

Be/Leaving also involves looking back, the courage to see, to be disillusioned, which is "not optional, not tidy, and never finished." Looking back is how Mary Daly avoids the coerced choice between erasure and assimilation and instead offers her readers "an open-ended conversation with her earlier selves/texts," how she sees through disillusionment to become a Pirate, how she develops a Pirate's insight and Pirates her Thomistic training, how we see Mary Daly in process, how she re-members her past, how we understand that she is never too far removed from where she last exited, how we understand that she Spirals. Mary Daly looks back; that's how she is able to Be/Leave and not just disassociate. As Debra Campbell puts it, Mary Daly could not believe in academia, for example, but rather Be/Leave in it.

For Debra Campbell, Mary Daly's departures are among her most important contributions: "Discovering, exploring, expanding biophilic space has been Mary Daly's major achievement for three decades."

One central tool for Be/Leaving is naming. Wanda Warren Berry argues that naming is a root metaphor for Mary Daly. Indeed, "naming" is Mary Daly's primary metaphor for the owning and transforming of language, the mobilizing of new symbols and creation of meaning. Some commentators have scoffed at Mary Daly's new namings, considering them insignificant as a mode of radical symbolic and political change. In her paper, Molly Dragiewicz implicitly poses the question, If a simple naming is insignificant, why is there such a huge backlash when we do it? The magnitude of the political power of naming is clearly demonstrated in her tracking and analysis of feminists' introduction of the name "acquaintance rape" and the backlash discourse mobilized in the U.S. mass media within a few years of the term's first public appearance (and general *acceptance* by the media)—an example of one element of the sado-ritual (i.e., erasure of responsibility) that Sheilagh Mogford articulates. Such analyses are crucial because, as Debra Campbell argues, being disillusioned and seeing in the mode of dis/illusionment is the way to become a Pirate.

Molly Dragiewicz argues that Mary Daly's exploration of language provides a vocabulary with which to speak from subjugated positions. Language is important to a woman who has been raped because she needs to name that experience in a way that encodes its significance and makes it intelligible to her and to others. Names which name it *assault* and locate her as a victim of an assault do not, as some have argued, reduce her to her victimization; such names enable her to be a subject naming her experience, and they correctly locate responsibility for harm done. Molly Dragiewicz's exploration of the logic of popular discourse on rape and the power of naming illustrates how language is a site of power and hence of contest. She develops her analysis of the backlash discourse through analytic categories of mindbinding articulated by Mary Daly—erasure, reversal, false-polarization and divide-and-conquer. With this investigation Molly Dragiewicz shows that "dominant discourses are established [and maintained] in part by the inclusion, and exclusion, of specific words in the cultural vocabulary."

Pointing out that "naming," in Mary Daly's work, must be read as metonymy, Frances Gray takes on the difficult job of explaining Mary Daly's politics of language and ontology, how it is articulated and how it is performed. Language is the vehicle for our potentialities, our becoming. There has been misunderstanding of Mary Daly's notoriously extreme and lively inventions of words, her giving new meanings to words, her play with spelling, and her often flamboyant metaphors. One claim that has had some currency is that her wordplay is limited in its effectiveness because it is "merely" subverting isolated signs rather than subverting discourse. Molly Dragiewicz illustrates and Frances Gray theorizes that there is no such thing as subverting isolated signs and that Mary Daly is obviously aware of this—such a notion is as foreign to her as it is critically rejected by poststructuralists. Mary Daly's strategy is not one of subverting isolated signs, but of displacing supposedly neutral (but men's) discourse in order to produce a women's discourse whose function is to articulate women's Be-ing: "[Mary Daly's] emphasis on process underscores her approach to language as an oceanic whole: vast, interrelated and everchanging."

Frances Gray explains the relations Mary Daly sees between language and ontology, particularly women as constituted through language practice, and how Mary Daly's writing is an ontologically creative performance that opens up possibilities for women's naming themselves and their worlds for themselves. Frances Gray organizes her exposition around three crucial interconnected elements which elaborate Mary Daly's notion of the language/ontology connection: (1) She discusses the strange alchemy of using language against itself, undermining extant "neutral" language (that erases women's possibilities) to make women's language possible. (2) She describes the role of "Naming," in the sense of active process, as a metonymy for the whole active appropriation and invention of language. And, complementing Wanda Warren Berry's and Marja Suhonen's arguments, (3) she describes metaphor as the central creative process of Be-ing, leading to an open-ended understanding of women. Thus, for example, "Goddess" is not the name of a superbeing but is a metaphor by which Daly animates possibilities for women. We see that in Mary Daly's hands language is performance/active/animate.

Mary Daly's use of metaphor seems to confound some of her readers. Her metaphorical naming of women with re-figured terms such as "Gossips" and of journeyers' ethics in such terms as "Virgin Virtues" and her use of Goddess images, tempt some readers to interpret her as essentialist. Frances Gray explains that Mary Daly's metaphors appeal to the idea of women as constituted through their own language practices, which are not themselves neutral. Mary Daly (not alone among feminists) believes that there can be no sex-neutral subject or language, and if women are to have language it will be women's language. Critics have thought that because Mary Daly rejects neutrality and engages in producing a radically creative and subversive Woman's discourse, her work is essentialist. Frances Gray argues that this is a non sequitur facilitated by imposing a modernist reading on the text and by missing entirely Mary Daly's critique of neutrality (a critique which with its own playfulness exposes postmodern seriousness).

Thus Mary Daly's ontological work, her Otherworld journeying, the journey of women becoming, does not conform to the boundaries of either modern or postmodern thinking. She does not invoke a substance/attribute and essence/accident ontology, nor would she accept feminist critiques of the category *women* under the banner of a supposedly antiessentialist postmodernism which reinscribes a patriarchal "neutrality" that is really the erasure of women. But the always-ongoing processes of women's be-ing, as meaning-making, are and can only be social, communal processes. This raises the question for journeyers of how to meet and connect with other women, how to recognize other women journeying, and geographically, where we anticipate such meetings. A neutralizing antiessentialism which erases women does not promote or theorize such meetings and connections, and even though it is sometimes presented as intrinsically anti-racist and anti-colonialist, it does not recognize the radicalness of the women of color who engage Mary Daly with these questions.

Raising questions of language, territoriality and sociality, María Lugones explores dictionaries that are political, contestatory. She offers us a discussion of two dictionaries of political contestation: *Wickedary* and *El Libro de Caló*, a dictionary of Pachuco slang.

Noting that meanings are always negotiated, María Lugones argues that a sense of linguistic interaction, the dialogical political history, is absent from most dictionaries. For example, the editors of the *Oxford English Dictionary* liken the lexicographer to the naturalist. Significantly, before about 1500 English did not exist as a single language but only as a variety of dialects, and words belonging to those various dialects are included in the modern *OED*. However, from 1500 on the *OED* includes only words of the dialect that was becoming a national language, and subsequent dialogic development and contestation is erased in favor of a naturalized portrait of English. The dictionary, then, recapitulates the correlation of linguistic unification and establishment of the nation state. "The question of politics and the question of mastery over words are not separate." Both dictionaries María Lugones discusses challenge our relationship to conventional dictionaries, which most of us enter looking for authoritative guidance in proper use.

The *Wickedary*, an explicitly political performance of linguistic resistance and transgression, is a counter-dictionary: an undoing of propriety and rules. Its strategies dismantle the being that is held linguistically captive. Reading through the *Wickedary*, women become conscious of their own relation to the contradiction between the values of the foreground and the Background. Engaging in practices of transgression and metamorphosis, Mary Daly and Jane Caputi problematize who is the master of words as only tricksters can. However, while the *Wickedary* constructs a context for women travelers, María Lugones questions the sociality and spatiality of this linguistic contestation/adventure. The *Wickedary's* anticipation of the arrival of others includes no sense of the relations of power with other weavers or webs, and no move to evaluate its overall relation to Anglicity. Its territoriality remains at the conceptual level, and as a result, its sociality does too.

Asking the question, What if one recognized the world outside domination to be more complex than a sister-world? María Lugones next explores *El Libro de Caló*. Each alphabet section begins with a placa, thereby telling us where this meaning is made—on the streets of L.A. *El Libro's* method contests territory, and documents the disruption of Anglicity in a world it introduces you to, showing its disregard for how reality is conceived Anglo-centeredly. Although formatted like a dictionary, *Caló* is not a translation tool; and upon entering *Caló*, one becomes self-conscious: resistance to colonization necessitates problematizing the arrival of others. Who you are and why you come matter in the words you take up. Confronting those who approach the dictionary, these words deride and destabilize colonial relations at every turn.

Having explored the logic of both these transgressive performances, María Lugones puts aside a bilingual's temptation to translate, to mediate. Seeking unmediated communication conversation speakers must struggle for, fashioned through lived connections, she laments the impossibility of a "wicked caló." The *Wickedary* doesn't take to the streets but stakes its domain in the Background, and thus it cannot meet with marimachas who, while needing to contest the limits of *Caló*, nevertheless must take up its spatial emphasis. And so she reaches for an everyday vocabulary that contests patriarchies and colonialism simultaneously, a territory where marimachas and gossips meet and converse.

María Lugones laments that certain conversations are not happening. Amber Katherine presents a collection of "stories of context" which place Audre Lorde's immensely influential "An Open Letter to Mary Daly" (1979) historically, politically, and in Amber Katherine's own life and her developing radical feminist politics. She forms the project around the question of why Mary Daly never answered the letter "in kind." (She believes that there is a response in Mary Daly's work after *Gyn/Ecology*—but not the kind that emerges from dialogue). The four "stories" are (1) the use of Audre Lorde's letter by white academic feminist theorists, (2) the events which led to Amber Katherine's own serious engagement with the letter, (3) the common ground of Audre Lorde and Mary Daly just before the publication of *Gyn/Ecology*, and (4) radical movement politics of the 1960s and 1970s—Civil Rights, Black Power, the New Left, and Radical Feminism.

Building up a sort of cognitive structure out of elements of these contexts, Amber Katherine demonstrates a "logic of the moment" which would have made it very unlikely that Mary Daly would be able to hear "the multiplicity in Audre Lorde's voice," as Audre Lorde both acknowledges that women's oppression knows no racial, ethnic, or religious boundaries and simultaneously demands recognition of difference and dialogue across them. In particular, Amber Katherine articulates the "root thinking" that was widely accepted in radical politics of the late 1960s and 1970s that required commitment to one root cause of oppression and saw demands for recognition of other forms of oppression as a betrayal. The recognition that we can be strengthened by our differences is new, and has only developed as a result of this and related struggles.

Amber Katherine speculates that Mary Daly heard the letter as signaling a fundamental shift in perspective that would have seemed like a betrayal, and that Mary Daly did not hear the shift in orientation from "sisterhood through commonality of oppression and resistance" to "sisterhood wherein our differences are strengths." Perhaps as a result of this she did not see as Audre Lorde did the significance of the fact that women of non-Western cultures are not only victims but (like women of Western cultures) are survivors with their own indigenous sources of female power.

As Frances Gray notes, language and ontology are intertwined. So metaphors functioning only in the semantic field of the English language will generate meaning and being that remains white/Anglo-bound. María Lugones suggests that the *Wickedary*'s lack of a critical consciousness of its own white/Anglo locatedness supports a certain vacancy of imagination about the locations and languages of the "other gossips" its participants may expect to encounter and converse with. Amber Katherine suggests Audre Lorde was pointing out that the very fact that patriarchy is indeed global means that women in various locations experience different practices of male domination *and* access different repertoires of gynocentric meanings, myths, and powers—different Backgrounds of female creativity and be-ing. However, the context for deep understanding of all this did not exist in 1979. It emerged as a result of heated and painful dialogue (which often was not interactive) among radical feminists. Amber Katherine argues that the meaning of Audre Lorde's letter may seem obvious now, but in 1979 Audre Lorde was one of the first to begin articulating a perspective which was not fully formed until the publication two years later of *This Bridge Called My Back*, and to this day may not be as fully grasped as the ubiquity of the academic jargon of "difference" may imply.

She concludes with the suggestion that the more important question may be why other radical white feminists have not responded to Audre Lorde's letter first by really engaging it and analyzing it and subsequently by developing a pluralist and radical white feminism. She points out (following María Lugones) that the demand from Audre Lorde was not a demand for a change in theory as postmodernists have treated it, it was an interactive demand. Such a politic is not born out of a particular theoretical framework but rather through interaction fueled by a desire to make connections under complex systems of oppression. It is the possibility of such connections that motivates María Lugones's refusal to translate for gossips and marimachas.

In a second paper, Amber Katherine articulates an insider/outsider distinction to explore how European-American radical feminists can develop a double or plural consciousness recognizing ourselves, through a re-reading of *Gyn/Ecology*, as both insiders and outsiders: outsiders to patriarchy and insiders to Anglo-European dominant tradition. Exploring Virginia Woolf's influence on Mary Daly, Amber Katherine traces a tradition of outsiders—women living/thinking outside of male/patriarchal authority and control. It is their independence which threatens the beneficiaries of patriarchy. However, if the Crone-ology of European-American radical feminists goes back through Virginia Woolf, Matilda Joslyn Gage, and the European witches, where does that leave radical feminists who trace their Background tradition through Africa, China, India, but as Sister Outsiders to (European-American) radical feminism?

One response to this awareness is to advocate the inclusion of women of other traditions. But such a solution ignores the patterns of relation between women as well as the values enacted in those patterns. Amber Katherine argues that, however inadvertently, Mary Daly replicates historical patterns of relating to women of non-Western cultures characteristic of Western women and men. For example, as portrayed by Mary Daly, *satī* is a matter of helpless victims with no independent gynocentric resources that might explain the patriarchal forces pitted against them. As a result, in constructing the independence of wild women, Mary Daly simultaneously constructs the outsider (and victim-only) status of women not of the European tradition, to radical feminism.

While the tradition of outsider women Mary Daly draws on enacts the value of *independence*, the value more prominently enacted by women of color is one of *interdependence*. Further, drawing on María Lugones's challenge to individualist notions of responsibility, Amber Katherine argues that Mary Daly's commitment to being a responsible decision-maker and naming patriarchal oppression at all its sites invokes a conception of the responsible agent as both independent (not dependent on patriarchal authority or swayed by deceptive revolutionary rhetoric) and unitary. This, Amber Katherine suggests, blocks Mary Daly's ability to see that her actions have multiple meanings and multiple effects. She may have been right to speak out about *satī*, but her speaking did not give voice to Indian women.

Debra Campbell focuses on Mary Daly's invocation of her many selves, looking back to understand how she was caught in patriarchy, trying to avoid new coercions. Amber Katherine draws on María Lugones's idea that we are multiply constituted (rather than being unitary) and points out that those of us located as insiders to a dominant structure may be able to detect our multiplicity only by means of the reflections of other Others who are erased by those structures. This is one reason that the value of interdependence, not just independence, is so important for radical feminists.

Citing Mary Daly's use of "suttee," instead of *satī*, and arguing that to see women's subjectivity and agency we need to contextualize it, Renuka Sharma and Purushottama Bilimoria address complex postcolonial questions of resistance. Debra Campbell talks of the power of presence, and Renuka Sharma and Purushottama Bilimoria raise questions of how U.S. and Indian women can be present to each other.

Agreeing with Mary Daly that *satī* is a particularly troubling phenomenon and needs a radical feminist response, Renuka Sharma and Purushottama Bilimoria question her success. For example, while Mary Daly rightly criticizes Western Orientalist scholarship's erasure of Indian women's subjectivity and agency, they argue that Mary Daly doesn't provide a means for retrieving the erased subjectivity and agency of Indian women. They argue that she conflates two projects: (a) searching for evidence of the global reach of patriarchal religion's oppression of women; and (b) locating the agency and subjectivity of women in sado-ritual torture in particular contexts. As a result, the absence of women's agency is taken as evidence of patriarchy's totalizing destruction, and Mary Daly fails to suggest how it would be possible to reinscribe women's subjectivity and agency.

Caught between resurgent religious fundamentalism and the modern trend of re-writing autonomy in terms of ungendered individual agency, Indian feminists simultaneously resist not only male dominance but also Western colonialism. While making it clear that a Western woman trying to defend the oppressed in another part of the world does not necessarily commit the fallacy of Orientalism, they resist the construction of *satī* as an object of outsider speculation in the process of colonial formation: we need to see the resistances that take place in oppositional discourse. Their point is not to reductively classify *satī* as suicide nor to allow the opposite category of crime, but to focus on "erased possibilities and potentials in an alternative discourse."

There is significant resistant subjectivity within the regime of sacred-making, even though Indian women are also subject to oppressive practices. Renuka Sharma and Purushottama Bilimoria illustrate how the process of patriarchal oppression reveals contradictions and counter-movements. They offer a brief history of *satī* and two examples of female potency, among other things, contrasting the very present and active Kali with the "cool image of the Virgin Mary."

Part of Audre Lorde's criticism is that while Mary Daly draws on many traditions to show that patriarchy and women's victimization are global phenomena, she only summons European goddess images when envisioning power and resistance. This then leaves a message that European tradition is the only source of strength for women. Advancing the discussion of the importance of ontology and the metaphor of goddesses developed in other papers in the anthology, AnaLouise Keating takes on the question of the value for feminists and feminism of prepatriarchal origin stories, projection of mythic female heroic or sacred figures, prepatriarchal woman-centered communities and other forms of revisionist myth-making, all of which are necessarily culturally located.

Amber Katherine lays out the commonality between Audre Lorde and Mary Daly of both understanding the Goddess as a symbol of female power and wanting to move beyond lives governed by a father god, and Laurel Schneider reminds us that in Mary Daly's journey beyond God the father noun passed through a verb, Be-ing, metaphorically inscribed as Goddess. AnaLouise Keating brings together Mary Daly, Paula Gunn Allen, Gloria Anzaldúa, and Audre Lorde in a significant discussion of their efforts to destabilize, or destroy, dominant metaphors, rituals, and epistemology. As do other contributors to this volume, AnaLouise Keating suggests that misunderstandings of Mary Daly have arisen because she is read literally and not performatively; the readings are oblivious to the workings of her transforming metaphors. All four of the writers AnaLouise Keating discusses use metaphor and myth, activating language's performative ability to bring about change, and all work in the belief that maintaining/constructing a relationship to a prepatriarchal past can transform our lives in the present. This is the activity of what Mary Daly calls re-membering. Disagreeing with those postmodernists who debunk origin myths on the grounds that they reinscribe existing patriarchal definitions of woman, she shows that all four break the Western dualism between male transcendent and female immanent.

AnaLouise Keating argues that transcultural models of feminist mythmaking demonstrate the possibility of writing the "feminine" in open-ended, nonexclusionary ways that revise previous notions of the universal. She argues that Paula Gunn Allen, Gloria Anzaldúa and Audre Lorde develop metaphoric representations of Woman that neither erase their own cultural specificities nor require those who would connect with the images to abstract themselves from *their* own specificities. She suggests that the similarity between the latter three writers and Mary Daly has been missed in part because Mary Daly has been read primarily as a philosopher and evaluated according to conventional academic standards that rigidly bracket out the creative performative dimensions of her revisionary mythmaking, and fail to engage with their visionary, ethical dimensions. But she also sees elements of Mary Daly's work that may encourage this misreading and contribute to the notion that she is projecting a normative, homogenizing mythic image of Woman that erects barriers to many women's participation.

Discussions of the mythmaking of Paula Gunn Allen, Gloria Anzaldúa, and Audre Lorde demonstrate that like Mary Daly, these theorists place the mythic images and narratives in nonlinear time, which contributes to their functioning to support a sense of continuation rather than nostalgia. However, echoing a concern of María Lugones, AnaLouise Keating argues that Mary Daly's mythmaking is unlike that of the others in that she associates the "Other-centered context" with an ethnically unmarked prepatriarchal (or metapatriarchal) tradition, and because of this abstractness, the oral performative dimensions of her writings do not work as interactively, as invitingly, for many readers as they do in these others' works.

Paradoxically, AnaLouise Keating's discussion suggests that one can be more inclusive and universal by being more particular. Mary Daly's images seem to require those who would participate in them to abstract themselves and restrict themselves to that which is "common," whereas the others' images, being overtly ethnically marked, represent themselves as particular, and invite a kind of relating to them that involves relating one's own ethnicity, one's own particularity, to them. Mary Daly's focus on commonality may be exclusionary (though that is certainly not her intention) for it compels readers to undergo a restrictive process of normalization—not just adopting but internalizing representations of the human subject. Mary Daly transcribes these means of knowing in gender-specific yet highly generalized terms such as "ancient Racial memories." She doesn't entirely ignore differences among women, but for instance she uses "witch" as an unmarked category to unify all women into a single elemental race. Mary Daly's universal offers readers a single subject position, downplaying difference; thus gender alone offers women grounds for authentic female existence. AnaLouise Keating suggests that the work of Paula Gunn Allen, Gloria Anzaldúa, and Audre Lorde indicates new concepts of *universal*—open-ended and potentially dialogic. As she understands these writings, they don't universalize the particular, they pluralize the universal, allowing a variety of culturally specific forms to coexist in dynamic interaction. They use difference to redefine the existing universal.

Finally, AnaLouise Keating underscores the open-ended possibilities of the project of using this "feminine" as an imaginative universal. "Because the 'discovery' of Woman as an ethical standard occurs within mythic metaphors, it defies literal, monologic interpretation, thereby making possible a proliferation of meanings, meanings that must be invented and lived out by each reader."

AnaLouise Keating thus suggests that we attend to cultural specificities to fully comprehend and enact transformational possibilities. Drawing on Irish sources which have informed Mary Daly's own ethnic tradition, Geraldine Moane addresses herself to the possibilities of transforming psychic damage, discussing women's psychic liberation and resistance in the Irish context. As a feminist psychologist she seconds Mary Daly's arguments against therapy and adds some of her own; but she believes there are worthy practices which can be identified in Mary Daly's work and grounded in political analysis, which link the personal and the political, involve a developmental process of radical change in consciousness, and result in taking action to bring about change.

Evoking a tradition of women who have been resisting oppression for hundreds of years, Geraldine Moane uses Mary Daly's foreground/Background distinction to explore the Irish context of colonialism and postcoloniality. In the foreground is a legacy of patriarchal institutions, including the Catholic church which stepped into the power vacuum created in the postcolonial context. In the Background are strong women's traditions of today and dating back through Celtic and Gaelic cultures to Neolithic culture, evidenced by thousands of stone structures all over Ireland. The best known is Newgrange, part of Brugh na Bonnie, where at Winter Solstice the rising sun lights the inner chamber, coming to rest on boulders inscribed with goddess symbols.

Geraldine Moane's double-edged desire is to re-member the earth-centered gynocentric existence of ancient Ireland and to dismantle patriarchal destruction of women through forced motherhood, violence, and poverty. Drawing on interviews and conversations with Irish women, she sketches women's practices which help us realize our own power, or as Marja Suhonen might say, reinscribe the divine in ourselves and facilitate biophilic choices. Confronting the foreground by demystifying patriarchal institutions such as catholicity and Anglicity (in this case, in contrast to the Irish language), joining the race of women by joining other women in solidarity, particularly in the Irish Women's Camp, to which women from both North and South come as well as from England, and journeying into the Background by creating new consciousness, all contribute to women's creative engagement and resistance. And so she ends with an account of Sistership, a splendid story of women's collective action.

Finally, as we address the millennium, in a Christian marking of time, Anne-Marie Korte reminds us of Mary Daly's postchristian theoretical situatedness by taking us on a brief journey to her 1998 book *Quintessence . . . Realizing the Archaic Future* and exploring her work/play with temporality. While Sheilagh Mogford reads Margaret Atwood's future into our present, Anne-Marie Korte shows us how Mary Daly vigorously resists the threat of that future/present by madly spinning/conjuring/spelling a story of a different future. While AnaLouise Keating explores Mary Daly's ways of re-membering the past, Anne-Marie Korte considers Mary Daly's ways of re-membering the future.

Visiting many different depictions of time, Anne-Marie Korte explains that the fundamental element in Mary Daly's approach to time is expecting/conjuring change that manifests itself in a new era. Noting that *Quintessence* does not explain how the world got from this present to that "Lost and Found" Future, Anne-Marie Korte suggests that *Quintessence* is not about continuity (steps from here to there, a political program) but rather constructs the Future as a way of setting up a significantly discontinuous point of view from which to critique the (more or less simultaneous) evils of the present and past. And, as she has done throughout her philosophical development, in *Quintessence* Mary Daly expresses the profound qualitative difference between phallocratic reality and the "otherworld" of Be-ing in terms of a metaphor of different eras. "New" awareness is located in a different *time:* women's own time.

"Women's own time" or "Life-time," Anne-Marie Korte explains, is not the time of dailiness, bodily functions, and cycles that other feminists have constructed. Mary Daly is not talking about time as a limiting factor at the level of the individual (mortality, busyness), and she sees moves toward cyclicity as constructing closed systems that stamp out difference—the endless repetition of the same. Instead, Mary Daly's radical feminism calls for a departure from a dangerous, perverted, patriarchal present, achieved through the development of a critical distance from which to look back at obstacles to women's transformation. For Mary Daly, time is a dimension of transformation and renewal, a dimension women need more fully to occupy with history and future of our own making.

Anne-Marie Korte argues that in Mary Daly's work, temporal discontinuity and play with time also connect memory and vision. In "flashbacks, foresight, and temporal contractions," boundaries thought to be absolute, such as time, place, and species, are transgressed, while boundaries of individuals, transgressed through practices of rape, remain intact. Opportunities are created for encounters among different beings of different eras which spark creativity and change. Time, for Mary Daly, is a dimension of extension and realization. Existing in time takes more than endurance, it requires an agency: to be present and do more justice, one must reinterpret the past and shape the future. 'Quintessence' is a new way of expressing what Mary Daly earlier called 'Verb' and 'Goddess' and involves "throwing her life as far as it will go."

And indeed, "going far" is something all the contributors to this volume do. Aside from the enormous contribution they make to re-reading the works of Mary Daly and to radical feminism, they offer many suggestions for continuing re-search:

- turning the conversations to women while understanding the relevant "species" category as biophilic, not biological
- the question of subjectivity understood as an ongoing process of becoming
- contrasting postmodern play with Mary Daly's playfulness
- how/why postmoderns are susceptible to a(n exclusively) modernist or a literal rather than a performative reading of Mary Daly
- strategies of Mary Daly's such as Be/Leaving, reversing reversals, and pirating through a patriarchal symbolic, by which separation is a practice of disrupting the logic of that symbolic
- exploring Mary Daly's concept of transcendence as the capacity to be an agent by shaping our conceptual framework
- the multiple focus involved in seeing women's resistance/subjectivity within a situation, detecting patterns of violence against women normalized by the context of those situations, and imagining otherworld possibilities
- the ambiguity of the need for feminists of colonial nations to speak out about violence against women in other parts of the world while that speaking carries with it traces, if not the stamp, of a colonial location
- how naming atrocities against women can inscribe women's victim status and foreclose women's possibilities, and how it can provide for the re-cognition of women's resistance and name a ground of action
- the territoriality of lesbian and women's space
- the power of conceptually moving to the Background and the power of taking to the streets to re-cognize by contextualizing other women's subjectivity, resistance, agency; the sociality of both of these strategies
- complex explorations of radical white feminist focus on independence from men and men's conceptualizing, and radical women of color's focus on the interdependence of women
- the logic of exploring boundary violation as rape with a focus on integrity of self, in relation to the logic of boundary crossing (colonial,

racialized, class, ethnic) that requires entering other women's contexts, seeing the self as plural or multiple and oppressions as interlocked

- complexing rather than neutralizing identity politics
- exploring ways we are multiply constituted: the many selves through time involved in the process of be-coming that Mary Daly develops as well as the co-temporaneous plural selves suggested by María Lugones's work, both in contrast to postmodern fragmented selves
- continuing to develop a pluralist radical feminism
- the struggle for conversations not facilitated or mediated by bilingual translators, exploring the different logics and sociality of approaching others with and without a bilingual translator
- as colonial racial patriarchy metamorphoses into yet another shape, how to resist and how to find and re-cognize re-sisters
- language as contested territory and meanings as negotiated, often through political struggle
- the theological dimensions of twentieth-century Western philosophy
- the facing of evil as exploring not just ethical values but the realm of rituals and sacred-making
- how to pluralize the universal, rather than universalizing the particular, making it open-ended dialogic, conjuring dynamic interaction and engagement
- the practice of philosophy/theory as performing, conjuring, animating, casting spells, entering the play

And more. And this work calls not for distanced academic proclamations but for a continuing, engaged feminist practice. There are so many sparking and sparkling ideas to play with.

We want to encourage you to play with Mary Daly's works. For example, getting students engaged in Mary Daly's language/ontology can be enormously biophilic. One of the editors, Sarah Hoagland, taught a language course during which she had the students write a description of an old woman and read it in class. There were fine discussions, amid grasping of limits of language, of women and old age and ageism. When that was done, she had them rewrite their descriptions using at least fifteen words from the *Wickedary*. The result was astounding. While the first writing left the students more thoughtful about old women, the second took the students into conversation with the old women; they saw the old women as agents capable of talking back to them, challenging them. "I had to picture her as a subject, a protagonist in her own destiny," wrote Rosibel

Cruz. "The words took me to a place where I couldn't speak for her, she had to speak for herself."

Mary Daly is a spinner and weaver, a performer, a wicced player throwing her life into the creation of new time. She works, to a great extent, as a magician of meanings—breaking words into syllables which release their etymologies or pun them into parody, re-"spelling" them to give them new powers in new environments, displacing words into new contexts, renaming patriarchal events and constructs to reveal their hidden connections and patterns, naming women's Selves, lives, knowledge, and Naming—in other words, re-metaphoring—the world. Since one can only begin such work with the words and meanings at hand, she is often "using old words with new meanings"—literally doing so, for example, when she uses 'female' in a way that detaches it from the discourse of biology and places it in a metaethical discourse of biophilia/necrophilia, and also metaphorically, when she uses old ideas, categories, analytic strategies and organizing frameworks (e.g., from Aquinas), information and disinformation, cultural artifacts of many sorts to craft new collages, new gadgets, new vehicles, new powers that give meaning to and get meaning from radically Other places, times, and possibilities.

When a reader encounters texts which say something new, she has to be able to hear the new in spite of and through the concrete form of the old that is presented to her senses. If one cannot do that, such texts seem simply full of mistakes and "misuses." Thus, creative, sometimes cross-linguistic, street slang just sounds ignorant to the hearer who cannot follow the creators' play into new meanings. The authors in this anthology, to a woman, have hearkened to the new in Mary Daly's new/old words and thus can play along with her as she breaks through the apparently and supposedly impenetrable and total structures of the patriarchal symbolics in rage, celebration, and cosmic creativity (i.e., creating a cosmos, or, if you please, socially constructing an other reality). And as players along, they can recognize the formative role Mary Daly has had in creating the space and possibilities feminists have been occupying and expanding in the past three decades.

These authors are encouraged, not frightened or offended, by the rage which is one of the motivating forces of Mary Daly's work. Offense at women's anger is partly a matter of the etiquette of the academic class—women's anger is unseemly and "inappropriate." But also, members of oppressed groups are taught to fear their own anger both because its expression is routinely punished and because it is, supposedly, cosmically destructive. Many women in our (the editors') academic and nonacademic communities say that if they let their anger "go" they would become monsters of rampaging destruction, and their ways of expressing this reveal a sort of superstitious sense that their rage would destroy not just some dishes, domestic peace, or a male ego, but the world. To access Mary Daly's work, one has to grasp that it is not *women's* anger that fuels the planetary destruction going on around us. We may be grateful that, notwithstanding her erudition and scholarly skill, and to the detriment of her reputation among academic feminist theorists, Mary Daly has not been assimilated into the professional academic class and her uncouth anger is available to her analysis and her vision.

Perhaps the other most significant motivator of Mary Daly's philosophy is another very un-cool, low-class passion: hope. In spite of, or because of (or both) Mary Daly's unremittingly clear and courageous perception of evil, she has never followed that evil to its logical conclusion of nihilism—a conclusion to which much postmodern poststructuralist feminist theory comes perilously close. We read the dynamic between the a-mazing analyses of atrocity and the blatantly Futuristic fiction in *Quintessence* to be the latest performance of the dynamic sparking interplay of rage and hope so characteristic of Mary Daly's life and work. We are familiar with such a dynamic in our own lives and work, even in the motivation and process of editing this anthology—our weary anger at dismissive, superficial, inaccurate, and astoundingly unimaginative readings of Mary Daly that are peppered almost ritually through a great deal of academic feminist theory, and our energizing hope that this anthology has given space and respect to theorists (Other academics, of course) whose work will re-open issues the others have foreclosed, and restimulate angry, hopeful, mythic, poetic, ontologically creative feminist philosophy and theory—not mimicking Mary Daly, but authorized by the liberties she brashly takes.

The project before us—women's continued be-coming, women's confrontation with oppression and movement toward transcendence—is a collective process. It will not be promoted by dismissing each other to distance ourselves from criticisms, and it will not be promoted by retreating to abstract theory severed from everyday practice and activism. It will be promoted by the trickster who mirrors us, in the case of radical feminists of the European-American tradition, perhaps by the play of the challenge of who we are when trying to enter the geography of such as *El Libro de Caló*, with all the mistakes entwined in entering a "foreign" territory not as an abstract colonial conqueror but as a sister seeking re-sister travelers.

This anthology is open-ended. Mary Daly is hardly through producing work, and so this anthology can hardly aspire to give a successful summary picture of it. And the questions raised by those feminists engaging with Mary Daly in her projects hardly have pat answers or easy solutions or pills subsequent feminists can swallow to get on with things. Radical Feminism is a continual work in progress. And the possibility of movement we have all inherited as a result of Mary Daly's work is awesome. We offer this volume in the hopes that women seeking to do dissertation work on Mary Daly's works and the criticisms and new territory it inspires will be encouraged, and that women committed to the embodiment of theory and practice will more easily benefit from the fertile ground we have to walk on.

Notes

1. Margaret A. Simon, introduction to *Feminist Interpretation of Simone de Beauvoir*, ed. Margaret A. Simon (University Park: Pennsylvania State University Press, 1995), 6.

2. Jeffner Allen, "A response to a letter from Peg Simons, December 1993," in Simon, *Feminist Interpretations of Simone de Beauvoir*, 132–33.

1

Feminist Theology: The "Verbing" of Ultimate/Intimate Reality in Mary Daly

Wanda Warren Berry

1. Mary Daly and the Feminist Theologians

Contemporary feminist theory is a richly varied phenomenon; sometimes it seems that only two convictions are shared by all feminists: (1) that women have suffered severe disadvantages historically, and (2) that humanity must find ways to erase these disadvantages and their continuing effects. Within the plethora of feminist publications of the past fifteen years, helpful studies of the diversity of feminist frameworks have been assembled (see, e.g., Jaggar and Struhl, 1978). These studies make it clear that feminist theories have been developed within most of the major alternative contemporary philosophical strategies. For example, there are Marxist feminists who remain within a socio-economic, historically-determined sense of reality. There are also pragmatist feminists, who do not indulge any far-reaching "ontological thirst," since they have confidence only in human ability to test the truth by social and individual results. In addition, there are more or less traditional religious feminists, who assume an unchanged theism as the revealed model for interpreting ultimate reality and meaning. The aim of this study is not to survey explicit or implicit views of ultimate reality and meaning in the wide variety of feminist theorists. Instead, I will work in the arena of contemporary American feminist theology, focusing primarily on Mary Daly, whose orientation differs from any of the positions thus far indicated; Daly is decisively ontological as well as non-traditional. In order to bring to the surface some of the issues raised by Daly for contemporary religious thought I also will analyze Sallie McFague and, briefly, Rosemary Radford Ruether as well as Starhawk.

Daly, Ruether, and McFague are all from the same generation of feminists in the United States of America. Their professional educations were received prior to the contemporary women's movement and their works show the changes wrought by the subsequent emergence of feminist theory in the 1970s. Mary Daly, born in 1928 in Schenectady, New York, USA, has been on the faculty at Boston College, Chestnut Hill, Massachusetts, since the middle of the 1960s. Her undergraduate degree (B.A., 1950) is from the College of St. Rose in Albany, New York. Her graduate degrees include an M.A. from Catholic University, Washington, D.C., U.S.A. (1952) and two doctorates, one in theology and one in philosophy, from the University of Fribourg, Switzerland (1963 and 1965), to which she went during an era when "there was no place in the U.S. where a female was allowed" to pursue the degrees normative for work in Catholic theology (Daly 1975a, 8).

Sallie McFague (TeSelle) was born in 1933 and holds degrees from Smith College, Northhampton, Massachusetts, and Yale University, New Haven, Connecticut, U.S.A. McFague has authored four books dealing with theology, religion, and literature. She teaches at The Divinity School, Vanderbilt University, in Nashville, Tennessee, where she has also served as Dean. Rosemary Radford Ruether (b. 1936) is the Georgia Harkness Professor of Applied Theology at Garrett Theological Seminary, Evanston, Illinois; she holds degrees from Scripps College and Claremont Graduate School in California. A leading influence in contemporary theology and in the development of women's studies in religion, Ruether has authored some twenty-three books and numerous articles. Starhawk (whose earlier name was Miriam Simos) is somewhat younger than the others (b. 1951). Her undergraduate degree is from the University of California at Los Angeles and she has done graduate studies there and at Antioch West University. Now the author of three popular books, Starhawk is presented in her book (1982) as "a writer, teacher, counselor, political activist, nonviolence trainer and witch . . ."

Daly's feminist authorship, with its brilliant imagistic formulations, has greatly influenced the development of feminist theology, a movement which since 1970 has transformed scholarship and publication in religious studies, at least in the U.S.A. Many in this movement no longer identify with Daly in the current developments of her position; but most are either consciously grateful for her painful pioneering of the movement or they are unconsciously dependent upon her analyses and phrases. The two main branches of contemporary feminist religious thought are both indebted to Daly's early work. But those called "reformers" as well as the "revolutionaries" need to read Daly to find the rebirth of their concerns in the last third of the twentieth century, a century which had managed to submerge the works of nineteenth-century religious feminists such as Elizabeth Cady Stanton and Matilda Jocelyn Gage. "Reformist" feminist theologians are those who believe that certain religious traditions were not oppressive of women in their original insights although they became agents of such injustice as they developed within patriarchal cultures. These feminist theologians work actively to reform institutions, sometimes calling for quite radical change to erase sexism. On the other hand, the "revolutionaries" consider all inherited institutions, especially those which are religious, as "irreformably sexist." Nevertheless, they see the women's movement as of deep religious significance. Some "revolutionaries" or "radical religious feminists" seek ancient woman-centered or "pagan" traditions as sources of symbols and rituals. They focus upon Goddess imagery, looking to alternative traditions such as witchcraft. Others seek new religious symbols emerging out of women's present experience (Christ and Plaskow 1979, 10ff.).

Mary Daly is of special interest to those who ask whether the liberation of women's powers from historical oppression will make any difference in human views of ultimate reality and meaning. More than any other feminist I know, she is explicitly ontological in her own orientation. More than any other ontologist I know, her books have had unprecedented popular influence, making reflection on what it means "to be" relevant to the lives of persons normally inaccessible to new concepts of ultimacy.

I believe that her powerful imagery and linguistic strategies have so shocked and delighted readers that they have opened radically new insights, for example, into envisioning reality as "process" rather than unchanging substance. This may not seem remarkable to those familiar with modern philosophy, theology, and science. But the unusual fact is that Daly's imagery has brought such a view into existential effectiveness for people formerly shaped by traditional assertions. One of Daly's favorite lines from Virginia Woolf expresses her project: "it is only by putting it into words that I make it [reality] whole" (Daly 1984, 173). Daly's authorship is a self-conscious, spiralling search for her own expression on the part of one who knows well the irony of trying to use linguistic strategies for revolutionary change, since language is a socially transmitted system. If one goes back to the more conventional style of her second book, one finds an early prophecy that Daly will need to make language and imagery a primary tool of her feminism. "It requires a kick in the imagination, a wrenching of tired words, to realize that feminism is the final and therefore the first cause, and that *this* movement is movement. Realization of this is already the beginning of a qualitative leap in be-ing. For the philosophers of senescence 'the final cause' is in technical reason; it is the Father's plan, an endless flow of Xerox copies of the past. But the final cause that *is movement* is in our imaginative-cerebral-emotional-active-creative be-ing" (Daly 1973, 190).

The shape of Daly's authorship dramatizes "the qualitative leap in be-ing" to which she here refers. Her first book, *The Church and the Second Sex* (1968), addresses Simone de Beauvoir, showing how de Beauvoir's criticism of Roman Catholicism for its oppression of women is justified, but defending the potential of the Church to change and reverse its undeniable sexism. Daly has been unable to authorize second and third editions of this book without adding layers of new introductory materials which, with imaginative irony, make it clear that she is no longer the same person who wrote the original book, however cathartic and pioneering it might have been. In 1975 she added an "Autobiographical Preface" as well as a "Feminist Postchristian Introduction," both of which testify to what her important article of the same year calls "The Qualitative Leap Beyond Patriarchal Religion" by which she left behind the stance of "feminist reformer" to become a feminist "revolutionary." In the third edition, her "New Archaic Afterwords" (1985) demonstrate the on-going transformations, particularly of her style/language, which have unfolded with continuity from the time of that "qualitative leap."

The second book, *Beyond God the Father* (1973), is central in terms of both style and theory; its revolutionary stance stimulates pungent new images and word-play in the course of a recognizably conventional outline and argumentation, so that by the end of the book a new dynamic is emerging. While Daly still identifies with herself as author of this book, its second edition required an "Original Reintroduction" (1985) which testifies to changes in language, style, and symbolism correlating with her epigenesis after the qualitative leap from "reform" to "revolutionary" feminism.

These new prefaces and introductions to the first two books mean that each incorporates in its new edition summaries of the developments in *Gyn/Ecology* (1978) and *Pure Lust* (1985). *Gyn/Ecology* contains explicit discussion of Daly's principles for forging a new linguistic style which "kicks the imagination" and "wrenches tired words." It also develops powerful historical studies of world-wide atrocities against women. *Gyn/Ecology* begins to "spin" new visions of an alternative creativity available through the bonding of women who separate from the oppressions of patriarchy. *Pure Lust* carries this task forward by taking up again the more ontological approaches of *Beyond God the Father*, while it continues Daly's analysis of the sickness of the sadomasochistic patterning of patriarchy, particularly in its religious symbolism. This book develops more fully the psychological, philosophical, and religious potentialities which she believes are the "Original" nature of "women and other biophilic creatures." (After the present essay was developed, Daly published *Websters' First New Intergalactic Wickedary of the English Language* [1987], reinforcing recognition of her emphasis on "verbalizing" as feminist methodology.)

In spite of the explicitly recorded qualitative as well as epigenetic changes in Daly's authorship, I will be arguing that her work is self-consciously an authorship not only in her insistence that each new edition of earlier works carry her own testimony to her development, but also in a continuity of fundamental concerns and images. A central concern of all four books is expressed as the explicit purpose of *Beyond God the Father:* she says that she aims to show that the women's revolution "is an ontological, spiritual revolution, pointing beyond the idolatries of sexist society and sparking creative action in and toward transcendence. The becoming of women implies universal human becoming. It has everything to do with the search for ultimate meaning and reality which some would call God" (Daly 1973, 6).

The later articles and books show Daly deciding that the word "God" is no longer available for feminist usage since it has proved to be impossible to break its connections to male/masculine imagery and meanings which block women from full participation in ultimate meaning (Daly 1985b, xxiv). Nevertheless, she continues to be oriented primarily by the quest for ultimate reality and meaning which she herself identified with "God-talk" in *Beyond God the Father* (Daly 1973, 7). Although she has leapt beyond not only "Father" imagery for Supreme Reality, but also beyond "God-talk," Daly still speaks of the project of *Pure Lust* as "radically metaphysical" (Daly 1984, 28). This approach continues her earlier testimony that "feminism is cosmic in its dimensions" (Daly 1973, 189). Daly's whole authorship is motivated by the conviction that she can best stimulate transcendence of patriarchal *social* realities by offering visions of *ultimate* reality and meaning which liberate women's original potential. In other words, she is still under the star of Elizabeth Cady Stanton, the nineteenth-century American feminist whom she quoted at the outset of the foundational chapter of *Beyond God the Father:* "The first step in the elevation of women under all systems of religion is to convince them that the great Spirit of the Universe is in no way responsible for any of these absurdities" (Stanton, quoted in Daly 1973, 13).

Virtually all feminist theorists share modern awareness of the sociology of knowledge and call for radical criticism of assumptions in the light of their relativity to patriarchy's prolonged conditioning of the human mind. Daly's powerful historical studies of such culturally-defined ideologies are directed, however, by her ontological orientation, rather than by the prevailing epistemological relativism. Unlike relativists, Daly believes that we can reach the original natural "Background" of our own potential, if we "exorcise" the patriarchal demons which possess our mind in the "Foreground." Her spatial/scenic images for the relationship between the ontological (Background) and historically-determined realities (Foreground) can introduce certain peculiarities of her feminist theory as well as her conscious use of metaphor to establish meaning.

2. Metaphor in Feminist Methodology

I have long believed that Daly's special intellectual powers were unleashed during the writing of *Beyond God the Father* as she first experimented with brilliant new imagery and startling linguistic reversals and coinages in order to express feminist experience. This liberation of potential was contagious; religious feminist readers of the book found it exhilarating. For example, traditionally conditioned Jewish or Christian women can hardly forget the delightful jolt to consciousness, back in the 1970s, which was caused by Daly's talk of "the sisterhood of man." Not only did that phrase humorously challenge patriarchal reality, it suggested possible renewal through the "bonding of those who are oppressed by definition" (Daly 1973, 9 and 59). Although such phrases have been left behind long ago by Daly's own development, she created sparks which facilitated liberation for many. As Daly's radical feminist authorship has developed, her style has become more and more imagistic, metaphoric, and poetic—and, of course, her images no longer are built from those inherited within patriarchal traditions. Many complain, as she herself predicted, that "Daly has now gone off the deep end" (Daly 1975a, 48) and that she has made herself impossibly difficult to read. Indeed, traditionally educated readers may need to remind themselves of how they felt when first coming to terms with others who tried to express radically new visions: for example, one of my students compared the effort required to read Daly to the way she felt when first reading Nietzsche. However, perhaps more than Nietzsche, Daly interweaves into even her later books what she calls "the honed logic of traditionally rational discourse" as well as "the deep Spinning power of Metaphor." Although Daly has been spinning new metaphors for feminist "be-ing" since such a modality was discovered in *Beyond God the Father*, she finally becomes explicit about the relationship between imagery and feminist philosophy only in the introductory methodological section, "Metaphors of Metabeing," in *Pure Lust*. "Since this first philosophy is about Elemental be-ing, it is radically metaphysical, concerned with ontological potency, knowledge, passion, virtue, creation, transformation. Given this complexity, our thinking must be not only imaginatively intense and concrete, but also intellectually extensive and abstract. The deep Spinning power of Metaphor is essential, and so is the honed logic of traditionally rational discourse" (Daly 1984, 28).

During the following exposition of Daly I will take my cue from this consciously expressed methodology, paying attention both to Daly's dominant metaphors for ultimate reality and to some traditional "logical" explanations of their meaning. I will here and there juxtapose Daly's views with those of Sallie McFague, a feminist "reform" theologian, whose work, *Metaphorical Theology*, can provide a perceptive supplement to Daly's work on metaphor as well as treatments of Daly which, while inadequately attentive to Daly's metaphors, nevertheless will help to surface some of the theological issues.

Returning, then, to the section on "Metaphors of Metabeing" in *Pure Lust*, part of which is quoted above, it is significant that Daly opens with a brief discussion of the role of symbols and metaphors which is developed largely through her agreement and disagreement with Paul Tillich. Tillich's formative influence upon Daly's intellectual development was both conscious and unconscious. The early books frequently echo with Tillichian concepts and language. Even in the later books (as here) she uses Tillich, as she does other nonfeminists, as a "springboard" or jumping-off point for her own analysis. In this passage Daly starts with Tillich's distinction between signs and symbols, saying that metaphors are like symbols in that they "participate in that to which they point. They open up levels of reality otherwise closed to us and they unlock dimensions and elements of our souls which correspond to these hidden dimensions and elements of reality" (Daly 1984, 25).

As we have seen, she strongly asserts that symbols are essential to the development of feminist philosophy. The truth of metaphors is to be tested by whether they "ring true" to "Prudes," i.e., to "Proud," "wise," and "good" women (Daly 1984, 14). Acceptable symbols also will be open to diversity, recognizing both individual and "tribal" differences.

Daly's brief sketch of the meaning of metaphor goes beyond Tillich by arguing that, while metaphor includes the power of symbol, it involves more than symbol, especially the power "to evoke action, movement." Daly elaborates upon the importance of metaphor by citing both Julian Jaynes and Susanne Langer's views that metaphor (in Jaynes' language) is "the constitutive ground of language." Those who find Daly's style puzzling, because of its constant word-play, will want to notice that such "ludic cerebration" is a deliberate linguistic strategy, aimed to affect reality. She says of metaphors: "They Name/evoke a shock, a clash with the 'going logic' and they introduce a new logic. Metaphors function to Name change, and therefore they elicit change. . . . They transform/transfer our perceptions of reality, enabling us to 'break set' and thus to break out of linguistic prisons" (Daly 1984, 25–26).

Although Daly employs discussion of the etymological roots of "metaphor" (*metapherein:* to transform, change, i.e., to carry/bear with), she does not even hint at the extensive analysis of the nature of metaphor which has been developed in contemporary thought, in philosophy, theology, hermeneutics, linguistics, and comparative literature. Her primary interest in metaphor, it seems, is ontological; discussion of it is introduced to emphasize the view of reality and meaning which we will find stressed by her root metaphors. "Metaphors are necessary for Elemental feminist philosophy, for this is about and *is* transformation, movement" (Daly 1984, 26).

In her "Spinning" style she jumps off the "springboard" of Aristotle's view that our minds are rooted in wonder (Daly 1984, 8), saying: "Women who lust for wisdom become astonished/astonishing, Wondering. As Muses of our own creation, Wonderlusters re-member our Original Powers. Unlike the frozen 'philosophy' that is packaged and stored within academic refrigerators, Wonderlust moves us always. Our vehicles are often Metaphors. Our destinations are the Realms of Metabeing" (Daly, 1984, 26).

From here Daly spins into a paragraph which places in order the primary metaphors which I will argue weave her view of ultimate reality and meaning.

"The word *Metabeing* is used here to Name Realms of active participation in the Powers of Be-ing. Be-ing, the Verb, cannot without gross falsification be reified into a noun, whether that noun be identified as 'Supreme Being,' or 'God,' or 'Goddess' (singular or plural). When I choose to use such words as *Goddess* it is to point Metaphorically to the Powers of Be-ing, the Active Verb in whose potency all biophilic reality participates" (Daly 1984, 26).

In this section Daly wants to introduce the neologism "Metabeing" as a summary name for her picture of feminist existence. A bit later she develops that orientation through three connotations of the Greek preposition *meta:*

1. meta = *after*/"occurring later." Feminist be-ing is possible only after thorough understanding of "the blockage" of women's powers within phallocracy. (Daly 1984, 27)
2. meta = "situated behind." Women emerging from patriarchy experience their own be-ing not simply as something entirely new, but as entrance into "Realms of our ancestral memories."
3. meta = "change in/transformation of." Feminist experience is of being as a "continuing process" of metamorphosis.

It is interesting that "Metabeing," which sums up Daly's orientation to feminist reality, involves the usual steps of temporal process: it starts by recognizing the *present*/the Foreground as dangerously shaped by patriarchy. It experiences disaffiliation with the present as opening transcendence through a new relation to the *past*, by "re-membering" women's "Original Powers." It also is oriented toward transcending the present in a continuing *future* process of transformation. Thus "Metabeing" functions to indicate feminist reality in terms of temporal process in a way which correlates in its first two steps with the scenic/spatial imagery of "Foreground" and "Background."

I do not deny that the recent coinage of "Metabeing" is an important step in Daly's implementation of her own humanity in terms of the definition of human existence in the often quoted line from *Beyond God the Father:* "To exist humanly is to name the self, the world, and God. The 'method' of the evolving spiritual consciousness of women is nothing less than this beginning to speak humanly—a reclaiming of the right to name" (Daly 1973, 8).

Moreover, I am convinced that "Naming"/"verbalizing" is Daly's root-metaphor for feminist method, a metaphor peculiarly powerful for women because they for so long were expected to accept being named by others. Nevertheless, the explanation of Metabeing quoted above, as well as the subtitle "*Metaphors* of Metabeing," reveal that this term is not itself adequately imagistic/metaphoric to replace her more fundamental metaphors: her root-metaphor for ultimate reality is "the Verb"/Be-ing; and for ultimate meaning, it is "verbing"/participation in be-ing. While she herself has not noted the delicious correlation of these images with her method (i.e., "verbalizing"/Naming), "honed logical analysis" added to metaphoric perceptiveness can reveal this to be the case.

While Daly's later books virtually explode with new images, many of which are introduced by pungent, ironic linguistic analysis, I am convinced that the root-metaphor for reality has continued to be 'the Verb' from the time of her first introduction of "God the Verb" in *Beyond God the Father*. Increasingly, from that time, she epitomizes the point of the metaphor by hyphenating "Be-ing" as well as other present participles. At the same time, her favored form of thought becomes "ludic cerebration" which involves use of word-play (Daly 1978, 23). It is interesting that originally "verb" meant "word," rather than only the specific kind of word given as its first meaning in modern dictionaries. Nevertheless, it is the modern usage which establishes Daly's view of reality; at the same time, her method connects with the still listed "obsolete" meaning ("a word"). In modern usage, a verb is "that part of speech by which an assertion is made, or which serves to connect a subject with a predicate (*Oxford English Dictionary*). The ramifications of Simone de Beauvoir's analysis of patriarchy's denial of subjectivity/agency to women can be seen as still operative in Daly's root-metaphor.

Before going further to develop Daly's meaning in her "verb" imagery, it is important to clarify more thoroughly the meaning of metaphor and, specifically, the meaning of "root-metaphor." It will be convenient to do so through some attention to a work by a very different feminist theologian who has always focused upon the uses of parable and metaphor. In *Metaphorical Theology* Sallie McFague, like Daly, distinguishes symbol from metaphor and finds "metaphorical statement" religiously "more powerful" than "symbolical statement." She explains this power through the special nature of metaphorical statements.

> Most simply, a metaphor is seeing one thing *as* something else, pretending 'this' is 'that' as a way of saying something about it. Thinking metaphorically means spotting a thread of similarity between two dissimilar objects, events, or whatever, one of which is better known than the other and using the better-known one as a way of speaking about the lesser known . . . Symbolical statements, on the other hand, are not so much a way of knowing and speaking as they are sedimentation and solidification of a metaphor. For in symbolical or sacramental thought, one does not think of 'this' *as* 'that,' but 'this' as *a part of* 'that.' The tension of metaphor is absorbed by the harmony of symbol. (McFague 1982, 15–16)

While McFague is here much more precise than Daly about how metaphor works and makes it clear that she shares Daly's preference for metaphorical thinking, there are hints in her way of talking about symbol of what will emerge as a different emphasis. Although Daly says that she prefers metaphorical analogy to the *analogy of being* in classical metaphysics, the image involved in her talk of "participation in be-ing" (i.e., "this" is *a part of* "that") suggests what McFague decides is less meaningful: sacramental/symbolical meaning (see note Daly 1984, 26).

Nevertheless, in many respects Daly and McFague agree. Like Daly, McFague expresses agreement with Langer's view that there is a metaphorical foundation of all thought and language, whether in religious or ordinary statements: "human thought is of a piece, it is indirect, and it involves judgments" (McFague 1982, 17). Nothing can be "known or thought of directly or literally"; when it seems to us that it can, we "have simply acquired a way of looking at it which is acceptable to us" (McFague 1982, 16). Such "ways of looking" are rooted in finding similarities/similes between discrete, particular experiences. To recognize that all religious thought (i.e., all "interpretations of the meaning of experience at its most profound level" [McFague 1982, 153]) is metaphorical, is to affirm both what we know and what we do not know. It "is 'positive' as well as 'negative,' giving license for speech about God as well as indicating the limits of such speech" (McFague 1982, 19).

Even McFague's Protestant skepticism here, however, cannot rule out the question of ultimate reality which concerns Daly so centrally. Insofar as the metaphors/models through which experience is interpreted "are well on the way to systematic thought," "they implicitly raise questions of truth and reference," since they are "comprehensive ways of envisioning reality" (McFague 1982, 25). McFague defines "models," whether in science or in religion, as "dominant metaphors" which are "substantive" and "organizing" and which mediate between simple metaphor and systematic thought (McFague 1982, 25, 28, 65). To preserve realization of the metaphorical basis of all "models," McFague also uses Stephen Pepper's term "root-metaphor" when referring to radical models: "a root-metaphor is the most basic assumption about the nature of the world or experience that we can make when we try to give a description of it" (quoted in McFague 1982, 28).

As a feminist Christian theologian, McFague is concerned not only to analyze and chart the root-metaphors of her own tradition, she also wants to "investigate possibilities for transformative, revolutionary models" (McFague 1982, 28). Her goal is to justify "dominant, founding metaphors as true but not literal" (e.g., God as Father) as well as to discover other appropriate metaphors which "have been suppressed" particularly by patriarchalism and its absolutization of only one way of imagining the relationship between humanity and reality/meaning. McFague, like Daly, thinks that father-imagery is unavoidable for God within her tradition, but that it must be "reconstructed" to be rid of patriarchalism. And it must be relativized by the use of other images (e.g., feminine/womb/Goddess-images as well as "God the Friend") which balance its picture of ultimate meaning by additional concrete pictures of meaningful relationships (see McFague 1982, chapter 5). In McFague's view, radical feminists like Daly have mistakenly taken patriarchalism as the root-metaphor of

Christianity. She agrees with the analysis of the schizophrenia which Daly and others have seen as intrinsic to this model: "At the heart of patriarchalism as root-metaphor is a subject-object split in which man is envisioned over against God and vice versa. God, as transcendent being, is man's superior Other and woman in this hierarchy becomes man's inferior other. From the basic dualism of a righteous God and sinful man, other dualisms develop—mind/body, spirituality/carnality, truth/appearance, life/death—which are projected upon men and women as their 'natures' " (McFague 1982, 148).

This diagnosis of humanity's sickness under patriarchy is derived both from Ruether and from Daly, and is of great influence in feminist thought. Sharing with Daly this view of our sickness, McFague nevertheless joins Ruether's hope to reform the dominant religious traditions rather than Daly's "qualitative leap beyond patriarchal religion," because she believes that the root metaphors of the tradition can be discovered actually to be communal (Kingdom) and mutual (covenant). For example, McFague argues that, as used by Jesus, God the "Father" emphasized the relational, personal, intimate character of the divine/human bond, rather than the oppressive and dichotomized patterns of domination mistakenly adopted by the tradition through much of its history.

Nevertheless, McFague aims at a theology which preserves the tension in metaphor between the "like" and "unlike," the "is" and the "is not"; she wants transformation of the tradition, rather than just to "baptize" it again (McFague 1982, 29). If "God" is "like" a father, but also "unlike" a father, aspects of the meaning intended by "God" can be better imagined through other metaphors. McFague sees the special power of metaphorical thought as to interpret life in terms of "veins of similarity," as well as in terms of "the region of dissimilarity." Metaphorical theology, in her view, is peculiarly appropriate for contemporary minds with their skepticism about claims to know reality. It formulates interpretations of life's meaning at the same time as it systematically recognizes that, as images, these are not identical with some objective, uninterpreted "given." She says, "What we do not know, we must simulate through models of what we know" (McFague 1982, 25). This epistemological orientation manifests a self-consciously Protestant orientation of the relation of faith to reason.

Daly, on the other hand, is deeply concerned that human thought be liberated from the paralyzing skepticism of the modern West so that it can confidently "participate in be-ing." Her metaphors aim to grasp through similes what we do know by immediate participation. She urges feminists "to trust intuitions and the reasoning rooted in them" and "to be intellectual in the most direct and daring way, claiming and trusting the deep correspondence between the structures/processes of one's own mind and the structures/processes of reality" (Daly 1984, 152). Daly sees the modern loss of ontological reason as a consequence of the subject-object split conditioned in us by patriarchy and calls for thought and language which reject nominalism in order to participate in "Realizing reason." "Realizing reason is both discovering and participating in the unfolding, the Self-creation, of reason" (Daly 1984, 162).

The possibility of such reasoning is rooted in the community of women and in commitment to ecological harmony: "The correspondence between the minds of Musing women and the intelligible structures of reality is rooted in our *promise*, that is, our potential and commitment to evolve, unfold 'together,' in harmony with each other and with all Elemental reality" (Daly 1984, 163).

To summarize these brief expositions of Daly and McFague on metaphorical method: their most important agreement seems to be on the importance of metaphor as a vehicle of transformative power which enables transcendence of the subject-object dichotomy characteristic of our patriarchal inheritance. Both are concerned, as well, about the tendency of religious images to become reified absolutes which reenforce pre-existing social structures. McFague agrees with Berger in seeing this tendency as intrinsic to unreflective religious processes. She says: "As Peter Berger and other sociologists have pointed out, we human beings, unfinished at birth, construct our world, which is then objectified over against us as 'reality.' . . . By reifying our constructions into objective realities, however, we make them resistant to change and we become prisoners of our own creations. Religion is one of the most powerful legitimators of our social constructions because it grounds our precarious constructions in ultimate reality" (McFague 1982, 150).

Within McFague's orientation, this tendency in religious thought is best offset by metaphorical theology, which self-consciously recognizes the non-literal character of images at the same time as it embraces the human necessity for such interpretations of the meaning of our existence. On the other hand, while Daly's extensive treatments of Berger in *Beyond God the Father* constantly criticize his blindness to sexism at the same time as they use his sociological insights, they are mostly concerned to rescue ontological reasoning from sociological relativism. Agreeing with

McFague that it is important to recognize the cultural relativity of symbols, Daly's emphasis, nevertheless, is upon "the sense of transcendence and the surge of hope" experienced as "rooted in the power of being" by women who face honestly their non-being within existing cultures. In language still under the influence of existentialism she says, "all human hope is ontological, that is, it requires facing nothingness" (Daly 1973, 28). But for Daly the next step, accomplished through separation from that which denies your being, is the new being enabled by sisterhood with all life-affirming be-ings, i.e., it is participation in Be-ing. It is interesting that McFague—in spite of the fact that she is centrally concerned to avoid "Catholic," sacramental, symbolic, "participation" language—does not address such usages in Daly. McFague is very concerned to define her own position by contrast with efforts to revitalize religious language for contemporary minds through sacramental consciousness. She says: "The crisis is too deep for patchwork solutions, for the problem lies in our most basic sense of 'how things hold together.' That is, many of us no longer believe in a symbolic, sacramental universe in which the part stands for the whole, the things of this world 'figure' another world, and all that is is connected by a web of being" (McFague 1982, 10). Given the recurrence of this theme in McFague, one wonders why her treatment of Daly later in her book fails to address the Dalyan emphasis on "participation in Be-ing." Perhaps McFague too quickly assimilated Daly into her own generalizations about radical feminism, which she sees as characterized by unmitigated immanentalism and "exclusively feminine" sources. McFague thus ignores both the complexity of Daly's resolution of the dialectics usually called transcendence/immanence and the fact that Daly's fundamental metaphors are not "exclusively feminine." Daly proposes through her "Verb" (a gender-neutral image) an experience of transcendence through participation in something resembling McFague's rejected "web of being," wherein, for Daly, be-ings participate in Be-ing without any dichotomy between "this world" (immanence) and some "other world" (transcendence).

3. Verbing Ultimate/Intimate Reality and Meaning

When Daly first introduces the metaphor "God the Verb" in *Beyond God the Father*, it is clear that its meaning is at least partially established by what it denies; thus we will first pursue what it means to say ultimate reality is like a "verb" by noticing a kind of *via negativa* in which Daly uses this image to deny characteristics traditionally attributed to ultimate reality and meaning. Early in her work Daly forged radical feminism in part through claiming it to constitute a new way to point to transcendence by showing what it is *not:* i.e., the ultimately real can*not* be the culturally relative aspects of patriarchy which deny participation in reality to women, who are treated as objects rather than subjects of their own being. The bonding of women in terms of such awareness increases consciousness "of the limitations on thought and creativity that inbreeding of the power-holding group involves" (Daly 1973, 38). Choosing not to belong to this limited world, and realizing that they have been excluded from "the world-building processes" of humanity, women systematically doubt the pictures of reality from which their own power to predicate has been excluded. As women begin to separate themselves through such doubt, their consciousness is directed "outward and inward toward as yet unknown Being that some would call the hidden God" (Daly 1973, 38). Therefore, if "God"/"Being" has been imagined in patriarchy as *a* Being, *an* Ultimate Reality, which is separate from women's being, it becomes possible to ask "Why indeed must 'God' be a noun? Why not a verb—the most active and dynamic of all?" (Daly 1973, 33). By saying "God is a Verb," Daly dramatized the possibility that women could embrace their own "unfolding" without losing the sense of transcendent meaning, a loss which static, substantial notions of a Noun-God require.

What are the traditional characteristics of ultimate reality which Daly takes pains to deny as she explains the import of "the Verb"? First in Daly's concern is to deny that ultimate reality should be reified. Daly sees the dichotomizing reifying consciousness as deriving family from societal dualism, the primary source of which is sexism. "The dichotomizing reifying projecting syndrome has been characteristic of patriarchal consciousness, making 'the Other' the repository of the contents of the lost self" (Daly 1973, 33).

As Simone de Beauvoir made clear, women have been the recurrent victims of processes which establish meaning by separating oneself from the Other. Therefore, for a feminist to say ultimate reality is best imagined as a Verb is to stress that it is not separate from one's own being. Daly believes that the new emergence of "sororal community consciousness" in women who have become aware of the universal sexual caste system within which they do not really exist, offers "clues and intimations of the God who is without an over-against—who is Be-ing" (Daly 1973, 36).

Daly here affirms a transcendence which is not hypostatized, not "Objectified" (Daly 1973, 19). Such a denial of "wholly Other" Reality means to offset understanding ourselves in relation to either an ultimate Object which subjects us to Itself, or an ultimate Subject to which we are objects. This complete rejection of the subject-object dichotomy is reenforced by Daly's brilliant reiteration that ultimate reality is not only "the Verb," but "intransitive Verb" (see Daly 1973, 34; 1978, 23; 1984, 423). "This Verb—the Verb of Verbs—is intransitive. It need not be conceived as having an object that limits its dynamism. That which it is over against is nonbeing" (Daly 1973, 34). Ultimate Reality is, then, expressed in the hyphenated present participle "Be-ing," an intransitive verb which, in not "taking an object," is not a reified substance, but that in which all being participates.

Coordinated with this denial that reality should be imagined in a way which allows reification is Daly's specification that it *not* be thought of as "controlling" other beings (Daly 1973, 18). Inasmuch as we participate in being, we need not deny our own powers in order to affirm the Verb, Be-ing. Neither need we think of reality as "arbitrary will" other than our own (Daly 1973, 1). Even more important to re-member our own being is the denial that ultimacy is "other worldly." As Verb, reality is neither pictured as separate from this world nor as asking that it be denied for the sake of some other world (Daly 1973, 30–31).

In addition to all of these traditional ideas denied by de-reification of ultimacy, to compare reality to a verb is to say that it is not static, but changing. Only the need to deny centuries of discourse about divine immutability makes it necessary to assert that reality is process rather than stasis, since change is manifest in our experience. The visualizing of this as "Verb" rather than noun is helpful to feminist theory, which must either embrace the ultimacy of revolutionary and evolutionary change or lack ontological grounding for women's own becoming.

As Daly's thought develops "beyond" *Beyond God the Father*, she more and more wants to deny as well the traditional need to image ultimate reality in terms of a strict monism/monotheism. She becomes more sensitive to the importance of respecting a plurality of ways of participation in be-ing for women, and begins to speak of the "Powers of Being." Nevertheless, she does continue to speak of *the* Verb, explaining in an important note in *Pure Lust* the relationship between the Verb, the Goddess, and the noun 'God':

> The symbol, God as Verb, was an essential step in my intellectual process to the Metaphor, Goddess as Verb. Often feminists try to eliminate this step, with the unfortunate result that "The Goddess" functions as a static symbol, simply replacing the noun *God*. In writing *Beyond God the Father*, I also used the expression *Power of Be-ing* to refer to ultimate/intimate reality. This emphasized the Verb, but I now think that it gives less than adequate emphasis to the multiple aspects of transcendence. I therefore now use the plural, *Powers of Be-ing*.
> . . . Some feminists, with good reason, prefer to use the singular Name, *The Goddess*. Others, also with good reasons, prefer to speak of *Goddesses*. Although the latter choice is motivated by understanding of the necessity for, and fact of, multiplicity and diversity in symbols/metaphors of the Goddess, there is, it seems to me, an unresolved problem, if one ignores the principle of unity: the One. When Be-ing is understood as Verb, the focus of the discussion changes. It would be foolish to speak of "Be-ings." But women can and do speak of different Powers and manifestations of Be-ing, which are sometimes imaged as Goddesses. (Daly 1984, 423)

This important passage is useful for several reasons. It carefully applies Daly's distinction between symbol and metaphor. It also reveals clearly the primacy of "the Verb" as image in her thought, at the same time as it reveals her development toward a multivalent picture of ultimacy which denies the monism which sometimes seems to have been the central traditional characteristic of transcendence.

Daly's *via negativa* also takes pains to deny traditional ways of relating human values to ultimate reality. "Verb" imagery coordinates with her denial of the imagery of God as "judge," rejected because it tends to support the "rules and roles of the reigning system," imposing false guilt on those whose need is self-respect (Daly 1973, 31). In an explicitly *via negativa* section of *Beyond God the Father* she also denies imagining transcendent reality as an "explanatory hypothesis" with its corollary attempts through theodicy to defend "a divine plan," which "is often a front for man's plans and a cover for inadequacy, ignorance, and evils" (Daly 1973, 30).

In addition, Daly through her emphasis on the Verb denies that transcendence needs to require the traditional dichotomy between nature and history. She favors picturing transcendence as "the process of integration and transformation"; this affirmation is explained in terms of a denial that it requires one either to be a-historical because one affirms the "holiness of what is" or a-ontological because one affirms the "holiness of what ought to be" (Daly 1973, 26ff.). Insofar as patriarchal thought has suggested a need to choose between a "God" acting in historical-social processes and a "God" who is the eternal "home" to which being returns unchanged, it has failed to apprehend "the Verb." As Verb, ultimate reality is *not* either a-historical or a-ontological. As Be-ing, it is inclusive of both historical and natural development.

The traditional rational discourse by which we have noted what Daly means to deny by saying ultimate reality is a Verb has implied much that she means to construct through this metaphor by an affirmative path. Nevertheless, she does communicate additional meanings through "the Verb" beyond that which is denied by saying "not a noun." The central affirmation in the image is that reality is ultimately dynamic, active, transforming Powers of Be-ing, shared in by all organically unfolding natural processes (Daly 1973, 33–34; 1984, 87; 1985a, xiv). In various places Daly characterizes Be-ing as "creative," "unfolding," and transformative—emphasizing its capacity for "metamorphoses" and movement toward new forms. It is interesting that even in the first edition of *The Church and the Second Sex*, i.e., before her "qualitative leap beyond patriarchal religion," her keenest theological interest was in questioning the traditional idea of immutability and its corollary, the "static worldview" (Daly 1968, 180ff.).

But Daly wants to affirm more than that reality is changing and open to change. She pictures it as purposive; increasingly she develops this through embracing "final causality" as apprehended by ontological reason.

> I suggest that the rejection of ontological final causality . . . has often really been a kind of metaphysical rebellion, even on the part of those philosophers who have been most disdainful of metaphysics. It has been an effort to overthrow the tyranny of the allegedly "supernatural end" that seemed to block the dynamics

> of thought and action. But this "block" was often a shadow and reified conception of the final cause. When those doing the rejecting have had no deep awareness of the dynamism in being, that is of the ontological force of final causality, the reified Block has not wholly disappeared. It has tended to reappear in various ways. (Daly 1973, 186–87)

Final causality as an aspect of ultimate reality is best developed through Daly's picture of ultimate meaning as "verbing." She speaks of the "profound meaning of final causality" as the "unfolding" of be-ing." "The inspiring, moving reality of final causality—the centralizing force/focus within the Self and within all be-ing—is spirit-force. This becomes inaccessible, or 'out of sight,' when the spiritual/philosophical imagination is dried up and reasoning banalized, routinized, reduced to the elementary realm" (Daly 1984, 155).

Such affirmation of purpose in Be-ing draws out also the fact that as Verb, Reality is "connecting," "communicating," "cosmic" process (Daly 1975b, 207; 1984, 30). "Today, in the light of feminist philosophy of Being, we are aware of the deep connection between women's becoming and the unfolding of cosmic process which some would still call 'God' " (Daly 1975a, 18).

When discussing her disagreement with religious reformers, Daly claims that, nevertheless, feminists who are religious, both reformers and revolutionaries, tend to have in common "a sense of becoming in cosmic process" (Daly 1975b, 207). To have a sense of "cosmos" is to apprehend a "world order" rather than ultimate absurdity.

Daly admits early in her usage of "the Verb" that she is not alone in emphasizing "process" as the key image of reality. She discusses not only Tillich, but also Whitehead and Bergson. Nevertheless, her work aims to "speak the dynamics of women's experience" rather than to work extensively with "prefabricated molds" (Daly 1973, 37). Moreover she questions why such thinkers never addressed the oppression of women.

In saying ultimate reality is like a verb, Daly does not mean to rule out affirming it as "personal," although she clearly wants to rule out any anthropomorphism. When she first introduced the metaphor, she clearly expected to be criticized for losing the sense of "God as Person." She argued that only the reifying consciousness needs "to anthropomorphize or to reify transcendence in order to relate to this personally" and asked: "is not the Verb infinitely more personal than a mere static noun?" (Daly

1973, 33; see also 1975b, 205). Daly continues to characterize be-ing in relation to Be-ing in terms of "depth," as well as to speak of it as "spiritual" and, occasionally, "personal." Although her emphasis is clearly not on what might be called the "one on one" personal relation to the divine, she still does adopt personal address to ultimacy as a possible feminist mode, as in the dedication to *Pure Lust*,

> To the Spirit
> who lives and breathes
> in all Elemental be-ing

which in subsequent stanzas addresses the Verb through two personified images: "the Lady of Words of Power" manifest in goddesses, and "the Muse in Metamorphosing women" (Daly 1984, v).

Whenever Daly uses "spirit/spiritual" to affirm aspects of Being, she, like many other feminist theologians, is careful to insist that affirmation of the spiritual does not deny the ultimate reality of the material/physical. "Several meanings of the word *Elemental* converge for the conjuring of Elemental feminist philosophy. An 'obsolete' definition is 'material, physical.' The philosophy here unfolded is material/physical as well as spiritual, mending/transcending this deceptive dichotomy" (Daly 1984, 7).

The most dramatic evidence thus far of Daly's affirmation of an image of ultimate reality which is both spiritual and physical is her discussion of "physical ultimacy" in *Pure Lust*. Not only does her orientation want to affirm both sense experience and the physical aspects of our humanity, she wants to talk of "physical ultimacy" in order to emphasize our capacity for connections which are ultimate in the sense of "farthest," "extreme," indeed "to the farthest stars." "Physical ultimacy suggests the possibility of relations with others as well as with one's Self that are far-reaching, demanding that we stretch our physical, imaginative, psychic powers beyond the limitations that have been imposed upon them" (Daly 1984, 80). Within such affirmation of the physical and spiritual she speaks of "ultimate intimacy."

In *Pure Lust* Daly invents a new word/image for Metabeing in a section which sums up much that has been indicated affirmatively about the significance of "the Verb": she speaks of the *Archimage* (to be pronounced so as to rhyme with *rage* and to be distinguished from her use of the same word with the "regular" pronunciation for the figure of Mary in the Christian tradition).

> Lusty women can reclaim the name *Archimage*, Naming the fact that she is the Witch within our Selves. She is a verb, and she is verbal—a Namer, a Speaker—the Power within who can Name away the archetypes that block the ways/words of Metabeing.
>
> Archimage is a Metaphoric form of Naming the one and the many. She is power/powers of be-ing within women and all biophilic creatures. She points toward Metabeing, in which all Witches/Hags/Weirds participate, and in which we live, move, and have our be-ing. (Daly 1984, 86–87)

In subsequent paragraphs Daly develops the meaning of Archimage as "Active Potency" in terms of transformative power, healing, and natural connectiveness. Woven together in the above quotation are the three concrete images which I am arguing constitute a kind of trinity expressing Daly's ultimate concern. She explains the meaning of her new coinage (Archimage) by relying upon something more familiar/concrete to her readers, that is, the meaning of the word "verb," to say something about that which is less known. As Reality, Archimage is "verb"/Power/powers of Be-ing. As Meaning, she is "verbing"/participation in be-ing. As Method for realization, she is "verbal"/a Namer, a Speaker.

In *Pure Lust* Daly highlights the ontological concern which I have argued is fundamental to her view of feminist meaning by Naming three "metamorphospheres" by the hyphenated participles: Be-Longing, Be-Friending, and Be-Witching. In each case, the words not only cut away from patriarchal connotations, they cut toward new affirmations, each of which through the prefix indicates "the ontological Lust" which enables participation in Be-ing. In all of this Daly seeks a way beyond the culturally conditioned splits, dichotomies, dualisms, and skepticisms which polarize the self and the world, the individual and the community, the social and the cosmic, history and nature, material and spiritual, passion and reason, etc.

4. The "Verb" and the Dialectics of Transcendence/Immanence

One of the dialectics of existence which has been dichotomized at certain points in Western traditions is indicated by debates over the transcendence and/or immanence of ultimate reality and meaning. Daly's talk of "ultimate/intimate Reality" provides imagery aimed to prevent this dichotomy between that which is "far" and that which is "near." By "writing/verbing" (Daly 1978, 22) Daly aims to stimulate "women and other biophilic creatures" to respond to their own original call in "all ways, now, to Be" (Daly 1984, 411), so as to make ultimacy intimate. Power/s of Be-ing, therefore, must be pictured as wed to our own powers of being, rather than as a separated transcendent potency. Such picturing is accomplished, I would argue, through the primacy of verb/verbing/verbalizing imagery which denies reification to Be-ing. When Daly utilizes Goddess-talk or personal pronouns to invoke "Archimage," her concern is to express a positive relation to that which is not simply one's own in the "power/s of Be-ing"; at the same time, such feminine imagery enables women to find this ultimate "beyond-the-self"/transcendent source intimately woven in their own being.

Feminist theology characteristically joins some other contemporary theologies in seeking ways to embrace the earthly/worldly/bodily aspects of being which were identified with the feminine and devalued in most traditions. Like Daly, many others see the recovery of immanence as essential if we are to overcome what she powerfully analyzes as the "sado-masochistic syndrome" which is manifest in suicidal/necrophilic nuclearism. Indeed some powerful feminists, like Starhawk, argue for a "religion of immanence." Starhawk urges us to choose an attitude by which our human quest for meaning "remains here" (*immanere*): "I am talking about choosing an attitude: choosing to take this world, the people and creatures on it, as the ultimate meaning and purpose of life, to see the world, the earth, and our lives as sacred" (Starhawk 1982, 11).

For Starhawk the 'normative image of immanence' is "the Goddess" (Starhawk 1982, 9). Rosemary Radford Ruether, usually classified as a reformer rather than with Daly or Starhawk as a revolutionary feminist, prefers the written symbol "God/ess," but in recent works still uses feminine pronouns to invoke the "Holy One" and often manifests comparable concerns for immanence. Indeed her historical studies prepared the way for feminist diagnosis of the dualisms/dichotomies of patriarchal consciousness. Ruether criticizes all "world-fleeing agendas" and seeks images by which "we discover the blessedness and holy being within the mortal limits of covenantal existence. This is the Shalom of God that remains the real connecting point of all our existence, even when we forget and violate it. Redemptive hope is the constant recovery of that Shalom of

God/ess that holds us all together, as the operative principle of our collective lives" (Ruether 1983, 256).

I want to suggest that Daly's position with regard to transcendence/immanence has been oversimplified and mis-classified by McFague. As we have noted, McFague treats Daly together with other "radical"/"revolutionary" thinkers like Starhawk as emphasizing immanence (as well as goddess imagery). But there are aspects of Daly which do not square simply either with Starhawk's earth-Goddess religion of immanence or with Ruether's recovery of Hebraic prophetic life-affirmation, in spite of the fact that all three share a concern that we recover the ultimate significance of this life/this world/our powers.

Starhawk's decision to call for a 'religion of immanence' means that she avoids any use of "transcendence." Nevertheless, she does not identify only human powers as sources of meaning; her affirmation of religious connection to the resources of nature/Earth apprehends meanings which some would consider "transcendence." Nevertheless, Starhawk suggests that we deal with death's threat to meaning by placing confidence in the cyclical rhythms of nature; she asks for no meaning beyond Gaia/Earth, causing one to wonder how to ask about ultimate meaning beyond the death of this solar system.

On the other hand, "transcendence" is a term which characterizes Daly's vocabulary much more than "immanence." In *Beyond God the Father* her well-known argument for the continued relevance of "God-talk" emphasizes our relation to transcendence by saying, "we have no power over the ultimately real," and that our authentic power derives from "participation in ultimate reality." The importance of "God" is to maintain awareness of such transcendence so that we do not become idolatrously fixated "upon limited objectives." In the important article of 1975, her language changes as well as her emphasis: "the 'self-transcending immanence,' the sense of giving birth to ourselves, the sense of power of being within, which is being affirmed by many women, does not seem to be denoted, imaged adequately pointed to, or perhaps even associated with the term 'God' " (Daly 1975b, 208).

During the period of *Gyn/Ecology* (1978) transcendence still means to Daly the power of "integration and transformation" identified in *Beyond God the Father*, but there is more emphasis on the sources of transformation "within." It is interesting that McFague's analysis of Daly was developed on the basis of *Gyn/Ecology*, before *Pure Lust* (1984) was available. Nevertheless, even in *Gyn/Ecology*, Daly argues for "hearing forth cosmic tapestries, remembering the Original creation of the Goddess," making it clear that the "within" is neither a disconnected subjectivity nor isolated will power. She still calls for "successive acts of transcendence and Gyn/Ecological creation," although the "metaethical" project of this particular book leads to an emphasis on our powers "to spin" meaning more than we will find in *Pure Lust*'s re-emphasis of ontological participation in meaning (Daly 1978, 414ff.). In the Preface to *Pure Lust* she identifies her orientation as "metapatriarchal consciousness" which is concerned for "elemental participation in Be-ing. Our passion is for that which is most intimate and most ultimate, for depth and transcendence, for recalling original wholeness" (Daly 1984, ix).

We have seen that "transcendence" is peculiarly important to Daly to indicate that ontological grounding liberates transformative activity. We have noticed her discussion of the primacy of "the Verb" image as a resolution of the traditional problem of "the one and the many." This root-metaphor also resolves the tension between transcendence and immanence. If reality is dynamic, active process, one's own active potency is not "other than" it so much as "participation in" it.

Nevertheless, there are aspects of the traditional dialectics between transcendence and immanence that reformers like McFague and Ruether would find it important to preserve. While Daly's usages, in speaking of transcendence as the Verb, preserve the religious sense of meaningful connection to sources/realities not simply identical with the self, her "ontological lust" in later work leads her to deny the importance of correlating transcendence/immanence with infinite/finite. The biblical emphasis, with which McFague and Ruether agree, is to express the dialectics of human existence, rather than to claim knowledge of Being Itself. This emphasis stresses an awareness of the finitude of all human meanings and powers, an emphasis which decreases in Daly's apprehension of transcendence after *Beyond God the Father*. By the time of *Pure Lust* Daly is explicit in criticizing thinkers like Tillich whose thought originates in the questions arising from finitude or "possible nonbeing" (Daly 1984, 29). She has not yet really addressed the need for a perspective on death and seems to identify such concerns with unnatural necrophilia which is alien to "women and other biophilic creatures."

One of Ruether's real accomplishments in *Sexism and God-Talk* is a feminist perspective on eschatology, i.e., on ultimate or last things. Her chapter on "Eschatology and Feminism" contains the affirmation of mortal existence; it joins Daly and Starhawk in calling for "immanence," i.e., for "remaining here" in confidence that our responsibility for human meaning is to be realized here through social, political, and ecological activities. But she also characteristically joins McFague in emphasizing the dangers of an idolatrous equation of human knowledge with the ultimate. Indeed, Ruether goes beyond McFague's more epistemological concern to existential expression of a religious sense of finitude: "We can do nothing about the 'immortal' dimension of our lives. It is not our calling to be concerned about the eternal meaning of our lives . . . Our responsibility is to use our temporal life span to create a just and good community for our generations and for our children. It is in the hands of Holy Wisdom to forge out of our finite struggle truth and being for everlasting life. Our agnosticism about what this means is then the expression of our faith, our trust that Holy Wisdom will give transcendent meaning to our work, which is bounded by space and time" (Ruether 1983, 258).

Other feminist theologians are also beginning to express the need for reflective biophilic creatures to think about their finitude, at the same time as they affirm their "infinitude," their freedom and powers of be-ing (see Gross 1986, as well as Berry 1978).

It is interesting to me that Daly's own hope has been expressed in terms of a faith in transcendence which separates her emphasis from that of Starhawk. At the end of the 1985 "Original Reintroduction" to *Beyond God the Father* she quotes the last lines of the book's first edition with its invocation "of the Good Who is self-communicating Be-ing, Who is the Verb from whom, in whom, and with whom all true movements move." Then she goes on to conclude: "The Journey can and does continue because the Verb continues—from whom, in whom, and with whom all true movements move" (Daly 1985b, xxix and 198).

This line can lead me to a conclusion which is a new beginning. In it we find a poetic affirmation of a religious resolution of immanence/transcendence which pervades not only Daly's writing, but other feminists, and which derives from traditional liturgy. The biblical source is Paul's speech on the Areopagus in Acts 17, 27–28. In the context of his discussion of the Athenian shrine to the Unknown God, Paul presents a line from a Greek poet in order to affirm universal divine activity in nature and history: "Yet he is not far from each one of us, for 'In him we live and move and have our being" (Revised Standard Version). In Augustine as well as in traditional liturgies, the line becomes a prayer, by taking the form of personal address. In Book VIII of his *Confessions*, Augustine says, "it is in you that we live and move and have our being."

In the Anglican Service of Morning Prayer, the "Collect for Guidance" opens, "O heavenly Father, in whom we live and move and have our being." The rhythm of this traditional phrase recurs at important moments in a number of Daly's evocative passages, some of which have been quoted earlier. An example of this early in *Beyond God the Father* is: "Women now who are experiencing the shock of nonbeing and the surge of self-affirmation against this are inclined to perceive transcendence as the Verb in which we participate—live, move, and have our being" (Daly 1985b, 34).

This same language is used in *Pure Lust* in speaking of Archimage as metaphor of Metabeing in which feminists "participate, and in which we live, move, and have our being" (Daly 1984, 87). It is interesting to find that Ruether also ends her central work with an invocation of the Holy expressed in the same rhythmic line: "The Shalom of the Holy; the disclosure of the gracious *Shekinah*; Divine Wisdom; the empowering Matrix; She, in whom we live and move and have our being—She comes; She is here" (Ruether 1983, 266).

By the feminine pronoun Ruether here makes explicit what was always present in the imagery and may account for the religious power of the ancient line: the expression of faith in transcendence through mother-imagery. The mother, after all, is the parent "in whom" we, for a time, literally "have our being." While feminists like Ruether and McFague question parental imagery which stresses only dependency, they agree with the tradition that such imagery has value to express relation to a creative source beyond one's own self. At the same time, such theologians agree with Daly in affirming the importance of taking responsibility for active companionship in divine activity (see McFague 1982, 177ff., and Ruether 1983, 68ff.). Daly's recurrent conjunction of "the Verb" with this traditional line is a beautiful refutation of any oversimplification either of her use of imagery or of her resolution of transcendence/immanence. She continues to function in terms of a gender-neutral root-metaphor for ultimate reality: the Verb. She continues to call for ultimate meaning to be accomplished immanently through our "verb-ing." And she continues to "verbalize" all this methodically and effectively. However, the next step in feminist reflection which some of us would ask her to consider would involve finding a gynecological, woman-and-life-affirming way to formulate not only our participation in Power/s-of-Being, but our experienced limitations. We need not only the challenge to be-ing, but also forgiveness when we fail in this task. Perhaps some further explication of Daly's trust that "the Journey can and does continue, because the Verb continues" will find a biophilic way to "verbalize" our finitude as well as our infinitude.

References

Berry, W. W. 1978. "Images of Sin and Salvation in Feminist Theology." *Anglican Theological Review*. 60:25–54.

Christ, C. P. and J. Plaskow, eds. 1979. *Womanspirit Rising: A Feminist Reader in Religion*. San Francisco: Harper and Row.

Daly, M. 1968. *The Church and the Second Sex*. Boston: Beacon Press.

———. 1973. *Beyond God the Father: Toward a Philosophy of Women's Liberation*. Boston: Beacon Press.

———. 1975a. *The Church and the Second Sex. With the Feminist Postchristian Introduction by the Author*. Boston: Beacon Press.

———. 1975b. "The Qualitative Leap Beyond Patriarchal Religion." *Women and Values*, edited by M. Pearsall, 198–210. Belmont, Calif.: Wadsworth Publishing Co.

———. 1978. *Gyn/Ecology. The Metaethics of Radical Feminism*. Boston: Beacon Press.

———. 1984. *Pure Lust. Elemental Feminist Philosophy*. Boston: Beacon Press.

———. 1985a. *The Church and the Second Sex. With the Feminist Postchristian Introduction and New Archaic Afterwords by the Author*. Boston: Beacon Press.

———. 1985b. *Beyond God the Father. Toward a Philosophy of Women's Liberation: With an Original Reintroduction by the Author*. Boston: Beacon Press.

———. 1987. *Websters' First New Intergalactic Wickedary of the English Language*. Boston: Beacon Press.

Gross, R. 1986. "Suffering, Feminist Theory, and Images of the Goddess." *Anima*. 13:39–46.

Jaggar, A. M., and Paula A. Struhl, eds. 1978. *Feminist Frameworks: Alternative Theoretical Accounts of the Relations Between Women and Men*. New York: McGraw-Hill.

McFague, S. 1982. *Metaphorical Theology: Models of God in Religious Language*. Philadelphia: Fortress Press.

Ruether, R. R. 1983. *Sexism and God-Talk: Toward a Feminist Theology*. Boston: Beacon Press.

Starhawk. 1982. *Dreaming the Dark: Magic, Sex and Politics*. Boston: Beacon Press.

2

The Courage to See and to Sin: Mary Daly's Elemental Transformation of Paul Tillich's Ontology

Laurel C. Schneider

Mary Daly is a student of Paul Tillich in the profound sense that her work has been influenced and informed by his. The growing scope and depth of her thinking is due in no small part to Tillich's pathbreaking analysis and vision of culture, symbol, existentialism, and ontology. Daly's use of Tillich as a "springboard" for her postchristian feminist philosophy[1] also entails a profound and invaluable critique of the limitations and distortions embedded in his thinking.

Few students of contemporary theology identify Daly in terms of her reliance upon and contributions to the fields of systematic theology or philosophy. Most often, her name is invoked as the delimitation of "radical" in relation to whatever view is in question, regardless of the applicability of the comparison or appropriateness of the categorization.[2] In what follows, I shall examine some of the similarities and differences between Tillich's and Daly's methods. I shall identify several of Tillich's central theological concepts that Daly has accepted, developed, and in some cases, moved beyond. Finally, I shall suggest that the radical aspect of Daly's work lies not in her rejection of the Western epistemological and theological traditions but in her creative and critical use of these traditions to begin building a systematic project.[3]

For the purpose of this study, I have made use of Tillich's *Systematic Theology* and his *The Courage to Be* not because they are exhaustively representative of his thought, but because they appear to be the writings most closely related to Daly's work. Mary Daly's thought develops through the course of her writing, and it is perhaps appropriate from a psychological standpoint to treat all of her books, even though she herself has gently distanced herself from the first, *The Church and the Second Sex*, claiming it to be the work of a "foresister whose work is an essential source and to whom I am indebted but with whom I largely disagree."[4] I agree with Daly that this first book differs fundamentally in character from her later works, and I will not refer to it here.

Method

Paul Tillich wrote in an era of growing religious skepticism and popular faith in what Daly calls contemporary secular theology.[5] In his work he seeks to bring estranged culture back into the "theological circle" by treating the questions he perceives as fundamental to all humans (to whom he refers as men). In *Systematic Theology* Tillich employs the "method of correlation." In his words, this method "makes an analysis of the human situation out of which the existential questions arise, and it demonstrates that the symbols used in the Christian message are the answers to these questions."[6] In using this method, Tillich hopes to maintain a transcendent integrity in his theological answers yet link them effectively to existential questions.

The existential question that precipitates out of his analysis of the human situation is "man himself." Being, or rather the "shock of nonbeing," is what causes "man" to ask the existential question of "himself."[7] The theological answer, in brief, is that Christ is the manifestation of "New Being," the one who reassures "man" that there is meaning in existence. Thus (in grossly oversimplified terms) Tillich claims to correlate theological answers with existential questions.

The method of correlation is not so much a means by which Tillich attaches theological answers to questions he deems universal, but a means by which he argues for the complete *interdependence* of god-answers (being-itself) and human questions (being or nonbeing). Tillich acknowledges that the method of correlation is itself a "theological assertion."[8]

Mary Ann Stenger has made a convincing argument that in *Beyond God the Father* at least, Daly appropriates Tillich's method of correlation and some of his central theological terms. She notes correctly that Daly extracts existential questions of being from the real-life location of women in patriarchal cultures.[9] Daly argues in *Beyond God the Father*, for example, that the question of transcendence is critical for women seeking ways of overcoming present oppression. In addition, the question of courage in the face of patriarchal alienation and New Being as a goal of feminism constitute ultimate concerns distilled from the experience of patriarchy.[10] It is quite true that Daly's propositions of women "be-coming" are meaningless apart from her in-depth critique of patriarchal influences, institutions, and distortions.

Stenger is critical of Daly's appropriation of the method of correlation, citing her "tendency to absolutize the feminist experience of becoming in her move beyond patriarchal religion."[11] This criticism is one expression of the most common argument against Mary Daly's work. The fear of feminist absolutization represents a concern that feminist claims constitute a new authoritarianism in drag. The concern is in part a good one, in part obfuscating—it is tempting and dangerous to project a simple reversal of power without deep critical analysis of the nature of power in patriarchy. To suggest that Daly does so is to ignore the depth of her analysis. It is worth asking whether feminism in its broadest sense could possibly result in a simple reversal of power when one of its central critiques, shared across (and within) the feminist spectrum of cultures and communities, concerns the nature and articulation of power itself. Feminist scholars, however, spend an inordinate amount of time dealing with this question.

It is true that Daly is not willing to deconstruct her own (and other feminist women's) experiences of marginality far enough to be able to make judgments about shared aspects and differences in feminist experience. Throughout her work, the idea of the experience of oppression as *informative* and therefore authoritative in the sense of *real* needs to be carefully distinguished from the idea of oppression as normative. The former allows the experience of oppression to be taken as valid enough for revolt and for transformation, without turning the experience of oppression into a new domination that erases differences between women. The latter suggests a flat grammar of experience that equates femaleness with oppression, eliminating any philosophical foundations for liberation, and hence any foundations for Daly's ultimate goals. The idea that oppression is normative is, Daly might argue, a phallacy of the victim, and she is decidedly not interested in victims who valorize (and hence want to remain in) their position. It also erases complex distortions that occur between women by making their experiences all functionally the same, hence privileging those most in the position to name and make their experiences known. Women's various experiences of oppression as information, on the other hand, provide a foundation for critique and for transformation rooted in an elemental existence that, she believes, is prior to patriarchal distortion. Theoretically, this is an idea that has room for all of the variety of women's voices, cultures (what Daly calls tribes), and experiences without entirely relinquishing a political and social ontology regarding the status of woman. There is room for infinite variety, except for those (fembots) who flatly deny or wholly collude with the oppressive erasures of patriarchy.

Daly is something of a latter-day Gnostic, insisting not only that feminist vision reveals the ugly fabrications and fallacies (phallacies) of patriarchal domination, but also, and more so, that this knowledge is itself powerful and revolutionary. The special knowledge that women hold is their own experience, authoritative not only in that it need not be authenticated by external, male-dominated norms, but also in that it is cultivated from the peculiarly insightful position of the margin. Like Sandra Harding, Daly believes that standpoint epistemologies, especially from the margin, are more comprehensive and therefore more reliably descriptive.[12] For this reason, they cannot congratulate themselves for perceiving a hidden text when they claim that Daly absolutizes feminist experience, because Daly has already clearly expressed this "preferential option" for them.[13] Daly taps feminist women as the bearers of New Being (*Beyond God the Father*) and of MetaBe-ing (*Pure Lust*) because of their boundary perspective. She distances her work from Tillich's notion of "working on the boundary between philosophy and theology. The work [of *Beyond God the Father*] is not merely on the boundary *between* these (male-created) disciplines, but on the boundary *of* both (because it speaks out of the experience of that half of the human species which has been represented in neither discipline)."[14]

Daly does not explicitly claim to be using the method of correlation, and she is suspicious of arguments that are too concerned with issues of method. She warns against "methodolatry," arguing that "it commonly happens that the choice of a problem is determined by method, instead of method being determined by the problem."[15] Stenger does note that Daly's work is not without method altogether. She bases her criticism, however, on the assumption that Daly is agreeing to operate with a single method, and that a unitary method is essential to the work of systematic theology or philosophy.

Daly's work is not without method, but it is easy to overlook the extent to which method discernible in Daly can be characterized as *movement*.[16] In *Beyond God the Father*, a book in which Daly's reliance on Tillich is far stronger than in her later works, a method of correlation is arguably present, even though Daly herself prefers to call it a "method of liberation."[17] *Gyn/Ecology*, *Pure Lust* and even *Outercourse* build upon the work of *Beyond God the Father* and chart distinct courses that seek biophilic new "Metabeing" in the context of (and therefore correlated to) the culture and tradition of patriarchy.

The method discernible in Daly's work is similar to that found in Tillich's *Systematic Theology*. Part of the limitation of Stenger's criticism of Daly lies in her own apparently uncritical acceptance of Tillich's absolutized universal "human" existential dilemma over Daly's explicit discussion of *feminist* insight.[18] Stenger clearly regards Tillich's discussion of human ultimate concerns as more careful and less essentializing than Daly's discussion of the ultimate concerns of women who have identified patriarchy as the root oppression in society. But Tillich's use of the more universal term "human" does not necessarily give more universal meaning to his text. Daly acknowledges that "Tillich's way of speaking about God as ground and power of being would be very difficult to use for the legitimation of any sort of oppression,"[19] but she also argues that "if God-language is even implicitly compatible with oppressiveness, failing to make clear the relation between intellection and liberation, then it will either have to be developed in such a way that it becomes explicitly relevant to the problem of sexism or else dismissed."[20]

Both Paul Tillich and Mary Daly find the methods of classical theology insufficient for explaining and dealing with the evils and the possibilities of contemporary life. Both make use of philosophy, sociology, psychology, and other secular theologies to chart a course toward a better, more whole, and healed existence. Tillich sees an anthropocentric "New Being," Daly a biophilic cosmic one, but both see all of culture as source and resource for revelation. *What* is revealed turns out to be rather different, depending on whether the presupposition is christocentric or biophilic-feminist. If a method of correlation is common to both thinkers, it is the deductive correlation of the preferred option (Christ, for Tillich; biophilic be-ing, for Daly) with the perceived data and means of culture (post-Enlightenment, existentialist "man" and "his" desires and anxieties for Tillich; patriarchal culture and its boundary representatives—feminist women—for Daly). I suggest that neither truly starts with analysis of culture and ends with theological answers. Both have answers in mind when they ask the questions, both presuppose a path of hope for those who perceive the anxieties/oppressions of contemporary life, namely systematic New Being/elemental Metabe-ing.

Theological Issues: The Power of Being-Itself and of Be-ing

One of the primary theological concepts in both Tillich and Daly is the notion of being. Tillich orients his entire corpus around the claim that "our ultimate concern is that which determines our being or not-being. Only those statements are theological which deal with their object in so far as it can become a matter of being or not-being for us."[21] Daly fundamentally agrees with Tillich, although her thinking changes across the course of her work. In *Beyond God the Father,* she sees Tillich's notion of being-itself as essentially static but accepts the ontological category as the best descriptive metaphor for transcendence.[22] Being-itself by itself is detached, abstract, and uncritical of the oppression of patriarchy. Daly's solution in *Beyond God the Father* is to cast being-itself into motion as a verb, as Be-ing.

Tillich developed the concept of being-itself as metaphor for God partly out of profound respect for the power of symbols. Foreshadowing feminist critiques of patriarchal theology, he wrote that "if a segment of reality is used as a symbol for God, the realm of reality from which it is taken is, so to speak, elevated into the realm of the holy. . . . If God is called the 'king,' something is said not only about God but also about the holy character of Kinghood."[23] Tillich's words are echoed in Daly's famous line "If God is male, then the male is God."[24]

Despite this similarity, there is a deeper divergence. Tillich stops short of offering a critique of the appropriateness of kinghood as a symbol for God. More important, his critique cannot speak to the ramifications of holy kinghood in contemporary society. Daly takes that extra step. The impact of theological systems on the organization of power in society is central to her entire program. If God is called Male, then something is said not only about God but also about the holy privilege of maleness. Daly sees quite clearly that there is more than coincidence in the relation between the maleness of God and the rapacious stature and power of males in history. Tillich opens the door, Daly takes the lead. "It is true that Tillich *tries* to avoid hypostatization of 'God' (though the effort is not completely successful) and that his manner of speaking about the ground and power of being would be difficult to use for the legitimation of any sort of oppression. However, the specific relevance of 'power of being' to the fact of sexual oppression is not indicated. Moreover, just as his discussion of God is detached, so is the rest of his theology."[25]

By casting "transcendent reality" into motion as the verb be-ing, Daly hopes to avoid hypostatization of "God" and affirm the "Verb in which we participate—live, move and have our be-ing."[26] In *Beyond God the Father* she refers to God as verb ("the Verb of Verbs") but by the time of *Pure Lust,* she does not speak of God at all, but only of Verb.[27] Like Tillich, she recognizes that the logical end of the deconstruction of god-talk is the awareness that, as Tillich puts it, "the truth of a religious symbol has nothing to do with the truth of the empirical assertions involved in it."[28]

Daly moves into her radical systematic program by warning that "Be-ing, the Verb, cannot without gross falsification be reified into a noun, whether that noun be identified as 'Supreme Being' or 'God,' or 'Goddess' (singular or plural)." Having recognized the vast historical potency of the reified metaphor "God" in both *Beyond God the Father* and *Gyn/Ecology*, Daly continues sparing use of the term "Goddess" (which she capitalizes in contrast to the patriarchal "god") in *Pure Lust* as metaphor for "the Powers of Be-ing, the Active Verb in whose potency all biophilic reality participates."[29] In acknowledgment of diversity within feminist consciousness and becoming, Daly also alters Tillich's power of being to the plural Powers of Be-ing.

Non-Being

According to Tillich, Socrates made it clear "that the courage to die is the test of the courage to be."[30] Non-being is the threat before all that has being. Awareness of this threat results in fundamental anxiety against which profound courage, and ultimately the Christ event, is required. Ultimate concern, or anxiety, "expresses the awareness of being finite, of being a mixture of being and non-being, or of being threatened by non-being."[31]

Daly fully accepts non-being and the consequent necessity of courage in the face of "the shock of non-being" as appropriate to feminist theological work. The meaning that Daly gives to non-being, however, is quite different and more specific than that given by Tillich. She finds it essential to place non-being squarely within the experience of structural evil and the oppression of women under patriarchy. Non-being as an amorphous existential fear of finitude is a particularly privileged, and one might suggest spoiled, anxiety.

True non-being, Daly suggests, is the alienation and degradation of women inherent in oppressive social, political, and economic structures. The critical existential conflict, she asserts, is not between the self and abstracted nothingness, but "between the self and the structures that have given such crippling security. *This* requires confronting the shock of non-being with the courage to be."[32]

The clear concern with existentialism and security betray Daly's early uncritical elitism in *Beyond God the Father*. Critical supporters such as Audre Lorde challenged Daly on her assumptions of essential feminist concerns and her lack of explicit acknowledgments of difference based on race and class experiences.[33] *Pure Lust* attempts a greater inclusivity and demonstrates a heightened awareness of difference. Perhaps in part as a result of her struggle to continue to speak with a *feminist* (albeit still white feminist) voice while attempting to account for difference in her philosophical conceptualization of biophilic woman, Daly began to suspect that "the questions [of non-being, or finitude] have been framed/confined within parameters that fail to express biophilic intuitions."[34] She cites Tillich's question "Why is there something, why not nothing?" as a particularly insidious example of patriarchal fascination with death. Equating "phallicism" with necrophilia, she suggests that Tillich's conflation of two quite different questions is one example of the way that biophilic thinking can be undermined.

> A wonderlusty woman might imagine that the question thus posed corresponds to her own ontological experience, to her Lust for Be-ing. She might imagine that the ontological question thus posed expresses an attitude identical to her own Wonder and gratitude that things *are*. Caught up in this Wonder, she might fail to notice anything suspect about the second half of Tillich's question: "why not nothing?" Musing women would do well to ask ourSelves whether this question would arise spontaneously in biophilic consciousness.[35]

The question of non-being for Daly develops across her work. She begins by accepting Tillich's idea that "all human beings are threatened by non-being" but suggests that he misunderstands the location of non-being in human life. She places non-being in a liberationist framework. It refers not to the bored pathos of the privileged male who suddenly realizes that he is not omnipotent, but to the crushed nothingness of women written out of existence altogether. The "shock of non-being" is the woman waking up to the awful reality of her mutilated life.

Women's non-being in patriarchal culture is so deep and vast that Daly ended up devoting an entire volume to it. The title, introduction, structure, and conclusion of *Gyn/Ecology* indicate an intention on Daly's part to write of "exorcism and ecstasy"—a glimpse into a postpatriarchal ethical system. However, the content of women's non-being overtakes the book. Perhaps because she accepted non-being as an essential category of Be-ing in *Beyond God the Father*, Daly could not escape the numbing totality of women's non-being when she moved on to ethics. She attempts to deal with this problem early in *Pure Lust* by raising the question of the appropriateness of non-being as a *necessary* opposition to Be-ing. Daly calls her suspicion biophilic intuition and suggests that the profound philosophical depth of the question "Why is there something?" is not appropriately completed by "Why not nothing?" Her revisionist stance thereby transforms into a critique of non-being itself as the necrophilic fascination of patriarchal "sado-spirituality."

Non-being, in Daly's feminist theological system, is finally of value only to the extent that it describes the ontological consequences of patriarchal oppression. The courage to be in the face of non-being is "women's confrontation with the structural evil of patriarchy."[36] Women numbed by patriarchal degradation to the point of acquiescence participate in non-being. Men and male institutions in patriarchal society, we might go so far as to say, are the bearers of non-being.

Courage

Courage is a crucial concept both to Tillich and to Daly. Tillich begins his book *The Courage to Be* with the statement that "few concepts are as useful for the analysis of the human situation. Courage is an ethical reality, but it is rooted in the whole breadth of human existence and ultimately in the structure of being itself."[37] Courage is the human response to the threat of non-being. It is the only positive human response possible. Taking into account the differences in their understandings of non-being, Daly fully agrees. To *be* in the face of patriarchal annihilation is an act of true courage.

Once again a notion originating with Tillich follows the transforming and deepening course of Daly's thinking. In *Beyond God the Father* Daly sees courage perhaps more simplistically than does Tillich. Where Tillich presents courage as an ontological stance, Daly initially sees it more as the bravery of a woman willing to attempt to break out of societal norms, willing to "emerge into a world without models."[38] "Courage," Tillich argued, "needs the power of being."[39] In *Beyond God the Father* Daly implies more simply that the power of being requires courage. She claims that the "courage to be is the key to the revelatory power of the feminist revolution."

The fact that Daly wrote *Gyn/Ecology* after *Beyond God the Father* makes sense in this light. If the Powers of Be-ing require courage because of the death-dealing grip of patriarchy on every woman, then *Gyn/Ecology* as an exposé on the horrors of patriarchy is an expression of this courage and a necessary step in Daly's evolution toward her more ontological understanding of courage in *Pure Lust*.

Tillich sees the courage to be as more than bravery. He argues that the "ethical question of the nature of courage" is one way of asking the ontological question of the nature of being, and involves a profound self-affirmation as well as risk. Daly only fully develops the implications of this insight for feminist systematics in *Pure Lust*. Having identified non-being as the structural evil of patriarchy, she begins to see the nature of courage in a feminist sense as a profound identification with whatever is "not" in patriarchal society. To do so requires the twin "courage to see" and "courage to sin."

The courage to see is perceiving and naming what is unseeable in patriarchy: the non-beings, especially the "primordial aliens: women." According to Tillich, courage is revelatory, for it reveals being on the brink of non-being.[40] But the courage to see is also the courage to see *past* patriarchy. Daly argues that a "patriarchal theological/philosophical analysis of anxiety has no way to Name the way past these, which is the Elemental Realizing of participation in Metabeing."[41] Seeing past is also re-membering, and here she begins to develop a more ontological understanding of courage. Pulling past, present, and future out of linearity implies a notion of being that integrates all three.

The courage to sin is the companion to seeing and can be expressed as the constructive side of courage. The courage to see unmasks the historicity and atrocity of patriarchy and also recalls other possibilities, even if those possibilities survive not as memories but only as questions. The courage to sin is the fundamental self-naming of women, the courage to say no to any and all norms of patriarchy and yes to actions, identities, and attributes deemed sinful in patriarchal culture. Describing her own process of discovery, Daly writes that she "came to See more of the previously hidden connections among Courageous Acts themselves." What she calls the Courage to Sin became, for Daly, the core insight and feminist ethical challenge, rooted in a Tillichian courage to be because, for women, to be in any real sense is to sin under patriarchal norms. "I am not alluding here to the petty sort of sinning which is forbidden and therefore deceptively incited by the 'major religions' of phallocracy. I am talking about Sinning Big. For a woman on this patriarchally controlled planet, to be is to Sin, and to Sin is to be. To Sin Big is to be the verb which is her Self-centering Self."[42] The courage to see, therefore, presages and illuminates the consequent sin of self-affirming existence.

Daly leads the way through a dance of etymology, retrieving the power of language used for millennia to control women. For readers new to Daly, her use of archaic words such as witch, hag, crone, spinster, and the like are jolting, especially when it becomes clear that the origins of these commonly derisive labels lie in a pre-Christian Anglo-European culture and refer to long suppressed strengths in women. The idea and promise of latent power residing in any term formerly used to beat down women is enormously gratifying. White Anglo-American feminists are discovering a desperate paucity of words with which to build themselves up, more so even than the women of African American or other ethnic descents. As Alice Walker has pointed out, for a young black girl to be chastised for "acting womanish," she is being put down with a term that equates femaleness with audacity, independence, responsibility, outrageousness.[43] For a white girl to receive chastisement for the same crime, she would have to be called "mannish" (as indeed some are).

With her concept of the courage to see and to sin Daly conditionally accepts Tillich's argument that "the courage of confidence says 'in spite of' even to death."[44] Death, however, is the crucial word. Tillich is content to keep death isolated from the structural evil of which he is a privileged part. Daly concretizes this idea of death not as the natural end process of life in balance, but as the necrophilic fascination of patriarchy in all of its manifestations. For a woman to risk her life to say no to death is courageous in the deepest sense. "The Courage to Sin, to be Elemental through and beyond the horrors of The Obscene Society, is precisely about being true and real ontologically, and about refusing to be a player of the [patriarchal] female part."[45]

The Culture of New Being: From Transcendent to Elemental

New Being is Tillich's metaphoric, optimistic answer to non-being: "a reality of reconciliation and reunion, of creativity, meaning and hope."[46] For Tillich, Jesus Christ is the bearer of New Being for humankind. He is both the ultimate and the final location of New Being because "if there were no personal life in which existential estrangement had been overcome, the New Being would have remained a question and an expectation and would not be a reality. . . . only if the existence is conquered in *one* point—a personal life, representing existence as a whole—is it conquered in principle."[47] Although Daly does not refer to this text in her writing, her critique of New Being relates to the assumptions apparent here. Tillich's acceptance of "personal life" as the location for New Being hints at Daly's notion of women's experience, but his limitation to "*one* point" is puzzling. Tillich assumes that principles require crystallized, abstracted, representational examples in order to maintain their claims to truth. Were more than one personal life to manifest New Being, difference might sully the principle, or negate it altogether.

It is not surprising that Daly fully rejects Jesus Christ as the manifestation of hope to those literally wiped out by patriarchal evil. In *Beyond God the Father* she argues a range of points against "christolatry" that are now familiar to feminists but that in 1973 were revelatory. Beyond the metaphorical power of Jesus' maleness in the hands of ecclesial authorities, she points to the convenient interchangeability of historicity and ahistoricity in the uses of Jesus' maleness to oppress women ("Jesus was a man, therefore women cannot be ecclesial or spiritual leaders" and "the maleness of Jesus is unimportant; women cannot identify oppression in him"). In addition, Daly identifies the "scapegoat syndrome," the sacrificial "female" posture of Jesus, the power of naming Christ as He, and finally the silencing "compensatory glory" of Mary. All of these issues and many more have since been examined more deeply, particularly by white feminist theologians benefiting from Daly's early work. Daly predicted in *Beyond God the Father* that the "problem" of christology would only grow as "woman-consciousness" grows. Some contemporary white feminist theologians who are attempting to work with christology are admitting to uncertainty that anything can be left after the "paring down of phallacies."[48]

In addition to the maleness of Jesus, the transcendent singularity of Jesus as the "final revelation"[49] severs the organic process of revelation required by the concept of being-itself as Verb, making Tillich's exclusivist christology further incompatible with Daly's transformation of a christocentric New Being into biophilic Metabeing. If language about transcendence is language about the verb be-ing, and if the threat of non-being is the threat posed to all life by the necrophilia of patriarchy, then New Being must define an ongoing process of liberation from patriarchy/non-being.

Nevertheless, Tillich argues that New Being is an "involved" experience,[50] and once again, Daly takes him seriously. Just as Tillich upends the transcendent notion of God as above and locates it in the underlying "ground," so Daly has taken the ahistorical particularity of Christ as New Being and concretized it in the experience of feminist women. As Stenger points out, "instead of Tillich's norm of ultimate meaning and reality being manifest in Jesus as the Christ, Daly sees ultimate meaning and reality manifest in the feminist experience of becoming."[51] It is a mistake to read "feminist becoming" as a purely anthropocentric vision. Daly "grounds" the notion of being far more completely than Tillich, and transforms the transcendent into an "elemental" understanding of the biosphere as a whole.

As a result of biophilia, the concept of New Being becomes too confined in linearity and anthropocentrism and so Daly replaces it in *Pure*

Lust with Metabeing. Metabeing is an involvement in the forces of life rather than the death-oriented severance of old from new in New Being. "The word Metabeing is used . . . to Name Realms of active participation in the Powers of Be-ing."[52] In fact, Daly's definitions of Metabeing provide the basic structure of her systematic (or Elemental) philosophy. The structure of *Pure Lust* is significant not only in terms of the flow of her arguments but also as illustration of the nature of her philosophical/theological project. It would be (and often is) too easy to classify Daly's work as mere commentary on Tillich or as a radical critique of patriarchy. It is also too simple to classify it as utopian in a futuristic, unrealistic sense. Metabeing, as one of the maturing concepts in Daly's thought, is itself a notion developed through stages, from Tillich's being, to be-ing, to new Being, to Metabeing.

The maturation of Daly's thought is evident not only in terms of the mobility of her concept of being but also of its multivalent historicity. She transforms the stasis of being into the motion of be-ing as verb, implying an evolutionary understanding of the nature of the immanent *and* the transcendent. But she develops this evolutionary understanding still further in her shift from New Being to Metabeing. Evolution as a linear history is insufficient for Metabeing. While Tillich strove to endow his concept of New Being with involvement *in* the nonstatic present, its dependence on the "one point of Jesus" as New Being valorizes the new and points a penile trajectory out over the actual and into the nonpresent transcendence of the future.

Daly structures *Pure Lust* around the four meanings of the prefix *meta* in Metabeing. A closer look at these four meanings reveals that her notion of "realms," of "foreground" and "background" are not aspects of some weird taxonomy but an integrational conception of nonlinear historicity. The first definition of *meta,* to "occur later" indicates the "knowledge of participation in Elemental Powers of Be-ing [occurring] *after* a woman has understood that the blockage of her powers within phallocracy . . . is insufferable."[53] A promise of power results from the courage to "see" phallocracy and to "see" women without hatred for perhaps the first time. Second, *meta* as "situated behind" re-covers the ancient past of probable female power (traced through despised but not-lost female terminology) and makes that past present through "lusty" linguistics and stories, a task she begins in her ambitious linguistic project *Webster's First New Intergalactic Wickedary of the English Language*.

Third, *meta* as "change in, transformation of" makes Metabeing a reweaving process that pulls together women's "frozen bits of being." The marginal though persistent resilience of witchcraft, of resistance, of Lesbianism, of biophilia, of traditions of independence and audacity still evident everywhere in unexpected places, and particularly in nonwhite women's cultures, are the "tiny bits of being" waiting like seeds for fertile ground.

Finally, *meta* as "beyond, transcending" gives to Metabeing its inclusive "times/spaces of continuing transcending of earlier stages of shedding the shackles of body/mind that fix women as targets of phallic lust."[54] Transcendence here is a mobile reality giving to courage the ability to see and sin. It is not a reality that can in any way be unlinked from immanence. Immanence for Daly is elemental: the spoken word, the entities of fire, air, earth, and water, the cosmos and intelligence.[55] Transcendence cannot transcend these—*that* is necrophilia, the switch to the question "Why not nothing?"

Metabeing forms the basic ontological structure of Daly's system. Being as a verb entails motion, either linear or organic, and Metabeing encompasses motion and presence. None of these meanings of Metabeing can therefore be called prior to any other. Daly speaks of a spiral as the visual metaphor for her work and claims that there is no starting point. Tillich glimpsed this possibility when he argued that his system presupposes *both* Christ *and* being, but he did not possess the courage to develop interdependence in the immanental way that Daly has done. He ends up with a fundamentally irreconcilable discontinuity between his single-point answer of Christ and his multiplex suggestion of being. Daly has made multivalence her method, with motion and multiplicity her outcome, resulting in both greater elemental comprehensibility and greater philosophical consistency.

Conclusions

Like Tillich, Mary Daly has embarked on a monumental project. She is attempting to explain the possibilities for "being" human in a way that correlates critical questions of experience and being with theological answers. What begins as a more or less simple feminist critique of Tillich's more promising notions (being, non-being, courage, New Being, and others) develops into a far-reaching attempt to construct a philosophy and theology that is consistent in its methods as well as its message. *Beyond God the Father* and *Gyn/Ecology* form a prolegomenon to *Pure Lust*, providing the foundation for her creative systematics of Metabeing.

I suggest that it is a mistake to speak of Daly as a utopian or to dismiss her corpus as hopelessly essentialist. Although visionary and even at times dogmatically resistant to accommodation, her work is not primarily future oriented, nor does it project a dislocated society of cloned feminists. Not all utopias are futuristic, but they tend to be "impossibly ideal schemes" especially when viewed from under the canopy of phallocratic patriarchy.[56] Instead, Daly offers a descriptive analysis of Tillich's more limited notion of New Being that is fully accountable to the daily conditions of grinding patriarchy with a deliberately optimistic, if uncompromising, view beyond. Her point, really, could hardly be more pragmatic. Utopia in its fantastical sense, I suspect, is finally as unacceptable as New Being in that it implies a discontinuity with the present that is once again necrophilia under wraps.

Daly herself as a philosophical separatist does not make separatism monolithic, reactionary, or normative, except when it implies removal from the most damaging centers and sources of phallocratic culture (to which she might now add Jesuit colleges!). She assumes a critical nature to femaleness and to patriarchy, but sees difference as fully compatible with (even, dare we say, essential to) these natures. Her work should not be placed in complete opposition to the critical skepticism of postmodernism except insofar as she absolutizes and hypostatizes the evils of patriarchal domination. Although she is fond of sweeping proclamations, such as "patriarchy itself is the prevailing religion of the entire planet,"[57] it is not possible to say that Daly finally essentializes women into a single nature or cultural construction and thereby erases difference. She is pragmatic in that she takes the category of "woman" as a given, bearing in itself both possibility and limitation as historically and culturally constructed, but is open to the fluidity of the category to individual, cultural, and even biological diversity. But Daly is impatient with words that do not lead to liberative action. "I want to blast out of bore-dom, every way, every day. 'That's so extreme,' they say. 'It's High Time to be Extreme,' I say. While we wade knee deep in the blood of women shall I chat about Freud, Derrida, and Foucault? No, I don't think so."[58]

Nevertheless, Daly is in love with words and with the power of naming, and wants to claim that power while guarding against the colonization that the act of naming historically bears. Again drawing on Tillich, she argues that symbolization is essential to the work of liberation in that symbols "open up levels of reality otherwise closed to us and they unlock dimensions and elements of our souls which correspond to these hidden dimensions and elements of reality" (*PL*, 25). In this she does not forego the possibility of an ontological or essential core that "responds" and she does not take up the postmodern question of the status of being altogether. But it is inaccurate and simplistic to suggest that Daly, in all of her work to unmoor Being-itself from hypostatization, turns and hypostatizes the essence of women in a single cultural construct. There is "no way" she argues, "that Elemental feminist philosophy can speak adequately to the realms of Wild be-ing without symbols. . . . Of course, there can be no One Absolutely Right symbol for all Lusty women, for we belong to different tribes and have great individual diversity. Despite this fact, and also because of it Prudes[59] prudently heed our intuitions about which symbols ring true, listening to the sounds of their names and to the rhythms of the contexts in which this Naming occurs" (*PL*, 25). To the extent that they are alive, women and men bear life, and therefore possess the potential for biophilic and elemental be-ing. If there is essentialism in Daly, this is it. She fully demands and depends upon the critical idea of profound social construction and uses the metaphor of a mirror for the deconstruction of identity necessary for everyone caught in patriarchy.

> Having learned only to mirror, they would find in themselves reflections of the sickness in their masters. They would find themselves doing the same things, fighting the same way. Looking inside for something there, they would be confused by what at first would appear to be an endless Hall of Mirrors. What to copy? What model to imitate? Where to look? What is a mere mirror to do? But wait—how could a mere mirror even frame such a question? The question itself is the beginning of an answer that keeps unfolding itself. The question-answer is a verb, and when one begins to move in the current of the verb, of the Verb, she knows that she is not a mirror.[60]

Daly affirms that there *is* something beyond the mirrors. But she does not presume to define what that something is, nor does she suggest that something involves unchanging sameness. Carol Christ supports Daly, arguing that "ambiguity is necessary to feminism. We acknowledge the perspectival nature of all truth claims, but we are not thoroughgoing relativists [which is] . . . *essential* to post-modernism."[61]

If Mary Daly cannot be neatly categorized as an essentialist utopian, the seriousness of her work *in continuity* with the patriarchal tradition of Western theology and philosophy becomes more significant. It is even possible to argue that she more than acknowledges the patriarchal epistemological tradition by engaging it as she does, both as source of argument and as springboard for her own elemental system. I suggest that the truly radical aspect of her work is not its extrapatriarchal, alien nature, but rather its metapatriarchal, engaged nature. Indeed, for beneficiaries of the "sado-state" and "sado-spirituality," to confront Daly as a true daughter of the tradition may mean to accept a threat to patriarchy that is much closer to home, and ultimately more damning.

Notes

1. Mary Daly, *Pure Lust: Elemental Feminist Philosophy* (Boston: Beacon Press, 1984), 29n. Hereafter referred to as *PL*.

2. I have most often witnessed this uncritical categorization of Daly's work in classrooms and in personal discussions, unfortunately from feminist professors as well as students.

3. I use the term "systematic" to describe Daly's project. She does not use this term herself, probably because it carries too much of a patriarchal burden. Part of my contention, however, is that her work is systematic/realistic and not merely utopian, so I employ the term with that conclusion in mind.

4. Mary Daly, *Beyond God the Father: Toward a Philosophy of Women's Liberation* (Boston: Beacon Press, 1973), xiii. Hereafter referred to as *BGF*.

5. See primarily Mary Daly, *Gyn/Ecology* (Boston: Beacon Press, 1978) for references to contemporary psychiatry and science practitioners as secular theologians (e.g., 93).

6. Paul Tillich, *Systematic Theology*, vol. 1 (Chicago: University of Chicago Press, 1941), 62. Hereafter referred to as *ST*, 1.

7. Tillich, *ST*, 1:62.

8. Tillich, *ST*, 1:8.

9. Mary Ann Stenger, "A Critical Analysis of the Influence of Paul Tillich on Mary Daly's Feminist Theology," in *Theonomy and Autonomy: Studies in Paul Tillich's Engagement with Modern Culture*, ed. John J. Carey (Macon: Mercer University Press, 1984).

10. Stenger, 246.

11. Stenger, 250.

12. See Sandra Harding, *The Science Question in Feminism* (Ithaca: Cornell University Press, 1986), especially chapter 6.

13. I use the liberationist phrase "preferential option" not because Daly uses it but because it is an appropriate loan/overlap from the liberation theology lexicon.

14. Daly, *BGF*, 6.

15. Daly, *BGF*, 11.

16. In *Pure Lust*, Daly explicitly describes her method as "movement," presumably as her attempt to maximize the room in her work for "metamutation" and the ongoing influences of new insights.

17. Daly, *BGF*, 8.

18. It is important to note that Daly does *not* attempt to speak for all women, nor to ascribe to all women a feminist consciousness of patriarchal oppression. She does, however, imply that there is an essential truth in the oppressive experience of women, however it is discovered or named, and in whatever terms it is analyzed. There is a kind of Gnostic essentialism concerning oppression in Daly's presuppositions, but feminist critics must be careful to identify it as such and not as an absolutizing of women per se. See *PL*, 27 and 344.

19. Mary Daly, "After the Death of God the Father" *Commonweal* 94 (March 12, 1971): 9.

20. Daly, *BGF*, 21.

21. Tillich, *ST*, 1:14.

22. Beginning in *BGF*, Daly is wary of the name God. She uses it only sparingly (and harshly) in *Gyn/Ecology* and abandons it altogether in *Pure Lust* (where only references under "god" are listed.) This movement reflects her own prediction in *BGF* that "it is probable that the movement will eventually generate a new language of transcendence. There is no reason to assume that the term 'God' will always be necessary, as if the three-letter word, materially speaking, could capture and encapsulate transcendent being" (*BGF*, 21–22).

23. Tillich, *ST*, 1:241.

24. Daly, *BGF*, 19.

25. Daly, *BGF*, 19.

26. Daly, *BGF*, 34.

27. See Daly's own description of her movement away from "God" in *Pure Lust*, 423 n. 24.

28. Tillich, *ST*, 1:240.

29. Daly, *PL*, 26.

30. Paul Tillich, *The Courage to Be* (New Haven: Yale University Press, 1953), 169. Hereafter *CTB*.

31. Paul Tillich, *Systematic Theology*, vol. 2 (Chicago: University of Chicago Press, 1957), 34. Hereafter *ST*, 2.

32. Daly, *BGF*, 24; emphasis mine.

33. See Audre Lorde, "An Open Letter to Mary Daly," in *Sister Outsider: Essays and Speeches* (Freedom, Calif.: Crossing Press, 1984).

34. Daly, *PL*, 29.

35. Daly, *PL*, 29.

36. Daly, *BGF*, 23.

37. Tillich, *CTB*, 1.

38. Daly, *BGF*, 24.

39. Tillich, *CTB*, 155.

40. Tillich, *CTB*, 178–81.

41. Daly, *PL*, 223. See also Mary Daly, "The Courage to See," *Christian Century* 88 (September 22, 1971): 1108–11.

42. Mary Daly, *Outercourse: The Be-Dazzling Voyage* (San Francisco: Harper San Francisco, 1992), 198.

43. Alice Walker, *In Search of Our Mothers' Gardens* (New York: Harper and Row, 1983).

44. Tillich, *CTB*, 168.

45. Daly, *PL*, 152.

46. Tillich, *ST*, 1:49.

47. Tillich, *ST*, 2:98.

48. Carter Heyward is one such theologian attempting to deal with christology, but who admits to the difficulty (personal conversation, Cambridge Mass., May 1990). See Carter Heyward, *Speaking*

of Christ: A Lesbian Feminist Voice (New York: Pilgrim Press, 1989). Rita Nakashima Brock has also made an important contribution in revisioning feminist christology. See her *Journeys by Heart: A Christology of Erotic Power* (New York: Crossroad Press, 1992).

49. See Tillich's discussion of the history of revelation (*ST*, 1:137–39) in which he attempts to incorporate both the multiple revelations of "humanistic theology" and the claim of ultimacy of "neo-orthodox and allied liberal theology" by speaking not of a sole revelation in Christ but a "final" one.

50. Tillich, *ST*, 1:137–39.

51. Stenger, 250.

52. Daly, *PL*, 26.

53. Daly, *PL*, 27.

54. Daly, *PL*, 27.

55. Daly, *PL*, 7–11.

56. *Oxford English Dictionary*, compact ed., s.v. "utopia."

57. Daly, *Gyn/Ecology*, 39.

58. Daly, *Outercourse*, 340.

59. "Prude, *n* [derived fr. F *prudefemme* wise or good woman, fr. OF *prode* good, capable, brave + *femme* woman—*Webster's*]: Good, capable, brave woman endowed with Practical/Passionate Wisdom; one who has acquired the E-motional habit of Wild Wisdom, enabling her to perform Acts which, by the standards of phallicism, are Extreme; Lusty Woman who insists upon the Integrity, Self-esteem, and Pride of her sex; Shrewd woman who sees through the patriarchal norms of 'good' and 'evil,' constantly Re-membering the Good. . . . *N.B.*: Prudes note with Pride that the word *proud* is etymologically akin to *prude*. Both are derived from the OF *prode*" (Daly, *Websters' First New Intergalactic Wickedary of the English Language. Conjured by Mary Daly in Cahoots with Jane Caputi* [Boston: Beacon Press, 1987], 157).

60. Daly, *BGF*, 197.

61. Carol Christ, "Embodied Thinking: Reflections on Feminist Theological Method," *Journal of Feminist Studies in Religion* 5 (Spring 1989): 14; emphasis mine.

References

Brock, Rita Nakashima. *Journeys by Heart: A Christology of Erotic Power*. New York: Crossroad Press, 1992.

Christ, Carol. "Embodied Thinking: Reflections on Feminist Theological Method." *Journal of Feminist Studies in Religion* 5 (Spring 1989).

Daly, Mary. "After the Death of God the Father," *Commonweal* 94 (March 12, 1971): 7–11.

———. *Beyond God the Father: Toward a Philosophy of Women's Liberation*. Boston: Beacon Press, 1973.

———. "The Courage to See," *Christian Century* 88 (September 22, 1971): 1108–11.

———. *Gyn/Ecology*. Boston: Beacon Press, 1978.

———. *Outercourse: The Be-Dazzling Voyage*. San Francisco: Harper San Francisco, 1992.

———. *Pure Lust: Elemental Feminist Philosophy*. Boston: Beacon Press, 1984.

———. *Websters' First New Intergalactic Wickedary of the English Language. Conjured by Mary Daly in Cahoots with Jane Caputi*. Boston: Beacon Press, 1987.

Harding, Sandra. *The Science Question in Feminism*. Ithaca: Cornell University Press, 1986.

Heyward, Carter. *Speaking of Christ: A Lesbian Feminist Voice*. New York: Pilgrim Press, 1989.

Lorde, Audre. "An Open Letter to Mary Daly" in *Sister Outsider: Essays and Speeches*. Freedom, Calif.: Crossing Press, 1984.

Stenger, Mary Ann. "A Critical Analysis of the Influence of Paul Tillich on Mary Daly's Feminist Theology." In *Theonomy and Autonomy: Studies in Paul Tillich's Engagement with Modern Culture*, edited by John J. Carey. Macon: Mercer University Press, 1984.

Tillich, Paul. *The Courage to Be*. New Haven: Yale University Press, 1953.

———. *Systematic Theology*. Vol. 1. Chicago: University of Chicago Press, 1941.

———. *Systematic Theology*. Vol. 2. Chicago: University of Chicago Press, 1957.

3

Deliver Us from Evil: Bad Versus Better Faith in Mary Daly's Feminist Writings

Anne-Marie Korte

Translated by *Mischa F. C. Hoyinck*

Mary Daly's later writings tend to make late twentieth-century feminist readers uncomfortable. Her later works are sometimes praised for their poetic, visionary, or "destabilizing" style and imagery.[1] Far more often, though, these works are sharply criticized for containing essentialist and dualistic concepts of gender and ahistoric and undifferentiating analyses of patriarchy.[2] Why do scholars in women's studies so often choose Daly's works to expose faults and slips in radical feminist thinking? I believe this is mainly due to the many religious connotations and reminiscences that permeate her work. For what are we to think of "patriarchy as a worldwide religion," for example, or of invoking "elemental faith" to resist the "spells of male demons"?

Critiques of Daly's writings have repeatedly suggested that her controversial feminist concepts are related to her adherence to traditional theological and philosophical frameworks.[3] Indeed, classic Christian theology and philosophy undeniably inform Daly's feminist writings, and her later, so-called post-Christian, works are still rife with religious concepts and imagery, which is no doubt due to Daly's Roman Catholic upbringing and theological training. However, this angle offers little challenge as a research perspective, for it almost inevitably points to the question Did Mary Daly Really Leave Christianity?[4] At best, this question leads to contemplation of classic christian views of 'virtues' or 'passions' at the heart of Daly's later work. But more often than not, it calls Daly's credentials into question. The narrow scope of the "Did-She-Really" question precludes a more refined view of the complex role of religious faith in Mary Daly's oeuvre, a complexity which is the focus of this article.

That Daly's work is so well suited to what Teresa de Lauretis has called "upping the anti [*sic*] in feminist theory" is, I believe, closely connected to the problematic status of religious faith in the frameworks of critical Western science that feminist reflection draws upon.[5] I see feminism as a movement that, in a practical and political sense, strives for the emancipation and liberation of women, while at the theoretical level historifying and deeply problematizing gender. It is a movement that unmistakably continues to propagate the ideals of the Enlightenment.[6] The Enlightenment ideals intrinsic to the feminist agenda are emancipation, self-determination, democratization and (historic) relativization of (religious) traditions. These are all matters that encourage the processes of secularization. Philosopher Alice Jardine has suggested that feminism, with its battle against what are perceived as "false images" of women, may be seen as the final secularization of the West. Feminism "is necessarily bound to some of the most complex epistemological and religious contradictions of contemporary Western culture."[7] Feminism has prompted many women to distance themselves from religious traditions, but it has also engendered a passionate struggle to liberate and renew religious faith.

Quite early on, in *Beyond God the Father* (1973), Daly observed that it was far from evident to most feminists why one should care about God or religious faith at all.[8] But to her, as a theologian, these were all-important issues. Through all her writings, she has held a certain religious faith very dear. Although her theoretical frameworks and her language changed drastically, she described this faith in various contexts as "a passion for transcendence." In *Pure Lust*, for example, she wrote: "[O]ur struggle and quest concern Elemental participation in Be-ing. Our passion is for that which is most intimate and most ultimate, for depth and transcendence."[9] She is convinced that this passion for transcendence is of great importance for the continuing development of a feminist attitude and conduct.

As a feminist and a theologian, Mary Daly's position on religious faith changes through the course of her oeuvre. In this chapter, I explore these changes. With this approach, I hope to achieve two things. First, I aim to analyze the meaning of religious faith and theology in Mary Daly's work while avoiding the usual prejudices and interpretations applied to her work. To understand and value the role that religious faith plays in Daly's feminist writings, we need to raise issues that can deconstruct established modes of interpretation, such as "feminism versus traditional Western theology and philosophy," issues that can uncover conflicts and differences that resist subsumption into these standard approaches. Second, I will contribute to the discussion of what religious faith means to feminism. These two aims are interrelated; identifying the many, often contradictory, meanings of religious faith to feminism and to the women's movement may contribute to a (re)valuation of Mary Daly's feminist theological project—and vice versa.

Knowledge of God

Looking back on her college years in Fribourg, Switzerland (1959–67), Mary Daly described her experiences there as bizarre:[10] like Alice in Wonderland, she found herself in a totally clerical world, devoted to neoscholasticism—the study of Saint Thomas Aquinas's texts to defend Roman Catholicism against the philosophy of Modernity. However, Daly's de facto marginalized position in Fribourg—as a non-European, a layperson in the Roman Catholic church, and above all, as a (young) woman—must also have given her a certain intellectual advantage. She could engage in modern philosophy and liberal theological debate with relatively little to fear, because she was outside the Roman Catholic power structure and thus could not be punished for deviating from "official" views. Evidence of this relative freedom can be found in Daly's two neoscholastic dissertations dating from the early 1960s.[11]

In these studies, Daly not only showed her capabilities in neoscholastic "logic," but also gave voice to contemporary concerns in a remarkably strong and consistent way. But Daly did not attempt to reconcile Christianity and modernity on the level of neoscholastic discourse itself, as some other young Roman Catholic theologians tried to do at that time.[12] She alternated expressions of religious faith in an "Infinite Being" with skepticism toward the complacency of people who continued to speak in theological terms as though nothing had changed since the Middle Ages. Her notions of God, theology, and religious faith were neoscholastic. At the same time, she spoke for a new generation in the increasingly secular Western world: the men and women who were interested in religion, but uninspired—or even turned off—by traditional Christian language and logic. In this context, Daly also openly discussed the specific problems faced by women like herself. In the abridged version of her theological dissertation, Daly explicitly pointed out her own exceptional position as a woman striving for a theological doctorate.[13] In this publication, she also discussed the meaning of theology to "non-clerical people" and criticized the exclusion of women from higher theological education.[14]

In her theses, Daly argued in favor of "speculative theology," an inductive method based on "positive knowledge of God through creatures." Neither the explanation nor the proclamation of the content of biblical revelation *for* modern people, but rather gaining access to God oneself *from* the position of "modern man" formed her line of approach. By reflecting upon their own "sense of being," their self-awareness and their actual existence, human beings can grasp, by way of analogy, God's Being. According to Daly, this Thomistic view of theology was "fundamentally open to historic reality and to the experiential world." Daly hereby placed a remarkable emphasis upon the rational moment in theology. Unlike her young male colleagues who were increasingly coming to regard the immense abstractness of neoscholastic theology as a problem, she did not consider this to be an obstacle to the vitality or relevance of Thomistic theology.

I believe that Daly emphasized the rationality of theology because she reasoned from the position of all women and those laymen and modern believers who lack the philosophical and historical education necessary for independent theological reflection. In various ways, the emphasis on "speculative theology," on the rationality of theology, gives women the opportunity to participate in theology: "positive knowledge of God through creatures" supposes an understanding of theology in which nobody is excluded, either as a subject or as an object of theology. With these views, Daly was clearly thinking along different lines from those of most other advocates of women's emancipation in the Catholic church around that time. Daly's primary concern was not the equal access of women to ecclesiastical offices, but an autonomous, unmediated access to the "knowledge of God," for as many people as possible.[15]

For the Sake of Their Souls

Daly made a plea for speculative theology as positive knowledge of God through creatures and for participation in this theology by men and women who are not part of the clergy. In terms of content, this plea is akin to the sixteenth- and seventeenth-century humanist and emancipatory debates on opening up the study of theology to women. It was not until the twentieth century that women were admitted to theological studies at the university level, and Roman Catholic women had to wait until the 1960s before they were allowed in. However, many women did not see the importance of being permitted to study theology. It was especially their nonscholarly interaction with religion that earned them the praise of church and society. In her research on learned women in European history, historian Patricia Labalme concludes: "(Not until the twentieth century was there a female doctor of theology.) . . . The world of the university was beyond the reach of women. There was a world, however, always within the reach of women, the world of eternal truth. Piety might be a highroad to religious wisdom. . . . Religious endeavor both encouraged and limited the literary productivity of learned women. But none wrote on theology: that is for the Doctors, said St. Teresa."[16]

In the Middle Ages and Renaissance, there was a great respect for a number of women who gave voice to religious matters in the devotional, rather than the scholarly, genre. As a rule, these women belonged to religious orders and their orthodoxy was unquestioned. The church authorities emphatically promoted their prayers and visions, and in their introductions to these women's writings "invariably emphasized the woman's talents for prophesy, inspiration, Christian devotion, and genuine religiosity, not her acuity, erudition, or literary gifts."[17] The church stressed that these women were merely a vehicle of divine inspiration (something that many women were eager to corroborate) and that God had chosen the weak to confound the strong. This was how the phenomenon of lay and female mystical inspiration could be explained "away."

Underlying this explanation is an ancient belief in women's abilities as mystics, prophets, and oracles and in their proclivity for religious fervor.

Women's access to theological studies did not become a public issue until the seventeenth century. It coincided with another question that divided academia at the time: the (in)dependence of philosophy and science from religious tradition (Descartes, Pascal, Spinoza). Sparked off by the Querelle des Femmes—the Renaissance polemics about "the nature of women"—women's participation in theology became the subject of debate. As a result of the humanist ideal and the Renaissance cult of erudition, women—often clergymen's daughters, sisters, or cousins—began entering the field of theology. Among scholars of theology, both in the Reformation and the Counter-Reformation, pleas were heard for opening the study of theology to women (Anna Maria van Schurman, Sor Juana Ines de la Cruz).[18]

Those who formulated these arguments, written mostly by women themselves, take the position that intellectual development and religious perfection go hand in hand. They therefore recommend the study of theology, but are clearly detached from the question of whether women should be able to practice a profession, acting as, for example, a clergywoman or a teacher of religion. Studying theology would simply contribute to women's personal religious education and facilitate its transfer to children and other members of the family.[19]

The Enlightenment itself did not give rise to debates on whether women should be allowed to study theology. In religious terms, women seem to have felt more appreciated and included in counter-Enlightenment movements: Pietism and Romanticism. Religious women did not take Mary Wollstonecraft's and John Stuart Mill's rational feminist line. The nineteenth century saw wide acceptance of the idea that women were "by nature" religiously and morally superior, a notion held even by women themselves. As a result, women started to actively take part in congregations, missionary work, church-run social welfare work, and charities. This involvement also led to calls for admitting women to the ministry. However, the thought that women would become "better" people and Christians through education and studies, by developing their mental powers and enriching their minds, did not reappear in the nineteenth- and early twentieth-century discussion about women and theology.[20] In terms of content, Mary Daly's plea for speculative theology as positive knowledge of God through creatures is a continuation of the sixteenth- and seventeenth-century appeals for women to be allowed to study theology; according to these arguments, since women were given a brain they should not be denied "the bliss of understanding the highest, divine insights."

I think it is too reductive to attribute this point of view solely to Daly's Roman Catholic background. After all, some of Daly's contemporaries, including Roman Catholic women, were calling for allowing women into the priesthood. I think that Daly's humanist and emancipatory approach reflects a modern awareness of the value of higher education and that it is part of the belief in the American dream that must have been of great importance in Daly's Irish Catholic immigrant family. Daly's approach also shows her to be one of a new generation of well-educated Roman Catholics who had outgrown their traditional religious upbringing because of their academic education[21] and were looking for a more intellectual religious life. In addition, I think her neoscholastic education itself contributed to her point of view, since Thomistic theology presupposes "fides quaerens intellectum," religious faith that searches for insight.

Mary Daly's early writings criticize institutions, people, and (theological) ideas that hamper a "well-developed" and individual approach to God. However, Daly does not question religious faith as such. Her views on faith and theology are derived from the internal neoscholastic debate and do not confront or deal with the modern suspicion of religious faith that was highlighted by the Enlightenment. In her dissertations, Mary Daly manages to find a positive connection between the neoscholastic concepts of theology and religious faith, and women's and laypeople's emancipation. She continues this line in *Beyond God the Father* when she starts speaking about God as Be-ing and Verbing from a feminist perspective. She assumes a close and mutual link between "sense of being" and "knowledge of God," between "being" and "participation in Be-ing." "When women take positive steps to move out of patriarchal space and time, there is a surge of new life. I would analyze this as participation in God the Verb who cannot be broken down simply into past, present, and future time, since God is form-destroying, form-creating, transforming power that makes all things new."[22] In her later work, we find the same idea cloaked in the term "elemental faith," religious faith that promotes feminist awareness and women's independent action. But Daly's later writings contain numerous attacks on "patriarchal religion" and the "phallocratic belief system" that hampers women's ability to have faith in themselves. Modern suspicion of religious faith gained a firm foothold in Daly's later work and brought her to sharply demarcate and distinguish between "good" and "bad" faith. How did this change of viewpoint come about?

Exemplary

From an in-depth analysis of Mary Daly's oeuvre, I conclude that Simone de Beauvoir's existentialist feminism, and particularly her gendered concept of 'bad faith' must have had a major impact on Daly's concept of religious faith.[23]

As Daly said many times, Simone de Beauvoir's *The Second Sex* (1949) greatly influenced her feminist thinking.[24] However, in Daly's first feminist study, *The Church and the Second Sex* (1967), her resistance to Beauvoir's feminist analyses outweighed her admiration. She felt the need to dispute Beauvoir's feminist attack on the Roman Catholic church. But in repudiating Christianity in the name of women's autonomy, and accusing the Roman Catholic church of overt misogyny, Beauvoir had turned to historical facts, which Daly could hardly deny. Daly's only way out was to point to impending "historical changes" in the Roman Catholic church of the 1960s.[25]

At the same time, Daly discovered that Beauvoir had been inconsistent in her indictment of Christianity and the Roman Catholic church as active oppressors of women. In *The Second Sex*, Beauvoir made several references to women "achieving transcendence through religion." For example, she stated that the power of religious orders had brought women such as Teresa of Avila to "heights that few men ever reached."[26] Daly interpreted Beauvoir's remarks to mean that the church as a social institution could provide "the needed condition for a St. Teresa to rise above the handicap of her sex."[27] Daly also noticed Beauvoir's pronounced admiration for Teresa of Avila. Beauvoir praised Teresa for "living out the situation of humanity" in an exemplary fashion. "As for the psychological leverage which produced this phenomenon, Beauvoir does not explain further," Daly remarked. "The one indisputable fact is that Teresa of Avila was a Christian mystic."[28]

Daly was well aware of the discrepancy between Beauvoir's merciless portrayal of someone like the French mystic Marguerite Marie Alacoque—whom she described as neurotic, overemotional, and narcissistic—and her almost "lyrical" description of Teresa of Avila, whom she credited with "achieving transcendence." Daly seemed, however, not to be interested in exploring the reasons behind this discrepancy. In fact, she seemed only too happy to accept Beauvoir's suggestion that Teresa of Avila somehow took up an exceptional position in the ranks of Christian mystics. In *The Church and the Second Sex*, Daly turned Teresa into a precursor of modern Bible interpretators and of proponents of women's emancipation. "Apparently, as a consequence of mystical experience, Teresa's understanding rose above the common interpretation of Pauline texts concerning women," Daly concluded, echoing both Beauvoir's views and her language.[29]

Gendered Concept of Bad Faith

In contrast to Daly, I am very interested in possible reasons for the ambivalence in Beauvoir's views on Christian religion and women's autonomy, or "transcendence," as expressed in *The Second Sex*. Beauvoir wrote this comprehensive antiessentialist study with the intention of demythologizing opinions on women and "femininity" commonly held in her own social and intellectual milieu. She exposed and analyzed the androcentric bias with which women are classified as "the other" and as subordinate to men. She argued that this phenomenon pervaded not only the Western literary canon, but also myths, morals, and rituals worldwide. Beauvoir showed that both Western, Christian, "enlightened" civilizations and "primitive" cultures were rife with prejudice against women. Yet she also stressed the historical and contextual nature of "femininity"; in her view, women are not "feminine" by essence or nature. On the basis of many examples, she identified the social and psychological processes whereby women learn to act "feminine."

For a critical interpretation of these processes she turned to the central analytical frameworks of the existentialist philosophy that she and Jean-Paul Sartre had developed. *L'être et le néant* (1943), the first major product of their collaboration, and which appeared solely under Sartre's name,[30] described in great detail how individuals shrink from reaching their full potential and thus give up their freedom. Instead of striving to transcend a given situation, they cling to certain positions and states of mind that prevent them from taking their freedom and from "actualizing the self." This "inauthentic" or "self-deceptive" way of living was termed *mauvaise foi*, or bad faith.[31] But whereas *L'être et le néant* only discussed the individual factors that act as impediments to self-actualization, in *The Second Sex* Beauvoir argued that women's failure to achieve transcendence also had its roots in a shared social situation. Women's social position seemed to engender an almost inevitable, permanent condition of bad faith.

According to Beauvoir, women's position was characterized by the fact that they grow up, live, and make their choices in a world where men have cast them as the other. "They propose to stabilize her as object and to doom her to immanence since her transcendence is to be overshadowed and forever transcended by another ego which is essential and sovereign."[32] Beauvoir eventually linked this subjection to the other to women's reproductive role, or more precisely, to their complete immersion in the sustenance of life itself.

In terms of religion, *The Second Sex* also expands upon the frameworks of the existentialist philosophy set out in *L'être et le néant*. Although *L'être et le néant* firmly denounced religious faith (or, to be precise, God's existence) because of its incompatibility with the individual's radically infinite freedom,[33] Beauvoir's *The Second Sex* offered a far more complex view. Beauvoir endorsed the existentialist "rational" refutation of God's existence,[34] but also admitted—albeit with mixed feelings—that religious faith sometimes made women autonomous and helped them transcend the gender-related boundaries imposed on them. It is quite remarkable that religion was the only field where Beauvoir found examples of "self-actualized" women, as Mary Daly was quick to observe in 1967. Therefore, it seems appropriate to investigate in more detail why religious women such as Joan of Arc, Catherine of Siena, and Teresa of Avila were given such special status in *The Second Sex*.

Religion of Love

In *The Second Sex*, there are two distinct trains of thought about women and religion. First and foremost, there is Beauvoir's main point of view: a strong conviction that religion affirms and legitimizes women's "immanence." She points to the blatant way in which Roman Catholicism achieves this: it provides saintly role models and uses symbols and rituals of kneeling and of women/mothers who are subservient to, and bow for, men/fathers representing God, the Almighty Father. Besides deepening women's dependency and powerlessness, religion also mystifies their fundamentally lower social status by granting them the illusion of transcendence. Christianity does this in a particularly ingenious way: ostensibly, it grants women an equal status: as creatures of God, both men and women possess eternal souls, bound to heaven. Simultaneously, Christianity, and particularly Roman Catholicism, offers women a magic universe filled with objects and activities to occupy their time and resign them to their fate: "Religion sanctions woman's self-love: it gives her the guide, father, lover and divine guardian she longs for nostalgically; it feeds her daydreams; it fills her empty hours. But, above all, it confirms the social order, it justifies her resignation, by giving her the hope of a better future in a sexless heaven. This is why women today are still a powerful trump in the hand of the Church; it is why the Church is notably hostile to all measures likely to help in woman's emancipation. There must be a religion for women; and there must be women, 'true women,' to perpetuate religion."[35]

But these mechanisms are at work not only in historical Roman Catholicism. According to Beauvoir, even contemporary Christianity has the same effect: "In modern civilisation which—even for woman—has a share in promoting freedom, religion seems much less an instrument of constraint than an instrument of deception. Woman is asked in the name of God not so much to accept her inferiority as to believe that, thanks to Him, she is the equal of the lordly male; even the temptation to revolt is suppressed by the claim that the injustice is overcome. Woman is no longer denied transcendence, since she is to consecrate her immanence to God."[36]

The second train of thought on women and religion in *The Second Sex* concerns the idea that (certain) women can achieve transcendence through religion. Both girls and adult women can gain autonomy through religious faith.[37] It is significant that, in this context, Beauvoir speaks of "mysticism" or "mystical experience" rather than religion. She is not interested in mysticism as a special religious experience, but rather as a special sort of erotic love. Beauvoir devotes an entire section to "the woman mystic."[38] This section forms the conclusion of an analysis of the ways in which women practice bad faith.[39] In Beauvoir's view, narcissism, erotic love, and mystical love have common characteristics. The gender specificity in how women forsake freedom lies in their rendering themselves—actually or imaginarily—totally dependent on men. Women practice a disastrous "religion of love":[40] a boundless devotion to divine men and masculine gods.[41]

> Love has been assigned to woman as her supreme vocation, and when she directs it toward a man, she is seeking God in him; but if human love is denied her by circumstances, if she is disappointed or overparticular, she may choose to adore divinity in the person of God Himself. To be sure, there have also been men who burned with that flame, but they are rare and their fervour is of a highly refined intellectual cast; whereas the women who abandon themselves to the joys of the heavenly nuptials are legion, and their experience is of a peculiarly emotional nature. Woman is habituated to living on her knees; ordinarily she expects her salvation to come down from the heaven where the males sit enthroned.[42]

Love of God can bring women to extremes of self-denial and self-abasement. Some female mystics even practiced automutilation, or physical self-neglect. But somehow this did not apply to Catherine of Siena and Teresa of Avila. In their cases, mystical experience rendered them autonomous; it empowered them and opened the gate to self-actualization in projects as important as those of men of power. "But the story of St. Catherine of Siena is significant: in the midst of a quite normal existence she created in Siena a great reputation by her active benevolence and by the visions that testified to her intense inner life; thus she acquired the authority necessary for success, which women usually lack."[43] Why are these women so exceptional? Why did Beauvoir consider them the only women to transcend their gender-specific boundaries and, what is more, to reach heights few men ever reached?

Resisting Subjection to Mortal Men

Beauvoir remained rather vague about the "self-actualization" of her great women mystics. She confined herself to stating that these women held their own against their male peers. I believe that Beauvoir's appreciation of these mystics' transcendence and self-actualization' is not based on an interest in their spiritual life or their actual social achievements. I think she held these women in high esteem because, as religious women, they were not bound by masculine authority, or at least they did not consider themselves to be. They did not recognize male authority and acted with amazing authority themselves.[44]

To Beauvoir, the importance of these mystics lay not only in their lack of ties to men, but also in their total lack of interest in men. In *The Second Sex,* one of Beauvoir's main concerns is the way in which women assent to their subjugation and objectification by men. In her quest for autonomy, independence, and self-actualization, the women mystics serve as paragons of womanhood, since they remained free of the bonds of earthly love and did not devote their entire lives to the sustenance of life itself.

Their unique status in Beauvoir's eyes results from her belief that the struggle for autonomy and the effort to resist subordination to men are intertwined with religious faith in a very concrete way. This link is evident not only in *The Second Sex,* but also in Beauvoir's *Memoirs* and other autobiographical texts. In one of the latter texts, there is an explicit reference to the direct link between the search for autonomy and self-awareness, and the experience of denying God's existence.[45] When asked in an interview what had made her aware of her position as a woman, Beauvoir answered by describing the time and place when she discarded her belief in God.[46] In interviews and in her *Memoirs,* Beauvoir confessed that her relation with Sartre had given her a fundamental security in life and a justification of her existence that she had previously only experienced in her relationship with her father and with God.[47] In *The Second Sex,* Beauvoir widened the scope of this interchangeability of father, God, and lover, and put the role they play in the process of "becoming a woman" in a wider context.

According to Beauvoir, a young girl's father "incarnates that immense, difficult, and marvelous world of adventure: he personifies transcendence, he is God." The girl's relationship with the eternal father is based on her relationship with her real father. All her life she may "longingly seek that lost state of plenitude and peace" that came from her father's affection. "The emotional concern shown by adult women toward Man would of itself suffice to perch him on a pedestal."[48]

The unique status of the women mystics in *The Second Sex* can be clarified by regarding the following two interrelated paradoxes as the core issues of Simone de Beauvoir's reflections on women and religion: (1) even women who have ceased to believe in God the Father may still put their faith in men as if they were gods; (2) by loving God "as a woman" women can radically break with their dependence on and subjugation to "mortal men." The first paradox describes Beauvoir's own position, while the second describes the position occupied by the great women mystics.

Joan of Arc

In *The Church and the Second Sex,* Mary Daly steered clear of the hazardous topic of women's autonomy, love, and religion as explored by Simone de Beauvoir. Nevertheless, there are some indications that Daly did not miss Beauvoir's point after all and took good note of her conclusions and dilemmas. In the final chapter of *The Church and the Second Sex,* titled "The Second Sex and the Seeds of Transcendence," Daly assessed the results of her attempts to "disprove" Beauvoir's rejection of Roman Catholicism. She chose a curious epigraph for this chapter, a statement she borrowed from Joan of Arc: "I do best by obeying and serving my sovereign Lord—that is God."[49]

This epigraph seemed to contradict all the issues Daly had presented and emphasized in the preceding chapters; she had previously argued in favor of a religious language that refrains from gendering God and had advocated total equality and "partnership" between men and women at all levels of church and society. Terms such as *obeying* and *serving* hardly fit into this scheme. However, the epigraph does make sense in light of Beauvoir's double paradox. It fits in well with the second paradox, which is that women could make a radical break with their dependence on men and their subordination to men, by loving God as a woman. By quoting Joan of Arc, Daly affirmed Beauvoir's argument, supporting autonomous religious women; and yet in the very same breath, she distanced herself from Beauvoir by declaring that she, Daly, did not need to turn her back on Christianity and the Roman Catholic church.

With this epigraph Daly confirms Joan of Arc's religious faith and autonomy toward earthly lords and sovereigns, as well as her own. Daly did not identify with the great women mystics, such as Teresa of Avila, whose outspoken, erotic mysticism Beauvoir had paid much attention to. By quoting Joan of Arc, Daly allied herself with a strong religious woman who was neither a member of a monastic order, nor involved in a (heterosexual) "mysticism of love." Joan of Arc was a sort of maverick: her autonomy was extreme and her actions were radical, as was her interpretation of a divine vocation. But unlike any of the other female mystics Beauvoir mentioned, Joan of Arc had had to pay a high price for her "radical transcendence": she was burned at the stake.

Daly later assessed this element of autonomy in her epigraph. In her 1975 "Post-Christian Introduction" to *The Church and the Second Sex*, she commented on her choice of epigraph (writing about herself in the third person): "It struck me as curiously fitting that the lead citation was from Joan of Arc. Joan had at least made a partial escape from patriarchy (as had Daly, in her own way.) . . . Of course, Daly's attention was focused not upon this ultimate "obeying and serving" but upon Joan's escape from the earthly masters."[50]

Patriarchy as a Religion

Simone de Beauvoir criticized Christian faith in general and Roman Catholicism in particular for having a negative impact on women's emancipation. Although Daly initially resisted this point of view, she eventually adopted it herself. I believe that she came to accept it precisely because Beauvoir had recognized that religious faith had an ambiguous impact—both positive and negative—on women's autonomy. Beauvoir's frame of reference allowed Daly her first opportunity to embrace modern criticism of religion in the name of feminism. This criticism, dating back to the Enlightenment, boils down to a renunciation of religious faith on the grounds that it, by definition, blocks people's autonomy. In this view, religious faith requires people to subject themselves to a higher being and to institutions claiming to represent this being. A concern of modern criticism of religion is to be free and protect human autonomy from the heteronomy intrinsic to religious faith in general and to institutionalized religion in particular.

As I mentioned before, existentialist philosophy strongly supported this criticism. It explicitly called any betrayal of one's own autonomy and self-actualization *mauvaise foi*, or bad faith. Daly took this modern criticism of religion much further: for example, to the point where she concluded that patriarchy as such was a religion. She put Beauvoir's remarkable comparison between (heterosexual) romantic love and religious faith as instruments of oppression at the core of her notion and critique of patriarchy. In a nutshell, Beauvoir had found that both love and religion force women to accept their status as the other in relation to men and to become "objects" instead of "realizing their potential." Deep veneration for divine men and masculine gods is women's particular—and particularly disastrous—form of bad faith.

Daly's later, rigorous critique of patriarchy in all its manifestations the world over is essentially an elaboration of this existentialist-feminist construction of gender-specific bad faith, culminating in the controversial thesis that "[p]atriarchy is itself the prevailing religion of the entire planet."[51] In tracing the development of this thesis through Daly's writings, one finds that Daly, in her initial definition of patriarchy, mainly stressed the wider social processes responsible for the imbalance in power between the sexes.[52] In *Beyond God the Father* (1973) Daly started to use the term patriarchy to describe a feminist analytical concept and defined patriarchy by comparing it to India's caste system:

> [T]here exists a worldwide phenomenon of sexual caste, basically the same whether one lives in Saudi Arabia or in Sweden. This planetary sexual caste system involves birth-ascribed hierarchically ordered groups whose members have unequal access to goods, services and prestige and to physical and mental well-being. Clearly I am not using the term "caste" in its most rigid sense, which would apply only to Brahmanic Indian society. I am using it in accordance with Berreman's broad description, since our language at present lacks other terms to describe systems of rigid social stratification analogous to the Indian system.[53]

However, Daly's declaration that patriarchy is "the number one religion of the entire planet" is not a simple extension of her critical sociological observations about religion. In *Gyn/Ecology*, Daly worded her point of view as follows:

> Patriarchy is itself the prevailing religion of the entire planet, and its essential message is necrophilia. All of the so-called religions legitimating patriarchy are mere sects subsumed under its vast umbrella/canopy. They are essentially similar, despite the variations. All—from buddhism and hinduism to islam, judaism, christianity, to secular derivates such as freudianism, jungianism, marxism and maoism—are infrastructures of the edifice of patriarchy. All are

> erected as parts of the male's shelter against anomie. And the symbolic message of all the sects of the religion which is patriarchy is this: Women are dreaded anomie. Consequently, women are the objects of male terror, the projected personifications of "The Enemy," the real objects under attack in all the wars of patriarchy.[54]

Here, one of Beauvoir's observations is taken to the extreme: that women are turned into the other in relation to men, emphasizing that patriarchy functions and legitimizes itself in exactly the same way that religion does.

Daly presented a further development of her analytical concept of patriarchy as a religion in *Pure Lust* (1983). She wrote of a "phallocratic belief system" and a "universal religion of phallocracy" that prevents both men and women from believing in women's power and holiness.[55] The results are continued objectification and rape of women.

In discussing the effects of patriarchy as a religion, Daly pointed to Simone de Beauvoir's analysis of women's religious masochism. Beauvoir used the exalted and extreme acts of self-denial by the French Roman Catholic mystic Marguerite Marie Alacoque to exemplify how patriarchal religion fosters feelings of guilt and brings women to "masosadism."[56] According to Daly, Roman Catholicism is not unique in this respect; every type of patriarchal religion, in fact patriarchy as such, is guilty of the same. Continual objectification causes a nagging doubt at the core of woman's mind, identity, and self. Women consumed by this doubt are prone to masosadism in a "sadosociety." Neither they, nor anyone else, are able to believe in the power and holiness of women's lives.

Emerging Two-Track View of Religion

Simone de Beauvoir's ambivalence about the impact of religion on women's autonomy also offered Daly the opportunity to maintain her positive stance toward religious faith, based on a neoscholastic concept of God. Beauvoir's ambiguous views allowed Daly to remain a theologian and to develop her theological insights further. In *Beyond God the Father*, Daly processed Beauvoir's ideas in a way that is still quite similar to classical Christian theology. Daly sees feminist criticism of religion as criticism of idolatry—a well-respected and important Judeo-Christian point of view. This criticism of idolatry serves to liberate and innovate religion itself:

> The passive hope that has been so prevalent in the history of religious attitudes corresponds to the objectified God from whom one may anticipate favors. Within that frame of reference human beings have tried to relate to ultimate reality as an object to be known, cajoled, manipulated. The tables are turned, however, for the objectified "God" has a way of reducing his producers to objects who lack capacity for autonomous action. In contrast to this, the God who is power of being acts as a moral power summoning women and men to act out of our deepest hope and to become who we can be.[57]

In *Beyond God the Father*, feminist criticism of religion is inseparable from a dynamic interpretation of religious faith that supports feminism; these are two sides of the same coin. Later, when Daly renounced Christian theology altogether, feminist criticism of religion and feminist religious faith became increasingly separate topics in her work. From *Gyn/Ecology* onward, she voiced sharp criticism of any type of faith—religious or otherwise—that turns women into "objects under attack." At the same time, but on a different track, she continues to develop a thea-logy which supports women's autonomy and "self-realization."

In 1990, Iris Marion Young characterized Daly's *Gyn/Ecology* both as a repudiation of femininity along the lines of Beauvoir's brand of "humanist feminism" and as an example of the type of gynocentric feminism that Young considered the antithesis of humanist feminism. She regarded the two as irreconcilable because women either want to be like men or they do not, but they cannot dwell in between. Young therefore classified *Gyn/Ecology* as a transitional work: "In it Daly asserts an analysis of the victimization of women by femininity that outdoes Beauvoir, but she also proposes a new gynocentric language."[58]

I find Young's solution of calling *Gyn/Ecology* a transitional work rather inadequate. After all, the same "contradiction" is present in Daly's 1983 publication *Pure Lust* and other later writings. *Gyn/Ecology* is not an inconsistency in Mary Daly's work. I believe that it is consistent with Beauvoir's ambivalent view of religion in relation to women's independence. In *Gyn/Ecology*, Daly uses Beauvoir's gendered concept of bad faith to demonstrate how women are turned into the other and how, acting in bad faith, they turn themselves into objects and shrink from realizing their potential. Daly's subsequent comparison of patriarchy to religion is still in keeping with Beauvoir's concept, but it provides Daly with a framework that allows her to do more than just analyze women's victimization and compliance: it also enables her to design strategies for resistance to and escape from patriarchy.

In line with Beauvoir's ambivalence toward religion, Daly starts to outline a "feminist faith" that supports this struggle. Basically, this faith is an unconditional affirmation of women's autonomy, transcendence, and self-actualization. Daly endorsed Beauvoir's finding that women have neither a history nor a religion of their own. She therefore reinvented this feminist faith by deconstructing patriarchal religious myths and imagery and reclaiming the fragments of women's lost or suppressed religious heritage in a gynocentric context. Daly's feminist faith is about establishing a subject position to counteract the objectification, silencing, and crushing of women. Hence, this faith both shapes, and is shaped by, a gynocentric language and context. Gynocentrism is necessary because women had been denied the power to name, as Daly concluded from her struggle with classic Christian discourse in *Beyond God the Father*. In Daly's post-Christian feminist writings this feminist faith manifests itself as an impressive amount of recaptured religious and mythical imagery rendered in an overwhelming, "scholarly" newspeak. In *Pure Lust*, Daly defined this feminist faith as "elemental faith." "Elemental" refers to all spiritual and material realities that have been attacked, suppressed, erased, or annihilated by the "phallocratic belief system."

Daly's seemingly contradictory combination of antiessentialist and gynocentric views can be accounted for by her ambiguous stance toward the role of religion in women's struggle for autonomy and "self-actualization." This brings her time and again to discern sharply between bad and good faith, between religion as an addiction ("opium") or a mystical experience (transcendence) and between religion's power to tempt women into total subjection or its role in empowering them to occupy a subject position. Her positive or affirmative view of religious faith enables her to emphasize women's subject position (gynocentrism), while her negative or critical view of religion allows her to put forward a cultural and religious critique (antiessentialism).

Subjectivity

Rather than exploring the (possibly contradictory) notions of gender and gender differences, I would like to focus on the various notions of subjectivity present in Daly's later writings. I think that this angle might best highlight Daly's unique significance as a theologian.

In Daly's later works, the affirmation of religious faith is used mainly to empower women as subjects. To describe what she means by such empowerment, Daly borrows terminology from her study of theology and philosophy (subject/object, self/other, being/nonbeing, being/Be-ing), as well as from popular psychology (power, energy, center, life, integrity, authenticity) and from her own, mythical female language (Hag, Crone, Spinster, Voyager, Witch, Goddess). Daly describes women's becoming-subject first and foremost as self-realization, which raises the question of whether this is anything but an uncritical adoption of the androcentric notion of the autonomous self as embraced by existentialist philosophy.[59] Daly thought of many equivalents for women's "Self" and a variety of qualifications with reference to this self; these show us that Daly's notion of female self-awareness can be equated neither with self-determination ("being independent") nor with autonomy ("being free of foreign authority"). She speaks of the Self, the subject, being, presence, awareness, soul, source, force, integrity, wholeness, strength, centering, and so on.

Women's Self as evoked in *Gyn/Ecology* is characterized by the fact that it is not a given or state of being. It must (still) be actualized; it is a matter of becoming. Daly's point of departure is the absence and fragmentation of the Self. This point is further elaborated in *Pure Lust*. Here, Daly raises the question of to what extent women have "something of their own," a self, despite patriarchy's crushing and deadly effects. Some claim that women have nothing of their own; Daly disagrees.[60] She does not believe that women have been oppressed to the point where they have no self left. The problem is that they are obstructed from realizing this, from realizing their self. Among the obstacles are violence against women and "patriarchal lies," but Daly also mentions the lack of solidarity among women (violence among women, the token woman) and individual women's inner fragmentation ("patriarchy's presence in our own mind").

In *Pure Lust*, however, Daly provides a more profound exploration of women's lack of self-actualization. This text provides a consistent, multifaceted inquiry into what constitutes and reinforces inner cohesion. Daly discusses three aspects of inner cohesion: consciousness, power, and "lust/longing," or, in other words, identifying one's self, asserting the self and extending the self. These aspects are dealt with in three major parts or "Spheres" of *Pure Lust*, focusing on reason, passion, and lust, respectively. Daly also establishes a strong correlation between achieving inner cohesion and naming the self, the world, and God.[61]

But where exactly should we place this treatment of women's self that hinges on achieving and promoting inner cohesion? Is this a continuation of the androcentric philosophical notion of the autonomous subject, or a break with it? In some respects, Daly's approach resembles that of feminist philosophers such as Luce Irigaray, who aligned themselves with the poststructuralist attack on the dominant Western notion of the subject.[62] This resemblance is evident mainly in the importance assigned to the level of language, to deconstruction, to deviant readings and different semantic connotations in order to establish and affirm oneself as a woman.[63] Daly refers to Monique Wittig's works, but actually gives them a very different twist.[64] Wittig argues that it is impossible for women to say "I" in phallocentric discourse; Daly regards this as an example of the fragmentation of women's self-awareness. In line with Virginia Woolf, Daly believes this fragmentation is healed only in "moments of being," in epiphanous experiences during which an I is created when the severed parts of the individual suddenly and fleetingly come together.[65] Unlike the French feminist philosophers, Daly does not consider the unity and identity of the subject problematic as such. To her, rather, the main problem is the absence of focus and the lack of re-membering; she considers the moments when women experience the constitution of a Self to be "revelations."

Daly's later writings contain two different and seemingly contradictory notions of subjectivity. In her criticism of patriarchy and religion, she argues that women need to construct an autonomous Self. But what she actually does and achieves and calls for in her writings, while naming, punning, and associating, constitutes a dismantling of this notion of subjectivity. She sings and associates, speaks in different voices, places herself outside any system, shows anger, pleasure, and analytical depth, draws on and cites Western theology, philosophy and mythology as well as contemporary culture; in so doing, she spins and weaves new tapestries of meaning. Insofar as Daly identifies and names her way of thinking, she provides new images of the Self as an intricate knot, consisting of many threads/links:[66] a thinking, feeling, listening and naming entity, which both integrates and reaches out, is self-supporting but also connected to others. These are concepts of the Self that are no longer caught in the opposition between the androcentric notion of the autonomous self and the criticism of this notion by feminists and French deconstructionists.

Daly is definitely not out to adopt this androcentric autonomous self, as she herself explains most lucidly in her treatment of the difference between her own "elemental feminist philosophy" and the androcentric ontology of Western philosophy and theology. Daly describes this ontology as follows: "The ontological question, the question of being-itself, arises in something like a 'metaphysical shock'—the shock of possible nonbeing. This shock often has been expressed in the question: 'Why is there something; why not nothing?' "[67] Daly considers the opposition generated in the second half of this ontological question unjustified: why would amazement about "being" be linked to bewilderment at the thought of "non-being"? Daly feels this automatic link points to a static notion of being, to a reified ontology which first and foremost sees being as the ability to stave off nonbeing. According to Daly, this idea reflects the position of phallic thinkers who sense the terror of the negation of everything that *is*—and therefore of their own, privileged position as well. The ontology that informs the primary questions of biophilic women is not based on this fear of nonbeing, but on the quest and longing for being (more).[68]

Daly posits a notion of subjectivity that resides in the tension between "being" and "Be-ing more." This tension does not arise from the shocking, distressing, or "impinging" experience of finiteness, individuality, and exclusiveness, but from the "unlocking," affirmative experience of "broadening," participation, and belonging.[69]

I believe that Daly derived this definition of subjectivity—which is not based on a modern, individualist, and androcentric opposition between autonomy and heteronomy—from premodern Thomistic religious ontology. This religious ontology assumes that there are various degrees of fullness or intensity of being. An increase in intensity means that people or matters are more involved in an all-transcending or encompassing reality: the fullness or completion of all that is in God. In this view, the way a being actualizes herself (more) is not by resisting or avoiding this all-encompassing reality, but by opening herself up to this reality and knowing herself to be part of it.

Conclusions

Mary Daly's post-Christian writings have been interpreted in very different ways. On the one hand, her later work is often characterized as shying away from the actual ongoing conflicts, political issues, and difficult battles the women's movement faced after the euphoria of the first successes.[70] On the other hand, Daly's *Gyn/Ecology* formed the basis for Sonia Johnson's green, leftist political program for Johnson's U.S. presidential campaign in the early 1980s.[71] Daly's later work is interpreted as an unconditional and unmediated affirmation of "the feminine": the body, emotions, "the natural."[72] But Daly's later writings have also been interpreted as expressing a disdain for the actual lives of women and an overemphasis on rationality.[73] In the same vein, it has been concluded that immanence and "*Diesseitigkeit*" characterize the religiosity that Daly's work has testified to since *Beyond God the Father*,[74] while it has also been maintained that her work stresses transcendence.[75] Similarly, there are those who believe that Daly's writings since *Beyond God the Father* hinge on female spirituality and the rewriting of "matriarchal religious imagery,"[76] whereas others point to the fact that Daly, in her later writings, no longer identifies the divine with the female.[77]

I believe this polysemic ambiguity is characteristic of Mary Daly's later writings and that it is of little use to try to reduce her work to one unambiguous statement. I have shown that her work contains two widely divergent positions on religion, which are inspired by the ambivalent views of Simone de Beauvoir on religion's importance to the women's movement. I find Daly's work especially intriguing in those places where the positive and negative aspects of religion cause tension and friction. I have given an example of this by showing how Daly, as a theologian, remained faithful to a premodern notion of religious faith. This notion allows her to define subjectivity without getting caught in the modern androcentric opposition between autonomy and heteronomy in which the subject is represented as "the Self in juxtaposition with the Other" and as "the Self inferior or superior to the Other." Neoscholastic theology has provided her with another concept of subjectivity that, in some respects, better defines what happens when women occupy a subject position. This concept hinges on the absence of subjectivity and lack of inner cohesion rather than an opposition between Self and Other. It is more closely connected to Thomistic religious ontology than to modern androcentric existentialist ontology, which—through Sartre and Beauvoir—has also informed much of feminist theory.

Incidentally, I find Daly's work interesting not only because of these new feminist interpretations of her old, theological inheritance, but also because of her ongoing critical interpretations of Christian discourse. I choose the word interpretations because Daly reinterprets classical theological themes incorporated in texts of a postmodern signature—in itself an unusual mode for theological discourse. Daly's later writings are characterized by the use of more than one kind of logic and several voices directed at different readers.

As I mentioned earlier, some critics—such as Young—consider Daly's post-Christian writings a catalog of women's victimization. For example, her detailed descriptions in *Gyn/Ecology* of the atrocities that women all over the world are subjected to have been interpreted as an overstatement to prove women's victimization. However, I believe that Daly had something more in mind than proving that women are victims. I believe that *Gyn/Ecology* is Daly's multilayered way of revealing, reflecting, and meditating on physical violence against women. As such, this book discusses suffering, sin, evil, and (the hope of) salvation from a woman's perspective—a well-known theological track from an unusual angle.

It is remarkable that Daly's self-declared farewell to Christian theology and philosophy coincided with the introduction of the theme of violence against women in her writings. She had touched upon this theme earlier. In *Beyond God the Father*, she included it in her discussion of the necessity of replacing phallic morality. In her attempt to deconstruct androcentric Christian morality, she mentioned the unholy trinity of rape, genocide, and war as the three-headed monster to be faced and fought. To write of rape in the academic, theological context of 1973 was an act of true courage because Daly thereby presented herself as a professional theologian who openly took women's experiences seriously. However, the manner in which she dealt with the subject in *Beyond God the Father* was still very impersonal and abstract.[78]

In *Gyn/Ecology*, this had radically changed. Here, she described every physical detail of various, systematic acts of violence against women, such as rape, genital mutilation, foot-binding, widow-burning and hysterectomy. I read *Gyn/Ecology* primarily in light of this fascination with the violation of women's bodies. Feminist theologians have suggested that *Gyn/Ecology* is a women's tale of salvation or a female version of the Passion of Christ. Instead of Jesus, women are nailed to the cross. I agree that *Gyn/Ecology* deals with this central christian story, but I believe that it does so in a very profound and dialectical way. One of Daly's distinguishing characteristics is precisely that she rejects any direct or positive correlation between the Passion of Christ and women's suffering. She is truly scandalized by the suffering caused by violence. Therefore, she is shocked to the core by the fact that Christian theological discourse does acknowledge suffering due to physical violence in the case of Jesus—or God incarnate—but is often oblivious to women's suffering from physical violence. Christian theological discourse seems not only to be indifferent to women's suffering; it is also unable to recognize how the discourse itself propagates this suffering. It condones the hidden violence toward women that is central to many of its own religious images and parables. Therefore, a feminist reinterpretation of Christian passion stories does not suffice. The discourse needs to be altered by the inclusion of other stories of passion and resurrection, in particular of those who have been excluded from and hurt by androcentric theological discourse.

In her introduction to *Gyn/Ecology*, Daly stated that she had exchanged theology for ethics. According to her, *Gyn/Ecology* contains the "Meta-Ethics of Radical Feminism." However, besides it being a feminist exploration of ethics, I consider this book as much an extraordinary form of theology. Daly's self-confessed reversal to ethics seems to me an epistemological move inherent in a shift in feminist position. As Sandra Harding commented in a 1986 publication: "For feminists, it is a moral and political, rather than a scientific, discussion that serves as the paradigm of rational discourse."[79] In my opinion, *Gyn/Ecology* deals directly with the moral and political discussion that, from a feminist point of view, must be included into theological discourse, the main issue being "How can we ensure that women are done more justice?" rather than "What can we know about women?"

One might argue that this is precisely the point where theology turns into ethics. I disagree; the way in which *Gyn/Ecology* deals with "evil" is every bit as religious as it is ethical. One need only consider the book's central premise: the act of turning women into objects to be abused, or even destroyed, far too often goes unrecognized as fundamentally wrong or evil. And Mary Daly considers this, the deliberate obfuscation of what should be regarded as evil, one of the main "sins" of all patriarchal religions and societies. A call for ethics alone will not do, because ethics has been distorted by phallic morality. In this situation, "deliver us from evil" seems to be an indispensable prayer for women.

Certainly, women have always cried and struggled for "justice." The thwarting of this longing and struggling gives rise to the birth pangs of radical feminist awareness. But only when the knowledge that something is not "right" evolves into uncovering the invisible context of gynocide and, beyond this, into active participation in the Elemental context of biophilic harmony and power can there be great and sustained creativity and action. To Name this active Elemental contextual participation, which transcends and overturns patriarchal "justice" and "injustice," Other words are needed. Nemesis is a beginning in this direction.[80]

. . . [U]nlike "justice," which is depicted as a woman blindfolded and holding a sword and scales, Nemesis has her eyes open and uncovered—especially her Third Eye. Moreover, she is concerned less with "retribution," in the sense of external meting out of rewards and punishments, than with an internal judgment that sets in motion a kind of new psychic alignment of energy patterns. Nemesis, thus Named, is . . . a relevant mysticism which responds to the tormented cries of the oppressed, and to the hunger and thirst for creative be-ing.[81]

Notes

1. See Catherine Keller, *From a Broken Web: Separation, Sexism, and Self* (Boston: Beacon Press, 1986), 207–12; Carol P. Christ, "Embodied Thinking: Reflections on Feminist Theological Method," *Journal of Feminist Studies in Religion* 5, no. 1 (1989): 7–15; Rita Nakashima Brock, *Journeys by Heart: A Christology of Erotic Power* (New York: Crossroad, 1989), 50; Sharon D. Welch, *A Feminist Ethic of Risk* (Minneapolis: Fortress Press, 1990), 1–10; Welch, "Sporting Power: American Feminism, French Feminisms, and an Ethic of Conflict," in *Transfigurations: Theology and the French Feminists*, ed. C. W. Maggie Kim et al. (Minneapolis: Fortress Press, 1993), 171–98; Mary McClintock Fulkerson, *Changing the Subject: Women's Discourses and Feminist Theology* (Minneapolis: Fortress Press, 1994), 46–47.

2. Audre Lorde, "An Open Letter to Mary Daly," in *Sister Outsider: Essays and Speeches* (Trumansburg, N.Y.: Crossing Press, 1984), 66–71; Hester Eisenstein, *Contemporary Feminist Thought* (London: Unwin Paperbacks, 1984); Beverly Wildung Harrison, *Making the Connections: Essays in Feminist Social Ethics*, ed. Carol S. Robb (Boston: Beacon Press, 1985); Chris Weedon, *Feminist Practice and Poststructuralist Theory* (Oxford: Basil Blackwell, 1987); Linda Alcoff, "Cultural Feminism Versus Post-Structuralism: The Identity Crisis in Feminist Theory," in *Feminist Theory in Practice and Progress*, ed. Micheline R. Balson et al. (Chicago: University of Chicago Press, 1989), 295–326; Jean Grimshaw, "Autonomy and Identity in Feminist Thinking," in *Feminist Perspectives in Philosophy*, ed. Morwenna Griffiths and Margareth Whitford (Bloomington: Indiana University Press, 1988), 90–108; Morwenna Griffiths, "Feminism, Feelings, and Philosophy," in Griffiths and

Whitford, *Feminist Perspectives in Philosophy*, 131–51; Elizabeth V. Spelman, *Inessential Women: Problems of Exclusion in Feminist Thought* (Boston: Beacon Press, 1988), 123–25; Amy Hollywood, "Violence and Subjectivity: *Wuthering Heights*, Julia Kristeva, and Feminist Theology," in Kim et al., *Transfigurations*, 81–108, especially nn. 14 and 108.

3. Rosemary Radford Ruether, *Sexism and God-Talk: Toward a Feminist Theology* (Boston: Beacon Press, 1983); Elisabeth Schüssler Fiorenza, *In Memory of Her: A Feminist Theological Reconstruction of Christian Origins* (London: SCM Press, 1983); Sheila Greeve Davaney, "The Limits of the Appeal to Women's Experience," in *Shaping New Vision: Gender and Values in American Culture*, ed. Clarissa W. Atkinson et al. (Ann Arbor: UMI Research Press, 1987), 30–48; Davaney, "Problems with Feminist Theory: Historicity and the Search for Sure Foundations," in *Embodied Love: Sensuality and Relationship as Feminist Values*, ed. Paula M. Cooey et al. (San Francisco: Harper and Row, 1988), 79–96; Ruth Großmaß, "Von der Verführungskraft der Bilder: Mary Daly's Elemental-Feministische Philosophie," in *Feministischer Kompaß, patriarchales Gepäck: Kritik konservativer Anteile in neueren feministischen Theorien*, ed. Ruth Großmaß and Christiane Schmerl (Frankfurt and New York: Campus Verlag, 1989), 56–116; Ellen T. Armour, "Questioning 'Woman' in Feminist/Womanist Theology: Irigaray, Ruether, and Daly," in Kim et al., *Transfigurations*, 143–70.

4. See also Ruether, *Sexism and God-Talk;* Mary Jo Weaver, *New Catholic Women: A Contemporary Challenge to Traditional Religious Authority* (San Francisco: Harper and Row, 1985); Großmaß, "Von der Verführungskraft der Bilder."

5. Teresa de Lauretis, "Upping the Anti [*sic*] in Feminist Theory," in *Conflicts in Feminism*, ed. Marianne Hirsch and Evelyn Fox Keller (New York: Routledge, 1990), 255–70.

6. The lasting impact of these Enlightenment ideals on feminism is evident in the prevalent categorization of feminist positions into the main political movements based on these ideals: liberal (or emancipatory) feminism, social (or sociological) feminism, and radical feminism (cultural criticism). See Ruether, *Sexism and God-Talk: Toward a Feminist Theology*, 214–34; Weedon, *Feminist Practice and Poststructuralist Theory* (Oxford: Basil Blackwell, 1987); Rosemary Tong, *Feminist Thought: A Comprehensive Introduction* (London: Routledge, 1989); Carolyn Merchant, "Ecofeminism and Feminist Theory," in *Reweaving the World: The Emergence of Ecofeminism*, ed. Irene Diamond and Gloria Feman Orenstein (San Francisco: Sierra Club Books, 1990), 100–105.

7. Alice A. Jardine, *Gynesis: Configurations of Woman and Modernity* (Ithaca: Cornell University Press, 1985), 100–101.

8. Mary Daly, *Beyond God the Father: Toward a Philosophy of Women's Liberation* (Boston: Beacon Press, 1973), 28–33.

9. Mary Daly, *Pure Lust: Elemental Feminist Philosophy* (Boston: Beacon Press, 1984), vii. See also Mary Daly, *The Church and the Second Sex* (London: Chapman, 1968), 223; and Daly, *Beyond God the Father*, 28–29.

10. Mary Daly, "Autobiographical Preface to the Colofon Edition," and "Feminist Postchristian Introduction," in Daly, *The Church and the Second Sex: With a New Feminist Postchristian Introduction by the Author* (New York: Harper and Row, 1975), 5–14, 15–51; Daly, "Vorwort zur deutschen Ausgabe von Beyond God the Father," in Daly, *Jenseits von Gottvater, Sohn & Co: Aufbruch zu einer Philosophie der Frauenbefreiung* (Munich: Frauenoffensive, 1980), 5–10; Daly, "New Archaic Afterwords," in Daly, *The Church and the Second Sex: With the Feminist Postchristian Introduction and New Archaic Afterwords by the Author* (Boston: Beacon Press, 1985), xi–xxx; Daly, "Original Reintroduction," in Daly, *Beyond God the Father: Toward a Philosophy of Women's Liberation; With an Original Reintroduction by the Author* (Boston: Beacon Press: Beacon Press, 1985), xi–xxix; Daly, "New Intergalactic Introduction," in Daly, *Gyn/Ecology: The Metaethics of Radical Feminism: With a New Introduction by the Author* (Boston: Beacon Press, 1991), xiii–xxxv; Daly, *Outercourse: The Be-Dazzling Voyage* (San Francisco: Harper, 1992).

11. Mary Daly, "The Problem of Speculative Theology: A Study in Saint Thomas" (Ph.D. diss., University of Fribourg, Switzerland, 1963); Daly, *Natural Knowledge of God in the Philosophy of Jacques Maritain* (Rome: Officium Libri Catholici, 1966).

12. Edward Schillebeeckx, "Het niet-begrippelijke kenmoment in onze Godskennis volgens Thomas van Aquino," *Tijdschrift voor Philosophie* 14 (1952): 411–53; Schillebeeckx, "Het niet-begrippelijke kenmoment in de geloofsdaad: probleemstelling," *Tijdschrift voor Theologie* 3 (1963), 167–94; Schillebeeckx, *Openbaring en theologie* [Theologische Peilingen; 1] (Baarn: Nelissen, 1964). Johan Baptist Metz, *Christliche Anthropozentrik: Ueber die Denkform des Thomas von Aquin* (Munich: Koesel, 1962).

13. In the summary of her theological dissertation Daly states: "[The author] would like also to acknowledge her debt to all of the professors of the Faculty of Theology, who by opening for a woman the door to a doctorate in theology expressed openness of mind and spirit." Mary Daly, acknowlegdments to *The Problem of Speculative Theology*, (Boston: Thomist Press, 1965). In her philosophical dissertation, Daly focused particularly on the philosophical and theological writings of women. Daly referred to the writings of Raissa Maritain—wife of Jacques Maritain, whose writings are the subject of her second dissertation, and to Raissa's role in her husband's philosophical development. Raissa Maritain, *Les grandes amitiés: Les aventures de la grâce*, vols. 1 and 2 (New York: Editions de la Maison Française, vol. 1, 1942; vol. 2, 1944); Maritain, *Situation de la poésie* [in cooperation with Jacques Maritain] (Paris: Desclée de Brouwer, 1948). Daly also praised Laura Fraga de Almeida Sampaio C. R. for her interpretation of Jacques Maritain's philosophical works, titled *L'intuition dans la philosophie de Jacques Maritain* (Paris: Vrin, 1963): "This enlightening and scholarly work is a most important aid to understanding Maritain's thought" (Daly, *Natural Knowledge of God*, 32 n. 76). Also, Daly favorably reviewed Sister M. Elisabeth I.H.M.'s publication "Two Contemporary Philosophers and the Concept of Being," *Modern Schoolman* 25 (1947/48), 224–37. "The author makes an interesting comparative analysis of Fr. Garrigou-Lagrange and Maritain" (Daly, *Natural Knowledge of God*, 20 n. 34). In addition, Daly pointed out yet another publication, by Sister Aloysius S.S.J., "The Epistemological Value of Sense Intuition," *Philosophical Studies* 5 (1955): 71–78.

14. Daly, *The Problem of Speculative Theology*, 41–47.

15. For a further elaboration of the central thesis of Mary Daly's theological dissertation about the importance and relevance of "speculative theology," based on (rational) "knowledge of God through creation," see Anne-Marie Korte, *Een passie voor transcendentie: Feminisme, theologie en moderniteit in het denken van Mary Daly* (A passion for transcendence: Feminism, theology, and modernity in the thinking of Mary Daly) (Kampen: Kok, 1992), 55–59, 82–85.

16. Patricia H. Labalme, introduction to *Beyond Their Sex: Learned Women of the European Past*, ed. Labalme (New York: New York University Press, 1984), 3–4.

17. Katharina M. Wilson, ed., *Medieval Women Writers* (Manchester: Manchester University Press, 1984), xvii.

18. See Elisabeth Gössmann, ed., *Das Wohlgelahrte Frauenzimmer* [Archiv für philosophie- und theologiegeschichtliche Frauenforschung; 1] (Munich: Indicium, 1984); Gössmann, ed., *Eva—Gottes Meisterwerk* [Archiv für philosophie- und theologiegeschichtliche Frauenforschung; 2] (Munich: Indicium, 1985); Anna Maria van Schurman, *Opuscula Hebraea, Graeca, Latina, Gallica, Prosaica et Metrica* (Leiden: Ex Officina Elseviriorum, 1648); Beatriz Melano Couch, "Sor Juana Inés de la Cruz: The First Woman Theologian in the Americas," in *The Church and Women in the Third World*, John C. B. Webster and Ellen Low Webster, eds. (Philadelphia: Westminster Press, 1985), 51–57; Rosemary Radford Ruether and Rosemary Skinner Keller, eds., *Women and Religion in America*, vol. 2, *The Colonial and Revolutionary Periods* (San Francisco: Harper and Row, 1983), xv–xvi, 46, 65–68.

19. See Anne-Marie Korte, "Een gemeenschap waarin te geloven valt: Over de spirituele en de politieke betekenis van het geloof van vrouwen aan de hand van de 'ommekeer' van Anna Maria van Schurman en Mary Daly" (M.A. thesis, University of Nijmegen, The Netherlands, 1985), 41–57.

20. See Moltmann-Wendel, ed., *Frau und Religion*, 11–38; Rosemary Radford Ruether and Rosemary Skinner Keller, eds., *Women and Religion in America*, vol. 1, *The Nineteenth Century* (San Francisco: Harper and Row, 1981).

21. This issue was raised by Mary Daly herself in the short version of her theological dissertation. Mary Daly, *The Problem of Speculative Theology*, 41–43.

22. Daly, *Beyond God the Father*, 43.

23. Korte, *Een passie voor transcendentie*, 86–187.

24. Daly's first reference to Simone de Beauvoir appeared in a 1965 issue of *Commonweal*, a North American Roman Catholic journal: "Simone de Beauvoir, in *The Second Sex*, manifested a strange mixture of insight and understanding when she wrote that Mary kneeling for her own Son represents the supreme victory of the male over the female. Catholic readers, shocked by this, protest that Mlle. de Beauvoir simply does not understand. It may well be true that she does not have a sympathetic understanding of Catholic theology, but in fact she understands its abuses only too well. It is unfortunately not difficult to find examples in Catholic writings about women which manifest the vision of man-woman relationship which Simone de Beauvoir is talking about. (The tortured use of symbolism can be seen in Gertrud von le Fort's *The Eternal Woman*, which has sold hundreds of thousands of copies, as well as in countless other places.) We might well ask where the true culpability lies for Simone de Beauvoir's misunderstanding of Marian doctrine, and incidentally be grateful for her insight into the perversion thereof." Daly, "A Built-in Bias," *Commonweal* 81 (January 15, 1965): 509–10.

In 1984, Daly wrote:

> In the late 1940s the publication of Simone de Beauvoir's great feminist work, *The Second Sex*, made possible dialogue among women about their lives. For many years this work functioned as an almost solitary beacon for women seeking to understand the *connections* among the oppressive evils they experienced, for they came to understand the fact of otherness within patriarchal society.
>
> There were other feminist works in existence, of course, but these were not really accessible, even to the "educated" women. *The Second Sex* helped to generate an atmosphere in which women could utter their own thoughts, at least to themselves. Some women began to make applications and to seek out less accessible sources, many of which had gone out of print. Most important was the fact that de Beauvoir, by breaking the silence, partially broke the Terrible Taboo. Women were Touched, psychically and e-motionally. Many women, thus re-awakened, began to have conversations, take actions, write articles—even during the dreary fifties. (Daly, *Pure Lust*, 374)

See also Daly, *The Church and the Second Sex*, 56 and Daly, "Feminist Postchristian Introduction," 16.

25. Daly, *The Church and the Second Sex*, 192–223.

26. Simone de Beauvoir, *The Second Sex* (New York: Vintage Books, 1989), 130.

27. Daly, *The Church and the Second Sex*, 68.

28. Ibid., 69.

29. Ibid., 100.

30. Jean-Paul Sartre, *L'être et le néant: Essai d'ontologie phénoménologique* (Paris: Guillimard, 1943). For a recent critical study of Beauvoir and Sartre's collaboration, see Kate Fullbrook and Edward Fullbrook, *Simone de Beauvoir and Jean-Paul Sartre: The Remaking of a Twentieth Century Legend* (New York: Harvester Wheatsheaf, 1993).

31. Sartre, *L'être et le néant*, 93–108.

32. Beauvoir, *The Second Sex*, xli.

33. See also Jean-Paul Sartre, *L'existentialisme est un humanisme* (Paris: Nagel, 1946).

34. Beauvoir, *The Second Sex*, 632.

35. Ibid., 624.

36. Ibid., 621.

37. See ibid., 104; 622, 673–74, 678.

38. Beauvoir, "The Mystic," in *The Second Sex*, 670–78.

39. Beauvoir, "Justifications," in *The Second Sex*, 629–78.

40. Dorothy Kaufmann McGall has shown how Beauvoir in *Le deuxième sexe* outlines the pitfalls of romantic love for women by comparing it to religious devotion: "If every man, for Malraux and for Sartre after him, dreams of being God, woman, as Beauvoir portrays her in this chapter, dreams of being His beloved. For Beauvoir it is the woman most avidly seeking transcendence who is often most vulnerable to the religion of love. Denied the transcendence of action and adventure offered to the male, she seeks transcendence by losing herself in a man who represents the essential which she cannot be for herself." For the origins of this comparison Kaufmann refers to Beauvoir and Sartre's existentialist philosophy and to Beauvoir's personal history: her Catholic upbringing and her relation to her father, God, and Sartre. However, Kaufmann's reconstruction largely ignores the ambivalence in Beauvoir's comparison between love and religion. Dorothy Kaufmann McGall, "Simone de Beauvoir, *The Second Sex*, and Jean Paul Sartre," *Signs: Journal of Women in Culture and Society* 5, no. 2 (1979): 209–23, especially 216.

41. In *Die fröhliche Wissenschaft*, Friedrich Nietzsche ironically compared women's (heterosexual) love to religious faith, "the only faith women have." For a detailed analysis of the mainly Marxist and existentialist philosophical origins of Beauvoir's gendered comparison between heterosexual love and religious faith, see Korte, *Een passie voor transcendentie*, 149–54.

42. Beauvoir, *The Second Sex*, 670.

43. Ibid., 104.

44. See also ibid., 622.

45. Beauvoir herself considered religion a primary influence on her life and on her growing awareness of her position as a girl and a young woman. She stated that girls from southern Europe grow up with a religion that has an importance in their lives incomprehensible to women from an Anglo-American background. See "Une interview de Simone de Beauvoir par Madeleine Chapsal," in Claude Francis and Fernande Gontier, *Les écrits de Simone de Beauvoir: La vie—L'écriture. Avec en appendice: Textes inédits ou retrouvés* (Paris: Gallimard, 1979), 381–96.

46. "Une interview de Simone de Beauvoir," 383.

47. Dorothy Kaufmann McGall investigated Beauvoir's opinions on love and autonomy in light of her real life relationship with Sartre. She concluded: "Her ties to Sartre, however, have been as knotted and difficult in meaning as any tie to husband or family." Kaufmann McGall, "Simone de Beauvoir, *The Second Sex*, and Jean Paul Sartre," 223. For research on heterosexual and lesbian love in *The Second Sex*, see also Judith Butler, "Variations on Sex and Gender: Beauvoir, Wittig, and Foucault," in *Feminism as Critique: On the Politics of Gender*, ed. Seyla Benhabib and Drucilla Cornell (Minneapolis: University of Minnesota Press, 1987), 128–42; Jo-Ann Pilardi, "Female Eroticism in the Works of Simone de Beauvoir," in *The Thinking Muse: Feminism and Modern French Philosophy*, ed. Jeffner Allen and Iris Marion Young (Bloomington: Indiana University Press, 1989), 18–34; Toril Moi, *Feminist Theory and Simone de Beauvoir* (Oxford: Blackwell, 1990); Karin Vintges, *Filosofie als passie: Het denken van Simone de Beauvoir* (Amsterdam: Prometheus, 1992).

48. Beauvoir, *The Second Sex*, 287–90, especially 288.

49. Daly, *The Church and the Second Sex*, 220.

50. Daly, "Feminist Postchristian Introduction."

51. Mary Daly, *Gyn/Ecology: The Metaethics of Radical Feminism* (Boston: Beacon Press, 1978), 39.

52. The concept of religion Daly used in *Beyond God the Father* is derived primarily from critical sociologists such as Peter Berger and Herbert Marcuse. In their definition, religion's main function is to stabilize dominant social structures and to uphold norms and values that confirm the social status quo. Religious imagery and rituals make people "remember" and "internalize" the behavior expected of them. According to Daly, women in particular are socialized to consume and internalize religious images.

53. Daly, *Beyond God the Father*, 2.

54. Daly, *Gyn/Ecology*, 39.

55. Daly, *Pure Lust*, 31, 35–77; 170, 339.

56. Ibid., 57–66.

57. Daly, *Beyond God the Father*, 32.

58. Iris Marion Young, *Throwing Like a Girl and Other Essays in Feminist Philosophy and Social Theory* (Bloomington: Indiana University Press, 1990), 82.

59. Griffiths, "Feminism, Feelings, and Philosophy," 131–51; Weaver, *New Catholic Women*; Grimshaw, "Autonomy and Identity in Feminist Thinking," 90–108; Grimshaw, *Feminist Philosophers*, 146–61; Jean Grimshaw, " 'Pure Lust': The Elemental Feminist Philosophy of Mary Daly," *Radical Philosophy*, no. 49 (1988): 25.

60. Daly, *Pure Lust*, 136–38.

61. The term "Self" ("Self is capitalized when I am referring to the authentic center of women's process" [Daly, *Gyn/Ecology*, 26]) is introduced in *Gyn/Ecology* in close connection with a number of other, new expressions: gynocentric terms for God, consciousness and "living as a woman," namely "ultimate be-ing," "integrity of be-ing," and "gynocentric be-ing" (Daly, *Gyn/Ecology*, xi–xviii). This interrelatedness points to the fact that women's "Self" cannot be reduced to one of these three key notions; what is at stake is a *woman's* affirmation of her self, which is related to all three of these aspects of Be-ing. Compare the use of the term Self in the following instances:

> "The finding of our original integrity is re-membering our Selves." (Daly, *Gyn/Ecology*, 39)
> "The murder/dismemberment of the Goddess—that is, [of] the Self-affirming be-ing of women." (111)
> "Our refusal to collaborate in this killing and dismembering of our own Selves is the beginning of re-membering the Goddess—the deep source of creative integrity in women." (111)
> "The Goddess within—female divinity, that is our Selves." (111)

62. Luce Irigaray, *Speculum: De l'autre femme* (Paris: Minuit, 1974); Irigaray, *Ce Sexe qui n'en est pas un* (Paris: Minuit, 1977).

63. See for example Johanna Hodge, "Subject, Body, and the Exclusion of Women from Philosophy," in Griffiths and Whitford, *Feminist Perspectives in Philosophy*, 154, 167 n. 7.

64. See Daly, *Gyn/Ecology*, 19, 327, 350; Daly, *Pure Lust*, 177.

65. Virginia Woolf, *Moments of Being: Unpublished Autobiographical Writings*, edited, introduced, and annotated by Jeanne Schulkind (New York: University Press Sussex, 1976), 86–100.

66. Daly, *Gyn/Ecology*, 406.

67. Daly, *Pure Lust*, 159–60. Here, Daly refers to Paul Tillich, *Systematic Theology*, vol. 1 (London: Nisbet, 1953), 181.

68. Daly, *Pure Lust*, 30.

69. For descriptions of this ontological experience, Daly turns to Virginia Woolf's writings ("moments of being" as ontophanies [Daly, *Pure Lust*, 171–78]) and Sonia Johnson's work (the "breaking open process" as an epiphany [236–37]).

70. Jean Bethke Elshtain, "Feminist Discourse and Its Discontents: Language, Power, and Meaning," in *Feminist Theory: A Critique of Ideology* ed. Nannerl O. Keohane et al. (Chicago: University of Chicago Press, 1982), 135; Schüssler Fiorenza, *In Memory of Her*, 21–26.

71. Ynestra King, "Healing the Wounds," in *Gender/Body/Knowledge: Feminist Reconstructions of Being and Knowing*, ed. Alison M. Jaggar and Susan R. Bordo (New Brunswick: Rutgers University Press, 1989), 124, 136–37 n. 22.

72. Joan L. Griscom, "On Healing the Nature/History Split in Feminist Thought," in *Women's Consciousness, Women's Conscience: A Reader in Feminist Ethics*, ed. Barbara Hilkert Andolsen et al. (San Francisco: Harper and Row, 1985), 85–98.

73. Wildung Harrison, *Making the Connections*, 231; Weaver, *New Catholic Women*, 170–78.

74. Sallie McFague, *Metaphorical Theology: Models of God in Religious Language* (London: SCM Press, 1982), 155–59; Elisabeth Moltmann-Wendel, introduction to Moltmann-Wendel, ed., *Frau und Religion: Gotteserfahrungen im Patriarchat* (Frankfurt am Main: Fischer Taschenbuch Verlag, 1983), 14; Susan Brooks Thistlethwaithe, *Sex, Race, and God: Christian Feminism in Black and White* (New York, Crossroad, 1989), 16.

75. Brooke Williams, "The Feminist Revolution in 'Ultramodern' Perspective," *Cross Currents* 31 (1981): 311; Weaver, *New Catholic Women*, 176–77.

76. Großmaß, "Von der Verführungskraft der Bilder," 56–116; Anne Kent Rush, *Moon, Moon* (New York: Random House, 1976), 355.

77. Wanda Warren Berry, "Feminist Theology: The 'Verbing' of Ultimate/Intimate Reality in Mary Daly," in *Ultimate Reality and Meaning* 11, no. 3 (1988): 212–32; Korte, *Een gemeenschap waarin te geloven valt*, 162–65.

78. Daly, *Beyond God the Father*, 98–131. See also Korte, *Een passie voor transcendentie*, 284–90.

79. Sandra Harding, *The Science Question in Feminism* (Milton Keynes: Open University Press, 1986), 12.

80. Daly, *Pure Lust*, 275.

81. Ibid.

References

Alcoff, Linda. "Cultural Feminism Versus Post-Structuralism: The Identity Crisis in Feminist Theory." In *Feminist Theory in Practice and Progress*, edited by Micheline R. Balson et al., 295–326. Chicago: University of Chicago Press, 1989.

Allen, Jeffner, and Iris Marion Young, eds. *The Thinking Muse: Feminism and Modern French Philosophy*. Bloomington: Indiana University Press, 1989.

Aloysius, Sister, S.S.J. "The Epistemological Value of Sense Intuition." *Philosophical Studies* 5 (1955): 71–78.

Armour, Ellen T. "Questioning 'Woman' in Feminist/Womanist Theology: Irigaray, Ruether, and Daly." In *Transfigurations: Theology and the French Feminists*, edited by C. W. Maggie Kim et al., 143–70. Minneapolis: Fortress Press, 1993.

Atkinson, Clarissa W., et al., eds. *Shaping New Vision: Gender and Values in American Culture*. Ann Arbor: UMI Research Press, 1987.

Beauvoir, Simone de. *The Second Sex*. New York: Vintage Books, 1989.

Butler, Judith. "Variations on Sex and Gender: Beauvoir, Wittig, and Foucault." In *Feminism as Critique: On the Politics of Gender*, edited by Seyla Benhabib and Drucilla Cornell, 128–42. Minneapolis: University of Minnesota Press, 1987.

Christ, Carol P. "Embodied Thinking: Reflections on Feminist Theological Method." *Journal of Feminist Studies in Religion* 5, no. 1 (1989): 7–15.

Cooey, Paula M., et al., eds. *Embodied Love: Sensuality and Relationship as Feminist Values*. San Francisco: Harper and Row, 1988.

Daly, Mary. "Autobiographical Preface to the Colofon Edition," 5–14 and "Feminist Postchristian Introduction," 15–51. In Daly, *The Church and the Second Sex: With a New Feminist Postchristian Introduction by the Author*. Boston: Beacon Press, 1975.

———. *Beyond God the Father: Toward a Philosophy of Women's Liberation*. Boston: Beacon Press, 1973.

———. "A Built-in Bias." *Commonweal* 81 (January 15, 1965): 509–10.

———. *The Church and the Second Sex.* London: Chapman, 1968.

———. *Gyn/Ecology: The Metaethics of Radical Feminism.* Boston: Beacon Press, 1978.

———. *Natural Knowledge of God in the Philosophy of Jacques Maritain.* Rome: Officium Libri Catholici, 1966.

———. "New Archaic Afterwords." In Daly, *The Church and the Second Sex: With the Feminist Postchristian Introduction and New Archaic Afterwords by the Author,* xi–xxx. Boston: Beacon Press, 1985.

———. "New Intergalactic Introduction." In Daly, *Gyn/Ecology: The Metaethics of Radical Feminism: With a New Introduction by the Author,* xiii–xxxv. Boston: Beacon Press, 1991.

———. "Original Reintroduction." In Daly, *Beyond God the Father: Toward a Philosophy of Women's Liberation; With an Original Reintroduction by the Author,* xi–xxix. Boston: Beacon Press, 1985.

———. *Outercourse: The Be-Dazzling Voyage.* San Francisco: Harper, 1992.

———. *The Problem of Speculative Theology.* Boston: Thomist Press, 1965.

———. "The Problem of Speculative Theology: A Study in Saint Thomas." Ph.D. diss., University of Fribourg, Switzerland, 1963.

———. *Pure Lust: Elemental Feminist Philosophy.* Boston: Beacon Press, 1984.

———. "Vorwort zur deutschen Ausgabe von Beyond God the Father." In Daly, *Jenseits von Gottvater, Sohn & Co: Aufbruch zu einer Philosophie der Frauenbefreiung,* 5–10. Munich: Frauenoffensive, 1980.

Diamond, Irene, and Gloria Feman Orenstein, eds. *Reweaving the World: The Emergence of Ecofeminism.* San Francisco: Sierra Club Books, 1990.

Eisenstein, Hester. *Contemporary Feminist Thought.* London: Unwin Paperbacks, 1984.

Elisabeth, Sister M., I.H.M. "Two Contemporary Philosophers and the Concept of Being." *The Modern Schoolman* 25 (1947/48): 224–37.

Elshtain, Jean Bethke. "Feminist Discourse and Its Discontents: Language, Power, and Meaning," In *Feminist Theory: A Critique of Ideology,* edited by Nannerl O. Keohane et al., 127–45. Chicago: University of Chicago Press, 1982.

Fraga, Laura de Almeida Sampaio C. R. *L'intuition dans la philosophie de Jacques Maritain.* Paris: Vrin, 1963.

Francis, Claude, and Fernande Gontier. *Les écrits de Simone de Beauvoir: La vie—l'écriture. Avec en appendice: Textes inédits ou retrouvés.* Paris: Gallimard, 1979.

Fullbrook, Kate, and Edward Fullbrook. *Simone de Beauvoir and Jean-Paul Sartre: The Remaking of a Twentieth Century Legend.* New York: Harvester Wheatsheaf, 1993.

Gössmann, Elisabeth, ed. *Eva—Gottes Meisterwerk.* [Archiv für philosophie- und theologiegeschichtliche Frauenforschung; 2]. Munich: Iudicium, 1985.

———. *Das Wohlgelahrte Frauenzimmer.* [Archiv für philosophie- und theologiegeschichtliche Frauenforschung; 1]. Munich: Iudicium, 1984.

Greeve Davaney, Sheila. "The Limits of the Appeal to Women's Experience." In *Shaping New Vision: Gender and Values in American Culture,* edited by Clarissa W. Atkinson et al., 30–48. Ann Arbor: UMI Press, 1987.

———. "Problems with Feminist Theory: Historicity and the Search for Sure Foundations." In *Embodied Love: Sensuality and Relationship as Feminist Values,* edited by Paula M. Cooey, 79–96. San Francisco, 1988.

Griffiths, Morwenna. "Feminism, Feelings, and Philosophy." In *Feminist Perspectives in*

Philosophy, edited by Morwenna Griffiths and Margareth Whitford, 131–51. Bloomington: Indiana University Press, 1988.

Griffiths, Morwenna, and Margareth Whitford, eds. *Feminist Perspectives in Philosophy*. Bloomington: Indiana University Press, 1988.

Grimshaw, Jean. "Autonomy and Identity in Feminist Thinking." In *Feminist Perspectives in Philosophy*, edited by Morwenna Griffiths and Margareth Whitford, 90–108. Bloomington: Indiana University Press, 1988.

———. " 'Pure Lust': The Elemental Feminist Philosophy of Mary Daly." *Radical Philosophy*, no. 49 (1988): 24–30.

Griscom, Joan L. "On Healing the Nature/History Split in Feminist Thought." In *Women's Consciousness, Women's Conscience: A Reader in Feminist Ethics*, edited by Barbara Hilkert Andolsen et al., 85–98. San Francisco: Harper and Row, 1985.

Großmaß, Ruth. "Von der Verführungskraft der Bilder: Mary Daly's Elemental-Feministische Philosophie." In *Feministischer Kompaß, patriarchales Gepäck: Kritik konservativer Anteile in neueren feministischen Theorien*, edited by Ruth Großmaß and Christiane Schmerl, 56–116. Frankfurt and New York: Campus Verlag, 1989.

Großmaß, Ruth, and Christiane Schmerl, eds. *Feministischer Kompaß, patriarchales Gepäck: Kritik konservativer Anteile in neueren feministischen Theorien*. Frankfurt and New York: Campus Verlag, 1989.

Harding, Sandra. *The Science Question in Feminism*. Milton Keynes: Open University Press, 1986.

Hilkert Andolsen, Barbara, et al., eds. *Women's Consciousness, Women's Conscience: A Reader in Feminist Ethics*. San Francisco: Harper and Row, 1985.

Hirsch, Marianne, and Evelyn Fox Keller, eds. *Conflicts in Feminism*. New York: Routledge, 1990.

Hodge, Johanna. "Subject, Body, and the Exclusion of Women from Philosophy." In *Feminist Perspectives in Philosophy*, edited by Morwenna Griffiths and Margareth Whitford, 152–68. Bloomington: Indiana University Press, 1988.

Hollywood, Amy. "Violence and Subjectivity: *Wuthering Heights*, Julia Kristeva, and Feminist Theology." In *Transfigurations: Theology and the French Feminists*, edited by C. W. Maggie Kim et al., 81–108. Minneapolis: Fortress Press, 1993.

Irigaray, Luce. *Ce Sexe qui n'en est pas un*. Paris: Minuit, 1977.

———. *Speculum: De l'autre femme*. Paris: Minuit, 1974.

Jaggar, Alison M., and Susan R. Bordo, eds. *Gender/Body/Knowledge: Feminist Reconstructions of Being and Knowing*. New Brunswick: Rutgers University Press, 1989.

Jardine, Alice A. *Gynesis: Configurations of Woman and Modernity*. Ithaca: Cornell University Press, 1985.

Kaufmann McGall, Dorothy. "Simone de Beauvoir. *The Second Sex*, and Jean Paul Sartre." *Signs: Journal of Women in Culture and Society* 5, no. 2 (1979): 209–23.

Keller, Catherine. *From a Broken Web: Separation, Sexism, and Self*. Boston: Beacon Press, 1986.

Kent Rush, Anne. *Moon, Moon*. New York: Random House, 1976.

Keohane, Nannerl O., et al., eds. *Feminist Theory: A Critique of Ideology*. Chicago: University of Chicago Press, 1982.

Kim, C. W. Maggie, et al., eds. *Transfigurations: Theology and the French Feminists*. Minneapolis: Fortress Press, 1993.

King, Ynestra. "Healing the Wounds." In *Gender/Body/Knowledge: Feminist Reconstruc-*

tions of Being and Knowing, edited by Alison M. Jaggar and Susan R. Bordo, 115–41. New Brunswick: Rutgers University Press, 1989.

Korte, Anne-Marie. "Een gemeenschap waarin te geloven valt: Over de spirituele en de politieke betekenis van het geloof van vrouwen aan de hand van de 'ommekeer' van Anna Maria van Schurman en Mary Daly." Master's thesis, Catholic University of Nijmegen, The Netherlands, 1985.

———. *Een passie voor transcendentie: Feminisme, theologie en moderniteit in het denken van Mary Daly* (A passion for transcendence: Feminism, theology, and modernity in the thinking of Mary Daly.) Kampen: Kok, 1992.

Labalme, Patricia H., ed. *Beyond Their Sex: Learned Women of the European Past*. New York: New York University Press, 1984.

Lauretis, Teresa de. "Upping the Anti [*sic*] in Feminist Theory." In *Conflicts in Feminism*, edited by Marianne Hirsch and Evelyn Fox Keller, 255–70. New York: Routledge, 1990.

Lorde, Audre. "An Open Letter to Mary Daly." In *Sister Outsider: Essays and Speeches*, 66–71. Trumansburg N.Y.: Crossing Press, 1984.

McClintock Fulkerson, Mary. *Changing the Subject: Women's Discourses and Feminist Theology*. Minneapolis: Fortress Press, 1994.

McFague, Sallie. *Metaphorical Theology: Models of God in Religious Language*. London: SCM Press, 1982.

Maritain, Raissa. *Les grandes amitiés: Les aventures de la grâce*. 2 vols. New York: Editions de la Maison Française, vol. 1, 1942; vol. 2, 1944.

Maritain, Raissa [in co-operation with Jacques Maritain]. *Situation de la poésie*. Paris: Desclée de Brouwer, 1948.

Melano Couch, Beatriz. "Sor Juana Inés de la Cruz: The First Woman Theologian in the Americas." In *The Church and Women in the Third World*, edited by John C. B. Webster and Ellen Low Webster, 51–57. Philadelphia: Westminster Press, 1985.

Merchant, Carolyn. "Ecofeminism and Feminist Theory." In *Reweaving the World: The Emergence of Ecofeminism*, edited by Irene Diamond and Gloria Feman Orenstein, 100–105. San Francisco: Sierra Club Books, 1990.

Metz, Johan Baptist. *Christliche Anthropozentrik: Ueber die Denkform des Thomas von Aquin*. Munich: Koesel, 1962.

Moi, Toril. *Feminist Theory and Simone de Beauvoir*. Oxford: Blackwell, 1990.

Moltmann-Wendel, Elisabeth, ed. *Frau und Religion: Gotteserfahrungen im Patriarchat*. Frankfurt am Main: Fischer Taschenbuch Verlag, 1983.

Nakashima Brock, Rita. *Journeys by Heart: A Christology of Erotic Power*. New York: Crossroad, 1989.

Pilardi, Jo-Ann. "Female Eroticism in the works of Simone de Beauvoir." In *The Thinking Muse: Feminism and Modern French Philosophy*, edited by Jeffner Allen and Iris Marion Young, 18–34. Bloomington: Indiana University Press, 1989.

Ruether, Rosemary Radford. *Sexism and God-Talk: Toward a Feminist Theology*. Boston: Beacon Press, 1983.

Ruether, Rosemary Radford, and Rosemary Skinner Keller, eds. *Women and Religion in America*. Vol. 1, *The Nineteenth Century*. San Francisco: Harper and Row, 1981.

———. *Women and Religion in America*. Vol. 2, *The Colonial and Revolutionary Periods*. San Francisco: Harper and Row, 1983.

Sartre, Jean-Paul. *L'être et le néant: Essai d'ontologie phénoménologique*. Paris: Gallimard, 1943.

———. *L'existentialisme est un humanisme*. Paris: Nagel, 1946.

Schillebeeckx, Edward. "Het niet-begrippelijke kenmoment in de geloofsdaad: Probleemstelling." *Tijdschrift voor Theologie* 3 (1963): 167–94.

———. "Het niet-begrippelijke kenmoment in onze Godskennis volgens Thomas van Aquino." *Tijdschrift voor Philosophie* 14 (1952), 411–53.

———. *Openbaring en theologie*. [Theologische Peilingen; 1]. Baarn: Bilthoven, Nelissen, 1964.

Schüssler Fiorenza, Elisabeth. *In Memory of Her: A Feminist Theological Reconstruction of Christian Origins*. London: SCM Press, 1983.

Schurman, Anna Maria van. *Opuscula Hebraea, Graeca, Latina, Gallica, Prosaica et Metrica*. Leiden: Lugd. Batavor.: Ex Officina Elseviriorum, 1648.

Spelman, Elizabeth V. *Inessential Women: Problems of Exclusion in Feminist Thought*. Boston: Beacon Press, 1988.

Tillich, Paul. *Systematic Theology* Vol. 1. London: Nisbet, 1953.

Tong, Rosemary. *Feminist Thought: A Comprehensive Introduction*. London: Routledge, 1989.

Vintges, Karin. *Filosofie als passie: Het denken van Simone de Beauvoir*. Amsterdam: Prometheus, 1992.

Warren Berry,Wanda. "Feminist Theology: The 'Verbing' of Ultimate/Intimate Reality in Mary Daly." In *Ultimate Reality and Meaning* 11 no. 3 (1988): 212–32.

Weaver, Mary Jo. *New Catholic Women: A Contemporary Challenge to Traditional Religious Authority*. San Francisco: Harper and Row, 1985.

Webster, John C. B., and Ellen Low Webster, eds., *The Church and Women in the Third World*. Philadelphia: Westminster Press, 1985.

Weedon, Chris. *Feminist Practice and Poststructuralist Theory*. Oxford: Basil Blackwell, 1987.

Welch, Sharon D. *A Feminist Ethic of Risk*. Minneapolis: Fortress Press, 1990.

———. "Sporting Power: American Feminism, French Feminisms, and an Ethic of Conflict." In *Transfigurations: Theology and the French Feminists*, edited by C. W. Maggie Kim et al., 171–98. Minneapolis: Fortress Press, 1993.

Wildung Harrison, Beverly. *Making the Connections: Essays in Feminist Social Ethics*. Edited by Carol S. Robb. Boston: Beacon Press, 1985.

Williams, Brooke. "The Feminist Revolution in 'Ultramodern' Perspective." *Cross Currents* 31 (1981): 307–18.

Wilson, Katharina M., ed., *Medieval Women Writers*. Manchester: Manchester University Press, 1984.

Woolf, Virginia, *Moments of Being: Unpublished Autobiographical Writings*. Edited, introduced, and annotated by Jeanne Schulkind. New York: University Press Sussex, 1976.

Young, Iris Marion. *Throwing Like a Girl and Other Essays in Feminist Philosophy and Social Theory*. Bloomington: Indiana University Press, 1990.

4

Toward Biophilic Be-ing: Mary Daly's Feminist Metaethics and the Question of Essentialism

Marja Suhonen

In feminist discussion, essentialism is understood as a belief in sexually differentiated essences (Humm 1990, 64). Sexually differentiated behavior is assumed to reflect either biological or metaphysical essences. A biological determinist locates sexual difference in biological reality. To a biological determinist 'nature' is biological nature, to a metaphysical essentialist it is metaphysical nature. On the one hand, essentialism is either biological or psychological determinism; on the other hand, it is a notion of the unchanging structure of subjectivity (Grosz 1990, 334; Braidotti 1992, 77).

Criticizing essentialism has been a significant theme in feminist theory and politics. However, within feminist discussion the term "essentialist" has often been used as a pejorative label without showing that the theorist who is called an essentialist actually presupposes a sexual essence. Calling alternative theories essentialist is often a way of putting forward one's own theory as a more advanced one (Braidotti 1992, 77). Mary Daly, for example, and also Luce Irigaray, Julia Kristeva, and other so-called French feminists, have often been criticized as essentialist without adequate argument.[1]

This essay deals with Mary Daly's understanding of sexual difference as linked to her metaethics.[2] I will claim and show evidence that essentialist interpretations have no basis in Daly's thinking. My thesis is that, rather than being an essentialist, Daly is an existentialist in the broad technical sense that she believes that existence, acting and doing, precede essence.

Daly's name is most often associated with radical feminism and lesbian separatism. What is not so often remembered is that she was one of the first and the most influential feminist theologians. She started her career as a Roman Catholic theologian and philosopher. Even though she later left the church, it is easier to understand her work if one understands it in its relation to Aristotelian-Thomist thinking. Other significant influences include Simone de Beauvoir's existentialist ethics and Paul Tillich's existentialist theology, although Daly's ideas are more closely connected to so-called process theology.[3]

One central point in process theology is the idea that actuality is being-in-process (Cobb and Griffin 1977, 14). Human existence is understood as a becoming. Thus, to be human means that one is open to the future, and consequently the future is seen as an open field of possibilities. This remains the existentialist thesis according to which existence—acting and doing—precedes 'essence'. Thus one creates one's essence. Daly shares this basic understanding of being with process theologians and existentialists (see [1968, 1973] 1985b, 188; 1977).

The starting point in my reading is the principle of charity. It can be called a methodological attitude according to which we assume that the writer is reasonable and that her project is cogently related to the discourses she references. According to the principle of charity, if an interpretation attributes obvious contradictions to the text, we should question the interpretation rather than accept it as a given. So when we are trying to undertand Daly's thinking and her concepts, we should not accept easily an interpretation that claims, contrary to her explicit statements, that her thinking is "essentialist," and does not take into account her relation to existentialist-phenomenological philosophy, or to process theology.

Equality

Those who call Daly essentialist refer to her later phase of thinking. I will show that such claims are based on insufficient readings of her texts. However, I will first take a look at Daly's earlier works, *The Church and the Second Sex* (1968) and *Beyond God the Father* (1973). In both of these one of the main themes is criticism of an essentialist understanding of "woman" and sexual difference.

Daly's first work, *The Church and the Second Sex,* was written in a Roman Catholic context.[4] She illustrates the implausibility of the metaphysical, essentialist notion of woman that prevails in the Christian tradition. She argues for equality between men and women. The church must acknowledge the importance of striving for equality, otherwise it will look as if Christianity is an enemy of human progress (Daly [1968, 1975] 1985a, 219).

At the end of the 1960s, Daly argued for the fundamental equality of women and men in theological terms. She looks at Thomas Aquinas's concepts of woman and soul. She interprets Thomistic principles as liberating for women, despite Aquinas's understanding of women's natural subordination to men, which is based on alleged weakness in the intellectual soul.[5] Daly claims that Aquinas is contradictory in that his theory allows arguments both for and against equality between the sexes. According to Aquinas, the intellectual soul is infused directly by God and therefore the human being is made in the image of God. Daly states that, according to Thomistic principles, there cannot be an essential difference between woman's and man's intellectual souls because, to Aquinas, the possession of an intellectual soul is natural and essential to both men and women. She concludes that Aquinas's notion of the soul seems to support the argument for equality between the sexes, contrary to his explicit claim about man as the principle and the end of woman (Daly [1968, 1973] 1985a, 91–95; cf. S.Th. I 92–93).[6]

In her second feminist work, *Beyond God the Father* (1973), Daly continues to criticize the essentialist concept of woman.[7] She still sees equality between the sexes as an important goal, even though women's autonomy is primary. However, she no longer thinks in terms of equality, but rather in terms of difference, and she describes her position as radical feminism. She is now more interested in symbols and metaphors and their meaning than in anthropology. Her understanding of Christianity has changed; she claims that it is an inherently sexist religion. Feminists should reject Christianity and create a new form of spirituality outside of the church.[8] We should also accept that the radical feminist walking away from the church may be a man as well as a woman. Men are welcomed to her radical feminist movement (see Daly [1973] 1985b, 169–74).

Daly uses the notion "sexual caste system" to describe the oppressed situation of women. She sees this as plausible because the caste system is pervasive, yet amenable to change. The sexual caste system can be maintained only as long as both the oppressed and the oppressors consent to it. This consent is obtained through the process of sex-role socialization, which starts from the moment a child is born. However, women and men live in a reciprocal relation. This means that if women change, men will change too (Daly [1973] 1985b, 2–3). Thus, first, Daly points to the social constraint that maintains the sexual caste system, and second she thinks that we can change this system.

Daly's understanding of the reciprocal relationship between the sexes resembles Simone de Beauvoir's views. Beauvoir thinks that men and women exist in mutual dependence; one can attain independence only within this existential dependence. She assumes that women accept their subordinate situation because they do not have an identity *as women* (Beauvoir [1949] 1988, 17–20; Lundgren-Gothlin 1995, 10). Daly accepts this assumption, and her feminist project is to create/discover this identity.

The sexual system that divides people into two categories presupposes that the subject denies her/himself the characteristics that are thought to belong to the "opposite" sex. Daly tries to develop a way of thinking that goes beyond this division, and that enables the subject to be her/himself. Her ideal is an *integral being*, and in *Beyond God the Father* the metaphor for this is the androgyne who denies the stereotypical opposites of femininity and masculinity and thus transgresses or rejects her/his gender role and breaks the patriarchal order. When people develop toward an integral being there is a radical change in consciousness and behavior. Old religious symbols and phallic morality lose their meaning and their power. By "phallic morality" Daly means morality that glorifies characteristics demanded from the oppressed, and especially from women, such as selflessness, sacrificial love, and humility. She calls the theory of phallic morality a passive ethic, since for a woman to act in accordance with phallic morality is for her to submit to her lot (Daly [1973] 1985b, 14–16, 98–131).

In *Beyond God the Father*, Daly argues for a new kind of normativeness in sexual ethics. According to her, an ethics that claims that heterosexuality is more valuable than homosexuality is patriarchal. Even the opposition between heterosexuality and homosexuality is a patriarchal classification. The oppression of women and hostility toward homosexuality are connected: this hostility and fear of " 'homosexuality' reflects anxiety over losing power that is based upon sex role stereotyping." Therefore, in phallic morality, homosexuality is a problem, and lesbian and gay relationships are not seen as authentic relationships. Daly wants to deny heterosexist morality, but she also thinks that feminists should avoid all other "dogmas" concerning sexual behaviour. Thus, while noting the interconnectedness of sexism and heterosexism, she dismisses the idea that feminists must reject heterosexuality (Daly [1973] 1985b, 124–26).

According to Daly, phallic thinking gives both 'lesbian' and 'homosexual' a negative value. Using 'lesbian' as a derogatory label is a way of keeping women under patriarchal control. She thinks that because women are afraid of this label, they also often repress their nonsexual feelings of love toward other women. Feminists should use the terms 'lesbian' and 'homosexual' to mean "a deep and intimate relationship with a person of the same sex, with or without genital activity." The same criterion should be applied to heterosexuality as to homosexuality: what is important in a relationship is not one's sex or the possibility to reproduce, but the level of intimacy and communication. Consequently 'homosexual' and 'heterosexual' are irrelevant characterizations when considering the quality of a relationship (Daly [1973] 1985b, 126).[9] Daly's attempts to change the evaluative connotations of these "labels" is one example of her effort to turn around patriarchal meanings, to confront external judgments and to name oneself, as she puts it. Perhaps Daly's notion of patriarchy is best understood as a symbolic universe (see Berger and Luckmann [1966] 1972, 112–22); she sees patriarchy as a theoretical tradition that legitimizes women's subordinate status. It is a totality in the sense that all human experience takes place within it. Daly argues, however, that it is possible to escape from patriarchy. Her understanding of patriarchy and necessity is existentialist, and as such dynamic, allowing for change.[10]

Daly points out that heterosexism is just one form of sexism. To achieve equality one has to understand other patriarchal forms of oppression, such as economic oppression (Daly [1973] 1985b, 126–27).

As a summary, it can be said that, in her earlier phase, Daly criticizes both metaphysical and biological determinist forms of essentialism as they relate to sexual difference, and that she starts her criticism from the traditional Christian understanding of "woman." She sees equality between the sexes as a goal. Her ideal for being is integrity, which she thinks is realized in the androgyne who transgresses the dichotomic sex-role system.

Separatism

My claim is that Daly has never given up this antiessentialist and antideterminist notion of sexual difference, and that she is true to her basic principles in her later writings too. Even though there are obvious changes in her thinking, there is no reversal. Rather, there is a continuum in her themes and her philosophical and theological understanding—including her antiessentialist understanding of sexual difference.[11] As she wrote in 1985, she has never abandoned the basic ideas of *Beyond God the Father*.

Daly already sees naming as a central part of her project in *Beyond God the Father*. She writes: "To exist humanly is to name the self, the world, and God. . . . The liberation of language is rooted in the liberation of ourselves" ([1973] 1985b, 8). This project of liberating the language is even stronger in her later work: her language changes, and she starts to create her own, to spell her own words (see Daly [1987] 1988). One aspect of this new language is the central position given to symbols and metaphors. According to Daly, symbols "participate in that to which they point" and "open up levels of reality otherwise closed to us." That is why the use of symbols is necessary to her feminist project. These attributes refer to metaphors too, but in addition, "metaphors evoke action, movement." Metaphors name and invoke the change. Since Daly sees her feminist philosophy of being as concerned with movement and transformation, metaphors are necessary in the process of naming (Daly 1984, 24–26; [1987] 1988, 82).

There are three terminological changes that indicate alterations in Daly's thinking. First, she discards the term 'God' and replaces it with 'Goddess'. She does this because she believes it is impossible to erase masculine imagery from the word 'God'. However, it is not enough to start to speak of 'Goddess'; if 'Goddess' remains a noun, divinity is still understood in patriarchal terms as a stable, permanent being. Goddess, whom she prefers to call Be-ing, is Verb calling for action (Daly 1977, 89–96; [1978] 1991a, xlvii–xlviii; cf. [1973] 1985b, 13–43).

Second, Daly abandons androgyne as an unsuccessful attempt to express the integrity of be-ing. She points out that if we were living in an androgyne society, there would not be any point in speaking of androgyny because people would not have notions of stereotypic sex roles that should be united. Her new expression for women's integrity is a woman-identified woman who is committed to women's becoming and liberation. Such a woman shows solidarity to all women regardless of their race, ethnic background, class, or nationality.[12] The third term she rejects is 'homosexuality', because it excludes lesbians just as the term 'man' excludes women (Daly 1977, 87–89; [1978] 1991a, xlviii).

Abandoning these terms is part of a larger change. Daly radicalizes her feminism and changes her strategy of criticizing patriarchy. Her critical approach resembles that of Luce Irigaray: Daly reads Thomas Aquinas's and Paul Tillich's texts similarly to the way Irigaray reads Plato or Freud, using mimicry and parody to problematize the functioning of the system. In an interview given in 1975, Irigaray says that the task of feminist research is to "disrupt" philosophical discourse, and she explains further that mimicry is a method by which we can do this. She wants to point out how the philosophers separate their concepts and ideas from the body, the passions, and the maternal, how they put their system together and how this system works. For her it is an examination of "the operation of the 'grammar,' " of the figures of discourse and also what is not articulated but what is supposed: the unspoken conditions of the discourse (Irigaray [1977] 1985, 74–76, 150–51; Heinämaa 1991). Daly's approach can also be described this way. She writes that "words, sentences, paragraphs *carry* meanings" that are not openly stated or even thought by the writer. By this strategy of mimicry and parody Daly shows how the theologians have a masculine bias in their thinking (Daly 1984, 155–60; [1987] 1988).

The changes in language also show that Daly is moving toward a mode of discourse that has often been called separatism. Her project is a feminist ethical one, but she emphasizes ontology, be-ing. She argues that if a woman cannot *be* herSelf, she is still in an oppressive situation. As indicated above, her ideal is an integral be-ing. In a patriarchal world, a woman's self becomes fragmented; she becomes alienated from herSelf.

Daly distinguishes between Original, integral Self and false self.[13] False self is "any of the many false identities inflicted upon women under patriarchy; the internalized possessor that covers and re-covers the Original Self." The process of liberation from patriarchy is the process of becoming one's integral Self. This integral Self is "the Original core of one's be-ing that cannot be contained within the State of Possession." It is "living spirit/matter" and "the psyche that participates in Be-ing" (Daly [1987] 1988, 95). However, the Original Self is not a static essence, but a constantly changing be-ing.

To Daly, separatism means "expanding room of our own." It is parting oneself from everything that causes fragmentation, everything that separates one from "the flow of integrity within her Self." The core of separatism is to destroy everything that creates false selves and that alienates one from one's Self (Daly [1978] 1991, 380–82; 1984, 370; [1987] 1988, 96). Thus, for her, separatism is not so much a goal to be achieved, as a means for making it possible to be in touch with oneSelf.

Metamorphosis

In *Beyond God the Father*, Daly proposes that salvation happens when the fragmented—that is, oppressed—Self becomes integrated.[14] It is hardly an overstatement to say that the process of becoming integrated is the core of Daly's feminist thinking. In her later phase, especially in *Pure Lust*, she speaks about Metamorphosis, which directs woman's consciousness toward final liberation from patriarchy. Women who are in the process of freeing themselves from patriarchy are moving toward further evolution.[15] Power for this evolution comes from the soul, which Daly calls the "Telic Focusing Principle." As the term indicates, she uses the Aristotelian notion of the soul as a springboard. Aristotle's thinking is teleological. What serves the purpose of a being's being seeks to be realized. If a being is not in a state in which it realizes its *telos*, *potentia* breaks out. If there are no obstacles, *potentia* realizes itself as a movement toward *telos* (Sihvola 1994, 40). Thus, in teleological thinking, *telos* directs a movement, while in causal thinking the cause determines what happens. Daly seems to accept this basic idea but she criticizes Aristotle's concept of soul for being too static: according to Aristotle, there may be accidental, but not essential, changes in the soul (Daly 1984, 344–50). She is trying to break this essentialist characterisation of the soul by putting it into a movement. Here we can see her existentialism: the constant essence is replaced by a changing be-ing.

According to Thomas Aquinas, there is one soul in a person, and this soul is a unity. Because the soul is the form of the body, it is present in each part of the body.[16] Daly substitutes the word 'Self' for the word 'soul'. She writes: "There are not many Selves in one woman, but rather, one Self, wholly present in that woman." She does not claim that 'Self' and 'soul' are equivalent terms. Soul is just one word to describe different aspects of Self. Another word may be 'body' or 'spirit'. Her point is to emphasize that there is an essential integrity at the very core of a woman's Self while neither "core" nor Self is conceived as a fixed Aristotelian substance (Daly 1984, 345).

To be free and happy involves the unfolding and realization of this integrity. Happiness and be-ing free are interconnected: a free woman is a happy woman. Happiness has an ontological meaning. Happiness is a life of activity. It is activity of the mind, or contemplation.[17] Thus Daly's notion of happiness is Aristotelian. Integrity is realized when a woman is present in all her activities. If woman's Self is integrated there is consistency in her behavior, because the Self's energy is focused, and fragmented false selves do not have power over her. Thus Happiness is "intensely focused ontological activity" (Daly 1984, 345–46; [1987] 1988, 64, 78).[18]

As indicated above, even though she uses the Aristotelian concept of the soul as a metaphor for integrity of the Self, Daly criticizes it for being too static and essentialist. Another aspect of Aristotelian understanding of human nature, which Daly criticizes, is the notion of sexual difference. According to Aristotle, sexual difference is accidental, nonessential; it does not categorize individuals in different species. According to Daly, Aristotle considered women human in theory, but they were less than human in society. "Women were said to belong to the fixed species called MAN." Daly states that women who are in the process of freeing themselves from patriarchy are quite horrified at such a blanket notion of belonging because they experience that they do not "belong" (Daly 1984, 350).[19]

There seems to be a contradiction: first Daly criticizes the notion of the soul for being essentialist and thus static, and then she criticizes the notion of sexual difference for being accidental. This does not prove, however, that her own concept of sexual difference is essentialist: she is simply stating that in a society in which women are not treated as "wholly human" it is paradoxical and not to the point to claim that they are as human as men.

Daly's criticism goes further than sexual difference: she wants to reject the whole traditional thinking in terms of species. This is why she speaks of macroevolution and metamorphosis.

Macroevolution is defined as "evolutionary change involving large and complex steps as transformation of one species to another" (Daly 1984, 350; [1987] 1988, 79). According to Daly, macroevolution is needed because "metapatriarchal" women—women who go beyond patriarchy—"experience as ineffably accidental" the connection "with the species" that has among its accomplishments witch-hunts, death camps, torture, and racism. In this evolution she differentiates two "species": biophilic, or life-loving; and necrophilic, death-loving. "This differentiation is affirmed by a series of conscious choices" (Daly 1984, 350–52, 413–14). Thus, be-ing constitutes essence. That is, we construct our essences through the choices we make.

Biophilic creatures constantly choose to differentiate themselves from necrophilic species, and these chosen differences are essential. Daly thinks that the traditional concept of the species blurs the difference between the biophilic and the necrophilic, whose lives are differently oriented. She rejects the whole idea of a unified human species. There is no such thing because the "lived decision" constitutes a difference which is greater than any species difference. In fact, biophilic creatures cannot be called a static species, because their essences are changing—essences that it may be helpful to think of as (in Maurice Merleau-Ponty's words) "a certain manner of being, in the active sense, a certain *Wesen*, in the sense that, says Heidegger, this word has when it is used as a verb" ([1964] 1975, 115). The difference between biophilic and necrophilic be-ings is confirmed by conscious choices or lived decisions. Daly writes about "differently oriented lives." There is not only one choice; be-ing biophilic (or necrophilic) is a continuous process (Daly 1984, 351–52). Consequently, values and meanings are constitutive to the Self.[20]

It seems that 'species' in the Dalyan sense should be understood as an attitude toward life: Daly gives ontological meaning to ethical activity and attitude toward life. The subject chooses either a biophilic or a necrophilic way of life. Here Daly's thinking resembles the philosophy of Levinas, Beauvoir, and Irigaray, where ethics precedes ontology.

In short, Daly first rejects the traditional concept of 'human species', and second, she claims that because the essences of biophilic creatures are changing, they cannot be said to form one static species. The soul of a person does not confine her/him within a 'species'; it is rather a principle of her/his uniqueness and diversity.[21]

Essentialist?

Daly writes that the distinction between biophilic and necrophilic essences is not based on sexual difference. Patriarchy is harmful not only to women's but also to men's consciousness (Daly 1984, 350–51, 351n). To insist that her notion of sexual difference is still essentialist is to assume that all women are biophilic and all men necrophilic.[22] This does not succeed because there are examples in her texts of both necrophilic women and biophilic men.

Woman-identified women are certainly biophilic, but there are nonbiophilic women too, such as so-called token women. According to Daly, tokenism is a patriarchal phenomenon allowing some women to succeed in social and cultural hierarchies to create an illusion of improvement in women's situation. A token woman identifies with men, and thus is willing to betray other women. Through betrayal she feeds hatred of women in women (Daly [1978] 1991a, 333–36; 1984, 109–11; [1987] 1988, 231).

Clearly, token women are not biophilic. It is of course possible to claim that Daly assumes that token women will at some point in time recognize their tokenism and then change the direction of their actions. However, I do not find such an assumption in her texts. Even if it were there, one question remains: If biophilic consciousness is essential to women, how is it possible for a woman to live in a necrophilic manner?

Further, most of the men Daly writes about are patriarchal and necrophilic. It could be said that, even though Daly is not essentialist in her view of women, she is so in her view of men. My first objection to this is that Daly's project is primarily to make room for women, not for men. In any case, not all men are patriarchal. Jesus of Nazareth, for example, seems to have been a victim of patriarchy (see Daly 1984, 131).[23]

In her autobiography Daly writes of her friend's death, and that he was "an extraordinarily sensitive and Life-loving person." Thus, according to Daly he was Life-loving, that is, biophilic (1993, 310). It can always be said that this man is an exception in Daly's thinking, but if even one man can be biophilic, then being a woman is not a necessary condition for being biophilic. Similarly, being a man is not a necessary or sufficient condition for being necrophilic.

Sex/Gender Paradigm and Sexual Difference

I have argued that the claim about Mary Daly's essentialism is incorrect. If I am right, if it is so clear that Daly is not an essentialist, then why is she accused of it so often?

It seems to me that one reason for this reading is the so-called sex/gender paradigm. The sex/gender paradigm is a view of the constitution of sexual identity, and it is widely accepted in feminist literature. Sometimes it is even assumed that it is necessary for feminist thinking. The problem arises when a critic assumes that the writer bases her/his work on the sex/gender paradigm and interprets the text accordingly (see Chanter 1993).

The core of the sex/gender paradigm is in the conceptual distinction between biological sex and social gender.[24] Here sex refers to biological nature or the biological body, and gender is the socially constructed interpretation of that body. If a critic reads sex/gender concepts into the text but the writer does not base her discussion on the distinction, then the interpretation made by the critic is likely to be problematic. My claim is that this is exactly what happens in Daly's case. Daly does not use the sex/gender concepts but begins her criticism with fundamentally different points.

For example, Daly writes that "those who are in possession of a penis" are the oppressors within the sexual caste system (1984, 232). If this is interpreted within the sex/gender paradigm, 'penis' would refer to anatomical sex, and thus it would seem that Daly sees the cause of women's oppression in biology. First, I will argue below that Daly does not explain woman's situation causally. Second, her comments on the penis should not be reduced to anatomy and biology. Penis as such is not the main point but rather the *possession* of a penis: in a patriarchal system, to possess a penis gives one privileges, and to lack one means missing out on these privileges.

In sex/gender paradigm, becoming gendered is understood as a causal process: gender is described as the combined effect of social and biological causes (Heinämaa 1996a, 119–29; 1996b, 295). Daly's texts do not present a causal explanation for women's oppression, or a causal understanding of women's and men's relationship. The focus is not on efficient causes, but on meanings and their constructions, in the open future. When Daly opposes biological determinism, she states that the male is the oppressor "by virtue of his rationalizing supremacy on the basis of biological difference" ([1973] 1985b, 125). She sees this rationalizing as a choice and an act of signification.

There are some instances in Daly's texts that clearly indicate that she rejects the sex/gender paradigm. For example, there is a passage in *Gyn/Ecology* on separatism where she discusses differences between women. She refers to the relations between women and men, and writes that "the basis of woman-identified relationships is neither biological differences nor socially constructed opposite roles" ([1978] 1991a, 382). Thus she rejects both biological determinist and constructionist theories of sexual difference. Difference is based neither on biological sex, nor on social gender. In the following passages I will explain her original understanding of its nature.

On the terminological level, Daly's thinking also differs from the sex/gender paradigm in which the terms 'female' and 'male' refer to sex, 'feminine' and 'masculine' to gender, and 'woman' and 'man' to both sex and gender. In Daly's texts, 'female' or 'male' does not refer to biology any more than 'woman' or 'man' does. For example, when she writes about the 'female Self', it would be misleading to interpret this as a biological self, since she has written that the body, like the soul or the spirit, is just another way of discussing different aspects of the Self. Nor should this body, which is one way of discussing the Self, be interpreted as bioscientific, but rather as the *lived* body, in the sense that existentialists have given to it. 'Feminine' and 'masculine' are patriarchal stereotypes, both of which should be rejected.[25] When she criticizes Aristotle, Daly uses the concepts 'sexual differentiation', 'sexual difference', and 'the difference of gender' synonymously. If these are synonymous, then it is obvious that the sex/gender distinction is not something she finds useful. She later uses the terms 'female' and 'male' in a note to refer to 'gender' (Daly 1984, 350–51, 351n). Thus, analyzing Daly's texts through the sex/gender paradigm does not do justice to her way of thinking.

My proposal is that Daly's view of sexual difference becomes more understandable in the context of theories of sexual difference that see the body as constitutive to the subject and part of her/his situation. I am particularly thinking of Simone de Beauvoir's phenomenological-existentialist project.[26] She distinguishes the body as described by the biosciences from the body as the lived reality and the starting point of our actions. She argues that causal explanations fail to make understandable the relation between women and men. She calls her perspective "existentialist ethics," and emphasizes that it is a study of *values* and *meanings* (see Heinämaa 1996a, 1996b; cf. Beauvoir [1949] 1988, 28). In this theoretical approach, sex and gender appear as theoretical abstractions that are developed in the specific practices of explaining and predicting human behavior. They are based on the feminine and masculine styles of being. Sexual difference appears primarily on the level of *the lived body*, not on the level of bioscientific description (Heinämaa 1997, 32). Like Beauvoir's, Daly's interest is in the *lived experiences* of women.

Summary

Whether 'essentialism' is used to refer to biological or metaphysical determinism or fixed, unchanging subjectivity, Daly is not an essentialist. Nor does it make any difference whether the focus is on her earlier or later works. If one wants to criticize Daly, one has to look for something other than essentialism.

For example, the distinction between biophilic and necrophilic may seem not unlike moralist thinking. My interpretation is more positive, however: in speaking of the biophilic and the necrophilic, Daly emphasizes the subject's responsibility in relation to either maintaining or destroying life on earth. 'Biophilic' and 'necrophilic' refer primarily to moral choices or values. Because ethics precedes ontology, moral choices provide the basis for essences. These essences depend on values and are open to change.

It could be said that, for Daly, uncovering the Original and integrated Self is the *telos* of the subject. However, like essences, the Self is changing. The biophilic Self is in a continuous process. Instead of being an essentialist, Daly seems to be a thinker who shares the basic ideas of process theology. In her thinking, the future is always open.

Abbreviations

HA	History of Animals
NE	Nikomakhoksen etiikka
S. Th.	Summa Theologiae

Notes

1. Daly is an essentialist according to, e.g., Elshtain (1981, 209–10), Grimshaw (1986, 120–22, 126), and Humm (1990, 64). Her essentialism is often taken for granted. For example, Humm in her feminist dictionary merely uses Daly as an example of an essentialist feminist without giving any evidence. Elshtain's claims are interesting, because she notes that essentialism does not really fit into Daly's theory, but she still insists that Daly is an essentialist.

On Luce Irigaray's claimed essentialism, see Heinämaa 1993, 26–27 and Grosz 1989, 112–13. Tina Chanter claims that there is a feminist fear of women's bodies behind such claims with regard to Irigaray and Kristeva. At least, in calling Kristeva an essentialist, sex/gender paradigm is used as an instrument (Chanter 1993, 181, 185–86).

2. I am grateful to Sara Heinämaa, Simo Knuuttila, Eva Lundgren-Gothlin, Tuija Pulkkinen, Martina Reuter, and the editors of this book, Marilyn Frye and Sarah Hoagland, for helpful comments on earlier versions of this essay.

3. My point is not to reduce Daly's thinking to any of these, but to find perspectives that are helpful in trying to understand her. Her texts are not at all simple, and in order to avoid simplistic interpretations it is necessary to be aware of her philosophical and theological roots. Simone de Beauvoir's existentialist-phenomenological project is particularly illuminating in the context of Daly's understanding of sexual difference.

One reason why interpretations of Daly's texts are not always definitive may lie in the education and background of the interpreter. One example of this is Rosi Braidotti's interpretation, in *Patterns of Dissonance* (1991). Braidotti sees Daly as not being able to move away from phallocentrism (versus Irigaray). During her visit to Finland at the beginning of 1994 I asked her why. She told me that I was not the first theologian to criticize her interpretation of Daly. In fact, all her theologian friends had said she was totally wrong about Daly. Braidotti also admitted that she had had a negative attitude toward theology when she was writing *Patterns of Dissonance*, which also affected her interpretation. Her view changed in *Nomadic Subjects* (1994): now she sees the similarity between Daly's and Irigaray's projects.

4. Daly started to write her book after visiting II Council (1962–65) in Rome. For radical and liberal Roman Catholics, this council occurred at a time when they believed and hoped that the church would change, as Daly herself stated ([1968, 1975] 1985a, 9).

5. Aquinas based his understanding on Aristotle's theory. According to Aristotle, woman's practical intellect does not have authority over the desires of the so-called vegetative and sensitive soul. Because man's intellect has this authority, woman is naturally inferior to man and he should have authority over her. However, woman's theoretical reason is as good as man's; females may even be more ready to learn, and more intelligent, than males (Sihvola 1994, 190; see HA VIII(IX) 1. 608a24–26).

6. In her post-Christian introduction, Daly points out that Aquinas is not liberating from the radical feminist point of view. However, what the "Daly of 1968" liked was "his ontological sense, his intuition of being" (Daly [1968, 1975] 1985a, 23). Thus, Thomas Aquinas's thinking is one source in Daly's radical feminist "philosophy of Be-ing."

7. For her views against biological determinism see, e.g., Daly ([1973] 1985b, 125).

8. Daly often seems to be almost hostile toward Christian feminists. Despite her conviction that it is not possible to reform Christianity, she also points out that it is a personal choice whether or not to stay within a patriarchal tradition, and there is no easy answer, and no rule according to which everyone should act (1991b, 335).

9. I think this rejection of heterosexist ethics is as important a change as the rejection of Christianity. As far as I know, Daly was the first theologian to claim that heterosexuality is by no means more valuable than homosexuality. Even though most feminist theologians nowadays agree with Daly, almost all official Christian statements concerning sexuality are heterosexist. See, e.g., "Congregation for the Doctrine of the Faith" (1988).

10. See Daly ([1987] 1988, 87–88). There is a universalist tendency in Daly's notion of patriarchy that may be seen as problematic. Contrary to what Daly ([1973] 1985b, 2) assumes, it makes a huge difference whether one is a woman living in Saudi Arabia or in Sweden. However, universalism is not the same as essentialism, as, e.g., Grimshaw (1986, 120–22) assumes it is. Grimshaw supposes that because Daly's notion of patriarchy is universal, she also thinks that there are universal male needs or desires, and that these comprise the male essence. However, it is not necessary to draw these conclusions. Daly rather assumes a universal patriarchy that is hostile toward women and in which we all live either as women or as men. As Grosz has pointed out, universalism "may be conceived in purely social terms." It suggests that there is something common in all women, and "it can only assert similarities . . . what homogenizes women as a category" (see Grosz 1990, 333–35).

11. Anne-Marie Korte sees *Beyond God the Father*, *Gyn/Ecology*, and *Pure Lust* as "Daly's 'systematic-theological' triptych," which can be compared with Paul Tillich's three-part *Systematic Theology* (see Tillich 1978). According to Korte, Daly takes a two-sided approach to "liberation from theology" in these books. On the one hand she describes how traditional theology has oppressed "woman" and "femaleness," and on the other hand she tries to make these terms more liberating (Korte 1992, 416).

12. Daly's move from androgyneity to woman-identified woman is part of the Northern American radical feminist discussion of the 1970s, when radical feminists tried to create ideals that would help to loosen women's subordination. One such ideal was the androgyne; another was based on the idea of woman-centeredness. Shulamith Firestone ([1970] 1988), for example, developed the idea of androgyne, and Adrienne Rich (1980) that of woman-centeredness. See Tong 1989, 95–109.

13. One way of pointing out the distinction between the false self and the integral Self is the capitalization in integral Self. Capitalization points to the meaning of the word. See Daly ([1987] 1988, xxi–xxii). Thus, "Self" refers to integral self and "self" to the false self.

14. There are many things that seem to connect Daly's and Luce Irigaray's thinking, and one of them is the idea of salvation, which should not be understood only as religious salvation. At the beginning of *Ethics*, Irigaray claims that if we could rethink sexual difference, it could be our "salvation" (*salut*). Pia Sivenius points out that the French word *salut* is also salutation, and so salvation is not a permanent state but a place of meeting and doing (Irigaray [1984] 1993, 5; Heinämaa 1996a, 164). For Daly, at least some of a person's oppression is due to "sex-role stereotyping." She thinks that sex as we live it in patriarchy is a site of a fragmentation of ourselves. But sex could also be a locus of integration, and it would contribute to our salvation.

15. Of course, Daly is not using the term "evolution" in its Darwinian sense, and her use of it shows the continuity of her thinking. While she was writing *Gyn/Ecology*, she also wrote about "new sensibility," which is "ontological mutation" (1977, 97).

16. Aristotle rejected both the material and the dualistic notion of soul. The soul is neither bodily nor separate from the body (Sihvola 1994, 44). When Daly accepts the Aristotelian-Thomist notion of soul, she rejects the substantial use of sex/gender paradigm, which reproduces the dichotomy between nature and culture. See Heinämaa 1996a, 114–17; 1996b, 292–93.

17. According to Thomas Aquinas, humans have, first, a natural *telos* that is Aristotelian, and

second, a supernatural *telos* that becomes realized through God's help. Daly criticizes Aquinas's notion that a human being cannot attain final happiness through her/his natural powers. She feels that Aquinas changed the Aristotelian notion of happiness as an activity of the mind and body into passivity after death (Daly 1984, 337–40; see NE X, 6–7; S.Th. I q. 12 a. 5; Työrinoja 1990, 122–26). Daly's critique of Aquinas may be compared with the difference between Plato's and Aristotle's notions of happiness. According to Plato, good, toward which beings are striving, is transcendent and one cannot attain it in earthly life. Aristotle thought that good is immanent, within beings (Alanen 1985, 22). Daly's notion of happiness is Aristotelian, while Aquinas sees final happiness as transcendent.

18. Simone de Beauvoir also discusses the relationship between happiness and freedom, as well as a person's happiness, which is characterized by freedom. However, she makes a point of the problem with "happiness": it is possible to picture as "happy" a situation in which one person wants to put another. Thus "happiness" can be a tool of oppression (Beauvoir [1949] 1988, 28–29). This resembles Daly's critique of passive ethics. Beauvoir's "transcendence" and Daly's "life of activity" seem to be similar.

19. English language is significant in Daly's critique. Aristotle wrote in Greek, which has separate words for human being (*anthropos*), man (*aner, andros*), and woman (*gyne, gynaikos*).

20. Here Daly comes close to Beauvoir's—and Maurice Merleau-Ponty's—phenomenological notion of the lived body. They regarded the body as a sediment of values and meanings created by its earlier acts. People realize these values and meanings in their acts. Sara Heinämaa argues that Beauvoir meant this sediment of acts when she wrote that "one is not born but rather becomes (*devient*) a woman" (Heinämaa 1995, 33–34; 1997). Daly does not claim that sex would determine how to "become"; quite the opposite, she emphasizes the choice within becoming.

21. Daly makes a reference to Thomas Aquinas's doctrine of angels. According to Aquinas, every angel is his/her own species. The difference between Daly and Aquinas is that he thought that the relationship between angels was hierarchical, but she considers biophilic creatures equal (Daly 1984, 352–53; S.Th. I q. 50, a. 4).

22. Gatens (1991, 80) claims that Daly understands women as biophilic and men as necrophilic, but she does not give any proof of this apart from Daly's claim that patriarchy is necrophilic.

23. When Daly speaks of Jesus as a person, she seems to be sympathetic, but when speaking of him as a Christian symbol she discards him.

24. On analysis and criticism of the sex/gender paradigm, see Gatens 1992 and Heinämaa 1995, 37–38; 1996a, 110–31; 1996b.

25. This use of "feminine" and "masculine" can be seen as reminiscent of the idea of androgyne. Going beyond "feminine" or "masculine" is going toward an integral be-ing.

26. Only recent research on Beauvoir has acknowledged the phenomenological trait in her thinking. It has been shown that her existentialism is not like Sartre's, but rather closer to Maurice Merleau-Ponty's phenomenology of the body. See Le Dœuff (1977) 1980; Kruks 1990, 1992; Lundgren-Gothlin 1991, 1995, 1996; Heinämaa 1995, 1996a, 1996b, 1997; Vintges 1996; Bergoffen 1997.

References

Alanen, Lilli. 1985. "Naisen asema valtiossa Platonin ja Aristoteleen mukaan." In *Nainen, järki ja ihmisarvo,* edited by Lilli Alanen, Leila Haaparanta, Terhi Lumme, 15–70. Porvoo: WSOY.

Aristotle. 1989. *Nikomakhoksen etiikka* (The Nicomachean ethics). Translated from the Greek by Simo Knuuttila. Helsinki: Gaudeamus.

———. 1991. *History of Animals: Books VII–IX*. Edited and translated by D. M. Balme. London: Harvard University Press.

Beauvoir, Simone de. (1949) 1988. *The Second Sex*. London: Pan Books.

Berger, Peter L., and Thomas Luckmann. (1966) 1972. *The Social Construction of Reality*. London: Penguin Books.

Bergoffen, Debra B. 1997. *The Philosophy of Simone de Beauvoir: Gendered Phenomenologies, Erotic Generosities*. Albany: State University of New York Press.

Braidotti, Rosi. 1991. *Patterns of Dissonance: A Study of Women in Contemporary Philosophy*. Oxford: Polity Press.

———. 1992. "Essentialism." In *Feminism and Psychoanalysis: A Critical Dictionary*, edited by Elizabeth Wright, 77–83. Oxford: Blackwell Publishers.

———. 1994. *Nomadic Subjects: Embodiment and Sexual Difference in Contemporary Feminist Theory*. New York: Columbia University Press.

Chanter, Tina. 1993. Kristeva's Politics of Change: Tracking Essentialism with the Help of a Sex/Gender Map. In *Ethics, Politics, and Difference in Julia Kristeva's Writing*, edited by Kelly Oliver, 179–95. New York: Routledge,

Cobb, John B., Jr., and David Ray Griffin. 1977. *Process Theology: An Introductory Exposition*. Belfast: Christian Journal. "Congregation for the Doctrine of the Faith." 1988. [Letter to the Bishops of the Catholic Church on the Pastoral Care of Homosexual Persons.] In *The Vatican and Homosexuality: Reactions to the "Letter to the Bishops of the Catholic Church on the Pastoral Care of Homosexual Persons,"* edited by Jeannine Gramick and Pat Furey, 1–10. New York: Crossroad.

Daly, Mary. 1977. "The Courage to Leave: A Response to John Cobb's Theology." In *John Cobb's Theology in Process*, edited by David Ray Griffin and Thomas J. J. Altizer, 84–98. Philadelphia: Westminster Press.

———. 1984. *Pure Lust: Elemental Feminist Philosophy*. Boston: Beacon Press.

———. (1968, 1975) 1985a. *The Church and the Second Sex: With a New Feminist Postchristian Introduction by the Author and New Archaic Afterwords*. Boston: Beacon Press.

———. (1973) 1985b. *Beyond God the Father: Toward a Philosophy of Women's Liberation With an Original Reintroduction*. Boston: Beacon Press.

———. (1987) 1988. *Websters' First New Intergalactic Wickedary of the English Language*. London: Women's Press.

———. (1978) 1991a. *Gyn/Ecology: The Metaethics of Radical Feminism with a New Introduction*. London: Women's Press.

———. 1991b. The Spiritual Dimension of Women's Liberation. In *A Reader in Feminist Knowledge*, edited by Sneja Gunew, 335–41. London: Routledge.

———. 1993. *Outercourse: The Be-Dazzling Voyage. Containing Recollections from My Logbook of a Radical Feminist Philosopher (Be-ing an Account of My Time/Space Travels and Ideas—Then, Again, Now, and How)*. London: Women's Press.

Elshtain, Jean Bethke. 1981. *Public Man, Private Woman: Women in Social and Political Thought*. Princeton: Princeton University Press.

Firestone, Shulamith. (1970) 1988. *The Dialect of Sex: The Case for Feminist Revolution*. London: Women's Press.

Gatens, Moira. 1991. *Feminism and Philosophy: Perspectives on Difference and Equality*. Cambridge: Polity Press.

———. 1992. "A Critique of the Sex/Gender Distinction. In *A Reader in Feminist Knowledge*, edited by Sneja Gunew. London: Routledge.

Grimshaw, Jean. 1986. *Feminist Philosophers: Women's Perspectives on Philosophical Traditions*. London: Harvester Wheatsheaf.

Grosz, Elizabeth. 1989. *Sexual Subversions: Three French Feminists*. London: Allen & Unwin.

———. 1990. "Conclusion: A Note on Essentialism and Difference." In *Feminist Knowledge: Critique and Construct*, edited by Sneja Gunew, 332–44. London: Routledge.

Heinämaa, Sara. 1991. "Naisellisen menetelmän mahdollisuudesta: Kysymyksiä ja mielleyhtymiä." *Naistutkimus-Kvinnoforskining* 4, no. 1:32–35.

———. 1993. "Paikka tutkimuksessa: Henkilökohtaisen paikanmäärityksen vaatimus naistutkimuksessa." *Naistutkimus-Kvinnoforskning* 6, no. 1:22–34.

———. 1995. Sukupuoli, valinta ja tyyli. Huomautuksia Butlerin ja Beauvoirin ongelmanasettelun yhteyksistä. *Tiede & edistys* 20, no. 1:30–43.

———. 1996a. *Ele, tyyli ja sukupuoli: Merleau-Pontyn ja Beauvoirin ruumiinfenomenologia ja sen merkitys sukupuolikysymykselle*. Helsinki: Gaudeamus.

———. 1996b. "Woman—Nature, Product, Style?" In *A Dialogue Concerning Feminism, Science, and Philosophy of Science*, edited by Lynn Hankinson Nelson & Tack Nelson. Amsterdam: Kluwer.

———. 1997. "What Is a Woman? Butler and Beauvoir on the Foundations of the Sexual Difference." *Hypatia* 12, no. 1:20–39.

Humm, Maggie. 1990. *The Dictionary of Feminist Theory*. Columbus: Ohio State University Press.

Irigaray, Luce. (1977) 1985. *This Sex Which Is Not One*. New York: Cornell University Press.

———. (1984) 1993. *An Ethics of Sexual Difference*. New York: Cornell University Press.

Korte, Anne-Marie. 1992. *Een passie voor transcendentie: Feminisme, Theologie en Moderniteit in het Denken van Mary Daly*. Kampen: J. H. Kok.

Kruks, Sonia. 1990. *Situation and Human Existence: Freedom, Subjectivity and Society*. London: Unwin Hyman.

———. 1992. "Gender and Subjectivity: Simone de Beauvoir and Contemporary Feminism." *Signs* 18:1, 89–110.

Le Dœuff, Michèle. [1977] 1980. "Simone de Beauvoir and Existentialism." *Feminist Studies* 6, no. 2:277–89.

Lundgren-Gothlin, Eva. 1991. *Kön och Existens: Studier i Simone de Beauvoirs "Le Deuxième Sexe."* Göteborg: Daidalos.

———. 1995. "Gender and Ethics in the Philosophy of Simone de Beauvoir." *NORA* 3, no. 1:3–13.

———. 1996. *Sex and Existence: Simone de Beauvoir's "The Second Sex."* London: Athlone; Hanover: Wesleyan University Press.

Merleau-Ponty, Maurice. [1964] 1975. *The Visible and the Invisible*. Evanston: Northwestern University Press.

Rich, Adrienne. 1980. "Compulsory Heterosexuality and Lesbian Existence." *Signs* 5, no. 4:631–60.

Sihvola, Juha. 1994. *Hyvän elämän politiikka: Näkökulmia Aristoteleen poliittiseen filosofiaan*. Helsinki: Tutkijaliiton Julkaisusarja 76.

Tillich, Paul. 1978. *Systematic Theology*. Vols. 1–3. London: SCM Press.

Tong, Rosemarie. 1989. *Feminist Thought: A Comprehensive Introduction*. London: Unwin Hyman.

Thomas Aquinas. 1952. *Summa Theologiae: Pars Prima et prima Secundae*. Torino, Italy: Marietti.

Työrinoja, Reijo. 1990. "Opus Theologicum: Luther ja skolastinen teonteoria." In *Evankeliumi ja sen ulottuvuudet*, edited by Antti Raunio, 117–60. Suomalaisen teologisen kirjallisuusseuran julkaisuja (Helsinki) 172.

Vintges, Karen. 1996. *Philosophy as Passion: The Thinking of Simone de Beauvoir*. Bloomington: Indiana University Press.

5

The Murder of the Goddess in Everywoman: Mary Daly's Sado-Ritual Syndrome and Margaret Atwood's *The Handmaid's Tale*

Sheilagh A. Mogford

Margaret Atwood's *The Handmaid's Tale* is, indeed, a frightening vision of a potential future. When I use the novel in my introductory women's studies classes, my students are usually split in terms of their reactions: some feel that it is far too fantastic to believe that Gilead could ever become a reality, and others react with fear while critically examining the features of our current society that could, in fact, lead to Gilead's manifestation. I believe that our analysis of this novel should not concentrate only on whether or not it is telling us our future; rather, our analysis should concentrate on examining it in terms of the politics of women's lives *now*. I also believe that, more than a decade after the novel's publication, we as a society are even closer to dealing with the big questions that Atwood raises: Are women gaining power? Does the society fear this power? How is the social system reacting to this power? What manifestations of global abuse and torture are we seeing as a result of women's (supposedly) gaining power? Once we realize that we can view Atwood's fictional account of a society where women are held hostage within a social and political structure designed to maintain the power of a few privileged men as an analysis of women's real, lived experiences in the United States and globally, we also realize that the answers to these kinds of questions present us with a very disturbing reality of our current situation. Indeed, the gains made by the feminist movement of the past forty years seem to be causing those in power to react out of fear of change. And those who fear women holding any kind of power will do whatever it takes to stop the feminist movement, whether by overt actions such as violence, rape, murder, and so on or by covert actions such as refusing to hire women, sexually harassing women, not paying women as much as men for the same job, not listening to women, and dismissing women's words if they don't conform to the status quo.

Since Atwood's postapocalyptic novel was published in 1985, much has been written about its Orwellian prediction of the future, as well as about its warnings for those of us living in the last years of the twentieth century, a time reflected in the novel as paving the way to the fictional Gilead. We can read from many different angles Atwood's dystopic vision of the United States being taken over by religious fundamentalists following a military coup. For example, we can marvel at the author's brilliant command of the language as illustrated in the linguistic gymnastics she performs to explain a "new society" that does not function on a literate level; we can dissect the biblical analogies and extrapolations in order to determine whether, in fact, the Bible does legitimate that sort of society; or we can view the novel as a feminist or postfeminist critique of a society designed to oppress in order to maintain patriarchal order. All of these views have been approached by critics in various permutations and combinations.[1]

It is no secret that the extremely active "pro-life" movement in the United States is strongly supported by the Christian Right, and the individuals and groups claiming biblical justification for their attitudes, beliefs, and actions feel that they are doing "God's work." The belief that women do not have the right to control their own bodies pervades the current abortion debate. It is true that the Supreme Court decision *Roe v. Wade* asserted a woman's right to an abortion within the early stages of pregnancy, but the Court's decision was not based on a belief that a woman had a right to control her body; rather, it was based on the constitutional right to privacy. Twenty-five years after the landmark decision, we are still living with a legacy of tradition and custom in this country with adherents who truly believe that women cannot be trusted to make decisions about their bodies or, for that matter, their lives.

The influence of the Christian Right in this country is not limited to issues about abortion. The Christian Coalition factors very strongly in the political arena, from tapping and supporting candidates for school board elections on the local level, to endorsing candidates for top-level national positions. The Christian Right is active in attempting to maintain its vision of "family values"; to the Christian Right, any attempt to legitimize a social structure/organization that is not centered on heterosexual, monogamous, legal marriage where the male in the family is viewed as the head of the household would lead to men losing power, and that would fly in the face of their reading of "God's word." These attitudes not only ultimately prevent women from finding and developing their own power, but also punish those women who do venture out of the prescribed social role, whether the punishment is at the hands of individual men, individual women, or society as a whole.

Many young women today intone the mantra that "things are getting better." In my women's studies classes, I often hear female students respond with this kind of rationalization after they have been exposed to literature and women's studies scholarship that discusses women's lives in contemporary U.S. society. The attempt to rationalize is, indeed, a defense mechanism, since it is psychically, emotionally, and spiritually painful to stare down the reality of women's lives related to economics, education, poverty, violence, and so on. But we must remember that this reality of women's lives, as amply evidenced in Susan Faludi's *Backlash: The Undeclared War Against American Women,*[2] clearly demonstrates that things are, in many arenas, actually getting worse. The reality of women's lives is that they are still viewed within the larger society in terms of their reproductive abilities, in much the same way as are the Handmaids in Atwood's tale, and the social structures and institutions within which women interact on a daily basis continue to operate upon the foundation of women's biology. Whether, how, and in what venue women will bear children remains the focus of society's attention.

The central issue of women having control over their reproductive choices and thus their bodies and lives is, I believe, the main point being raised in Atwood's novel. In these last few years of the twentieth century, we are witnessing a backlash against the strides made by women over the past one hundred years in this country. The backlash takes many forms on the personal and societal levels, but its goal remains the same: to discredit, dismiss, or dispel the validation and power that women have fought for and, in some cases, achieved. The men of Gilead who take power after the coup create a society that not only clearly defines women's roles, but does so according to women's abilities to reproduce. It's as if Atwood envisioned a society where the "family values" presented by the Christian Right of the 1990s are taken to their ultimate conclusion. The attitudes about women's value that run just below the surface of our current society are brought to fruition in Gilead, and they are the attitudes that form the cornerstone of women's roles: beliefs, attitudes, and social policy are structured around the biology of reproduction. The difference in Gilead is apparent in that the misogyny and contempt for women is spoken out loud, rather than only whispered in locker rooms, as it is today.

The new society of Gilead achieves several objectives, objectives that fit right in with many people's attitudes today. I don't believe it is a coincidence that Atwood chose this latter part of the twentieth century, when women have achieved some level of independence, to illustrate the extreme form of backlash presented in Gilead. Much of the current right-wing, backlash rhetoric points directly at the strides made by women in the twentieth century and names these strides as *responsible* for the "social ills" that surround us all. Whereas many women view issues such as participation in the workforce, participation in politics, some level of reproductive control, and some level of independence from the legal marriage contract as positive moves forward, many conservative religious and political leaders view them as setbacks, as anathema to their vision of the way things are "supposed to be."

The reaction against women in the novel points to the reality that the men who seize power in Gilead create the new society in such a way as to insure that women are kept in their places. The notion of women stepping out of bounds is not a new one. But I continue to wonder where this attitude of keeping women in their place originates. I believe that Atwood's novel illustrates that men fear women gaining power; the structural organization of Gileadean society clearly demonstrates that most of the changes are about controlling women.

This patriarchal desire to keep women in line, to control their movements, is not new. Indeed, it has ancient cultural roots. Mary Daly's analysis of what she terms "Sado-Rituals" facilitates a clear understanding of what is at work in a culture when patriarchal society attempts to keep women from discovering their own power, individual and collective. By using Daly's theoretical framework to analyze the Gileadean society, as well as our own, we can see a pattern in the tapestry of women's lives throughout centuries of experience. What we might at first consider random, unrelated experiences in our own society—in other words, issues about abortion, work, education, violence, and so on—and what we might at first consider random, unrelated experiences in other societies—in other words, female genital mutilation, Chinese foot-binding, the European witch trials (all examples discussed by Daly)—are really all different threads that make up the same pattern. An analysis such as this can bring us to a point of understanding what is truly simmering beneath the surface of our own society, and it can permit us to see that virtually every belief and practice that surrounds women's lives is a part of the Sado-Ritual Syndrome. Everything women are encouraged to do in this society is designed to maintain male dominance and female submission.

Daly's theoretical framework of the Sado-Ritual Syndrome will provide the structure for my analysis of the society of Gilead and for our current society. My analysis here will illustrate that Atwood and Daly tell very much the same story, a story about the destruction of women in an attempt to maintain patriarchal order, a story in which U.S. women today play starring roles.

Mary Daly begins her discussion of the Sado-Ritual by discussing the so-called importance of ritual, in general, to all of our lives. The Myths of the Masters, those myths upon which our society is built, are perpetuated through ritual. The continuous repetition of the myth functions to provide common experiences that will help tie the members to one another and to all those members of the group who came before. Additionally, the ritual comes to illustrate the values of the group. And we must keep in mind that the performance of the ritual becomes nonelective. Some examples of groups that perform rituals include religions, the military, fraternities and sororities, gangs, families, school communities, and the government. It may be difficult for us to know what the rituals mean, even if we know that they exist. Without an understanding of the rituals, we might decide to dismiss them as just part of the way things are, and we lose the opportunity to see the interconnection between all of the groups' rituals, namely the repetition of a practice meant to point to the "mythic" Truth, with the assumption that such a thing exists. Additionally, only through analysis of the behaviors in our own lives that seem unconnected will we see that our lives are highly ritualized, and the rituals we perform are designed to point to the mythic Truth of the patriarchal society in which we all live: men are superior, and women are inferior.

Daly uses the prepatriarchal and the patriarchal myths to demonstrate how the myth is "designed" to *model* social expectation and attitude, and it is "repeated" in order to *affirm* the desired social expectation and attitude; thus, those who act in accordance with the myth are rewarded, and those who defy the myth are punished.

Many of the cultural myths upon which patriarchal society is built demonstrate the need to take over women's power, to, in effect, destroy all that might be seen as powerful in woman. Daly provides us with several examples, such as the "Babylonian creation myth . . . wherein the god Marduk slays a marine monster, the Goddess Tiamat, and dismembers her body, splitting it in two, in order to create the cosmos."[3] Daly then refers to Mircea Eliade's work relating to the function of myth within a culture: " 'What is essential is periodically to evoke the primordial event that established the present condition of humanity' [read: gynocidal patriarchy] [*sic*]" (110).

For centuries, the social system that divides us into categories of man and woman, and that allots opportunity and access to resources according to which category we fit into, has justified the split by citing "biological differences." These biological differences are "natural," and therefore we are only following nature when we say that women can't do the same jobs as men, or women can't perform in sports like men, or women don't need to be educated and have meaningful work of their own because their "natural" role is to bear children and raise them while taking care of their husbands.

The Judeo-Christian morality that points to the mythic Truth of the Father, the Son, and the Holy Spirit provides the basis for viewing women as subservient to men. The mythical world is that to which we aspire, and the rituals we perform in our lives are meant to point to that mythical world. If the supreme beings of the mythical world are presented as male, and the value system of the society says that our lives and behaviors are meant to illustrate that value system, then women learn and perform rituals that reinforce male supremacy. The more we perform the ritual—in other words, live the value system of male superiority—the more we, ourselves, begin to believe in both the ritual and the mythical value to which it is pointing.

According to Daly, the patriarchy that murdered and dismembered the Goddess in order to design a mythology of male domination must reenact the murder of the Goddess as the "evocation of the primordial event" to which Eliade alludes. This reenactment of Goddess-murder does not take place on the mythological level alone. The reenactment of the murder of the Goddess takes place by murdering or dismembering anything which resembles women's power, women's divinity, the Goddess in every-woman, "the Self-affirming be-ing of women" or by murdering/maiming/dismembering actual living women. Turning in the face of this belief, Daly asserts that through radical feminism, we can "[remember] that as long as we are alive the Goddess still lives" (111).

Daly also alludes to the punishments that are meted out by those in power to those who defy the myth of male domination, of Goddess-murder: "Continual complicity in the crime of Goddess-killing is mandatory in the Man's world," but she also demonstrates that defiance of the myth will be women's salvation: "Our refusal to collaborate in this killing and dismembering of our own Selves is the beginning of re-membering the Goddess—the deep Source of creative integrity in women" (111).

This notion of "refus[ing] to collaborate" forms the core of how I believe Daly's theoretical framework can merge theory and practice in our lives. Once we are able to see the pattern (by viewing experiences in women's lives through the lens of the Sado-Ritual Syndrome framework), to really discern the picture formed by all of the seemingly unrelated threads, then we will be able to finally say, "No more!" No more will we participate in the rituals; no more will we help to maintain a social system that views us as inferior; no more will we turn against other women in an attempt to gain male recognition or attention. Once we can say this, we will then be in a position of developing our own power and supporting other women as they develop their power. Once we can say this, we will finally be able to unquestioningly support other women on their Journeys. Once we can say this, we will finally learn that our connections with our women friends are valuable and necessary to our own survival. And we won't spend time worrying about whether we risk losing the approval of men. This change in thinking requires a great deal of energy and commitment, and it requires that we open up to the awareness of what's really going on in our lives. Daly's framework, I believe, provides the map that will bring us to this awareness.

Daly has designed a framework through which she has unmasked the Sado-Rituals in the lives of women. These Sado-Rituals are, in fact, the "evocation of the primordial event" to which I allude above, and they "unmask the very real, existential meaning of Goddess murder in the concrete lives of women" (111). Without this pattern-detecting framework, the atrocities we witness on a daily basis (the rapes, the murders, the dismemberments, the mutilations, and the beatings of women all around the globe) might seem unrelated—or at least we try to convince ourselves of their randomness. The pattern demonstrates the "intention" of the male-dominated patriarchy to reenact the murder of the Goddess in women at all levels so that the social system will be maintained, and so that women will be convinced that the social system is meant to be because, after all, the cultural mythology says it is so.

By using Daly's Sado-Ritual Syndrome as a framework for viewing Atwood's novel, I believe, we can un-cover the pattern that is intrinsic in this cautionary tale, as well as intrinsic in the reality of women's lives. The Sado-Ritual, once unmasked, demonstrates common patterns across women's experiences; we see ourselves and our sisters in the reflection of the various components that Daly addresses. Seeing *The Handmaid's Tale* in this light, and perhaps seeing in it the realities of our own lives, can help all women see our own complicity in the maintenance of the myth that demands that all women's power be destroyed, or at least controlled.

Daly's discussion illustrates how each of the seven components works in terms of a specific social practice or ritual. In using Daly's framework to view Atwood's novel, however, we see that the seven components permeate the very fabric of life in Gilead, not only specific cultural practices. This discussion of *The Handmaid's Tale* will move one step beyond what Daly does in her analysis of specific cultural practices. The value of looking at an entire *society* in this way, beyond a specific ritual *from* that society, is that we can get a clearer picture of how the Sado-Ritual Syndrome is evident in our own society. An analysis such as this will uncover the pervasiveness of the Syndrome in our own lives, and it will demonstrate that the workings of the Sado-Ritual Syndrome have become a part of our own unconsciousness, as women; we have inherited the Syndrome from our foremothers, and our society today perpetuates it. This analysis will also illustrate that the experiences we often try to dismiss as random are really part of a pattern. Once we unmask the pattern, perhaps we can rework the tapestry so that we leave a different legacy to the women coming after us.

I

The first component in Daly's Sado-Ritual Syndrome is "the obsession with purity" (131). Intrinsic to this component is the overall belief that the ritual *must* be practiced in order to "purify" the society, to rid it of something altogether undesirable. This obsession with purity is carried out throughout the ritual in terms of practice and goals. We see this obsession carried out in Atwood's novel in many instances. The notion that the Handmaids (who are assigned to the Military Commanders in order to bear children, since an unnamed apocalyptic event has left large numbers of people sterile) are assigned *only* to the Commanders, and that the Handmaids must keep themselves pure for their role as breeder, illustrates this desire/rationalization for purity.

The bath scene is a very clear example of the obsession with purity. Once a month, the Handmaid is to bathe herself ceremoniously in preparation for the Ceremony wherein the Commander attempts to impregnate her. The ritualization of the Ceremony is necessary in order to make it tolerable, and finally to make it seem natural. The Ceremony itself will be discussed later, in terms of its role in the Sado-Ritual. It is, however, clear that the Handmaid must be clean prior to going to the Commander: "The bath is a requirement, but it is also a luxury."[4] Everything about how the Handmaids act, behave, and live reflects this obsession with purity. As Offred (the Handmaid whose story we are reading) is undressing for her ceremonial bath, her thoughts offer commentary about her situation. As she removes the "loose cotton pantaloons," she muses: "Pantyhose give you crotch rot, Moira used to say. Aunt Lydia would never have used an expression like *crotch rot. Unhygienic* was hers. She wanted everything to be very hygienic" (82). While she is in the bath, Offred again thinks about the obsession with purity, although she does not name it thus: "I wish to be totally clean, germless, without bacteria, like the surface of the moon. I will not be able to wash myself, this evening, not afterwards, not for a day. It interferes, they say, and why take chances" (84)? This obsession with purity has been so successfully drilled into Offred's mind that she no longer questions it, nor does she even think about why she feels this way.

The notion of purity permeates everything that the Handmaids think. They wear red robes with white winged headdresses. This way, they are easily identified, and the headdresses prevent them from looking at people if they are walking in the town. Offred refers to her clothing as "regimented . . . robes of purity" (251). The traditional connotation of the color red is reversed here. Often, red symbolizes *impurity* and leads us to think of "wanton" women, rather than purified vessels. The red robes worn by the Handmaids serve as constant reminders that the women are, by nature, impure, and only by perpetuating the rituals that now comprise their lives will they attain the ideal of purity as designed by those in power.

This same notion is evident in the attitudes toward women's bodies today. As Daly discusses in detail in her analysis of the institution of American Gynecology, U.S. society and culture view women's bodies as naturally unclean. Similar attitudes about women's bodies can be seen on a global scale in other types of rituals, but to provide an example, Daly discusses U.S. women. Women's uteruses, breasts, and vaginas (those physical, "biological" aspects by which the society defines us as "women") are sites for "potential" disease. The medical establishment "treats" women from this belief system. How many women undergo unnecessary hysterectomies or mastectomies when cancer is detected at even very early stages and might be treated with alternatives to radical surgery? It seems as if the medical establishment's answer to the slightest indication of disease is to remove the offending body part. This belief that women are naturally "impure" goes back to the Old Testament, which includes teachings that women are unclean after they give birth (Lev. 12:2–8) as well as during and after menstruation (Lev. 15:19–30).

In and of itself, this obsession about the impurity of women's bodies may seem an isolated belief that really doesn't have anything to do with the lived experiences of women today. But when we realize that this belief has been so successfully ingrained in women's minds, we must also realize that the end result of the belief is contempt for one's body. Young girls in this society learn very early to feel shame where their bodies are concerned. They learn that menstruation is something to hide, that it is the "curse" that all women must experience. The responses to the shame vary among girls and women.

Very recent research on eating disorders among adolescent girls shows that their refusal to eat is sometimes a way to prevent the physical development of their bodies, as if the breasts and hips of a normal adult female are something to avoid, even at the high cost of starvation. Other adolescent girls might respond to this societally dictated shame by rebelling, which could take the form of tatoos or body-piercings (especially when the specifically "female" body parts are pierced, i.e., the nipples or the labia). Whether girls and young women hide their bodies, flaunt their bodies, scar their bodies, or try to prevent their bodies from growing, the underlying pattern is that they are reacting to the myth that their bodies are impure. The unconscious message sent to women in this society is that it's only a matter of time before the disease happens, since you have a female body, after all.

Perhaps one of the most insidious examples of our society's obsession with the notion of women's (im)purity is the long-running commercial campaign for feminine sprays, douches, and powders designed to keep women "fresh," with the underlying meaning stressing that women's bodies cannot *naturally* be fresh (since we need products to make it happen), and this freshness is something the society values. Not only are these products *physically* damaging to women's bodies, but they are also spiritually and psychically damaging to women's minds. Being constantly bombarded with the message that there's something dirty about the body, something so awful as to require floral-scented perfumes to mask it, can ultimately result in women believing in the mythic Truth of their impurity. Again, the repetition of the ritual, in other words, the constant reminder of their uncleanness, can lead women to believe in it as a natural fact.

II

The second component of Daly's Sado-Ritual Syndrome is the "total erasure of responsibility for the atrocities performed through such rituals" (132). Very often, we hear men (and women) say, "Men can't help it. They were born that way," or, "It's not men's fault that women decide to do these things for/to themselves." In *The Handmaid's Tale*, the erasure of male/societal responsibility is evident at many levels. One of the first instances is when Nick, the Commander's Guardian, speaks to Offred, and she is reminded of something Aunt Lydia ("teaching" the new Handmaids at the reeducation center) would say: "He isn't supposed to speak to me. Of course some of them will try, said Aunt Lydia. All flesh is weak. . . . They can't help it, she said, God made them that way but He did not make you that way. He made you different. It's up to you to set the boundaries" (60). Aunt Lydia's response is similar to the age-old double standard with which generations of women in this society have grown up: it's up to the woman to control the man's sexual appetites (without the power or legitimacy to do so), and if sex occurs and she doesn't want it, she merely fails to be strong enough in her refusal. Once again, we see the erasure of male responsibility.

Another example of this component is Offred's monthly appointment at the gynecologist's office. The point of the appointment is to make sure the Handmaids are still menstruating and still able to get pregnant. When Offred reacts to the doctor's "offer" to help her (by trying to impregnate her and letting her claim that the child belonged to the Commander), she is shocked because he claims, "Most of the old guys can't make it anymore. . . . Or they're sterile." Offred realizes that he has said "the forbidden word. *Sterile*. There is no such thing as a sterile man anymore, not officially. There are only women who are fruitful and women who are barren, that's the law" (79).

Here we see that the entire society has been redesigned to deal with the fact that many people have been adversely affected by some type of toxin or disease. Therefore, those in power decide that they must increase their chances of reproducing a child. In reality, most of the Commanders are sterile, so for survival's sake, the Handmaids often find other ways to become pregnant (at the suggestion of the Commanders' Wives). But in order to maintain the ideology of male supremacy, and to rationalize the Handmaids' not getting pregnant, the blame must be put on the women.

When the Commander takes Offred to Jezebel's (the local brothel set up for high-ranking officials) for a night of entertainment, the Commander offers his own rationalized explanation for the events leading up to the formation of Gilead. Just as Offred has internalized her own situation to the point where she no longer questions it, the Commander's response to the New Order is similar: "The problem wasn't only with the women, he says. The main problem was with the men. There was nothing for them anymore. . . . I mean there was nothing for them to do with women" (Atwood, 272). The Commander refuses to acknowledge that the system prior to the Gilead regime was designed by men. Men were the leaders, men held the power, and men decided how things would be set up. Although the Commander begins his explanation by saying that the "problem was with the men," and although it at first it appears that he is acknowledging his own complicity in the situation, he still manages to place the blame for the new social order squarely on the shoulders of women: "[T]he sex was too easy. Anyone [read any *man*] could just buy it. There was nothing to work for, nothing to fight for" (273). The implication here is that it is *women's* fault (since they were too sexually available) that *men* were unhappy in the system that *men* created.

We see this notion of the erasure of male responsibility running through the fabric of current society. Again, since the society supports the mythic Truth of male superiority, it must also support ways of acting and thinking that insure the continuation of this belief, while drawing the attention away from the men, so it will seem as if the male superiority is, once again, "natural." Knowing that the point of rituals is to enact, in some physical way, the values of the society, we can see that there are many current social practices that can be seen in a new light if viewed through Daly's analytical component of "erasure of male responsibility." If men are absolved of any accountability for the rituals, the truth about the ritual becomes masked. While the ritual is designed to maintain male power and dominance, this truth remains hidden because the focus is not on the men; the men are absolved of the responsibility of enacting the ritual, yet they benefit from what the ritual means. One such example of this erasure of responsibility might be young women's obsession with dieting to attain the "super-model" look or the continuous rise in instances of anorexia and bulimia in adolescent women. On the one hand, young girls and women are actually "doing" the dieting; mothers teach their daughters to diet in order to be considered attractive; most adolescent girls in this country have been on a diet; girls keep each other in line where food and weight is concerned; and girls and women continue to look at fashion magazines for the ideal image of how they are to look. On a large scale, men learn not to take responsibility for this, since girls and women are the ones who choose not to eat. But on the other hand, politicizing this phenomenon forces us to question why girls and women diet, and who is served by girls and women dieting? Focusing the responsibility on girls and women for their own obsession with thinness leaves men in the clear, even if they actively support the cultural barometer of beauty, which focuses on unattainable thinness.

Another example of this component's pervasiveness in our society might be some men's (and women's) view that there is no such thing as date rape—if a woman gets into a situation that leads to sexual intercourse, it can't be rape because she should know that men are going to want sex. Again, the mythical Truth that "men can't control themselves," or "it's men's 'nature' to want and need sex all the time" places all of the responsibility on the shoulders of women. What better way to reinforce the belief in male superiority than by giving them carte blanche where sex is concerned. In general, our society still holds fast to the belief that an unmarried pregnant girl or woman is a social pariah: she is "bad"; she couldn't control herself; she will end up being a drain on the taxpayers because of course she'll end up on welfare, and the good taxpayers of this country certainly don't want to reward a girl or woman who breaks the rules; and, perhaps the worst sin, she had the gall to behave in a sexual manner outside the "bonds" of matrimony. No such treatment is given to the boys and men who actually view sexual behavior, and promiscuity, as a measure of their masculinity. Once again, the ritual is repeated, in other words, men and women engaging in sexual activity, yet the translation of the ritual helps to enforce the belief in male superiority by removing the responsibility for the behavior from the men. And again, male sexuality is seen as a "natural," "uncontrollable" force that women just have to learn to live with. If women hear this enough times, and experience the societal pressures and punishments, they will begin to believe that yes, it's their fault that they got pregnant, it's their fault that they can't control their sexuality, and it's their fault if they forfeit male approval because of their sexuality.

Perhaps one of the strongest forces present in current U.S. society that illustrates the erasure of male responsibility is, once again, the Christian Right. The goal of "family values," which stress heterosexual, monogamous, legal marriage with the male as head of household, uses biblical precedent, often the letters of Saint Paul, to justify its belief system. What better way to justify male superiority than by saying, "We can't help it if this is God's intention"? What better tactic than to say that women must be subservient to men, and men are just following the orders that are laid out in the Bible? Again, it makes it appear as if male superiority is natural law, and men are removed from all accountability.

III

Daly explains the third component of the Sado-Ritual Syndrome by asserting that "gynocidal ritual practices have an inherent tendency to 'catch on' and spread" (132). The very notion that Gilead was able to become reality in a relatively short time, and the notion that its occurrence did not come about by means of any completely unbelievable methods, point to Daly's notion of catching on and spreading. Here, we can view the entire Gilead society, and all of the rituals, practices, and beliefs necessary to develop and maintain it, through the lens of the Sado-Ritual Syndrome. The reality of Gilead spread geographically—from what we translate to be Boston (the Heart of Gilead) to Florida, Detroit, North Dakota, and Appalachia (all battle sites mentioned throughout the novel)—as well as psychically; people became convinced that the social framework was both desirable and normal.

Just as Daly notes that the invention of the printing press contributed to the geographic "spread" of the witchcraze, so too do we see technology contributing to the spread of Gilead both through increasing the physical territory within its borders and through colonizing the minds of the citizens of what was once the United States. Technology served this purpose by making it possible to wipe out of all of the women's CompuCard accounts, wiping out their economic independence. Other events contributed to the "catching on and spreading" of Gilead as well: the "military" moved in quickly to maintain order; those in power had the biblical teachings to support the new society; and the Constitution was suspended by those in power, so the average citizen did not feel qualified to question what was happening.

As Offred reminisces about her days in the reeducation center, she realizes that something was happening to the way she viewed things: "Already we were losing the taste for freedom, already we were finding these walls secure. In the upper reaches of the atmosphere you'd come apart, you'd vaporize, there would be no pressure holding you together" (172). After a certain period of time, after a certain amount of reeducation, many people might end up feeling the same way. In her story, Offred relates her recollection of how the social transition took place without anyone knowing what was happening. In reference to the CompuCard accounts (which bear a striking resemblance to today's credit cards), she relates, "I guess that's how they were able to do it, in the way they did, all at once, without anyone knowing beforehand. If there had still been portable money, it would have been more difficult" (224).

While at Jezebel's with the Commander, Offred meets up with Moira, her friend from the days before the Gilead regime, and Moira relates her own story of what brought her to the brothel. Moira had escaped from the Reeducation Center and, after a series of events, ended up at Jezebel's. Offred learns that initially the movement toward the Gileadean society was small and involved very few people. Moira relates her understanding of how it all happened: "What I didn't know of course was that in those early days the Aunts and even the [Reeducation] Center were hardly common knowledge. It was all secret at first, behind barbed wire. There might have been objections to what they were doing, even then. So although people had seen the odd Aunt around, they weren't really aware of what they were for" (319).

In current society, we see how this notion of catching on and spreading applies to us personally in our inability to see the connections between seemingly disparate experiences and phenomena in our lives. We may not realize that the ritualization of our lives does, indeed, catch on and spread over time and in terms of the numbers of women affected by the rituals. For example, we see the ritualization of women's obsession with thinness in terms of this component as well. The waiflike model is only a recently developed standard of beauty. In the 1950s, the standards of beauty were Marilyn Monroe and Jane Russell, both at least a size fourteen. Some feminist theorists have forwarded the notion that the (male) desire for women to become smaller coincides, time-wise, with the beginnings of the second wave of the feminist movement.[5] As consciousness-raising groups sprang up all over the country, designed to encourage women to actually find their voices and take up more space, so too did Weight-Watchers facilities flourish, designed to get women to take up less space. The point is that every culture has standards of female beauty, the standards are made up by men, and women are encouraged to strive to reach the standards. But the standards are designed to serve men, and the patriarchal society, in some way. In order for women to feel that they fit it, they will attempt to follow the standard, and they will encourage other women to follow it as well. Again, the rituals required to achieve that standard, in other words, in the U.S., dieting, shaving legs and underarms, applying makeup, having plastic surgery, and working out in a gym for three hours every day, help to reinforce the societal belief that the standard of beauty is naturally occurring, that men are born with the desire for skinny women. This belief obscures the fact that men "learn" to be attracted to a certain standard of beauty.

Especially today, because of the technology that allows information to spread across the country at an alarmingly fast rate, it is possible to inform masses of the population very quickly about "new" fashions, fads, and so on. The print media puts fashion advertising in the hands of millions of women and girls every month, so it is easier to inform people of the "new" standards of beauty. Likewise, all other forms of media, including commercials, television shows, films, music, and music videos, help to reinforce in a very short time the messages and values that the society holds about women's roles within the society. And since all of the media is controlled by a relatively small number of companies, we can see that there is a small concentration of people who control what is sent out, yet the audience that receives the information is incredibly vast. Thus, things can spread very quickly and efficiently.

IV

The fourth component of Daly's Sado-Ritual Syndrome is that "women are used as scapegoats and token torturers" (Daly, 132). This is perhaps the most insidious of the seven components. We must remember that the ritual is designed in order to maintain a mythological idea of male superiority. Again, the patriarchs in power set up the ritual so that women end up "doing it to each other," to further remove the men from responsibility. This also allows us and those in control to rationalize: "Well, even if it's something women don't like, it's other women who are doing it, so they can't blame anyone but themselves."

One of the major ways that this component works is by employing what Daly calls one of the "sins of the fathers": the divide-and-conquer technique (8). This technique enables the men to sit back and watch the women psychically, physically, and spiritually sever the relationships they have with one another, thus eliminating whatever force might come from women joining together as a united front. In today's society, we see many examples of women being used as token torturers. It is evident in the practice we continue to see here in the United States of pitting women against one another in virtually every circumstance. For example, we encourage women to compete with one another for men; we encourage women to compete with one another over who can be thinner and more "beautiful"; we perpetuate the cultural mythology that women will stab one another in the back if given a chance; and we encourage women to never trust one another. And much of this "training" that women receive as they grow up often comes from their mothers and other women.

Using women as token torturers is evident in many instances in Atwood's novel. One of the first ways in which we see the manifestation of token torture is through the Aunts at the Reeducation Center. The role of the Aunts is to indoctrinate the new Handmaids into the life they must now lead. Each category of women is set up against another category in order to prevent women from connecting with one another. For example, at the Reeducation Center, Aunt Lydia tells Offred, "It's not the husbands you have to watch out for. . . . it's the Wives. You should always try to imagine what they must be feeling" (61). In the household, the women function in their own roles, and antagonism between the groups of women is almost encouraged: "[Rita] is thinking she could have done [the shopping] better herself. She would rather do the shopping, get exactly what she wants; she envies me the walk. In this house we all envy each other something" (63).

Perhaps most frightening about the interactions between the women in the novel is that they sound all too familiar. Do we not learn to envy one another in this society? We learn to envy the woman with the "perfect" life: husband, children, house, and so on, and we also learn to encourage one another to attempt to achieve this perfection. Our own skills as token torturers are developed very early in life as we attempt to control one another's behavior (with whom we should be friends, whom we should see, what activities we should engage in, how we should dress, how much we should weigh, and so on), and these skills become honed as adults as we compete for the right husband, the right neighborhood, the right kind of house, and so on.

At the Reeducation Center, when Janine tells all of the new Handmaids about her experience being gang-raped, the Aunts very carefully turn the blame around in order to reinforce the male domination and the blame on women:

> But *whose* fault was it? Aunt Helena says, holding up one plump finger.
> *Her* fault, *her* fault, *her* fault, we chant in unison.
> *Who* led them on? Aunt Helena beams, pleased with us.
> *She* did. *She* did. *She* did.
> Why did God allow such a terrible thing to happen?
> Teach her a *lesson*. Teach her a *lesson*. Teach her a *lesson*. (93)

Again, the frank reality of women's interactions with other women is clearly evident in this passage. How often do we hear of a woman who reports an assault, a rape, or harassment, and other women immediately respond with, "I wonder what she did to let that happen," or some such statement to question the woman's story. So often, a case of assault or harassment comes down to "her word against his." But are women encouraged to immediately support other women in a situation such as this? More often than not, we find that we must dissociate ourselves from a woman who is either assaulted or harassed in order to preserve what we think is our sense of security. Our defense mechanism kicks in to assure us that we are different from "that" woman, so we figure that she *had* to have done something to warrant the assault or the harassment. If we did not have this defense mechanism, we would have to admit that we could *be* that woman, that she is no different from us, that we are as much at risk for assault and harassment as she is. And that reality is often just too much to bear.

During the Ceremony presented in the novel, which is a literal reenactment of the biblical story of Rachel and Bilhah, we see yet another example of women as token torturers. The biblical quotation refers to Rachel's inability to bear a child for her husband, Jacob. Rachel's response is, "Behold my maid Bilhah, go in unto her; and she shall bear upon my knees, that I may also have children by her" (Gen. 30: 1–3). This scene is carried to the literal extreme during the Ceremony, which is conducted every month, presumably when the Handmaid is most fertile.

During the Ceremony, the Handmaid is on her back, "fully clothed except for the healthy white cotton underdrawers" (120). Above her is the Wife; in Offred's case, this is Serena Joy. "Serena Joy is arranged, outspread. Her legs are apart, I lie between them, my head on her stomach, her pubic bone under the base of my skull, her thighs on either side of me." This position is, indeed, intended to reflect that any child produced from the union between the Commander and the Handmaid will belong to the Wife, but Offred senses something different—token torture: "My arms are raised; she holds my hands, each of mine in each of hers. This is supposed to signify that we are one flesh, one being. What is really means is that she is in control, of the process and thus of the product" (121).

After the Ceremony, Offred steals back to her room to rub her body with butter that she had hoarded from her dinner tray: "There's no longer any hand lotion or face cream, not for us" (124). Something that might be inconsequential, like hand lotion, takes on a different meaning when it is part of a system, part of a larger whole that is instituted to keep women apart: "This was the decree of the Wives, this absence of hand lotion. They don't want us to look attractive. For them, things are bad enough as it is" (125).

When Offred secretly begins to meet with the Commander to play Scrabble and read outdated magazines, she begins to worry about Serena Joy's reaction should she find out about the relationship. The system of fear built up between women carrying out and women suffering from this ritual is effective enough to bring Serena Joy to Offred's mind as soon as she feels she has transgressed: "If she were to find out, for instance. [The Commander] wouldn't be able to intervene, to save me; the transgressions of women in the household, whether Martha or Handmaid, are supposed to be under the jurisdiction of the Wives alone. She was a malicious and vengeful woman, I knew that." (208). Here, we see that using women as token torturers is quite effective in perpetuating the ritual and thus perpetuating women's oppression. Rather than risk Offred and Serena Joy's possibly getting together, befriending one another, questioning the nature of both of their lives, and possibly posing a threat to the power structure, the Sado-Ritual Syndrome requires that they maintain an adversarial relationship.

This notion of women maintaining adversarial relationships is evident today, as well, in the way we raise our daughters to relate to other women as competition for male attention. Women being used as token torturers is evident in virtually every situation where women interact with one another. In the workplace, we see the manifestation of the "Queen Bee," where a woman in power may use that power to insure that no other women move up the corporate ladder. Women with a certain amount of power have been successfully indoctrinated to believe that power for women is a finite commodity, and another woman gaining power is a threat. We fail to learn that this "power" that we are taught to protect is not real power. Women, as a group, gaining "real" power—power to self-determine and control our own lives—is an absolute threat to the current social structure. In reality, the "power" that some women have is nothing more than a compensatory illusion designed to insure that women will do the work of keeping other women in line.

In the United States, we see the token torture and the divide-and-conquer techniques in the relationships between mothers and daughters. Mothers raise their daughters with the hope that the daughters will have happy lives. Built into the societal model of the Mother-Daughter relationship, however, is that the mother knows she must teach her daughter what the patriarchy wants her to know so the daughter will have as little conflict as possible. Mothers do not want their daughters to be rejected by the society, and rejecting the model of expected social roles for females will, indeed, cause conflict for the daughter. Therefore, mothers teach their daughters to wear makeup, to wear high heels, to sit with their legs together, to walk a certain way to attract male attention, to shave their legs, to be submissive, to avoid confrontation with men, to desire male attention and approval, to view relationships with men as more important than relationships with other women (rather than viewing all relationships as potentially valuable in and of themselves), and, above all else, to never question the system, for questioning the system is decidedly unfeminine. Daughters who fit into the desired model of female behavior will be accepted by the male-dominated society, while daughters who go against this model will often be rejected by the society (as well as by the mother because the daughter is not doing what the mother taught her).

V

The fifth component of Daly's Sado-Ritual Syndrome is "compulsive orderliness, obsessive repetitiveness, and fixation upon minute details, which divert attention from the horror" (Daly, 132). There are several instances in *The Handmaid's Tale* where we see this type of compulsive orderliness being carried out, and we do, in fact, see the main function of this component: it diverts the participants' attention from what is really going on. One example of this is the time when Offred is taken to her monthly gynecological appointment. The process and procedure of the event illustrate Daly's point:

> After I've filled the small bottle left ready for me in the little washroom, I take off my clothes, behind the screen, and leave them folded on the chair. When I'm naked I lie down on the examining table, on the sheet of chilly crackling disposable paper. I pull the second sheet, the cloth one, up over my body. At neck level there's another sheet, suspended from the ceiling. It intersects me so that the doctor will never see my face. . . . When I'm arranged I reach my hand out, fumble for the small lever at the right side of the table, pull it back. Somewhere else a bell rings,

> unheard by me. After a minute the door opens, footsteps come in, there is breathing. He isn't supposed to speak to me except when it's absolutely necessary. But this doctor is talkative. (Atwood, 78)

The details presented in this scene demonstrate how this component of Daly's framework fits in with the others to form a superstructure designed to destroy women's power, to murder the Goddess within. Here we see how the minutiae of details and procedures is taking the place of the real horror that the Handmaid is experiencing. In reality, she is being tested for her breeding capability, but all she is concerned about is proper placement of sheets and insuring that the doctor does not see her face.

Another example of this compulsive orderliness appears when Offred is preparing to participate in the Ceremony and all of the ritual that precedes it. The point of this scene is that the entire household must assemble in the sitting room while the Commander reads passages from the Bible. The members of the household then meditate and pray that the Ceremony to follow will be successful and the Handmaid will become pregnant. When Offred goes into the sitting room, she doesn't think about the horror and violation that is about to take place. She has been conditioned to believe that it's all just a part of life. Rather, she offers us two full pages of description of the room, from curtains and rugs to furniture and draperies (103). She allows some of the bric-a-brac to remind her of the "time before," but beyond a quick note of nostalgia, she ponders the room as if disconnected from the experience.

The Ceremony is rife with reminders of the need to be orderly and attend to detail. When thinking about the entire household assembling to participate, Offred states, "But they need to be here, they all need to be here, the Ceremony demands it. We are all obliged to sit through this, one way or another" (104). When the Commander knocks on the door to the sitting room in preparation for the Ceremony, Offred recalls, "The knock is prescribed: the sitting room is supposed to be Serena Joy's territory, he's supposed to ask permission to enter it" (111). Again, these examples demonstrate the attention to detail and orderliness that draws the participants' attention away from what is really going on.

In current U.S. society, women's lives are, indeed, highly ritualized, and many of the rituals are designed to encourage women to focus on the ritual, rather than on the overriding reason for the ritual, or the value that the ritual is meant to reinforce. For example, we once again see this component played out in the beauty industry. Women are encouraged from a very young age to spend a great deal of time and energy focusing on how they look. We are encouraged to think about makeup, hair products, clothing, accessories, how we look, how we smell, how our skin feels, what color eye shadow to wear, what color to dye our hair, what shoes to wear with a specific dress, and so on. The ritual of preparing our bodies to be seen in public takes up a significant amount of a woman's day, yet we are never encouraged to question why we participate in the ritual. The ritual, itself, seems to be a naturally occurring phenomenon: women are *supposed* to spend this much time trying to appear "as good as they possibly can" for the people (specifically men) with whom they come in contact on any given day. But underlying the ritual is the real belief that women are unacceptable they way they are. They must spray, powder, dye, cover, highlight, and mask their real selves in order to be considered attractive or even "acceptable" to others. And most women will probably admit that they perform the ritual in the same way every morning. Again, the point is that the ritual is, indeed, meant to point to a mythic Truth, a value of the society (in the case of women's beauty rituals, the Truth is that women must "fix" themselves to be acceptable to men, but we never really talk about this), and fixating on the performance of the ritual will focus our attention away from that Truth, while at the same time forcing us to internalize its message.

VI

Daly explains the sixth component of the Sado-Ritual Syndrome by asserting that "behavior which at other times and places is unacceptable becomes acceptable and even normative as a consequence of conditioning through the ritual atrocity" (Daly, 132). This aspect of the Sado-Ritual illustrates how the society or culture carrying out the ritual can learn to accept a practice, behavior, or belief that in any context outside of the ritual would be unacceptable by those enforcing the ritual. A key to this component of the Sado-Ritual is the idea that generally unacceptable behaviors, practices, or attitudes become acceptable only within the context of the ritual. In the case of Atwood's Gilead, virtually everything surrounding daily life centers on this concept of the unacceptable becoming acceptable. A clear example of this is the Ceremony. This highly ritualized practice is only acceptable within the context of the ritual. It is not acceptable for Offred to interact with the Commander at any time, under any circumstances, outside of the ritual: she knows she may pay dearly if her nightly Scrabble games with him are discovered. But *within* the context of the ritual, it is acceptable for the Commander to "have sex" with her, to engage in what appears to be a highly personal interaction. This component of the Sado-Ritual rationalizes a situation where it seems quite logical for the sexual act to take place, but a Scrabble game could carry extreme punishment.

Another aspect of this component of the Sado-Ritual is understanding how a ritual, a belief, or a practice can become acceptable and accepted over time. If people are successfully conditioned, they might learn to accept anything, especially if the alternative is forced expulsion from the group carrying out the ritual. Offred gives us various examples throughout her narrative that demonstrate this aspect of the Ritual. At one point, Offred remembers Aunt Lydia saying, "Ordinary . . . is what you are used to. This may not seem ordinary to you now, but after a time it will. It will become ordinary" (45). So even if the Handmaids resisted the indoctrination at the Reeducation Center, the Aunts were ready with the response. Those who designed the new society knew that it would meet with resistance, so they determined ways to counter it.

When Offred wonders how things were in the "time before" and how things managed to change so quickly and completely, she states, "Whatever is going on is as usual. Even this is as usual, now. We lived, as usual, by ignoring. Ignoring isn't the same as ignorance, you have to work at it. Nothing changes instantaneously: in a gradually heating bathtub you'd be boiled to death before you knew it" (74). These statements indicate at least a partial awareness that unacceptable things become acceptable quite quickly. Within the context of the new society, all of the new practices and rituals, as well as the new thinking into which citizens were conditioned if they hoped to stay alive, became accepted.

In current U.S. society, the notion of the acceptance of things previously considered unacceptable informs many aspects of women's lives. The acceptance is evidenced in the way in which we learn to view specific aspects of our lives. For example, in the United States, domestic violence is the number-one cause of injury to women. In the context of how U.S. citizens view civil behavior, it is not acceptable to physically abuse other citizens: legally it is viewed as a crime, in other words, assault. When the violence is in the context of a male/female relationship, however, especially one where the involved parties know each other, our mindset allows us, even encourages us, to view the violence in a different manner. The conditioning we receive throughout our lives brings us to see domestic violence as part of the fabric of the society; we learn not to question it.

Another example of our acceptance of something previously considered unacceptable is the pornography industry in the United States. Within the context of what is viewed as "normal" behavior among citizens in the United States, custom and tradition assert civil and equitable relationships. We are taught from a very early age that our nation is founded on the principle of the protection of each individual's civil rights. But within the context of pornography, where sexuality hinges on the concept of exploitation and objectification, we have been successfully conditioned to suspend the basic premise of this country's Constitution. The magazines, videos, cyberlinks, and TV shows in this country that use women to satisfy male sexual desires have somehow been removed from the purview that we are conditioned to believe functions as a totalizing philosophy.

VII

The final component of Daly's Sado-Ritual Syndrome is "Legitimization of the ritual by the rituals of 'objective' scholarship—despite appearances of disapproval" (Daly, 133). This component of the Ritual can be used to describe the final section of Atwood's novel. Here we have "The Historical Notes," supposedly written many years after the action of the rest of the novel has taken place, which precisely illustrate what happens in the academy, in "objective" scholarship, when atrocities such as Gilead or the conditions of women's lives around the world are discussed.

"The Historical Notes" functions as almost a postscript to the story that we have understood, up to this point, to be occurring in real time. Not until we enter the Twelfth Symposium on Gileadean Studies are we jarred from our (mis)understanding about how the story came to be told. From this postscript, we are to surmise that the Gilead offered in Offred's account has somehow evolved into a society that uses the Gilead regime as fodder for academic analysis. Are we also to surmise that the people of a later time, noted as the year 2195, have moved so far away from Gilead that they "objectively" study it from a historical or anthropological approach?

This type of objective study, conducted by academics and scholars throughout history, provides the material from which Daly's final component of the Sado-Ritual comes. Daly asserts that the process and language with which scholarly study is accomplished function as the final piece of the ritual atrocities suffered by women over time: "The basic cultural assumptions which make the atrocious ritual possible and plausible remain unquestioned, and the practice itself is misnamed and isolated from other parallel symptoms of the planetary patriarchal practice of female maiming and massacre." Daly cites Jan Raymond, who suggests that "scholarship should be called *meta-ritual.*" Daly feels that "the name is accurate, for this kind of writing not only 'records' (erases) the original rituals but also provides 'explanations' and legitimizations for them, purporting to see beyond their materiality into their 'soul' or meaning" (133).

"The Historical Notes" in *The Handmaid's Tale* functions as this kind of "record," and the notes clearly illustrate how scholarship and the academy "gloss over" much of what really happens in any given situation in an attempt to "legitimate" not only that which is being studied, but also their own "objectivity." Arnold E. Davidson analyzes this attempt at legitimization: "The historical notes, like any scholarly afterword, also serve to validate the text that they follow, and there is something ominous in that claiming of the right to have the last word."[6]

Davidson alludes to some of the problems inherent in "The Historical Notes": "After an appalling story of tyranny, genocide, and gynocide in late twentieth century America, we are, in effect, brought fast-forward to June 25, 2195, to the University of Denay in Nunavit and an International Historical Association's rather placid (if pompous) intellectual foray back into Gilead Regime" (Davidson, 114). This attempt to "legitimize," that is, to find a way to explain and analyze, a woman's account of the ritual atrocities suffered by her and many other women demonstrates the scholars' belief that what they have to say about a certain situation is of much more importance than what the original participants have to say.

Throughout his keynote address at the Gilead Symposium, Professor James Darcy Pieixoto concentrates on some key questions that *he* feels are the *core* issues to discuss in relation to Offred's story. He offers a detailed analysis of his attempt to authenticate the audiotapes that contributed to his transcription of *The Handmaid's Tale*. He offers a detailed analysis of his understanding of audiotape technology available at the approximate time during which the tapes were made. He also demonstrates to his audience that no scholarly stone was left unturned, that he is, indeed, a proficient scholar: "[W]e had to make some decision as to the nature of the material we had thus so laboriously acquired. Several possibilities confronted us. First the tapes might be a forgery" (Atwood, 383).

Pieixoto proceeds with another detailed account of his attempts to identify the narrator of the tapes, which would have offered much more evidence for the authenticity of the tapes. He is sure to inform the other scholars in attendance that he did his homework and tried to "identify the inhabitants of the house that must have occupied the site of the discovery [the locker containing the tapes]." He also offers a detailed account of the leads that the researchers followed, which, "unfortunately, . . . led nowhere" (384).

Pieixoto's discussion continues with his explanation of how he and his research team attempted to identify other key participants in the Gilead presented in the tapes, and he offers suggestions for the identity of the Commander (these suggestions are, of course, taken from other "objective" historical accounts).

Another technique used by scholars to legitimize the Sado-Rituals is the use of the passive voice. Daly discusses how the linguistic patterns of "objective" scholarship remove agency from those committing the ritual, and place the agency on those at whom the ritual is aimed (128). In other words, the very language used to record or analyze these situations is designed to remove blame from the perpetrators and place it squarely on the shoulders of the victims. Pieixoto clearly demonstrates this tendency when he discusses the composition of the narrator's name: "[I]t was patronymic, composed of the possessive preposition and the first name of the gentleman in question. Such names *were taken by these women* upon their entry into a connection with the household of a specific Commander, and *relinquished by them* upon leaving it" (emphases mine) (387). This type of language assumes that the women involved "chose" these names, when it is clearly evident that this is not the case. Passive voice here assigns agency to the women and leads readers to conclude that women, not men, were the active agents of this naming.

In general, the final component of the Sado-Ritual functions to hold the other components together. Scholarship reinforces the legitimacy of the practices that take place, and it erases the reality that we are talking about women's lives, in this case, the women of Gilead. Davidson refers to the dangers of this type of scholarship: "Do we, as scholars, contribute to the dehumanization of society by our own critical work, especially when, as according to the distinguished professor of the novel, 'our job is not to censure but to understand' " (115).

In current society, it is not only academic "scholars" who might fit into this component of Daly's framework. Indeed, any "authority" who asserts a right to translate and explain women's experiences, roles, desires, and so on would fall under this component. In addition, if we accede to that person's assertion, and buy into that notion of "authority," then we become complicitous. For example, when a woman is sexually assaulted, and she chooses to go to the police, it is up to the district attorney to determine if charges will be filed and if a suspect will be prosecuted. If that district attorney decides there is no case, does that mean that the assault never took place? Do we fall into the trap of believing the district attorney and questioning the woman who made the initial accusation because, after all, the DA is an educated person, and wouldn't he know whether or not the assault took place? Many of us are encouraged to think this way, and we must guard against always believing what a person in an "authority" position tells us.

We are encouraged to view our newscasters as people whom we can trust. They are seen as authority figures and "experts," people who know what's going on and who will fill us in on the "truth." But if we believe that the "truth," the real, lived experiences of people across the world, can be boiled down to what we hear in a thirty-minute news broadcast, we will have a very skewed view of the world. This is the point that Daly is making with the final component of the Sado-Ritual Syndrome. We must guard against imbuing authority figures with all of our confidence, for they are not necessarily the ones with our interests in mind when they translate and decipher their vision of the world.

It is true that *The Handmaid's Tale* is a work of fiction, and any attempt to use a piece of fiction as "prescriptive" in terms of social conditions becomes problematic at best. Using works of fiction to un-cover "patterns" about our lives, however, can be extremely beneficial. Daly's framework of the Sado-Ritual Syndrome might offer us a means by which we can read not only works of fiction such as Atwood's, but also instances in our own lives that reflect the components and thus complete the pattern of the Sado-Ritual Syndrome. It is also true that current sociopolitical situations in the United States, including a relatively new Republican

Congress and an active Christian Right that campaigns nationwide about the need to return to "traditional family values," might cause us to wonder about the potentiality of the Gilead portrayed in *The Handmaid's Tale*.

We might be tempted to say, "Oh, that could never happen here," or, "This is not the same as the world Atwood describes," but I believe that the challenge is not necessarily trying to find out what pieces of our society might turn into Gilead at some future date. Perhaps our time would be better spent looking at the pieces of Gilead that already exist in our society and trying to confront the forces that are, indeed, fully invested in creating a world where women are under complete control of men, body and soul. The strides in the feminist movement of the past twenty or thirty years are being challenged by factions throughout the world, and we are certainly in danger of moving back instead of moving forward.

When looking at these strides made in the feminist movement and trying to gain strength from what we might think are advances, it is critical to understand that the factions challenging women's power, those invested in making the backlash a reality, permeate every institution within the society. We are currently witnessing the development of practices in U.S. society and around the globe that on the surface appear to be designed to benefit women, but once we peel away the layers, we might see that the practice is once again set up to maintain the dominant-subordinate relationship.

Much of Atwood's novel focuses on how women's bodies and women's reproduction form the center of their power: those designing the new society feared this source of power, so they summarily co-opted it for their own benefit, thus taking the power from women. In current U.S. society, we see a similar phenomenon occurring in the guise of new reproductive technologies, such as in vitro fertilization, donor insemination, surrogate motherhood, and so on. On the surface, it appears that these technologies offer power to women. We might read these medical advancements as ways for women to have increased choices about their lives, and thus as advances that could move us away from the dominant-subordinate social structure. Some current feminist scholarship, however, advises caution before wholeheartedly embracing these new technologies as "liberating" technologies for women. Janice Raymond, for example, suggests that the availability of additional "avenues" for bearing children does nothing to expose the underlying problem, namely that the society continues to define women according to their reproductive abilities.[7] Raymond also suggests that it is impossible to "freely choose" within the current social makeup (especially given the economic framework, which stipulates that choice depends on one's ability to pay), so the notion of "additional choices" is but an illusion.[8]

An analysis of some of the instances in our own society that I feel can be viewed through Daly's analytical framework, and understood for how the instances affect women's lives, points most definitely to patterns surrounding women's lives. As stated at the beginning of this paper, seemingly disparate phenomena might be dismissed as random events if we don't look for the patterns. This is one of the main points of the feminist movement in the United States and across the globe. We must look at the macrocosm of women's lives, as women; what are some of the things that women experience within patriarchal society "because they are women"? It is true that it is frightening to see the full pattern laid out before us, to see all of the pieces of our lives that contribute to the maintenance of a system designed to keep men superior and women inferior. But if we don't force ourselves to look at it, we will simply continue on, helping to bring this mythic "truth" to fruition, and we will continue to believe that this social structure is "natural."

It is also true that anytime a woman or a group of women "makes a fuss" or claims that there are issues that we need to critique, in other words, education, standards of beauty, pay inequity, violence, and so on, an attempt to dismiss the discussion shortly follows. It is not in the best interest of those who hold power in this society to find commonalities among the experiences of women. The system is much better served if we all think our experiences are random, or accidental, or isolated. Perhaps the legacy we have inherited from our foremothers who fought for the vote, who fought for women's right to be educated, who fought for women's rights in the workplace is, indeed, the imperative for the new generation of women to see that their experiences are connected with one another, and they must act to insure that the backlash does not succeed.

If a woman meets resistance when she raises her voice about an injustice that she witnesses, her first reaction is to stop talking: women in this society are raised to avoid confrontation at all costs, especially if that confrontation could cause any sort of discomfort for men. And if the confrontation might result in a woman losing the approval of men, she must definitely cease that confrontation. But we must resist that reaction and realize that if we meet resistance, it is because we have hit a nerve, and it's a sign that we must yell even louder than ever before.

Similarly, when women voice concerns about injustice, they often meet the accusation of being "paranoid." The notion of paranoia raises hints about conspiracy theories as well as the suggestion of emotional instability. The goal in using the accusation of paranoia is to silence women, to dismiss their concerns, and to trivialize any connection or pattern they may have detected in their own lives. To Daly, however, the quality of paranoia can be a successful strategy for women who have begun to detect the patterns: "This pattern-detecting—the development of a kind of positive paranoia—is essential for every feminist Searcher, so that she can resist the sort of mind-poisoning to which she must expose herself in the very process of seeking out necessary information" (125).

The only way that we can prevent the Ritualistic Murder of the Goddess, the ritualistic murder, dismemberment, and destruction of women everywhere, is by "re-invoking the Goddess within, which involves 'forgetting' to kill the female divinity, that is, our Selves" (Daly 111).

Notes

1. For discussions of these critical approaches, see Arnold E. Davidson, "Future Tense: Making History in *The Handmaid's Tale*," in *Margaret Atwood: Vision and Forms*, ed. Kathryn VanSpanckeren and Jan Garden Castro (Carbondale: Southern Illinois University Press, 1988), 113–21; Dorota Filipczak, "Is There No Balm in Gilead?—Biblical Intertext in *The Handmaid's Tale*," *Journal of Literature and Theology* (June 1993): 171–85; Peter Fitting, "The Turn from Utopia in Recent Feminist Fiction," in *Feminism, Utopia, and Narrative*, ed. Libby Falk Jones and Sarah Webster Goodwin (Knoxville: University of Tennessee Press, 1990), 141–58; W. J. Keith, "Apocalyptic Imaginations: Notes on Atwood's *The Handmaid's Tale* and Findley's *Not Wanted on the Voyage*," *Essays on Canadian Writing* 35 (Winter 1987): 123–34; and Reingard M. Nischik, "Back to the Future: Margaret Atwood's Anti-Utopian Vision in *The Handmaid's Tale*," *English American Studies* (March 1, 1987): 139–48.

2. Susan Faludi, *Backlash: The Undeclared War Against American Women* (New York: Crown, 1991).

3. Mary Daly, *Gyn/Ecology: The Metaethics of Radical Feminism* (Boston: Beacon Press, 1978), 110. Subsequent references to this work are cited parenthetically.

4. Margaret Atwood, *The Handmaid's Tale* (New York: Fawcett Crest Books, 1985), 81. Subsequent references to this work are cited parenthetically.

5. See, for example, Kim Chernin, "The Tyranny of Slenderness," in *Race, Class, and Gender in the United States: An Integrated Study*, 3d ed., ed. Paula Rothenberg (New York: St. Martin's Press, 1995), 238–45.

6. Davidson, "Future Tense," 114. Subsequent references to this work are cited parenthetically.

7. Janice G. Raymond, "Connecting Reproductive and Sexual Liberation," in *Radically Speaking: Feminism Reclaimed*, ed. Diane Bell and Renate Klein (Melbourne: Spinifex Press, 1996), 231–46. Subsequent references to this work are cited parenthetically.

8. Raymond, "Connecting Reproductive and Sexual Liberation," 242.

References

Atwood, Margaret. *The Handmaid's Tale*. New York: Fawcett Crest Books, 1985.

Chernin, Kim. "The Tyranny of Slenderness." In *Race, Class, and Gender in the United States: An Integrated Study* 3d edition, edited by Paula Rothenberg, 238–45. New York: St. Martin's Press, 1995.

Daly, Mary. *Gyn/Ecology: The Metaethics of Radical Feminism*. Boston: Beacon Press, 1978.

Davidson, Arnold E. "Future Tense: Making History in *The Handmaid's Tale*." In *Margaret Atwood: Vision and Forms*, edited by Kathryn VanSpanckeren and Jan Garden Castro, 113–21. Carbondale: Southern Illinois University Press, 1988.

Faludi, Susan. *Backlash: The Undeclared War Against American Women*. New York: Crown, 1991.

Filipczak, Dorota. "Is There No Balm in Gilead?—Biblical Intertext in *The Handmaid's Tale*." *Journal of Literature and Theology* (June 1993): 171–85.

Fitting, Peter. "The Turn from Utopia in Recent Feminist Fiction." In *Feminism, Utopia, and Narrative*, edited by Libby Falk Jones and Sarah Webster Goodwin, 141–58. Knoxville: University of Tennessee Press, 1990.

Keith, W. J. "Apocalyptic Imaginations: Notes on Atwood's *The Handmaid's Tale* and Findley's *Not Wanted on the Voyage*." *Essays on Canadian Writing* 35 (Winter 1987): 123–34.

Nischik, Reingard M. "Back to the Future: Margaret Atwood's Anti-Utopian Vision in *The Handmaid's Tale*." *English American Studies* (March 1, 1987): 139–48.

Raymond, Janice G. "Connecting Reproductive and Sexual Liberalism." In *Radically Speaking: Feminism Reclaimed*, edited by Diane Bell and Renate Klein, 231–46. Melbourne: Spinifex Press, 1996.

6

Be-ing Is Be/Leaving

Debra Campbell

> The sermon was dedicated to the subject of Bingo, and as I gazed around at the blank-faced, lily-white congregation in easter attire I experienced an overwhelming desire/need/decision to leave.
>
> We were sitting near the front. Just as I stood up and strode alone down the long aisle to the exit, the organ began to play. Unbelievably, the hymn that resounded through the church as I departed was "Daily, Daily, Sing to Mary," that paean which my teacher had found it amusing to tease me with in my childhood. I had considered the joke unfunny and boring. At this Moment of Be/Leaving, however, I Heard the hymn take on dimensions of cosmic hilarity. For years I had been struggling to avoid church. This, however, was a Great Departure and Debut. I was Moving Out—Leaving/Leaping further in this First Spiral Galaxy of Outercourse
>
> —Mary Daly, *Outercourse: The Be-Dazzling Voyage*

Mary Daly, the self-proclaimed Radical Feminist Pirate, has made a career out of writing about leaving. There is a sense in which her entire corpus deals with departures of one kind or another. Some of Daly's departure narratives, such as the account of easter 1968, quoted above, could have happened to almost anybody. (Didn't most catholic feminists lose patience with traditional worship services during the late sixties?) Yet even the narratives that start out as almost anybody's story can take a wild turn in midstream when a much more evolved Mary Daly who is doing the Re-membering enters the scene from an Other vantage point and interprets it for the reader. Then we encounter Be/Leaving as only Mary Daly experiences it. A formerly irksome traditionalist hymn gives way to a cosmic joke; an impulse to leave an embarrassing sermon becomes a theaphany; a mundane walk down the aisle of a Saint Petersburg parish church ends in a new mode of be-ing.

Daly's many stories about leaving fit into a larger framework, her own highly idiosyncratic discourse on life as a Be-dazzling Journey, Outercourse, a "Voyage of Spiraling Paths, Moving Out of the State of Bondage" (Daly 1992, 3). This framework, which Daly constructed in stages in *Gyn/Ecology* (1978), *Pure Lust* (1984), and *Outercourse* (1992) provides women with New Time and New Space on the Boundary where women's Power of Presence and Archaic Futures are Realized (Daly 1987, 84). The central axis around which the Spiraling Galaxies and the New Space and Time revolve is Be-ing: "the Final Cause, the Good who is Self-communicating, who is the Verb from whom, in whom, and with whom all true movements move" (Daly and Caputi 1987, 64). In order to embark upon the Be-Dazzling Journey, however, one must cross a threshold, the first in the endless series of thresholds encountered on the Voyage. Crossing thresholds constitutes Be/Leaving (Daly 1992, 94, 121), the performance of Originally Sinful Acts that question and challenge the patriarchal order and display "a Prude's Self-centering Lust" (Daly and Caputi 1987, 84).

In this essay, I maintain that Mary Daly's many carefully negotiated departures, described in painstaking detail in published works that have appeared since the early seventies, constitute one of her most important contributions. Much of what Daly represents as a feminist teacher and scholar is conveyed in these departure narratives, which return again and again to two central themes: (feminist) women's protracted, sometimes complicated, extremely personalized process of Be/Leaving, and the challenge of be-ing (participation in Be-ing), for the sake of which all Be/Leaving takes place. Amid all of the developments in Daly's style and subject matter over the past quarter century, and throughout her evolution from pioneer catholic feminist philosopher/theologian in 1968 to Nag-Gnostic Pirate in 1992, Daly's focus on these two issues has been constant. The dynamic created by the relationship between these two aspects of Daly's life and thought has shaped her Self-consciousness and profoundly affected her approach to Self-disclosure/Hagography in her writings.

I believe that Daly's willingness to write about the issues of be-ing and Be/Leaving honestly and concretely with reference to her own life may be among her most abiding legacies. The courageous, often outrageous, improvisations/performances that appear most prominently in Daly's works from *Gyn/Ecology* onward may be as important to the future of feminism as the (far more widely acknowledged and appreciated) feminist analysis of patriarchal institutions and language in her first two books: *The Church and the Second Sex* (1968) and *Beyond God the Father* (1973). Each reader can decide to make or to eschew such comparisons. I will not pit the two Dalys (more accurately: the many Dalys) against one another and make them compete for top honors. Instead, I will pay attention, as Daly herself does, to some of the relationships (and internal consistencies) among the many Selves Daly discloses to us in her autobiographical works, as well as to the ways in which the terms be-ing and Be/Leaving provide Daly with the means to Name, claim, and take seriously the expanding cast of Mary Dalys who serve as protagonists in her autobiographical writings. I will focus upon what Daly has shown us about the fundamental connections between be-ing, Be/Leaving, and Hagography, and upon why that demonstration is so important and sustaining. In so doing, I hope to answer the pundits who continue to ask, from a variety of ideological positions, just what Mary Daly has done for us lately.

Be-ing and Be/Leaving

In the *Wickedary* (1987), the place where Daly honed and refined the expanding webs of Dis-covered words that she had been Spinning for almost a decade, she included the following definition of Ontological Courage: "the Courage to Be through and beyond the State of Negation which is patriarchy; participation in the Unfolding of Be-ing—continuing on the Journey always" (Daly and Caputi 1987, 69). This definition, conjured by Daly in her Third Spiral Galaxy, provides a good place to begin to explore the dynamics of Be-ing and Be/Leaving in Daly's life and work. The inclusion of both the negative aspect of Be/Leaving (movement "through and beyond the State of Negation") and its positive aspect ("continuing the Journey always") within Daly's definition of Ontological Courage merely makes explicit what close readers already know: in Daly' s cosmology, be-ing and Be/Leaving are inseparable.

An individual's commitment to and participation in Be-ing necessarily means that she is a Be/Leaver. For to embrace be-ing wholeheartedly one must become a Pirate, a Spinster, always on the move, pursuing life as a

"Wild-Goose Chase," a "Be-Laughing lark; a fruitful, hopeful, ecstatic Quest" (Daly and Caputi 1987, 180). Spinning and Sparking never end. There is always another threshold to cross. Daly's frequent recourse to metaphors of movement and travel, her way of describing the feminist vocation (the Call of the Wild), provides important insights into her vision of separatism. In a helpful footnote in *Outercourse,* Daly explains why it is always necessary to discuss separatism within its larger context, why Be/Leaving needs to be understood in relation to be-ing. Separatism, Daly affirms, is "an essential prerequisite" of the "ontological Metamorphosis" that Radical feminism makes possible. But here she adds a crucial caveat: the name *separatist* is "inadequate" unless it is used "in a context of Lusty words" to connect it with the final cause, "Biophilic communication/participation in Be-ing" (Daly 1992, 445 n. 15).

The vital connection between Be/Leaving and be-ing shines through clearly in Daly's personal narratives. Since 1975 Daly has incorporated autobiographical narrative into her philosophy along with her growing lexicon of New Words Dis-covered in the Third and Fourth Spiral Galaxies. Daly has experimented with a mixed genre that interweaves philosophy/Pyrosophy and autobiography/Hagography because of her conviction that crossing thresholds (Be/Leaving, Original Sinning, asking Nonquestions) is a recurring event, a major component in the lives of those who are "Furiously focused" on the Final Cause, Be-ing (Daly 1985e, xxvii). Personal narratives that capture Moments of Be/Leaving lend shape and substance to Daly's philosophy. Even if Ontological Courage sounds like an abstraction, there is nothing abstract about *living a life* grounded in Ontological Courage.

By 1975, when she wrote the "Autobiographical Preface" and "Feminist Postchristian Introduction" to the second edition of *The Church and the Second Sex,* Mary Daly knew that if she really wanted to become a philosopher, she would have to become a Hagographer. Three years later, in *Gyn/Ecology,* Daly introduced her New Word *Hagography*. Like Ontological Courage, Hagography has both negative and positive aspects. Its negative aspect is related to its function as a corrective. It addresses the need to replace the "moldy 'models' " for women featured in christian hagiography, which extolls "the masochistic martyrs of sadospiritual religion," with the real lives of Great Hags found in "woman-identified writing" (Daly 1990, 14). While associated with the negative process of removing from circulation plastic patriarchal models of virtuous womanhood, Hagography is primarily a positive, future-oriented enterprise. Daly elaborates: "For women who are on the journey of radical be-ing, the lives of the witches, of the Great Hags of our hidden history are deeply intertwined with our own process. As we write/live our own story, we are uncovering their history, creating Hagography and Hagology" (Daly 1990, 14–15).

Here Daly touches upon some of the features of Hagography that make it an effective antidote to christian hagiography. She reclaims a "so-called obsolete" definition of the noun *haggard* found in *Merriam-Webster*. A *haggard* is "an intractable person, especially: a woman reluctant to yield to wooing." This reclaimed meaning becomes the basis for Daly's vision of Hagography: "Haggard writing is by and for haggard women, those who are intractable, willful, wanton, unchaste, and, especially, those who are reluctant to yield to wooing. It belongs to the tradition of those who refuse to assume the woes of wooed women, who cast off these woes as unworthy of Hags, of Harpies" (Daly 1990, 15–16).

Because Daly writes in a very distinctive style that has become her trademark, it is possible to overlook the fact that she situates herself, as a writer and a Radical Feminist Philosopher, within this larger tradition of Hagographic discourse. Leigh Gilmore has coined the term *autobiographics* to refer to the hidden tradition of women's personal narrative, which should be distinguished from the (supposedly) generic category of life-writing associated with the term *autobiography*[1] epitomized by patriarchal works such as Augustine's *Confessions*. Gilmore describes autobiographics as a specifically feminist mode of self-representation whose primary strategies include "interruptions and eruptions, . . . resistance and contradiction" (Gilmore 1994, 42). Within this framework a feminist writing her life is engaged in an improvisation performed by a Hagographer in her capacity as Spell-Weaver: a "Creative Crone who weaves contexts in which Wonders can happen" (Daly and Caputi 1987, 167). Hagographers engaged in autobiographics do not merely write their lives; they create new contexts, new Space and Time, in which New Selves Weave Spells.

In her three most explicitly Hagographic works, the "Autobiographical Preface," "Feminist Postchristian Introduction"—both in the 1975 edition of *The Church and the Second Sex*—and *Outercourse*, Daly provides us with glimpses of her girlhood, young womanhood, and formal education. These glimpses constitute carefully prepared/shared Moments placed within their own contexts. Their purpose is to depict Daly's growing Self-consciousness, and the process by which she Named herSelf a radical feminist, a Hag, a Pirate, and so on. Although these Moments are presented within specific temporal frameworks (within one of the four Spiral Galaxies), they do not represent merely a linear series of events. In the Prelude to the Second Spiral Galaxy of *Outercourse*, Daly asserts, almost in passing, "Of course, I had already been a Pirate all my life, accumulating treasures of knowledge that had been hidden from my Tribe." In this same section, Daly refers to Piracy as a Call, an identity, a career (Daly 1992, 129). Piracy represents one way in which Daly participates in Be-ing, pursuing her Final Cause. The Pirate's life is an endless Journey punctuated by Moments of Be/Leaving, in which be-ing is increasingly realized.

When one reflects upon the Moments Daly Re-calls in the First Galaxy of *Outercourse*, it is striking to see how many of them serve to recount and reaffirm Daly's Passion to become a philosopher, "a woman who could think, write and teach about the most fascinating of questions and earn her living by doing just this" (Daly 1985a, 8). Some of the Moments describe mystical "intuitions of be-ing," for example, the summer day in early adolescence when Daly, lying on the grass near a favorite swimming hole, had "an encounter with a clover blossom." For Daly, the Moment had tremendous ontological significance. The blossom "Announced its be-ing" to her (Daly 1992, 23, 41). These Moments of epiphany continued into womanhood. There was the Dream of Green that interrupted Daly's study of medieval literature at Catholic University in the early fifties and reinforced her earlier conviction that she was *meant* to study philosophy (Daly 1992, 48–49). There was the hedge at Saint Mary's, Notre Dame, where she received her first doctorate in theology. When the hedge said: "continued existence" (Daly 1992, 51–52) directly to Daly, it provided her with a whole new set of questions to pursue as a philosopher and reminded her that the philosopher's Quest is personal as well as professional.

Re-calling these Moments sustained Daly's (initially subliminal) Ontological Courage throughout a whole series of disappointments related in the First Galaxy of *Outercourse*. Daly grew frustrated with the catholic secondary school and college she attended, where women were steered away from science and philosophy and toward literature and the arts. She recoiled at the "enforced narrowness of horizons" and only decades later did she decode the "all-pervasive subliminal message" that had repeated itself in a variety of ways throughout her undergraduate years. The message, disconcertingly clear in her Re-membered Moments, was that "we were not destined for greatness" (Daly 1992, 43).

In a master's program in English literature at Catholic University, Daly disobeyed the unwritten rules and wrote a thesis on literary theory. When a priest who served as a reader for the thesis dismissed her ideas and declaimed her "lack of philosophical *habitus*," this only strengthened Daly's determination to earn a doctorate in philosophy (Daly 1992, 49). For an American catholic woman in the fifties, the best way to realize this goal was to study theology first. The pioneering doctoral program for women at Saint Mary's, Notre Dame (Mandell 1997, 183–88), seemed like a godsend, a door in the wall. But even at Saint Mary's, in a program explicitly designed to nurture a new cadre of female catholic theologians, Daly felt like "a cognitive minority of one."

She welcomed the mental challenge posed by the philosophy of Saint Thomas Aquinas (1225–74), the centerpiece of the neoscholastic curriculum taught at even at the most progressive catholic institutions in the period before the Second Vatican Council (1962–65). She Re-calls Moments of complete happiness and satisfaction studying Aquinas's theology, Moments when she "felt something like pity for people who did not understand the theology of 'the Trinity.' " But there were Other painful Moments when Daly first articulated some of the Nonquestions raised by the scholastic texts. One day, studying Aquinas's *Summa theologiae* (I, q. 92, a. 1 ad 1), she Dis-covered a passage that depicted women as "defective and misbegotten," the result of a "defect in the active force [male seed] or from some material indisposition, or even from some external influence such as that of a south wind, which is moist." When Daly approached another ("considerably older and somewhat intimidating") woman in her program about the passage, her concerns were dismissed with a statement of the catholic party line: "That's no offense to *your* dignity." Daly could not agree. She "filed away" the Moments of isolation, invisibility, and inaudibility for future reference. Years later, when she wrote *Outercourse,* she Names them "Moments of Prophecy and Promise" (Daly 1992, 51–53, 6).

Even in the early fifties, Daly began to appreciate the bittersweet sensation of Be/Leaving, at least subliminally. She learned more about it in the spring of 1954, a few months before she received her doctorate from Saint Mary's. At first her prospects had looked promising. She had applied to the doctoral program in theology at the University of Notre Dame, and Sister Madeleva, President of Saint Mary's, had offered her a teaching position that would help pay her tuition. But then Notre Dame denied Daly admission because of her sex and Sister Madeleva withdrew her offer after Daly had joined a student movement to reform her pet project, the theology program for women (Daly 1992, 53).

When Daly left Saint Mary's for five bleak years teaching at Cardinal Cushing College (and secondary school) in Brookline, Massachusetts, she left a part of herself behind, the part that had wanted to believe the "hidden broken Promise" undergirding the all-female catholic educational system (Daly 1992, 44–45) to which she had been confined by the circumstances of her birth, sex, and background. Daly soon discovered that her doctorate from Saint Mary's opened very few doors, and her final spring at Saint Mary's had taught her what catholic women's colleges did to the outspoken, the marginal, the "uppity" students without funds and family connections (Daly 1992, 53). Daly realized that she would have to seek patrons and opportunities beyond the semicloistered world assigned to catholic women. In seeing this, she caught glimpses of an Other Galaxy that she could only reach by continuing her Journey, and learning more.

Daly set her sights on the most prestigious catholic advanced degree, the doctorate from a pontifical faculty of sacred theology. When Catholic University, the only such program in the United States, rejected her because of her sex, Daly found universities in Germany and Switzerland that offered the same degree and accepted applications from women. With financial help from John Wright, Bishop of Pittsburgh and a well-known patron of (male) lay theologians, Daly set out in 1959 for the University of Fribourg, where she spent seven years, and earned the highest degrees in theology and philosophy available in the catholic world. Daly thrived at Fribourg, and later called her graduate study there "a seven years' ecstatic experience interspersed with brief periods of gloom, . . . a sort of lengthy spiritual-intellectual chess game" (Daly 1985a, 9).

The object of the game was to master the writings of Thomas Aquinas (and his intellectual heirs, the neoscholastics) and apply and interpret them in new ways appropriate to the modern context, all the while remaining within the bounds of orthodoxy. Daly's two dissertations, "The Problem of Speculative Theology" and "Natural Knowledge of God in the Theology of Jacques Maritain," attest to her grasp of scholastic and neoscholastic theology. She survived the awkwardness of studying with seminarians who avoided sitting next to her and eschewed eye contact.

Indeed, some of these same European seminarians broke into applause when Daly passed an especially grueling set of examinations and compared her to the astronaut John Glenn (Daly 1992, 62).

At Fribourg, Daly showed (herself and others) that she could meet the challenges posed by the most demanding catholic doctoral programs and simultaneously teach American undergraduates studying abroad. Her adventures in Europe, Great Britain, and the Middle East laid the foundations for the pervasive travel metaphors underlying her later Radical Feminist writings.

Daly's European sojourn released her from a bondage she had only begun to acknowledge, and taught her the meaning as well as the *sensation* of Be/Leaving: "The Stunning thing about my early travels in Europe was the utterly surprising phenomenon of having all the magical images that had populated my imagination since childhood actually materialize and come alive. In Rome, for example, when I first saw the Forum and the Colosseum at night I was transported. I had seen pictures in my Latin textbooks in high school. Now they really existed! So I was Space/Time traveling, participating in the Fourth Dimension."

In the same passage in *Outercourse* Daly captures the sense of liberation, the positive aspects of Be/Leaving, that she Dis-covered in Europe in the early Sixties with a whole array of images already familiar to readers of *Pure Lust:* "It was as if I had lived imprisoned in a sort of disneyland and was suddenly released into the real world. I was like someone who had known only plastic trees and flowers and who was now let loose in a verdant place—a forest or a jungle. Countless doors and windows in my brain were thrown open and I gulped the fresh exhilarating air. I had been suffocating in a state of sensory deprivation, and that state was behind me" (Daly 1992, 64).

These sensations associated with the Fribourg years survived, and perhaps even catalyzed, Daly's departure from the catholic church in the late sixties. For Daly, studying Aquinas and the neoscholastics was not merely a matter of mastering *content;* the neoscholastic curriculum suggested a way of being in the world. Daly calls her forays into Thomistic metaphysics "an exhilarating ride." She was attracted to the order, clarity, and "exquisitely complex" logic of Thomas (Daly 1992, 59–60). She cherished *the way it felt* to be part of the neoscholastic enterprise at Fribourg. Writing her second (philosophy) dissertation on intuition in the works of the neoscholastic philosopher Jacques Maritain, Daly "learned to trust [her] own intuitions while demonstrating their implications rigorously, and to articulate [her] own arguments in a way that is inherently clear in itself—which is quite a different matter from being a good 'debater' who argues only to score points but does not seek the truth" (Daly 1992, 75).

Daly was drawn to the study of catholic neoscholastic theology, in part, because it promised that truth was available to those who were properly trained in the use of reason and intuition in the pursuit of truth. Historian Philip Gleason suggests that by the middle of this century, neoscholasticism was more than a school of philosophy or theology. It was an ideology that pervaded the entire mental world inhabited by catholic intellectuals. At the center of this ideology, Gleason maintains, was "the breathtaking assertion" that "human reason alone was sufficient to establish with certainty that God exists, that the divine nature was such that God always spoke the truth and had in fact spoken to humankind, proposing definite truths for their belief" (Gleason 1987, 169).

Daly imported some of this ideology into her postchristian Radical Feminist Philosophy. One sees this on a superficial level in the many references to neoscholastic/Thomistic terminology (especially central concepts such as Be-ing and the Final Cause) in Daly's works written in all four Spiral Galaxies. In her account of the history of catholic feminist theology in *New Catholic Women,* Mary Jo Weaver addresses the question of how Daly's neoscholastic education shaped her Radical Feminist Philosophy. Weaver maintains that amid all of the stylistic and substantive changes in Daly's writings over the years, one thing remains constant. In Daly's first article published in *The Thomist* (Daly 1965) and in *Pure Lust,* which appeared nineteen years later, one finds " 'a consistent search for transcendence or what [pre-Vatican II neoscholastic] theologians called Being," along with an emphasis upon the need "to strive 'toward a higher level of human existence' " (Weaver 1995, 176).

Weaver asserts that what changes for Daly, the postchristian feminist, is "the location of the source of transcendence." This crucial change of location is signaled by the new hyphenated spelling of Be-ing. Weaver explains:

> In *Beyond God the Father* [Daly] argued that it was impossible to leave God behind and therefore necessary to destroy the "myth of God the Father" in order to be empowered by God the Verb. In *Pure Lust*, feminism, not God, is the Verb, a process that continues and draws us along with it. The Verb has the same function,

> to encourage belief in the self, community, and a new age; but it is no longer perceived as outside women. . . . The spirit of transcendence rests within women, yearning for activation. (Weaver 1995, 177)

Daly does not deny the fundamental continuity that Weaver describes, but she revels in the discontinuities and departures. In true Pirate fashion she later Named Thomistic philosophy her Labrys that "[enabled her] to cut through man-made delusions to the core of problems" (Daly 1992, 75). For this reason, she Re-members her "Quest through the mazes of academia" as a "Rite of Passage on [her] Piratic enterprise of Plundering treasures stolen by phallocratic thieves and Smuggling them back to women within academia itself" (Daly 1992, 78). Still, as Weaver has observed, throughout the Journey, the search for transcendence, which Daly calls participation in Be-ing, remains the dynamic central axis of Daly's Radical Feminist Philosophy. What changed was the context, the way in which she envisioned Be-ing and its place in her expanding cosmos.

This process of Re-calling and Re-vision happened gradually during the final years of the sixties, and it became Daly's driving Passion by the first half of the seventies. In the early seventies, spurred by her recent encounter with phallocracy in the fight for tenure at Boston College, Daly began to explore the possibility of addressing ontological questions outside the church and beyond the christian tradition. In her second book, *Beyond God the Father*, she argues that women's liberation hinges upon women's discovery of a new Space "on the boundary" beyond the christian realm, a Space where wholeness and participation in Be-ing were possible. Daly Named this new Space the "exodus community" or "Cosmic Covenant" of Sisterhood (Daly 1985b, 132–78), experimental, transitional terminology still informed by her christian heritage and training. Nonetheless, readers familiar with the conciliatory tone and language of even the most critical sections of *The Church and the Second Sex* could not help but see Daly's second book as a sharp and Self-conscious departure.

Starting with its title, *Beyond God the Father*, and Robin Morgan's quotation on the first page ("I want a women's revolution like a lover. I lust for it."), Daly's second book breathed the spirit of the radical flank of the American women's movement of around 1973. Her treatment of ontology, arguably the central theme of the entire volume, was also deeply informed by the feminist rhetoric of the early seventies. She calls for the "castrating of language and images that reflect and perpetuate the structures of a sexist world." She does not shrink from asserting that among the candidates for castration are the fatherly God of the christians and Jews, and all traditional religious institutions. Daly explains why castration is not an unduly harsh or violent method of women's liberation: "As aliens in a man's world who are now rising up to name—that is, to create—our own world, women are beginning to recognize that the value system that has been thrust upon us by the various cultural institutions of patriarchy has amounted to a kind of gang rape of minds as well as bodies" (Daly 1985b, 9).

"Why indeed must 'God' be a noun?" Daly asks in *Beyond God the Father*. "Why not a verb—the most active and dynamic of all?" Drawing upon the ideas of other feminist theologians in her own circle of friends, especially Nelle Morton and Janice Raymond, and generalizing from the mutuality and support available to her within that circle, Daly posits that wherever "sororal community-consciousness is present," there, too, is God, the Verb, Be-ing. The women's movement (and individual women who are agents within the movement) participate in the evolution of Be-ing: "The unfolding of woman-consciousness is an intimation of the endless unfolding of God" (Daly 1985b, 33, 35–36).

Almost twenty years later, in *Outercourse*, Daly acknowledged the "Overwhelming Oversight" in *Beyond God the Father*: her retention of the word "God." It was not a "simple oversight," Daly explained. "No: it was a complex acrobatic process/problem, . . . engendered by a great desire to save *God*." Daly vividly Re-called her intense, unquestioned need to keep God in the picture, albeit reconstituted and castrated, the ultimate intransitive Verb, Be-ing (Daly 1992, 161). For all of her new-found Ontological Courage, she could not yet conceive of Be-ing without its connection to the christian God. Daly's account of the Overwhelming Oversight, which appears in her autobiography, written almost two decades later, preserves for us a Self-portrait of Daly, the Novice Nag, in the midst of a painful Moment of Be/Leaving, still instinctively clinging to a vestigial fragment of her past: "I was unconsciously afraid of losing my true Self and/or forgetting my intuition of Be-ing, in which I and all Others participate. In traditional language, *God* represented this, although inadequately. The grip of the word *God* was strong: its tentacles were tenacious. After a short time, however, when I did make the "Qualitative Leap" and dispense with "him," I found that Be-ing the Verb was very much alive and well, and so was I. I had lost Nothing" (Daly 1992, 161).

We have already seen that in the early seventies Daly had begun to make connections between her bent for thinking ontologically and her own evolving woman-consciousness. After the grueling tenure fight with the jesuits at Boston College (1968–69), Daly's public exodus from the church in 1971, and her Dis-covery of her Lesbian identity during this same period, Daly found herSelf on the Other Side, in a new Space/Time. In *Outercourse* she captures the change in a Re-membered Moment/Metaphor/intuition: "I Re-Call looking out my office window at trees whose branches met and having an overwhelmingly powerful intuition that expressed itself in the words 'The trees came together.' I would Now call that experience 'an intuition of Elemental integrity' " (Daly 1992, 144). This experience of "Dis-covering . . . an Other dimension of [her] identity" transported Daly into a new mode of be-ing. Suddenly she found herSelf "several woman-light years" away from the author of *The Church and the Second Sex,* on the Other side of a "journey in time/space that . . . could not be described adequately by terrestrial calendars and maps" (Daly 1992, 144; Daly 1985a, 5). Daly would not, and could not, compartmentalize herSelf. She had to honor her intuition of Elemental integrity, which she now recognized as her participation in the cosmic unfolding of Be-ing.

With this in mind, it is illuminating to take a closer look at the spirit in which Daly, the postchristian feminist author of *Beyond God the Father,* approached her former Self, the catholic feminist who had launched *The Church and the Second Sex* eight years before "with a great sense of pride, anger, and hope" (Daly 1985a, 5). The opportunity for the two Mary Dalys (1968 and 1974) to meet in print arose when Daly's publisher proposed a second edition of *The Church and the Second Sex.* At first, Daly considered both of her options "odious." She could publish a revised edition, knowing that no revisions, however extensive, could make her first book speak for (or from) her current position, or she could simply refuse to issue a second edition, silence her former Self, and deprive potential readers of access to a pivotal, if dated, early feminist text.

Almost twenty years later, in her autobiography, Daly explained why she had rejected both of these alternatives. She had felt compelled to choose between two of the Seven Deadly Sins (assimilation and elimination) as she had renamed (and augmented) them in *Pure Lust.*[2] Then, just in time, Daly discovered "a Transcendent Third Option" that allowed her to avoid "the twin perils of tokenism/assimilation and Self-erasure/ elimination" and in the process, create "something entirely New." She decided to provide readers with both "the early Daly's book and the radical critique—a tangible record of Intergalactic Travel" (Daly 1992, 186). In the process, Daly showed what Be/leaving looked like, and even, on occasion, what it *felt* like.

Daly was immediately comfortable with her decision in favor of the Transcendent Third Option and made several subsequent decisions based upon this precedent. In 1985 she published a second edition of *Beyond God the Father*, with an "Original Reintroduction" explaining her relationship to the book and its author. The same year she added the "New Archaic Afterwords" to the third edition of *The Church and the Second Sex*. In 1990, she issued a second edition of *Gyn/Ecology*, with a "New Intergalactic Introduction" that bridged the gap between her present and former Selves. For the *Wickedary*, her radical feminist lexicon, which appeared in 1987, Daly devised a set of symbols based on the phases of the moon to denote the sites, or Word-Works, where she had first introduced her Dis-covered words (Daly and Caputi 1987, xv, 59–60, 285 n. 2). In *Outercourse*, Daly incorporated these same symbols into her footnotes, and provided contextual remarks as well as more recent perspectives on all of the new prefaces and introductions. The dialogue between Daly and her earlier Selves/texts continues in *Quintessence*, published in 1998 (Daly 1998, 13–24).

The process of writing these assessments and explorations of her former Selves and works has prompted Daly to cultivate a deep and rich awareness of the relationships among her multiple Selves. It is significant that she chose not to issue revised versions of her original texts/Selves, nor did she attempt to airbrush the transitions to make them appear smoother. Instead she sought to provide readers with direct access to her own open-ended, unexpurgated conversations with her earlier texts/ Selves. She did not want to be complicit in the patriarchal sins of assimilation and elimination. She did not want to isolate herSelf or her readers from earlier Selves and Spiral Galaxies. For it would be impossible to write about her central/ontological concern with Be-ing within the kind of two-dimensional, static framework that a conventional revised version of her texts would create. Daly simply could not consign herSelf, even an earlier and very different Self, to what she would later call the foreground past, sealed off from the new sisterhood coming "into be-ing" where women's hearing/healing presence made New Space and Time possible.

Despite everything, and even after all that had transpired to separate them, Daly circa 1974 could still empathize with Daly circa 1968. ("I felt as if this were the journal of a half-forgotten foremother, whose quaintness should be understood in historical context and treated with appropriate respect.") Yet, she was shocked in 1974 by some of the proposals she had made in 1968. She openly confessed her sense of alarm and disorientation: "Why, I wondered, would anyone want 'equality' in the church? . . . Why did she say 'we' when she meant 'I' and 'they' when she meant 'we'?"(Daly 1985a, 6). After a thorough, chapter-by-chapter critique of her 1968 book and Self, Daly circa 1974 submitted the following measured, but enthusiastic, judgment:

> As critic, what have I managed to say of this work? It has made me alternately exasperated and joyful. The biographical data accessible to me concerning the author indicates that she was not an overly modest person, so I don't think she would mind my saying that she helped to build a tradition in which I now participate. I would be less than just if I failed to acknowledge this. I have found the work worth studying at this time, and I recommend it to scholars who wish to understand *the process of the feminist movement*. (Daly 1985d, 47; italics mine)

It is worthwhile to linger over Daly's use of the word "process" here. "Process" was a buzzword of the seventies, but in Daly's prose the term always refers back to ontology and ultimately to Thomas Aquinas. While many of Daly's teachers and fellow students at Saint Mary's and Fribourg found in the theology of Aquinas a static textbook description of the perfections of God, the eternal, unchanging, unmoved mover, Daly, the Alchemist, found the raw materials for a radically dynamic theology/philosophy of becoming, an ontology which envisions individuals actively striving to amplify the Be-ing that gives Life its very Life. Gradually Daly introduced her own Metaphors of Spiraling and Spinning to convey a sense of the dynamic ontology she had first Dis-covered and embraced within the philosophy/theology of Aquinas.

Thomistic ontology remained Daly's foundation, her touchstone, no matter how many thresholds she crossed. Daly, the Be/Leaver, took Thomas with her on her Spiraling Journey. Even as recently as 1992 Daly could still state unequivocally that "for decades" the thirteenth century, the century of Aquinas and the scholastics, "has been the century in which I have felt at home" (Daly 1992, 3). Elsewhere in *Outercourse* she clarifies why she continues to capitalize the terms Thomist and Thomistic (as well as the name Thomas Aquinas) when the rest of her capitalization has become "capitally irregular," depending upon the "ever changing contexts which [she has] created." She capitalizes these terms to acknowledge the ways in which her Thomistic training "[prepared] the way for the creative work that was to come" (Daly 1992, 60).

Daly clarifies her debt to Aquinas in a Re-membered Moment in the "Feminist Postchristian Introduction," written during the summer of 1974. She revisits her treatment of Aquinas in *The Church and the Second Sex*, bringing with her a new set of questions and Nonquestions. She declares the "critique of medieval biology . . . too restrained" (in other words, she should have been far more appalled by Thomas's appropriation of Aristotle's biology and misogyny). Daly does not need to belabor her point. The single reference to Thomistic biology will do. Then Daly turns to a much more subtle, more revealing kind of exegesis. She treats her 1968 analysis of Aquinas as a palimpsest.

Once again in this passage, we see Daly herSelf in process. Daly scours the text with a new set of personal questions, an outgrowth of Be/Leaving and her new/Archaic Radical Feminist context. What interests Daly most is what she had *almost* written in her first book, risks she had *almost* taken, hopes she had *almost* expressed. She pores over her old text in search of the faint outlines of the text that she had not yet dared to write but can still perceive between the lines, even in a much more recent re-reading of her first book. She provides an analysis of two pages of the original text of *The Church and The Second Sex* (Daly 1985c, 94–99) paying special attention to ontological questions:

> I think I can detect in Daly's defense of Aquinas's "radically liberating principles" a quality different from her lip service to the single "liberating" Pauline text [Gal. 3:27–28] and even quite different from her general defense of "basic Christian doctrine." In the latter case, . . . she seems to be avoiding the threat of a radical break from Christianity. But in her plea for Aquinas there is, it seems to me, a kind of positive passion. . . . I think it fair to say that she was struggling to find ontological roots for what we know today as the feminist philosophy of Be-ing. In the better parts of Aquinas's work she found hints of what a philosophy of be-ing/becoming could begin to say. . . . The ontological process which

> Daly so ardently sought could only be found in the women's revolution, which had not yet surfaced. Consequently, she took starvation rations from the best of the Christian philosophers. In her time, when sisterhood had not yet emerged, moving too far ahead would have meant venturing into an endless desert, into a state which an uncomprehending world would have called "madness" and treated as such. It is important for our historical sense, I think, that we try to comprehend this situation. (Daly 1985c, 23–24)

I have quoted Daly at length to convey both the seriousness of her tone and the pains she takes to provide a close textual analysis of a portion of the original book that most of her readers were in no position to appreciate without guidance. By the time Daly wrote this passage in the summer of 1974, she was already living a Life of Ontological Courage. She had crossed a threshold to radical feminism and was well on her way to a separatist position. She could have simply Moved On, with a firm resolve not to look back. Why did she want to Re-member and share the Desire and Need with which she had approached the writings of Aquinas? Why did she want to Re-call her old fears of the desert, of standing on the Boundary, looking/feeling like a cognitive minority of one, maybe even a madwoman?

Daly takes the trouble to show her readers (and perhaps remind her-Self) that Be/Leaving is not optional, not tidy, never entirely finished. Even in another Galaxy, Daly continues to participate in the process of Be/Leaving she had begun several woman-light-years before. This participation provides Daly with a special gift she calls the Courage to See: "the courage to become dis-illusioned, to See through male mysteries, to become a Seer, envisioning an Archaic Future" (Daly and Caputi 1987, 69). The negative aspect of Be/Leaving plays a crucial role in developing the Pirate's sight. See-ing *through* disillusionment is the only way to become a Pirate.

Daly's recourse to two contrasting descriptions of Be/Leaving in *Outercourse* parallels her definitions of Ontological Courage and the Courage to See in the *Wickedary*. The contrast between the positive and negative examples suggests the range of emotions and experiences Named by the verb "to Be/Leave." It also underscores the varying degrees of resistance against which and beyond which one chooses to Be/Leave. The first reference to Be/Leaving, quoted at the beginning of this essay, describes Daly's joyful departure from the world of catholic liturgy. The second reference, which examines Daly's expanding awareness of the "hidden broken Promise" of academic life, is far more painful to read.

Daly provides the full account of her unsuccessful bid for tenure in 1968–69, including the student protests and news coverage, in the "Autobiographical Preface" to the second edition of *The Church and the Second Sex*. She relates, how, after the students had left for vacation, and she for a summer-school post on the West Coast, Boston College's administration had reversed their decision in the wake of the negative media attention they had received the previous spring. Then Daly received a telegram from the president of Boston College, "informing [her], without congratulations, that [she] had been granted promotion and tenure." Daly's description of her reaction to the news is analogous to her account of leaving during the bingo sermon on easter day 1968. It is infused with the same undercurrent of anticlimax and finality, and ultimately the same sense of be-ing in a New Place, but it lacks the feelings of lightness and celebration. "It was a strange victory," writes Daly, in an effort to reproduce the complicated feelings she experienced upon receipt of the telegram. "Apparently the book which had led to my firing had generated the support which forced my rehiring. . . . But something had happened to the meaning of 'professor,' to the meaning of 'university,' to the meaning of 'teaching' " (Daly 1985a, 13).

As in the earlier narrative of her final departure from mass, Daly reflects upon the two-sideness of life. Just as the hymn that had been a taunt became her processional out of penarchy, the book that had closed the door to tenure had miraculously reopened it, and the promotion that Boston College had so grudgingly granted alerted her to the "pre-possession" in store for "successful" academic women. In *Outercourse*, Daly explained that it was in response to this ambiguous victory in the tenure process that she first clarified the meaning of be-ing and Be/Leaving and consciously chose life "on the Boundary." "As I came to understand more about academia," Daly maintains, "I still wanted to be in that world, as it were, but not of it—to be there still, but unconstrained. I wanted academia to support my real work in the world."

This is where Boundary Living came in. Through her grueling experience with the tenure process (and a similar ordeal when she was denied promotion to full professor in 1975), Daly Dis-covered that "although [she] could no longer believe in academia/academentia, [she] could Be/Leave *in* it." Buoyantly, she concluded: "In Other words, I could be a highly qualified Pirate" (Daly 1992, 121). This Moment of Dis-covery informs all of Daly's subsequent strategies as a separatist. Daly understood that be-ing and Be/Leaving did not entail making discrete "either/or" decisions (for example, leave academia or stay and assimilate). She felt called upon to make Other plans, to build New Space where she and Other women could explore the meaning of their Power of Absence and embrace the Prance of Life, "the large and complex steps required for Macroevolution; the springing, capering, frisking, frolicking, cavorting, romping, gamboling" style of Wild Creatures (Daly and Caputi 1987, 89). Daly chose to adopt this style as a philosopher and a public Presence on the margins of academia. In so doing she came to epitomize the Non-questions at the heart of her philosophy.

Although the first-person accounts in the "Autobiographical Preface" and the "Feminist Postchristian Introduction," might seem, implicitly, to suggest otherwise, Daly did not negotiate her way to boundary living alone. She made the journey in the company of women: the transtemporal community of Hags and Spinsters that she originally Named the "antichurch" or "cosmic covenant" of sisterhood (Daly 1985b, 132–78) and later conjured by the word "Presence" (Daly and Caputi 1987, 88–89; Daly 1992). The new postchristian feminist ontology first introduced in *Beyond God the Father* was grounded in Daly's proliferating experiences of Elemental integrity and her expanding woman-consciousness. It grew out of Daly's successful struggle to accept her Life on the Boundary as a positive development, her deepening Realization that she had Nothing to lose. What did it matter if Daly had Plundered her Boundary metaphor from the Harvard theologian Paul Tillich, about whom she was deeply ambivalent? Being a Pirate requires a variety of approaches to recycling Smuggled Goods, including the skills of the Prospector and the Alchemist. Daly "sorted out nuggests of partial, i. e., patriarchally distorted, knowledge and placed these in a Metapatriarchal context, so that they could radiate richer meanings." She insisted that "the secret of [her] Alchemical powers lay in [her] ability to Dis-cover and create an entirely Other setting for these treasures, that is, Radical Feminist Philosophy" (Daly 1992, 148, 157). Once freed from Stag-nation, Daly's Plundered Metaphors and gems of knowledge become part of an endless process of Re-membering, Re-calling the connections binding Elemental beings (Daly and Caputi 1987, 92–93).

The Other setting that Daly Dis-covered on the Boundary was a separatist vision of community among Hags and Spinsters. In the Third Passage of *Gyn/Ecology*, Daly examines what happens to Spinsters' Selves in the new Space on the Boundary. She contrasts the claim that J. Glenn Gray makes about male friendship ("[It] seeks to expand [the] walls [of self] and keep them intact") with her growing experience of female friendship. Daly explains that sisterhood is about "burning/melting/vaporizing the constricting walls imposed upon the Self." She elaborates: "Female friendship is not concerned with 'expanding walls and keeping them intact,' but with expanding energy, power, vision, psychic and physical space." In Other Words, female friendship/Sparking, which is only fully Realized on the Boundary, is all about be-ing. Separatism, or Life on the Boundary, requires "paring away the layers of false selves from the Self" so that "the Self's original movement" can be set free. These unbound Selves are not clones, they're Crones. Daly insists that "the variety which Crones respect in each other has as its basic precondition and common thread the endurance/fortitude/stamina needed for persevering on the Journey" (Daly 1990, 380–81).

Daly's Words Re-call the spirit, energy, and wisdom of the Third Spiral Galaxy. While Be-ing remains her Final Cause, Be/Leaving, a never ending process, demands even more endurance/fortitude/stamina the longer the Journey Spins On. Freeing the Self's/Selves' original movement is not a task that can be completed once and for all. The more Hags See, the more challenging be-ing becomes. Hags' lives are complicated by the Boundary's location on the edge of patriarchy. Not even the most Outrageously Original Sinning, not even the most intense and sustained Be/Leaving can bring about the total eclipse of phallocracy, or even one Hag's complete escape from the sado-state. This situation is a given; Spinning Hags work/Spiral around it. Radical feminism, even separatism, does not mean escapism and the abdication of responsibility. Commitment to Biophilic Energy entails endless forays into dangerous territory.

The further Daly pursues her Journey, the more Spiral Galaxies she explores, the keener her awareness of phallocratic necrophilia becomes. Pirates can create Separate Spaces, Other Settings for their Plundered gems of knowledge. Crones can crack their own jokes about the noxious gases of patriarchy. Still, the noxious gases have not dissipated. Daly's Hagographic writings from the eighties and nineties are more insistent than ever that "phallocracy does not and in fact cannot essentially change. It cannot reverse its destructive mechanisms that massacre women and nature, for these are essential to its necrophilic existence. They are its vital, i.e., lethal functions" (Daly 1985e, xv).

It is not surprising then to see Daly expand upon the timeliness of the Courage to Leave in the 1985 "New Archaic Afterwords" to *The Church and the Second Sex.* Daly herSelf has Named patriarchy and the dangers of patriarchal religion, but she is by no means indifferent to the plight of the women who remained "lost/trapped inside its gynocidal, spirit-deadening maze" (Daly 1985e, xii). She retains a strong sense of empathy for the Self who had written *The Church and the Second Sex* and for others who had yet to encounter its message. It is to this audience that she writes:

> From the perspective of 1985 A. F. [Anno Feminarum] it can be seen clearly, and more clearly than ever, that a tragic error/terror manages to lock women within the prisons of blind/blinded faith.
>
> Acceptance of this error gives rise to terror of Leaving. This terror is itself a major cause of spiritual death. . . . The terror and the belief system to which it is attached are exorcised only when women break through to the Elemental Realization that we owe the church Nothing, since the church has given us precisely Nothing. We then see that we have Nothing to lose by Leaving. Indeed the loss of Nothing posing as Something brings almost inexpressible relief. (Daly 1985e, xii–xiii)

Daly refused to forget the "terror of Leaving" that had kept her in the church and then in a state of limbo, on the verge of Be/Leaving, from the late fifties through the late sixties. The fear of "an endless desert" and of being treated as a madwoman (Daly 1985c, 23–24) stayed with her as vivid memories of a still recountable, but no longer frightening, nightmare. In the "New Archaic Afterwords" Daly drew upon the power of this nightmare that had almost paralyzed her and still terrorized women of the Eighties. Thus she reassures women that "We have Nothing to lose by Leaving" and that the loss of "Nothing posing as Something" opens up new possibilities.

The "New Archaic Afterwords" provides a concrete example of what it means for Daly to be a Pirate. Daly's Journey and her dedication to exorcising the patriarchal demons are endless and boundless. The Spiral Shape of her Journey ensures that Daly is never too far removed from where she has made her latest exit. Her Home on the Boundary, in a subsequent Spiral Galaxy, simply affords her an enhanced perspective from which to speak. The Daly who revisits her 1968 text and Self in 1985 is a very different Daly from the one who took such pains in 1975 to explain the relationship between her commitment to Aquinas's theology and her radical feminist ontology. Daly circa 1985 assumes that we understand the roots of her ontology. She brings this Hagography with her to the text but her chief concern remains the women who are locked within the prisons of blind/blinded faith.

Daly speaks directly to the women of the "dulled-out mid-eighties" who are being "force-fed" media images of Nancy Reagan and Sunny von Bulow and parallel images of catholic women kneeling at the feet of john paul two (Daly 1985e, xviii, xx). Daly finds New Words befitting the Third Galaxy to describe the connection between be-ing and Be/Leaving: "The timelessness of recession/procession into archetypes which characterizes the mid-eighties a. d. is a pathological mirror image of the Elemental shedding of patriarchal time that is essential to movement into and creation of an Archaic Future. As women move more and more into Living Archaic Time, our Original Creative Time, we Realize ourSelves and realize that the year of the lord—any year a. d.—is *archetypal deadtime*" (Daly 1985e, xviii).

For all that has changed—the Words, the Setting, Daly herSelf—the message is familiar: "Original Women, in touch with our Origins, bring forth Original thoughts, words, deeds. Forgetting to remember old creeds, we conjure new and ancient Faith. Ignoring false promises/premises, we hop with Living Hope. Riding the Tides of Present Promise, we bond in the chorus of Be-ing" (Daly 1985e, xxviii). Daly's message here should be read within the framework of her central Metaphor, the Spiraling Journey. Hags partake of Original Time and Space by simultaneously looking backward into archetypal deadtime and Spinning forward into the Archaic Future. Original Movement, by definition, proceeds toward the Final Cause, the Good (Daly and Caputi 1987, 152).

Even from the Third Spiral Galaxy Daly can smell the noxious gases of patriarchy smoldering on. She does not embrace an ontology or a separatism that functions as a nosegay, keeping the stench just out of range. Just as Be-ing is not a static destination but a Final Cause, Be/Leaving is not escapism but movement that expands the Space for Biophilic be-ing. *Pure Lust* and *Outercourse* Be-speak the truth: the Journey does not get easier, less dangerous, in Spiral Galaxies Three and Four. The rewards and intuitions of be-ing deepen and expand with each Pirate raid, but the raids themselves Re-call the proximity of normative non-being, phallocracy. Toward the end of the Second Realm of *Pure Lust*, Daly sketches out the delicate ecology of Life on the Boundary, as gleaned from the Third Galaxy:

> It is difficult to avoid the conclusion that when women are most true to our Selves, we are *distemperate*, that is, "out of order, not functioning normally." As supernormally functioning Scolds, Sylphs, Shrews, Wantons, Weirds, and company, Pyromantic women are definitely "out of order." Breaking Out of the male-ordered catalogs of virile virtues is not a tidy affair. Rather, this is achieved through movements that may be compared to tidal waves, and it involves invoking Muses and confronting demons. (Daly 1984, 288)

The Fourth Galaxy of *Outercourse* models for us some of the untidiness of tidal change. In the New Time of the Fourth Galaxy, Daly finds herSelf at the Beginning of her Journey as well as at the culmination of the three preceding Galaxies. The Fourth Galaxy sounds Different from its predecessors. Daly speaks more directly, more urgently to her readers, and frequently stops to question and challenge herSelf. Sometimes she appears to be answering questions that readers cannot hear. At one point the discussion leads back to a Moment in Cork, Ireland, in 1984, when someone had asked Daly why she continued to teach at Boston College. Daly's impromptu answer, "I choose to Stand my Ground," had since become a kind of mantra for her. It Be-spoke to her the deeper meaning of separatism. In her account of the defining Moment in Cork eight years before, Daly explains some of the insights her one-line response had brought to the surface: "I was choosing to Fight/Act (Stand my Ground) at that precise location on the Boundary between Background and foreground where the demonic patriarchal distortions of women's Archaic heritage are most visible and accessible to me, where my Craft can be most effective in the work of Exorcism—reversing the reversals that blunt the potential for Realizing Ecstasy" (Daly 1992, 284).

In the Fourth Galaxy, Daly returns to this Moment with new concerns and an Archaic consciousness. Her spontaneous answer, which had clarified so much for her in Galaxy Three, now poses difficult questions for her in Galaxy Four.

> The important question is: Is my Ground, in the deepest sense, on the Boundaries of patriarchal institutions? The answer is no, not Now.
>
> Oh, yes, I still Fight/Act there, on those Boundaries. But my true Ground, the Ground of that Ground, so to speak, is farther Out, farther Back. Back in the Background . . .

Daly concedes that she can be distracted by what transpires on the other side of the Boundary, inside patriarchal institutions, but this distraction is weaker in the Fourth Galaxy than in Galaxies One through Three. In Galaxy Four, which she entered in 1987, Daly's life is centered on the "pull of the Verb—the intransitive One." She explains that the pull, or attraction, is "so overwhelming that I fly sometimes, fly into the Unfolding, Enfolding arms" (Daly 1992, 340).

The Daly of the Fourth Galaxy describes herSelf as a commuter to earth who lives with Wild Cat and Catherine the Cow on the Other side of the moon. She senses the Presence of Other Crones in nearby craters and mountain ranges, although she has never actually seen them. "Really, there's been no Time for a conference," she relates. "But everyone is aware of everyone else" (Daly 1992, 346–47). The last section of *Outercourse,* labeled "Concluding—Beginning" is Named "The Great Summoning and the Great Summation." It starts out with Daly, Catherine, and Wild Cat poring over clippings from earth, apocalyptic warnings in true-to-life news stories about silicone breast implants, depleting ozone, lethal ultraviolet rays. It ends with Daly addressing the multitude, thousands of Cronies and Familiars, sharing the podium (a moon rock) with celebrated Hags of yore, including Granuaile, the sixteenth-century Pirate from Ireland; Hypatia; Harriet Tubman; Susan B. Anthony; and Spider Woman.

This passage, a controversial personal narrative in which Daly shares her soul and her dreams, poses problems for many feminists. Is Daly coopting the women she mentions, denying the particularities of their lives and words? Is she appropriating their voices and authority for herself, in order to promote an essentialized middle-class, white, Euro-American version of womanhood, which fails to understand the power of difference? Or is this visionary passage just another example of what New Time/Space can mean in Daly's Fourth Galaxy? My reading suggests the third alternative. In this fantasy placed near the end of *Outercourse,* Daly constructs the Metaphor of an intergalactic conference of Hags to dramatize what Hagography and the Power of Presence have meant to her, and to underscore the vital role community plays in be-ing and Be/Leaving. Daly has maintained that Pirates' Spiraling Journeys are intertwined with those of the Great Hags of all times, whose life stories have been stolen and hidden from us (Daly 1990, 14–15). In the Great Summation scene Daly paints a portrait of women's community, what she calls the Power of Presence: the "flow of healing energy experienced by women who are Present to each Other in New Time/New Space" (Daly and Caputi 1987, 88).

Daly closes her autobiography with a portion of a speech very similar to the ones she has made all over the world. We see Daly, the Nag-Gnostic inspirational speaker in top form. Daly's "Great Summation" is a distillation of her Radical Feminist Philosophy, familiar words, but in an Other Setting. "*Together, Moonstruck Metamorphosing Intergalactic Voyagers* can *change our world. The Great Summation requires cumulative negation of the nothingness of the state of necrophilia (patriarchy). The Great Summation* is *following our Final Cause, Realizing our participation in Be-ing. It* is *cumulative affirmation and celebration of Life*" (Daly 1992, 407–15).

Daly, the Radical Feminist Philosopher takes huge risks in *Outercourse*, especially in this final section that takes place in a New Space/Time on the Other side of the moon. The subtitle to the Fourth Spiral Galaxy prepares us to accompany Daly to the "BE-DAZZLING NOW," a Galaxy "Off the Calendar, Off the Clock." An illustration reassures us that the urtext is indeed the nursery rhyme about the cow jumping over the moon. The Prelude to the Fourth Galaxy, interwoven with Moments of Momentous Re-Membering, is driven by two of Daly's mantras ("Keep going Mary, Go!" and her mother's urgings "Go do your own work, dear"). It ends with a passage that reminds us that Daly inhabits a world of unceasing motion, Spiraling movements that bring Daly, Catherine, Wild Cat, and us, her readers, that much closer to the Unfolding, Enfolding Arms of Be-ing: "Run right into the Now. There is so much room (no room for gloom). It is so open here, there, everywhere. So full of the sweet, fresh smells of earth and air. Just dare!" (Daly 1992, 331–36).

In *Quintessence* Daly continues the Journey into the Fifth Spiral Galaxy, "the Expanding Here," (Daly 1998, 27–55) where she finds herSelf in the midst of a postpatriarchal Radical Elemental Feminist Movement called the Anonyma Network. The setting has shifted to the Lost and Found Continent in the year 2048 B.E. (Biophilic Era) but the message comes as no surprise to readers of *Outercourse*. Daly, still commuting between the margins of patriarchy in the 1990s and an Other extraterrestrial environment beyond the influence of the "nectech nasties" (Daly 1998, 220) writes with a growing sense of urgency. She calls *Quintessence* "a Desperate Act performed in a time of ultimate battles between principalities and powers." The apocalyptic imagery accurately reflects Daly's assessment of the stakes of the battle between "Boundary-violating necrotechnologists" and Daly's Cronies, whom she Names "Biophilic Bitches" (Daly 1998, 1–3, 119).

The battle is about Space, both inner and outer Space. "The space-rapists say they intend to strip-mine the moon," Daly warns. "They are invading and destroying the genetic wilderness and space wilderness." For Biophilic Bitches, "faced with the reality of hideous manipulation and the probability of ultimate extinction, not only of our bodies/minds (ourSelves), but all of nature," Daly maintains that the only option is to explore the Archaic Future. The Archaic Future is the new frontier, accessible by "Time-Space Travel beyond archetypal deadtime and . . . deep in our Memories, our Deep Past" (Daly 1998, 2–3).

In *Quintessence* Daly uses the word *diaspora* to describe the situation of women in the 1990s. For the term evokes the "state of dividedness and dispersion of women under patriarchy," both our "external dispersion" and "internalized oppression—the exile, scattering, and enforced migration of consciousness—which cuts us off from deep and focused Realizing of the Background" (Daly 1998, 37–38). Daly, proficient at reversals, suggests that Elemental Feminists can still transform their diaspora into a positive, biophilic Movement. "The workings of Elemental Feminist Genius can almost be invisible at first: one woman Sparks insight in another, and so on. The process, seemingly slow at first, is contagious. Then, apparently all of a sudden, it takes cumulative Quantum Leaps across Time and Space. That's how our Genius works—by Expanding Here" (Daly 1998, 77).

Mary Daly and the Ecology of Women's Space

The above discussion of the evolution of Be-ing and Be/Leaving in Daly's works shows what Mary Daly has done for us lately. She has provided New Space for us to think about some of the fundamental questions and challenges that face women and other Biophilic inhabitants of planet earth. Daly started to provide this New Space subliminally and implicitly in her first book, *The Church and the Second Sex,* where she juxtaposed two categories, the unchanging and eternal catholic church and the demands of feminists of the fifties and sixties, encapsulated in Simone de Beauvoir's unforgettable phrase, "the second sex." When she experimented with this juxtoposition, Daly Dis-covered an entire range of human discourse: the posing of Nonquestions, which became her life's work. Daly's Nonquestions opened up a new frontier analogous to the expanding Galaxies of Outer Space, a frontier that Daly, the christian feminist theologian, set out to explore in the late sixties. This open frontier is what attracted Daly—who had doctorates in both philosophy and theology—to theology; theology seemed to provide more space in which to promote social change and challenge the status quo (Daly 1992, 84).

Daly's first book captured the imaginations of catholics and feminists of the late sixties because it opened up vast spaces of the christian past, present, and future to hopeful and courageous scrutiny. The popularity of the book (as well as its notoriety in conservative catholic circles) showed Daly still more New Spaces, an expanding universe where she had never thought to look for it: beyond God the Father. In her second book, *Beyond God the Father,* Daly unveiled brave new worlds of feminist philosophical discourse that combined quite naturally with her commitments as an activist for feminist causes. During the early seventies, when she was writing *Beyond God the Father,* and the "Feminist Postchristian Introduction" and "Autobiographical Preface" for the second edition of her first book, Daly Dis-covered still another realm of discourse in which feminist philosophy and personal narrative/Hagography flow together. Since Daly's personal experience within the confines of academentia had shown her that life and work were *never really separate,* even for phallocrats, Daly was prepared for this new insight, but not for the experience of light and space and boundarylessness that greeted her in the "newly founded invisible counter-university, the Feminist Universe" that she and her Nonquestions helped to create. Daly was Be-Dazzled. This New Space became and remains Daly's Home.

Starting in 1978 with *Gyn/Ecology,* Daly has envisioned the growth of her Life/Philosophy (her Radical Feminist Metaethics) as an Otherworld Journey, a Spiraling Voyage of Exorcism and Ecstasy. What makes the Journey possible is "the radical be-ing of women" (Daly 1990, 1). The goal of this neverending, always uncompleted Journey is "both discovery and creation of a world other than patriarchy." On the last page of

Gyn/Ecology, we see what the Spiraling Journey has wrought: Spinsters hearing themSelves and eachOther into be-ing (Daly 1990, 424). In Other words, New Space can produce Otherworldly acoustics with remarkable ontological implications. *Pure Lust*, the *Wickedary*, and *Outercourse* continue the Journeys that Daly embarked upon in *Gyn/Ecology*, and in the Course of these Voyages Daly shows how Metaphor and the Spinning of New Words provide still more expanding Space and Time in which women can Dis-cover themSelves and participate in the Unfolding of Be-ing. As we have seen in the case of the Fourth Galaxy of *Outercourse*, Daly's Metaphors have expanded beyond the Boundaries that the rules of rhetoric have assigned to them. These rules do not apply on the Other side of the moon, a place where even the Boundary appears infinitely spacious, far closer to the Enfolding arms of Be-ing than to the sado-society that sent Daly and her Cronies to the Boundary in the first place.

Since 1968 Mary Daly, the theologian, the Radical Feminist Philosopher, the Nag-Gnostic Pirate has been Creating, Dis-covering, and Be-speaking the existence of Space for women to pursue their own survival and other Bio-philic causes. Much of this Space lies in the Realm of the feminist imagination, but all of it is Real (or can be Realized). Thanks to Daly, women can conceive of the possibility of Be/Leaving; they know that there is Life beyond each threshold, and that all Life participates in Be-ing. Thanks to Daly's Hagographies, women can embark with confidence upon Journeys through Spiraling Galaxies, and find vantage points within the various Galaxies where Hags can realize their past and future Selves. Thanks to Daly, women know about the Boundary, that it is not a two-dimensional line but a four-dimensional Space that expands infinitely toward Be-ing. Finally, thanks to Daly and her courageous, outrageous escapades and experiments, women who challenge constraints placed upon Space (Real and imagined), or who refuse to be tidily consigned to their place, can approach their own challenges without having to reinvent the wheel. They can muster some confidence from the fact that Daly has been in that place before (and somehow found Space). Discovering, Exploring, Expanding Biophilic Space has been Mary Daly's major achievement for three decades. Daly found the Space necessary for be-ing long before her fellow phallosophers were willing to admit that being could occupy space (or that women could participate in be-ing). Feminists whose Journeys began after Daly's have been beneficiaries of the Space Daly has Dis-covered and Expanded, whether they have been aware of it or not. At the end of one of the more disheartening moments in the Fourth Galaxy of *Outercourse*, Daly, ever resilient, reveals her latest plan: "Blast a hole in the wall between the foreground and the Background—a whole so big that everyone who is really Alive can get through." Daly adds: "I decided that the way to do that was just to be my Natural Self, who is extreme" (Daly 1992, 341). Daly, Pirate and Hagographer, shows us the clear and concrete meaning in Leigh Gilmore's enticingly abstract maxim "autobiography provokes fantasies of the real" (Gilmore 1994, 16).

Notes

1. In this essay I use the word *autobiography* as a synonym for *life-writings* and *personal narratives*. This is in keeping with Daly's use of the word *autobiography* in *Outercourse* (Daly 1992, 11). Nonetheless, it is clear that Daly's writings belong within the tradition of feminist personal narratives that Gilmore examines in *Autobiographics*.

2. To her expanded version of the first seven deadly sins (Professions/pride, Possession/avarice, Aggression/anger, Obsession/lust, Assimilation/gluttony, Elimination/envy, and Fragmentation/sloth), Daly added an eighth: Processions/deception (Daly 1984, x).

Works Cited

Daly, Mary. 1965. "The Problem of Speculative Theology." *Thomist* 29: 177–216.

———. 1984. *Pure Lust: Elemental Feminist Philosophy*. Boston: Beacon Press.

———. 1985a. "Autobiographical Preface to the 1975 Edition." In *The Church and the Second Sex*. 3d ed., 5–14. Boston: Beacon Press.

———. 1985b. *Beyond God the Father*. 2d ed. Boston: Beacon Press.

———. 1985c. *The Church and the Second Sex*. 3rd ed. Boston: Beacon Press.

———. 1985d. "Feminist Postchristian Introduction [to the 1975 Edition]." In *The Church and the Second Sex*. 3d. ed., 15–51. Boston: Beacon Press.

———. 1985e. "New Archaic Afterwords." In *The Church and the Second Sex*. 3d. ed., xi–xxx. Boston: Beacon Press.

———. 1990. *Gyn/Ecology: The Metaethics of Radical Feminism*. 2d ed. Boston: Beacon Press.

———. 1992. *Outercourse: The Be-Dazzling Voyage*. San Francisco: Harper San Francisco.

———. 1998. *Quintessence . . . Realizing the Archaic Future: A Radical Feminist Manifesto*. Boston: Beacon Press.

Daly, Mary, and Jane Caputi. 1987. *Websters' First New Intergalactic Wickedary of the English Language*. Boston: Beacon Press.

Gilmore, Leigh. 1994. *Autobiographics: A Feminist Theory of Women's Self-Representation*. Ithaca: Cornell University Press.

Gleason, Philip. 1987. *Keeping the Faith: American Catholicism Past and Present*. Notre Dame: University of Notre Dame Press.
Maritain, Jacques. 1966. "The Intuition of Being." In *Challenges and Renewals*, edited by Joseph W. Evans and Leo R. Ward, 119–33. Notre Dame: University of Notre Dame Press.
Mandell, Gail Porter. 1997. *Madeleva: A Biography*. Albany: State University of New York Press.
Stanley, Liz. 1992. *The Auto/biographical I: The Theory and Practice of Feminist Auto/biography*. Manchester: Manchester University Press.
Tillich, Paul. 1936. *On the Boundary*. New York: Charles Scribner's Sons.
Weaver, Mary Jo. 1995. *New Catholic Women: A Contemporary Challenge to Traditional Religious Authority*. 2d ed. Bloomington: Indiana University Press.

7

Women's Voices, Women's Words: Reading Acquaintance Rape Discourse

Molly Dragiewicz

From Experience to Enunciation

Empowering women to speak demands the provision of an adequate vocabulary to describe and construct our experiences. This means struggling to change the ways in which existing language is used and creating new terms when necessary. Mary Daly's explorations of language provide a vocabulary with which to speak from subjugated positions, as well as tools to facilitate alternative readings of dominant discourses. In this essay, I utilize one set of Daly's tools to expose (and oppose) some of the tactics used to inhibit the introduction of oppositional vocabulary and meanings into mainstream discussions of rape.

Discourses are specific ways of talking about the world and events. In these discourses, conventions of style and a shared vocabulary of terms and concepts are employed. For example, those in the legal and medical fields approach rape from different perspectives. As a result, they talk about it in different ways. For doctors, rape is a medical problem. For police officers, it is a crime. Ways of talking about rape reflect ways of thinking about it. Popular discourses on rape are important because they provide us with resources to describe and define sexual assault. The manner in which we discuss rape at the community level affects (and reflects) the meaning of rape, shaping the individual's experience of sexual assault and the community's response to it.

Since the 1980s, the terms "acquaintance rape," and "date rape" have come into use to describe sexual assaults that differ from stereotypical Rape concepts.[1] The existence of these terms reveals the substance of dominant ideas about rape. If rape were popularly defined as nonconsensual sex, there would be no need to distinguish between "kinds" (often interpreted as "degrees") of rape, according to the relationship between the rapist and the victim, or the degree of physical force involved. If acquaintance rape were not part of the cultural vocabulary, however, women would currently have no term available to them to describe any rape that differs from dominant connotations of Rape (usually a violent rape committed by a stranger). As a result, many women are forced to use terms that perpetuate the distinction between kinds of rape in order to identify the crime enacted against them as rape at all.

I am inclined to endorse the use of any term that allows women to name rape as rape, even as I recognize the danger of perpetuating distinctions between "kinds" of rape. That danger stems from the belief that different "kinds" of rape are different in degree as well as in circumstances. The introduction of acquaintance rape into the cultural vocabulary is a move away from definitions of rape that focus on the context of the crime toward definitions that focus on whether the sexual encounter was consensual. The institution of a consent-based idea of rape is a step toward more effectively fighting rape: identifying it as equally deplorable in all of its forms. Thus, the term "acquaintance rape" is presently useful and necessary, even as anti-rape efforts work toward the institution of a consent based rape concept which would eventually render the term obsolete.

Women's accounts of sexual assault demonstrate the need for a consent-based definition of rape. The following excerpts from narratives recorded as part of a psychology research project illustrate women's struggles to come to terms with unwanted sexual experiences.[2] The difficulty stems from a variety of factors including prior involvement with the rapist, consensual participation in some intimacy prior to the rape, and the relationship between the rapist and perpetrator.

- I never thought of anything he ever did as sexual assault because I was his girlfriend and . . . I just felt like I had to do what was expected of me, and he made it seem like this is all perfectly normal.
- . . . I ended up sitting on his lap and kissing him which was fine with me, actually, and, and that's part of the reason that it's been really hard for me to . . . really call it rape or call it a violation.[3]
- But in the act itself I felt raped. . . . I felt raped and I didn't have any place to go at the time, or anybody I could talk to about it. I had no place I knew I could turn to with it.

Some women talk about how the term acquaintance rape was not available to them at the time of the assault, but became useful to them when it later became available.

- I realized . . . that this was . . . an acquaintance rape sort of situation, which I think at the time . . . that phrase wasn't really out and I just thought, oh, I'm so stupid.
- I never realized that I had been raped until much later. When people started talking about date rape, I realized that's what it was.

Women who claim acquaintance rape as part of their vocabularies find that it facilitates talking about the unwanted sexual experience.

- It was more of a date rape than anything else.
- I know that it was rape (a woman who was raped by her boyfriend).
- This guy at work asked me out, so this was a date rape and an acquaintance rape.
- . . . And it was a date rape.
- The closest thing . . . I would say was kind of a date rape situation, although it wasn't a date.

The last woman does not have the term acquaintance rape available to her, but she uses the closest available term—"date rape"—in order to describe the experience as accurately as possible. Her naming the experience rape, but also distinguishing it linguistically from Rape, is important. This is evidence that she is aware of the limitations on the use of the word "rape." Her use of the term 'date rape' is evidence that the concept of acquaintance rape is useful to her, despite her not knowing the specific name for it. These quotations exemplify the primacy of language to the ways in which women understand and communicate about nonconsensual sexual experiences.

Discourse analysis provides an insight into cultural values, fictions, and realities. Dominant discourses "[prescribe] the boundaries of the lives we might imagine and will ourselves to live."[4] Dominant discourses institute the perceptual reservoir in relation to which we can give meaning to our experiences.[5] Mary Daly identifies four tactics that illuminate the ways in which discourses can be used to maintain existing power relations:

- Erasure
- Reversal
- False Polarization
- Divide and Conquer[6]

All of these tactics are visible in backlash discourse on acquaintance rape.

The History of Acquaintance Rape Discourse

The introduction of the term acquaintance rape into the American cultural vocabulary offered the promise of a reformed understanding of rape; one that was more useful to more women in describing rape experiences. News discourse on acquaintance rape is marked by a radical reversal that began in 1990. Before then, scattered coverage of what was variously called "nonstranger rape," "confidence rape," "social rape," "date rape," and "acquaintance rape" appeared in popular magazines. Acquaintance rape coverage proliferated following the publication of "The Scope of Rape: Incidence and Prevalence of Sexual Aggression and Victimization in a National Sample of Higher Education Students," in 1987.[7] Initial media reactions to the study included shock that more rapes were apparently being committed by acquaintances than by strangers, and surprise that such large numbers of female students reported having been victims of assaults matching the legal definition of rape. Mainstream print news media responded to the "Scope of Rape" study with calls for action. Writers of news stories aimed to educate and offered analyses of the causes of acquaintance rape. While conservative publications refused to accept the results of "The Scope of Rape" study all along, many mainstream periodicals concluded that date rape was a problem in need of a solution. It was in mainstream periodicals that the prevalence of rape, and the reality that it is most often perpetrated by acquaintances, was presented to the general public.

Since the initial spate of coverage, there has been a reversal of mainstream news opinion on acquaintance rape. This reversal may be viewed as a backlash because it occurred despite the fact that no contradictory research emerged in the period between the initial positive reaction to the "Scope of Rape" study and the ensuing negative coverage. In fact, backlash articles often attack the same study that they cited as definitive a short time earlier. This suggests that the change in coverage of acquaintance rape was not based on new information, but on the political and cultural climate in the United States. Both sides of the debate attribute the backlash to the introduction of the Violence Against Women Act into Congress in 1990. Conservatives such as Neil Gilbert, who call anti-rape efforts "rape hype," have openly stated that their aim was to discredit research on acquaintance rape in order to prevent federal funding of rape-related services.[8] *Newsweek*, *Time*, and the *New York Times* provide clear illustrations of the reversal of position on acquaintance rape—they all featured articles seeking to educate the public about "date rape" in the mid to late eighties and ran backlash articles in the early nineties.

The initial articles on acquaintance rape validated the research on rape and applauded efforts to decrease rape occurrence. " 'Acquaintance Rape' Comes into the Open" appeared in a February 1986 edition of *Newsweek*. The bold type below the headline read, "Colleges work to solve—and stop—a shockingly frequent, often hidden outrage." From there, a brief acquaintance rape scenario was recounted ("Paul ran into his classmate Karen at a dorm party"), followed by a definition of acquaintance rape ("forcible sexual assault in which the victim knows her assailant"). Next came arguments about the cause and nature of the crime, and consultations with various experts:

> Newsweek On Campus has obtained the final results of a three year survey of 6,104 students at 33 colleges, the work of Mary P.

> Koss, of Kent State. . . . Because women often fail to think of forcible sex as rape, Koss asked "behavioral" questions about what men had done to them, then used legal definitions to reach her final figures. . . . The Koss study indicated that 15 percent of the college women surveyed had been raped, according to strict legal standards. In 84 percent of these attacks the women knew their attackers.[9]

" 'Acquaintance Rape' Comes into the Open" cites other studies supporting Koss's findings. It also asks why acquaintance rape occurs ("Researchers are looking for the causes. Prof. Barry Burkhart of Auburn says our culture 'fuses sexuality and aggression,' and so tolerates or even encourages rape")[10] and discusses rape prevention programs positively. The article notes with regret that some male students and law officers are reluctant to recognize acquaintance rape as real rape. The article closes with a quote from Barry Burkhart, who says that ending acquaintance rape is "tantamount to changing the culture." Burkhart observes with optimism that "the social climate appears to be changing."[11] In this *Newsweek* article, acquaintance rape is presented as a crime that is contributed to by American culture and that needs to be dealt with. The article is based on information from several scientific studies and its major conclusions are drawn from evidence provided by these studies.

Another positive article, "When Date Turns into Rape," appeared in the March 23, 1987, issue of *Time*. Like the *Newsweek* feature, it included a subtitle that hinted at the urgency of the problem, "Too often the attacker is the clean-cut acquaintance next door."[12] The format here is the same as *Newsweek*'s: the date rape scenario is followed by an analysis of the problem. *Time* cites the same "Scope of Rape" study, and the same 15 percent figure, noting Koss's use of "behavioral" questions and legal definitions to get her numbers. The *Time* feature also quotes Barry Burkhart, confirming Koss's assertion that women are unlikely to name acquaintance rape as Rape, and to report the crime: "Because it is such a paralyzing event, so outside the realm of normal events, they literally don't know what happened to them. . . . And because they don't see it as rape. . . . They are left without a way of understanding it, so they bury it, feeling guilty and ashamed." Like *Newsweek, Time* notes that "the judicial system is not quite ready for acquaintance rape." "When Date Turns into Rape" applauds the increasing number of rape prevention programs on college campuses. The article ends by remarking that "times may be changing" and describing a fraternity poster of *The Rape Of The Sabine Women*, featuring the words "Today's Greeks call it Date Rape: Against Her Will is Against the Law." Like " 'Acquaintance Rape' Comes into the Open," "When Date Turns into Rape" presents acquaintance rape as an all too prevalent problem that needs to be dealt with.

The *New York Times* printed its own version of the acquaintance rape story, "The New Realities of 'Date Rape,' " in 1985.[13] This article also begins with an acquaintance rape scenario and appears to have an educational intent. It provides a discussion of what acquaintance rape is, why it occurs, and what is being done about it. Like the other articles, "The New Realities of 'Date Rape' " suggests that acquaintance rape is a problem in need of a solution. This story was followed by a more general feature on rape, "A Bias Crime," in 1990. "A Bias Crime" names rape as a bias crime against women, comparing it to racially motivated hate crimes, and criticizes discourses that obscure the gendered character of rape. "Let's get it straight," the author says, "sexual assault is mainly about gender. It is about how some men feel about women. . . . It is about believing that women like to have sex against their will. . . . This is our number one bias crime."[14] "A Bias Crime" also addresses "another infuriating part of this discussion. . . . Deterrence centers on the victim. Take self-defense classes. Get good locks. Strike out with your keys in a clenched fist. . . . No, change the rapists." Ultimately, the author demands that men take on the responsibility for ending rape. Perhaps this article hit too close to home, calling for changes in patriarchal culture and behavior, such as teaching little boys that "women are equals, that sex demands consent, that violence is unconscionable, that rape is one of the gravest crimes of all." This was the last article printed in the *New York Times* challenging traditional conceptions of, and responses to, rape prior to the backlash.[15]

In 1991, the *New York Times* led the backlash against efforts to address acquaintance rape, printing Katie Roiphe's Op-Ed piece "Date Rape Hysteria" as a "Voices of a New Generation" feature. The publication of this article provided the backlash with momentum and media attention. Other periodicals (including *Time* and *Newsweek*) soon followed suit. The *New York Times* also printed an expanded version of the Roiphe article "Rape Hype Betrays Feminism" as the cover story for the June 13, 1993, *New York Times Magazine*. Writers of these and other backlash articles use the four tactics identified above to subvert the newly emergent discourses on acquaintance rape, which threatened to incite discussion on related, controversial topics. An awareness of the erasure, reversal, false polarization, and divide-and-conquer tactics allows readers an opportunity to identify and resist them in discourses on rape and other topics.

Erasure

The first tactic utilized in backlash discourse is erasure. Erasure is manifested in five key ways:

- The dismissal of anti-rape efforts as "sexual correctness"
- The sequestering of the issue of consent
- The naturalization of rape
- The denial of high rape rates
- The subversion of women's authority

First, much backlash discourse feeds on the stigma of "political correctness." A 1993 *Newsweek* cover story on acquaintance rape, titled "Sexual Correctness: Has It Gone Too Far?" appropriates the stigma of political correctness in order to circumvent further discussion on acquaintance rape. The charge of sexual correctness, like that of "political correctness," arises in a reaction against impending changes in the (sexual) status quo, and is intended to derail discussion of the issue at hand.[16]

The second type of erasure is the erasure of consent, which forces a return to context-based definitions of rape. Focusing on the relationship between the rapist and the victim, on the "character" or past conduct of either, or on the amount of physical violence used during the rape renders the victim's nonconsent a nonissue. Erasure of consent leads to the validation of relationship- or context-based definitions of rape over consent-based definitions. According to context-based definitions of rape, what matters is whether the two people involved knew each other, if they have ever dated, if they have ever had sex before, or if the victim is visibly bruised or injured, all of which are irrelevant to determining whether or not both people consented to a particular sexual encounter.

The erasure of consent is evident in the insistence that we reserve the use of the word rape to describe only stereotypical Rapes, and reject any other definition of rape as "highly original and unacceptably broad,"[17] a "paranoid metaphor," an "overused word . . . [a] cliche, drained of specificity and meaning,"[18] or a "trendy anti-man, women-as-victim, anti-individual responsibilities P.C. policy."[19] In an attempt to abrogate the significance of consent, backlash discourses describe consent-based definitions of rape as something that "radicalized victims justify flinging around as a political weapon, referring to everything from violent sexual assaults to inappropriate innuendoes," or a "metaphor, its definition swelling to cover any kind of oppression to women."[20] The dismissal of consent-based definitions of rape on the grounds that they are biased in a way that more traditional "objective" definitions of Rape are not is evidence that phallocentric, stereotypical Rape definitions are so prevalent as to be invisible.[21] To dismiss women's right to refuse sex as unacceptable, "paranoid," "anti-man," or "anti-individual responsibilities," is to make a powerful statement about men's absolute authority to define sex and rape, and to present the view that women's consent is largely irrelevant.

Through the erasure of the issue of consent, acquaintance rape itself is erased, and context-based definitions of rape are reaffirmed. Diana Russell discusses the harmful side effects of context-based ideas about rape in her book *The Politics of Rape*. "In cases of rape by friends, it is usually assumed that the victim colludes in her own victimization. It is frequently suggested that the word 'rape' be confined to cases where the woman is raped by a stranger and that another word be invented for cases in which the woman is raped by a friend, acquaintance, lover, or husband. . . . Using the relationship between the rapist and victim as *the* basic distinction between rape experiences can perpetuate . . . the myth of collusion."[22] Russell's observation illustrates the importance of the availability of the term acquaintance rape, given the existing cultural vocabulary. It also explains the dangers of using that term.

The third type of erasure is the naturalization of rape. Timothy Beneke notes that "rape signs" serve to erase rape by including it in our ideas of what is natural or normal. They "stand between us and the reality of rape, obfuscating and numbing our vision and sensitivity. . . . They tell us false stories about rape, men, and women without our consciously hearing the stories."[23] The denial that acquaintance rape is Real Rape is a rape sign, according to Beneke's definition. It naturalizes rapes that do not fit the stranger rape stereotype. The 1991 *Time* article on acquaintance rape exemplifies the naturalization of rape. In response to a statement from Dr. Mary Koss demanding that men be held accountable for committing rape, the *Time* writer argues: "Historically, of course, this has never been the case, and there are some that argue that it shouldn't be—that women too must take responsibility for their behavior, and that the whole realm of intimate encounters defies regulation from on high. Anthropologist Lionel Tiger has little patience for trendy sexual politics that make no reference to biology. Since the dawn of time, he argues, men and women have always gone to bed with different goals."[24] Tiger's assertions naturalize rape by depicting it as a "biological" part of reality. The implication is that if rape has been around since the "dawn of time," it must be natural and therefore normal and acceptable. Tiger's attempt to dismiss anti-rape efforts as merely the product of a "trend" is an attempt to erase debate on rape altogether by juxtaposing anti-rape discourses with the authoritative discourses of science. Likewise, the assertion that rape is merely a product of "different goals" establishes rape as a nonissue. It naturalizes rape through an assumption that the rapist's notions of rape are definitive, and that the horror of acquaintance rape comes from the naming alone. As women's narratives of rape demonstrate, this is not the case.

The fourth manifestation of the erasure tactic is the denial of high rape rates. By denying the validity of rape research, backlash discourses are an attempt to deny that rape is really a problem. A 1993 *Newsweek* article reads, "In the rape-crisis mentality, the numbers keep being bloated." The writer notes that this "bloating" is unnecessary, since even the most "conservative, yet trustworthy" numbers are "horrifying."[25] *Newsweek* picks a one-in-seven statistic from the National Victim Center Survey as the most credible approximation of rape occurrence, but notes that that statistic does not include rapes where intoxication was a factor. The fact that alcohol has been shown to be a statistically significant factor in acquaintance rape, as argued in the same article by prosecutor Linda Fairstein, is not addressed by *Newsweek*. In response to the one-in-seven statistic, the *Newsweek* writer says, "That's a lot. But it doesn't mean all women are victims—or survivors, as we are supposed to call them. And it sure doesn't mean all 'suffering' warrants attention or retribution, or even much sympathy."[26] From this malicious reaction against an imagined claim that all women are rape victims (and perhaps the imagined assertion that all men are rapists), the *Newsweek* writer leaps from rape to sexual harassment, hinting that the two share a "gray area" where it is impractical, if not undesirable, to know what consent is.

In her articles in the *New York Times*, Katie Roiphe also distorts the research findings to downplay the prevalence of rape. Roiphe quotes research indicating that one in four college women have been victims of rape or attempted rape, then confuses that statistic by asking, "If 25 percent of my women friends were being raped—wouldn't I know it?"[27] This question transforms the statistic of one in four women being victims of rape or attempted rape to one in four being victims of completed rape. It also changes the breadth of the statistic from a representative sample of college women to Katie Roiphe's friends.[28] This manipulation is apparently an attempt to discredit the study, despite the irrelevance of Roiphe's remark to the validity of the research.

The fifth way in which acquaintance rape is erased is through the denial of the female voice. The authority of the female voice is undermined when nonverbal "cues," which women supposedly emit, are considered to be more valid than what women say. Here, the "no doesn't really mean no" myth surfaces. Those who do not consider women's voices to be legitimate insist that it is OK to ignore a woman's words in favor of these "cues." By erasing women's words, backlash proponents can deny that acquaintance rape is really rape. An important consequence of the erasure of women's words is that it allows any aspect of a woman's behavior to be read as consent to any sexual act, regardless of her verbal communication. This makes it easy for lawyers, jurors, and rapists to deny that a rape has occurred. It also makes it virtually impossible for a woman to press charges for anything other than a violent stranger rape and difficult to press charges even in the case of a violent stranger rape. Timothy Beneke notes that this kind of erasure is an important part of victim blaming. He argues, "In all cases where a woman is said to have asked for it, her appearance and behavior are taken as a form of speech . . . the woman's actions . . . are given greater emphasis than her words."[29]

An example of this form of erasure appears in a 1991 *Time* article. In "When Is It Rape?" the writer describes a rape case that was dropped due to lack of evidence because, as the victim said, "Who's gonna believe me? I had a man in my hotel room after midnight," despite her attacker's admission that he heard her say no.[30] This is an obvious case of ignoring (erasing) the woman's voice in favor of irrelevant nonverbal cues. This particular rape case was dropped despite the fact that the man acknowledged that the woman had verbally refused consent. She said, "He says he didn't know that I meant no. He didn't feel he'd raped me." Clearly, in this case and others like it, the woman's consent or nonconsent is erased, allowing the rapist to define what rape is. College students are frequently quoted in backlash articles denying the validity of the female voice. One student said, "[If you're drunk and she] says no sometime later, even in the middle of the act, there still may be some kind of violation, but it's not the same thing. It's not rape. If you don't hear her say no, if she's playing around with you—oh, I could get squashed for saying it—there is an element of say no, mean yes."[31] Here, female autonomy and the issue of consent are erased. The student's choice of words is telling: "If you don't hear her say no" suggests that the rapist's *hearing* nonconsent is what matters, not what the woman actually says. The student's statement that "there is an element of say no, mean yes," suggests that "hearing" consent has less to do with auditory perception than with his judgment of what (and *if*) women's words really mean. According to this logic, women have no right to judge whether a rape has occurred, since their refusal or consent is entirely superfluous. The erasure tactic denies women the power to define rape in general and denies women the authority to name rape even when it happens to them.

Reversal

The second tactic used in backlash discourse is reversal. The two main reversal tactics are

- Placing the responsibility for all manifestations of sexuality, including rape, on women (victim blaming)
- Defining consent-based definitions of rape as repressive to women.

Reversal comprises the misappropriation of blame, responsibility, and victim status. According to the rhetoric of reversal, women cause rape. Moreover, reversal implies that consensual sex and consent-based definitions of rape are repressive to women, implying that rape itself is not harmful, only naming it is. Thus, the rapist is the true victim. He is victimized by women who impinge upon his exclusive right to determine what sex and rape are.

The first part of reversal is the placement of the responsibility for all sexuality, including rape, on women. Diana Russell summarizes this phenomenon in *The Politics of Rape:* "Women often take responsibility when men treat them as prey. This isn't just an odd female quirk. The attitude is deeply entrenched in the thinking of men, as well. Women are taught to make themselves attractive to men. Those who don't are ignored by men or incur their displeasure. But if they become victims of sexual assault, they are immediately suspected of collusion. No man is ever guilty. If he did something bad, it must have been invited."[32] The idea that rape is more justifiable if a woman does not know, or adhere to, "the rules" is also a part of this tactic. Reversal tells us that women who "should have known better" than to let a man into their home, to wear a certain outfit, or to have sex outside of marriage are responsible for rape by men. Holding women to special rules, such as *Don't go out alone at night*, is blatant reversal, especially when her "transgression" is used to divert blame from the rapist, or when a woman who breaks these rules is viewed as inviting rape. As Beneke puts it, "If a woman trusts a man and goes to his apartment . . . or goes out on a date and is raped, she's a dupe and deserves what she gets. 'He didn't *really* rape her' goes the mentality—'he merely took advantage of her.' "[33] By breaking the rules, women lose all of the "protection" afforded women by patriarchal culture (defense of her virtue, integrity, and so on). Women who break the rules are therefore rendered unrapeable. By unrapeable I do not mean that women who break the rules are safe from rape, but that their "misbehavior" is taken as unconditional and unlimited consent not only to sex but also to physical violence and other forms of abuse.

The reversal of blame often appears in backlash discourse as the displacement of blame for rapes away from the men who rape. Apparently, the media are not willing to blatantly blame rape victims for causing rape, but they still want to. A less straightforward way of blaming the victim is *not* blaming the rapist, or diverting the responsibility for rape away from men and onto women. *Time* magazine prints the comment "Those who view rape through a political lens tend to place all responsibility on men to make sure that their partners are consenting."[34] The *Time* writer is quick to point out that even some "feminists . . . protest the idea that the onus is on the man."[35] It is interesting that this *Time* journalist is eager to use feminist views as "proof" that men are not responsible for rape, when in the rest of the article feminism is discussed in venomous terms.

Newsweek joins the protest against holding men responsible for rape with the comment "Thanks to nature, he's got the weapon,"[36] suggesting that rape is an inevitable, natural fact, and that men are the victims of anti-rape discourse because they have penises. With this statement the author ignores that fact that women *are* the usual victims of rape and men are the usual perpetrators, while using the same fact to naturalize rape. The logical implication of assertions that men are not responsible for rape is that women are responsible for it and that nonconsensual sex is "natural" and so there is nothing to be responsible *for*. As Roiphe suggests, if women are responsible for causing nonconsensual sex, it isn't really rape at all. "If we assume that women are not all helpless and naive, then they should be held responsible for their choice to drink or take drugs. If a woman's 'judgment is impaired' and she has sex, it isn't necessarily always the man's fault; it isn't necessarily always rape."[37] First, it is important to mention that no one ever suggested that all sex when one partner's "judgment is impaired" is rape. The issue in determining if a rape occurred is whether the sex was consensual. Clearly, a person who is unconscious is unable to consent to sex. I doubt that any reasonable person would confuse an unconscious person's failure to refuse consent or resist rape with consent itself. Roiphe suggests that women are merely confusing consensual sex with rape. By simultaneously suggesting that women are incapable of determining whether they consented to sex and asserting that women are completely responsible for preventing rape, Roiphe puts women in a double bind: one with no authority and total responsibility, not just for their own actions, but for men's actions as well. The flip side of this is that men are absolved of responsibility for rape, and rapists are endowed with the authority to equate consent with failure to successfully resist rape.

Reversal takes men's innocence one step further. Not only does backlash discourse encourage men to abdicate responsibility for rape, it also presents men as the victims of acquaintance rape discourse. The *Newsweek* writer says, "Who is the victim and who is the victimizer here? In the ever morphing world of Thou Shalt Not Abuse Women it's getting mighty confusing."[38] Here, men are presented as the victims of consent-based definitions of rape, and this victimization negates the victimization of the women who are being raped. The *Time* writer says, "Taken to extremes, there is an ugly element of vengeance at work here. Rape is an abuse of power. But so are false accusations of rape."[39] In *Time* the example is cited of a college student who said he was falsely accused of raping a woman who was very drunk. "I felt violated . . . I felt like she was taking advantage of me when she was very drunk. I never heard her say 'No!' 'Stop!,' anything."[40] Troubled by his story, the writer muses, " If rape is sex without consent, how exactly should consent be defined and communicated, when and by whom?" That the failure to verbally refuse consent *does not equal consent* is lost on both the *Time* writer and the accused rapist. Their common perspective seems to be that it is safer if men determine consent, since women cannot be counted on to do so accurately. That the absence of a verbal no in this case is seen as proof that no rape occurred, while the verbal no in the "When Is It Rape?" story was regarded as irrelevant, is an example of the tendency of backlash discourses to entrust the male involved with the authority to determine whether rape occurred.[41]

The second reversal tactic is the assertion that consent-based definitions of rape are repressive to women. Roiphe writes, "Let's not reinforce the images that oppress us, that label us victims, that deny our own agency and intelligence, as strong and sensual, as autonomous, pleasure seeking, sexual beings."[42] What Roiphe implies is that merely discussing acquaintance rape does all of these things. According to Roiphe, talking about acquaintance rape, educating students about occurrence rates, and speaking out about rape is more oppressive than rape itself. Unfortunately, ignoring the reality of acquaintance rape does not make it go away. As women's rape narratives illustrate, language is very important to rape victims not because it *makes* them victims, but because it allows them to name a rape experience in a way that makes sense to them and to others. By definition, nonconsensual sex is not liberating or pleasurable for women. Pretending that it is forces women to seek sexual pleasure on someone else's terms and denies them both sexual agency and autonomy.

Roiphe is not alone in suggesting that acquaintance rape is merely a matter of semantics. An article by Mary Matalin in *Time* suggests that acquaintance rape prevention efforts and rape research, which Matalin names "feminist P.C. policy," teach us that "women are powerless innocent victims; men are overpowering, sex-crazed barbarians; both are infants who, without written instructions, are incapable of mature communication."[43] Like Roiphe, Matalin ignores the research on acquaintance rape occurrence in favor of ignorance and disbelief. She does not address research that has been done on acquaintance rape, opting instead to repeat Roiphe's misleading statements. Like Roiphe, Matalin asserts that feminism is what is *really* victimizing women. *Newsweek* seconds this opinion, noting that: "It does seem ironic that the very movement created to encourage women to stand up and fight their own battles has taken this strange detour, and instead is making them feel vulnerable and in need of protection."[44] This attempt to make anti-rape policies appear paternalistic is followed in the *Newsweek* article by the suggestion that feminism is not only repressive and paternalistic, it is also turning women into "sissies." "They're huddling in packs, insisting on a plethora of rules on which to rely, and turning to authority figures to complain whenever anything goes wrong. We're not creating a society of Angry Young Women. These are Scared Little Girls."[45] The implication is that big girls wouldn't let themselves be raped, and if they did, they wouldn't tattle. *Time* agrees. The writer of the cover story "When Is It Rape?" says, "It demeans women to suggest that they are so vulnerable to coercion or emotional manipulation that they must always be escorted by the long arm of the law."[46] Of course, it also demeans women to deny them the use of the word rape to describe rape experiences.

Reversal rhetoric implies that consensual sex is unnatural and distasteful as well as repressive to women. Roiphe calls it neopuritan and Victorian.[47] *Time* quotes Stephanie Gutmann as saying: "How can you make sex completely politically correct and completely safe? . . . What a horribly bland, unerotic thing that would be! Sex is, by nature, a risky endeavor, emotionally. And desire is a violent emotion. These people have erected so many rules and regulations that I don't know how people can have erotic desire or desire driven sex."[48] The implication is that sexual pleasure for women means sex on men's terms, or not at all. The "many rules and regulations" to which Gutmann refers are, apparently, the insistence that women have the authority to choose to consent to or refuse sex and the assertion that men should be held accountable when they choose to disregard that choice. It is important to reiterate that women have long been held to unwritten sexual codes of conduct that have accorded others the power to define their experiences and desires. What consent-based rape laws do is apportion some sexual responsibility to men. Contrary to backlash rhetoric, this does not repress women, but authorizes them to be sexual on their own terms.

In the same *Time* article, Andrea Parrot says, "Too bad that people think that the only way you can have passion and excitement and sex is if there are miscommunications, and one person is forced to do something he or she doesn't want to do."[49] However, Parrot's comments are all but dismissed in the context of the article. Directly after her comments, *Time* switches to a focus on the "battle between the women," away from the issue of acquaintance rape itself. *Newsweek* also joins in the condemnation of consent-based rape policies: "The much publicized rules governing sexual intimacy at Antioch College seem to stultify relations between men and women on the cusp of adulthood,"[50] confirming the *Time* writer's, Roiphe's, and Gutmann's ideas about the repressiveness of consensual sex.

The rejection of consent-based definitions of rape by the mainstream *Time, Newsweek* and *New York Times* parallels right-wing sentiments about acquaintance rape. The *National Review* quotes Neil Gilbert, who has never conducted any original scientific research on rape, as a sociologist who has nonetheless made a "scrupulous analysis" of "this theory" and the "phantom 'epidemic of sexual assault' to which it has led."[51] The "theory" in question is actually not theory at all, but the results of several studies on the incidence of rape. The *National Review* endorses Gilbert's statement that under consent-based definitions of rape, "the kaleidoscope of intimate discourse—passion, emotional turmoil, entreaties, flirtation, provocation, demureness—must give way to cool-headed contractual sex: 'Will you do it, yes or no? Please sign on the line below.' "[52] The message is the same in *Time, Newsweek,* and the *New York Times. Time* says, "At the extreme, sexual relations come to resemble major surgery, requiring a signed consent form.[53] *Newsweek* is more verbose. Directly following a misrepresentation of Antioch's stance on acquaintance rape, in which a statement by an individual woman is presented as school policy, *Newsweek* expresses its opinion about attempts at acquaintance rape prevention. "How silly this all seems; how sad. It criminalizes the delicious unexpectedness of sex. . . . What is the purpose of sex if not to lose control? . . . The advocates of sexual correctness are trying to take the danger out of sex, but sex is inherently dangerous. It leaves one exposed to everything from euphoria to crashing disappointment. That's its great unpredictability. But of course, that's sort of what we said when we were all made to wear seat belts."[54] The seat belt comment hints that consent-based rape laws might be a good idea even if they make some people uncomfortable. However, this passage suggests that the worst outcome of nonconsensual sex is "crashing disappointment," not rape. Earlier on the same page, *Newsweek* equates acquaintance rape with "romantic disappointment" and "bad sex," asserting that "Everyone had bad sex back then [in the early seventies] and, to hear them tell, survived just fine."[55]

The problem is that women have never survived rape "just fine." Without the term acquaintance rape, women *couldn't* name their experiences for what they were: *rape* experiences. In fact, to hear them tell it, women have long been highly aware of the inadequacy of the language surrounding rape. Meg Nugent, who was raped by an acquaintance in 1976, says that she may not have identified what happened to her as rape then, but it was still a "terrifying experience," and it was still rape. Despite the fact that she was drugged and raped by her date, Nugent said, "I had to have outside confirmation to recognize that it was rape."[56] The discussion of acquaintance rape in Robin Warshaw's *I Never Called It Rape* was the outside confirmation that allowed her to identify the incident as really rape. The term acquaintance rape made it directly possible for her to name, understand, and communicate about her rape experience for what it was. Thus, despite *Time*'s attempts to trivialize acquaintance rape as a figment of the overactive imaginations of victimhood-inducing feminists, the term acquaintance rape allows women to name their rape experiences and get on with the recovery process, a necessity that, to the detriment of women, was previously denied.

False Polarization

False polarization is the creation and maintenance of artificial divisions between things that are not inherently opposite. In backlash discourse, this tactic works by means of a differentiation between "rape" and "Rape." This includes decisively distinguishing rapists from regular men, and distinguishing "rapeable" women from "normal" women.[57] As I mentioned above, attempts to limit the use of the word rape to the description of stereotypical Rapes are part of backlash efforts to keep acquaintance rape from becoming part of the cultural vocabulary. It is a form of erasure as well as an example of false polarization. The division between rape and Rape is an important one. It serves to limit the concept of rape to extremely violent rapes by strangers. This kind of rape represents the minority of actual rape cases. The false polarization of rape and Rape discourages women who are raped by acquaintances, boyfriends, or husbands from reporting the rape, or even calling it what it is. False polarization is used to reinforce rape myths at the expense of effectively addressing the realities of sexual assault.

Time creates a distinction between Rape and rape by commenting that a student named Ginny Rayfield "was really raped when she was 16," as opposed to other women quoted in the same article, who apparently merely thought they had been raped.[58] Katie Roiphe also has definite ideas about what rape is and is not. She expresses indignation that women dare to name acquaintance rape 'rape,' writing, "While real women get battered, while real mothers need day care, certain feminists are busy turning rape into fiction."[59] In her article in the *New York Times Magazine*, Roiphe reveals her definition of real Rape: "It's hard to watch the solemn faces of young Bosnian girls, their words haltingly translated, as they tell of brutal rapes; or to read accounts of a suburban teen-ager raped and beaten while walking home from a shopping mall."[60] Roiphe's idea of Rape is as stereotyped as can be, involving brutality, beatings, innocent young victims, foreigners, and strangers.[61] Roiphe rejects the notion that consent divides rape from sex, writing, "It [a consent-based definition of rape] is measuring her word against his in a realm where words barely exist. There is a gray area in which one person's rape may be another's bad night."[62] *Newsweek* agrees. A 1993 *Newsweek* article says, "Rape and sexual harassment are real. But between crime and sexual bliss are some cloudy waters."[63] True, the scarcity of vocabulary surrounding rape does indeed create some "cloudy waters." Backlash writing suggests that this cloudiness in inevitable, and best left alone. However, what consent-based definitions of rape do is attempt to clear up this cloudiness by conceding the authority to consent to or refuse sex to individual women. This represents a radical reversal of power relative to context-based definitions of rape.

By limiting the use of the word 'rape' to the description of violent assaults perpetrated by a stranger, the majority of rapes are designated *not* rape and are defined as a lesser offense. This limitation is important because it labels rape as a freak occurrence—something perpetrated by a few crazy or sick men. It also falsely and decisively divides the rapist from "normal" men. The implication of such a division is that "regular" guys don't rape. This assumption reinforces women's fears of not being believed about having been raped by someone they know, and their feelings of guilt about not having identified him as a rapist prior to the rape. This polarization suggests that men who can get a date, or are attractive or popular, couldn't possibly rape—they are too normal. *Time* quotes a student who was accused of rape, and "angry and hurt" at the charges, saying, "Rape is what you read about in the *New York Post* about 17 little boys raping a jogger in Central Park."[64] Clearly, under that definition, he could never do anything remotely resembling rape, even though he acknowledges that the woman who accused him of rape did not consent, and was "very drunk." The false polarization of rapists and normal men (and Rape and rape) also capitalizes on differences that are already culturally loaded, such as race and class. For example, *Time* recounts one woman's story of how the race of her assailant made it a Rape in the eyes of the police. "The first thing the Boston police asked was whether it was a black guy," she said. "So, you were really raped," was their reaction upon hearing that it was.[65]

In addition to distorting the picture of who rapes, the false polarization between Rape and rape distorts the image of who gets raped. Under the stereotypical Rape definition, the women who get raped are usually those who don't play by the rules: women who go out after dark alone, women who hitchhike, women who dress "provocatively." This polarization serves to assure ordinary women that they can't be raped as long as they are careful. It also stigmatizes all rape victims in accordance with the idea that women who are raped are really just getting what they asked for. Limiting the use of the word rape to "Real Rape" sends the message that nonconsensual sex is acceptable unless it is especially violent, and with a stranger. Of course, assurances based on myths are empty. Women are most often raped by someone they know.[66]

Divide and Conquer

The last tactic Daly names is divide and conquer. This tactic is an attempt to discredit efforts to fight acquaintance rape by suggesting that such efforts are the work of an overzealous fringe of "radical feminists" that most women, and even some feminists, oppose. By using this tactic, backlash discourses divert attention away from what anti–acquaintance rape efforts are fighting for and against. Anti–acquaintance rape efforts work to promote equality by authorizing women to determine whether they consented to a specific sexual act. One objective of this work is to hold men accountable for their actions when they choose to disregard that authority. Thus, anti–acquaintance rape efforts oppose the status quo that suggests that a variety of circumstances can mitigate a woman's right to refuse sex. Divide-and-conquer rhetoric creates the illusion that the only thing feminists are fighting is other women. The divide-and-conquer tactic obscures sexism and the problems caused by it, and it impedes efforts to address issues such as rape by persistently changing the subject.

The divide-and-conquer tactic is a highly visible part of backlash discourse on acquaintance rape. Women who are willing to speak out against feminism receive lots of coverage, and many publications play up the conflicts between individual women. For example, the *New York Times* ran a piece on acquaintance rape that was originally written by Katie Roiphe for her school newspaper. In the the article, "Date Rape Hysteria," Roiphe asserts that the research on acquaintance rape is "rape hype" and suggests that feminists limit women's sexual freedom by talking about acquaintance rape.[67] The *New York Times* ran an expanded version of this article in 1993, as the cover story for the *New York Times Magazine*.[68] This article was an excerpt from Roiphe's book *The Morning After: Sex, Fear, and Feminism on Campus*. It is important to note that, unlike the peer-reviewed research that Roiphe attacks as "hype," the book is based on Roiphe's personal experiences. As such, it is hardly a valid criticism of the body of scrupulous research on rape.[69] Nonetheless, the *New York Times* responded enthusiastically to her message and reviewed the book favorably—twice. First, it was reviewed in the newspaper, on September 16, 1993. Then, two days later, it was reviewed on the cover of the *New York Times Book Review*. The *Times* did not run any articles in defense of the acquaintance rape research that Roiphe dismisses as "hype." Dr. Mary Koss (one of the researchers whose work Roiphe attacks) attempted to answer Roiphe's accusations by writing letters to the editor, but these were not printed. The *Times* eventually relented to print a 125-word response from Koss only after she contacted the publisher of the newspaper and insisted that she had a right to defend her work from slander.[70] The disparate handling of Roiphe and Koss by the *New York Times* indicates that the editors were very eager to print material attacking feminists and rape research, but reluctant to air the views of the feminists or researchers themselves. By directing attention toward Roiphe's work, which positions feminism as an enemy of women, the *Times* avoids the issues raised by anti–acquaintance rape efforts altogether.

Newsweek was less subtle in pitting woman against woman in its 1993 cover feature "Sexual Correctness: Has It Gone Too Far?" This feature was printed under the heading "Society," indicating that "sexual correctness" was a bigger concern than date rape had been earlier. The 1986 and 1987 articles on acquaintance rape were printed under the headings "College Life" and "Sexes," indicating a more limited sphere of concern. Neither of the earlier *Newsweek* articles were cover features. This apportionment of space indicates that *Newsweek* had a bigger stake in reacting against the threat of anti–acquaintance rape efforts than it did in addressing rape. "Sexual Correctness: Has It Gone Too Far?" consisted of a four-page feature followed by one-page articles by Susan Faludi, Mary Matalin, and Susan Estrich. All of these articles were printed under the heading "Sexual Correctness," which explicitly positions them as part of a debate on sexual correctness, not rape.

"Whose Hype?" by Susan Faludi, is a factually based rebuttal of specific assertions that acquaintance rape has been blown out of proportion by feminists. The article includes a photo of Faludi and a comment below the picture, in bold print, that says, "Stand-tall new feminists use wit, not whining, to make their point."[71] Apparently, this quote was selected to heighten the contradictions between Faludi and Matalin's views. It is also the only sentence in the article that could possibly be taken to indicate division between feminists.

Mary Matalin's article, "Stop Whining!" follows Faludi's. The caption beneath Matalin's photo is "Get those moody girls a prescription of Motrin and water pills, quick."[72] The article does not focus on acquaintance rape, nor does it directly address the issue. Instead, it consists of an attack on "some feminists" and is liberally sprinkled with the stigmatizing term "political correctness." Matalin simply dismisses the research on acquaintance rape as hype, and like Roiphe, distinguishes between "real" women's issues and "hyped" ones. Matalin's intent in this article is clearly to attack "some feminists," and to inform the reader that "these women do not represent people like us." Matalin's assertions are not backed up by facts, nor are they made in response to any specific person, study, or statement about rape. Instead, in the article she makes vague accusations against "extremist feminists," playing up the conflict between what she calls "people like us" and feminists, and fitting very nicely into the *Newsweek* layout, which does the same thing.

The last part of the *Newsweek* feature is Susan Estrich's article, "Balancing Act." Estrich focuses on the issue of acquaintance rape itself and brings the discussion back to the issue of consent. However, her article also appears beneath the "Sexual Correctness" heading, which reduces her understated argument to part of the debate about sexual correctness, not rape. Estrich's article is decidedly sympathetic to anti-rape efforts and ends with a comment about how there needs to be a balance between protecting women and men in acquaintance rape cases and the observation that it is good that it is difficult to prosecute rapes because this protects men. In the context of the other articles, this sounds like a warning not to let the anti–acquaintance rape policies go too far, as the *Newsweek* feature suggests they do. It also suggests that anti-rape efforts include encouragements to women to falsely accuse men of rape. Estrich carefully distinguishes herself from "radical feminists" and "neo-feminists" who she says have asserted that all heterosexual sex is rape. This comment seems uncalled for, since proponents of anti–acquaintance rape efforts have never been interested in naming anything but nonconsensual sex as rape.[73]

The layout of the *Newsweek* feature highlights the dissension over acquaintance rape policies. It does not focus on the issues presented by "The Scope of Rape" study or by the emergent discourses on acquaintance rape to which charges of "sexual correctness" were supposedly a response.[74] The divide-and-conquer tactic helps to keep acquaintance rape discourse away from a discussion of rape and focused on the sexual correctness debate, obscuring the reality that rape is common enough to demand serious attention, not to mention broad social changes. Divide-and-conquer tactics also distance the issue of acquaintance rape from women and men who don't consider themselves to be feminists, addressing the issue as if it were irrelevant to them. If readers believe that acquaintance rape is not an issue, and political correctness is, they are apt to be less likely to recognize the realities of rape, and thus less convinced of the necessity and feasibility of preventing its occurrence. By pitting woman against woman, the media harms both anti-rape efforts and the people they could help. Divide-and-conquer tactics are attempts to divide feminists and women so that it is more difficult to effectively address sexism and the problems it engenders.

Conclusion

Language is central to our individual attempts to understand and communicate our experiences. The availability of adequate vocabulary with which to enunciate our experiences is crucial to our constructions of ourselves and our understanding of the world in which we live. Since discourse, knowledge, and power are so closely interrelated, language is a site of contest. Dominant discourses are established in part by the inclusion, and exclusion, of specific words in the cultural vocabulary.[75] The interjection of terms from subjugated discourses into dominant ones can effect significant[76] changes to the existing episteme or horizon of meaning.[77] As a result, changes in the cultural vocabulary can have a powerful impact on both the way in which we conceptualize our experiences and the conditions in which we live. "It is in language that differences acquire meaning for the individual. . . . Language differentiates and gives meaning to assertive and compliant behaviour and teaches us what is socially accepted as normal."[78] Discourses about rape are attempts to delineate which sexual behaviors are normal and which are deviant. Oppositional possibilities for changing rape-related language and ideas exist because "dominant meaning can be contested, alternative meanings confirmed."[79] These possibilities include the potential to ratify a consent-based concept of rape, authorizing women to consent or refuse to engage in specific sexual acts.

As I argued earlier, women's statements about the rapes they have experienced illustrate the necessity for the term acquaintance rape. Backlash discourse on acquaintance rape is potentially damaging to women, since it stigmatizes the term acquaintance rape. Stigmatizing the term could effectively remove acquaintance rape from the cultural vocabulary, despite its usefulness, by designating it a product of sexual correctness. The erasure of acquaintance rape through sexual correctness rhetoric is an attempt to silence discourse on rape and contiguous issues, including gender roles and sexual norms. By learning to read rape discourses through a feminist lens, guided by the categories Daly names, women can maintain the usefulness of the term acquaintance rape despite backlash efforts. Identifying erasure, reversal, false polarization, and divide and conquer as backlash tactics provides an opportunity for undertaking oppositional readings of popular discourses on rape. Most important, this methodology may also be applied to other areas of discourse, facilitating oppositional readings of discourses on many issues across various forms of media.

Notes

1. In this essay, I use the capitalized term "Rape" to denote rapes that match the stereotyped concept of rape as a violent attack perpetrated by a stranger. While such rapes do occur, they do not represent the majority of occurrences. Stranger rapes comprise a small portion of all rape cases, and

the threat of violence often precludes physical violence beyond the act of rape itself. Thus, this concept of rape is inaccurate and inadequate. I chose to capitalize this usage in recognition of its current prevalence and to mark dominant Rape concepts as a distortion of what rape means and is.

2. All quotations are taken from the Women's Life Experiences Project, research funded by the National Institute of Mental Health, Violence and Traumatic Stress Research Branch with Mary P. Koss as the principal investigator. Overall, the study's participants (253 women) were urban working women who were educated (6 percent had less than a high school education), white (89 percent), middle income (14 percent had household incomes greater than $50,000, 19 percent had household incomes less than $15,000). The average age of participants was thirty-eight, and the average time since the rape was fifteen years.

3. This quote is taken from the woman's explanation of why she did not feel entitled to call a specific incident of forced sexual intercourse rape.

4. Penelope, xiv.

5. Ibid., 38.

6. "First, there is *erasure* of women. (The massacre of millions of women as witches is erased in patriarchal scholarship.) Second, there is *reversal*. (Adam gives birth to Eve, Zeus to Athena, in patriarchal myth.) Third, there is *false polarization*. (Male defined 'feminism' is set up against male defined 'sexism' in the patriarchal media.) Fourth, there is *divide and conquer*. (Token women are trained to kill off feminists in patriarchal professions.)" Daly, 8.

7. Koss, Gidycz, and Wisniewski, 162–70.

8. Paula Kamen, "Erasing Rape: Media Hype on Sexual-Assault Research," *Extra!* November/December 1993, 10.

9. Schwartz et al., 12.

10. Schwartz et al., 14.

11. Schwartz et al., 15.

12. Pelton, 77.

13. *New York Times*, October 23, 1985.

14. "A Bias Crime," 1990.

15. At the time this essay was written, in 1995, there were no other articles on rape indexed by the *New York Times* between the printing of "The New Realities of 'Date Rape' " and Katie Roiphe's 1991 piece.

16. National Council for Research on Women, 7.

17. "When No Means No," 12.

18. Roiphe, "Date Rape Hysteria."

19. Matalin, 62.

20. Gibbs, 49.

21. Phallocentrism is "a discursive or representational form of women's oppression," wherein the two sexes are "conflated into one 'universal' model which . . . is congruent only with the masculine," as defined by Grosz, 93–96.

22. Russell, 87.

23. Beneke, 7.

24. Gibbs, 53.

25. Crichton, 56.

26. Ibid.

27. Roiphe, "Rape Hype Betrays Feminism."

28. "When No Means No," an article in the conservative *National Review* (June 10, 1991) uses the same tactic, asserting that "a new feminist theory of rape . . . suggests that it afflicts as many as one woman in two and is generally perpetrated by men known to the victims." Ironically, this same *National Review* article refers to the *New York Times* as one of the "great institutions of the liberal media," and criticizes "this feminist theory which most newspaper staffers [at the *New York Times*]

have absorbed through the customary process of ideological osmosis." Apparently, the institutions of the "liberal media" share backlash tactics and perspectives on rape with far-right publications.

29. Beneke, 30.

30. Gibbs, 52.

31. Ibid.

32. Russell, 44.

33. Beneke, 30.

34. Gibbs, 52.

35. Ibid., 53.

36. Crichton, 52.

37. Roiphe, "Rape Hype Betrays Feminism."

38. Crichton, 52.

39. Gibbs, 52.

40. Ibid.

41. Laura Flanders comments on the portrayal of accused rapists as the real victims in "Rape Coverage: Shifting the Blame," *EXTRA!* March/April 1991, 4.

42. Roiphe, "Date Rape Hysteria."

43. Matalin, 62.

44. Crichton, 56.

45. Ibid.

46. Gibbs, 53.

47. Roiphe, "Date Rape Hysteria."

48. Gibbs, 53.

49. Ibid.

50. Crichton, 52.

51. "When No Means No," 12.

52. "When No Means No," 13.

53. Gibbs, 53.

54. Crichton, 54.

55. Ibid.

56. Olen and Ostrow, 1991.

57. As I mentioned in the section on reversal, there is a complex constellation of mitigating factors that determine whether a woman will be considered (by others and even herself) to have been raped. These factors influence the opinions of jurors, journalists, people reading the news, the woman and man involved, etc., and have a broad impact on a community's various responses to rape.

58. Gibbs, 51.

59. Roiphe, "Date Rape Hysteria."

60. Roiphe, "Rape Hype Betrays Feminism."

61. It is important to note that this kind of stereotyping does harm some men (for instance, minorities or immigrants) by labeling them as potential rapists while protecting other men (such as young white men) from being named as rapists regardless of their actions.

62. Ibid.

63. Crichton, 54.

64. Gibbs, 52.

65. Ibid., 51.

66. Warshaw, 11.

67. Roiphe, "Date Rape Hysteria."

68. Roiphe, "Rape Hype Betrays Feminism."

69. It is also significant that where Roiphe does address that research, she misrepresents its results. See the section on erasure for a discussion of Roiphe's misreading of the "Scope of Rape" study.

70. Koss, personal communication, July 17, 1997.

71. Faludi, 61.

72. Matalin, 62.

73. Some feminists have questioned the notion of meaningful consent in the context of a patriarchal and hierarchical culture in which many heterosexual women are financially dependent upon their husbands. This may be a valid question; however, mainstream discourses on rape have not broached this subject, and this question is decidedly absent from consideration of rape law or policy at this time.

74. Koss, Gidycz, and Wisniewski, 1987. This remains the most extensive study on rape occurrence among college students, and several similar studies have produced results that agree with it. No original research has ever been conducted by those who assert that the study is unreliable.

75. By cultural vocabulary I mean the vocabulary in popular usage within a given community. It is the vocabulary of the dominant culture, that which is institutionalized in authoritative discourses such as news and law, and for which members of that community are held accountable.

76. "Significant" here means both important and relating to signification.

77. Teresa de Lauretis defines the horizon of meaning as the set of terms, concepts, rhetorical strategies, shared assumptions, interpretive paths, and unstated premises contained within existing "discursive boundaries . . . [not] simply constraints but also configurations, discursive configurations—[which] delineate a set of possible meanings," 4.

78. Weedon, 76.

79. Ibid.

Works Cited

Beneke, Timothy. *Men on Rape*. New York: St Martin's Press, 1982.

"A Bias Crime." *New York Times* (May 6, 1990).

Carlson, Margaret. "The Trials of Convicting Rapists." *Time*, October 14, 1991, 11–C8.

Crichton, Sarah. "Sexual Correctness: Has it Gone Too Far?" *Newsweek*, October 25, 1993, 52–56.

Daly, Mary. *Gyn/Ecology: The Metaethics of Radical Feminism*. Boston: Beacon Press, 1978.

de Lauretis, Teresa, ed. *Feminist Studies/Critical Studies*. London: Macmillan Press, 1986.

Estrich, Susan. "Balancing Act." *Newsweek*, October 25, 1993, 64.

Faludi, Susan. "Whose Hype?" *Newsweek*, October 25, 1993, 61.

Gibbs, Nancy. "When is it Rape?" *Time*, June 3, 1991, 48–54.

Grosz, Elizabeth. "The In(ter)vention of Feminist Knowledges." In *Crossing Boundaries*, edited by B. Caine and E.A. Grosz. Sydney: Allen and Unwin, 1988.

Kamen, Paula. "Erasing Rape: Media Hype an Attack on Sexual-Assault Research. *Extra!* November/December 1993, 10–11.

Koss, Mary P., Christine A. Gidycz, and Nadine Wisniewski. "The Scope of Rape: Incidence and Prevalence of Sexual Aggression and Victimization in a National Sample of Higher Education Students." *Journal of Consulting and Clinical Psychology* 55, no. 2 (1987): 162–70.

Matalin, Mary. "Stop Whining." *Newsweek*, October 25, 1993, 62.

National Council for Research on Women. *To Reclaim a Legacy of Diversity: Analyzing the "Political Correctness" Debates in Higher Education*. New York: National Council for Research on Women, 1993.

Olen, Helaine and Ronald Ostrow. "Date Rape Gains Attention After Years as Taboo Topic." *Los Angeles Times*, April 23, 1991.
Pelton, Charles. "When the Date Turns into Rape." *Time*, March 23, 1987, 77.
Penelope, Julia. *Speaking Freely: Unlearning the Lies of the Fathers' Tongues*. New York: Teachers College Press, 1990.
Roiphe, Katie. "Date Rape Hysteria." *New York Times*, November 20, 1991.
———. "Rape Hype Betrays Feminism." *New York Times Magazine*, June 13, 1993.
Russell, Diana E. H. *The Politics of Rape: The Victim's Perspective*. New York: Stein and Day, 1975.
Schwartz, John, Karen Goldberg, Asra Nomani, and Irene Tucker. " 'Acquaintance Rape' Comes into the Open." *Newsweek*, February 1986, 12–15.
Sherman, Beth. "The New Realities of 'Date Rape.' " *New York Times*, October 23, 1985.
Warshaw, Robin. *I Never Called It Rape: The Ms. Report on Recognizing, Fighting, and Surviving Date and Acquaintance Rape*. New York: HarperCollins, 1994.
Weedon, Chris. *Feminist Practice and Poststructuralist Theory*. Oxford: Basil Blackwell, 1987.
"When No Means No." *National Review*, June 10, 1991, 12–13.

8

Elemental Philosophy: Language and Ontology in Mary Daly's Texts

Frances Gray

You are the icon of woman sexual
in herself like a great forest tree
in flower, liriodendron bearing sweet tulips,
cups of joy and drunkenness.
You drink strength from your dark fierce roots
and you hang at the sun's own fiery breast
and with the green cities of your boughs
you shelter and celebrate
woman, with the cauldron of your energies
burning red, burning green.
—Marge Piercy, "The Window of the Woman Burning"

In *The Church and the Second Sex*, originally published in 1968, Mary Daly took seriously the place of language in the social production of women and their experiences. She did this within a theological context. Her denunciation of the Eternal Feminine, an essentializing conception of women that held that women had a fixed, unchanging nature, was accompanied by a strong stand for a social constructionist perspective that was an attempt to refocus and rethink the idea of Woman. Her work was and remains blatantly political and strategic, a deliberate search to reconceive the ideas of Woman and divinity within her own divisive and destabilizing discursive framework.

Central to her concerns is her desire to create discourse(s) specific to women which represent their interests. Daly's explicit assumption is that language is not sex/gender neutral: rather, language is sex/gender specific. She maintains that all languages carry implicit symbolics and semantics. In Western societies, the symbolics and semantics of the dominant language are that of white, middle-class men who have created a master discourse. For such men, language serves the function of maintaining hegemonic masculinity with its associated power and sanctioned pseudo-neutrality. On the whole, women accept this alleged neutrality. Daly claims, however, that women find themselves victims within this purportedly neutral system that seeks to define and name them. It is in this context that one should understand Daly's claim that women have had the power of naming stolen from them. And it is in this context that Daly elaborates the idea that language use is subversive: Daly's use seeks to overthrow the purported neutrality of patriarchal discourses and to claim a ground on which women can create their own sex-specific discourses.

Daly's subversive use of language is also strategic. By this I mean that she acknowledges that language always operates within sociopolitical contexts and that language is therefore implicitly perspectival. But she challenges men's discursive hegemony by making language work for her in an attempt to produce and initiate women's discourses. So, at one level, she uses the rules and plays of the master language with its apparently irresistible claim to neutrality as her own theological springboard. At another, she deliberately subverts that master language by undermining its foundations. She takes a pre-existing condition of language—that it is not neutral, but sexed/gendered and monopolizes those who are constituted within its sphere—and then she manipulates that condition in order to subvert its supposed neutrality. Daly's intention is to be divisive and to destabilize language to show that women and their experiences are produced through men's discursive practices, in which women cannot name for themselves. But she also intends to re-conceive language to enable women to name for themselves once more.

Note that Meaghan Morris, in writing about *Gyn/Ecology*, has argued that Daly uses language strategically.[1] When she uses the term "strategy"[2] Morris refers to the way in which Daly deploys "punning, alliteration, word-play, allegory, and the Great Metaphor of the Voyage"[3] to achieve her revolutionary ends. For Morris, however, Daly's strategy is unsuccessful. She maintains that Daly confines her critique to "a politics of subverting isolated signs, not one of transforming discourse" (71) or "language in use" (73).

What Morris means by 'discourse' is spelled out in her lengthy "digression on discourse" which she argues that Daly is concerned with semantics and not with contextual matters, "with the semantics of the said, rather than the enunciative strategies of saying." Her main claim is that Daly situates meanings *in words* instead of *in contexts* (74). Because Daly does this, then according to Morris, Daly fails to acknowledge that "a context—in particular, at least an image of an audience—plays a part in what is said and how it's said. Mary Daly's approach can imply quite the opposite: because you have 'true meanings' to articulate, you are likely to say the same thing in the same way in the same language in any circumstances to anyone to whom you accept to speak politically. It is then up to the audience to situate itself/themselves accordingly" (75).

On this view, Daly's preoccupation with nouns and their meanings renders hers a project that cannot be transformative, because *énonciation* should be the primary site of transformative discourse. To support her reading, Morris cites Pym's view of discourse as " '*constraints* on semiosis,' semiosis being defined as the production of meaning by signs *in continuous action* [*sic*]" (77; Morris' italics) and Benveniste's idea of discourse as the " 'product of a speaking position' " (90).[4] Morris's stress then is on *énonciation*, the activity of language, what "everybody does every time that they open their mouths (to good or evil effect)."[5] In her view, Daly is not concerned with discursive action at all.

I am not persuaded by Morris's argument. It is not clear to me that Daly is unconcerned about either "speaking position" or the "production of meaning by signs in continuous action." Daly's desire to destabilize discourse is situated in her belief that patriarchy constitutes itself through the semantic position that Morris describes so well (and ascribes to Daly). Daly's focus on nouns, on radicalizing their meanings, depends for its success on *énonciation:* without a speaking position, without acknowledging that meaning is produced precisely as Morris suggests, there is little point to Daly's critique of the meaning/reference of nouns and discourse in general.[6]

Further, and this follows from what I have just claimed, Morris's contention about Daly's subverting isolated signs is strange given the postmodern culture in which she situates herself. Both Ferdinand de Saussure and Derrida argue that no sign can be isolated: that a sign is always a sign *within* a system and that to change one sign is to change the system as a whole.[7] I will argue, contrary to Morris, that Daly, cognizant of structural analysis, is successfully strategic and that her ontological concerns could not be articulated in any other way. Hence I will argue that Daly's is not a strategy of subverting isolated signs at all, but an attempt to displace supposedly neutral (but men's) discourse in order to produce a women's discourse, the function of which is to articulate women's Be-ing.[8] Punning, alliteration, wordplay, and allegory are all integral to the transformation of discourse and are not acts of terrorism against isolated linguistic signs: there can be no isolated aspects of, no isolated signs in, language. Daly's speaking position emerges from the oppression of women. Her choice of which aspects of language/discourse to subvert reveals a deep-seated commitment to producing new meanings by rethinking discourse as continuous activity.

Daly's early works, *The Church and the Second Sex* and *Beyond God the Father*, neither used nor appropriated language in a divisive and destabilizing manner. Daly's work with language begins in *Gyn/Ecology* and develops in earnest in the subsequent births of *Pure Lust*, *Wickedary*, and *Outercourse*. Daly's primary task in *The Church and the Second Sex* was to argue for the equality of women and men as church members, to expose the masculine bias of Christian theology, and to demonstrate the explicit iniquitous practical and psychological consequences that this theology had (and continues to have)[9] for women in the church. She saw the Catholic church as an oppressive, man-dominated institution which failed to reconcile its opposing views of women (as virgin and whore), but that used that opposition to revere, regulate, and revile the lives of its women adherents. In Daly's view, the movement to equality between women and men was anathema (70) to the church hierarchy, who resisted and opposed any change to the status of women within the church. "Those engaged in the struggle for the equality of the sexes have often seen the Catholic Church as an enemy. This view is to a large extent justified, for Catholic teaching has prolonged a traditional view of woman which at the same time idealizes and humiliates her" (107).

Informed as her work was by *The Second Sex* (107), her writing took on much of Simone de Beauvoir's critique of the socio-ontological arrangements that constitute, encompass, and entrap women. Indeed, Daly's book can be seen as a Catholic response to Simone de Beauvoir's critique of the Catholic church's oppression of women. Daly was keen to reveal the history and social circumstances of women in the church. With this disclosure would come an admission that women have been tied to immanence, tied to materiality and symbolized as the embodiment of temptation, lust, and sin. Daly was committed to arguing for some favorable outcomes once the problems were identified and acknowledged. With identification and acknowledgment, women could begin to overcome the historical and social contingencies that had cast them as secondary beings.

> The fundamental difference between Simone de Beauvoir's vision of the Church and women and that which motivated this book is the difference between despair and hope. For this reason our approach is fundamentally far more radical than that of the French existentialist. De Beauvoir was willing to accept the conservative vision of the Church as reality, and therefore has had to reject it as unworthy of mature humanity. However, there is an alternative to rejection, an alternative which need not involve self-mutilation. This is commitment to radical transformation of the negative, life-destroying elements of the Church as it exists today. The possibility of such commitment rests upon clear understanding that the seeds of the eschatological community, of the liberating humanizing Church of the future, are already present, however submerged and neutralized they may be. Such commitment requires hope and courage. (70)

Daly could, therefore, be seen as an apologist for the Truth that she believed the Catholic church manifested and revealed and this is a position quite contrary to Simone de Beauvoir's (172). However, there is a significant and fundamental point on which Simone de Beauvoir and Daly agree. Like Simone de Beauvoir (171), Daly attacked the essentializing notion of the Eternal Feminine, the Eternal Woman, the idea that there is a "fixed human nature" (155) peculiar to women. Daly's critics have wrongly argued that she does not persist with her exposure, that she ultimately retrieves an idea of feminine essence which revalorizes universalizing concepts of women. On this view, Daly retreats from her agreement with Simone de Beauvoir, and instead, revalorizes and reinscribes the Eternal Feminine in *Gyn/Ecology* and *Pure Lust*. Elisabeth Schüssler Fiorenza, for example, argues that Daly "brilliantly . . . uses an ontological-linguistic strategy to articulate such an alterity. It is a process of Be-coming instantiated by the Wild, Original, Self-actualizing woman who has made the leap from phallocracy into freedom, into the Otherworld of Be-ing" (155).

Schüssler Fiorenza argues that Daly reconstructs the category of Woman as a superior, natural category over and against Man. She describes Daly's position as just one of the many that come "dangerously close to reproducing in the form of deconstructive language traditional cultural-religious ascription[s] of femininity and motherhood, ascriptions all too familiar from papal pronouncements, which have now become feminist norms."[10] Schüssler Fiorenza's claim is strange, to say the least, when one considers Daly's complete refusal of fixed categorization and her vehement rejection of essentialism and the Eternal Feminine.

Note that Daly continually emphasizes the idea that Woman is in process, that women do not have a fixed, immutable nature. The (potential) creation of new Woman is the acknowledgment of that process. As social circumstances and conditions will change and change again, so too will women in their searches for Be-ing. The Otherworld Journey in which women should be engaged points to potentiality rather than actuality. So Daly is not appealing to the actuality of an Eternal, essential Woman at all. She is signposting the idea that women are in process, redefining their potentialities, re-claiming their own naming and thus their be-ing.

It should be stressed that in *The Church and the Second Sex* Daly extensively analyses and subsequently dismisses the concept of women's essence. Her reading identifies the Eternal Woman as the essential Woman: she is that which makes a woman truly Woman. It is this idea of essential womanhood that Daly passionately rejects. Daly remarks:

> The characteristics of the Eternal Woman are opposed to those of a developing, authentic *person*, who will be unique, self-critical, self creating, active and searching. . . . By contrast to these authentic personal qualities, the Eternal Woman is said to have a vocation to surrender and hiddenness; . . . Self-less, she achieves not individual realisation but merely generic fulfillment in motherhood, physical or spiritual. . . . She is said to be timeless and conservative by nature. She is shrouded in mystery because she is not a genuine human person.[11]

She argues that the Eternal Feminine and the Eternal Woman are symbols that operate at a normative level in society.[12] Hence the concepts of the Eternal Woman and the Eternal Feminine, although symbolic, are not merely descriptive. They *prescribe* how a woman ought to behave in order to count as a Woman. Women, on this account, are genuinely women by virtue of their "passive, dependent, totally relational"[13] qualities, which are embodied by the idea of the Eternal Woman. But, Daly maintains, these symbolic qualities are "radically opposed to female emancipation"[14] for they evince a perception of women that both describes and prescribes their individual natures as inferior human beings. Paradoxically, anything falling outside this model fails to count as a woman. The Eternal Feminine is, in other words, the essence of individual women: "The formula is very simple: once the *a priori* norms of femininity have been set up, all the exceptions are classified as 'defeminised.' "[15] Note the relationship, reminiscent of Plato, between the idea of universal Woman and individual women: one is an individual woman in virtue of participating in the ideal form of Woman.

So Daly argues that in a strong sense individual women were expected to derive the idea that they were women from the symbolic Eternal Feminine and the idea of "pure" or "brute" biological nature. The Eternal Feminine is an a priori given; women's sex remains a biological brute fact. Daly saw the Eternal Feminine as an evil which should be exorcised from the church as well as from the lives of women. While the grip of the Eternal Feminine persisted, little could be achieved for women. However, in highlighting the flawed nature of essential Womanhood, Daly resolved to launch on a project designed "to minimize biological differences"[16] in order to change how, and the conditions under which, women should be symbolized.[17] In this context, one must acknowledge that Daly's project was devoted to elaborating an idea of androgyny.

It is important to acknowledge that Daly was then concerned for women to remain within the church and that she believed that it would be possible to transform the church into the kind of institution in which women would have equality. For her the idea of androgyny suitably expressed the neutrality of the subject. Both women and men, if they were to throw off the shackles of essentializing theory, should see androgyny as an ideal. The last two chapters of *The Church and the Second Sex* are concerned with "some modest proposals" about how this might come about. Daly's optimism witnesses her belief in the liberal feminist commitment to full participation in the pre-established (sex-neutral) forms of hierarchical institutions. For her, acceptance of women as equal partners in an androgynous church would lead to the transformation of the institution itself, wherein "(m)en and women, using their best talents, forgetful of self and intent upon the work, will with God's help mount together toward a higher order of consciousness and being, in which the alienating projections will have been defeated and wholeness, psychic integrity, achieved."[18]

That meant that women and men must abandon the dominant image of women as the embodiment of the Eternal Feminine. In turn, that meant the traditional roles ascribed to women (in which the Eternal Feminine is honored) would need to be re-evaluated so that women could be given the freedom to move into new space(s). Daly contended that men also must go through a process of transformation and come to terms with the ways in which society had imposed values on, and expectations of, them. "The eternal masculine" traps and limits men as much as the Eternal Feminine has women.

> What is more the "eternal masculine" itself is alienating, crippling the personalities of men and restricting their experience of life at every level. The male in our society is not supposed to express much feeling, sensitivity, aesthetic appreciation, imagination, consideration for others, intuition. He is expected to affirm only part of his real self. Indeed, it may be that a good deal of the compulsive competitiveness of males is rooted in this half existence. . . . It is the nature of the disease, therefore, to inhibit the expansion of the individual's potential, through conditioned conformity to roles, and through a total identification of the individual with them.[19]

Thus although at the time of writing *The Church and the Second Sex* Daly had as her primary concern the liberation of women from archaic theory and the social practice built upon that theory, her concern was also for the liberation of all humans, women and men alike. She believed that women and men must fracture the stereotypes by which they are characterized and that the 'real'[20] self somehow exists apart from sexual identity. She took up this theme in *Beyond God the Father,* where she explored notions centered around androgynous being and in which she generated a trinity: language, transcendence, and androgyny. The relationship among these three is implicit: together they produce the ontological foundations for human becoming to ultimate, authentic Be-ing. Note that later, in *Gyn/Ecology*, Daly remarked that along with the terms 'God' and 'homosexuality', 'androgyny' is a term she will never use again. Daly situated these terms within the masculine paternal canon. They represent men's interests, not women's.

What I do want to emphasize here is that regardless of what patriarchal intellectual commitments Daly attacks and attempts to refute, her underlying commitment to women's liberation remains couched in terms of language and ontology. Daly uses the patriarchal centeredness of dominant language and ontology ingeniously, as we shall see.[21] Overwhelmingly, she appropriates and exploits patriarchal language and ontology to make political statements, to address what she considers to be socially and morally corrupt practices, and to redefine the enterprises of theology and philosophy. She reconstitutes language and ontology as her own Elemental Feminist Philosophy in *Gyn/Ecology* and *Pure Lust,* the works in which she develops her cosmic odyssey, her gynocratic vision.

In *Beyond God the Father* for example, Daly is very taken by the idea of process theology because it does not present us with a static world view. She obviously admires the work of Charles Hartshorne, who, she says, believes that "process is creative synthesis."[22] But she is dubious about the social worth of theory such as his and is also suspicious about that which is ready-made (man-made) and can apparently be readily appropriated by feminists. Her enterprise is to make new philosophy and create new language out of the experience(s) of women. "The essential thing is to hear our *own* words, always giving prior attention to our *own* experience, never letting theory have *authority* over us. Then we can be free to listen to the old philosophical language (and all philosophy that does not explicitly repudiate sexism is old, no matter how novel it may seem)."[23] Her endeavors, to create out of the old, to renegotiate the relation between ontology and language, should be seen in this light.

From the time of *Gyn/Ecology*, language is, categorically, the ontological groundwork of Daly's sex-specific women's discourse; in other words, language *becomes* ontology for Daly: language is the material out of which ontology is constructed, it is the being or *esse* of ontology. *Contra* Morris's argument, Daly's strategy involves more than isolating some signs. She seeks to highlight the idea that language and ontology are so related that language is a condition, not just for the articulation of ontology, but for the very possibility of ontology. For her then, the key to directly affecting change in women's lives is through radically re-viewing discourse. Daly's work with nouns begins this change. She is unequivocally committed to transforming discourse in an endeavor to create a space for women, in terms of language and ontology. Hence hers is subversive linguistic activity. By this, I mean that her strategy is to destabilize, refigure, and transform not only discourse, but the way in which one conceives of ontology and one's life, one's be-ing. But of necessity for Daly, the master discursive framework of patriarchal philosophy is the origin of her project.[24]

So what is the language/ontology relation which Daly affirms? There are three crucial, interconnected elements of Daly's work that elaborate her notion of the ontology/language relation. The first is the idea that women's meanings, the symbolization of their experiences and of women's discourses, must be produced out of existing discourses. The second is that naming is foundational to the creation of meanings; and the third is Daly's use of metaphor.

Daly argues that all language establishes and comes out of an ontologically committed context which is not neutral (as I argued earlier).[25] Put simply, language constructs ontology: language establishes the conditions of being. However, there is a reciprocal relationship involved here. Not only does language construct ontology, but the limits of language are set by our ontological understandings and commitments. Language is a condition for the construction of ontology, which in turn is a condition for language. For Daly, the production of be-ing, which participates in Be-ing, is grounded in displacing patriarchal meanings, in appropriating language, in acknowledging becoming, in shape shifting.[26] It presupposes an extant discourse. In a similar vein, Mark C. Taylor argues: "While philosophy's other always slips through the structures imposed by conceptual reflection, the unthought can only be evoked through the language of philosophy itself. The postphilosophical thinkers must strategically use language *against* language. 'In order to make the attempt of thinking recognizable and at the same time understandable for existing philosophy, it could at first be expressed only within the horizon of that existing philosophy and its use of current terms.' "[27]

Daly commits herself to using language against language: to looking at its etymological sources, using them, abusing them, drawing out their implications for women and doing that within the horizon, which necessarily must change, of existing philosophical and theological discourses. She is, therefore, engaged in a double project: exploring and using the present/past terrain of philosophy, while at the same time shifting the boundaries it imposes on itself and in particular upon women. The subverting of discourse is a strategy Daly deliberately embraces when she disfigures extant discourse in order to highlight the possibility of women's ontology/language. Hers is a political task that depends upon undermining (purportedly neutral) language. Daly understands language as a whole, as a dialogical, transformative means of achieving a radically altered society for women.[28] Given this kind of interpretation of Daly's work, Morris' allegation that Daly merely subverts isolated signs, rather than re-shaping discourse as a whole, should be seen as the dubious rendering that it is.

In the *Wickedary* Daly talks of elemental ontology, "the philosophical quest for Be-ing; rooted in the intuition that Powers of Be-ing are constantly Unfolding, creating, communicating; philosophy grounded in the experience of active potency to move beyond the foreground of fixed questions and answers and enter the Radiant Realms of Metabeing."[29] Such an understanding reinforces her belief that there is an intimate fundamental relation between language and ontology. Her term 'Metabeing', "(r)ealms of active participation in Powers of Be-ing, State of Ecstasy," is intended to convey the necessary conjunction of discourse and be-ing. For her Be-ing, "Ultimate/Intimate Reality, the constantly Unfolding Verb of Verbs which is intransitive, having no object that limits its dynamism; the Final Cause, the Good who is Self-communicating who is the Verb from whom, in whom, and with whom all true movements move,"[30] is an energizing process. 'It' is not fixed and determined as essence would be: the play of Be-ing scampers with delight in its boundlessness and constant shape changing.

This gives voice to the Heracleitan resonances we find in Daly's work. She stresses that language is primarily "performative/active/animate" activity, potentially alive with meaning. Her emphasis on process underscores her approach to language as an oceanic whole: vast, interrelated, and ever changing. On this basis, Daly proposes a re-orientation of language that will highlight the fluidity of verbs. And this brings us to the second element in her elaboration of the ontology/language relation.

In discussing the activity of naming which she understands as the locus of power, Daly argued:

> In order to understand the implications of this process it is necessary to grasp the fundamental fact that women have had the power of *naming* stolen from us. Women have not been free to use their own power to name themselves, the world, or God. The old naming was not the product of dialogue—a fact inadvertently admitted in the Genesis story of Adam's naming the animals and the woman. Women are now realising that the universal imposing of names by men has been false because partial. . . . To exist humanly is to name the self, the world and God.[31]

She identifies naming as a functional process which can oppress (as it has women) or liberate. In short, Daly believes that because men have named, they have controlled. Hence men have power. Language is therefore necessarily political: it provides the foundations for control and power. Language, then, has been, and continues to be, oppressive to women. In this sense, naming functions as a metonym for all of language.[32] Naming, in other words, is but one part of language. Yet the fact that naming plays such a decisive role in the productions of meanings and the construction of our worlds affirms the idea that the whole of language is engaged in some way with the process of naming. Naming—language as an activity that implies, and is implied by, discourse—is a prime mover in both the construction and understanding of Being. But, to reiterate, the concept of naming is not meant to be understood in a literal, narrow sense. Naming embraces the whole of discursive practice. In *Beyond God the Father*, Daly had denounced the monopolistic practice of naming in which men have engaged. She argued that what she calls "old naming" as a function of language has assumed an oppressive role within, and is constitutive of, patriarchal structures including discursive practice(s). So, Daly believed, "new naming" can creatively constitute a world in which all sexual oppression will disappear.

The power of naming, highlighted in *Beyond God the Father*, is a crucial feature of Daly's work in *Gyn/Ecology* and by the time of *Pure Lust* had developed into a highly sophisticated network of critical exploration of language, play on words, neologism, and re-definition. But Daly re-orients what we might think of as 'usual' in the practice of naming. Predominantly, we associate naming with nouns: with sorting, categorizing. Daly is scathing about this practice and emphasizes the importance of verbs over nouns. This is where naming as a metonym becomes a clear strategic device for Daly. The shift from noun-naming to verb-naming swings naming to a new position within language. It is not just that one must find suitable nouns to use in naming: it is that with an emphasis on verbs and their open-endedness—the Heracleitian resonances to which I alluded above—the idea of new-naming becomes an idea of what all language is about: referring, expressing, disclosing, creating, and so on. In this sense, language is action, performance, process, being. Language is the embodiment of creation, the condition for the possibility of anything.

The stress on the role of verbs is no better highlighted than in Daly's discussion of the idea of God. In *Beyond God the Father* Daly argues: "Why indeed must 'God' be a noun? Why not a verb—the most active and dynamic of all? Hasn't the naming of 'God' as a noun been an act of murdering that dynamic Verb? And isn't the Verb infinitely more personal than a mere static noun? The anthropomorphic symbols for God may be intended to convey personality, but they fail to convey that God is Be-ing. . . . This Verb—the Verb of Verbs—is intransitive. It need not be conceived as having an object that limits its dynamism."[33]

Daly's concern with the term 'God' as a noun is not simply grammatical. 'God' either as a proper name or as a mere noun poses a problem for Daly because of her onto-theological concerns and mistrusts. That is to say, Daly ultimately refuses the androcentric term 'God', preferring instead 'Goddess'. This term however, is not intended to convey the idea of a female super-person with whom women might have a personal relationship. Instead, Daly's use is metaphorical. The term 'Goddess' represents potential, possibility: it evokes an idea of what women might become.

According to Daly, that God is construed as a fixed definable thing, that God is reified, is a Deadly Deception. Be-ing, with which she identifies the Goddess, is not a thing at all. In reifying, in making things into objects when that should not be the case, the Divine is essentialized, cast into rocklike solidity that does not change; but Be-ing should not and cannot be contained as nouns contain. (This is what patriarchy practices. Witness Daly's claim that 'God' "represents the necrophilia of patriarchy.")[34] Daly argues that reification is a masculine engagement with which she refuses to identify. According to her, the term 'God' and what it represents is irredeemably masculine. Daly also acknowledges the possibility of falling into the trap of reifying the Goddess, treating the Goddess as an object named by a noun as 'God' has been. But for her, 'Goddess', properly used, "affirms the life-loving be-ing of women and nature"[35] and is the embodiment of the Verb of verbs.

In refiguring the Divine in terms of concentrating on the "verbness of Be-ing," Daly is following a long theological tradition that situates discourse in ontology and ontology in discourse. The Old Testament story of the revelation of the Divine Name is enshrouded in cosmic mystery and linguistic difficulties:

> Moses then said to God, "Look, if I go to the Israelites and say to them, 'The God of your ancestors has sent me to you,' and they say to me, 'What is his name?' what am I to tell them?" God said to Moses, "I am he who is." And he said, "This is what you are

> to say to the Israelites, 'I am has sent me to you.' " God further said to Moses, "You are to tell the Israelites, 'Yahweh, the God of your ancestors, the God of Abraham, the God of Isaac and the God of Jacob, has sent me to you.' This is my name for all time, and thus I am to be invoked for all generations to come."[36]

Commentators on this biblical passage point out that there are etymological and interpretative worries concerning the text, both of which have bearing on Daly's concerns. Etymologically, they argue, *Yahweh* is archaically related to the Hebrew verb 'to be'. But they also acknowledge that it may be the causative 'he causes to be' or 'he brings into existence'.[37] In any case, the emphasis is on the activity (being, causing, or both) signified by the word. The interpretational question is, in part, one of how the word functions, for it apparently has a naming role.[38] What is pertinent for us is that the naming takes place through the use of the present indicative (a verb function), not through the isolation of properties, characteristics, or features (a noun function in terms of modification and qualification). In other words, God's pronouncement, "I am he who is," if we do take it to be a case of naming, is a verb-naming rather than a noun-naming. Needless to say, its origins and the rules of Hebrew grammar indicate that it is tied up with the verb 'to be' and hence is revelatory of God's Being (as Being).[39] Verb-naming according to Daly seeks not to reify, but to characterize the divine as active principle, as elemental, which is precisely what is happening in this Hebrew text.

The impetus for producing a peculiarly women's discourse lies precisely in theological quandaries such as that represented by the Yahweh debate. Daly uncovers the prejudice toward anthropomorphism that she maintains patriarchal use/discourse exhibits in its theological language. She realizes that language constitutes our understandings and conceptualizings, particularly because many of our concepts are "trapped" in nouns. By "playing around" with language, her intention is to create not only a conceptual shift, but an ontological shift: a shift that will make possible the discovery of the (metaphorical) Goddess in the experience of women.

Note that Mary Daly is concerned with "playing around." Much of her writing is a joyful playing with concepts, ideas, etymologies, and breaking up of syllables to re-emphasise new and different meanings. Daly's writing is the performance of that play. The divine is found not only in the deep and serious matters of the mind. The divine is found in unfolding the contorted layers of meaning that have fabricated women's lives as well as at times of bliss. Humor and play are restored to philosophy.

The mystery that is the divine is exposed in Yahweh's own playfulness, Yahwistic humor—I tell you who I am: I am. The Hebrew story, which historically speaking is assuredly counter-hegemonic and thus already antithetical to dominant Hebrew-inspired patriarchal conceptions of the divine, exhibits a deep religious bias toward acknowledging the Be-ing and mystery of divinity that falls outside noun-naming processes. So, in identifying noun-naming as a problem for "God," Daly reiterates part of a tradition that she puts superbly to work in her performing of feminist theology. The centrality of verbs, the stress on their processive function, signifies the open-endedness of Be-ing toward which women can move, marking the re-emergence of the Goddess. And this idea of the Goddess as Verb of Verbs should not be read through patriarchal modernist categories.

Daly's notion of the Goddess points "metaphorically to the Powers of Be-ing, the Active Verb in whose potency all biophilic reality participates."[40] Notice Daly's use of the word 'metaphorically' here. The recognition of this term and its cognates brings us to the third element in Daly's elucidation of the language/ontology relation: her use of metaphor. Just as naming functions as a metonym for the whole of language use and practice, so metaphor guides the explosion of language which occurs with the transference of energy from nouns to verbs. The role of metaphor becomes political. It is the means by which transcendence will be made possible. In other words, the Goddess is an expression of the possibility of women's transcendence, of women's gracious movement. Thus use of metaphor, the idea of the Goddess and transcendence are intimately linked.

Daly's chapter "Bewitching: The Lust for Metamorphosis" in *Pure Lust* contains a substantial elucidation of both the role and significance Daly wants to give metaphor. There, she argues that metaphors are not mere symbols nor mere abstractions. Metaphors are, as she notes in the *Wickedary*, "words that carry Journeyers into the Wild dimensions of Other-centred consciousness by jarring images, stirring memories, accentuating contradictions, upsetting unconscious traditional assumptions."[41] In *Pure Lust* she also maintains that the Great Mother is one of the "myriad possibilities for naming transcendence"[42] (and that some women can become fixated on images such as the Great Mother, an example of reification of the Goddess).

> A metapatriarchal metaphor "works" precisely to the extent that it carries a woman further into the Wild dimensions of other-centered consciousness—out of the dead circles into Spiralling/Spinning motion. Be-witching metaphors transmute the shapes of perception. They do this by jarring images, stirring memories, accentuating contradictions, upsetting unconscious traditional assumptions, evoking "inappropriate" laughter, releasing pent-up tears, eliciting gynaesthetic sensings of connections, arousing Dragon-identified Passions, inspiring acts of Volcanic virtue, brewing strange ideas.[43]

Daly's concern is with developing a metaphorical understanding of Woman and divinity that is open-ended. In this sense it is essential that one understands her project as non-literal. Daly situates herself within a tradition of metaphorical discourse of which she is simultaneously subversive.[44] She alleges: "Metaphors function to Name change, and therefore they elicit change. . . . Thus the very task of naming and calling forth Elemental be-ing requires metaphors."[45] For Daly, change necessitates the use of metaphor.[46]

The echo that rebounds in Daly's exegesis of metaphor resonates with the playfulness to which I alluded above. In using metaphor, one plays; that play constitutes performance, challenging and subverting the categories that subtend language. *Énonciation* occurs in the written text! For example, she speaks of women's bodies as "transmutable to and from energy" and of "[t]he spiration of the Archimage within Lusty women, who speak women's words, heals broken connections between words and their Sources, reconnecting women with their elemental origins."[47] As Daly showed in her analysis of essentialism, this is not the patriarchal way of thinking about women or their bodies. If women in patriarchy are lusty, they are whores; if there is spiration within women, it is the Word of God speaking to a (compliant) Virgin Mother to whom an announcement is made (that she will be the Mother of God). The change in metaphor brings about a change in thinking: Virgin Virtues do not revolve around the idea of submission; Virgin Virtues are "life affirming habits of Uncaptured/Unsubdued women";[48] to Gossip is "to exercise the Elemental Female Power of Naming, especially in the presence of other Gossips."[49]

Ironically, Daly's use of (seemingly stereotypical?) "female" metaphors tempts commentators to interpret Daly as essentialist. But Daly's metaphors appeal to the idea of women as constituted through their own language practices, which are not themselves neutral. This cannot be stressed enough, especially since the claim that there can be no sex-neutral subject is discussed widely in feminist literature and Daly's work highlights this assertion.[50] But there is a great deal of confusion about what is actually going on when feminist theorists call for a female subject and most of this confusion collapses into debates surrounding essentialism. In other words, the idea that there should or could be a female subject is almost always read as a reaffirmation of the idea of a female essence, even when a theorist taking such a stand identifies herself as a social constructionist and denounces essentialism. This is the case with Mary Daly and her critics.[51]

Rosi Braidotti, for instance, has maintained that Daly has a "conceptual tendency to naturalize the feminine"[52] and thus to reinstate essentializing notions of women. Braidotti's accusation stems from her analysis of Daly's (metaphorical) Goddess imagery, which she misreads as invoking essentialist images. Furthermore, she agrees with Morris, whom she interprets as accusing Daly of "re-naming at the level of lexicon, of the vocabulary, leaving unchanged the syntax of representation."[53] Let me revisit Morris, who writes: "One focus of Daly's interest in *Gyn/Ecology* is the possibilities offered by changing *particular words* (those items in the dictionary, ie. the available code—or *langue*—of patriarchal English). She de-constructs and de-forms them in their inert state as signs whose only context *is* the dictionary, and then puts them to work in the discourse. . . . Her strategy is to warp the words of the patriarchal dictionary, to bend the code back against itself until it snaps to their shrieks of derision" (her italics).[54]

To reiterate the point I made earlier in this essay, this interpretation charges that Daly deconstructs terms within language, without deconstructing the corpus, language in use, and her own speaking position. On this misreading, Daly valorizes Woman as she has been understood through the texts of Western philosophy, ascribing to Woman an essence that depends upon the implicit acceptance of the categories of Western thought. Morris's and Braidotti's readings of Daly are, however, literal rather than metaphoric. They fail to let Daly "mess with their minds,"[55] to let her metaphors dislodge patriarchal meanings and re-orient their thinking. They read her through a modernist lens.

Daly does not reinscribe Western philosophical ideas of Essential Woman at all. To recapitulate, her language is metaphorical and seeks to explore the previously unexplored: the possibility of women's discourse. It is important to stress that both Morris and Braidotti assume that Daly essentializes the Goddess and women because she boldly dismisses neutrality as a construction of patriarchy. It is possible that Morris and Braidotti do not recognize the link Daly makes between patriarchy and neutrality. However, that Daly holds that patriarchy constructs the idea of neutrality is apparent. Her rejection of androgyny, tied as it is to the idea of a gender-neutral "best possible subject," (" 'John Travolta and Farrah Fawcett-Majors scotch-taped together' ")[56] states her point sharply and shortly. Daly's underlying argument is always that language is sex specific: there is no gender-neutral sex and, therefore, there can be no gender-neutral language. Since language constructs subjectivities, identities, it follows that there can be no gender-neutral subject. The elimination of the idea of androgyny is couched in these terms.

Daly rejects androgyny; Morris and Braidotti revalorize neutrality. Braidotti's affirmation of neutrality in this text emerges when she argues: "So Daly falls into what I consider one of the worst traps besetting feminism today: the replacement of the masculine subject by the feminine subject. . . . The latent dogmatism in Daly's thought, quite as much as its reactionary nature, seems to me potentially dangerous for current feminism, insofar as it subverts the signs, not the codes."[57]

But Daly replies to her critics who choose the concept of neutrality over that of woman:

> Particularly insidious is the pseudo-feminist usage of the term *essentialist* to label and discredit all feminist writing that dares to Name and celebrate the Wild and Elemental reality of women who choose to think beyond the prescribed parameters of patriarchal mandates. . . . It elicits the patriarchally embedded Self-censor in women attempting to create in women-identified ways. . . . In other words, the expression of Original Powers and of the Ecstatic existential experience of women breaking free from patriarchal mindbendings is stigmatized by the label "essentialist," leaving only the grimness of oppression as that which women have in common. Ultimately this reversal/usage functions to negate Hope for Life that transcends the illusion of inclusion in forever male-identified "humankind."[58]

The development of Woman's Be-ing, Elemental Woman's Be-ing, is dependent ultimately on the rejection of masculine discourse, men's discourse, commonly thought of as neutral discourse. Daly's intuition about the role of discourse is sound. Her belief is that the Divine, the Goddess, is mirrored through language practices and therefore the Divine is the mirror of women. The claim that discourse must be sex/gender specific, and that Daly is creating the context for metapatriarchal discourse, is a superb strategy. But it is more than a strategy.

Earlier I remarked that a member of Daly's trinity in *Beyond God the Father* was the idea of transcendence. The relation between metaphor and transcendence is intimate. Indeed for Daly, metaphors are "the language/vehicles of transcendent spiraling."[59] Metaphors promote transcendence: they embellish the possibilities for women to participate in Be-ing, to persist with the Journey. But what it means to transcend is elusive. And again, the idea of neutrality looms ominously, this time in the context of Simone de Beauvoir.

In her existentialist philosophy Simone de Beauvoir promoted the idea of transcendence, thought of as a peculiarly male interest. Man achieves transcendence in his own subjectivity, "the male recovers his individuality intact at the moment he transcends it."[60] Women do not achieve transcendence: they fail to develop as subjects, for they never transcend their own individuality. Women fail to create value: they make babies instead and remain immanent in the species.[61] This does not mean that women have no values. But it means that they subscribe to values that are produced externally to them and that are believed to be neutral.

Now, by appropriating men's discourse and developing the triadic relation between ontology and language, naming and metaphor, Daly shifts away from transcendence conceived of as a peculiarly men's project. She denies that women cannot achieve transcendence, cannot make their own values and seek their own autonomy. The play of metaphor evokes the Goddess. And it is in the Goddess, the Verb of Verbs, that transcendence moves to liberate. Transcendence thus becomes a function of women's process, of women's movement, and metaphor its expression. Transcendence is not to be reified, as a thing that can be defined. Transcendence is the process in which women are engaged as they name themselves, make and re-make themselves in performing their divinity, their participation in the Goddess. The language of transcendence and the Goddess is the language of metaphor. In Daly's hands, metaphor is the language of the Goddess, the language of divine politics, the language of Be-ing.

When one looks at the claim made against Daly—that she is essentialist because she launches a project that attempts to seek out Woman and that Daly's language betrays her—one wonders how closely her detractors have read her. Daly has not claimed to define, to categorize women. Daly works to find a way for women to become Wild, to be Lusty, to be Strong. Her belief that women can have no ontology, no being without women's language, recommends an analysis of the idea of Woman such as Daly has produced. If one can accept that women are on a Journey and that the Journey is within language, then the possibility of Elemental ontology opens before one. It is dangerous, the Journey, the Journey to ontology, for it is to be on the Outercourse, toward transcendence and Be-ing.

I have been arguing that Mary Daly's work is primarily directed towards the re-creation of women through the dis-membering and re-construction of discourse. I have argued that far from her project's being a mere changing of isolated signs as Morris has argued, Daly is concerned to produce a radically creative and subversive Woman's discourse. Implicit in that project is the development of an ethic that valorizes women without reinscribing real essentialist accounts (such as the Eternal Woman) of Woman. I have also argued, using Schüssler Fiorenza's terminology, that this strategy is ontological-linguistic, meaning that for Daly, a strong relationship exists between ontology and language, indeed that the two are so intertwined that language becomes ontology for Daly in the sense I have outlined above. She calls into question the idea that the dominant discourses of theology and philosophy are sex neutral. Because these discourses are masculine paternal discourses, Daly believes that women should develop their own language in which they can articulate their own be-ing. In other words, Daly seeks to re-vision the idea of women and their experiences, ontology and the divine. In so doing, she creates a politics of divinity that is not sex neutral but is an expression of women's transcendence because it involves the idea that women should reclaim the power of naming for themselves. Her work creates divinity as politics because she seeks to subvert hegemonic conceptions of language, the divine, and transcendence. In her work she seeks to subvert men's ownership of, and the imposition of boundaries on, the divine. Daly's work systematically defies the canons of men's theology and philosophy, within which is the myth of neutrality. While that myth preserves patriarchal—that is, masculine paternal—hegemony, women will not have the words with which they might name for themselves, a women's language. In new naming is new ontology, women's transcendence, and the Goddess. This is be-ing for women, Be-ing in women. This is women's participation in the Verb of Verbs. This is a women's politics of the divine. And this is Mary Daly's legacy to philosophy and theology.

Notes

I would like to thank the following women for their encouragement and helpful discussions, insights, and editorial comments in relation to this paper: Marilyn Frye, Sarah Hoagland, Heather Thomson, Angela Bouris, Jan Preston-Stanley, Natalie Stoljar, Cynthia Freeland, and Philippa McLean.

1. Meaghan Morris, "A-mazing Grace: Notes on Mary Daly's Poetics," *Intervention* 16 (n.d.): 71–73.

2. Grosz and other commentators on Irigaray use the term "strategy" in discussing Irigaray's work. See Elizabeth Grosz, *Sexual Subversions: Three French Feminists* (St. Leonards: Allen & Unwin, 1989).

3. Morris, "A-mazing Grace," 73.

4. Morris here refers, in a footnote, to Pym's work, a 1980 honors thesis at Murdoch University, and notes that the definition was passed on to her by Anna Freadman.

5. Morris, "A-mazing Grace," 76.

6. One also might consider that in the early days of "second wave" feminism, there were howls of protest from women who realized that terms such as 'man' and 'mankind' for instance, were meant to be inclusive and gender neutral. But in being inclusive, feminists argued, the terms denoted a disregard for the individuality and sexed subjectivity of women. There was, therefore, a push to subvert what might be thought of as "isolated signs" in the writing of public documents. The infamous replacement of "chairman" by "chairwoman" and then its replacement by "chairperson" and the introduction, in English, of the marriage-status-neutral term "Ms." for women, instead of the two choices "Miss" (unmarried woman) or "Mrs." (married woman) are examples of this practice of apparently subverting isolated signs. It is manifest however, that the subversion of isolated signs was, and is, only apparent. Such apparently minor changes have called attention to a problem endemic in many languages and have caused a rethinking of how particular nouns are used and when. I think that this is, in part, what Daly is addressing. I talk further about language neutrality later in this essay.

7. See Ferdinand de Saussure, "Course in General Linguistics" (1916), trans. Wade Baskin, in *A Critical and Cultural Theory Reader*, ed. Anthony Easthope and Kate McGowan, 8–13 (St. Leonards: Allen & Unwin, 1992): "[T]o consider a term as simply the union of a certain sound with a certain concept is grossly misleading. To define it this way would isolate the term from its system. . . . Language is a system of interdependent terms in which the value of each term results solely from the simultaneous presence of the others" (8, 9); and Jacques Derrida, "Différence," in Easthope and McGowan, *A Critical and Cultural Theory Reader*, 108–32: "[T]he signified concept is never present in and of itself, in a sufficient presence that refers only to itself. Essentially and lawfully, every concept is inscribed in a chain or in a system within which it refers to the other, to other concepts, by the systematic play of differences" (115). See also Vincent Descombes, *Modern French Philosophy*, trans. L. Scott-Fox and J. M. Harding (Cambridge and New York: Cambridge University Press, 1980), chap. 3, "Semiology." His discussion of structural analysis, initially using Molière's "Le Bourgeois Gentilhomme" is particularly insightful here. See 82–100. Descombes also refers to Saussure's remark " '*In a language there are only differences*,' " going on to note, "That is why knowledge of any one element is conditional upon knowledge of the system," 87.

8. Daly uses the hyphenated forms Be-ing and be-ing to emphasize their "verbness" so that the reader will not be tempted to reify, as she might if she were to read them as nouns.

9. Although topics such as those raised by Daly about women and the church are commonplace discussion today, little in the sacramental life of the Catholic church (the official position of which remains as it has been for hundreds of years) has changed regarding the understanding and role of women. See John Paul II's apostolic letter *Ordinatio Sacerdotalis* (1994) for evidence of this.

10. I have used the past tense here, in spite of the fact that this remains true of Catholic hierarchy and many devout men (and some women) Catholics. Arguments against ordination of women to the Catholic priesthood for example are based upon an assumed inferiority of women developed from Pauline texts in particular. The "different but equal" sentiments that condemn women to lesser positions of power in the church are also an example of this.

11. Daly, *The Church and the Second Sex*, 53.

12. Simone de Beauvoir, *The Second Sex*, trans. H. M. Parshley (London: Picador Books, 1949).

13. Daly, *The Church and the Second Sex*, 221.

14. In the "Post Christian Introduction" in *The Church and the Second Sex*, Daly speaks of the position she had taken in the first edition in terms of dis-ownership. That is to say, she speaks of herself in the third person, dissociating from and critiquing the views of the earlier Daly.

15. See Simone de Beauvoir, *The Second Sex*, Part III, in particular her discussion of the Mother and the Virgin Mary, 170ff. It is beyond the scope of this essay, however, to explore in great depth the relationship between Simone de Beauvoir's work and Daly's.

16. Daly, *The Church and the Second Sex*, 70.

17. See in particular Daly's chapters "Demon of Sexual Prejudice: Exercise in Exorcism" and "Roots of the Problem: Radical Surgery Required" in *The Church and the Second Sex*, 166–91.

18. Ibid., 223.

19. Ibid., 193–94.

20. Throughout this essay, where the term 'reality' is obviously contested, I use single quotes. Where it is not necessarily contested, I omit the quotes.

21. The irony here is that according to Meaghan Morris, this very point was made by Layleen Jayamanne at what Morris calls "the Mary Daly event" in Sydney in 1981. But in that scenario, it is a point made against Daly, rather than for her. See Morris, "A-mazing Grace," 70.

22. Daly, *Beyond God the Father*, 188.

23. Ibid., 189.

24. Nancy Fraser, discussing Foucault's work, also makes this point. She says: "Now, the fact that Foucault continues to speak (or at least to murmur) the language of humanism need not be held against him. Every good Derridean will allow that there is not, at least for the time being, any other language he could speak. . . . Foucault himself acknowledges that he cannot simply and straightforwardly discard at will the normative associations with the metaphysics of subjectivity." Nancy Fraser, *Unruly Practices: Power, Discourse, and Gender in Contemporary Social Theory* (Cambridge, U.K.: Polity Press, 1989), 57.

25. See, for example, her discussion of titles and roles within a workplace context: "In women one notices 'accommodation attitudes,' that is, a self-abnegating and flattering manner that is almost 'second nature.' Conditioning to such accommodation attitudes is intensified by such customs as nonreciprocal first naming, common even when the boss (Mr. Jones, Father Jones, Professor Jones or Doctor Jones) is thirty years of age and the secretary, who is sixty, is called 'Sally.' A similar custom is reference by 'the boss' to 'Sally' as 'the girl' in the office. A young male 'executive assistant' doing essentially the same work as Sally, for a much higher salary, is of course not referred to as a " 'boy.' " See Daly, *Beyond God the Father*, 136.

26. Daly, "Be-witching: The Lust for Metamorphosis," in *Pure Lust*, especially 390ff.

27. Taylor's comment occurs in a discussion of Heidegger in Mark C. Taylor, "Cleaving: Martin Heidegger," in *Alt∇rity* (Chicago: University of Chicago Press, 1987), 42–43. In response to the

interjector at the "Daly event" in Sydney in 1981, I would cite a claim such as this. Given that one grows up in a culture, how else can one speak except within its terms? Daly is challenging this and attempting to dissipate (a little) the boundaries. Taylor's quotation from Heidegger is Martin Heidegger, "Letter on Humanism," in *Basic Works*, ed. and trans. D. Krell (New York: Harper and Row, 1977), 235.

28. This point is reinforced in Daly, *Pure Lust*. See "On Lust and the Lusty," passim.

29. Daly, *Wickedary*, 86.

30. Ibid., 64.

31. Daly, *Beyond God the Father*, 8.

32. I thank Marilyn Frye for this insight.

33. Daly, *Beyond God the Father*, 33–34.

34. Daly, *Gyn/Ecology*, xi.

35. Ibid.

36. *Exodus* 3:13–15 New Jerusalem Bible (New York: Doubleday, 1985). The "I am has sent me to you" is the translation from the New Jerusalem Bible. For example, the sentence is also translated as "I am who I am." See RSV, Catholic ed. (Nelson, 1966).

37. New Jerusalem Bible, 85 n. g.

38. In the footnotes, the translators discuss the question of whether or not the intention of God is to give "his" name. They assume (not argue) that "he" does intend so doing and that is the context in which I am writing.

39. *Exodus*, New Jerusalem Bible, n. g.

40. Daly, *Pure Lust*, 26.

41. Daly, *Wickedary*, 82.

42. Daly, *Pure Lust*, 403.

43. Ibid., 405.

44. Ibid., 407–8.

45. Ibid., 25.

46. Ibid., 408.

47. Ibid., 91.

48. Daly *Wickedary*, 99.

49. Ibid., 133.

50. See Moira Gatens, "A Critique of the Sex Gender Distinction," in *A Reader in Feminist Knowledge*, ed. Sneja Gunew (New York: Routledge, 1991); and see Grosz, *Volatile Bodies*.

51. A recent example of this is in Lesley Instone's essay "Denaturing Women," in *Contemporary Australian Feminism 2*, ed. Kate Pritchard Hughes (South Melbourne: Addison Wesley Longman, 1997). Instone accepts Carlassare's diagnosis of Daly as essentialist, noting that Carlassare qualifies her position by arguing that Daly's essentialism is progressive rather than regressive. Such essentialism is strategic as it is "seen as contextual and emerging from specific historical and social situations" (155).

52. Braidotti, *Patterns of Dissonance*, 206.

53. Ibid.

54. Morris, "A-mazing Grace," 72.

55. Thank you to Sarah Hoagland for this expression.

56. Daly, *Gyn/Ecology*, xi.

57. Ibid., 207.

58. Daly, *Wickedary*, 251.

59. Ibid., 82.

60. Simone de Beauvoir, *The Second Sex*, 54.

61. Ibid., 54–56.

References

Daly, Mary. 1973. *Beyond God the Father: Toward a Philosophy of Liberation*. Boston: Beacon Press.

———. 1978. *Gyn/Ecology: The Metaethics of Radical Feminism*. London: Women's Press.

———. 1984. *Pure Lust: Elemental Feminist Philosophy*. Boston: Beacon Press.

———. 1985. *The Church and the Second Sex*. Boston: Beacon Press.

Daly, Mary, in cahoots with Jane Caputi. 1988. *Websters' First New Intergalactic Wickedary of the English Language*. London: Women's Press.

de Beauvoir, Simone. 1949. *The Second Sex*. Translated by H. M. Parshley. London: Picador Books.

Descombes, Vincent. 1982. *Modern French Philosophy*. Translated by L. Scott-Fox and J. M. Harding. New York: Cambridge University Press.

Easthope, Anthony, and McGowan, Kate, eds. 1992. *A Critical and Cultural Theory Reader*. St. Leonards: Allen & Unwin.

Fraser, Nancy. 1989. *Unruly Practices: Power, Discourse, and Gender in Contemporary Social Theory*. Cambridge, U.K.: Polity Press.

Grosz, Elizabeth. 1989. *Sexual Subversions: Three French Feminists*. St. Leonards: Allen & Unwin.

———. 1994. *Volatile Bodies: Toward a Corporeal Feminism*. Bloomington: Indiana University Press.

Gunew, Sneja, ed. 1991. *A Reader in Feminist Knowledge*. New York: Routledge.

Heidegger, Martin. 1977. "Letter on Humanism," in *Basic Works*. Translated and edited by D. Krell. New York: Harper and Row.

John Paul II, 1994. *Ordinatio Sacerdotalis*. http://www.knight.org/advent.

Morris, Meaghan. N.d. "A-mazing Grace: Notes on Mary Daly's Poetics" *Intervention* 16:70–92.

Piercy, Marge. 1990. *Circles on the Water*. New York: Alfred A. Knopf.

Pritchard Hughes, Kate, ed. 1997. *Contemporary Australian Feminism 2*. South Melbourne: Addison Wesley Longman.

Schüssler Fiorenza, Elizabeth. 1992. *But She Said: Feminist Practices of Hermeneutical Interpretation*. Boston: Beacon Press.

Taylor, Mark C. 1987. *Alt∇rity*. Chicago: University of Chicago Press.

9

Wicked Caló: A Matter of the Authority of Improper Words

María Lugones

I like dictionaries. I am also suspicious of them. I am politically discriminate, critical, active as I "look up words." I am particularly attracted to dictionaries of the linguistically improper. Keeping in mind questions of linguistic historicity, of the politics of everyday interaction in the creation of meanings and of the politics of compilation, I focus in this essay on dictionaries that in different ways contest the dominant linguistic order. In particular, as my attention is placed on strategies of linguistic resistance and on the possibilities of communication across different forms of linguistic resistance, I strive to politicize the practice of "looking up words."

I am interested in dictionaries that are contestatory in that they "capture" linguistic revolt and resistance as one might capture an image in a picture without denying either its ephemerality or historicity. Since linguistic contestation is ephemeral and vulnerable to the politics of co-optation, appropriation, and ossification, one facet of linguistic resistance is strategic. Linguistic resistance includes strategies to counter or survive co-optation, appropriation, and ossification. Linguistic contestation also refuses a "natural" conception of meaning, including a naturalized sense of linguistic "evolution." Many contestatory dictionaries include "philosophies" that perform a transformation of the politics of putting words together in networks of words. They unmask and upset domination through words in ways that mirror the transgressive lives and possibilities of those who create meaning and of those who compile the transgressions. Often, no distinction can be drawn between creating meaning and compiling it or between those who do the one or the other task. The lexicographer's presumed disengagement and political innocence are troubled in the process of politicization; or, maybe better expressed, the lexicographer ceases to be and joins the linguistic activist.

Here I will limit myself to reflection on two dictionaries of the improper: *El Libro de Caló/Pachuco Slang Dictionary*, compiled by Harry Polkinhorn, Alfredo Velasco, and Mal Lambert and published by Atticus Press in San Diego in 1983; and *Websters' First New Intergalactic Wickedary of the English Language*, conjured by Mary Daly "in cahoots" with Jane Caputi and published by Beacon Press in Boston in 1987. These dictionaries are very different from each other. The politics of their relation to English and "Anglicity" are markedly different. The networks of speakers in linguistic resistance are quite different. Their strategies/methodologies of "putting words together" are very different. They stand related in my linguistic practices as contemporary documents of linguistic resistance, as significant pieces of affirmation of improper speaking that are "destined" not to speak to each other by the politics of fragmentation. Putting them together does not put them in conversation, but rather it enables me to raise and consider questions that are otherwise outside of what can be thought or spoken in the politics of communication: questions of communication across resistances to linguistic domination.

The logic of linguistic domination requires that questions of communication across resistances to linguistic domination lie outside what can be thought or spoken. Though linguistic resistance is coexistent with linguistic domination, given that the logics of resistance and oppression exclude each other, linguistic domination conceptually hides linguistic resistance. Locating myself on the side of resistance and comparing dictionaries of the improper enables me to address questions of communication across resistances. Once linguistic resistance and strategies of resistance are in focus I can consider the barriers to communication across resistances.

A sense has developed in theorizing resistance to oppression that the conceptual place opened by subjecting binaries and dichotomies to critique and restructuring—a place understood in spatial terms as a boundary or border or a place in-between—provides the conditions for communication across resistances.[1] With my attention on both *El Libro de Caló* and the *Wickedary* and on their strategies of contestation of domination, I take up this sense and consider whether all resistance to oppression stakes a place that challenges fragmentation, the pulling apart and dismembering of live beings in their constructions as subjugated or outcast. Putting them together enables me to ask whether their strategies constitute in-between places, "third-spaces" for communication. Could a Wicked Caló be an in-between communicative tongue? These are complex questions in the politics of communication that I can begin to consider by putting these two resistant dictionaries "together," though as one quickly uncovers, there is deep discontinuity that marks the attempt at crossing between them.

Looking Up Words

When I look through dictionaries I consider the words I "look up" as inserted in networks of words. It is obvious that no word stands alone as meaningful. As I think of networks of words, I also think of meanings as devised, settled, negotiated in an infinitude of interactions.[2] I imagine the negotiations among very different folks, in very different geographies, standing in particular relations of power. I wonder whether the linguistic exchanges left room for challenges to the established order of things. This wondering leads me to look for traces of such challenges. I imagine who the interlocutors might have been and whether they would have been conceptually banished in the linguistic exchange. I look for clues of such banishment. I wonder about possibilities of infiltrating the linguistic history, influencing meaning.

Dictionaries, I have come to understand, are very significant in this history. As I think of geographies and relations of power in linguistic interactions, I think of metropoles and colonies, of houses of prostitution, and houses of government, of people garnering strength under brutal domination through words, of people exercising brutal power through their mastery over language. Which dictionaries contain which histories? Which dictionaries capture resistant meanings? Which dictionaries draw territorial boundaries with the power of the tongue? What is the exercise of looking up a word? In which dictionary? These I understand as questions of linguistic politics.

A sense of the history of linguistic interaction among politically and economically positioned linguistic agents is absent in most dictionaries. Words appear as historically unplaced with two familiar exceptions: the practice of providing a word's etymology and the practice of recording word usage. The politics of these practices is not often discussed in the dictionaries' philosophical or historical sections. Etymological comments mark frozen "original" evolutionary linguistic moments, disconnecting contemporary users from a linguistic relation to a history of significant power shifts, linguistic rebellions, linguistic banishments, linguistic domination. In this sense, etymology is not genealogy of meaning. It connects them instead to a pristine, depoliticized moment that makes the language user a historically dislocated participant in some grand tradition. The politics of the choice of tradition is left unspoken. In my experience of looking up words in dictionaries of Mapuche, Guarani, Pachuco Caló, and Lunfardo, the practice of offering etymologies in this sense of providing an original tie, a frozen linguistic moment, is absent.

The lexicographers' interest in etymologies is not an interest in unveiling political relationships lived through linguistic interaction. Rather, the etymological impulse ossifies a word's relationship to some language and geography that has been given a privileged status, an "original" linguistic standing. Consider the following as an example: *Webster's New Collegiate Dictionary* (8th ed.) gives several meanings for *black* including "having dark skin, hair, and eyes: swarthy" and "(1): of or relating to a group or race characterized by dark pigmentation; esp: of or relating to the Negro race (2): of or relating to the Afro-American people or culture." We find no traces of the highly political interactions fashioning these meanings in the etymology, nor are we given to understand the politics of meaning formation. Rather we are taken back to an original linguistic point: to the Latin *flagrare*, "to burn." The dialogical political history of the change from *negro* to *black* is not displayed in the etymological investigations in *Webster's*; the linguistic history of racialization is left outside of the question of origins. Rather, a lineage is traced that ties *black* to one of the classical European languages.

The politics of recording usage are equally underhanded. When we look at the *Oxford English Dictionary* we can see a clear tie between recording usage and the formation of a national language. Dialectal usages are noted only when they contribute to the formation of a national language. The politics that guides the selection of "usages" is not problematized. Why select some usages over others? What does that reveal about the political linguistic project expressed in that particular dictionary? Who does the selecting? What power does the lexicographer have to make the selections widely authoritative?

As one looks up words with these questions in mind, it becomes clear that the politics of compiling a dictionary intersect the negotiation of meaning in interactions among people in relations of power. Words are placed in networks of words that constitute dictionaries by people in particular linguistic and political relations to the compiling task. Much of the time the intersection is unmarked. The accounts of meaning that particular dictionaries perform may locate both meaning and the lexicographer's task in the realm of the "natural" rather than the "political." The lexicographer is of course understood as dealing not with a formal, but with a natural, language. There is no closed calculus with a closed semantics that the lexicographer can appeal to with precision. But the language is also conceived as natural in the sense of "not political." The lexicographer's task is not overtly declared as inscribed within, nor dictated by, political concerns and forces. The practices of compiling dictionaries and looking up words are understood as politically innocent.

The lexicographer is a personage in the politics of certain kinds of dictionaries: the dictionary's *compiler*, someone whose task is to "detail the signification of a word" (*OED*). The "lexicographer" may well be a committee delegated by a society dealing with the politics of words, with the mastery of words. In *Through the Looking Glass*, Alice gets irritated at Humpty Dumpty for changing the meaning of words in the course of argumentation. She declares to him that one cannot do that ("cannot" as in "it is logically impossible"). Humpty, shifting from logics to politics, informs her that it all depends on who is the master of words (Carroll, 269). I wonder who in this business of compiling words into dictionaries is the master of words and whether the "lexicographer" is such a person.

It is interesting and to the point that in the "Historical Introduction" in the *Oxford English Dictionary* we learn that the dictionary took seventy-one years, from 1857 to 1928, to compile and that the Philological Society resolved on December 8, 1859, that "a committee be appointed to draw up a set of Rules for the guidance of the Editor of the Society's new English Dictionary" (vi). Two years had passed since the dean of Westminster encouraged the society to make plans for a new dictionary and it took all of two years to resolve to set in motion the formation of a rule-drawing committee to guide the dictionary's eventual editor. So, it isn't simply a matter of working hard and authoring a scholarly book. The *OED* had many editors, subeditors, assistants, contributors, and helpers and a significant number of guidelines and policies as well as a philosophy regarding word mastery.

That the politics of compilation intersect the negotiation of meaning in interactions among people in relations of power is clearly exemplified in the *OED*'s philosophy, as explained in a section titled "Vocabulary." The master of words is to attempt the task of grasping the "vast aggregate of words and phrases which constitutes the Vocabulary of English speaking men . . . *as a definite whole*" (x). When this is attempted, the "whole" proves treacherous and must be conceived in naturalistic terms as akin to "one of those nebulous masses familiar to the astronomer" or "one of those natural groups of the zoologist or the botanist." In both cases there is "a clear and unmistakable nucleus" that shades off on all sides and is "linked on every side to other species, in which the typical character is less and less distinctly apparent, till it fades away in an outer fringe of aberrant forms." "So the English vocabulary contains a nucleus or central mass of many thousand words whose 'Anglicity' is unquestioned"; "they are the *Common Words* of the language. But they are linked on every side with other words which are less and less entitled to this appellation" (x). The lexicographer must, like the naturalist, draw the line somewhere in each divergent direction.

The philosophy of meaning in the "Vocabulary" also speaks about language and time. The living vocabulary does not stay still, making the whole yet more difficult to grasp. In this history, the lexicographer also has political decisions to make. It is not a matter of whether a use survives, but whether a use can be traced as part of the history of the central mass whose Anglicity is unquestioned. The *OED* aims at exhibiting the signification of English words within certain chronological limits: it contains words used since the twelfth century. The date was chosen so that the "Anglo-Saxon" vocabulary could be included. But up to the fifteenth century the language existed only in dialects, all of which had a literary standing. Words from these dialects are then included, up to the year 1500. Afterward, dialectal words are not admitted, revealing the connection between linguistic unification and the formation of the nation state, the modern English nation. After 1500, dialects are relegated as outside the living *English* language. There are "many claimants to admission" into the recognized vocabulary and some will be included if they become "Common Words." Others that are "current coin" with some speakers and writers may never make it to "good English" (*OED*, x). There is certainly a question of propriety: the question of politics and the question of mastery over words are not separate.

As I place dictionaries in relation to linguistic resistance, I politicize the practice of looking up words and unveil the politics of compilation. Resistance moves from a natural to a political understanding of meaning creation.[3] The move can be made by either the compiler or the one looking up words or both. Moving this way involves a reconceptualization of linguistic interaction. It involves attention to the network of speakers as located historically and socially in relations of power that have linguistic dimensions. It also involves looking closely at the methodology of putting words together in networks of words, in particular the methodologies of unveiling or hiding linguistic contestation, of unveiling or hiding alternative, intersecting, in-tension sense or worlds of sense. The practice of reducing linguistic history to original points while erasing the linguistic genealogy, and the erasing of particular linguistic strands toward linguistic unification, are methodological examples of hiding contestation and exhibiting a politics of domination in compilation that is necessarily unmarked. The necessity is political, not logical.

As I move to consider frankly contestatory dictionaries, I pay attention to the "compilers' " methodologies of unveiling contestation, that is, strategies of engagement with linguistic disruption and its possibilities. *As methodologies become strategies, compilers become activists*. My own way of moving as I participate in the politics of linguistic contestation at this level is marked by my own history of engagement with languages and communities of resistance, with radical lesbian living and theorizing, with Chicano life and politics in diverse locales, as well as by a troubled relation to both lesbian separatism and Chicano nationalism. I have maintained a willingness and ability to get inside the *Wickedary* and *El Libro de Caló* and activate their sense-making and sense-recording moves. I consider their relation in a fragmented political terrain at the level of methodology, the politics of putting the networks of words/speakers/writers together. My attention is not on critique, but rather on understanding and appreciation of both sets of strategies and on the difficulties of moving between them. Daly suggests a strategy of moving to other resistant word networks, a strategy of which I do become critical as I move from the *Wickedary* to *El Libro de Caló*. As I cross from one world of sense to the other—these are indeed very different conceptually—I find myself reversing the direction of engagement that Daly suggests. I find myself problematizing the spatiality of her reaching outside of her tongue. *El Libro de Caló* does not contain any parallel strategy. The attempt to cross places me in a deeply discontinuous linguistic space. My own way of moving as a linguistic activist, one cognizant of both tongues and of the lived environments within which their transgressive senses are enacted, places me in a very tense position, one in which discontinuity in linguistic transgression is experienced as disturbing. I experience discontinuity not only in moving between the two worlds of sense, but more profoundly, at the level of methodology/strategy. The compilers' strategies of contestation in the two dictionaries are discontinuous with each other. It is from this vantage point, dwelling in this disconcerting discontinuity, that I stake out a place from which to understand the possibilities of and barriers to communication across resistances to linguistic domination. These I understand as crucial issues in a politics of linguistic transgression.

The *Wickedary*

In the *Wickedary* there is a sustained theoreticopractical line of thought

created/conjured among women
in different emotive tonalities
in different dialogic ambiances
in different moments of their relationship
in different positionalities

The *Wickedary* is a linguistic political contemporary document of resistant lesbian relating, an explicitly and deeply interactive linguistic adventure that both theorizes and disrupts its own relation to patriarchal domination. In this book words are understood to be guides for women in a linguistic journey to a world other than patriarchy. The sociality of this network of words and its techniques of disruption and resistance stand in clear defiance of the rules of lexicography and call the reader/journeyer to an active, irreverent, transformative interpretation of the practice of looking up words.

Central to the logic of the *Wickedary* is the contradiction between the realities named by the guiding words "foreground" and "background." An articulate and elaborate consciousness of this contradiction permeates the movement of the book. Women and animals, captive in the logic of the foreground, are turned passive, tame, by it. The background understands women and animals as active, untamed, wild. It is central to the foreground that its sense be handled, heard, spewed as exhausting the possibility of sense, that those outside its sense are outside sense. Thus those in the foreground cannot comprehend the background or the very possibility of its sense. The juxtaposition of foreground and background or the journey from foreground to background cannot be conceived from the foreground. The logic of the background comprehends the move from foreground to background and the elaborate techniques of resisting the foreground's sense. The preoccupation and focus on the foreground in the negotiation of meanings in the naming makes clear the depth of fluency in the language of the foreground. The logical relation between foreground and background is the relation between the logics of oppression and resistance. The woman who reads the *Wickedary* becomes conscious of her being positioned with respect to this contradiction. Her working her way through the network of words changes her own relation to this contradiction and to other women who are also positioned in relation to it.

How and why would one use the *Wickedary?* As a user of conventional dictionaries the reader may not begin the book at the beginning. She may rather begin by looking up words. But then, what words would she look up? A scholar of Daly's work may have words to look up, but surely the *Wickedary* is not a book written to inform on the proper use of Daly's and Caputi's vocabulary. It is unlikely that the reader would be looking up a word she has on her tongue, rather she may open the book and become curious as to what "luster," "nag," "gossip," or "gooney" might "mean." Soon the reader comes to understand that this is not a dictionary in any conventional sense, but rather something like a counterdictionary, an undoing of propriety, of convention, of fixed meanings and rules, of standard morphologies. She may then become interested in the book's structure and philosophy. The *Wickedary* is not a dictionary but a philosophical work that is eminently practical, one that takes the philosopher reader in confidence on a series of strategies and techniques of dismantling the being held linguistically captive. The organization of the *Wickedary* is philosophically constituted as a practice of transgression and metamorphosis.[4]

The *Wickedary* is organized in three phases. The first phase both resembles and differs from conventional dictionaries' sections on history, pronunciation, capitalization—issues of "morphology," grammar, and history. In this section the language user/reader is introduced to a defamiliarizing of her own relation to words and to the task of looking up words as a normed and passive task. If she begins the *Wickedary* at the first phase, she will encounter a sense that she is embarking in a linguistic, philosophical, political, highly social journey. The sections on spelling and capitalization, for example, open the user/reader to an unfamiliar sense of these words and to the experience of breaking words up in an unruly way in a search for meaning. To spell is grasped as casting spells, a practice that is attentive to context (privileging a woman-centered context) and that is freely playful and detectivesque with word morphology—the material form of a word. Words are heard and looked at for what they might suggest without a particular set of restrictions on what suggestions to entertain and follow. The impulse to hear and see anew, see and hear different possible semantic directions, is what is encouraged, what one is prepped in. Similarly with the practice of capitalizing, the *Wickedary* mocks and puns on the German tradition of capitalizing.

The second phase contains the three core Webs or "tribes of words." The three Webs are interconnected as they constitute the "journey" that takes the philosopher reader—active journeyer—from the patriarchal conceptual and linguistic taming, trapping, fixing of women and animals to nonpatriarchal possibilities. The Webs are attentive to the positionality of women as conjurers of words, attentive to dialogic ambiances, to time in relations among women, to women's passions in the sociality of their linguistic resistance.

Word Web One includes philosophical words that both provide clues to the ways of the journey toward the discovery of a world other than patriarchy and that exorcise those who would keep the woman from journeying. The clues do not direct her on a linear path, but rather provide guidance "on many complex routes" (xviii). The practice of looking up words begins to be defamiliarized while retaining a touch of the familiar. With conventional dictionaries one looks up words purposefully to check out meaning, spelling, pronunciation, etymology: one is looking for authoritative guidance into proper use. One does not read a conventional dictionary from cover to cover. It is in this sense a reference work. But clearly one is passive in the looking up to the extent that one is looking for linguistic propriety.[5] The *Wickedary* recommends not reading the book from cover to cover in linear fashion, but rather going back and forth among the Webs. The practice of looking up words is transformed into an active one. If she is actively into the journey toward a world other than the patriarchy, the woman who goes into this journey possibly will herself metamorphose.

The work of "weaving" the word networks toward "a world other than the patriarchy" is one of constructing a context that provides footing for women word travelers and it provides a way of traveling, of "crisscrossing and connecting" with other women. This movement is also a movement in time that contrasts sharply with fixing a word's origin. Sometimes the *Wickedary* goes for the point-of-origin technique, but to spin a different possible history of meaning for the word based on extremely different interactions that pay very much attention to the positionalities of the interlocutors in patriarchal history. The whole book is extremely playful, ironic, parodic: it pokes serious and disrespectful fun at the cohort of meaning authorities by unveiling in an outrageous way their devious and overwhelming relations to power. "Who is the master of words?" is problematized over and over in the way that tricksters can problematize mastery, not by having it, but by ridiculing it, declaring it obsolete, untruthful (manipulative), by artfully, conspiratorially and wickedly twisting it around so that words can place one's imagination at a creative edge with respect to the use of any tongue, the master's tongue included.

Because in the *Wickedary* there is no erasure of the politics of interlocution, because it is clear who is talking to whom and why, it is possible to find oneself at odds with the imaginative narrowness of the network of guiding words for "gossips" of the *English* Language. That is, it is possible to engage in a political critique of the relations among those who conceive the journey (and those who don't), of the journey itself, and of the world other than patriarchy that is understood as the cause of the journey. Here I am more interested in critiquing the sociality that grounds the linguistic adventure than in quarreling with the presuppositions and characteristics of the journey and its destinations. Or to put it another way, I am interested in noting the sociality that constructs/conjures the *Wickedary* as a point of departure for a critique of its politics. But the critique itself rests on a taking up of the *Wickedary*'s understanding of linguistic resistance and transgression.

As I begin to move my attention from within the *Wickedary* to its network of speakers as located historically and socially in relations of power that have linguistic dimensions, I think about the complexity of the routes pointed to by the word-clues. When I skipped to the Webs that constitute the third phase of the *Wickedary*, I found a preoccupation with and an anticipation of the "arrival of Others," other word Webs and other weavers. But the anticipation is not accompanied by a sense of relations of power with other weavers of words or even with other possible Webs. This is a historical linguistic leap that I consider from the vantage point of my engagement with lesbian communities as a marimacha, someone whose tongue and spatiality are related when it comes to resistance. The *Wickedary*'s anticipation either excludes marimachas from the circle of gossips or excludes consideration of linguistic relation of Wicked English to, for example, Pachuco Caló, one of the languages that marimachas have on their tongues. It also excludes attention to the spatiality of linguistic resistance and of linguistic domination. There is an unacknowledged, unexplored, uncritical spatiality to the *Wickedary*. It is as if Lesbians lacked spatiality, while instead their spatiality is troubled. Lesbians inhabit domains problematically their own, contested domains where they may lay their heads and form their coalitions. The *Wickedary* does invite Others to the weaving of other Sister Word-Works. There is a recognition that Wicked English is "far from sufficient" in the journeys toward worlds outside of patriarchy. But there is no vocabulary and no conceptual move, considering its relation to Anglicity and the spatial imperiousness of English. As Daly does turn on English as the language of the foreground, she does not turn on its spatial greed.[6] I wonder, as an active user of the *Wickedary*, what constitutes another tongue, a tongue separate from both Standard English and Wicked English, and how the lines are drawn when one considers the practice of looking up words to be an active one toward a world beyond patriarchy. What does "English Only" mean within the "gossiping out" that constitutes the *Wickedary*? What work have the conjurers done in rebellion against the "Anglicity" of patriarchal English dictionaries?[7] How are the realities of social fragmentation "mirrored" in the circles of speakers, in the conceptual word-routes into the world of the Strange?

El Libro de Caló

Suppose that I consider the *Wickedary*'s anticipation of the "arrival of others" and the "invitation" to other word-works to be a wider one than

Daly means it to be, one that recognizes the "world" outside domination to be more complex than a sister-world. Suppose that I approach that complexity through the tongues of other improper speakers, where speaking is an elaborate, artful, both transgressive and contestatory intersubjective accomplishment. Suppose the speaking that is artfully disruptive of the Anglicity at the core of this society and that claims its space, its geographical domain, and rules from within its "outlaw" condition is Pachuco Caló. Suppose that I want to investigate the distance to be thoughtfully walked between the methodology—the strategy—of making sense theorized in the *Wickedary* and that one expressed in *El Libro de Caló*, a dictionary of Pachuco slang. Suppose that. If you turn the suppositions over enough you can see that I have to ask a set of questions: Why would I begin from that direction, from the *Wickedary*'s anticipation of the "arrival of others"? Why would anyone coming from that direction—the *Wickedary*'s resistance to domination—want to have any Pachuco Caló in their mouths? "Arrival of others" where? Arrival at the streets of Sidro, Tijuas, Los, Diego? Of course that is not what Daly could mean. How do I know that she means arrival of others to territories where she resides? Because that linguistic terrain—Tijuas, Sidro, Los, Diego—is contested in such a manner that "anticipation of the arrival of others" to it is a heavy matter. That linguistic terrain is occupied in defiance. But then you may not see that I have to ask these questions precisely because the linguistic geography of which *El Libro de Caló* is part, is unknown to you.

Have you ever entered a book geographically? Like walking the streets of a place where folks put the words up there for public recognition, for difficult communication, emphatically marking the particularities of their expressive style, as assertion and defiance? Have you ever entered a word-book—a book of meaning—where the words are of a place, constitutive of a geography, turf-taking in an anticolonial mode? Have you entered such a book? "Entered" for what reason and in what fashion? Like a colonial thief, like a wanna-be, like a culture-vulture scholar, like a vato loco looking for your words in yet another taken domain, taken in reverse, disrupted like, in a transgression? Like, who are you to put this meaning in your mouth? Like, do you hear how it comes out when you say it? Have you ever walked into a book looking for/looking up words that you may not be able to have in your tongue? Have you ever walked into a book dangerously, carefully?

Ese, vato, chuco, cuate, cholo, chingon—is that you? Or some gabacho, guero guerinchi colichi, tagging along for the ride, "cause it seems cool? Ese, chicote, pon la palabra justa pa" que sepan su lugar, their place, like since when can they come and walk into this language? Like this book is a barrio painted emphatically for careful use! Placas marking a territory; "placas" is the crucial word here, the clue to the "entrance." Placas define this book. Plaquear: a word in the mouth and on the wall, bouncing back and forth demanding, conferring, public recognition. Placas define a geography and a subjectivity, a who is where: Tijuas, Sidro, Calecia, Califas, Chicali, Aztlan, Duque, Diego, T.J. Caló is a literate/literary defiant language pa los que tienen corazón in the land of Aztlan. This space is taken C/S. "Con safos," "a barrio copyright, patent pending—anything you say against me will bounce back at you . . . whether you like it or not, this is my reality" (Burciaga, 6).

Each letter of the alphabet is introduced en *El Libro de Caló* con una placa, marking over and over the geography where sense is made, a place conceived politically both as the place of the Mexica, Aztlan, and as the place of survival and resistance de los cholos, both places inscribed en las placas C/S. The web of words en *El Libro de Caló* make up a world, a changing world, where meaning has been made interactively in the "San Diego–Tijuana extended community."[8] So you know where you are entering, las A's—placa style—says "abuson," "agringado," "aguas," "aguila," "a la brava." The place of which these words make sense and where their sense is made unfolds as the book takes us from word to word as a place of resistance. In the A's, assimilation into the white middle-class is rejected, the need for folks to tell each other to watch out, to be careful, is marked repeatedly, taking advantage of people is marked as an insult, daring is noted as necessary but not romanticized, the political importance and meaning of Aztlan are emphatically marked. The book expresses resistant moves. The meaning and the making are as ephemeral as resistant moves are ephemeral: you can anticipate their being turned dull and being given a new edge.

At first sight *El Libro de Caló* may appear to be a translation tool. It helps to understand its methodology to see why it cannot be such a tool. I want to argue that it appropriates the translation-dictionary format and disrupts it, changes its meaning by defying the linguistic relation as one to be described as between source and target languages. *El Libro de Caló* artfully documents the disruption of Anglicity in a world to which it introduces you. *El Libro*'s methodology—its strategy—is from within the geography and its intersubjective conceptualization as a contested territory. The strategy is to show up the world one is to deal with, live in, negotiate, appreciate if one is to participate in communication and to show it up in its territoriality, rather than as a system of thought. Speakers of Caló constantly disrupt English or Spanish or Spanglish with linguistic resistance, constantly politicize speaking. So you don't access the book with concepts in your mind from an Anglicity-centered construction of "reality" and look up how it is said in Caló. Caló shows up its disregard for how reality is conceived Anglo centeredly. So looking up *agringado* is very unlike holding the word *bottle* in one's tongue and going to see how that concept that one already contains is said in French. It is also very unlike encountering the word *bouteille* and looking up the English "equivalent." Why would one look up the word *agringado*? If you are looking it up who you are matters a lot. The relations derided by the word confront you as you are looking it up. The practice of looking up words is politicized; colonial encounters are troubled in the linguistic turn. And you may be put on your toes as it makes you real conscious that the words do not sit well on just anyone's tongue. It takes a life of transgression against colonialism to approach this argot from outside its linguistic borders con corazón.

In the Discontinuous Zone

El Libro de Caló is a document of linguistic strategy that does not begin from an articulate theory of oppression. The movement in *El Libro* is mimetic, it pulses with the movement of Caló. The movement in the *Wickedary* is the movement of weaving. This is conceived as a collective and dialogic activity. Yet the collective engagement is not one that moves outside of Daly's imagination even when the circle of gossips that she keeps in mind is quite real. The *Wickedary* rather maps Lesbian meaning creation by providing an articulate understanding of what is to be resisted and of the direction of resistance. Its central movement is not collective or dialogical. It is in this respect a work of philosophy that is put into practice. But the practice is tightly tied to the theoretical framework. Its vocabulary generates from the theoretical framework. The theoretical framework provides the generative themes for both the creation and the compilation of words. As a blueprint for linguistic transgression, the *Wickedary* requires that one share its philosophy.

El Libro de Caló participates instead in a collective strategy of territorial linguistic contestation that is not initiated from a theoretical blueprint. It looks at linguistic transgression as it is lived and enacted in a politics of linguistic confrontation against domination that is piecemeal. In this respect its methodology is deeply transgressive as it abandons the arrogance of mastery. *El Libro* acknowledges the impossibility of capturing live transgression with any permanence. In that sense it acknowledges its own necessary obsolescence. Yet it sees its contribution in its enabling us to look into a culture and "apprehend a style of expression the depths of which usually escape us in their very ephemerality" (vii). *El Libro* also strives to work against overgeneralization and thus emphasizes its territory as the San Diego–Tijuana extended community (viii). As it offers the sense of a word it cautions us to understand what it offers as "approximations." Its methodology of compilation emphasizes territory and uses interviews with speakers in the region. The book's format evidences a world whose geography is collectively taken through language. That is why I have emphasized the place given to the placa in *El Libro de Caló*. The value of affirming subjectivity and its connection to geography constitute a living strategy that *El Libro* takes up, a strategy of linguistic contestation that does not require a political program. The anticolonial tenor of the politics is deployed in a way that has certain values. This is clear in the connection between subjectivity and geography. But these values are not articulated beforehand in a philosophy that serves as a generative linguistic framework. The "mastery" over words is rather an artful occupation by Chucos that is particularly public, geographically located, and ephemeral. The possibility for significant departures from past creations is entirely conceivable here; you can predict more linguistic creativity, but its anticipation is guided by what has happened historically, what's happening in the barrio as met by the contestatory stance of the speakers/writers.

So as I think of the distance to be understood between the *Wickedary* and *El Libro de Caló*, I rethink the order of entrance, the possibility of anticipation, the communicative strategies of improper communication. I think of speakers in interaction, in tension. I think of linguistic erasure, of linguistic insurrection. As I dwell in the discontinuous space I put aside the temptation to mediate and appease and manage through translation. This is a temptation of bilinguals, people who have both resistant tongues in their mouths. But I am looking for unmediated communication. Translation in this context is a form of heroism, of managing and digesting resistant sense as if there were no lived connections to be fashioned, struggled for, in resistance to domination in a linguistic mode.

As I step into the discontinuous zone, I ponder whether I am stepping out or into a boundary/border/linguistic in-betweenness. Because the territoriality of Caló is not conceived in the anticipation of gossips I think of the impossibility, after all is said and done, of a "wicked caló" as an in-between tongue. As I juxtapose them, the rift between the wicked of the *Wickedary* and the Caló of *El Libro de Caló* yawns before me. The *Wickedary* doesn't take to the streets to learn its strategy but rather challenges a system of domination through conceptual maneuvering, while *El Libro de Caló* ties linguistic contestation to a collective holding of a territory. Caló does indeed constitute a linguistic restructuring of linguistic binaries in a spatial mode. An in-between tongue indeed, not captured by bilinguality, but obliterating it. The *Wickedary* is not at home in-between. It stakes its "domain" in the "background," dissociating from domination as if one could wash oneself clean—conceptually, linguistically, carnally clean—of the whole affair. Thus it cannot meet up with Caló and with marimachas who exercise themselves in an in-between linguistic style that defies spatial rulings.

That marimachas need to contest the terms of the limits with the power of the tongue is indeed a matter of importance that *El Libro de Caló* does not take up. No lengthy entry for *marimacha* that matches the conceptual importance of *Aztlan* in this book. But the linguistic contestation that it apprehends and furthers in its spatial emphasis is one that marimachas must take up in coming to speak up their many names in defiance of Caló's construction of subjectivity. "A critical spatial imagination" (Soja, 5) is and needs to be part of what they/we interject in the linguistic terrain with their/"our"[9] tongues.

As I stake my place in the disconcerting discontinuity between these two modes of linguistic transgression, I am moved as a linguistic activist to reconceive theorizing linguistic resistance as frankly wordly, spatialized, contestatory.[10] But I am also moved to theorize linguistic resistance as speaking what is conceptually banned by domination, including the wildness of lively subjects turning words in our mouths and hands that mock subjection, words molded out of foul clay. As I do so I feel the urgency of having on the tip of my tongue an everyday vocabulary that contests patriarchies and colonialisms in one mouthful: a marimacha's urge. But there is a danger of making up, fantasizing, heroic speakers who fantasize a blueprint that generates only imaginary socialities. Moving among those who contest through the tongue, with a sharp and heady tongue, requires listening to the echoes of one's own impropriety.

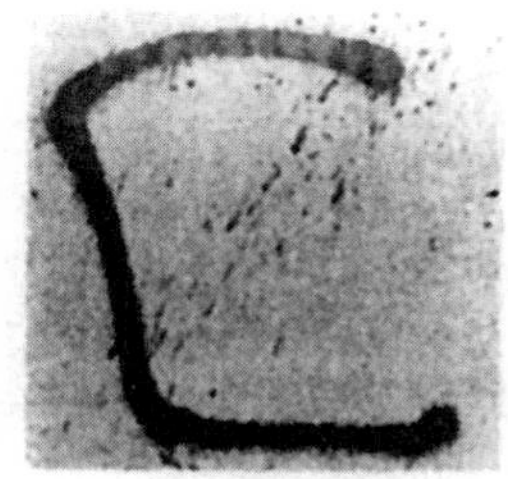

CON SAFOS

(*phrase*)

sm: None, except possibly from *zafo-a*, free; disentangled; exempt from danger.

nsm: Usually appears as "c/s" on walls and buildings in the *barrio*, meaning "Leave this alone" when written with something like "*Chato con Lupe*;" with luck; with a lot of "oomph;" doing something with a lot of force or feeling; "Whatever you say will bounce off me and stick to you;" similar to "safety" in English, when one child can hit another and say "safety," so that he can't be hit back.

Con Safos (C/S)

CORPOS

(*m.n.*)

sm: None.

nsm: Corpus Christi, Texas.

COTOREAR

Notes

1. See Gloria Anzaldúa, *Borderlands/La Frontera*; Homi Bhabha, *The Location of Culture* (in particular "The Commitment to Theory" and "The Postcolonial and the Postmodern: The Question of Agency"); Edward Soja, *Third Space*, Walter Mignolo, *The Darker Side of the Renaissance*, Guillermo Gomez Peña, *The New World Border*, as well my own "Purity, Impurity, and Separation."

2. See, for example, Volosinov/Bahktin's theorizing the interactive complexities in meaning formation in *The Dialogic Imagination, Marxism, and the Philosophy of Language*.

3. Think about the politics of linguistic purity in a multilingual society that has passed "English Only" laws. Think of the two men fired from their job in Texas for speaking Spanish, or of the woman ordered by a Texas court to speak English and not only Spanish to her daughter. See "Workers Fired for Speaking Spanish," *Santa Fe New Mexican*, August 15, 1997, A1 and A3.

4. Noting why the *Wickedary* is not really a dictionary defamiliarizes "real" dictionaries; it shakes the user of conventional dictionaries from a sense that particular conventional dictionaries exhibit linguistic facts and clues one in to their disguised politics.

5. One can, of course, engage in the practice of looking up words as an active and transgressive practice as one "uses" dictionaries of proper usage.

6. "Background" and "foreground" are spatial metaphors, conceptual spaces. The spatiality of the sociality is left at this metaphorical level.

7. Here I do not intend to emphasize Spanish/English code switching, but rather all code switching across any of the other worlds of sense linguistically contesting the colonialist and white supremacist tongue.

8. Though Caló contests English dominance in a much wider territory, *El Libro de Caló* "apprehends the style of expression" (see vii) of the San Diego-Tijuana extended community (viii).

9. I see "our" within quotes, because I am a marimacha and I am one of those outsiders to Caló and its territories who has carefully placed it in my mouth.

10. As I write this piece, Proposition 227 has passed in California. I heard on the grapevine that the passage of the proposition has also given agringado and pinchi gringo teachers, believers in English Only and linguistic "unity," the authority to tell children en East Los que "the proposition has passed, you cannot speak Spanish in California."

References

Anzaldúa, Gloria. 1987. *Borderlands/La Frontera*. San Francisco: spinsters/aunt lute.

Bakhtin, M. M. 1981. *The Dialogic Imagination*. Austin: University of Texas Press.

Bhabha, Homi K. 1994. *The Location of Culture*. London: Routledge.

Burciaga, Jose Antonio. 1993. *Drink Cultura*. Santa Barbara, Calif.: Joshua Odell Editions

Carroll, Lewis. 1960. *The Annotated Alice*, New York: Bramhall House.

Daly, Mary, in cahoots with Jane Caputi. 1987. *Websters' First New Intergalactic Wickedary of the English Language*. Boston: Beacon Press.

Gomez Peña, Guillermo. 1996. *The New World Border*. San Francisco: City Lights.

Lugones, María. 1994. "Purity, Impurity and Separation." *Signs* 19, no. 2: 458–80.

Mignolo, Walter. 1995. *The Darker Side of the Renaissance*. Ann Arbor: University of Michigan Press.

Polkinhorn, Harry, Alfredo Velasco, and Mal Lambert. 1983. *El Libro de Caló, Pachuco Slang Dictionary*. San Diego: Atticus Press.
Soja, Edward W. 1996. *Thirdspace*. Oxford: Blackwell.
Volosinov, V. N. 1986. *Marxism and the Philosophy of Language*. Cambridge: Harvard University Press.

10

"A Too Early Morning": Audre Lorde's "An Open Letter to Mary Daly" and Daly's Decision Not to Respond in Kind

Amber L. Katherine

> Reaching for you with my sad words
> between sleeping and waking
> what is asked for is often destroyed
> by the very words that seek it
> like dew in an early morning
> dissolving the tongue of salt
> as well as its thirst
> —Audre Lorde, "Sister, Morning Is a Time for Miracles" (1979)

One thing I have learned growing up politically and intellectually in the United States in the late twentieth century is that historical context matters. It doesn't just matter because it has become the correct alternative to essentialism and universalism. It matters because telling the truth matters and because radical and progressive change matters. And another thing, there are many ways to frame a context. I learned these things in the process of researching and writing my dissertation on Mary Daly's *Gyn/Ecology: The Metaethics of Radical Feminism* (1978), which I began with questions raised by Audre Lorde's response. In May 1979, Audre Lorde wrote a letter to Mary Daly offering her critical insights in response to *Gyn/Ecology*. Four months later, having received no reply, she published it as an open letter to the community of women.[1]

In the "New Intergalactic Introduction" in *Gyn/Ecology* (1990) Daly acknowledges Lorde's letter explaining that "for deep and complex personal reasons" she was "unable to respond to this lengthy letter immediately," and that it continues to be her "judgment that public response in kind would not be a fruitful direction" (xxx).[2] Still, I have wondered, *why* didn't Daly respond? This is also what my students most want to know after reading Lorde's letter. They move with vacuous speed to the conclusion that Daly was "just racist," a conclusion that at once presumes an understanding of Lorde's letter, dismisses historical understandings of Daly's decision, and situates them on the other side of racism. Likewise, I think, many feminist scholars, stepping around the ad hominem, have interpreted Daly's decision not to respond in kind as an admission of *Gyn/Ecology*'s inherent flaws. Whatever her personal reasons, I believe that there are deep and complex historical reasons that made it difficult for Daly to respond to Lorde's letter. In a poem, perhaps written to Mary Daly, Lorde also seems to have understood Daly's judgment in historical terms. The title of the poem, "A Too Early Morning," suggests that Lorde wrote the letter before the sun could illuminate her critical insights and before the possibility of fruitful dialogue became apparent. But what did Lorde say in the letter that dissolved like dew in the early morning? Why was the morning too early? I offer the following stories of context as perspective on feminist truth and change.

Lorde's Letter in the Context of Recent Academic Feminism

It is remarkable that Lorde's letter, the paradigmatic example of challenges to white feminist theory by feminists of color in the 1980s, has received, to my knowledge, no systematic analysis or criticism. Nevertheless, it has played a significant role in the development of academic feminist theory in the past ten years or so.

Linda Alcoff discussed both Daly and Lorde in her widely read and influential essay "Cultural Feminism Versus Post-Structuralism: The Identity Crisis in Feminist Theory" (1988). On Alcoff's reading of *Gyn/Ecology*, Daly "identifies a female essence, defines patriarchy as the subjugation and colonization of this essence out of male envy and need, and then promotes a solution that revolves around rediscovering our essence and bonding with other women" (Alcoff 1988, 410). Here Alcoff follows Alice Echols, who attributes this essentialist position to Daly on the basis of an inference from Daly's strategic emphasis on creating and discovering feminist culture. Alcoff concurs with Echols's inference on the grounds that "it is difficult to render the views of Rich and Daly into a coherent whole without supplying a missing premise that there is an innate female essence" (412). After reducing Daly's feminism to essentialism, Alcoff (again following Echols) renames Daly's position "cultural feminism" to separate it from "radical feminism," which was apparently not so inclined toward essentialism. (All of this without a word about the politics of naming or the subtitle of *Gyn/Ecology*.) Alcoff goes on to racialize the category "cultural feminism," suggesting, on her reading, that women of color, including Audre Lorde, had "consistently rejected essentialist conceptions of gender," and concluding, therefore, that cultural feminism is "the product of white feminists" (413, 412).[3] Thus, Alcoff situates Audre Lorde (and other Radical Womyn of Color) on the opposite side of the essentialist divide from Mary Daly (and the radical feminism of *Gyn/Ecology*) and then maps the essentialist divide onto the color line.

In "The Essence of the Triangle or Taking the Risk of Essentialism Seriously: Feminist Theory in Italy, the U.S., and Britain" (1989), Teresa de Lauretis attempts to reframe and critique feminist discussions of essentialism, Alcoff's in particular. De Lauretis makes a connection between the preoccupation in Anglo-American feminist theory with "typologizing, defining, and branding various 'feminisms' along an ascending scale of theoretico-political sophistication where 'essentialism' weighs heavy at the lower end" (4), and the "investments that feminism may have in the heterosexual institution" (32). In response to Alcoff's rendering of Daly's view into a coherent whole by supplying the "missing" essence, de Lauretis asks, "What is the purpose, or the gain, of supplying a missing premise (innate female essence) in order to construct a coherent image of feminism which thus becomes available to charges (essentialism) based on the very premise that had to be supplied?" (13). It is no coincidence, she argues, that the challenge to the social-symbolic institution of heterosexuality in the United States "has been posed, and most articulately by precisely those feminists who are then accused of separatism in their political stance and of essentialism with regard to their epistemological claims" (32). Interestingly, Mary Daly makes a similar connection in the *Wickedary* (1987). "Particularly insidious is the pseudofeminist usage of the term *essentialist* to label and discredit all feminist writing that dares to Name and celebrate the Wild and Elemental reality of women who choose to think and to be beyond the prescribed parameters of patriarchal mandates. Using this label, self-appointed thought police have campaigned to exclude Radical Feminists from possibilities of teaching and publishing and, indeed, surviving" (251). Both Daly and de Lauretis make connections between the charges of feminist essentialism and the interests some feminists may have in excluding lesbian/radical feminism from the field of feminist theory. What I want to suggest is that racializing the critiques/constructions of feminist essentialism, as Alcoff did, serves not only to exclude some feminist theories, but also to legitimize others. From the perspective of Alcoff's narrative, Lorde's letter reads like a forerunner of postmodern theory, not only dismissing the radical feminism of *Gyn/Ecology*, but also constructing postmodernism as the obvious theoretical preference of antiracist feminists.

In the opening essay of the anthology *Feminism/Postmodernism* (1990), titled "Social Criticism Without Philosophy," Nancy Fraser and Linda Nicholson call for feminist theory informed by the theoretical strengths of postmodernism and a postmodernism grounded in the strength of feminism's practical social criticism. In the process of making their case they offer the following narrative, which explicitly links critiques of racism (such as, and including, Lorde's) with a critique of what they call, appropriating the language of postmodern theorist Jean-François Lyotard, "quasi-metanarratives."

> In recent years, poor and working-class women, women of color, and lesbians have finally won a wider hearing for their objections to feminist theories which fail to illuminate their lives and address their problems. They have exposed the earlier quasi-metanarratives, with their assumptions of universal female dependence and confinement to the domestic sphere, as false extrapolations from the experience of the white, middle-class, heterosexual women who dominated the beginnings of the second wave. For example, writers like Bell Hooks [*sic*], Gloria Joseph, Audre Lord [*sic*], Maria Lugones [*sic*], and Elizabeth Spellman have unmasked the implicit reference to white Anglo women in many classic feminist texts. Likewise, Adrienne Rich and Marilyn Frye have exposed the heterosexist bias of much mainstream feminist theory. Thus, as the class, sexual, racial, and ethnic awareness of the movement has

> altered, so has the preferred conception of theory. It became clear that quasi-metanarratives hamper rather than promote sisterhood, since they elide differences among women and among the forms of sexism to which different women are differently subject. (33)

What Fraser and Nicholson suggest here is that implicit in the objections raised by marginalized women to mainstream feminist theories which "fail to illuminate their lives and address their problems" is a theoretical agenda, that is, "exposing quasi-metanarratives." The main lesson of the objections, then, is not to illuminate lives and address problems, but to expose bad theory. From the perspective of this narrative, Lorde's letter is, essentially, a postmodern critique that points the way to a theorizing that promotes sisterhood. What kind of theorizing is that? The kind informed by the theoretical strengths of postmodernism. Says who? Audre Lorde!

In "On the Logic of Pluralist Feminism" (1991), the only essay I have ever read that attempts to untangle the challenges raised by Radical Womyn of Color from the theoretical critiques they are said to advance, María Lugones explains how the two became confounded in the first place.

> In hearing the "What Chou Mean We, White Girl?" question, white/anglo women theorizers did not really hear an interactive demand, a demand for an answer. Looking at the resulting theoretical responses, it seems to me that what they heard was a radical attack on the activity of white women theorizing, an attack that seemed justified to them but also seemed to them to undermine fundamentally the possibility of any theorizing to the extent that it requires generalization. . . . Thus white theorizers interpreting the question saw a problem with the way they were theorizing: The "problem of difference" refers to feminist theories—these theories are the center of concern. (40–41)

From the perspective of Lugones's analysis, reading Lorde's letter as a critique of essentialism or quasi-metanarratives, rather than an interactive demand, generates a theoretical problem, but solving this theoretical problem does not answer the letter. Since Lorde explicitly says to Daly at the end of the letter, "as a sister Hag, I ask you to speak to my perceptions" (71), I believe that Lorde's letter should be read as a demand for an answer to the substantive issues raised therein rather than as a theoretical signpost.

Ironically, one of the substantive issues Lorde raises in the letter involves Daly's reading and use of her work. Lorde asks her, "Have you read my work, and the work of other Black women, for what it could give you? Or did you hunt through only to find words that would legitimize your chapter on African genital mutilation in the eyes of other Black women? And if so, then why not use our words to legitimize or illustrate the other places where we connect in our being and becoming? If, on the other hand, it was not Black women you were attempting to reach, in what ways did our words illustrate your point for white women?" (69). Might not similar questions be asked of feminist theorists who have cited Lorde's letter to legitimize their own theoretical projects? If Alcoff did read Lorde's work, then how could she situate Lorde and Daly on opposite sides of the essentialist divide based on an inference from Daly's strategic emphasis on creating and discovering feminist culture, since Lorde's work clearly and unambiguously shares this emphasis? How are the lives of poor and working-class women, women of color, and lesbians illuminated and how are their problems addressed in the pages of *Feminism/Postmodernism?* Did Fraser and Nicholson read the work of bell hooks, Gloria Joseph, Audre Lorde, María Lugones, Elizabeth Spellman, Adrienne Rich, and Marilyn Frye for what it could give them, or did they hunt for names that would legitimize their postmodern theoretical project, and in whose eyes?

Lorde's Letter in the Personal/Political Context of My Life

As an undergraduate at the University of Illinois in the early eighties I "came out" and took women's studies courses in search of lesbian feminist interaction and insight. After several courses cross-listed with women's studies that turned out to be academic business as usual, including an anthropology course that dismissed—without consideration—talk of matriarchal societies, I decided that academic feminism was more like aspirin than intellectual nourishment. In various feminist critiques of institutions and texts I found some relief from the headaches of patriarchal education, but I wanted more.[4] Having done diapers (I was *in* them) and Disney in the sixties and disco, dieting, and *Dallas* in the seventies, I was in search of an identity, a community, a movement—that is, anything to distinguish myself from my race- and class-privileged peers who were mostly buying an education as a ticket to corporate America. I wanted a *radical* education, one that would enable me to make connections and make a difference.

Mary Daly's *Gyn/Ecology*, assigned in a feminist theory course taught by graduate students, fed my imagination and provided my first practical instruction in radical thinking. Daly confirmed my suspicion that learning might involve more than consumption and regurgitation of what is said to be known. *Gyn/Ecology* promised insight into the processes of discovering and creating a new way of knowing and "Be-ing" in the world. *Gyn/Ecology* became my guidebook for "Metapatriarchal Journeying," introducing me to a "Crone-ology" that connected me with Western European women burned as witches, and authorizing the unthinkable (for example, that I might *become* something Other than a patriarchal Woman through identification with Witches and other Others). I was particularly attracted to her claim that radical feminists were all about making a world Other than patriarchy. The ones I found and joined in the mid-eighties, who were struggling to reinvent themselves along the lines of Daly's vision, were calling themselves Dykes and Separatists, and they were doing the most "A-mazing" things.

I do not remember my first reaction to Audre Lorde's "Open Letter" when I read it in the same feminist theory course along with other critiques of white feminist theory. What I thought generally about these critiques was that they did not have much to do with me, or I should say, I hoped they didn't. Understanding the connections between the challenges of Women of Color and my own life situation seemed beyond me.[5] At first, there was no imperative, no hunger for insight, built into my situation or my world that compelled me to figure out what they meant for me. My friend Jacqueline Anderson reminds me that this is the genius of segregation. It was only after leaving school, when I began to build my life around a radical lesbian feminist vision, that I remember becoming aware that there were implications in Lorde's letter for me on my Metapatriarchal Journey. It was among dykes and separatists that I learned about the lives of poor and working-class women, disabled women, survivors of incest and psychiatric abuse. I met the first women of color I could honestly call friends in the world of radical dykes and separatists. It was among these women that I began to understand the significant ways in which I wasn't as Other, as different, from my peers as I had intended to become. Ironically, by the late eighties, the charge of racism directed against the vision of radical lesbian feminist separatism I was living became a compelling reason to address the question of what the challenges, Lorde's included, had to do with me.

I signed up for a graduate course of study with Marilyn Frye, one of the few white radical lesbian feminist separatists I knew of with an explicitly antiracist perspective. After some more years of academic business as usual, including the feminist antiessentialist discourse above, I decided to write my dissertation starting from questions I had about the implications of Lorde's letter for Daly's *Gyn/Ecology*. When I began, I honestly did not know where the project would end. I knew, from the start, that I did not want to write an apologetic for Daly. (Even if I did feel Daly's work has been unfairly dismissed and that it deserved more engagement than it had received—at least until this anthology.) On the other hand, I did not want to write an indictment of Daly either. I choose not to establish myself as an antiracist by definitively establishing Daly as a racist. (Even if I did feel there were serious problems with *Gyn/Ecology*, especially in the Second Passage). I wanted to get beyond her guilt or innocence to something bigger, I did not know what. In my dissertation I argued that Lorde's letter was, among other things, an attempt to effect a shift in Daly's thinking that would strengthen her work and help realize the vision she and Lorde shared. I argued that Daly's radical feminist project in *Gyn/Ecology* should be reconstructed, rather than abandoned, especially by radical white European American feminists with an interest in pluralist feminist theory. Still, through much of the process of writing this dissertation I was bothered by what that something bigger was that I wanted it to be a part of.

The answer came, in the late fall of 1995, after black lesbian poet and community activist Terri Jewell, took her own life. The year before, when I had mentioned to Terri the subject of my dissertation, she was encouraging and affirmed the importance of the project. Her affirmation was vitally important to me because I loved her work and because of the kinship between her work and Audre Lorde's. I really wanted to ask her *why* my work was important, but I was afraid to reveal my own lack of clarity. In a personal tribute to her life and her work I reread Terri's poems. In the poem "Show You Here" I found an answer. The poem begins

among my people
it is rude
to listen to another
without making noises
of acknowledgment.

In the poem she names things racist and sexist people say that she suggests are dangerous to listen to "without sucking one's teeth." In the end she proclaims,

i am a black woman.
i am a lesbian.
now make a noise
of acknowledgment.

A light went on. Perhaps the importance Terri found in my project was the acknowledgment of Lorde's letter. Lorde had sucked her teeth in response to Daly's presentation of non-European women only as victims and preyers-upon of one another and proclaimed the power and strength and nurturance in the traditions of bonding among African women. Daly did not make a noise of acknowledgment in response to Lorde's letter. The bigger thing beyond Daly's guilt or innocence, I began to understand, was to show that I heard, regardless of what Daly did or ever does. It was, after all, an *open* letter to the community of women.

Lorde's Letter in the Context of Her Common Ground with Daly, 1977–79

The letter is unique among Lorde's political writings. Addressing Daly on a first-name basis, the letter is profoundly personal. In it she expresses gratitude, faith, and hope, which are rooted in the common political ground between them, as well as pain, frustration, and righteous anger, which emerge as she pieces together a picture of "a white woman dealing only out of a patriarchal western European frame of reference" (Lorde 1984, 68). In one of the paragraphs that begin the letter Lorde thanks Daly for having *Gyn/Ecology* sent to her and offers the insights of her letter in exchange for Daly's analyses, which she has found "full of import, useful, generative, and provoking" (67). In particular, when she began reading *Gyn/Ecology*, she reports, "I was truly excited by the vision behind your words and nodded my head as you spoke in your First Passage of myth and mystification. Your words on the nature and function of the Goddess, as well as the ways in which her face has been obscured, agreed with what I myself have discovered in my searches through African myth/legend/religion for the true nature of old female power" (67).

The researches Lorde is referring to here culminate in her seventh book of poetry, *The Black Unicorn* (1978), which Lorde would have been working on at the same time Daly was writing *Gyn/Ecology*. While the genres of these two books are different, the projects are very much the same. Both Lorde and Daly began from the impulse to generate radical woman-identified feminist insight through "deconstructing" patriarchal symbolic/mythological systems. While Daly's focus was on myths and symbols within the European tradition, primarily christian, Lorde's focus was on African myth/legend/religion, primarily from Abomey. Both understood the Goddess as a symbol of female power that had, for centuries, been obscured by and twisted into patriarchal myth. They shared a vision of women moving beyond lives governed by God the Father toward lives inspired by strong and life-affirming female symbolic figures. Indeed, Lorde and Daly understood this strategic emphasis on dis-covering and creating feminist culture as a necessary means to women's survival.

In 1977 Daly and Lorde both read papers on a Modern Language Association panel titled "The Transformation of Silence into Language and Action."[6] Daly read a paper containing sections from *Gyn/Ecology*, on Patriarchy as a State of Possession, as a State of War, and the "warrior element in Sisterhood." She argued, since "the Female Self is The Enemy under fire from the guns of patriarchy," a woman's survival depends on her resistance to assimilation. She must not be "tied back by old ligatures, old allegiances," Daly proclaimed.

She pledges allegiance to no flag, no cross. She sees through the lies of alleged allies. She re-veres no one, for she is freê-ing her Self from fears (8). Sisterhood is effective resistance to patriarchal assimilation. Unlike brotherhood, which involves the loss of individual identity to communal allegiances, Daly argued, sisterhood "has as its core the affirmation of freedom" (9). Under patriarchal fire, sisters must fight back as warriors, but Amazon bonding, Daly points out, "becomes truly dreadless daring only when it is focused beyond fighting," on the possibilities of female friendship which break the boundaries of the patriarchal "State of Possession" (9).

Following Daly's presentation, Lorde prefaced her paper with a poem from *The Black Unicorn* titled "A Song for Many Movements."[7] After the reading, which she dedicated to Winnie Mandela, Lorde reflected, "In listening to Mary I was struck by how many of the same words seem to come up. They did in her paper, and I know they do in mine, words such as *war, separation, fear* and the ways in which those words are intimately connected with our battlings against silence, and the distortions silence commits upon us" (1978b, 12). After explicitly stating the common themes in their work, she goes on in her paper to announce the discovery of a tumor in her breast. Although the tumor was benign, she explained how facing her mortality enabled her to see through the fear that "within the war we are all waging with the forces of death, subtle and otherwise, conscious or not, I am not only a casualty, I am also a warrior" (13). She attributes this knowledge, and the empowerment that it inspired, to her connections with women who shared a vision of "bridging our differences." In her words, "The women who sustained me through that period were black and white, old and young, lesbian, bisexual, and heterosexual, and we all shared a war against the tyrannies of silence. They all gave me a strength and concern without which I could not have survived intact" (13). Echoing Daly's call for resistance to the state of possession and false allegiances, she demands that "we not hide behind the mockeries of separations that have been imposed upon us and which we so often accept as our own" (14). In this moment, shortly before the publication of *Gyn/Ecology*, Lorde and Daly stood together raging against patriarchal oppression and calling for empowerment and resistance through sisterhood.

In the "Open Letter," Lorde charges, first, that in *Gyn/Ecology* Daly uses the tools of patriarchy against non-European women, African women in particular, by implying that all women suffer the same oppression. While Lorde agrees that "the oppression of women knows no ethnic nor racial boundaries," she insists that "that does not mean it is identical within those differences" (70). Beyond a sisterhood that fails to recognize different forms of patriarchal oppression, Lorde argues, there is still racism.[8] Second, she charges that excluding goddesses and other symbols of female power recoverable from nonwhite, non-European traditions on the presumption "that the herstory and myth of white women is the legitimate and sole herstory and myth of all women to call upon for power and background . . . serves the destructive forces of racism and separation between women" (69). Lorde argues that in making this presumption Daly has denied the "real connections" among women, that is, the spirit of resistance to patriarchal oppression through sisterhood evident in our unique histories and traditions. In this moment, shortly after the publication of *Gyn/Ecology*, Lorde took this stand against Daly, asking, "Should the next step be war between us, or separation?" and proclaiming, "Assimilation within a solely western european herstory is not acceptable" (69).

The Context of Radical Movement Politics of the Sixties and Seventies

From Civil Rights to Black Power

After the arrest of Rosa Parks in 1955, black activism in the United States took shape in the Civil Rights movement. In the late fifties and early sixties, a rainbow coalition of civil rights groups worked against segregationist policies using a variety of tactics, including economic boycotts, voter registration campaigns, sit-ins and mass demonstrations. Martin Luther King Jr. symbolized the vision of equality and justice for all regardless of skin color. In his "Letter from Birmingham Jail," King argued that Americans have a *moral* responsibility to break unjust laws. He claimed, "An unjust law is a code that a numerical or power majority group compels a minority group to obey but does not make binding on itself. This is *difference* made legal. By the same token, a just law is a code that a majority compels a minority to follow and that it is willing to follow itself. This is *sameness* made legal" (King 1963). The civil rights demand for an integrated, "color-blind" society was an effort to make white Americans act in accordance with the principle "equality and justice for all."[9] It was a challenge to the contradiction evident in the history of U.S. laws and programs conceived and justified on the basis of "real" or "biological" racial *difference*. Against this history of essentialist racism, it made sense to insist that people are all the *same* under the skin. This was the antiracist's position.[10]

By the mid-1960s the Black Power movement emerged, giving black activism a new shape and direction. To get a sense of this shift, consider how it is exemplified by developments in the political thought of Stokely Carmichael. An early advocate of the integrationist approach, Carmichael claimed that working in the Civil Rights movement had taught him that the problems associated with being black in the United States could not be solved by integration. In *The Black Power Revolt* (1968), Carmichael proclaimed that "integration is subterfuge for the maintenance of white supremacy," because for blacks it always meant assimilation (67). The problem, on this view, is not a few unjust laws, it is an entire system of injustice. "The reality is that this nation, from top to bottom, is racist," he insisted (70). Struggles for justice and equality must attack White Power, from social institutions and structural interests to the norms, values, and traditions that maintain white supremacy.

Effective resistance to white power, Carmichael insisted, would require "Black Power," achieved through self-determination, self-sufficiency, and cultural autonomy. At first, Carmichael worked with urban blacks in the Black Panthers to realize these ends "from a position of strength," within the U.S. context. At this point he argued that from such a position, "the masses could *make or participate in making* the decisions which govern their destinies, and thus create basic change in their day-to-day lives" (62). Cultural autonomy, he maintained, was strategically necessary to combat the psychological damage done to blacks in a society built on the distortion and denial of black experience: "Black people must redefine themselves, and only *they* can do that. Throughout this country, vast segments of the black communities are beginning to recognize the need to assert their own definitions, to reclaim their history, and their culture; to create their own sense of community and togetherness" (37).

They argued that redefinition could be accomplished through "the use of words." For example, "Negro" is a white term that blacks should reject because it has been associated with "lazy, apathetic, dumb, good timers, shiftless, etc." On the other hand, they suggest, "African-American" and "Afro-American" are terms that blacks can use to self-define as "energetic, determined, intelligent, beautiful and peace-loving" (37). A "common bond," a sense of community, is generated out of the practice of self-definition, such as that which is evoked when "people refer to each other as brother—soul-brother, soul-sister" (38). In addition, challenging white-identified self-understandings necessarily involved learning black history, since it was "not taught in the standard textbooks of this country." White supremacy maintained itself through the lie that blacks "had no culture, no manifest heritage, before they landed on the slave auction blocks in this country" (37). The Black Power movement was about fostering a new race consciousness and racial identity, one Carmichael and others sought to awaken among black people that was based on the unique histories and traditions of African-Americans and that gave rise to black interests, institutions, norms, and values. Notice the emphasis here is on racial *difference*, understood in social and historical, rather than essentialist, terms. Against the threat of assimilation, it made sense to insist that racial difference matters. In this moment, the antiracist called for a recognition of difference.

In 1971, reflecting on the lessons of political work within the U.S. context, Carmichael explained that he and other black activists soon learned, "our solution cannot be found within America, even though those of us who live in the United States may remain there physically" (1971, 177). As Carmichael's thinking developed, he adopted a global perspective by linking the plight of blacks in the United States with that of Africans on the continent. It was a mistake, he argued, to view slavery as the beginning of black history in the United States and colonialism as the beginning of black history on the continent. He pointed out that all Africans were connected by virtue of their land and civilizations prior to slavery and colonization: slaves were Africans who had been taken from their land and the colonized were Africans who had had their land taken from them (223). As a result of their losses, "Africans today, irrespective of geographical location, have a common enemy and face common problems. We are the victims of imperialism, racism, and we are a landless people" (222). Thus, Carmichael argues, "there is no way we can operate as an independent island surrounded by a hostile white community's police and military forces" (1971, 177).[11] He urged blacks in the United States toward separatism based on "the fact that we are an African people, that we must be about building a nation" (180), and in this work, he insisted, "we depend upon no one but ourselves" (196).

The Emergence of the New Left and Radical Feminism

The Civil Rights movement gave birth not only to Black Power, but also to the "New Left."[12] The emergence and development of the New Left was hastened by the shift in black activism away from coalitions toward separatist organizations. At first, this shift left many young white radicals, men and women, without a cause. In response to the idea that each oppressed group should organize autonomously, Students for a Democratic Society (SDS) produced a powerful indictment of American social and political values. The early theoretical positions of SDS, heavily influenced by the moral and political force of the Civil Rights movement, stressed the values of equality, brotherhood, and participatory democracy.[13] In contradiction with the commitment to these ideals, men on the Left maintained gender-role expectations consistent with those promoted in the larger mainstream culture. Leftist men saw themselves as the intellectual muscle behind the movement and relegated women to the less prestigious tasks, commonly referred to as the "shitwork." As social historian Todd Gitlin remembers it, "The fantasy of equality on the barricades shattered against the reality of the coffeepot and the mimeograph machine" (1987, 373). The competitive and aggressive intellectual mode that dominated the New Left, according to Sara Evans, excluded women from full participation and leadership roles and, at the same time, made it almost impossible for women to protest their exclusion. As Marlene Dixon pointed out, "Women had learned from 1964 to 1968 that to fight for or even sympathize with Women's Liberation was to pay a terrible price: what little credit a woman might have earned in one of the Left organizations was wiped out in a storm of contempt and abuse" (quoted in Burris 1971, 325).

As the New Left grew (tenfold between 1965 and 1967), and the Vietnam War escalated, concern with equality, participation, and process gave way to "a kind of macho stridency and militarist fantasy" (Evans 1980, 200). As Gitlin put it, "In the rush toward phantasmagorical revolution, women became not simply a medium of exchange, consolidating the male bond, but rewards for male prowess and balm for male insecurity" (1987, 372). Among the "revolutionary" leaders, Marge Piercy charges, "fucking a staff into existence" was only the extreme form of what passed for common practice in many places (Piercy 1969, 430). In addition to being pressured by "male heavies," movement women were kept from challenging their own exploitation, in a movement that claimed to be for "human liberation," by a concern for the "larger justice," which on Piercy's analysis, reflected the psychological damage of being raised to sacrifice one's own needs for the good of the patriarchal family (436–37).

After several years of failed attempts by women in the New Left to make their male comrades see the contradiction between their political ideals and practices, women began to organize autonomously. Women's farewell to the New Left was symbolized, on Robin Morgan's view, by the women's 1970 seizure of *Rat*, one of the major "underground" newspapers of the Left and the counterculture.[14] In the first women's issue, Morgan published her infamous "Good-bye to All That" (1970), which featured a detailed list of misogynist crimes committed by all of the important male leftist leaders and a demystification of their rhetoric (Morgan (1977) 1978, 122–30). In this open letter she says good-bye to the male *Rat* staff who had published articles on "pussy power" and "clit militancy"; good-bye to Charles Manson, Abbie Hoffman, and John Sinclair; good-bye to "the illusion of strength when you run hand in hand with your oppressors"; and good-bye to "the dream that being in the leadership collective will get you anything but gonorrhea" (124). "Good-bye" was widely reprinted and discussed, much to the dismay of those named. In response to this letter, Morgan reported, she received death threats from her "revolutionary" brothers. After *Rat* was seized, Morgan claims, the New Left was never the same again. Of course, feminists did not cause the fragmentation and dissolution of the New Left. According to Todd Gitlin, as early as 1967 the "tough-talking men of steel, committed to their revolutionary mirage, were losing their grip on reality" (1987, 373). For many reasons it was an agonizing time for leftist men. However, since women had been "the cement of the male-run movement, their 'desertion' into their own circles completed the dissolution of the old boys' clan" (374). Leftist men vented their resentment by scapegoating and guilt-tripping feminists.

Perhaps the most damaging leftist response to women's departure from the New Left was the accusation that radical feminists were just a bunch of "white, middle-class women." The charge was echoed by black male revolutionaries concerned that "their" women might follow suit, and by the mainstream media, which was working full time to distort feminism in a multitude of fiendish ways (Combahee River Collective, 1981). The use of the descriptive adjectives "white" and "middle class" were intended as a way to dodge the emerging analysis of patriarchal oppression and to undermine the possibility of a sisterhood that bridged the differences of race and class. As strange as it may seem now, after a quarter century of "second wave" feminism, the idea of an autonomous political movement of women resisting patriarchal oppression was new and extremely radical. As late as 1970 there was no such thing, but it was not beyond the imagination of the male political leaders who had just witnessed and helped mobilize the massive movements against racist oppression and war in the sixties. In response to the threatening prospect of sisterhood, men from the New Left and the Black Power movement fervently denied that the situation of women constituted oppression. They pointed to black women who prioritized the struggle against racism and to Vietnamese women who prioritized the struggle against capitalist imperialism. Most claimed any discussion of women's "oppression" was peripheral or a deliberate effort of privileged women to sabotage the real revolution, which was rooted in the struggle against race and class oppressions.

Radical feminists resisted these attacks with the bold claim that patriarchy, not racism or capitalism, was the root of oppression. For example, Robin Morgan claimed, "Sexism is the root oppression, the one which, until and unless we uproot it, will continue to put forth the branches of racism, class hatred, ageism, competition, ecological disaster, and economic exploitation" (1977, 9). From this perspective, another early radical feminist, Barbara Burris, challenged the accusatory label "white, middle-class women." She pointed out that, in fact, it was sex, rather than race or class, that determined women's primary "caste" position in society. If race was a primary determinant of one's social position, she reasoned, then *all* whites would share the same privileges and exercise the same powers. In fact, since white men exclude white women from the white power structure, she concluded, "whiteness does not overcome the caste position of being a woman in this society" (1971, 330). Any "incidental advantages" that a white woman accrues by virtue of being white or middle-class "come to her mainly in her affiliation with a dominant white male," and are "meaningless in terms of women's true caste position as a sex" (330). On this radical feminist analysis, the "white, middle class" label is only an effective weapon against feminists who have failed to identify their "true caste position as women" (331). Since "the Female Liberation Movement must cut across all (male-imposed) class, race, and national lines, any false identification with privileges that are really male (such as whiteness or class, etc.) will be fatal to our Movement" (332). This is the context within which Daly warned women against being "tied back by old ligatures, old allegiances."

In support of their claim that patriarchy was the root of oppression, radical feminists began to develop a global perspective. Barbara Burris argued, for example, that women around the world shared the repression of their female cultures within their national, ethnic, or racial cultures. Drawing support from "third world" women who resisted their subordinate status within their national liberation movements, she criticized nationalist revolutionary analysis that viewed women's oppression as a by-product of colonialism. For example, she quotes Algerian women in order to "show that a nationalist, anti-imperialist revolution does not free women because the dominant male culture is identified as the national culture, and male supremacy is never attacked" (351). This is the context within which Daly's 1978 project must be understood. In the "Prelude to the Second Passage" in *Gyn/Ecology*, Daly explains:

> In the following pages I will analyze a number of barbarous rituals, ancient and modern, in order to unmask the very real, existential meaning of Goddess murder in the concrete lives of women. I will focus upon five specific righteous rites which massacre women: Indian *suttee*, Chinese footbinding, African female genital mutilation, European witch-burning, American gynecology. In examining these, I will seek out basic patterns which they have in common, and which comprise the Sado-Ritual Syndrome. Those who claim to see racism and/or imperialism in my indictment of these atrocities can do so only by blinding themselves to the fact that the oppression of women knows no ethnic, national, or religious bounds. There are variations on the theme of oppression, but the phenomenon is planetary. (111)

These Radical Feminist theorists shared the logic which moved them from the belief that sexism was a primary form of oppression, through cross-cultural arguments for that belief, to the conclusion that women's solidarity must be grounded in a woman-identified politic that condemned any identifications on the basis of race, ethnicity, religion, or class.

Careful consideration of this radical feminist perspective and the seemingly disparate views of the men in the New Left and the Black Liberation movements reveal a connection in their ways of thinking about the relations among systems of oppression. Both radical feminists and revolutionary men were thinking that there was one system at the base or root of the others that acted as a causal determinant in the workings of the other systems of oppression that were said to spring from it. In addition, there is a strong family resemblance between, on the one hand, the *emergence* of the Black Power movement based on the view that race difference matters and that blacks must organize autonomously to resist assimilation *from* the coalition-based Civil Rights movement founded on a "color-blind" view; and on the other hand, the *emergence* of an autonomous feminist movement based on the view that women's survival depends on resistance to patriarchal assimilation *from* a leftist movement claiming to be founded on the values of equality, brotherhood, and participatory democracy, but that was, in fact, thoroughly male supremacist. Reflection on the logic of these radical movement politics of the seventies reveals a pattern of thinking and organizing whereby the root of oppression is assumed to exist in one base system (race supremacy or patriarchy) that is claimed to be a neutral, or universal, order of values, norms, and powers, and whereby resistance to assimilation within this system is achieved through identification with a difference (race or gender) that challenges and departs from the dominant order.

If it is not already obvious, the story I have been telling thus far says much more about the thinking and organizing of black and white men and white women than it does about black women.[15] So, where did radical black women stand in the seventies? Faced with two autonomous movements, male-dominated Black Liberation and white-dominated Women's Liberation, black women were often forced to choose between them. Choosing feminism meant dealing with the racism of white feminists. Choosing Black Power meant dealing with the sexism of black men, for example as in Stokely Carmichael's notorious comment that the only position for women in SNCC was prone. Most chose Black Power because of the long tradition of black women and men struggling *side by side* for the liberation of the race. A testament to this tradition, Angela Davis argued in "Reflections on the Black Woman's Role in the Community of Slaves" (1971) against the myth of the Black Matriarch, that through history the black woman "fought alongside her man, accepting or providing guidance according to her talents and the nature of their tasks" (214).[16]

In order to get a sense of the position of radical black women in the seventies, consider the perspectives collected by Beverly Guy-Sheftall in *Words of Fire: An Anthology of African-American Feminist Thought* (1995). There were those, such as Francis Beale in her widely anthologized essay "Double Jeopardy" (1970) and Linda La Rue in her essay "The Black Movement and Women's Liberation" (1970), who employed feminist arguments, but prioritized the struggle for black liberation. Both insist that a commitment to the Black Movement must include a critique of sexism. According to La Rue, the "black movement needs its women in a position of struggle, not prone" (171). And Beale chastises black men who exert "their 'manhood' by telling black women to step back into a domestic, submissive role" (148); and yet, she insists, "black women are not resentful of the rise to power of black men. We welcome it. We see in it the eventual liberation of all black people from this corrupt system of capitalism. Nevertheless, this does not mean that you have to negate one for the other. This kind of thinking is a product of miseducation; that it's either X or Y. It is fallacious reasoning that in order for the black man to be strong, the black woman has to be weak" (148). Here, in the same breath, she depends on and criticizes the logic of "root" thinking. She depends on it when she is attempting to unite black men and women against racism rooted in capitalism, and criticizes it when she is attempting to unite black men and women against sexism.

On the relationship of black women's struggles to the women's liberation movement, Beale and La Rue both claimed that fundamental differences in black and white women's experiences make an alliance unlikely. Despite the "surge of 'common oppression' rhetoric and propaganda," La Rue argues, "any attempt to analogize black oppression with the plight of the American white woman has the validity of comparing the neck of a hanging man with the hands of an amateur mountain climber with rope burns." (164). Furthermore, Beale claims that since black people are engaged in a life-and-death struggle, "the main emphasis of black women must be to combat capitalist, racist exploitation of black people." "While it is true," she admits, "that male chauvinism has become institutionalized in American society, one must always look for the main enemy—the fundamental cause of the female condition" (153). Notice that she grounds her commitment to prioritizing the black struggle against capitalist, racist exploitation, in the same logic that she condemns as "fallacious"—as requiring either X or Y. In this case, she reasons, either "male chauvinism" or racist capitalism is the most fundamental cause of the female condition.

Others, such as Mary Ann Weathers, in her essay "An Argument for Black Women's Liberation as a Revolutionary Force" (1970), argued for a revolutionary coalition. Weathers criticized black women who were "expounding all their energies in 'liberating' black men," who talked about "giving black men their manhood—or allowing them to get it," or who "chew[ed] the fat about standing behind our men" (Guy-Sheftall 1995, 158). On behalf of black women's liberation she proclaimed, "We do not have to look at ourselves as someone's personal sex objects, maids, baby sitters, domestics, and the like in exchange for a man's attention. Men hold this power, along with that of the breadwinner, over our heads for these services, and that's all it is—servitude. In return we torture him, and fill him with insecurities about his manhood, and literally force him to 'cat' and 'mess around' bringing all sorts of conflicts. This is not the way really human people live. This is whitey's thing" (160). Hence, she advances a feminist critique of black manhood and womanhood as they are constructed within the Black Liberation movement, but she does not reject the root thinking that views sexism as "whitey's thing." Unlike Beale and La Rue, however, Weathers insisted, "*All* women suffer oppression, even white women, particularly poor white women, and especially Indian, Mexican, Puerto Rican, Oriental, and black American women whose oppression is tripled by any of the above mentioned. But we do have female's oppression in common. This means that we can begin to talk to other women with this common factor and start building links with them and thereby build and transform the revolutionary force we are beginning to amass" (160–61). She resists the forces urging her to side with either black (men) or (white) women by proposing Black Liberation and women's liberation link up "with the entire revolutionary movement consisting of women, men and children" (158).

This is the context within which Audre Lorde's feminist work prior to the "Open Letter" must be understood. While critical of racism within the Women's Liberation movement, she dreamed of and worked for a world of women-loving-women "bridging our differences." In contrast with La Rue, Beale, and Weathers, Lorde believed in the power of women to change the world. On the basis of this vision, in this moment that demanded black women choose, Lorde's primary loyalties were to women.

In "Anger in Isolation: A Black Feminist's Search for Sisterhood" (1975), Michelle Wallace laments the absence of a movement that prioritized the struggle of black women. She argued that both the movements of Black and Women's Liberation failed black women, and she founded the National Black Feminist Organization to fill the gap. The organization folded when it was barely off the ground, because, she explains, "many of the prime movers in the organization seemed to be representing other interest groups and whatever commitment they might have had to black women's issues appeared to take a back seat to that." The problem, in her view, was that "we had no strength to give to one another" (226). Black women's commitments to Black Liberation, the New Left, and Women's Liberation functioned effectively to alienate black women from one another. Describing the plight of black feminists in the early seventies, she concludes, "We exist as women who are black who are feminists, each stranded for the moment, working independently because there is not yet an environment in this society remotely congenial to our struggle—because, being on the bottom, we would have to do what no one else has done: we would have to fight the world" (227).

Ironically, it was this situation of facing multiple systems of oppression, and of feeling alienated from the political movements of the day, that ultimately led to the disruption and overthrow of the political logic that dominated the seventies by the coalition calling themselves Radical Women of Color. But that story cannot be told until after we consider Lorde's "Open Letter" in the context sketched above, because Lorde's letter was a central force in creation of this coalition.

Why Didn't Daly Respond in Kind to Lorde's Letter?

The "too-early morning" of Lorde's poem is this historical context of movement politics that I have just sketched. In this moment, what Lorde was asking Daly for was destroyed "like dew in an early morning dissolving the tongue of salt." In this section, first I discuss what I think Daly *did* hear in Lorde's letter at the time she received it; and second, I suggest what I think Daly *did not* hear in Lorde's letter because the context needed to "hear her to speech" was just beginning to take shape.[17]

What did Daly hear in the criticisms of the "Open Letter"? When she first received the letter perhaps she thought back a year to the Modern Language Association panel, to Lorde's agreement with her claim that patriarchy is a *war* waged against *all* women, a war that *separates* women. Or maybe she remembered Lorde's call for women to bridge our differences in the name of sisterhood. In the context of this moment, which demanded that black women choose between movements, and in which most were choosing to prioritize the struggle against racism, Daly probably assumed that Lorde's priority was the radical feminist struggle against patriarchy. Daly assumed Lorde was a brave black feminist who shared the knowledge that in order to end racism, it was necessary to get to the root of the problem and therefore necessary to stand with her sisters in the struggle for women's liberation. It is likely that on the basis of these assumptions, what Daly heard when she read Lorde's letter was a fundamental shift in perspective and, perhaps, a betrayal.

Consider Lorde's charge that in *Gyn/Ecology* Daly had used the tools of patriarchy against women of color by implying that all women suffer the same oppression. What Daly probably heard in this criticism was a *denial* that black and white women, and women all around the world, alike suffer patriarchal oppression—denial that would have resonated with the claims about the need to recognize racial forms of oppression and racial difference that were being made by black radicals. Recall Carmichael's claim that Africans around the world have a common enemy and face common problems. And recall Beale's insistence that there are "quite basic" differences in the experiences of black and white women, and that the struggle of black women must be against the "main enemy." If Daly heard voices like these echoing in Lorde's letter, it would have sounded as though Lorde was shifting from the position she held at the panel the previous year to prioritizing the struggle against racism. From Daly's viewpoint, this sort of shift would only undermine the effort by radical feminists to establish the fact of a patriarchal system of oppression, because the argument for the claim was based on common patterns in practices and rituals across cultures designed to destroy the Self in every woman. Like other white radical feminists at the time, Daly thought the only logical response to the denial that patriarchy existed was to insist that racial and cultural differences were epiphenomenonal, that basically, all women faced a common enemy and common problems. Furthermore, since she believed patriarchy was the "root" of all oppressions, its demise would entail the end of racism too. Inside of the logic of this moment it would have been extremely difficult for Daly to hear Lorde *both* agreeing (with radical feminists) that patriarchy is a global system oppressing all women *and*, at the same time, denying (with radical blacks) that women suffer the same oppression as women.

Now consider Lorde's charge that by excluding female symbolic figures from nonwhite, non-European traditions and assuming that those recovered from white European herstory and myth could serve as a basis of identification for all women, Daly contributed to the forces of racism and separation between women. Some evidence that Daly could *not* hear the concern behind Lorde's suggestion that she should have included material on nonwhite, non-European female power and symbol dis-covered from a radical feminist perspective is found in Daly's reply (in the conversation she had with Lorde before the letter was published) that *Gyn/Ecology* was not intended to be a compendium of goddesses[18] (Daly 1990, xxx). This reply suggests that Daly did not hear Lorde's concern with assimilation. Assimilation, on Daly's radical feminist perspective in *Gyn/Ecology*, was what women must resist in the patriarchal State of Possession. Recall Daly's view that sisterhood is not subterfuge for the maintenance of a patriarchal power structure that demands identification with one tradition of goddesses, because, sisterhood, unlike brotherhood, "has as its core the affirmation of freedom." She was assuming that her refusal to pledge allegiance to any and all male-identified religions, nations, or political movements would free the feminist symbolic figures she dis-covered in *Gyn/Ecology* from any racial or ethnic identification. Daly replied, *Gyn/Ecology* is not a compendium, probably thinking that Lorde had misinterpreted her effort to recover female mythology from the European tradition as an effort to set up the new feminist symbolic order of allegiance. But Daly's reply misses Lorde's point, which was that by offering *only* material for a white European feminist symbolic, she does, in effect, offer it as the sole basis of identification for all women. The racism (in this case, a form of ethnocentrism) implicit in this effect, on Lorde's view, is the denial that women of African, Indian, or Chinese descent reading the chapters on the patriarchal crimes of genital mutilation, suttee, or foot-binding in *Gyn/Ecology* would need female symbols of power from their own traditions in order to identify themselves and their sisters who had been mutilated, not only as victims, but also as survivors, resisters, and warriors. Notice, this is how the female symbolic figures presented in *Gyn/Ecology* function for women of European descent reading the chapters on the patriarchal crimes of witch-burning and Western gynecology. In other words, Daly did not hear Lorde's effort to point out how this asymmetry in the text constituted a form of assimilation that conflicted with her intention to theorize a sisterhood based on the affirmation of freedom. If Daly did not hear Lorde on this point, perhaps it was due in part to the context within which what it meant to be radical was to pledge allegiance to the one movement which had identified the root of all oppression. If she heard Lorde's concern with assimilation at all, she probably heard it as more evidence of a shift in perspective and loyalty from radical feminism to black radicalism. In spite of Daly's insistence that radical feminists pledge no allegiances, I think she worried that Lorde's criticisms would only serve the interests of men by undermining the possibilities of female friendship that break the boundaries of the patriarchal "State of Possession."

What was Daly *unable* to hear in the criticisms of the "Open Letter"? Because Daly, like other white radical feminists at this time, shared with radical men the idea that systems of oppression stood in a relation like the branches of a tree to its roots, she could not hear Lorde's attempt to speak her radical black politics *and* her radical feminist politics with one voice. She could not hear the multiplicity in Lorde's voice as a challenge to the revolutionary-movement rhetoric that forced black feminists to choose only one dimension of their identities to prioritize in the struggle for liberation. Lorde's letter was not meant to undermine the radical feminists' case against patriarchy; in fact, she believed, like Daly, that there were common patterns in practices and rituals across cultures designed to destroy the Self in every woman. Lorde meant to articulate the existence of something that had not been said to date, or at least had not been amplified by a movement. She was trying to say that patriarchy *is* a global system oppressing all women but since it *intersects*, or *interlocks*, or *interacts*, with racism, colonialism, and imperialism in different places at different times, women do not suffer the same oppression as women.[19] This bold new claim, which undermined the idea that destroying patriarchy would necessarily entail the end of racism, spoke to the need for a radical politic that was not based on a hierarchy of oppressions. In this too-early morning, dominated by the political logic of "root thinking," Lorde was asking for a radical feminism that prioritized the differences in women's oppression as well as the commonalities. This would be a radical feminism which sought to dis-cover female symbols of power in the patriarchal traditions of Africa, India, and China, in order to resist the white European patriarchal view of nonwhite, non-Western women as victims incapable of standing up for themselves, and to acknowledge the need all women have for the knowledges and values of the many different female-identified traditions. Not a compendium, but a feminist symbolic that affirmed racial and ethnic diversity, because Lorde fathomed the radical potential of a movement of women who viewed their differences not as cause for separation, but as forces for change.

If the meaning of Lorde's letter, as I have presented it here, seems obvious now, it did not in 1979. From our historical moment, it is difficult to keep in mind that a context within which Daly might have heard the complexities of Lorde's letter did not yet exist. For a sense of how impossible Lorde's position sounded at the time, consider the reflection of one white feminist who heard her speak:

> I began as a graduate student in sociology in 1978. At the time, debate centered on the possibility of linking Marxist theories of class with feminist theories of gender. Could these theories be reconciled or were they in ontological conflict? Clearly, in asking those questions, race was not on the agenda. Also, around that time Audre Lorde came to the Amherst area to give a speech. I remember then a confusion I felt—and one she wished to teach the audience—about her multiple commitments. She discussed her participation in black community groups, in women's groups, and in gay and lesbian groups, but she wanted to stress, she was a whole person, one person across these settings. I asked her, nervously raising my hand in a large auditorium setting, how *can* you be and act all these things at once? My memory of her response to my question was that it didn't make any sense to her. (Kathleen Daly 1993, 59)

To those who felt alienated in the seventies, and who hoped, as Wallace did, that "perhaps a multicultural women's movement is somewhere in the future" (Guy-Sheftall 1995, 226), the question would not have made sense. If the message of Lorde's letter makes sense now it is because the multicultural women's movement that Wallace hoped for came into being in the early eighties through women calling themselves Radical Women of Color. Lorde's letter was one of the sparks that ignited what Daly calls in the new introduction to *Gyn/Ecology* an "Explosion of Diversity" (1990, xxx). What Daly had not realized, but acknowledges in the new introduction, is that "Explosions of Diversity do not happen without conflict" (xxx). The interaction between Daly and Lorde took the shape of an irresolvable conflict because it was a part of changing the world, of bringing a new world into being, the world of "Radical Women of Color."

To understand how Lorde's letter helped create the context that makes it possible now to hear her criticisms and vision in all their complexity, it is useful to consider the insights of some of the first women to identify as Radical Women of Color. Toni Cade Bambara introduces the women whose writings are published together in *This Bridge Called My Back* (1981): "Blackfoot amiga Nisei hermana Down Home Up Souf Sistuh sister El Barrio suburbia Korean The Bronx Lakota Menominee Cuban Chinese Puertoriqueña reservation Chicana campañera and letters testimonials poems interviews essays journal entries sharing Sisters of the yam Sisters of the rice Sisters of the corn Sisters of the plantain putting in telecalls to each other. And we're all on the line" (vi). Radical Women of Color first identified themselves as such on the basis of the experience of being "bridges" between various other movements. Cade Bambara is explicit about the foundation that Lorde's "Open Letter" provided for the development of this multicultural consciousness. In the foreword to the book she writes that

> though the initial motive of several sister/riters here may have been to protest, complain or explain to white feminist would-be allies that there are other ties and visions that bind, prior allegiances and priorities that supersede their invitations to coalesce on their terms ("Assimilation within a solely western european herstory is not acceptable"—Lorde), the process of examining that would-be alliance awakens us to new tasks ("We have a lot more to concentrate on besides the pathology of white wimmin"—davenport)
>
> and a new connection: US
> a new set of recognitions: US
> a new site of accountability: US
> a new source of power: US (vi)

In the preface of *This Bridge Called My Back* Cherríe Moraga struggles with the newness of this sisterhood that affirms differences. Listen as she describes her first visit to Boston to meet with Barbara Smith:

> By the end of the evening of our first visit together, Barbara comes into the front room when she has made a bed for me. She kisses me. Then grabbing my shoulders she says, very solid-like, "we're sisters." I nod, put myself into bed, and roll around with this word, *sisters*, for two hours before sleep takes on. I earned this with Barbara. It is not a given between us—Chicana and Black—to come to see each other as sisters. This is not a given. I keep wanting to repeat over and over and over again, the pain and shock of difference, the joy of commonness, the exhilaration of meeting through incredible odds against it. (xiv)

Moraga goes on to draw insight and guidance from Lorde's 1979 essay "The Master's Tools Will Never Dismantle the Master's House," which Lorde wrote shortly after the "Open Letter."

> When Audre Lorde, speaking of racism, states: "I urge each one of us to reach down into that deep place of knowledge inside herself and touch that terror and loathing of any difference that lives there," I am driven to do so because of the passion for women that lives in my body. I know now that the major obstacle for me, personally, in completing this book has occurred when I stopped writing it for myself, when I looked away from my own source of knowledge. Audre is right. It is also the source of terror—how deeply separation between women hurts me. How discovering difference, profound differences between myself and women I love has sometimes rendered me helpless and immobilized. (xvi)

One of the widely read papers in *This Bridge Called My Back,* titled "A Black Feminist Statement" written by black feminists calling themselves the Combahee River Collective, describes how they became disillusioned with movements that insisted on one order of allegiance, and how this created the need "to develop a politics that was antiracist, unlike those of white women, and antisexist, unlike those of black and white men" (Combahee River Collective 1981, 210). This paper provides a previously unavailable framework for understanding Lorde's criticisms in the "Open Letter." The insight of the collective that makes sense of Lorde's letter is that "the major systems of oppression are interlocking," rather than related as are the branches to the roots of a tree (209). They make the claim against the idea that *either* race and class *or* sex is the root of their oppression, that "there is such a thing as racial-sexual oppression which is neither solely racial nor solely sexual, e.g. the history of rape of Black women by white men as a weapon of political repression" (213).

In the absence of this context, which has emerged in part as a consequence of Lorde's "Open Letter to Mary Daly," and due to the conceptual grip that root thinking had on Daly's most passionately held beliefs, I have argued, Daly would have heard the letter as a shift in Lorde's perspective or a betrayal.[20] In addition, I have argued, Daly would not have been able to hear Lorde's letter as call for a new sisterhood based the recognition that patriarchy *intersects* with other systems of oppression, creating significantly different experiences of oppression and a commitment to dis-covering a diverse feminist symbolic that all women might draw from in our efforts to survive and thrive under oppression. In my view, it is reasonable to assume that Daly chose not to respond in kind because, at the time, as she read Lorde's criticisms they pierced the heart of radical feminism with an arrow dipped in the patriarchal poison of divide-and-conquer. If she could think of nothing to say in reply to Lorde except to make the countercriticism that it was not she, but Lorde, who was contributing to the forces of separation between women, then it is not hard to understand why Daly did not respond in kind. Such an exchange would not have been fruitful.

It may seem that my speculations about Daly's decision not to respond in kind to Lorde's letter only answer the historical question about why Daly did not respond in 1979. For those who care to look, I think there is a response of sorts in Daly's work after *Gyn/Ecology*, but it is not the kind of response that emerges from fruitful dialogue. Daly has not chosen the path of dialogue. As a result, I believe, her work has suffered and fallen short of its radical potential. However, in my view, the question we are left with is not Why hasn't Daly responded to Lorde's letter? but Why has no one else? The letter calls, not for the end of radical feminism, but for an antiracist, antiethnocentric radical feminism, for a radical *white European American* feminism. This sort of politic is not born out of a particular theoretical framework, it is achieved through interaction fueled by a desire to make connections under complex systems of oppression, the desire to show you hear.

Notes

1. The "Open Letter to Mary Daly" was first published in *Top Ranking* (1980). It was subsequently published in slightly different versions in *This Bridge Called My Back* (1981, 1983) and in Audre Lorde's *Sister Outsider* (1984). All references in this essay are to the version in *Sister Outsider*. Readers of this essay should read Lorde's letter in conjunction with this essay.

2. Daly reports here on a meeting she and Lorde had to discuss the letter on September 29, 1979 at the Simone de Beauvoir Conference in New York. This was the conference at which Lorde read "The Master's Tools Will Never Dismantle the Master's House."

3. Alcoff was not the first to make a categorical distinction between white radical feminists and radical women of color. See de Lauretis's note on the recent genealogy of the typological project in Anglo-American feminist theory, in "The Essence of the Triangle or, Taking the Risk of Essentialism Seriously: Feminist Theory in Italy, the U.S., and Britain" (1989, 33).

4. And I did get more from a few exceptional teachers, including Bernice Carroll, Ann Russo, Pat Cramer, and Cheris Kramerae.

5. The dilemma discussed by Marilyn Frye in "On Being White: Thinking Toward A Feminist Understanding of Race and Race Supremacy" (1983) conveys some of why the politics of white antiracism seemed impossible to me at the time.

6. All of the papers presented on this panel were published together in *Sinister Wisdom* 6 (Summer 1978). The panel, convened by Julia P. Stanley (Julia Penelope), was attended by seven hundred women in December 1977, in Chicago.

7. This paper was revised and reprinted in *Sister Outsider* with the title of the panel, "The Transformation of Silence into Language and Action" (1984).

8. The language of this criticism points directly to the following passage in *Gyn/Ecology*: "Haggard criticism should enable women who have been intimidated by labels of 'racism' to become sisters to these women of Africa—naming the crimes against them and speaking on their behalf—seeing through the reversal that is meant to entrap us all. It is truly racist to keep silent in the face of these atrocities, merely 'studying' them, speaking and writing deceptively about them, failing to see and name the connections among them. Beyond racism is sisterhood, *naming* the crimes against women without paying mindless respect to the 'social fabric' of the various androcratic societies, including the one in which we find our Selves imprisoned" (172).

9. In his dissenting opinion in the case of *Plessy v. Ferguson* (1892) Supreme Court Justice Marshall Harlan argued, "Our Constitution is color-blind." For an insightful discussion of "The Color-Blind Principle" see Bernard R. Boxill, *Blacks and Social Justice* (Rowman & Allanheld, 1984).

10. It is instructive to reflect on how the "color-blind" argument is being appropriated by conservatives today.

11. In the early seventies Carmichael was expelled from the SNCC (Student Nonviolent Coordinating Committee) and quit the Black Panther Party. He changed his name to Kwami Toure and moved to Conakry, Guinea, where he became a citizen and lived with his wife, South African musician Miriam MaKeba.

12. On some accounts the "Old Left"—made up of Communists, labor and religious activists, and pacifists—had burned out resisting the McCarthyism of the 1950s. The children of the Old Left, along with other middle-class youth of that generation, who joined the sit-ins, voter registration drives, and freedom rides in the early 1960s, revitalized and reinvented the Left in the form of the antiwar movement, student movement, and counterculture movement of the late 1960s. My account of this history is indebted to Sara Evans's *Personal Politics: The Roots of Women's Liberation in the Civil Rights Movement and The New Left*.

13. The SDS manifesto, the "Port Huron Statement," was written by Tom Hayden (New York: Students for a Democratic Society, 1962).

14. Evans dates women's departure to a meeting of women in Chicago in the aftermath of the 1967 National Conference for New Politics (NCNP). The women at this meeting wrote a manifesto declaring that women should organize their own movement (Evans 1980, 196–99).

15. It also says a lot more about blacks and whites than it does about other people of color. This is both a reflection of the state of racial politics at the time and a limitation of my narrative.

16. Lest there be any confusion about the relation between Davis's debunking of the black matriarch and Lorde's effort to reclaim the Black Mother (Goddess), I offer the following: I think the projects of both Davis and Lorde were responses to the urgent need to stand against this ideological warfare being waged directly against black women during in the sixties and seventies. The myth of the black matriarch advanced by racists such as Patrick Moynihan constitutes what Lorde would call a "distortion" of the difference represented by the archetype of the Black Mother. While Davis fought the distorted archetype from the ground of concrete historical circumstance, Lorde fought the distortion from the ground of possibility represented by black female symbolic figures reclaimed from patriarchal myth. One difference in their projects reflects the political alliance each was working to foster at the moment. Davis's project, which focuses on how the distorted myth threatens the common struggle of black people, was primarily intended to strengthen the ties between black men

and women. Lorde's project, as articulated in her open letter to Daly, focuses on how the myth is obscured and distorted by ethnocentric racism and was primarily intended to strengthen the ties between black and white women.

17. The kind of hearing I am thinking of is a complex process, which Daly names in *Gyn/Ecology* as "Depth Hearing" (412). Implicit in this idea of Depth Hearing is a critique of the commonly held view that in the beginning there is "the Word," that is, there is nothing to hear until something is said. Depth Hearing supposes the reverse, that is, there is nothing one can say until there is hearing. Depth Hearing takes place *before* speaking, in the sense that what is spoken is incoherent without a context within which it can be heard. Here is an example. In the preface to *This Bridge Called My Back* (1981), Cherríe Moraga relates how she experienced being heard into speech for the first time: "Months ago in a journal entry I wrote: 'I am afraid to get near to how deeply I want to love the other Latin women in my life.' In a real visceral way I hadn't felt the absence (only assumed the fiber of alienation I so often felt with anglo women as normative). Then for the first time, speaking on a panel about racism here in San Francisco, I could physically touch what I had been missing. There in the front row, nodding encouragement and identification, sat five Latina sisters. Count them! Five avowed Latina Feminists: Gloria, Jo, Aurora, Chabela y Mirtha. For once in my life every part of me was allowed to be visible and spoken for in one room at one time" (xvii). While she had spoken before, she had not been Heard because there was no context within which her words could make sense. What she found, in this moment, in the presence of her Latina-identified sisters who affirmed her whole Self, or all of her selves, was a context within which she could be Heard.

18. The reply I refer to here is the one Daly mentions in her 1990 introduction to *Gyn/Ecology* and that she made at the meeting of September 29, 1979, at the Simone de Beauvoir Conference in New York. While this is a reply to Lorde, it is not a reply in kind, since it was not part of an open, community dialogue.

19. The words in italics were the words Lorde needed to articulate her claim, but that she did not yet have.

20. Of course, there are limits to a contextual explanation such as mine, since there were white feminists who were beginning to articulate an antiracist radical feminist politic of the sort Lorde was urging Daly toward. See, for example, Adrienne Rich 1979.

References

Alcoff, Linda. 1988. "The Identity Crisis in Feminist Theory." *Signs* 13, no. 3: 405–36.

Beale, Francis. 1970. "Double Jeopardy." In Guy-Sheftall 1995.

Burris, Barbara. 1971. "The Fourth World Manifesto." In Koedt 1973.

Carmichael, Stokely. 1968. *The Black Power Revolt*, edited by Floyd B. Barbour. Extending Horizon Books.

———. 1971. *Stokely Speaks: Black Power Back to Pan-Africanism*. New York: Random House.

Carmichael, Stokely, and Charles V. Hamilton. 1967. *Black Power: The Politics of Liberation in America*. New York: Vintage.

Combahee River Collective. 1981. "A Black Feminist Statement." In Moraga and Anzaldúa 1983.

Daly, Kathleen. 1993. "Class-Race-Gender: Sloganeering in Search of Meaning." In *Social Justice* 20, nos. 1–2.

Daly, Mary. (1978a) 1990. *Gyn/Ecology: The Metaethics of Radical Feminism*. Boston: Beacon Press.

———. 1978b. Paper delivered at the 1977 Annual Modern Language Association Convention, December, Chicago, Illinois. Published in *Sinister Wisdom* 6:11.

Davis, Angela. 1971. "Reflections on the Black Woman's Role in the Community of Slaves." In Guy-Sheftall 1995.

de Lauretis, Teresa. 1989. "The Essence of the Triangle or, Taking the Risk of Essentialism Seriously: Feminist Theory in Italy, the U.S., and Britain." *Differences* 1, no. 2:3–37.

Evans, Sara. 1980. *Personal Politics: The Roots of Women's Liberation in the Civil Rights Movement and the New Left*. New York: Vintage.

Frankenberg, Ruth. 1993. *White Women, Race Matters: The Social Construction of Whiteness*. Minneapolis: University of Minnesota Press.

Fraser, Nancy, and Linda J. Nicholson. 1990. "Social Criticism Without Philosophy: An Encounter Between Feminism and Postmodernism." In Nicholson 1990.

Gitlin, Todd. 1987. *The Sixties: Years of Hope, Days of Rage*. New York: Bantam.

Guy-Sheftall, Beverly, ed. 1995. *Words of Fire: An Anthology of African-American Feminist Thought*. New York: New Press.

Jewell, Terri L. 1994. *Succulent Heretic*. Opal Tortuga Press.

King, Martin Luther, Jr. 1963. "Letter from Birmingham Jail." In *The Accommodating Reader*. McGraw-Hill, 1993.

Koedt, Anne, Ellen Levine, and Anita Rapone, eds. 1973. *Radical Feminism*. New York: Quadrangle/New York Times Book.

La Rue, Linda. 1970. "The Black Movement and Women's Liberation." In Guy-Sheftall 1995.

Lorde, Audre. 1978a. *The Black Unicorn*. New York: W. W. Norton.

———. (1977) 1978b. Untitled paper presented at Modern Language Association panel, published in *Sinister Wisdom* 6 (Summer).

———. 1982. *Zami: A New Spelling of My Name*. Freedom, Calif.: Crossing Press.

———. 1983. "Open Letter to Mary Daly." In *Sister Outsider: Essays and Speeches by Audre Lorde*. Freedom, Calif.: Crossing Press.

Moraga, Cherríe, and Gloria Anzaldúa, eds. 1983. *This Bridge Called My Back: Writings by Radical Women of Color*. New York: Kitchen Table Women of Color Press.

Morgan, Robin, ed. 1970. *Sisterhood Is Powerful: An Anthology of Writings from the Women's Liberation Movement*. New York: Vintage.

———. (1977). 1978. *Going Too Far: The Personal Chronicle of a Feminist*. New York: Vintage.

Nicholson, Linda J., ed. 1990. *Feminism/Postmodernism*. New York: Routledge.

Omi, Michael, and Howard Winant. 1986. *Racial Formation in the United States: From the 1960's to the 1980's*. New York: Routledge and Keagan Paul.

Piercy, Marge. 1969. "The Grand Coolie Damn." In Morgan 1970.

Rich, Adrienne. (1978) 1979. "Disloyal to Civilization: Feminism, Racism, Gynephobia." In *On Lies, Secrets, and Silence: Selected Prose 1966–1978*. New York: W. W. Norton.

Wallace, Michele. 1975. "Anger in Isolation: A Black Feminist's Search for Sisterhood," in Guy Sheftall 1995.

Weathers, Mary Ann. 1970. "An Argument for Black Women's Liberation as a Revolutionary Force." In Guy-Sheftall 1995.

11

(Re)reading Mary Daly as a Sister Insider

Amber L. Katherine

In response to Mary Daly's *Gyn/Ecology: A Metaethics of Radical Feminism* (1978), Audre Lorde wrote an open letter to her in 1979 in which she said:

> This letter has been delayed because of my grave reluctance to reach out to you, for what I want us to chew upon here is neither easy nor simple. The history of white women who are unable to hear Black women's words, or to maintain dialogue with us, is long and discouraging. But to assume that you will not hear me represents not only history, perhaps, but an old pattern of relating, sometimes protective and sometimes dysfunctional, which

> we, as women shaping our future, are in the process of shattering and passing beyond, I hope. (Lorde 1984, 66–67)

Audre Lorde's critique of *Gyn/Ecology* was, and continues to be, compelling. As a result of, and coupled with, Mary Daly's decision not to respond in kind to Lorde, there has been very little discussion of *Gyn/Ecology* by white feminists in the United States.[1] This is unfortunate because there is still much to be learned from reading and thinking about this book, especially with regard to unfruitful patterns of relating among women of different racial and ethnic orientations/identities. In this essay I offer a way of reading (for third wavers) or of rereading (for second wavers) Mary Daly's radical feminism that takes up Audre Lorde's open invitation to dialogue.

Outsiders and Insiders

The rereading that I propose is a project in becoming more conscious of how radical feminists in the European American tradition are, at once, outsiders and insiders. A genealogy of European American radical feminism can be a reflective starting point. In her aspirations to live as an "Outsider" to patriarchal reality, Mary Daly drew from Virginia Woolf; and before her, Matilda Joslyn Gage; and before her, those burned in Europe as "witches." The title of Audre Lorde's 1984 collection of essays, *Sister Outsider,* suggests among other things that she understood herself, in relation to her "sisters" inside this European American feminist tradition, as an Outsider. As Lorde's title implicitly points out, even though Daly, Woolf, and Gage chose to live as gender outsiders, they were raised as racially and geopolitically privileged insiders. In this paper I focus on two insider/outsider relations: that between patriarchal loyalists and radical feminists of the European American tradition, and that between radical feminists of the European American tradition and women of other traditions. In the former relation radical feminists such as Daly and myself are outsiders, in the latter, we are insiders.

I use the terms "insider" and "outsider" to refer to one's situatedness in relation to historically constituted, material axes of power. In a race-supremacist society, insiders are the ones who live with racial power or privilege and outsiders are those who must live with racism. In a patriarchal society, men are insiders, women are outsiders. The rich are insiders, the poor outsiders in class society. Insiders move through the world more comfortably and empowered than the outsiders they ignore, exploit, and oppress. An insider may have access to privileged knowledge or language, an authorized vantage point and/or the resources and/or the right to speak or act on behalf of others. Insiders are often judges, teachers, scholars, psychotherapists, gynecologists, bosses, and fathers. They are connected in power relations with outsiders who are often prisoners, students, patients, domestic workers, and daughters. Hence, in the way I am using the terms here, insiders are "in" dominant/privileged social/political groups, outsiders are "out" of these groups.

Insiders may share the benefits of power, and outsiders the burdens of oppression, but one's placement within a complex of power relations does not necessarily determine how one views their situation or that of others. However, there are patterns in the perspectives among both insiders and outsiders that do seem directly related to one's social/political placement. I have been influenced most in my thinking about the patterns in perspective among insiders and outsiders by María Lugones (1987, 1991, 1994; Lugones with Rosezelle 1992), but also by W. E. B. Du Bois and the discourse of feminist standpoint epistemology (Alcoff and Potter 1993). In general, insiders do not view themselves as insiders, nor do they see outsiders as such; rather, they claim to view everyone as individuals. Outsiders, on the other hand, are more likely to have a perspective from which they view themselves and others as excluded or included on the basis of their group membership. This outsider's perspective is often characterized as a "double consciousness" or a pluralist self-consciousness. Outsiders are more likely to know themselves from the insider's perspective *and* from their own outsider's perspective. In contrast, insiders usually lack awareness of themselves as multiply constituted selves, seeing themselves instead as unified individuals. One explanation put forth for this difference is the greater stake insiders have in maintaining or justifying their (unified) identity, practices, and projects in the world. The point is *not* that only outsiders have pluralist-consciousness and insiders only have single-consciousness, because all people are, in principle, capable of understanding themselves and others from more than one perspective. Rather, the point is that within a regime of oppressive power relations, insiders are less likely to be conscious of themselves and others as double or multiple because that would entail acknowledging their power/privilege over others. Within such a regime, outsiders motivated to resist have a stake in revealing the ways in which insider/outsider relations shape one's perspective. For example, I see myself as an Outsider, that is, one who rejects the patriarchal insider's perspective of me as a "woman," in favor of a radical feminist consciousness of myself as "Other." But when I look in the mirror and see the Outsider, the radical feminist who says no to the patriarchal scholar, I see only one of my selves. While maintaining this sense of self, I can also see myself through the eyes of Audre Lorde's "Sister Outsiders" as an insider. By cultivating this pluralist self-understanding I make a *choice* that enables me to contribute to an interruption in the dysfunctional patterns of relating that Lorde names in her letter, a choice that enables me to *hear* the words of women of color and to enter into dialogue with them.

Although I did not know Audre Lorde and have not met Mary Daly in person, both of them have been my teachers. What I found inspiring in their works when I first began to read them in college classrooms in the early eighties was a vision of feminist interaction and connection that they named "sisterhood." It is possible to read the title of Lorde's collection of essays *Sister Outsider* as Lorde's seeing Daly's omissions and assumptions in *Gyn/Ecology* as a betrayal because they construct Lorde as an outsider to the sister relation they both sought to affirm. Perhaps sharing something of Lorde's reaction, María Lugones argues that "sisterhood is neither an appropriate metaphor for the existing relations among women nor an appropriate ideal for those relations when put forth by white feminists" (Kramarae 1992, 406). She offers as a reason the absence of analysis or defense of the sister relation by white/Anglo feminists, who have nevertheless extensively critiqued the American family. I agree with Lugones's proposal of aspiring to a feminist ideal of pluralist friendship that begins with "compañerismo" rather than sisterhood. Yet I also believe that critical reflection on the sister relation is a necessary and fruitful place to begin.

I remain hopeful that Daly's work can be used to reflect on things that we do with little if any awareness—especially as radical feminist insiders—that, had we awareness, we might choose to do differently or not at all. I learned from both Daly and Lorde that history is present in our patterns of relating and, importantly, that by studying history we can dis/cover those oppressive foreground patterns side by side and intertwined with those inspiring and empowering patterns that Mary Daly calls the "Background." I have found the idea of the mirror in the work of María Lugones a most helpful strategy for becoming aware of this intertwining of patterns and how our many selves, or cultural identities, are historically and geopolitically constituted. In her essay "On the Logic of Pluralist Feminism," Lugones suggests that one way white feminists can begin to notice women of color is to "realize that we are mirrors in which you can see yourselves as no other mirror shows you" (Card 1991, 41–42). She says, "It is not that we are the only faithful mirrors, but I think we *are* faithful mirrors. Not that we show you as you *really* are; we just show you as one of the people you are. What we reveal to you is that you are many—something that may in itself be frightening to you. But the self we reveal to you is also one that you are not eager to know for reasons that one may conjecture" (Card 1991, 41–42). In the present case, this would be to look at Mary Daly's *Gyn/Ecology* in the mirror of Audre Lorde's criticisms. But I am not only, or even primarily, interested in what might be learned about *Gyn/Ecology* from an analysis at this level. I am more interested in what critiques by U.S. radical women of color, particularly Audre Lorde's, reveal about European American radical feminists in general. And I am most interested in learning about myself, and other white feminists, by looking at the historical tradition of European American radical feminism in the mirror of sister outsiders, like Audre Lorde. The trick, I think, is to develop the skills to (re)read Daly's *Gyn/Ecology* in a way that reveals *both* the feminist Outsider and the eurocentric insider. The challenge for those of us who trace, or re-member, a genealogy similar to that of Mary Daly is to maintain an awareness of ourselves as sister insiders and to always use that awareness, together with other self-awarenesses, to inform our feminist practices, discussions, and projects.

A Background History of Outsiders

The history of radical feminism, as Daly presents it, is a Crone-ology of Outsiders.[2] She *re-members* radical feminism by exploring its roots in a buried gynocentric tradition. On Daly's reconstruction, the witches of yesterday and the radical feminists of the late twentieth century are related in lines that run through Gage and Woolf. What unites the tradition is an allegiance to the standpoint of the Outsider in patriarchy.

Daly re-members Matilda Joslyn Gage as "a major radical feminist theoretician and historian whose written work is indispensable for an understanding of the women's movement today" (Gage [1893] 1980, vii). In her foreword to Gage's *Woman, Church, and State* ([1893] 1980), Daly identifies Gage as a "foresister of contemporary feminists" who dared to reveal and name the enemy (vii). In her book Gage brings together studies of matriarchal societies, female sexual slavery, witchcraft, and marriage, adding critiques of civil and ecclesiastical law, in order to reveal the systematic nature and consequences of patriarchal oppression. "The most stupendous system of organized robbery known has been that of the church towards women, a robbery that has not only taken her self-respect but all rights of person; the fruits of her own industry; her opportunities of education; the exercise of her own judgment, her own conscience, her own will" (238). This injustice led Gage to dedicate her book to "all Christian women and men, of whatever creed or name who, bound by Church or State, have not dared to Think for Themselves" (2). The standpoint of those who have dared is, in Daly's terms, that of the Outsider in patriarchy.

Gage's *Woman, Church, and State* is the primary source in Daly's chapter on the European witch-burnings. Among the scholars of the witchcraze whom Daly surveys in that chapter, only Gage exemplifies a "Hag-identified vision"[3] (Daly 1978, 216). In her chapter, Daly develops Gage's claim that many women were persecuted as witches because their independent thinking and their healing practices presented a threat to the patriarchal church. Daly's expanded thesis is that the witchcraze was a "primal battle" between "an aspiring 'intellectual' elite of professional men" and "a spiritual/moral/know-ing elite cross-section of the female population of Europe," which "was at heart concerned with the process of know-ing" (Daly 1978, 194). Following Gage, Daly argues that the witchcraze "masked a secret gynocidal fraternity, whose prime targets were women living *outside* the control of the patriarchal family, women who presented an option—an option of 'eccentricity' and of 'indigestibility' " (Daly 1978, 186; my emphasis). This is not to say, however, that either Gage or Daly held the view that only eccentric or scientifically minded women were persecuted. On the contrary, both were aware that the threat of being accused of witchcraft functioned to keep all women *inside* the control of the patriarchal church and family.

Undoubtedly Gage was the primary influence on Daly's "Re-membering" the witches as early modern Outsiders. And yet the term Outsider comes not from Gage but from Virginia Woolf. As important as Gage was with respect to Daly's thinking about witches, Virginia Woolf was equally important to the overall project of *Gyn/Ecology*. It is interesting to note that Virginia Woolf (1882–1941), who on Daly's reconstruction was a sort of symbolic daughter of Matilda Joslyn Gage, was eleven years old when Gage's *Women, Church, and State* was published in the United States; and that Daly, symbolic daughter to Woolf, was ten years old when *Three Guineas* (1938) was published in England. In my view, Woolf is the single most important influence on Daly's radical feminist thought. The index of *Gyn/Ecology* contains fifteen reference to Virginia Woolf, (three times as many as to Simone de Beauvoir), and Daly repeatedly identifies Woolf as her feminist foresister. Like Gage, Woolf sets a precedent for Daly's emphasis on daring and independent thought. But Woolf's influence runs even deeper than Gage's. It is there in the conceptual framework of *Gyn/Ecology*, in the Outsider's journey from the patriarchal "foreground" to the feminist "Background."[4] There are sources of Daly's thought in Woolf's *Moments of Being* (1976) and *Three Guineas*.[5]

In her essay "A Sketch of the Past," included in *Moments of Being*, Woolf writes, "Behind the cotton wool is hidden a pattern" of human connectedness (Woolf 1976, 72). "Cotton wool" is her term for "nonbeing," that level of existence constituted by the moments "one does not remember," moments "not lived consciously." For example, she says, "One walks, eats, sees things, deals with what has to be done; the broken vacuum cleaner; ordering dinner; writing orders to Mabel; washing; cooking dinner; bookbinding" (Woolf 1976, 70). In contrast, Woolf describes "moments of being" as engaged, satisfying, highly conscious experiences that are "embedded" in the "nondescript cotton wool." She offers the activities of her previous day, including enjoying her writing, walking along the river, noticing the country very closely, reading Chaucer with pleasure, and starting a book of memoirs that interested her as examples of "moments of being." Behind the "cotton wool" appearances of people who live "very much like the characters in Dickens," she finds "the scaffolding in the background," patterns of satisfying and highly conscious moments (73). Awareness of these patterns comes as a shock, as "a revelation of some order; it is a token of some real thing behind appearances" (72).

I find Woolf's influence on *Gyn/Ecology* in Daly's ontological vision of radical feminism as "the journey of women becoming." Like Woolf, Daly appears to be interested in the process through which women, enmeshed in the cotton wool, come to be fully conscious, engaged, inner-directed individuals able to see through the cotton wool existence. Daly announces this process of radical becoming, which she calls "Be-ing," as a journey from the world of the phallocentric "foreground" to the gynocentric "Background." On my view, then, Daly's "foreground" is developed from Virginia Woolf's "cotton wool," and Daly's "Background" as the "realm of the wild reality of women's Selves" develops from Woolf's "scaffolding in the background." A defining feature of this distinction is one's level of awareness in each arena. In the foreground one moves through the world mechanically, without thought, according to patriarchal norms; in the Background, one moves in a highly reflective, Self-centering way, which acknowledges the organic connections among all things. For example, in *Gyn/Ecology*, the African mother who silently, and without conscious awareness of what she is doing, subjects her daughters to excision and infibulation exemplifies foreground movement, while the American feminist who speaks out of her conscious interconnection with all women to challenge the conspiracy of silence upheld by "objective" Western scholars on the subject exemplifies Background movement.

Woolf provides further insight into this ontological distinction in her autobiographical reflections. On Virginia's telling, her mother, Julia Jackson, and sister Stella Duckworth were caught in the "cotton wool" of pouring tea for distinguished men. Virginia remembers them as sad and silent and notes that neither left anything to remember them by (Woolf 1976, 83–88). Her brothers and her father, on the other hand, were engaged in a lively existence that included the finest education money could buy and abundant opportunities for making a mark on the world as "a Headmaster, an Admiral, a Cabinet Minister, a Judge" (132). Woolf remembers her father, Leslie Stephen, as a Victorian patriarch who engaged in weekly breast-beating tirades over the accounting books, tirades vented in "brutal" rages against Virginia's sister Vanessa (125). Virginia's brother George, who took social responsibility for the family, was critical and domineering. In one instance, Woolf remembers, George criticized her dress. "He was thirty-six when I was twenty. He had a thousand pounds a year and I had fifty. Those were reasons that made it difficult to defy George that night. But there was another element in our relationship which affected me as I stood there that winter's night exposed to his criticism in my green dress. I was not wholly conscious of it then. But besides feeling his age and his power, I felt too another feeling which I later called the outsider's feeling" (131–32). Interestingly, in this encounter, Virginia identifies not only the financial inequality as a cause of her beholden situation, but also identifies the origin of her resistance in the standpoint of the "outsider." This riveting sketch, which was published in the midst of Daly's writing *Gyn/Ecology*, must have appeared to Daly as a time capsule from a radical feminist foresister. Although the details of Daly's life are very different from those of Woolf's, Daly's identification with Woolf is deep. Both understood themselves as outsiders emerging from the cotton wool, or patriarchal foreground, in search of engaged, satisfying, highly conscious life experiences: Woolf's "moments of being," which become Daly's "Background Be-ing."

In *Three Guineas* Woolf seeks a path for "the daughters of educated men," daughters who, for the first time in history, have the means to make a mark in the world. Woolf sums up the revolutionary potential of this new influence in the following way:

> The educated man's daughter has now at her disposal an influence which is different from any influence that she has possessed before. It is not the influence which the great lady, the Siren, possesses; nor is it the influence which the educated man's daughter possessed when she had no vote; nor is it the influence which she possessed when she had a vote but was debarred from the right to earn a living. It differs, because it is an influence from which the money element had been removed. She need no longer use her charm to procure money from her father or brother. Since it is beyond the power of her family to punish her financially she can express her own opinions. (1977, 32)

On Woolf's view, economic independence from men is the condition for women's independent thought and action. On this model, freedom is won with "the weapon of independent opinion based upon independent income" (73).

The question of *Three Guineas* is how women will use this new influence. Woolf asks, will they follow in the processions of ruling class men? She argues that there is a difference between the situations of women and men that could enable women to maintain their freedom without joining the patriarchal processions. The difference is not a social- or economic-class difference, she notes, because women and men of "the educated class" "speak with the same accent, use knives and forks in the same way; expect maids to cook dinner and wash up after dinner; and talk during dinner without much difficulty about politics and people, war and peace, barbarism and civilization" (9). Rather, the difference is a gendered one:

> Take the fact of education. Your class has been educated at public schools and universities for five or six hundred years, ours for sixty. Take the fact of property. Your class possesses in its own right and not through marriage practically all the capital, all the land, all the valuables, and all the patronage in England. Our class possesses in its own right and not through marriage practically none of the capital, none of the land, none of the valuables, and none of the patronage in England. That such differences make for very considerable differences in mind and body, no psychologist or biologist would deny. (Woolf 1938, 1977, 33)

This difference is the effect of having been excluded from all professions of the public sphere in the name of God, Nature, Law and Property, which gives one very little stake in "civilization" (119). Thus, Woolf famously declared, "as a woman, I have no country. As a woman I want no country. As a woman my country is the whole world" (197). In a similar vein Angela Davis (1995) and Adrienne Rich (1978) argued in the seventies that being disenfranchised endows one with a particularly unique and useful political perspective, ground for agency, and set of possibilities.

Rather than join the processions of educated men, Woolf argues, the daughters should work for liberty, equality, and peace as outsiders (Woolf 1938, 1977, 192). She calls for an "Outsider's Society," which would have no office, no committee, no secretary, and no meetings and would hold no conferences. It would have no oaths, nor ceremonies, nor pageantry. Outsiders would live by the lessons of their own "unpaid-for" tradition of education.[6] According to Woolf, this tradition offers four great teachers, "poverty, chastity, derision, and freedom from unreal loyalties" (145). Poverty teaches that one must earn enough money to maintain one's independence, but not a penny more (145). Chastity teaches that one must refuse to sell one's brain for money. Derision teaches to "refuse all methods of advertising merit, and that ridicule, obscurity and censure are preferable, for psychological reasons, to fame and praise" (146). Finally, freedom from unreal loyalties teaches one *not* to identify with people on the basis of nation, religion, college, family, and sex

(146). If we live by these lessons, Woolf promises, we "can join the professions and yet remain uncontaminated by them" (151).

In the introduction to *Gyn/Ecology* Daly singles out Woolf's *Three Guineas* as a particularly important source of inspiration (Daly 1978, 33). Daly charts the journey from the foreground to the Background on the basis of Woolf's strategic attempts to think about how the daughters of educated men can at once maintain their economic independence and break with the processions of their fathers. On Daly's development, radical feminism is about not only economic independence from the fathers, but independence in all its dimensions, mind/body/spirit, in the midst of the ever-present invitations of assimilation and tokenism. Daly insists that in the process of inventing/creating our Selves, we must embrace our Otherness by re-membering our Selves as members of the Outsider's Society, who pledge allegiance to no flag, acting only in the interest of our conscious freedom to move in the Background.

Through re-membering Gage and Woolf, Daly re-constructs a radical feminist tradition of strong, knowledgeable, resistant women linked "Crone-ologically" with the European women burned as witches. What unites the tradition is the independent standpoint of the Outsider in patriarchy.

"What We Reveal to You Is that You Are Many . . ."

In the mirror of Lorde's "Open Letter to Mary Daly," the history of radical feminism re-constructed by Daly can be read as a Crone-ology of Sister *Insiders*.[7] After reading *Gyn/Ecology*, and finding everywhere Witches and Outsiders from a European Background, Lorde asked, "Where was Afrekete, Yemanje, Oyo, and Mawulisa? Where were the warrior goddesses of the Vodun, the Dahomeian Amazons and the warrior-women of Dan?" (Lorde 1984, 67). If the European witches of yesterday and the radical feminists of the late twentieth century are related in lines that run through Gage and Woolf, where does that leave the radical feminist who traces her Background traditions through India, China, or Africa? Lorde insists that "assimilation within a solely western european herstory is not acceptable" (69). Since the only Background tradition remembered in *Gyn/Ecology* is European, a feminist from another tradition is constructed in the text as a racial/ethnic outsider, a *Sister Outsider*.

What unites the European American feminist tradition, from this perspective, is an implicit allegiance to the standpoint of a gender outsider who is also, without awareness, a racial/ethnic insider.

One response, perhaps the most widespread, by European American feminists who have become aware of the construction of the Sister Outsider, is to advocate inclusion. On this view, Daly should have included strong, resistant female symbolic figures and Background histories from the traditions of the women in all the patriarchal cultures she interrogates. While the inclusion solution might enable one to recognize important differences in Background traditions, it ignores the patterns of *relation* between women from different feminist traditions by making it appear as if all women are similarly situated geopolitically as Outsiders to patriarchy. It might appear, for example, as if African women can aspire to become Outsiders just like European women if there is no interrogation of the relation between the African and European women. Since the problem is not a failure to hear and dialogue about differences, but rather a failure to hear and dialogue about the *relations* that construct differences, I recommend a rereading of Daly's *Gyn/Ecology* that highlights the ways in which radical feminist Outsiders from the European American tradition are also Insiders in relation to Outsiders from non-European American traditions. Daly's *Gyn/Ecology* offers a case study in the construction of an Insider's perspective that lacks awareness of itself as such. The rereading I propose is a consciousness-raising project designed to enable European American radical feminists to choose a pluralist self-conception that can facilitate dialogue and connection across differences.

A Foreground History of Sister Insiders . . .

In response to Lorde's criticisms, I take to heart María Lugones's suggestion that U.S. white women block identification with their self that constructs the woman of color as the sister outsider. Lugones says white women block identification because "knowing us in the way necessary to know that self would reveal to you that we are also more than one and that not all the selves we are make you important. Some of them are quite independent of you. Being central, being a being in the foreground, is important to your being integrated as one responsible decision maker. Your sense of responsibility and decision-making are tied to being able to say exactly who it is that did what, and that person must be one and have a will in good working order" (Lugones 1991, 42). I propose a self-critical reflective investigation to reveal how those of us raised as racial/ethnic insiders have separated ourselves from women who were raised as racial/ethnic outsiders. Hence, I am suggesting a return to Daly's text as an exercise in unblocking identification with the historically and geopolitcally constituted insider self. The goal is to move beyond old patterns of relating that continue to cause pain and thwart feminist connection.

Mary Daly wrote in 1990, "I hope that in its richness, as well as in its incompleteness, *Gyn/Ecology* will continue to be a Labrys enabling women to learn from our mistakes and our successes, and cast our Lives as far as we can go, Now, in the Be-Dazzling Nineties" (Daly 1990, xxxiii). The task of the radical feminist who wishes to unblock identification with, or dis/cover, the patterns of relating that constitute her as an insider is to reread the history of radical feminism as a Crone-ology of Sister Insiders in relation to those it constructs as Sister Outsiders. Let us begin here with what Daly says about the relationship between the foreground and the Background. She suggests that much of what appears as foreground reality is a reversal of Background reality. For example, she suggests that the Christian myth of the trinity, Father, Son, and Holy Ghost, is a reversal of the Triple Goddess in early mythology, Maiden, Mother, and Moon (Daly 1978, 75–79). The work of radical feminists, she says, is to "reverse the reversals." "In order to reverse the reversals completely we must deal with the fact that patriarchal myths contain stolen *mythic* power. They are something like distorting lenses through which we *can* see into the Background. But it is necessary to break their codes in order to use them as viewers; that is, we must see their lie to see their truth" (Daly 1978, 47). I propose a self-reflective shift in European American radical feminist thinking. If we can see into the Background only through the distorting lenses of foreground phenomena, we must acknowledge that the Background we are re-membering is a reversed reversal, and therefore, inevitably bears traces of the foreground. The traces I am concerned with here are the racist and/or ethnocentric assumptions and practices of the patriarchal foreground. If Lugones is right that each of us is a multiply constituted (not univocal) self, then part of a European American radical feminist politic must necessarily include raising awareness about historical patterns of relations between women from traditions differently situated with regard to racial/ethnic and geopolitical axes of power. From Lugones's perspective, individualist notions of responsibility must be challenged regardless of whether the responsible one is a patriarchal loyalist or a radical feminist. One might frame Daly's Outsider with Lugones's words by saying: "Being central, being a being in the [Background], is important to your being integrated as one [who governs Hagocracy]. Your sense of responsibility and decision-making are tied to being able to say exactly [what men have done to women], and that [Outsider] must be one and have a will in good working order." With this shift in mind let us re-view Daly's history of radical feminism to dis/cover the Sister Insider.

What Matilda Joselyn Gage passed down to Mary Daly was a radical feminist vision of resistance and transformation based on the power of independent thought and judgment. Recall that Daly develops Gage's claim that many women were persecuted as witches because of the threat that their independence presented to the church. Daly's thesis is that the witchcraze was an epistemological battle between the rising class of professional men and "a spiritual/moral/know-ing elite cross-section of the female population of Europe" (Daly 1978, 194). Now consider how the central value of independence looks from the perspective of women whose survival and resistance was based on the power of *inter*dependence. According to Lorde, this was the case for women of African traditions whose struggle was, by necessity, based on the power of female bonding (Lorde, 69). Notice how this difference in values points to a different focus on relations. For women of European descent the focus has, historically, been on *independence from men.* This was clearly the case for Woolf, who understood the challenge faced by the daughters of educated men as a struggle to maintain economic independence from men. In contrast, for women from non-Western traditions, the focus has been *interdependence on women* in the extended family and community. The Sister Insider, in this case, is the one whose focus has been on independence from men to the exclusion of interdependence with at least some women. She is an insider insofar as she is loyal to the order of values of the fathers who have traditionally understood freedom as an independent rather than collective interest.

Daly is a case in point. Although she seeks to identify the global nature of patriarchal oppression, the focus of each chapter in the Second Passage of *Gyn/Ecology* is on the relation between the Western patriarchal scholar whose "objectivity" distorts and erases gynocidal intent and the feminist Searcher whose "gynaesthetic" perception reveals and names this same intent. The project of this Passage is not to detect the patterns of relation among the women from the diverse patriarchal locations she investigates, with the exception of establishing the relation between the European witches and contemporary feminists that I mentioned earlier. The project is to dis/cover and create a feminist Self by engaging the epistemological battle of early modern Europe, present today between radical (academic) feminists and patriarchal scholars. Daly does not ask, as Lorde suggests she might have, about the "real connections" among women from diverse traditions.

However inadvertently, Daly replicates historical patterns of relating to women of non-Western cultures characteristic of Western women and men. For example, in the chapter on Indian suttee, Daly champions Katherine Mayo as an independent feminist Searcher who has been discredited and erased for her "daring" efforts to name atrocities against Indian women.[8] However, adopting Mayo's perspective, Daly situates herself in the tradition of white women saving brown women from brown men, which provided the moral justification for British imperialism. Because Daly's focus is simply independence from patriarchal scholars, she fails to interrogate the pattern of relation between Mayo and Indian women. By siding with Mayo, Daly situates herself more in relation to imperialist men than Indian women.[9]

I have argued above that Virginia Woolf influenced Mary Daly's thinking about the Outsider's journey of consciousness and practice from the patriarchal foreground to the feminist Background. This influence is present in Woolf's distinction between "cotton wool" moments of nonbeing and conscious moments of being, which Daly echoes in her distinction between patriarchal foreground and feminist Background existence. In order to reveal the Sister Insider embedded in this distinction, consider it from the perspective of Mabel, the domestic servant who Woolf mentions in her examples of activities that constitute the level of existence she calls nonbeing. Recall her comment that among the things one does that are not remembered, "not lived consciously," is "writing orders to Mabel." From Mabel's perspective, the *relation* between Woolf's engaged, satisfying, highly conscious "moments of being" (enjoying her writing and reading Chaucer with pleasure) and Woolf's unremembered "moments of nonbeing" (writing her orders to cook and clean) is probably obvious. Not only is the power relation between them is obscured by Woolf's construction of Mabel's work as nonbeing, but more important, Woolf's freedom *depends* on Mabel's servitude. The foreground/Background distinction itself is forged and constituted on Mabel's back. Woolf is independent of the men of her own class, but she is not independent of the women of Mabel's class. Insofar as Woolf is unconscious of her relations with women outside her class she is a privileged insider. Here again, it is not the collective interests of all women, but only the individual interests of a privileged class of women that concern Virginia Woolf.

Similarly, Daly's insider self is revealed through an interrogation of the distinction she inherits from Woolf. Like Woolf, who constructs the distinction between moments of nonbeing and being on Mabel's back, Daly constructs the distinction between the foreground and Background in part on the backs of the women from India, China, and Africa. Consider the fact that the feminist Seacher (the descendent of the witch) makes her Background self through uncovering the victimization of women who, in the text, have no Background existence at all. Of course there are women, in America and beyond, who are victimized to such an extreme extent that they experience nothing on the order of a significant moment of be-ing. The problem in *Gyn/Ecology* is that Daly only sees women from non-Western cultures in these situations. Hence, the feminist Searcher discovers the following basic difference between women of European descent and those of non-Western cultures.

> The situation of those accused of witchcraft was somewhat different from that of the footbound Chinese girls and of the genitally maimed girls and young women of Africa, for these were mutilated in preparation for their destiny—marriage. It was also somewhat different from the situation of the widows of India, who were killed solely for the crime of outliving their husbands. For the targets of attack in the witchcraze were not women defined by assimilation into the patriarchal family. Rather, the witchcraze focused predominantly upon women who had rejected marriage (Spinsters) and women who had survived it (widows). The witch-hunters sought to purify their society (The Mystical Body) of these "indigestible" elements—women whose physical, intellectual, economic, moral, and spiritual independence and activity profoundly threatened the male monopoly in every sphere. (Daly 1978, 184)

The witchcraze was not a slaughter of helpless victims, but a "battle" over knowledge fought by men against daring independent "Outsiders." In contrast, suttee, foot-binding, and genital mutilation are represented as crimes against helpless victims with no gynocentric traditions that might explain the patriarchal forces pitted against them or from which they might draw the strength to resist. The point is that the identity of the feminist Searcher in *Gyn/Ecology* is constructed through and *dependent* on the representation of non-Western women as victims rather than as victims *and* as descendants of non-Western gynocentric Background traditions. The radical feminist Journeyer's Background existence *depends* on deconstructing, or in Daly's lexicon "A-mazing," the foreground, which is necessarily constituted only by perpetrators and victims of patriarchal violence.

Of course, on Daly's view, these non-Western women were only victims and, therefore, naming their situation is the responsible and daring thing to do. Consider Daly's position on the African woman who is silenced by pain, who is subject to a conspiracy of silence involving academics, Catholics, liberal reformers, population planners, and "politicos of all persuasions":

> I have chosen to name these practices for what they are: barbaric rituals/atrocities. Critics from Western countries are constantly being intimidated by accusations of "racism," to the point of misnaming, non-naming, and not seeing these sado-rituals. The accusations of "racism" may come from ignorance, but they serve only the interests of males, not of women. This kind of accusation and intimidation constitutes an astounding and damaging reversal, for it is clearly in the interests of Black women that feminists of all races should speak out. Moreover, it is in the interest of women of all races to see African genital mutilation in the context of planetary patriarchy, of which it is but one manifestation. (Daly 1978, 154)

On Daly's view, accusations of racism are intended to keep white Western women, such as herself, from speaking out. Because she does not attend to the history of relations between Western women and African women, the possibility does not occur to her that the feminist act of speaking out against patriarchal violence might, at the same time, be a racist or ethnocentric act. Although she is aware that others will be critical of her exposé, she is not aware of how racism and ethnocentrism are embedded in her radical feminist perspective. She cannot see how speaking *for* the African woman implicates her in a relation that contributes to their oppression and constitutes her as an insider. Part of what keeps Daly from seeing the racism and ethnocentrism of her perspective is the responsibility she feels as a Feminist Searcher who knows, to speak out. She understands this responsibility as one that transcends the foreground ethics of race and racism. In Lugones's terms, her commitment to being a responsible decision maker, to being able to name patriarchal oppression, blocks her ability to see the duplicitous meaning and effects of her actions.

In defense of Daly one might argue that her case is quite different from that of Virginia Woolf. While Woolf explicitly limits her project to discovering a liberatory path for the daughters of educated men with little concern for the liberation of working class and poor women, Daly on the other hand argues explicitly that radical feminism must concern itself with the plight of all women. And where Woolf's stake in not seeing her relation to Mabel is obvious, Daly's stake in not seeing her geopolitical relation to the non-Western women she represents in *Gyn/Ecology* is not so obvious, at least not to white women. In fact, forging the foreground/Background distinction on the backs of Indian, African, and Chinese women in the book only jeopardizes her intention to further the liberation of all women. It would be unfair not to acknowledge this difference, and yet acknowledging it only helps to illustrate my point further. Daly's Outsider who strives to break the silence and speak out against the crime of genital mutilation is *also* the Insider who silences the other by speaking on her behalf. By naming the crime of genital mutilation "barbaric," Daly inadvertently situates herself with the "civilized" men of the educated class who "use knives and forks in the same way; expect maids to cook dinner and wash up after dinner; and talk during dinner without much difficulty about politics and people, war and peace, barbarism and civilization," while simultaneously, and ironically, she does the right thing in refusing to be silenced by white Western critics charging her with "racism"! This is the very multiplicity Lugones suggests we must acknowledge in the interest of feminist friendship for change.

Global Feminism

Finally, let us re-view Woolf's Outsider declaration "as a woman, I have no country. As a woman I want no country. As a woman my country is the whole world" (Woolf 1977, 197). Recall that she makes this proclamation from the epistemological standpoint of one who has been excluded from participation in the public sphere. By systematically embracing this outsider status she attempts to maintain her independence from patriarchal values without losing the freedom secured by the economic privileges of carrying on in the patriarchal professions. Daly follows Woolf arguing that by re-membering our Selves as members of the Outsider's Society who refuse to pledge allegiance to any flag we affirm our freedom. How is the Sister Insider revealed in this seemingly noble declaration?

In a recent essay, Susan Friedman reminds us that Adrienne Rich answered this question in a critique of Woolf's ethnocentrism. Rich offers this critique in the context of a self-criticism advanced along the lines I have been suggesting are called for by the politics of feminist bridge-building. Whereas previously Rich had understood her feminism unproblematically in the tradition of Woolf's declaration, in 1984 she reflected, "As a woman I have a country; as a woman I cannot divest myself of that country merely by condemning its government or by saying three times 'As a woman my country is the whole world.' Tribal loyalties aside, and even if nation-states are now just pretexts used by multinational conglomerates to serve their interests, I need to understand how a place on the map is also a place in history within which as a woman, a Jew, a lesbian, a feminist I am created and trying to create" (Rich 1984, 22). The Sister Insider is revealed in the Outsider's declaration of having no country insofar as it constitutes a denial, or just a lack of awareness, about the ways in which one bears the history of imperialism in their present patterns of relation. According to Friedman, however, Rich's critique constitutes a misreading of Woolf that is the result of Rich's felt need "in the 1980s to define a locational politics that did not erase the differences among women in the service of a false global sisterhood that potentially obscures the structure of power relations between different groups of women at home and abroad" (Friedman 1998, 197). But, Friedman argues, since Woolf is advocating "a transnational oppositional identity that replaces patriotism," rather than "a global sisterhood where gender oppression links women everywhere in a common sisterhood," her work "exhibits an early feminist formulation of a locational politics, not a repudiation of it, as Rich implies" (198–99).

What's most relevant to my concerns in this paper is that Friedman offers the critique of Rich in the context of a larger effort to sever a genealogical link between Daly and Woolf. Friedman reads Daly in the same way she reads Rich, as author of a misguided attempt to "globalize feminism" (Friedman 1998, 181). Pointing to the problem with the global-feminist theory in this U.S. radical feminist tradition, Friedman says:

> The difficulties and dangers of such an internationalization are significant. Unless one's field is itself comparative, learning about women and gender systems in other parts of the world from one's base of specialization requires a considerable time investment to acquire sufficient contextual knowledge about other societies and histories. Feminist bricolage or patchwork so beautiful and provocative in the arts is not so beautiful in theory and scholarship. Plucking bits and pieces of women's lives and gender systems from here and there is seriously ahistorical, oblivious to the local overdeterminations of cultural formations. (Friedman 1998, 182)

In a footnote, Friedman suggests, "Mary Daly's *Gyn/Ecology* is the most notorious example of such decontextualized internationalization of feminism" (217). Without denying the mistakes Daly made as a Sister Insider, I think it is important to reflect critically on Friedman's dismissal. On Friedman's view, attempting to make global connections among gender systems is "dangerous" for anyone without a "base of specialization" or a "considerable time investment," in other words for those not in the most privileged knowledge/power positions. The language she uses here shares a family resemblance with the language that was used by the U.S. scholars in the seventies who tried to discredit the efforts of feminists who were attempting to make connections that revealed patriarchy as a planetary phenomenon. A large part of *Gyn/Ecology* is devoted to deconstructing the scholarship that attempted to persuade women that making such connections was itself racist or ethnocentric. For example, Daly argues, many female scholars use the deceptive language of "objective scholarship" because "the temptation to identify with the male viewpoint—which is legitimated by every field—is strong, and the penalties for not doing so often intimidate women into self-deception" (Daly 1978, 126). My point in highlighting this resemblance is to caution against trusting that scholars with "specializations" are better situated than others (for example, domestic workers, artists, people who listen to public radio, or even self-reflective Sister Insiders) to do the work of globalizing feminism.

I believe that if the goal is raising awareness of global patterns of oppression in the interests of changing of them, we should all be trying, in every way we can, using whatever resources and skill we have, to make the connections. Of course, we will not always get the picture right (if there is such a beast), but we will surely get it wrong if we fail to study mistakes we have made in the past for what they can teach us about historical patterns of relation that continue to thwart our best efforts to make connections across difference. Hence, the problem with severing the genealogical link between Daly and Woolf—as Friedman does by arguing that Daly's global feminism is decontextualized while Woolf's is not—is that it obscures the lessons that I have been arguing can be learned from a rereading of Daly in the radical feminist Outsider's tradition of Gage and Woolf. In other words, it does a serious disservice to the project of understanding the historical relations that have constituted radical feminism to deny, as Friedman implicitly does, that Woolf and Daly can and should be read together in the tradition of the Sister Insider.

Conclusion

In my view there is much to be learned from re-reading *Gyn/Ecology* with regard to moving dialogues forward among feminists across racial and ethnic differences. I have suggested that the work of María Lugones provides useful insights for developing a way to reread Daly's radical feminism that is responsive to Audre Lorde's criticisms. Part of what can be accomplished through such a rereading is a sense of one's self in relation to others, which makes a deeper kind of hearing possible. It is my hope that realizing this possibility will contribute to the practical development of a model for feminist relating across differences. I have recently experimented with and developed this rereading in the process of coming to know and befriend Debra Barrera Pontillo, a Chicana artist and teacher with whom I have had the good fortune (in a predominantly white academic context) to work. At times, this process had been harrowing and painful. However, coming to know myself as a radical feminist in relation to Debra, unblocking identification with my historically constituted ethnic/racial insider self, has enabled me to hear her more fully. It has also enabled us to engage fruitfully in dialogue across our differences. Some of these dialogues have made us an effective force for change within our academic community. My experience, informed by my rereading of radical feminism with an insider perspective, affirms Gloria Anzaldúa's proclamation "Caminante, no hay puentes, se hace puentes al andar (*Voyager, there are no bridges, one builds them as one walks*)" (Anzaldúa 1981, v).

Notes

This essay began as a chapter in my dissertation. It grew from my studies with Marilyn Frye, who has been my ally, respectful critic, and model of how to do philosophy since 1988. I am grateful to Claudia Card for her patience, thoughtful comments, and critical suggestions throughout the revision process.

1. Audre Lorde attached a note to the version of the open letter published in *Sister Outsider*, which said, "The following letter was written to Mary Daly, author of *Gyn/Ecology*, on May 6, 1979. Four months later, having received no reply, I open it to the community of women." Daly reports in the "New Intergalactic Introduction," in *Gyn/Ecology*, that she had a meeting with Lorde to discuss the letter on September 29, 1979, at the Simone de Beauvoir Conference in New York. She reports, "I explained my positions clearly, or so I thought. . . . Apparently Lorde was not satisfied, although she did not indicate this at the time." She concludes her brief comments on Lorde's letter, "It continues to be my judgment that public response in kind would not be a fruitful direction. In my view, *Gyn/Ecology* is itself an 'Open Book' " (Daly 1990, xxx). Audre Lorde died of breast cancer in 1992.

2. This is not the only historical re-construction of this sort. Another original effort is offered by feminist philosopher Claudia Card in "What is Lesbian Culture?" (1995).

3. According to Josephine Donovan, Gage is "the first to see the witches as bearers of alternative feminine traditions, which established them as community powers feared by the church" (Donovan 1992, 41).

4. At times I follow Daly's "irregular" practices of capitalization, which conform more to meaning than to common usage, as a way of both revealing her influence and engaging her work on her terms. She explains that "in writing of the deep *Background* which is the divine depth of the Self, I capitalize, while the term *foreground*, referring to surface consciousness, generally is not capitalized" (Daly 1978, 26).

5. The influence of Woolf's *A Room of One's Own* (1929) on Daly's *Gyn/Ecology* is also evident, although I have not explored it here. See, for example, "Separation: Room of One's Own" (Daly 1978, 380–84).

6. In order to reconstruct this tradition she consults the biographies of Florence Nightingale, Ann Clough, Emily Brontë, Christina Rossetti, and Mary Kingsley.

7. My thinking in this section has been most influenced by María Lugones, as indicated by the quote in the subheading. These are her words.

8. For insightful critical studies on this pattern of relation that implicate Daly, see Mrinalini Sinha, "Reading Mother India: Empire, Nation, and the Female Voice." *Journal of Women's History* 6 (Summer 1994); and Gayatri Spivak, "Can the Subaltern Speak? Speculations on Widow-Sacrifice." *Wedge*, nos. 7/8 (Winter/Spring 1995).

9. In many quarters revealing this pattern raises questions for feminists who are working for social change with women who are situated differently with regard to the dominant axes of power.

For example, at my college there is an emphasis on service learning that many of my feminist colleagues support. The pedagogical rationale that is often cited in support of service learning is the empowerment of the students. Through serving those in need, it is said, students realize their potential for making positive change. The focus here is on the establishment of an independent student capable of exercising her own judgment, her own conscience, her own will. Reflecting on the patterns of the sister insider prompts important questions: How often are service learning projects designed around the value of interdependence with the goal of restructuring power relations between those who "serve" and those who "need"? Who designs these projects? Who is served by them?

References

Alcoff, Linda, and Elizabeth Potter. 1993. *Feminist Epistemologies*. New York: Routledge.

Card, Claudia. 1991. *Feminist Ethics*. University of Kansas, 1995.

———. 1995. "What is Lesbian Culture?" In *Lesbian Choices*. New York: Columbia University Press.

Donovan, Josephine. 1992. *Feminist Theory: The Intellectual Traditions of American Feminism*. New expanded edition. New York: Continuum.

Daly, Mary. (1978) 1990. *Gyn/Ecology: The Metaethics of Radical Feminism*. Boston: Beacon Press.

Davis, Angela. (1971) 1995. "Reflections on the Black Woman's Role in the Community of Slaves." In *Words of Fire: An Anthology of African-American Feminist Thought*, edited by Beverly Guy-Sheftall, 200–218. New York: New Press.

Elspeth, Whitney. 1995. "International Trends: The Witch 'She'/The Historian 'He.' " *Journal of Women's History* 7, no. 3: 75–101.

Friedman, Susan. 1998. "Geopolitical Literacy: Internationalizing Feminism at 'Home': The Case of Virginia Woolf." In *Mappings: The Locations of Feminism in the Borderlands*. Princeton: Princeton University Press.

Gage, Matilda Joslyn. (1893) 1980. *Women, Church, and State: The Original Exposé of Male Collaboration Against the Female Sex*. Watertown, Mass.: Persephone.

Kramarae, Cheris, and Dale Spender, eds. 1992. *The Knowledge Explosion: Generations of Feminist Scholarship*, New York: Teachers College Press.

Lorde, Audre. 1984. *Sister Outsider: Essays and Speeches by Audre Lorde*. Freedom, Calif.: Crossing Press.

Lugones, María. 1987. "Playfulness, 'World'-Traveling, and Loving Perception." *Hypatia* 2, no. 2: 3–19.

———. 1991. "On the Logic of Pluralist Feminism." In *Feminist Ethics*, edited by Claudia Card. University Press of Kansas.

———. 1994. "Purity, Impurity, and Separation." *Signs* 19, no. 2: 458–479.

Lugones, María, in collaboration with Pat Alake Rosezelle. 1992. "Sisterhood and Friendship as Feminist Models," in Kramarae and Spender.

Moraga, Cherríe, and Gloria Anzaldúa, eds. (1981) 1983. *This Bridge Called My Back: Writings by Radical Women of Color*. New York: Kitchen Table Press.

Rich, Adrienne. (1978) 1979. "Disloyal to Civilization: Feminism, Racism, and Gynephobia." In *On Lies, Secrets, and Silence: Selected Prose, 1966–1978*. New York: Norton.

———. 1984. "Notes Toward a Politics of Location." In *Blood, Bread, and Poetry: Selected Prose, 1979–1985*. New York: Norton.

Woolf, Virginia (1938) 1977. *Three Guineas*. London: Hogarth.

———. 1976. *Moments of Being: Unpublished Autobiographical Writings*. Edited and with an introduction and notes by Jeanne Schulkind. New York: Harcourt Brace Jovanovich, 1976.

12

Where Silence Burns: *Satī* (suttee) in India, Mary Daly's Gynocritique, and Resistant Spirituality

Renuka Sharma and Purushottama Bilimoria

We wish to take this occasion to reread Mary Daly by revisiting (after Audre Lorde) Daly's astute critique of the practice and discourse of suttee (*satī*) in India.[1] The critique appears as chapter 3 of the Second Passage and is titled "Indian *Suttee*: The Ultimate Consummation of Marriage" in her by now legendary and authoritative work *Gyn/Ecology: The Meta-ethics of Radical Feminism* (1978). We are moved to focus on this particular treatment by Mary Daly for three critical reasons, each of which considers distinctive moves in the larger tapestry of the problematic and the disputations surrounding the specific discourse. So it is important to state these reasons at the beginning, as the questions raised under each also centrally guide and inform the analysis in the rest of the essay, although not in that order.

The reasons are the following: (1) *Satī* at the symbolic level continues to evoke a uniquely troublesome image of a particularly gratuitous facticity of suffering of women anywhere, or so the claim goes. As such this "transgression" against (Indian Hindu) women, a cause célèbre if ever there was one, demands a decisive, indeed a radical, response. But the story of the originary impulse, the history of the practice, and the accounts hitherto presented in the long chain of articulations, narrative representations, critical reflections, commentaries thereto, and so on, are far from conclusive, definitive, or complete. Why should the next-issued account or critique around the corner be thought to be so? More significant, what is crucially at stake? Is it universality of ethics, natural rights, self-preservation, cultural virtues, an individual's honor, a woman's dignity, women's empowerment, the moral right to life, duty of care, society's protective obligations, rightful spirituality, some or all of these, or much else? Further, what is the determinant question here? That of agency or of free will (the *satī*'s or another's), of submerged or erased subjectivity, of active or passive coercion, of voluntary homicide, or murder, or ritual sacrifice, or of a culture's portended suicide, and so on and so forth? The culture where the conundrum is located remains anguished or is still thinking through these and related questions. Let us call this the indigenous *angst*.

This leads us to the second reason: (2) It is an avenue for engaging with Daly on the range of issues that such a formation and its variegated treatments throws up for consideration. But these are the issues (sampled above), in some form or reformulations, that are also baited and championed as it were from outside of the historical-cultural context of its formation, or to be precise, in the broader context of the apparently stable and unbounded canons of positional criticism and indeed of 'metaethics.' (The subtitle of Daly's book enlists the "fourth critique," in other words, the prodromus of metaethics to the more generalized cause.) Our question to this intervention is, Do the issues substantially remain the same, or do they change, or are they different for being critical and metaethical, and thereby more urgent? And where, if anywhere, do the twain from the two directions of disputation meet? Where lies the locus of moral responsibility? Reason 1 and 2 together, then, form the pretext for the main thrust of the essay, which takes us to our third reason.

(3) We feel that there is a reflexive imperative to take on board alternative perspectives in respect to the debate on *satī* (recalling elements of (1) above) as well as the kinds of resistance and challenge that have

begun to emerge. The context is thus: at present there is a disjunctive confrontation of the discursive over-determination stemming largely from Western gynocritiques of "third world" morality against the tide of post-orientalist, postcolonial and postindologist *metaécrit* that is working through themes such as the praxis of traditional segregation, identity formations, colonial and nationalist (dis)empowerments, violence and sexuality, and so on. This tension is played out as much on the debate concerning *satī*, and the dominance of the former genre in particular is resisted and challenged. The resistance and challenges in part mark a repositioning of the lost or suppressed voices in the disputation and a space, albeit "third space," as a condition for the possibility of indigene women's spirituality. "Does the *satī* [subaltern] speak?" is the question made famous by Gayatri Spivak. That, though, is only one of the critical tropes; and it may even be a loaded question to ask, in some ways, because it trades on a tacit binary (*satī* and bipolar authorial another), and the implied inherent contradiction does not necessarily exhaust a nuanced hermeneutic of the much-touted erased subjectivity of the silent "victim," much less of the self-reflexive understanding of the culture in question. There is understandably a motive in resisting a straitlaced answer to this question, or in not being resigned to the assumed total passivity of the interred subjectivity. This cultural politics of resistance has ramifications for a feminist ethics. Given this scenario, compounded by the complexity of the subject matter in question, the bulk of the essay is devoted to this exploration. So as not to beg the question, our own position is situation not within the binary, nor quite in the discursive efforts indicated under (2), but rather on the margins of (3), and with a sensitive *epoché* towards (1). The refurbished critique and some gestures that we offer are far from being intended as a resolution to the whole question of the *satī*.

As said earlier, the analysis will proceed by our unpacking the motivations underpinning the three reasons; the connections among them are more contingent than logical, and for this reason the argument will only emerge more fully with the discussion of the third reason or motivation in Part II of the essay. So the first move in the argument responds counterfactually to (2), and the second move develops a positive response to (3), corresponding respectively to the two parts of the essay. It should be patently obvious that the issues we are called upon to examine are complex, extremely sensitive, and fraught with difficulties that require more than the modicum of acute methodological and theoretical groundedness than has usually been accessed in this debate, although we draw upon its wisdom too. Our analysis therefore has its own limitations, though we will have succeeded in the tasks set out if the boundaries of the discussion commenced by Daly are pushed in a direction that make it contemporaneously relevant. It might also open up a common space for negotiating solidarity of motivations between hitherto disparate (or for some critics, the unspeakably incommensurable) vectors of the postmodern feminist critique and the postcolonial critique of the phenomenon at hand. But that negotiation itself would be too large an undertaking, and we are not presently adequately equipped for it.

Part I: The Moral Menace

A. *Definitions and Descriptive Parameters*

Mary Daly is moved by a legitimate concern to bring to the attention of the global village a particularly worrying phenomenon that has bedeviled women in the Indian subcontinent for some centuries now. We will shortly ponder questions of definition and the setting up of descriptive parameters that best capture the phenomenon at issue and its associated practices as these are etched in Daly's treatment. But very generally Daly is perturbed, indeed incensed, by (in her own opening words) the "Indian rite of *suttee*, or widow-burning" (Daly 1978, 114). In the specific location of its enactment, "the hindu rite of *suttee* spared widows from the temptations of impurity by forcing them to 'immolate themselves,' that is, to be burnt alive, on the funeral pyres of their husbands" (115). To Daly's way of thinking this "ritual sacrifice," alien as it might appear to contemporary Western society, speaks hideously of an abominable and contemptible evil: it raises a universal moral and ontological problem concerning the subjugation of women, real or symbolic, to forces of oppression, violence, torture, tyranny, massacre, and death in any and all locations. This is a genuine and nonnegotiable concern, as it perspicuously arises from a caring attitude toward the welfare and survival of women *in concreto*, and not merely because the practice instantiates a form of patriarchal goddess-murdering sado-ritual or some such mythical or mystical felony.

In what looks to be a tendentious move, Daly next draws a complicitous link between "our" (meaning Western) rituals of patriarchal oppression and Western scholarship that participated in the enactment of this seemingly alien ritual by providing the resources and sanction for the particular "rite of female sacrifice" through this act of scholarship. Indeed, the latter intervention has been well documented in colonial literature. Bordering on the hermeneutic of suspicion, Daly has a two-pronged motivation for making recourse to Western scholarly sources on this social phenomenon, to wit: (a) a disinclination to research indigenous (Indian) scholarship, for its reliability would be questionable to the same degree on account of its patriotic/patriarchal defensive agenda (although Indian feminists would find this reticence a trifle offensive to their own endeavors and therefore epistemologically lacking); more interesting, (b) by using and examining the Western knowledge source she would paradoxically be able to reveal its own complicity in a regime of power that is both oppressive and deceptive (for knowledge is also power). Inverting (and thereby shaming) a scholarship from which something of importance nonetheless is gleaned, she can, in that most Nietzschean of moves, also help discern a pervasive, indeed a universal, tendency in the androcentric social order toward the depositioning of women. (Babou: *Truth is woman!*)

Whether the avowed latter strategy is by itself sufficient to demonstrate the global infestation of patriarchy with its common structures (sado-ritual syndrome) in different times and other cultures is of course a moot question, to which we shall return again in the context of orientalist and colonialist handling of this issue. The thrust of this motivation nevertheless is consistent with Daly's quest of underscoring a value ethics for women *qua woman* and to articulate a radical outrage against global patriarchy's violations of women's self-determination. (Although, it may be observed in passing, Daly is conspicuously silent on the vexed question of the universality of human rights or women's moral rights as being on a par with men's or human beings' natural rights, as in the classical liberal formulations; but this need not detract much from the exclusive gyno-ethic enterprise that she has been engaged in.) In this respect, Daly's poignant intervention in this erstwhile and benighted debate is most important as it carries a compelling message of care and responsibility. No contemporary humanly concerned beings worth their soul could afford to ignore the issue, without risking the opprobrium of antihumanism and other myopic or even divine excesses. And as an accomplished gynocritic, she succeeds admirably in this project, considered against the background of the various different (or diversely located) instances of violative practices against women and aligned issues that she addresses in her works in the horizon of contemporary and radical or postmodern critiques of a stridently patriarchal and androcentric-dominated world order despite (or in spite of?) the advances of (European) Enlightenment with its progressive ideals of an egalitarianism, representative/participatory democratic framework, liberties of the individual, and so on. (Although, again, Daly would not wish to bet *her* virtues of "Shenergy" (*Shakti*) on these promissory accomplishments.)

However, the articulations that Daly presents us with are not without their own problems and difficulties. We shall examine her analysis and the summation she draws from her study with a view to complementing her argument with the following suggestion. The phenomenon needs to be better contextualized in the historical and cultural specificities of the society in which it occurs, and a more fine-tuned epistemic archeology or anthropology is needed if we are ever to gain access to or reconstruct in (or from) hindsight the agency of the women involved in it. It is not that Daly is oblivious to these methodological and subject-positional issues, on the contrary; but given the period and context in which Daly was writing on this, and now with some twenty or so years behind her, one cannot ignore the wealth of recent scholarship and soul-searching that has gone on, especially with the entry of Indian feminists and postcolonial critics into the fray. And so anyone reading her work heretofore in contiguity with this intermediate ground stands to gain a better grasp of the phenomenon, even if the subcontinental critiques might not—as they clearly do not invariably—converge with nor directly reinforce Daly's judgment about the classification of *satī* as a crime or, in this context, her preeminent commitment to the inexorable universality of patriarchal macho-ritualism. Our critical reappraisal of Daly's position on *satī* has to be viewed in this light: it is an overture, not an oeuvre, and certainly not an "attack" on her laudable work. We shall begin by considering the basis of the sources of knowledge that Daly singles out for her treatment and interpretation of those very sources in the ambience of the larger principle and concerns about gynocidal practices in the Western and non-Western modalities that she has worked through in her writings.

Daly is at pains to present an understanding of the phenomenon by casting it in its social context. But what would this mean? The first point to note is that the descriptive terms deployed in part come out of a particular mode of representation, and they therefore betray various strata of covert constructs. Although this is not a major point, it may nonetheless be noted that the exclusive use of the orientalist/early colonial romanization of the Sanskrit and vernacular cognate as "suttee," in contrast to the current practice of translitering the same Sanskrit term as *satī* (which denotes a virtuous wife), makes one wonder about the current status of the sources used. The term "suttee" became widely used in written European and English literature in the early part of this century, and curiously it persists in popular pulp and other media as well. Either way, "suttee," or *satī*, certainly bears connection with marriage and wedlock, especially when conjoined with *Savitrī*, the name of a heroine from Hindu mythology who is likened to Sītā the princess-wife of Rāma in the epic *Rāmāyana*. But what is the connection of *satī*, so understood, with the clause in the subtitle of Daly's essay: "The Ultimate Consummation of Marriage"? Admittedly, its exclamatory insertion is intended to draw a rhetorical blush. But as a well-constructed consequent phrase separated from the antecedent by a colon, its meaning is ambiguous. For on the one hand it seems to want to impute a claim that for Indians all or most marriages end in the immolation of a widow, while on the other hand it appears to decode the male partner's entitlement to total sexual possession of the female partner in a patriarchal marriage institution. If we took the former as the intended meaning, then we would have to say this: While it is true that Sītā herself underwent an intolerably severe test to prove her chastity, it does not follow that her marriage would be consummated in *satī*. Protecting the chastity of women in the tradition and the feminine imaginary ascribed to Sītā precede any reference in the literature to *satī* or other forms of bridal destruction. *Satī*, in its literal trope as a wife enabled by great virtues, might be *implied* by a marriage; but a marriage does not necessarily entail *satī* in the Indian or in any institution, patriarchal or otherwise. However, this may not be Daly's intended reading of *satī*, in which case we could assume the latter reading, namely, *satī* ritually carries the theme of sexual ownership out to its "ultimate conclusion" and thereby, in a way, discloses the meaning of marriage in patriarchy as few other evidences she enlists do. The nonliteral reading then is quite acceptable.

On the specific question of the pervasiveness of the ritual act of *satī* itself, Daly is aware and rightly cautions her readers that this "ritual is largely confined to the upper caste, although there was a tendency to spread downwards" (Daly 1978, 115; and we shall have more to say on this under Part II). However, she points to numerous anecdotes about surviving widows and other forms of victimization of married women, girl-children, and women that occur generally in rural India, alongside dowry-deaths and suicide.

Now for a suspect definition of *satī* (under "suttee") Daly initially refers to *Webster's* (although the *Shorter Oxford English Dictionary* would have been a little less circumspect), and she is troubled by its underscoring of the free will and "devotion" on the part of the widow in committing herself to the deceased husband. The *Webster's* definition reads: "the act or custom of a Hindu woman *willingly* cremating herself or being cremated on the funeral pyre of her husband as an indication of her *devotion* to him" [emphasis is Daly's]. She comments, "It is thought-provoking to consider the reality behind the term *devotion*, for indeed a wife must have shown signs of extraordinary slavish devotion during her husband's lifetime, since her very life depended upon her husband's state of health." (Daly 1978, 116). She also returns to the question of the description of such barbaric practices of "human sacrifice" as "custom." We suppose the point Daly is making by pointing to this definition is that Western scholarship (in which *Webster's* presumably stands tall in the United States) remains complicit in this victimization of women. But Daly wants to scrutinize the wisdom of ascribing "willingness," in other words choice and agency, in the active voice, and "devotion," in other words unflinching conjugal commitment to the just-deceased husband lying on the pyre, on the part of the widow. For Daly this "agency" can only be a *deferred* agency, as it is not in respect to herself but only in respect to and in the sole interest of the husband. How can this be an "active agency?" This is a contentious point (to which we shall return again) and obviously the lexical scribes at *Webster's* did not sit up to examine the niceties of the definition they most likely adopted or adapted from an orientalist logbook. Daly is right in drawing our attention to the persistence of the rejected or dated material, as this source remains authoritative in many a library and on many encyclopedic shelves around the world. Daly has faith that by deconstructing such short-sighted descriptions it may be possible "to re-*cover* women's history." This may indeed be a noble motive, but a bad piece of scholarship can only be unhinged (if not also blocked) by a more reliable scholarship and, in this instance, a complex definition fitting to the occasion. Reference to both indigenous understanding of the phenomenon and current scholarship (both Western and non-Western) would certainly be indispensable for countering such simplistic resources. For a contrast precisely as concerns the complexity of the nuances involved in a such seemingly simple term as *satī*, one would do well to turn to Sutherland-Goldman (1999), Mani (1992), Spivak (1985), Courtright and Harlan (1995), and Hawley (1994, 11–15). Alas, all such works have emerged well after Daly's pioneering work.

Daly therefore has a general concern that the Western accounts that appear to be popular are already constrained by being located in the colonial discourse on the culture of alterity, because they make the victims appear as agents of their own destruction. As an example of this, Daly cites Benjamin Walker, a colonial scholar who wrote in the late 1790s on the apparently customary practice among the northern Indian warrior group of Rajputs whose wives, mistresses, sisters, mothers, sisters-in-law, and other female relatives would "burn themselves" along with their deceased master. Walter links this extended practice of *satī* (he uses the more acceptable romanization) to the rise of the practice of *jauhar,* purportedly common in wars (notably during the Muslim onslaught of India) and other perils, whereby whole communities of women would "immolate themselves" or commit suicide as a defiant act of saving the honor of their clan (on the presumption that their husbands would not return alive from the war). Daly, again, is correct in noting, and questioning, Walker's suggestion that the women's "choices" are wholly free and they actively and freely choose to die. For Walker, like numerous British administrators and writers of his ilk, was only permitted to observe such rituals from a distance, and so would have had very little knowledge of the intricacies of the intra-cultural negotiations that would have preceded this stage in the process. But it is instructive that Walker draws a connection between *satī* and other practices of self-initiated death that broadens the context in more complex ways than might otherwise appear, by hinting at the possible element of collective resistance in the face of social calamities. Perhaps Walker intended to generalize this resistance in the case of Indian women by ascribing a muted but active agency to the women in the face of other such predicaments. But this is not clear from Daly's discussion of Walker.

Likewise, Daly chastises Joseph Campbell's skewed judgment that it would be wrong of us to even try to imagine the psychological state and experience of the widow on the basis of our own imaginable reactions, as she is consumed by the fire along with the corpse of her husband on the pyre. Daly points out that Campbell's reasoning is that these widows were not in any manner distinguishable from the communal group, class, or clan of which they were a member and hence could not be said in any significant sense to be endowed with the "realization of a personal individual destiny or responsibility" (Daly 1978, 117).[2] Campbell virtually brackets out the question of individual agency; he might even think it to be a largely irrelevant issue here. Instead, he pleads to a mood of detachment, which, however, might be taken as ignoring the subjectivity of the women's suffering. Campbell also dilates on the philological root of the term *satī* to draw out an *ontological* dimension to the rite, whose metaphysical reaches, however, would distance the bearer from the mundane and social travails of living. Campbell's tone is apologetic, and in his effort to contextualize the agency and subjectivity relative to their historical and cultural locations, he refrains from blaming the women for their own destruction. It is immensely insightful of Daly to have picked out a representative orientalist characterization of *satī* that attempts to ground its definition in learned Sanskritic scholarship, although it raises the same sorts of issues for Daly as the other two definitions considered earlier. However, Campbell's self-confessed judgment is also the most instructive of the three sources Daly has examined, as it not only makes women's agency an issue to be grappled with, but also circumscribes an ontological *telos* by internalizing the social-moral responsibility, in other words, the normative culture, in the said "victim" and thereby distances her from the domain of the social order. Campbell might not have been careful in his choice of words, but there is a glimmer of the scope for an "altered state of spirituality," which some indigenist scholars have been moved to underscore, as we shall see a little later in the essay. It is worth re-citing Campbell's passage in question in full here. "*Satī*, the feminine participle of *sat*, then, is the female who really *is* something in as much as she is truly and properly a player of the female part: she is not only good and true in the ethical sense but true and real ontologically. In her faithful death, she is at one with her own true being" (Daly 1978, 117).

Daly does not offer an alternative positive critique of the broader contours of the traditional discourse to which Campbell is obviously making an appeal. As we just saw, Daly is quick in her dismissal of Campbell's oversight on the "ontological and moral problems surrounding female massacre" (Daly 1978, 119); in other words, he appears to ignore female suffering and exemplifies an "androcratically attached de-tachment from women's agony." It eludes the scholar that the pain and misery is of "a woman destroyed by Patriarchal Religion (in which he is a true believer), which demands female sacrifice." However, Daly does not provide a means for retrieving the erased *subjectivity* and *agency* of the individual women concerned in the specific locations.

B. *Mayo and the Question of Representation*

Daly believes, against the grain of popular Indian and current South Asian scholarly opinion, that there is one writer who is exceptional and shows a deep understanding of the situation in all its complexity. Here we are introduced to Katherine Mayo and her famously controversial work *Mother India,* published in 1927. But Mayo's account as Daly introduces it primarily underscores the horrors of child brides, and it is juxtaposed with anecdotal narratives from various other Western writers on gynocidal atrocities, notably by Van Bullough (*The Subordinate Sex*) and the defensive stance on *satī* taken by David and Vera Mace, writing in 1960.[3] Still, it is Mayo's account on which Daly relies most for the historical adoption of the "rite" of *satī* and its subsequent revival since its legal banning by the British governor William Bentinck, acting for the East India Company administration in 1829. Mayo wrote that it was a belief common in the Hindu community that the woman had to assuage and suffer for her husband's death because it was her sins from a former life that had determined this fate. There was no other course for meting out justice in such a dire situation but for her to succumb to the fires of her husband's pyre in order that both partners may be liberated into an unencumbered future existence. Mayo of course conflated a number of different beliefs and generalized another from a commendation, not an injunction, that has only existed among a minor fraction of the Hindu society at any one time and in only one or a few unrelated regions of the vast subcontinent. Daly does not question this overrepresentation.

While Daly notes candidly the plethora of articles and books that were issued in the wake of Mayo's purportedly realistic assessment of the situation, she remonstrates against the opposition to the latter's brilliantly demonstrated understanding of the phenomenon "*within the context of the entire culture*" (1978, 128; Daly's emphasis). But we are not given much insight into the "*context.*" Instead, she cautions feminist researchers to be aware of heuristic devices that accuse honest researchers of "one-sidedness" and other intimidation tactics intended to induce fear against criticizing "another culture." Of course, Daly is alluding to the discourse of orientalism and anthropological alterity, which together seek to check the projections of Western terms of reference and representations of the "other" in the image of one's own past history, glories, anguishes, and trajectory. This appeal is a common ruse on the part of gynocidal patriarchal regimes, it would seem, and it could lead to debilitation, erasure, and silencing of the feminist voice, as it attempts to articulate the plight of its oppressed sisters in the third world and other cultures. And so the Feminist Sisters/Spinsters and Hags (in her own words) are encouraged to "search out and claim such sisters as Katherine Mayo" (Daly 1978, 129).

We believe that Daly has conflated two different projects in her highly selective use of modernist resources. The two projects are (a) the search for evidence of the universality of patriarchal religious oppression of women, and (b) locating the agency and subjectivity of women in their most horrific torture or sado-ritual agony particularized in their historical and cultural contexts. Thus the erasure or even the absence (as in moments of silence) of women's agency—which she assumes must otherwise always be in the active state—and subjectivity (again, in active voice) is taken as an evidence of patriarchy's totalizing destruction. While there is much urgency in casting *satī* in a wider or global framework (a project we are sympathetic with), there are nevertheless less global and more particularist frameworks in which *satī* has to be recast if certain other questions about the feminine imaginary and women's role in its formation are not to be marginalized. Daly does not sufficiently distinguish between the two projects (and the subtleties within [b] in particular), nor argue for the necessary logical connection, indefeasibly and seamlessly, between the two moments. It is for this reason that we believe also that Daly fails to suggest a way in which it would be possible to inscribe the subjectivity and agency of the women in the condition of suffering, everywhere and anywhere. The Anglicized and colonial representation of *satī* as "suttee" presupposes the woman as being without agency and merely following out a destiny over which she has no real individual control. Although Daly will question it, this representation strikingly echoes the accounts Daly enlists for her own criticism and takeoff point, and appears therefore to support her summation for project (a). However, the "victims" are not the ones likely to benefit from this judgment; nor is the research likely to take more fruitful directions if this impasse is not overcome. In saying this we do not intend to suggest, as some writers do univocally, that white, middle-class, bourgeois scholars invariably commit the fault of orientalism when they attempt to speak about/for the oppressed and silenced in the power relations governing (externally or internally) people of other cultures. There are indeed different ways of negotiating this discursive space within the limits of its own epistemological tracking, if we are to learn anything of significance from the works of Fanon, Foucault, Levinas, and Spivak, among others. But where exactly has Daly overreached herself?

First, her preeminent problem with a/the planetary Patriarchal Religion and her programmatic schema to arrest *its* excesses in other but particularly Western societies is an unmistakable motif that speaks through her own defensive postures. To this end, the issue of *satī* seems to be contingently and therefore tendentiously connected (as the chapter on Chinese foot-binding and one or two others in Mary Daly's book might under closer scrutiny turn out to be). Even though her aim is to decode the commonality of patriarchal oppressiveness, such a swift pronouncement of homogenization and globalization, partly because it posits Indian women as Other, has the danger of leaving intact the very edifice of white-centered ethnophallocentrism it intends to demolish (cf. Mani 1992, 392.) In other words, as we shall say more in Part II, these pronouncements overlook the kinds of resistance and re-creations that emerge within particular and multiply located contexts of indigenous subjectivity. Second, and more important, Daly in an asterisked note only mentions the official outlawing of *satī* in 1929 (Daly 1978, 114) and subsequent legislation on other women- and child-related practices up to the time of the writing of the book, but she appears uninterested in engaging in the requisite detailed scholarship on their historical specificities. This historiography would entail tracing the chronological unfolding of the immensely fascinating and instructive (for her purposes too) events, bigendered indigenist resistances, campaigns and scholastic interventions (traditional and Indological, sanctioning prohibition), that surrounded the 1929 legislation and its aftermath. Again, it is no part of our thesis to commit orientalism by suggesting that Daly is disqualified from this undertaking by virtue of her location outside the Indian culture, but—as we have been at pains to stress—she has not sufficiently distinguished (within project [b], showing the complicity of Western knowledge sources) the epistemological authorial enactments from the discursive angst rubbing against the grain of colonial representations and stereotypes that prefigure in the very gestures toward such an analysis, criticism, and assessment that is supposed to take a stance on metaethics. By metaethics, as Daly invokes it in the subtitle of her book, we assume that we would be told what it means to say something is wrong or unjust, and further that the judgments that follow would not be privileged in any direction but would be fair to all parties in question. We shall reserve our own presentiment about whether metaethics is or is not part of a Western (Enlightenment) project, but if this strategy is offered, then the analysis and judgments made in the particular project in question would need to cohere to it. Let us try to tease out this structural problem in the following way.

The making of the *colonial* discourse on *satī* and its discursive underlays, which inform the assessment and accounts of each of the sources that Daly has brought to bear as testimonials in support of her own judgment, is as important a concern as the "unsnarling [of] phallocratic 'scholarship.' " One fallacy cannot be a surrogate for another; both kinds of discourses stand in need of deconstruction. What we are laboring to express here is the postcolonial hermeneutic of suspicion that no present-day discussions of a constitutive phenomenon as complex as *satī* is complete in the absence of much careful attention to and sifting through the discursive sedimentation of representations, arguments, and counterarguments, narrative and epistemic denouements, that have preceded this moment. For these inevitably impact on anything that we might want to—or indeed be moved to—pronounce on good moral grounds, but from our own location in a particular historical space in respect of the ontology of that Constitution. It is as Chandra Talpade Mohanty has cogently spelled out, the contextless binary of power versus being powerless reinscribing itself in the Western feminist representation of "third world" women as a homogenous category of "the oppressed," who are thereby never permitted within the bounds of this assumption to "rise above the debilitating generality of their 'object' status" (Mohanty 1991, 71). This coded "feminization" of the third world women-question could be viewed as another phase in the Western humanist dispersal of the Enlightenment *telos* of "civilizing the lawless natives" (cf. Kant 1983). Nevertheless, Daly's reliance on the apparently "neutral grounds" provided by metaethics is commendable, as it goes a long way toward setting down the parameters of a debate between those systems of morality that belittle, forget, and erase the gendered other, the female, and those intellectual insurgencies or resistances that are opposed to such ravages, whether they be of an overloaded patriarchy, androcracy, or the brute imperial force of colonialism, and so on. We have no problems with invoking metaethics to aid one in this task, even though philosophers nail metaethics (as with metaphysics) to the critique of moral judgments, in the pure and abstract.

However, we do not believe that Daly stays centered in this base, as she allows herself to be overcome by an emotive mood that generates a phantasm of ontological (read *gratuitous*, signifying "monstrously ill-willed") evils that she generically and unflinchingly ascribes to the subject male, to the phallocratic worldview, as Audre Lorde among others have pointed out. In the same move she predicates women as the "object" and, as if linguistically determined, "victim" of the *masculine* gender. And so where there is clear and demonstrable evidence of male injustices against the female, which it would be foolish to deny in the case of *satī* and dowry-related bride burning, Daly's polemical strategy, as evinced particularly in the overdetermination of her derisive judgments of "gynocidal ritual," the "rite of female sacrifice," the "meta-ritual of 'objective' scholarship" (Daly 1978, 132–33), detracts from rather than induces confidence in the overall faithfulness of the specific project. Much new research has been taking place and further factors hitherto unthought of have come increasingly into play in the manner and direction in which the analyses have hitherto proceeded. Needless to say, Daly could not have anticipated these lines of research, but her own work in an ongoing dialogue with indigenous and recent scholarship could have made a contribution to it; that it has in no small measure is a fact that should indeed not be overlooked, or this essay would be uncalled for. To move the analysis begun by Daly in this fruitful direction, in the remainder of the essay we shall draw on the recent writings of noted Indian women researchers to highlight these aspects, and especially the issues of "alert subjectivity" and resistant spirituality, in illustrating the third motivation, (3), (outlined at the beginning of this essay), which informs our second move in the argument. Since the literature is already vast, we shall be selective and brief in our treatment.

Part II: The Aporia of a Resistant Spirituality

A. Historical Contextuality

Indian feminists of late have aired doubts about the essentializing and totalizing representation of "woman" ("third world" or more specifically the "Indian/Hindu woman") that is a fundamental presupposition of and implicated in the range of critiques directed against the dominant modes of ideology or ideological imperatives (patriarchy, colonialism, capitalism) (Sunder Rajan 1993, 129). There might even be something coercive, they believe, in the very structuring of women's own self-representation, for femaleness, far from being an essential quality, is a construction whose every composition has to be examined at any given moment or in later interpretations, lest it itself become hegemonic, and a semiotic critique working more to control the construction of femaleness than to promote social change. Indian feminists likewise have been highly critical of casting the Indian woman's plight in binary terms and their ritualized opposition, a common tendency in Western criticism. However, at the same time Indian feminists express anxieties about the regressive moves within the society in India that not only legitimate "new" forms of orientalism—and fundamentalism, as demonstrated with the rise of the Hindu right—but also seek to sanction events such as *satī* (Sangari and Vaid 1989, 2; Mani, 405 n. 41). The public advocates and protagonists of *satī* in modern-day India are not upper-caste Brahmins—as was largely the case in nineteenth-century Bengal—but are to be found among the landed gentry and Marwadi business class from the middle-caste groups around the northwestern state of Rajasthan where incidents of *satī* have been reported to have increased steadily since Independence, though not more than forty in all. A widely reported incident of *satī* in September 1987 took place in the village of Deorala near Jaipur in Rajasthan, involving an educated eighteen-year-old, Roop Kanwar, who was widowed only seventeen months into her marriage (having spent five weeks in all with the husband in this period) (Sunder Rajan 1993, 16). This provoked widespread opposition in the society (and comments in the foreign press), leading to state legislation prohibiting the practice by the widows, and its abetting and glorification by those who would invest their faith in the practice (Commission of Sati [Prohibition] Act, 1987). But communal groups among the Rajputs have been active since before the incident in articulate defense of the *faith* in *satī*, not as a religious prescriptivism but rather as an erstwhile local custom consistent with a modern Hindu Indian ethos (contrasting it with the nineteenth-century Bengali "traditional" defense), which they embellish by erecting temples to the eponymous goddess Sati in popular locations. The living namesake is becoming a lucrative neo-*satī* icon attracting mass pilgrimage. Roop Kanwar as a child routinely visited one such shrine in her vicinity. The aftereffects of Roop Kanwar's action (presuming that all reported accounts are accurate) nevertheless have raised the same sorts of issues, becoming a site of contests for *either/or* solutions that structurally continue to control the discursive contours of *satī*: "Was it voluntary?" "Was she forced to die?" "Why was she not rescued?" "Was it murder by all hands?" "Is it tradition against modernity?" Rajeswari Sunder Rajan sums up the difficulties in the judgments one feels moved to make with the following comments: "To repudiate ancient scripture as a basis for modern practice is to invite the charge of alienation; to designate *satī* as a crime rather than ritual, and by such designation seek to intervene through legislative prohibition, is to merely replicate the move of the colonial ruler; to highlight the plight of the woman is not only to be insensitive to the identity of the Rajput community (which is defined by her [Roop Kanwar's] act), but also to be selective and hypocritical in the women's issues that one champions—and have one's bona fides questioned" (1993, 17). It may be remarked thus that Indian feminists too, not unlike their Western counterparts, are caught in this triple bind and are not free of risk of some kind of political or egregious ambivalence.

So what is at stake in all this? Several things, in terms of semiotic investments and analytical antinomies. We will sketch these through a summary of findings from the work of three Indian feminist writers. Gayatri Spivak from her extensive examination of colonial archives on *satī* in the nineteenth century (in the now famous essay "Can the Subaltern Speak? Speculations on Widow-Sacrifice," 1985), turns up some interesting insights, the most fundamental of which has to do with the rigid oppositional binary of "ritual versus crime" (tradition versus modernity), which is related to the aporia of "subject versus object-status" marking the colonial formulation of *satī*. Spivak is forthright in her assertion that it was a grave act of epistemic violence to reinscribe *satī* as a crime (culpable homicide), whatever else it could be conceived to be—superstition, martyrdom, morbid cultural praxis. For by so naming it the onus of crime falls on the victim, who is no longer there to defend her case or to reenact her agency and reveal for posterity her subjectivity and pain. This "epistemic violence"—which echoes in Mary Daly's use of the descriptives of "gynocidal atrocity," "murder" under project (a) discussed in Part I—cannot mitigate or lessen the violence implicated in the act itself.

Drawing from Gayatri Spivak, the following poignant points can be noted: The intellectual is complicit in the persistent constitution of the

Other as the self's shadow; Mary Daly's concern for the oppressed can hide both the privileging of the intellectual and the concrete subject of oppression (or victim); two premises of colonial discourse—"White men save brown women from brown men," and "The women wanted to die." These are dialectically interlocking, and Mary Daly has not produced an alternative to the first; protection of women becomes a signifier for the establishment of a good society (Spivak 1985, 280–98).

It is such occlusions and overdetermination that has concerned Indian postcolonial critics such as Gayatri Spivak, Lata Mani, and Rajeswari Sunder Rajan, among others. There is certainly coercion involved and other kinds of subtle persuasive implorations or intimidations and ideological indoctrination intended to accomplish the widow's ascent onto the pyre; but it is questionable whether the element of choice (as is present in the case of suicide) is so totally eclipsed, such that the *satī* is to be viewed inexorably "as a victim and thereby emptying her subjectivity of any function or agency" (Sunder Rajan 1993, 19).

Developing this line of scrutiny and noting that in contemporary discourse on *satī* there has been an absence of any discussion of the phenomenological dimension of *pain*, Rajeswari Sunder Rajan asks the following: Suppose *satī* was to be read as "suicide" ("voluntary culpable homicide by consent")—as indeed the colonial administration, in a later moment exhibiting its own deep ambivalence, had agreed to decree it[4]—would that admission of free will and "choice" in the individual decision taken not make the woman involved analogous to the religious martyr, the heroic male soldier, the ascetic, the monk, and the recent political activist Gandhi to Vinobha Bhave? (Sunder Rajan 1993, 18). Jain monks and nuns who are burdened with terminal illness or infirmity, which they deem would incapacitate them from making real spiritual progress toward the desired goal of liberation, voluntarily make the choice of fasting to death, the practice known as *sallekhana*. Very recently the highest judicial bench in India, in a judgment acquitting a man charged with attempted suicide, struck down the law in the penal code from colonial times that had made suicide a "crime punishable in law." An earlier bench of the Bombay High Court in its speculations adverted to the age-old religious practices of *sallekhana*, *jauhar*, and other forms of "suicide" where the integrity of free will was not at issue and that could even be subversive toward a community, regime, or state that was a potential threat or stood in the way of the individual's subjectivity (Bilimoria 1995, 160–61). What is of significance in the case of *satī* is to resist it as "the ground for speculations" (by the outsider, as in the colonial formulation; Mani 1992, 401), not to reductively reclassify it as suicide ("subject-status"), nor to allow for the opposite category of enforced felony/crime ("object-status"), but rather to focus on the erased possibilities and potentials in an alternative discourse. Let us develop this argument in yet another way.

Imperceptible in this imagery of *satī* is an incipient core of resistant intentionality of double transgression and self-transformation, whose perceptible vectors, however, do not cut across the immediacy of the act nor smother the fire, but are dispersed as traces in the multiple direction of the smoke from the pyre embers. *The process of patriarchal oppression reveals contradictions and complex countermovements*, which we would like to illustrate through two broad-stroked examples. But before that a brief historical background is apposite. Women's condition in India cannot be reductively homologized with *satī,* which could well be a practice that came into India from regions far to its northwest some two thousand years ago. As prominent Indian woman historian Romila Thappar has shown from her half century of research, the status of women varied vastly at different periods. For example, in early Aryan civilization "the position of women was on the whole free" (Thappar 1966, 40ff). Not only was remarriage of women not uncommon, it was required under certain circumstances by the more moderate law manuals of classical economy, notably, *Arthaśāstra* and *Naradīyaśāstra.* Even the conservative law codifiers, Manu and Yājnavalkya, had merely recommended a chaste life for the widow. *Satī* was more a symbolic performative than a realistic pursuit, until its repetitive symbolic enactments, hand in hand with the subordination of women from around C.E. 300–700, led to its translation into ritual enactment and its earliest recommendations in Dharma (a religious order) scriptures are recorded (as well as in Purānic literature, notably the Garuda). But even here the historical developments did not entirely foreclose the freedom of women and its subversion and subreption of the shifting political-religious hegemonies. Women chose to opt out of the "normal" repertoire of the female in society and became Buddhist nuns, Jain ascetics, actresses, courtesans, temple dancers, and prostitutes. The emblematic inversion of Hindu male divinities into Buddhist female deities ascribed to women unique kinds of liberties within the emergent tantric emphasis in Buddhism, especially after its spread into Tibet. Meanwhile, from C.E. 800–1200, feudalism in the Rajput states led to the glorification of military virtues that taught women "to admire men who fought well" and expected them to follow in the boots of the deceased husbands; in other words, undertake *satī* (Thappar 1966, 247). In due course, in the medieval period, the secular military intentionality conjoined with religious accoutrements to yield a sanitized ritual *satī*, which the Hindu community at large would appropriate in its own mythic tracts.

During Muslim rule, women had inferior status and were encouraged toward greater seclusion. Although the Moghul rulers viewed *satī* as suicide and were therefore strongly opposed to its practice under Islamic *sharia* law, which prohibited suicide as a violation of Allah's will, some permitted it among Hindu women, presumably out of respect for local custom. The Moghul emperor Akbar, however, tried to intervene to prevent incidents of *satī* (Thappar 1996, 292). We might note in passing that the appended semiotics of *satī* as suicide, forbidden as a rule (in Muslim law), stripped it of its perceived sacred-making power as a rite under the traditional Brahmanic code and then again bracketed it to avoid giving offence to the predominant Hindu community. But also stray interventionist plotting contributed to further destabilizing the bounds of moral propriety in the gaze assumed by the subsequent chain of rulers right up to the rigorous though equivocal encoding in the campaigns leading to the 1829 legislation.

B. *Two Examples of Feminine Potency*

(a) Iconic symbols of the feminine are taken, not unusually by women themselves, from traditional canonical leaves and rewritten to darkly mirror the invidious ploys of male heroes and players. Draupadī, in the epic *Mahābhārata*, storms into the court assembly when the "good guys" (Pandavas) lose her to the "bad guys" (Kauravas) in a game of dice. In self-defense she presses the legalistic challenge of whether her husband Yudhishthira was already a slave when he lost her, and she is able to resist her attempted disrobing through Krishna's empathetic intervention. To this day, in other ceremonial festivals in southern India there are vivid enactments of legendary narratives in which a menstruating Draupadī tramples over the body of Duryodhana (the Kaurava regal contender), her long, untied black hair mingling with the blood from the antihero's pierced thighs (Hiltebeitel 1991, 396). Draupadi here symbolizes regenerative potency as well as sexual revenge, with all its inversive tantric (esoteric, magical) connotations. *Shakti*, the gendered potency in Hindu cosmopsychology depicted in the variegated images of goddesses and aspects of feminine divinity, is a source of feminine virtue that can overflow into an excess of "good wifehood," domesticity, conjugal relationships, and eventually history and polity in the form of *satī* (or in its transempirical signifier of the iconic Satī too). And yet paradoxically, as Rajeswari Sunder Rajan puts it, "to envisage that such a virtue can prove excessive . . . is to give another dimension to 'good wifehood' " (Sunder Rajan 1993, 58). With a sense of irony, however, the Bhakti women poets, and some modern-day Indian women healers, shamanic mediums, priestesses, and tantric (sexo-orgasmic) adepts following in the steps of their medieval sisters, will shun the "good wifehood" syndrome, leave behind the kitchen *chula* (stoked fire), and explore other dimensions of devotion or their beloved craft. Thus, Mira Bai, the sixteenth-century Rajput princess-poet would muse:

> "I will sing to Giridhar (the lord Krishna)
> I will not be a *satī*."
> [She might have added: "Give us not this day our daily dread,
> lead us not into wild temptations,
> but deliver us from patri-evil and free us for all eternity—
> from ourselves too."][5]

Nevertheless, despite this temptation to opt out of the social-institutional structures, some feminist advocates urge service to various secular causes. Serving secular goals does not necessarily mean that one had condescended to the whims of Secular Patriarchy, given that in the Indian subcontinent women have carved out and assiduously guarded a niche for their activities in the care and welfare of the oppressed, disadvantaged, and marginalized. It is not always possible to succeed in these activities by opting out of existing structures and by shutting behind one the doors of an active, public-issue-orientated judiciary, legal and academic support groups, and available expatriate financial or diaspora postcard support. Besides, deployment of secular "means" need not have as its "end" simply a secular *telos*: it could have liberatory or emancipatory results that supplement a spiritual teleology.

The paradoxicalness that the powerful images of feminine divinity/goddesses, and gendered tutelary protector spirits, present amid socially oppressive conditions, however, is nothing like what is presented by the cool image of Virgin Mary. Unlike the denials entailed in the simulation of the latter in one's bodily dispositions (sensual, sexual, perhaps also maternal, desire-base), the Indian goddess, such as the tantric (ecologically vibrant) Bhairavī, by contrast evokes passionately celebratory, re-creative or regenerative, life-affirming dispositions, and when perfected with phronesis or disciplined intellect these are elevated to the status of exemplary virtues. In her less benign form of Kālī (or Durgā), perched on a lion, she presents the archetypal symbol of resistance, of gendered *destruktion* or dismantling of oppositional nodes, and steamrolling, albeit with extreme compassion and empathy, the conditions of oppression and their perpetrators alike. This semiotics embodies a powerful regime of sacred-making; and for its morally effective actualization, it does not require grounding in metaphysical theism or a theology of supernaturalism, especially one that is biased toward a "macho" nuanced transcendentalism.

(b) In times of major cultural and political crisis (or compounded crises), there is ferment that "magically" mobilizes a concerted response by womenfolk. In such moments gendered spiritual resources come into sharp focus under a collective canopy, with its energies and often vociferous resistance directed against oppressive regimes (male-based and institutional), and it may even be geared towards a secular *telos*, such as the nationalist cause of ousting an external imperial regime. Such a movement in recent times germinated as part of the early nineteenth-century "renaissance," with its revision of the traditional conceptions of woman and womanhood as championed notably by Raja Rammohun Roy (Rai) in his campaign for educational and social reforms. The reformist first "father" of modern India, Rammohun Roy, in his spectacular struggle, led the movement against the *satī* and pursued the case after some orthodox Hindus lodged an appeal all the way up to the British Privy Council in London, where the final verdict was cast, upholding the proscription a year later (Nandy 1980, 2–17).[6] Gandhi in his own inimitable way continued and built on this resource for the revolutionary freedom struggle, as this newly unleashed gendered energy perfectly complemented, and supplemented, his revamped principle of nonviolence, or noninjury (a disposition amenable to the nonconscriptable womenfolk). Gandhi had claimed that Indian women, the moral realism of truth, and an attitude of devotion and dedication, formed the backbone of the freedom movement, which had no equivalents in previous historical experience. After Independence eminent women leaders and peaceful fighters went on to establish or operate community-based hospitals, hospices, and other health-care centers, schools and colleges, centers for the arts and cultural experimentation, ashrams and retreats, village-industry collectives, trade unions, credit unions, and so on. Exactly fifty years after Independence, the legacy is celebrated and continued by women's groups, NGOs and individual women activists and academics in many parts of India and among the diaspora hyphenated-*desis* also.

That said, it must also be noted that there are feminists within India who echo Judith Butler's observation that both traditional and normative discourse are less sanguine about women's direct agency, especially as the latter supervenes on the assertorial exercise of individual rights and legal entitlements (Butler 1992, 13).[7] Certainly the resurgent religious fundamentalism and instrumentalist political exigencies have threatened to reverse the "modern" trend of rewriting autonomy in terms of ungendered individual agency. This tussle is a critical one and it raises a host of other issues in respect to negotiating communal/family practices constituted as personal law (which is gendered in various of its codes and recognized in the constitution) versus positive rights and entitlements of the individual citizen under the Constitutional Bill of (Fundamental) Rights. Space constraints do not permit us to go into this issue with all its contradictions here, but its bearing on the current debate on *satī* is certainly significant, a resolution of which *a fortiori* lies in attending to both strands of the contests without sacrificing or unwittingly compromising either, in the interest of the greater good. And, in the exploration of conceptual alternatives, as Susie Tharu reminds us, "the discourse of our times will constitute our worlds as much as they do our subjectivities, but it is necessary, all the same, that 'a historically informed analysis' be sensitive to the subversions, elaborations, hybridizations, transformations, realignments, or reappropriations that do take place within oppositional discourses" (Tharu and Lalitha 1989, 127).[8]

Conclusion

A proper epistemological treatment does not only ask "Who speaks and for whom?" but also scrutinizes the theoretical moral basis on which such and such judgments are made or adduced. In the case of *satī*, we wish to urge the following considerations in the abstract ethical calculus that we believe is as important as the historical analysis we have also urged.

If it could be established that the act of *satī* (call it x) was/is murder, defeasibly and unmitigatably, then the absolute moral prescriptivism of not doing x under any circumstances would apply. But if this code of universally acceded crime or "evil" proves difficult to legitimate in this context, then x would have to be relativized to a moral theory that either urges restraint in accordance with a categorical norm (for example of not administering y, z, f, that causes x), or compels intervention on the weight of the detrimental consequences compromising or counter to the greater common good. This difficulty was of course countenanced at least twice in the legal history of *satī*, when both the Moghul and British imperial powers encountered the practice. The best legal and scholastic minds could not agree or find clear evidence in any humanly known jurisprudence of how exactly to classify the palpable misdemeanour, and this resulted in equivocation. In any case, if the intentionality of gendered murder ("culpable homicide," "gynocide") were to go through, feminists have since reasoned, the woman would stand condemned twice over (by her community of relatives, and in the ensuing legal proceedings). Alternatively, she would be cast abjectly as the *victim* of a premeditated criminal process—or, even more alarmingly, the subject-object of both, and hence of a hideous crime, tantamount to a gendered holocaust, inconceivable outside of the Indian social context, as Katherine Mayo came close to suggesting. The evidence of the complicity of patriarchy at each stage of the act is unredoubtable; however, that does not necessarily mean that patriarchy alone and unmodified is generating this violence in all its locations.

This equivocation notwithstanding, an ethics that gives greater coherence to the set of social, moral, cultural, and economic factors and considerations in play on a given issue is surely more rationally illuminating than one that assumes a categorical deontic/transcendental imperative without regard to the complexity of historical epistemes beneath which lies buried repressed archetypes or semiotics of—which are also the clues to—its antecedents in mythic sacred-making rites, shifts in social, cultural, and political spaces that increasingly marginalized women, and the rise of institutional hegemonies. But our account in this regard must perforce remain incomplete until further archaeological digging (in the Foucauldian sense) yields more evidence to substantiate the speculations of the scholarly and advocacy groups. In this respect, Mary Daly's account, as in the case of numerous others, is one of overdetermination. However, this admission does not mitigate our responsibility to make a determined and concerted response to the practical considerations, that is, in the applied context. What is needed is not a "high altitude" moral stance that holds a universal Patriarchal Religion culpable for the alleged crime, but another kind of imperative: drawing on the cumulative reserve of energy and experience, and with wisdom taking control of the situation, and liberating it by reappropriating its sacred nuance, sublimating and transforming it from within.

Finally, we would like to take up the empty space (the invisible hyphen) in Mary Daly's descriptive conjunct of "female sacrifice" and insert the disjunctive of difference to set apart the two terms, registering (onto)-logically distinct but not morally separable moments. In "female/sacrifice" each side of the mark is accented differently in varying circumstances and conditions of production, so that in one given moment "sacrifice" made by women to subtly deflect male dominionship might be their calling (recall Joan of Arc, Draupadī, Sītā), while in another moment the assertion of the "female" calling upon sacrifice on the part of the male—as exemplified by Krishna, Akbar, Gandhi—would yield greater liberative potency. The female can control the amoral ontology of "sacrifice," even contribute to its sacred-making potency, but need not—indeed ought not—be consumed by it. Perhaps this is the fault in *satī* that Mary Daly, along with a galaxy of enlightened women in East and West, has rightly alerted us to. We differ on the question of its formation and contextualization, and on the effectively appropriate strategy for its de-mythologization, a/theologization, naturalization, and trans-formation.

Notes

We are grateful to Sarah L. Hoagland and Marilyn Frye for their very useful lengthy comments and for their perseverance despite the tardiness in completing the essay. A good number of Indian feminists, by contrast, dismissed returning to Daly's critique out of hand, characterizing Daly as a "dated and long-critiqued first world white separatist feminist" (!) (anonymous reader for *Hypatia*).

1. Audre Lorde, "An Open Letter to Mary Daly," in *Sister Outsider: Essays and Speeches* (Freedom Calif.: Crossing Press, 1984).

2. Daly is citing from his work *The Masks of God: Oriental Mythology* (New York: Viking Press, 1962), 62.

3. We presume that the sources Mary Daly cites are correct. Katherine Mayo's *Mother India* was published in 1927 by Blue Ribbon Press in New York.

4. The Bentinck Abolition of Sati Act of 1829 treated *satī* as homicide; however, it was amended ten years later in the Indian penal code as suicide, under the reintroduced category of "voluntary culpable homicide by consent," which was incorporated in the penal code of 1860 with minor modifications (Sangari 1989, 15–16).

5. We have cited the verse ascribed to Mira Bai from Sunder Rajan, 63 n. 49; the parenthetical addition is our own.

6. We believe that a more detailed historiography of the indigenist participants, advocates, and antagonists of *satī* reform led by Rammohun Roy is being carried out by Paul Courtright of Emory University in Atlanta, Georgia. We look forward to the results of this research. Meanwhile, see Courtright et al., in Hawley 1994.

7. Rajeswari Sunder Rajan cites Butler (138 and 146 n. 39).

8. I have used Rajeswari Sunder Rajan's rephrasing (143) here of Susie Tharu.

References

Bilimoria, Purushottama. 1995. "Legal Rulings on Suicide in India and Implications for the Right to Die." *Asian Philosophy* (Nottingham) 5 (October 1995): 159–80.

Butler, Judith. 1992. "Contingent Foundations: Feminism and the Question of Post-modernism." In *Feminists Theorize the Political*, edited by Butler and Joan W. Scott. New York: Routledge.

Courtright, Paul B., and Lindsey Harlan, eds. 1995. *From the Margins of Hindu Marriage: Essays on Gender, Religion, and Culture*. New York: Oxford University Press.

Daly, Mary. 1978. "Indian Suttee: The Ultimate Consummation of Marriage." In *Gyn/Ecology, The Metaethics of Radical Feminism*. Boston: Beacon Press.

Hawley, John Stratton, ed. 1994. *Satī, The Blessing and the Curse: The Burning of Wives in India*. New York: Oxford University Press.

Hiltebeitel, Alf. 1991. *The Cult of Draupadi 2: On Hindu Ritual and the Goddess*. Chicago and London: The University of Chicago Press.

Kant, Immanuel. 1983. *Perpetual Peace and Other Essays on Politics, History and Morals*. Translated and with an introduction by Ted Humphrey. Indianapolis: Hackett.

Mani, Lata. 1992. "Cultural Theory, Colonial Texts: Reading Eyewitness Accounts of Widow Burning." In *Cultural Studies*, edited and with an introduction by Lawrence Groosberg et al., 392–408. New York: Routledge.

———. 1993. "Contentions Traditions: The Debate on *Satī* in Colonial India." In *Recasting Women*, edited by Kumkum Sangari and Sudesh Vaid, 88–126. New Delhi: Kali for Women.

Mohanty, Chandra Talpade. 1991. "Under Western Eyes: Feminist Scholarship and Colonial Discourses." In *Third World Women and the Politics of Feminism*, edited by Chandra Talpade Mohanty, Ann Russo, and Lourdes Torres. Bloomington: Indiana University Press.

Nandy, Ashis. 1980. "Satī: A Nineteenth Century Tale of Women, Violence and Protest." In *At the Edge of Psychology: Essays in Politics and Culture*, 1–31. Delhi: Oxford University Press.

Ruether, Rosemary Radford. 1993. *Sexism and God-Talk: Towards a Feminist Theology*. Boston: Beacon Press.

Sangari, Kumkum, and Vaid, Sudesh, eds. 1989. *Recasting Women: Essays in Colonial History*. New Delhi: Kali for Women. (Reprinted 1993).

Sharma, Renuka. 1993. *Understanding the Concept of Empathy and Its Foundations in Psychoanalysis*. Lewiston/Lampeter: Edwin Mellen Press.

———. 1996. ed. *Representations of Gender, Democracy, and Identity Politics in Relation to South Asia*. Delhi: Satguru Publications for Indian Books Centre.

———, ed. 1999. *The Other Revolution: NGOs and Women's Movements in South Asia*. Naari Studies in Gender, Culture and Society, no. 3. Delhi: Satguru Publications for Indian Books Centre.

Spivak, Gayatri Chakravorty. 1985. "Can the Subaltern Speak? Speculations on Widow-Sacrifice." *Wedge* (Winter/Spring): 120–30.

———. 1985a. "The Rani of Simur." In *Europe and Its Other*, edited by Francis Barker et al. Vol. 1, *Proceedings of the Essex Conference on Sociology and Literature, July 1984*. Colchester: University of Essex.

———. 1988. *In Other Worlds: Essays in Cultural Politics*. New York: Methuen.

Sunder Rajan, Rajeswari. 1993. *Real and Imagined: Gender, Culture, and Postcolonialism*. London: Routledge.

Sunder Rajan, Rajeswari, and Zakia Pathak. 1992. "Shahbano." In *Feminists Theorize the Political*, ed. Judith Butler and Joan Scott, 257–79. New York: Routledge.

Sutherland-Goldman, Sally. 1999. "Sutte, Satī, and Sahagamana: Re-reading Narrative." In *Outside Theory: Negotiating Gender in South Asia (Sixth Feminist Book Fair, Melbourne 1994)*. Naari Studies in Gender, Culture, and Society, no. 4. Delhi and Melbourne: Satguru Publications and Open Wisdom, Ink.

Thappar, Romila. 1966. *History of India*. Vol. 1. Harmondsworth: Penguin.

———. 1987. *Cultural Transactions and Early India*. Delhi: Oxford University Press.

Tharu, Susie, and K. Lalitha. 1989. "Response to Julie Stephens." In *Subaltern Studies VI: Writings on South Asian History and Society*, ed. Ranajit Guha. Delhi: Oxford University Press.

———, eds. 1993. *Women Writing in India 600 B.C. to the Early Twentieth Century: An Anthology with Introduction*. London: Pandora HarperCollins.

13

Back to the Mother? Feminist Mythmaking with a Difference

AnaLouise Keating

> The change evoked on these pages is material as well as psychic. Change requires a lot of heat. It requires both the alchemist and the welder, the magician and the laborer, the witch and the warrior, the myth-smasher and the myth-maker.
>
> —Gloria Anzaldúa

> There is no arcane place for return.
> —Trinh Minh-ha

My title reflects an ongoing debate in U.S. feminist movement: the political (in)effectiveness of prepatriarchal origin stories and other forms of revisionist mythmaking. As Mary Daly has argued, accounts of a gynecentric culture can empower contemporary women in several interrelated ways. First, by positing a time *before* patriarchy, feminist origin stories suggest the contingent nature of female oppression and thus motivate women to challenge restrictive social systems. In the words of Daly, women are inspired to "transcend the trickery of dogmatic deception," reject the "distorting mirror of Memory," and "recognize the Radiance of our own Origins" (1984, 113). Second, by depicting nonpatriarchal egalitarian communities of women, these stories offer a new teleological perspective. And third, by replacing the (male) "God" with the (female)

"Goddess," feminist revisionary myths reject the hierarchical worldview that elevates men (who are made in God's image) over women (who are not). Thus in *Beyond God the Father*, Daly argues that genuine selfhood—which entails each individual's ability to name the self, God, and the world—has been "stolen" from women. By defining God as "the Father" and human beings as "mankind," conventional language has effectively silenced women; it has denied their existence. She maintains that in order to move from silence and "nonbeing" to self-affirmation and speech, women must establish a new relationship to language, one acknowledging their presence by recognizing their "Female/Elemental divinity" within.

Other theorists, however, are far less sanguine about the usefulness of these attempts to move beyond God the father. Often all such calls for female images of the divine are dismissed as regressive, essentializing strategies that inadvertently reinstate normative gender roles and exclusionary practices. According to Judith Butler, Donna Haraway, and other poststructuralist theorists, subversive strategies that imply an "irrecoverable origin" (Butler 1989, 78) in a prehistorical past or an "innocent and all-powerful Mother" (Haraway 1990, 218) are far less effective than Daly and other radical feminists suggest. Indeed, they argue that mythic accounts of a maternal origin are exclusionary, divisive, and politically conservative, for they lead to simplistic identity politics based on restrictive, ethnocentric notions of female identity. Butler, for example, maintains that although feminist origin stories are employed to destabilize the dominant representational system, they generally replicate existing conditions: "The postulation of the 'before' within feminist theory becomes politically problematic when it constrains the future to materialize an idealized notion of the past or when it supports, even inadvertently, the reification of a precultural sphere of the authentic feminine. This recourse to an original or genuine femininity is a nostalgic and parochial ideal that refuses the contemporary demand to formulate an account of gender as a complex cultural construction" (1989, 36). In other words, feminists' attempts to recover or re-create "prepatriarchal" forms of woman-centered communities inevitably rely on existing (phallocentric) definitions of "woman"; consequently, they reject conventional gender categories only to establish other (equally restrictive) heterosexist binary oppositions. Moreover, Butler maintains that focusing on a time supposedly prior to or beyond contemporary socioeconomic-political conditions inhibits feminist analysis and action in the present.[1]

For Teresa de Lauretis as well, there is no "going back to the innocence of 'biology' " or to biologically based descriptions of gender. She explains that because gender is produced by a wide range of discursive practices, it cannot be described as a "natural" attribute, as "something originally existent in human beings" (1987, 2–3). Such descriptions reify normative phallocratic definitions of "woman," as well as the hierarchical male/female binary system. Thus she rejects what she sees as

> some women's belief in a matriarchal past or a contemporary "matristic" realm presided over by the Goddess, a realm of female tradition, marginal and subterranean and yet all positive and good, peace-loving, ecologically correct, matrilineal, matrifocal, non-Indo-European, and so forth; in short, a world untouched by ideology, class and racial struggle, television—a world untroubled by the contradictory demands and oppressive rewards of gender as I and surely those women, too, have daily experienced. (20–21)

Donna Haraway makes a similar point in her "Manifesto for Cyborgs" when she claims that in today's fragmented, postmodern world, "[i]t's not just that 'god' is dead; so is the 'goddess' " (81). She maintains that all such "transcendental authorizations" lead to restrictive political agendas based on totalizing and imperialistic identity politics that prevent feminists from constructing effective coalitions in the sociopolitical/historical present. According to Haraway, "There is nothing about being 'female' that naturally binds women." Indeed, "[t]here is not even such a state as 'being' female, itself a highly complex category constructed in contested sexual, scientific discourses and other practices" (72). She too challenges feminists to reject all such naturalized identities and develop temporary strategic alliances based on situational choices.

Like Haraway, Butler, and de Lauretis, I am extremely suspicious of feminist identity politics founded on exclusionary accounts that reify "women's experience." I, too, question the political effectiveness of rallying around normative concepts of "Woman,"[2] or mythic/monolithic images of "*the* Goddess"; all too often such representations inadvertently reinstate phallocentric descriptions of "Womanhood" and reproduce heterosexist, racist gender systems. Yet I also know from personal experience that the recognition of female gods can be quite empowering. Moreover, to assume that we can (or even *should*) simply reject *all* origin myths, along with *all* references to "Woman" or the "feminine," seems rather dismissive—not to mention highly unlikely. These categories have become so deeply engrained in our personal and cultural meaning systems that we cannot simply reject them. Nor can we sort through the numerous images of women circulating in twentieth-century life and distinguish the truth from the lies.

As I see it, this debate over the (in)effectiveness of gynecentric origin stories is part of a larger debate concerning the possibility of positing, from *within* the currently existing juridical system, nonhegemonic feminist "beyond(s)": Can we affirm the "feminine" yet arrive at representations of "Woman" that are *qualitatively* different from phallocratic descriptions? Perhaps more importantly, can we do so without erasing the many material and cultural differences between real-life women? On the one hand, terms such as "Woman" and the "feminine" can be extremely divisive when they prevent us from recognizing that, because gender intersects with historical, economic, ethnic, sexual, and other axes of difference in complex ways, it is an unstable category with multiple meanings.[3] But on the other hand, to refuse all references to sexual difference risks reinstating the pseudouniversal human subject defined exclusively according to masculinist standards. Moreover, to ignore or actively deny the "feminine" perpetuates the currently existing sociosymbolic system; as Drucilla Cornell points out, "the repudiation of the feminine is part of the very 'logic' of a patriarchal order" (1991, 5).

In this essay, I explore the psycholinguistic implications of Daly's call for feminist spiritualities and female divines in greater detail, for I believe that her work opens new spaces where the creation of transculturally contextualized images of "feminine" spiritual power can occur. More specifically, I set Daly in dialogue with Paula Gunn Allen, Gloria Anzaldúa, and Audre Lorde. The similarities between these theorists' discussions of feminist spiritualities and revisionist mythmaking are, at times, quite striking. Yet scholars almost never discuss these women—one labeled "white" and the others "Native American," "Chicana," and "Black"—in conjunction; instead, each is relegated to discrete categories of feminist thought based on genre, culture, and "race." At most, scholars use Lorde's well-known "Open Letter to Mary Daly" to dismiss Daly's attempt to invent new images of female identity as far too exclusionary to be effective. However, by reading Daly in conversation with Allen, Anzaldúa, and Lorde, I argue that transcultural models of feminist mythmaking demonstrate the possibility of writing the "feminine" in open-ended, nonexclusionary ways that revise previous notions of the universal.

By locating themselves in the present yet going "back" to their Native American, Mexican Indian, and West African mythic origins, Allen, Anzaldúa, and Lorde invent new myths that both illustrate and extend Daly's call to move beyond God the Father. Like Daly, these self-identified lesbians of color redefine the past from their present perspectives, replacing patriarchal mythologies with self-affirming images of female identity. They develop metaphoric re-presentations of Woman that neither erase their own cultural specificities nor erect permanent barriers between disparate groups. Instead, their writings affirm what I call "feminine" mestizaje: "feminine" in its remetaphorized "Women"; mestizaje in its fluid, transformational, trans*cultural* forms. I borrow this latter term from Cuban literary and political movements where its usage indicates a profound challenge to hegemonic racial discourse. As Nancy Morejón explains, mestizaje transculturation defies static notions of cultural purity by emphasizing

> the constant interaction, the transmutation between two or more cultural components with the unconscious goal of creating a third cultural entity . . . that is new and independent even though rooted in the preceding elements. Reciprocal influence is the determining factor here, for no single element superimposes itself on another; on the contrary, each one changes into the other so that both can be transformed into a third. Nothing seems immutable.[4]

In various ways and to varying degrees, the writers I examine in this essay incorporate this ongoing cultural transmutation into their mythic metaphors of Woman. Drawing on the dialogic elements of verbal art, they utilize metaphoric language's performative effects and invite their readers to live out the "feminine" in new ways. They develop nondual epistemologies and embodied metaphysics that disrupt conventional boundaries between writer, reader, and text. Their transcultural affirmations of the "feminine" challenge readers to rethink the dominant culture's sociopolitical inscriptions, the labels that define each person according to gender, ethnicity, sexuality, class, and other systems of difference. Destabilizing the restrictive networks of classification that inscribe us as racialized, en-gendered subjects, their "feminine" mestizajes open up psychic spaces where alterations in consciousness can occur. They create what Trinh Minh-ha describes as "a ground that belongs to no one, not even to the 'creator' " (1989, 71). Unlike conventional identity politics' foundationalist justifications, this "ground" functions as a nonessentialized, constantly shifting location where new forms of identity can occur.

> The Mother, the Grandmother, recognized from earliest times into the present among those peoples of the Americas who kept to the eldest traditions, is celebrated in social structures, architecture, law, custom, and the oral tradition. To her we owe our lives, and from her comes our ability to endure, regardless of the concerted assaults on our, on Her, being. . . . She is the Old Woman Spider who weaves us together in a fabric of interconnection. She is the Eldest God, the one who Remembers and Re-members.
>
> —Paula Gunn Allen

> Archimage is a Metaphoric form of Naming the one and the many. She is power/powers of be-ing within women and all biophilic creatures. She points toward Metabeing, in which all Witches/Hags/Weirds participate, and in which we live, move, and have our be-ing. . . . She is shimmering Substance—Real Presence—that shines through appearances. She is root of connectedness in the female Elemental Race.
>
> —Mary Daly

Throughout her writings, Allen maintains that to alter current conditions, contemporary social actors must recognize their ties to the past. Origin stories and other precolonial narratives play important roles in this process, for they enable us to go "back" to the "past," thus transforming the present and creating new visions for the future. She suggests that "traditionals say we must remember our origins, our cultures, our histories, our mothers and grandmothers, for without that memory, which implies *continuance rather than nostalgia*, we are doomed to engulfment by a paradigm that is fundamentally inimical to the quality, autonomy, and self-empowerment essential for satisfying, high quality life" (1986, 214; my emphasis).

But what, exactly, is the difference between "continuance" and "nostalgia"? After all, both terms could be interpreted to indicate an escapist desire to recapture an earlier era.[5] Yet Allen's feminism, coupled with her belief that time is nonlinear and human beings are "moving event[s] within a moving universe" (1986, 149), make such interpretations untenable. In a dynamic, constantly changing world with no "beginning" or "end," we cannot go *back* to an earlier point in time. Instead, Allen explains, we can use the so-called past both to understand present conditions more fully and to direct future actions. For Allen, continuance implies the historical past's continuity, its constant *presence* and ongoing interaction with contemporary human life. As she explains in "The Ceremonial Motion of Indian Time," whereas western culture's exclusive emphasis on chronological time divides history into discrete segments and separates time itself from "the internal workings of human and other beings," Native American "ceremonial time" is achronological and "mythic"; events apparently located "outside" the temporal present—whether or not we "actually" experienced them—can have significant effects on our lives (1986, 149). Daly illustrates one form that this nonlinear convergence of past, present, and future can take in her 1985 "Original Reintroduction" to *Beyond God the Father* where she discusses her work during the thirteen years since first publishing this early text: "Since, however, this is not a flat, linear route but rather a spiraling journey, the beginnings cannot simply be left behind. Rather, they are taken up again and again, understood and heard more and more deeply, in an ever-evolving context" (xiii).[6] Similarly, in her "New Intergalactic Introduction" to *Gyn/Ecology* (1978) Daly underscores her desire to redefine the past from her present perspective by creating a new "Memory of the Future—a hope that Something Else could be" (xvi). As she goes "back" to earlier points in time—"Leaping through portals into the Background" (xxii)—Daly "Dis-covers" and invents a rich resource for contemporary women, or what she describes as "the Treasure Trove of symbols and myths that have been stolen and reversed by the patriarchal thieves" (xxvii).

According to Allen, continuance has additional implications for indigenous North American peoples. Indeed, given the specific types of oppression experienced for the past five hundred years—which include (but are not limited to) genocide and forced assimilation, sterilization, removal, christianization, and reeducation—continuance, survival, and recovery are almost synonymous. Allen's frequent references to the devastating effects of this ongoing material and ideological extermination make it difficult, if not impossible, to dismiss either her origin stories or her desire to recover the "feminine" in American Indian traditions as an escapist retreat into an impossible, highly idealized past. It is, in fact, almost the reverse. Her emphasis on the sociopolitical and cultural implications of indigenous mythic systems indicates an attempt to reshape contemporary and future conceptions of American Indians, feminism, and U.S. culture. Indeed, Allen's femininized, indianized "cosmogyny"[7] represents several significant alterations in currently existing systems of meaning. First, by describing preconquest North American cultures as gynecentric, Allen revises previous academic interpretations of Native traditions that relied on male-centered stories from christianized Native informants.[8] Second, by replacing these masculinist interpretations of Native cultures with interpretations emphasizing the centrality of "feminine" powers, she provides all U.S. feminists—whatever their cultural backgrounds—with new models of female identity. As she asserts in an interview, "[W]hat I'm really attempting to do is affect feminist thinking. Because my white sisters—and they have influenced the Black and Asian and Chicano sisters—have given the impression that women have always been held down, have always been weak, and have always been persecuted by men, but I know that's not true. I come from a people that that is not true of" (quoted in Ballinger and Swann 1983, 10). In both her academic and creative writings, Allen insists that these images of powerful Native women have important implications for women of all ethnicities. Third, by attributing the forms of oppression experienced by contemporary women to the "same materialistic, antispiritual forces . . . presently engaged in wiping out the same gynarchical values, along with the peoples who adhere to them, in Latin America" and other countries (1986, 214), Allen expands existing conceptions of feminism and challenges self-identified feminists to develop cross-cultural, cross-gendered alliances with other oppressed peoples. Finally, by associating a diverse set of Native mythic figures with a cosmic "feminine" intelligence, Allen develops an epistemological system that draws on the oral tradition's dialogical nature to redefine Enlightenment-based descriptions of the intellect.

Although Allen's revisionist mythmaking takes a variety of forms and draws from numerous tribal traditions, I want to focus exclusively on her stories concerning Thought Woman, because this Laguna Pueblo creatrix represents a remarkable departure from conventional western origin stories. In both her academic and her creative work, Allen associates Thought Woman with a cosmic intelligence that manifests itself through language. She opens *The Sacred Hoop: Recovering the Feminine in American Indian Traditions* by declaring: "In the beginning was *thought*, and her name was *Woman*" (1986, 11; my emphasis). Similarly, she begins *The Woman Who Owned the Shadows* with her version of the story of Old Spider Woman, whose "*singing* made all the worlds. The worlds of the spirits. The worlds of the people. The worlds of the creatures. The worlds of the gods" (1983, 1; my emphasis). And again in *Grandmothers of the Light* she attributes the creation of the entire cosmos—including nature, human beings, sociopolitical systems, literature, and the sciences—to the Laguna Keres' Grandmother Spider or "Thinking Woman," who "*thought* the earth, the sky, the galaxy, and all that is into being, and as she thinks, so we are. She *sang* the divine sisters Nau'ts'ity and Ic'sts'ity . . . into being out of her medicine pouch or bundle, and they in turn sang the firmament, the land, the seas, the people, the katsina, the gods, the plants, animals, minerals, language, writing, mathematics, architecture, the Pueblo social system, and every other thing you can imagine in this our world" (1991, 28; my emphasis).

I want to underscore the innovative nature of Allen's stories, where creation occurs through language and thought. These remarkable narratives have little in common with standard phallocentric creation accounts that conflate "Woman" with "womb" and reduce the "feminine" to the highly sexualized yet passive bearer of (male) culture. Nor are they similar to those feminist origin myths that valorize women's previously denigrated maternal role by identifying goddess imagery and female power primarily with childbirth.[9] As Daly argues in *Pure Lust*, western versions of the "Great Mother"—the "original parthenogenic Goddess" whose creative powers had her source in her own body and mind, with no need for male insemination—have been appropriated and reshaped by patriarchal cultures in ways that contain women's power and restrict their movement (1984, 82).

By redefining the maternal as transformational thought, Allen reappropriates and alters patriarchal categories of gender. She destabilizes the hierarchical dichotomous worldview that equates the "masculine" with transcendence, culture, and the mind, and the "feminine" with immanence, nature, and the body. Significantly, she does not simply replace one dualism with another. As "the necessary *precondition* for material creation," her remetaphorized Woman represents a dynamic all-inclusive intellectual/creative power that generates both "material and nonmaterial reality" (1986, 14–15; my emphasis). This "feminized" intelligence can be described as both *supernatural* (Allen equates it with Thought Woman) and *natural* (Thought Woman's "intelligence . . . permeates the land—the mountains and clouds, the rains and lightning, the corn and deer" [1991, 34]). By synthesizing the spiritual with the physical, Allen's remetaphorized Woman participates in what Daly describes as the "Super Natural"—"Unfolding Nature in degree and in kind" (1984, 336). As Daly notes, this unfolding Super Natural feminine power provides an important intervention into patriarchal versions of the supernatural, which replace reverence and respect for nature with masculinized transcendence of the physical. Unlike Athene, the Greek goddess of (patriarchal) wisdom whose divine intelligence entails the sacrifice of the mother,[10] Allen's mythic Woman "Unfolds Nature"; she represents a maternalized embodied intelligence, or what Luce Irigaray might describe as "a spirituality of the body, the flesh" (1993, 135).

As this emphasis on the embodied material dimensions of thought implies, Allen develops an epistemological system that avoids the Cartesian mind/body dualism. Establishing a reciprocal relationship between intellectual, physical, and spiritual components of life, she destabilizes classical western definitions of reason and rationality and invents what I call "embodied mythic thinking": A transformational, nondual epistemology where thoughts, ideas, and beliefs have concrete material forms and effects. In Allen's epistemology, language is transformational and thought gives us "magical"[11] power: just as Old Spider Woman thought and sang the material world and everything in it into existence, so real-life women of all cultural backgrounds can, by directing their thought and using language in new ways, alter their physical surroundings as well as themselves.[12]

Revisionist mythmaking plays a vital role in Allen's embodied mythic thinking. By associating Thought Woman with a cosmic "feminine" intelligence that manifests itself in mutually interchangeable, unfolding physical and nonphysical forms, Allen affirms women's intellectual and creative capacities. In her epistemology, thinkers are not passive receptacles waiting to be filled by a divine source of guidance; they are, rather, co-creators in an ever-changing reality. "Since all that exists is alive and must change as a basic law of existence, all existence can be manipulated under certain conditions and according to certain laws" (1991, 22). By focusing their thought and channeling its energy in specific ways, women can effect material change.

In many ways, Allen's embodied mythic thinking resembles Daly's gynocentric epistemology and what she describes as "Realizing reason." As Daly explains in *Pure Lust*, this "doubly-edged" term indicates both an action—"the *act* of Realizing (actualizing) reason"—and an intellectual power enabling women to transform their world. Whereas conventional forms of reason indicate a passive intellectual mode of thinking generally associated with rational, logical thought, Daly's Realizing reason does not. Instead, it indicates a holistic intellectual energy that combines perception with action. Like Allen, Daly insists that this nonpatriarchal mode of thinking enables women to bring about concrete material change: "As a consequence of Realizing her *realizing reason*, a woman participates in the actualization of the structure of the universe" (1984, 162–63; her emphasis).

Also like Allen, Daly associates this embodied thinking with previous forms of knowledge. When women recognize their Realizing reason, they draw on "the original force of words" and acquire a new source of power (1984, 173). Yet she stipulates that in order to do so they must re-member their "ancient Racial memories" (95). According to Daly, these ancient memories of elemental female power have been covered over, repressed, and in other ways denied by patriarchal culture. She urges her readers to begin using language differently; only then can they gain access to this "biophilic" power: "In their double-edged dimensions, . . . words wield/yield messages about the tragedy of women and all Wild be-ing confined within imprisoning patriarchal parameters. Besides/beyond this, they radiate knowledge of an ancient age, and they let us know that they, *the words themselves*, are treasures trying to be freed. Breaking the bonds/bars of phallocracy requires breaking through to radiant powers of words, so that by releasing words, we can release our Selves" (4; my emphasis). Distinguishing between the paralyzing effects of contemporary patriarchal words and the earlier, female-identified meanings they contain, Daly invents an origin myth that underscores language's transformational power. She argues that language provides women with a liberating mode of perception; by discovering "the *elixir* of words, . . . their quintessential transforming powers and life-fostering force" (90), women can reject the sexist implications of patriarchal language and "recognize the Radiance of our own Origins" (113). Because she believes that "truly focused purposefulness is rooted in deep Memory" (355), Daly maintains that this recognition of Radiant Origins gives women a new sense of agency:

"Singing into conscious awareness our childhood and ancestral memories, Sirens lure women into our Past and therefore into our Future, awakening Be-Longing" (360).

But while Daly describes these alternate ways of knowing in gender-specific yet highly generalized terms such as "ancient Racial memories" and locates language's transformational power within the words themselves, Allen does not. Instead, she associates her embodied mythic thinking with culturally specific traditions and thus more easily evades the charges of essentialism, superficiality, and ineffectiveness sometimes leveled at Daly. More specifically, by associating thought's transformational power with indigenous North American oral traditions, Allen creates the larger context that some critics find lacking in Daly's theory of language.[13] She uses revisionist myth to construct a dialogic epistemology that draws on language's performative effects to generate personal and collective change.

Based on a relational model requiring participation by both storyteller and listeners, oral narratives reinforce the communal, creative dimensions of thinking. As Richard Bauman points out, this conversational structure provides a transformational context leading to the creation of new social systems. He associates the "distinctive potential" found in oral narratives with a performative, interactive model of language use and explains that verbal art's communal nature potentially establishes a unique bond between performer and audience: "It is part of the essence of performance that it offers to the participants a special enhancement of experience, bringing with it a heightened intensity of communicative interaction which binds the audience to the performer in a way that is specific to performance as a mode of communication. Through his [*sic*] performance, the performer elicits the participative attention and energy of his audience, and, to the extent that they value his performance, they will allow themselves to be caught up in it" (1984, 43).

For Allen as well, oral narratives function simultaneously as the expression and the active fulfillment of individual and collective needs. Just as the mythic stories conveyed in oral narratives utilize participatory, performative speech acts to unify communities and bring about social change, her highly inventive, gynecentric myths function as "verbal ritualization[s]" designed to transform readers of all cultural backgrounds into "medicine women" (1991, 7). She explains that any reader who fully participates in the "ritual-magic-stories" she (re)tells experiences an alteration in consciousness; she learns to forego her usual reliance on empirical knowledge and rational, linear thinking and "moves into mythic space and becomes a voyager in the universe of power" (109). However, by incorporating her transcultural perspective into her description of oral traditions, she expands conventional academic definitions of the term. According to Allen, "The oral tradition of all tribal people—whether Native American, Hindu, Greek, Celtic, Norse, Samois, Roman, or Papuan is best seen as psychic literature. It cannot adequately be comprehended except in terms of the universe of power, for it speaks to the relationships among humans, animals of all kingdoms, supernaturals, and deities in a landscape that is subject to influences of thought, intention, will, emotion, and choice" (22). This broad-based description of tribal peoples underscores the inclusionary dimensions of Allen's embodied mythic thinking. Associating Native American oral traditions with those of a wide variety of other cultures, Allen points to a generally overlooked commonality shared by diverse peoples. Similarly, by redefining oral tradition as "psychic literature" and locating it in "the universe of power," she emphasizes its value for contemporary readers. In her work, reading becomes a participatory, transformational speech act.

Perhaps most importantly for my argument, Allen's innovative definition of oral traditions provides a useful model for more fully understanding Daly's work. Like Allen, Daly insists that oral traditions provide women with an alternate form of knowledge. As she explains in her preface to *Beyond God the Father*, her conversations with other women—which she views as an essential part of an ongoing gynecentric oral tradition—were a more valuable source of information than the scholarly books and articles she cites: "Having been denied equal access to the realm of the printed word, women still have primarily an oral tradition. My references to conversations are meant to be a reminder of that tradition, as well as an effort to set precedent for giving women some of the credit due to them, finally" (1973, xxxiii–xxxiv). Like Allen, then, Daly develops a linguistic context designed to transform her readers. Indeed, in her "Original Reintroduction" to *Beyond God the Father*, she insists that transformation does not occur with "a mere semantic shift in . . . vocabulary" but instead requires a nonpatriarchal speaking position (xix). Again in *Pure Lust* she maintains that it is not enough to use words in new ways, for it is "only in an Other-centered *context* that these can come Alive as instruments of Be-Witching, that is, as Metaphors of Metamorphosis" (1984, 404; her emphasis). However, because she associates this "Other-centered context" with an unmarked prepatriarchal tradition, or what she describes as the "glimmerings of our Archaic Elemental heritage" (1984, 117), readers often ignore its oral performative dimensions.

As Allen validates her truth claims with references to Thought Woman and as Daly calls on the "Archimage within" to justify their assertions, they draw on metaphoric language's performative effects to alter their readers' self/worldviews. Building on earlier descriptions of oral traditions, Allen provides the most extensive justification for this transformational linguistic process. She equates myth with metamorphosis and change by defining it as a unique mode of communication, "a language construct that contains the power to transform something (or someone) from one state or condition to another." She challenges western conceptions of mythic stories as falsehoods or lies and argues that they embody a mode of perception—"the psychospiritual ordering of nonordinary knowledge"—shared by all human beings, "past, present, and to come." According to Allen, this mythic perception has a direct bearing on how people conduct themselves in the physical world. By affirming each person's "most human and ennobling dimensions," she explains, mythic tales provide human beings with new possibilities for action (1986, 103–6). Allen's origin myths illustrate this transformational process. As she remetaphorizes Woman as Thought Woman, she offers her readers new ways to see themselves and new ways to act. Similar comments can be made about Anzaldúa, Daly, and Lorde as well. Although each writer uses different metaphors and myths, they too maintain that our ties with a prepatriarchal past can transform our lives in the present.

> I say mujer magica, empty yourself. Shock yourself into new ways of perceiving the world. Shock your readers into the same. Stop the chatter inside their heads.
>
> —Gloria Anzaldúa

> Only confirmation of one's own Reality awakens that Reality in another.
>
> —Mary Daly

For Anzaldúa as well, metaphoric language can have concrete material effects. She too draws on mythic metaphors embedded in culturally specific oral traditions as she writes her "feminine" mestizaje. Thus she identifies her task as a writer with that of the Aztec nahual, or shaman: She is a "shape-changer" who uses language to reinvent herself, her readers, and her world. In *Borderlands/La Frontera: The New Mestiza* (1987) and again in her preface to *Making Face, Making Soul/Haciendo Caras* (1990a), she insists that each reader is "the shaper of [her] flesh as well as of [her] soul."[14] Like Allen and Daly, Anzaldúa does not rely exclusively on academic arguments or western philosophical discourse to validate her truth claims concerning writing's transformational potential. Instead, she uses this ancient Nahuatl proverb and the nondualistic worldview it represents to develop an argument based on embodied metaphysical power, where the inner and outer dimensions of life are intimately related. For Anzaldúa, this interrelationship implies that all creative endeavors include a "spiritual, psychic component: synthesizing body, soul, mind, and spirit" (1990a, xxiv). She describes writing as "making face, making soul" to underscore language's transformational power, its ability to alter both the material and spiritual dimensions of reality.

Revisionist mythmaking plays an important role in Anzaldúa's transformational theory of language. By (re)claiming and (re)interpreting Coatlicue, an ancient Mesoamerican mythic figure, Anzaldúa invents a mythic narrative where historical and contemporary issues of gender, culture, sex, and class converge: As she traces Coatlicue's descent from her pre-Columbian role as an all-encompassing, multigendered divine being to her current status as the demonic Serpent Woman, she charts the transition to increasingly male-dominated, hierarchical social structures that occurred when the indigenous Indian tribes were conquered by the Aztecs and Spaniards. Stripped of her all-inclusive cosmic powers, this god/dess[15]—who originally "contained and balanced the dualities of male and female, light and dark, life and death"—was doubly divided, first feminized then split into two: as Tlazolteotl/Coatlicue, she was banished to the underworld where she became the embodiment of darkness, materiality, and female evil; and as Tontantsi/Guadalupe, she was purified, christianized, "desexed," and transformed into the holy virgin mother (1987, 32).

Anzaldúa's description of Coatlicue's mythic fall should not be read as the nostalgic desire to return to some utopian, gynecentric state of epistemological innocence—to what Haraway might skeptically call "a once-upon-a-time wholeness before language, before writing, before Man" (1990, 93). Nor does it imply what Butler might describe as a deterministic trajectory, "a necessary and unilinear narrative that culminates in, and thereby justifies, the constitution of the law" (1989, 36). Instead, Anzaldúa adopts this mythic figure to invent an ethnic-specific yet transcultural, transgendered symbol synthesizing cultural critique with the invention of new ways of thinking. She develops a complex narrative which she calls the "Coatlicue state" that associates Coatlicue's loss of elemental power both with the double consciousness she experiences as a dark-skinned woman in contemporary U.S. culture and with the hierarchical division between reason and intuition found in Enlightenment-based knowledge systems.

Anzaldúa associates the Coatlicue state with her own ambiguous position in contemporary U.S. culture. As she explains in *Borderlands/La Frontera,* the opposing Mexican, Indian, and Anglo worldviews she has internalized lead to self-division and shame. On the one hand, she is drawn to nonrational Native traditions that validate psychic, supernatural events; on the other hand, she has been trained to rely solely on reason and to dismiss such beliefs as "pagan superstitions." These two modes of perception—"the two eyes in her head, the tongueless magical eye and the loquacious rational eye"—seem to be mutually exclusive; they are separated by "an abyss that no bridge can span" (1987, 45). Yet she maintains that her willingness to confront, rather than reject, the cultural ambiguities and immerse herself in the Coatlicue state leads to the creation of an alternate mode of perception that synergistically combines rational and nonrational thought. Anzaldúa describes this synergistic energy as a "third element," which she names "mestiza consciousness." Drawing on her own experiences of alienation in the various cultures she interacts with, she explains that the new mestiza learns to live with conflicting Indian, Mexican, and Anglo worldviews "by developing a tolerance for contradictions, a tolerance for ambiguity. . . . She has a plural personality, she operates in a pluralistic mode—nothing is thrust out, the good the bad and the ugly, nothing rejected, nothing abandoned. Not only does she sustain contradictions, she turns the ambivalence into something else" (1987, 79).

As this emphasis on tolerance and ambivalence suggests, Anzaldúa's mestiza consciousness represents a fluid, transitional epistemology. She does not offer her readers a systematic, fully structured alternative to existing theories of knowledge. Instead, she provides us with a different perspective, a way to begin inventing new forms of thought. She maintains that "[a] massive uprooting of dualistic thinking is the *beginning* of a long struggle" (1987, 80; my emphasis). In Anzaldúa's mestiza consciousness, there is no single epistemological destination, no correct form of thinking we must strive to achieve, for its constant movement among existing categories of meaning defies fixed boundaries and final goals. The nondual energy she describes indicates an ongoing transformational process that continually breaks down the rigid, unitary elements in any new paradigm we construct.

Like Allen, Anzaldúa associates her transformational epistemology with culturally specific oral traditions. In *Borderlands/La Frontera*, for example, she reinterprets Aztec metaphysical beliefs from her contemporary perspective and incorporates them into her theory of writing. This synthesis of "western" and "nonwestern" practices serves two interrelated purposes. First, by insisting that tribal cultures' shamanic traditions represent the development of sophisticated, well-integrated aesthetic, religious, and political systems, Anzaldúa exposes the ethnocentric bias that dismisses native peoples' belief systems as "mere pagan superstition."[16] According to Anzaldúa, precolonial Mexican Indians believed that art should be "metaphysical" yet communal, participatory, and intimately related to everyday life (1987, 67). Consequently, art played a vital role in people's social and spiritual existence by validating their lives and empowering them to bring about individual, collective, and cosmic change. Second, by incorporating this dialogic, performative tribal perspective into her theory of writing, Anzaldúa emphasizes language's transformational role, its ability to revitalize individual and communal identities. Thus she describes her own work as "acts encapsulated in time, 'enacted' every time they are spoken aloud or read silently. I like to think of them as performances and not as inert and 'dead' objects (as the aesthetics of Western culture think of art works). Instead, the work has an identity; it is a 'who' or a 'what' and contains the presences of persons, that is, incarnations of gods or ancestors or natural and cosmic powers" (67). As "both a physical thing and the power that infuses it" (67), Anzaldúa's writing is, as it were, a complex mixed breed; just as the mestiza mediates between diverse cultures, her art synthesizes past, present, and future perspectives by mediating between political, personal, and spiritual dimensions of reality. It's this synthesis of apparently distinct categories of meaning that enables Anzaldúa to insist on writing's transformational power. She describes her own work as a series of mind/body-altering processes, or "[t]hought shifts, reality shifts, gender shifts: one person metamorphoses into another in a world where people fly through the air, heal from mortal wounds. I am playing with my Self, I am playing with the world's soul, I am in dialogue between my Self and *el espiritu del mundo*. I change myself, I change the world" (70).

As these highly metaphoric descriptions of writing suggest, Anzaldúa draws on indigenous North American oral traditions and employs metaphors of shape-shifters and shamanism to support her contention that writing and other forms of art can have concrete physical and psychic effects on both writers and readers. Like the Aztec shamans whose interaction with unseen forces enabled them to transform themselves and their people, she explains, the mestiza writer is "*nahual*, an agent of transformation, able to modify and shape primordial energy and therefore able to change herself and others into turkey, coyote, tree or human." She describes her own writing practice as "carving bone . . . creating [her] own face, [her] own heart—a Nahuatl concept" to emphasize the ways in which writing enables her to redefine herself and her interactions with others (1987, 74–75). Similarly, in "Haciendo caras" she adopts a Nahuatl saying—" '[*U*]*sted es el modeador de su carne tanto como el de su alma.* You are the shaper of your flesh as well as of your soul' "—to emphasize her readers' ability to attain personal and collective agency (1990a, xxv).

By associating her theory of writing with the Aztec shamans' ability to negotiate the apparent boundaries between spiritual and material worlds, Anzaldúa develops a theory of hybrid metaphors that unites visionary language with political intervention. She maintains that because "the spirit of the words moving in the body is as concrete as flesh and as palpable," metaphoric language can bridge the apparent gaps between writer and reader (1987, 71). In "Metaphors in the Tradition of a Shaman," she describes writing as a fluid process between the writer's body and the reader's mind. She explains that writers "attempt to put, in words, the flow of some of [their] internal pictures, sounds, sensations, and feelings and hope that as the reader reads the pages these 'metaphors' would be 'activated' and live in her" (1990b, 99). As in "Haciendo caras" and *Borderlands/La Frontera,* Anzaldúa defines herself as a "poet-shaman," a cultural healer or agent of change who uses metaphoric language to fight the diverse forms of oppression existing in contemporary North American societies. She describes the negative images, destructive stereotypes, and false information concerning oppressed groups as "dead metaphors" that have concrete personal and socioeconomic effects. People who see themselves continually referred to in derogatory terms internalize these negative images and begin acting them out. Anzaldúa insists that writers can replace such debilitating beliefs with "new metaphors": "Because we use metaphors as well as *yierbitas* and curing stones to effect changes, we follow in the tradition of the shaman. Like the shaman, we transmit information from our consciousness to the physical body of another. If we're lucky we create, like the shaman, images that induce altered states of consciousness conducive to self-healing" (1990b, 99–100). The poet-shaman Anzaldúa describes takes this transformational process even further: She makes what she thinks materialize in her readers. She "listen[s] to the words chanting" in her *own* body and attempts to inscribe them in the bodies of others (1987, 68–71).

According to Anzaldúa, then, metaphors can literally—physically and psychically—transform us; images communicate "with tissues, organs, and cells to effect change" (1990b, 99). As her phrase "making face, making soul" implies, she displaces the boundaries between spiritual, material, and textual worlds and destabilizes their conventional meanings. The rigid borders between writer, reader, and text dissolve: words have concrete physiological, ideological, and psychic effects as physical bodies are transformed into texts that the "poet-shaman" interprets and reinscribes. Thus she views her own writings as conversations between writer, reader, and text. In her introduction to *Making Face, Making Soul/Haciendo Caras*, for example, she describes her writing process as a "constant dialogue" between her selves, her readers, and the words on the computer screen: "Ultimately alone with only the hum of the computer, accompanied by all my faces (and often yours as well), the monitor's screen reflects back the dialogue among 'us.' I talk to myself. That's what writers do, we carry on a constant dialogue between language and hands and images, one or another of our identities trying desperately to get in a word, an image, a sound" (1990a, xxiv).[17]

In many ways, this conversation between writer, readers, and text resembles the "journey of women becoming" (1984, 1) that Daly enacts in her works. Take, for example, the ways in which she describes her use of language in the 1990 preface to *Gyn/Ecology*: "[T]he emergence of *Hag*-related words, as well as such Names as *Crone*, *Spinster*, *Harpy*, *Fury*, and other New Words, was an integral part of the writing process, and when I spoke these aloud to women I was committing Acts of Be-Speaking. I was speaking the words into be-ing. Nor was I alone in this process. Wild women Heard me into Be-Speaking, and together we were forging a Metalanguage that could break through the silence and the sounds of phallocratic babble" (xx). As Daly's emphasis on language's creative power indicates, she too insists that words can have concrete, shape-shifting[18] material effects. She rejects the conventional western dichotomy between language and action as inaccurate and maintains that there is "no authentic separation" between them. Similarly, in *Pure Lust* she associates metaphoric language—or what she describes as "Be-Witching metaphors" (1984, 405)—with alternate modes of perception that she invites her readers to share. She explains that the images she employs "stir the atmosphere E-motionally, awakening ancient connections not only with each other, but with winds, waters, rocks, trees, birds, butterflies, bats, cats, stars" (405). When readers are moved by these "Be-Witching metaphors," they experience a transmutation in consciousness. No longer confined to the paralyzing implications of patriarchal language, they "break out of linguistic prisons" (26) and begin defining reality for themselves.

Daly and Anzaldúa use metaphoric writing to activate language's performative effects, its ability to bring about individual and collective change. Yet scholars rarely acknowledge the performative dimensions of Daly's writing. Focusing on the specific metaphors she employs, they assume that she attempts to change only individual words—not underlying structures—and conclude that her linguistic tactics are ultimately ineffective. Thus for example Meaghan Morris argues that Daly replaces one form of (phallocentric) hierarchical thinking with another, equally hierarchical form (1988, 31–35). Such accusations oversimplify Daly's tactics, and she herself cautions readers against this superficial use of language. For instance, both in her "Original Reintroduction" in *Beyond God the Father* and again in her "New Galactic Introduction" in *Gyn/Ecology* she insists that it's not enough to replace the word "God" with "Goddess."[19] In order to be effective, this shift must occur in a larger context, which she describes as a "profound alteration of consciousness and behavior—that is, of the *context* in which words are spoken" (1973, xix; her emphasis). For Daly, this new context is postpatriarchal and entails a twofold process: first, the recognition that existing forms of discourse have been (mis)shaped by male-dominated pseudouniversal interests; and second, each woman's decision to begin naming reality for herself. As she explains in *Beyond God the Father*, "To exist humanly is to name the self, the world, and God. The 'method' of the evolving spiritual consciousness of women is nothing less than this beginning to speak humanly—a reclaiming of the right to name. The liberation of language is rooted in the liberation of ourselves. . . . [T]he liberation of language from its old context implies a breakthrough to new semantic fields" (1973, 8).

All too often, however, Daly's exclusive focus on the gendered implications of this contextual shift prevents Morris and other critics from recognizing the "new semantic fields" she enacts with her words. But by repeatedly incorporating a culturally specific dimension into her theory of metaphor, Anzaldúa more clearly demonstrates the radical possibilities opened up by performative language. Take, for example, her use of mythic metaphors to emphasize the transformational dimensions of her own writing process. In *Borderlands/La Frontera* she draws on revisionist myth to underscore the intense self-exploration she requires as a writer. When she writes, she explains, she must "jump blindfolded into the abyss of her own being and there in the depths confront her face, the face underneath the mask" (1987, 74–75). By identifying this hidden "face" both as the "alien other" and as her own "inner self, . . . the godwoman . . . *Antigua, mi Diosa*, the divine force within, *Coatlicue . . . Coatlalopeuh-Guadalupe*" (51), Anzaldúa displaces the conventional boundaries between inner/outer, subject/object, and self/other. She locates the "alien other"—the objectified outsider—within herself and dissolves the borders between writer, reader, and text. Writing becomes a series of perpetual rebirths in which her "soul . . . is constantly remaking and giving birth to itself through [her] body" (73).

This equation of writing with perpetual physical/spiritual self-(re)birth is disruptive. As Trinh observes, "a subject who points to him/her/itself as a subject-in-process . . . is bound to upset one's sense of identity—the familiar distinction between the Same and the Other, since the latter is no longer kept in a recognizable relation of dependence, deviation, or appropriation" (1989, 48). By deconstructing the image of a monolithic self and destabilizing the boundaries between writer, reader, and text, Anzaldúa's "feminine" mestizaje challenges readers to redefine their own borders and begin (re)writing themselves. Because she believes that "[n]othing happens in the 'real' world unless it happens in the image in our heads," she develops metaphoric configurations of psychic and political power such as the Borderlands, mestiza consciousness, and the Coatlicue state itself. These graphic metaphors are performative; they invite readers to imaginatively reconstruct their worldviews and envision alternate ways of living.[20]

Using mythic metaphors that "concretize the spirit and etherealize the body" (1987, 75), Anzaldúa's "feminine" mestizaje builds a new culture, una cultura mestiza. Her words incite us to actively create a complex mixed-breed coalition of "queers"—outsiders who, because of ethnicity, gender, sexuality, class position, or whatever, attempt to transform dominant cultural inscriptions. Although Daly's new culture is not as inclusive as Anzaldúa's,[21] she too uses mythic metaphors that break down the boundaries between the spiritual and material realms and invites readers to create revolutionary communities.

> The function of much of what I read about Africa and about Black women, that is meaningful to me, is frequently to keep me from feeling crazy. That's one of the horrors of being locked into the mouth of the dragon: not only do you not have any role models, but there's no resonance for your experience. That's what made me begin to think about writing what I've been writing. We (Black lesbian feminists) have been around a long time. . . . Yes, we do need role models. I wish I'd had some. It would have saved a lot of time.
>
> —Audre Lorde

> Having been a Pirate for many years, I have Righteously Plundered treasures of knowledge that have been stolen and hidden from women, and I've struggled to Smuggle these back in such a way that they can be seen as distinct from their mindbinding trappings.
>
> —Mary Daly

Like Anzaldúa and Allen, Lorde draws on precolonial mythic figures and epistemological traditions as she writes her "feminine" mestizaje; and she too associates her belief in writing's transformational power with her own culturally specific nonwestern worldview. In an interview with Claudia Tate, she defines art as "the use of living" and explains that, whereas the European worldview depicts life as a series of conflicts, "African tradition deals with life as an experience to be lived. In many respects, it is much like the Eastern philosophies in that we see ourselves as a part of a life force. . . . We live in accordance with, in a kind of correspondence with the rest of the world as a whole" (Tate 1983, 112).

As Lorde herself points out, this approach to life is not uniquely African. Yet by attributing her organic worldview to her African ancestry, she subtly emphasizes the political implications of her work. According to Patricia Hill Collins, black U.S. women activists' (re)creation of African cultural traditions has enabled them successfully to resist the dominant society's attempts to destroy their sense of community: "By conserving and recreating an Afrocentric worldview women . . . undermine oppressive institutions by rejecting the anti-Black and anti-female ideologies they promulgate" (1990, 144). I see Lorde's revisionist mythmaking as an important dimension of this ethnic-specific political activism. As she incorporates Yoruban and Dahomean orisha, or spiritual forces, into her poetry, fiction, and prose, she simultaneously reclaims and invents a gynecentric tradition that has been almost entirely erased by Judeo-Christian cultural beliefs.[22]

This mythological erasure parallels the experience of African American women who are dehumanized—both by the dominant U.S. culture and by their local communities—through a series of overwhelmingly negative stereotypes such as the matriarch, the welfare mother, and Jezebel, the sexually promiscuous woman. As Collins notes, although these doubly oppressive images make each woman "invisible as a fully human individual," many African American women have transformed their status as "invisible Other" into a source of tremendous inner strength (1990, 94). By developing a "private, hidden space of . . . consciousness," they successfully have defied the externally imposed labels and maintained their authority to define themselves (92–93). Indeed, one of Collins's main arguments throughout *Black Feminist Thought* is that African American women's ability to create unique self-expressed standpoints, or ways of knowing based on their personal experiences as black U.S. women, has been essential to their survival. However, because they often use a doubled consciousness and mask their inward resistance with outward conformity, this inner dimension of their lives has received little recognition (91). As Collins suggestively notes, "far too many black women remain motionless on the outside . . . but inside?" (93, her ellipses).

Lorde uses revisionary mythmaking to *externalize* the "inside ideas" Collins sees as a hallmark of black U.S. women's resistance to dominant groups (1990, 92–93). In Lorde's work, West African mythic images serve as vehicles for her "feminine" mestizaje, enabling her to establish new definitions of womanhood, definitions that affirm the culturally specific components of black female identity yet go beyond this affirmation to provide all women with new models of subject formation. By expressing her own self-defined standpoints through the figures of Aido Hwedo, Seboulisa, and other Yoruban/Fon orisha, Lorde critiques previous conceptions of womanhood modeled on European beauty standards and social roles, creates positive role models for other self-identified black women, and offers readers of all cultural/ethnic backgrounds new ways to perceive themselves and new ways to act. It's this trajectory from "inside ideas" to outer forms she refers to in the interview with Tate when she describes her attempt to develop a voice "for as many people . . . who need to hear what I have to say—who need to use what I know." When she writes, she explains, she "speak[s] from the center of consciousness, from the *I am* out to the *we are* and then out to the *we can*" (qtd. in Tate 1983, 105; her emphasis).

Lorde's "we" is performative; it enables her to establish a personal/collective voice and an alternate epistemology she invites her readers to adopt. In "Uses of the Erotic" she locates this "nonrational knowledge" in "a deeply female and spiritual plane" and describes it as "the erotic—the sensual—those physical, emotional, and psychic expressions of what is deepest and strongest and richest within each of us" (1984, 56). Like Allen's embodied thinking, Anzaldúa's mestiza consciousness, and Daly's Realizing reason, Lorde's "erotic" indicates a nondual, transformational mode of perception that draws on language's performative effects to bring about personal and societal change. She maintains that those who acknowledge their "erotic knowledge" gain access to a previously unrecognized source of wisdom, "an incredible reserve of creativity and power" with which to transform themselves and their world (37, 56). As she explains in the interview with Tate, the erotic makes it possible to develop "new ways of understanding our experiences. This is how new visions begin, how we begin to posit a future nourished by the past. This is what I mean by matter following energy, and energy following feeling. Our visions begin with our desires" (quoted in Tate 1983, 107). As this transition from feeling to energy to matter implies, Lorde's invention of the erotic indicates her attempt to integrate the material and nonmaterial dimensions of life. Just as Allen's embodied mythic thinking, Anzaldúa's mestiza consciousness, and Daly's Realizing reason enable them to synthesize spiritual, political, and material issues, Lorde's theory of the erotic enables her to integrate her Afrocentric spirituality with social protest and cultural change.

Lorde's theory of the erotic represents an innovative epistemological process that subverts patriarchally defined concepts by affirming previously denigrated ways of knowing. This synthesis of emotional energy with rational thought implicitly challenges the Cartesian mind/body dualism, the commonly accepted belief that ideas and insights arise exclusively from mental processes. Like several contemporary poststructuralists, Lorde replaces this binary knowledge system with an embodied theory of knowing that posits an affective foundation for thought.[23] In her epistemology, "thinking" represents an intimate, indivisible connection between body and mind. Ideas and insights have their source in physical, as well as intellectual, experiences. Locating this emotionally charged mode of perception within every individual, Lorde underscores the importance of personal agency. She maintains that

> when we begin to live from within outward, in touch with the power of the erotic within ourselves, and allowing that power to inform and illuminate our actions upon the world around us, then we begin to be responsible to ourselves in the deepest sense. For when we begin to recognize our deepest feelings, we begin to give up, of necessity, being satisfied with suffering and self-negation, and with the numbness which so often seems like their only alternative in our society. Our acts against oppression become integral with self, motivated and empowered from within. (1984, 58)

As this synthesis of deep feeling and external action indicates, Lorde associates her theory of the erotic with an agent-centered collective subjectivity uniting inner direction with outward change.

By identifying herself with Yemanja, Oshun, Oya, and other Yoruban/Fon orisha, Lorde invents new myths to incorporate her erotic way of knowing into a complex self-naming process that combines the rejection of negative images with the invention of new individual and communal identities. In "October," for example, she calls on Seboulisa to infuse her vision with power (1982, 108). By aligning herself with this Yoruban orisha, Lorde synthesizes language with action and memory with myth. She replaces the destructive stereotypes of Jezebel with an African-inspired tradition of strong women capable of transforming themselves and their world. Again in "The Winds of Orisha" Lorde borrows from Yoruban myth to invent new images of African-inspired female power. In this poem, she uses revisionist mythmaking to affirm her identity as a black woman warrior poet and lover of women. She creates an extended family of divine female figures, including Yemanja, mother of all the orisha; "the beautiful Oshun," orisha of beauty and love; and "Oya my sister my daughter," orisha of destruction and change. By associating her work as a writer with these West African spiritual forces, Lorde underscores the importance of her task, as well as her own creative power. Like Oya, who "destroys the crust of the tidy beaches," her words are forceful, designed to bring about positive change. And, by describing a sexual interchange between herself and Oshun, she affirms her own lesbian-identified, embodied erotic knowledge: "the beautiful Oshun and I lie down together / in the heat of her body truth my voice comes stronger." As this fluid shift from the orisha's "body truth" to the poet's voice suggests, Lorde's revisionist myth enacts the erotic. She depicts an embodied, transformational way of knowing where "[i]mpatient legends speak through [her] flesh / changing this earths [*sic*] formation / spreading" (1982, 48–49).

As she reinvents strong female images drawn from Yoruban and Fon mythic systems, Lorde invests her personal insights with collective, ethnic-specific meaning. Karla Holloway (1992) makes a similar point in her study of West African and African American women writers' use of nonwestern mythic material. As Holloway demonstrates, by incorporating metaphoric ancestral and goddess figures into their work, contemporary black women writers have created both a gendered, culture-specific voice and a "collective consciousness" (30). In their texts, mythology serves as a cultural and linguistic bridge: it is "the meta-matrix for all uses of language and the primary source of a literature that would recover a historical voice that is at once sensual, visceral, and real" (107). Women writers of the diaspora cannot physically reclaim the African cultures—the "language[s], religion[s], political independence, [and] economic polic[ies]"—lost during the Middle Passage and slavery; however, their revisionary myths enable them "spiritually" to re-member and reconstruct their cultural pasts (20).

Although Holloway restricts her analysis to the aesthetic dimensions of fictional narratives, her emphasis on the interconnections between mythic metaphors, voice, and "spiritual memory" (1992, 20) has important implications for Lorde's poetry. In *The Black Unicorn* (1978), Lorde's collection of poems thematically unified by references to Yoruban and Dahomean orisha, mythology serves as the "meta-matrix" for the invention of culture- and gender-specific voices. In the first section, Lorde reshapes West African myth to define herself as a black woman warrior poet. Throughout the remaining sections, she enlarges this original definition to encompass a network of mythic, historic, contemporary, and imaginary women extending from the Yoruban orisha—through the ancient Dahomean Amazons, her family, friends, and female lovers—to the "mothers sisters daughters / girls" she has "never been" (48). Because myth provides the basis for "the community's shared meanings [and] interactions with both the spiritual and the physical worlds" (Holloway

1992, 31), Lorde's retrieval of West African mythic figures enables her to intervene in existing systems of gendered meaning.

Throughout *The Black Unicorn*, Lorde uses revisionist mythmaking both to critique existing definitions of womanhood and to invent new definitions that more accurately reflect her own experiences as a woman of African descent. Replacing European-based, masculine images of a benign Mother Goddess with metaphors of Yoruban/Fon orisha, she simultaneously exposes the limitations in western ethnocentric concepts of womanhood and constructs an alternate model of female identity formation that begins at a specific cultural location yet moves outward. The title poem, for example, concludes with her "redefinition of woman, a necessary naming through unnaming, since in Western literature 'woman' has historically meant 'white' " (Annas 1982, 24). Lorde's revisionist mythmaking challenges other negative concepts of female identity as well. In "A Woman Speaks," she spurns the image of "womanly" power as a gentle nurturing force and warns readers to "beware [of her] smile": she is "treacherous" and angry, filled with "old magic" and "the noon's new fury" (1978, 5–6). And, like Allen's creatrix figures or Daly's "Unfolding Nature," Lorde's new metaphors of Woman combine transcendence with immanence. In "The Women of Dan Dance with Swords in Their Hands," she subverts the dualistic notion of a transcendent deity, a disembodied spiritual power that exists elsewhere, in a nonphysical, supernatural place. She declares that her power, although divine, is not otherworldly: she "did not fall from the sky," nor does she descend gently "like rain." Instead, she "come[s] like a woman"—like an Amazon warrior woman—with a sword in her hand (1978, 14–15).

Whether she refers to Amazon women warriors dancing with swords in their hands or to goddesses "bent on destruction by threat" (1978, 88), Lorde's mythic figures represent an innovative departure from those reclaimed by a number of Anglo cultural feminists. These differences reflect the specific conditions faced by many contemporary black women and illustrate Holloway's contention that "[t]he African deity imaged in black women's literature is very different from the highly romanticized versions of goddesses rediscovered by Western feminists. The African deity is a figure of both strength and tragedy—like the women whose lives echo hers" (1992, 154–55).[24] In both "Dahomey" and "125th Street and Abomey," for instance, Lorde revises conventional western images of a bountiful mother goddess with her depiction of Seboulisa—"one breast / eaten away by worms of sorrow and loss" (1978, 10, 12). Yet these poems are not elegies; they are, rather, assertions of power in the face of tremendous cultural deprivations. In the latter poem she names herself Seboulisa's "severed daughter," underscoring the cultural loss she has experienced in the diaspora, the personal loss she experienced after her mastectomy, and her reconstruction of personal/communal/mythic voices. In a stanza beautifully illustrating Collins's description of black women's "inside ideas," Lorde writes that, although separated by "[h]alf earth and time" from this single-breasted black goddess, her own "dream" reunites them. She has inscribed Seboulisa's image "inside the back of [her] head." This self-inscription demonstrates the performative, transformational dimensions of Lorde's revisionary mythmaking. Through imaginative reconstruction, she adopts the ravaged goddess's name as her own; she enacts the erotic, "the woman strength / of tongue" that empowers her work. Redefining herself as Seboulisa, she synthesizes individual and collective concerns; she projects her speech outward and boldly declares that she will laugh "*our* name into echo / all the world shall remember" (1978, 12–13; my emphasis).

For Daly as well, revisionist mythmaking plays an important role in the invention of alternate models of individual and collective female identity. Take, for example, her discussion in *Pure Lust* (1984) of the Archimage, or "the Muse within" (90). According to Daly, "[T]he true *Archimage behind* the simulators/reversers . . . is the Great Original Witch, who is *in* women and all Elemental creatures. As an Original Act of Exorcism, of dis-spelling the archi-magi's bad magic, Lusty women can reclaim the name *Archimage*, Naming the fact that she is the Witch within our Selves. She is a verb, and she is verbal—a Namer, a Speaker—the Power within who can Name away the archetypes that block the ways/words of Metabeing" (86–87; her emphasis). In many ways, this Archimage functions analogously to Lorde's theory of the erotic, for it provides women with an inner source of transformational power enabling them to rename themselves and their world. Thus Daly insists that when women gain access to this "Great Original Witch" within themselves, they will acquire new forms of personal and communal agency, empowering them to transcend patriarchal culture's "dogmatic deceptions" (113) and reestablish cross-cultural communities of women, or what she describes as "a Cosmic Commonality, a tapestry of connectedness which women as Websters/Fates are constantly weaving. The weaving of this tapestry is the Realizing of a dream, which Adrienne Rich has Named 'The Dream of a Common Language' " (26–27). According to Daly, this

"Dream" is already a reality—the "Real Presence—that shines through appearances" (113). But she stipulates that in order to recognize it as such, women must awaken this Archimage—the "root of connectedness in the female Elemental Race" (87)—within themselves.

There is, however, an important difference between the Archimage Daly describes and Lorde's mythic women: Daly's metaphoric images of Woman seem to lack the culturally specific dimensions found in Lorde's work. As her references to "female Elemental Race" and "Cosmic Commonality" imply, Daly often employs highly generalized terms in her attempt to transcend all culturally specific models of female power and create cross-cultural communities of women, or what she describes in her "New Intergalactic Introduction" to *Gyn/Ecology* as "biophilic Bonding with women of all races and classes, under all the varying oppressions of patriarchy" (1978, xxxi). To be sure, Daly does not entirely ignore the differences among women. Indeed, her "Great Original Witch" could be tied to earlier European traditions; however, Daly herself does not underscore this connection. Rather, she uses this Witch as an unmarked category to unify all women into a single originary "Elemental Race," a gynocentric form of "Metabeing" that supersedes the many differences among women; it is "a metaphysical way of Naming forth and Naming faith in this common bonding of Lusty women. For *Metabeing* names the Elemental participation in Powers of Being which is the source of authentic female bonding" (1984, 27). Although Lorde also attempts to create transcultural communities of women, her approach is quite different. She draws almost exclusively from Yoruban/Fon belief systems and remetaphorizes Woman in ways that are culturally specific yet nonexclusive. Thus for example in her letter to Daly she associates Mawulisa, Yemanja, and other orisha with "the female bonding of African women" but maintains that these "old traditions of power" are available to "*all* women who do not fear the revelation of connection to themselves." She urges Daly to acknowledge this connection, to "re-member what is dark and ancient and divine within yourself that aids your speaking" (1984, 69–70; my emphasis). Though it seems paradoxical, it is these culturally specific contexts that enable Lorde to create transcultural, transgendered communities that neither ignore nor reify the many differences among us.

Similar statements can be made about Allen and Anzaldúa as well. They too use culturally specific mythic metaphors of Woman to destabilize monolithic conceptions of female identity and create transcultural, transgendered communities.[25] But how do these movements from the particular to the transcultural occur? And what makes Allen's, Anzaldúa's, and Lorde's claims more effective for many readers than Daly's? After all, the four writers *all* employ a universalizing discourse to generate new bonds among women from diverse backgrounds, yet only Daly has been accused of creating exclusionary, pseudouniversal concepts of female identity. Although these issues require far more detailed exploration than I can provide in this chapter, we find important clues in the forms that their universalism takes.

Despite feminist and poststructuralist critiques of universalism, universals are a necessary fiction. As Ernesto Laclau argues, the universal represents "an empty but ineradicable place" (1995, 157)—a never attainable yet always necessary space that mobilizes social actors, providing them with new horizons of the possible. Allen, Anzaldúa, Daly, and Lorde expand existing horizons by appropriating and subverting Enlightenment-based concepts of the (masculine) universal; they invent new universals that they invite their readers to adopt. But Daly overlooks the role that differences among women can play in redefining the universal, whereas Allen, Anzaldúa, and Lorde do not. She uses references to specific ethnic/cultural traditions only to highlight what she sees as all women's shared "Elemental" power, a universal gynocentric form of sameness that she believes transcends the many differences between women.[26] As she explains in *Pure Lust*,

> it is clear that Lusty women are profoundly different from each other. Not only are there ethnic, national, class and racial differences that shape our perspectives, but there are also individual and cross-cultural differences of temperament. . . . But there is also above, beyond, beneath all this a Cosmic Commonality. The word *Metabeing* is a metaphysical way of Naming forth and Naming faith in this common bonding of Lusty women. For *Metabeing* names the Elemental participation in Powers of Being which is the source of authentic female bonding. (1984, 26–27)

Ironically, Daly's primary focus on women's commonality can be more exclusionary than she intends, for it compels readers to undergo a restrictive process of normalization. This process goes beyond external behavior and requires individuals to see themselves in a specific way. As Etienne Balibar explains, "Normality is not the simple fact of adopting customs and obeying rules or laws: it means internalizing representations of the 'human type' or the 'human subject' (not exactly an essence, but a norm and a standard behavior) in order to be recognized as a person in its full right, to become *présentable* (fit to be seen) in order to be represented" (1995, 63). To enter into Daly's "Cosmic Commonality," each woman must identify with her "Lusty women" and relinquish any claims to the particular that do not conform to the universal feminine she describes. Those who cannot or will not are excluded. In short, Daly's universalism interpellates readers into a single subject position. Downplaying the role that differences play in shaping women's identities, Daly implies that gender, in itself, offers women an adequate grounds for "authentic female bonding." This assertion of "*Metabeing*" prevents dialogue and revision: the common ground already exists; there is no space to redefine it according to individual desires and needs.[27]

Whereas Daly relies on a gender-specific universal that transcends differences among women, Allen, Anzaldúa, and Lorde do not. Instead, they create new concepts of the universal that negotiate between commonality and particularity *without denying the importance of either*. This negotiation serves two purposes. First, it enables them to redefine the universal in radically open-ended, potentially dialogic ways. Although they incorporate the culturally specific into their concepts of the universal, they do not simply universalize the particular. Instead, they pluralize the universal, allowing a variety of culturally specific forms to coexist in dynamic interaction. This dynamic coexistence makes further change—further transformations of the universal—possible. To borrow Lorde's words, difference becomes a "creative force for change" (1984, 45–46). Second, their negotiations between commonality and particularity offer readers a variety of subject positions within the universal. They create inclusionary communities of women. Individual women can acknowledge their sense of difference(s) from others without feeling excluded. It is, in fact, the reverse: They too can use difference(s) to redefine the existing universal.

The new universals that Allen, Anzaldúa, and Lorde invent serve another purpose as well: by highlighting and inventing gynocentric, culturally specific traditions, they redefine ethnic categories.[28] And, by incorporating these redefined categories into their ethnically marked images of female power, they transform their readers' ethnicities as well. If, as a number of contemporary theorists suggest, each subject is composed of multiple parts and located at the intersection of diverse—sometimes overlapping, sometimes conflicting—discourses, no identity is or ever can be entirely stable and fixed. As Chantal Mouffe states, there is always "a certain degree of openness and ambiguity in the way the different subject-positions are articulated" (1988, 35). It's this potential openness to redefinition that makes personal and cultural change possible. However, in order to bring about radical social change, these subject positions cannot simply be combined differently; they must be transformed:

> If the task of radical democracy is indeed to deepen the democratic revolution and to link together diverse democratic struggles, such a task requires the creation of new subject-positions that would allow the common articulation, for example, of antiracism, antisexism, and anticapitalism. These struggles do not spontaneously converge, and in order to establish democratic equivalences, a new "common sense" is necessary, which would transform the identity of different groups so that the demands of each group could be articulated with those of others according to the principle of democratic equivalence. (43)

In other words, in today's postmodern world, political unities must be consciously developed through a process of articulation.[29] We—no matter who "we" are—do not automatically unite on the basis of shared "natural" traits. Instead, shared identities must be created. By writing their "feminine" mestizajes, Allen, Anzaldúa, and Lorde invent new forms of ethnically marked yet transculturally shared identities. Their focus on particularity—seen for example in their use of culturally specific female mythic images—plays a vital role in this transformational process. In psycholinguistic terms, because their representations of Woman occur within metaphor, on an imaginary level, they potentially destabilize readers' ego-ideal identifications, the master signifiers or symbols that shape each person's self-conceptions in pivotal ways. When western readers of all colors identify the "feminine" in ourselves with the "feminine" in Thought Woman, Coatlicue, Yemanja, or the other mythic figures they employ, we experience a "metaphoric transference."[30] That is, we encounter a slippage within our current definitions of Woman and the "feminine" as we recognize a gap between what *is* and what *could* or *should be*. It's this slippage between competing definitions that enables us to act out the "feminine" differently. More specifically, because Woman and the "feminine" function as master signifiers in identity formation, this recognition produces a shift in self-perception. As Mark Bracher explains, "[W]hat happens to our sense of being or identity is determined to a large degree by what happens to those signifiers that represent us" (1993, 25).[31] To be sure, this slippage can also occur when readers encounter Daly's metaphoric Woman. However, because Daly does not openly incorporate ethnicity into her mythic metaphors, the effect is quite different. Whereas Allen, Anzaldúa, and Lorde invent new ethnic markers, Daly strips them away, inadvertently creating the illusion of a single gender-specific subject position that seems simply to replicate already-existing master signifiers of the "feminine." By indianizing, mexicanizing, or africanizing the master signifiers that represent "us" women, Allen, Anzaldúa, and Lorde indianize, mexicanize, or africanize their readers as well: they invent a variety of subject positions that they invite their readers to adopt.

As they excavate and re-create ethnic-specific gynecentric myths, Allen, Anzaldúa, and Lorde take Daly's injunction to move "beyond God the Father" to new levels. They replace Judeo-Christian traditions with Native American, Mexican Indian, and West African worldviews and develop new myths to transform themselves and their readers. I want to emphasize the highly inventive nature of the new myths they enact: Allen, Anzaldúa, and Lorde do not provide readers with authentic, gendered, ethnic-specific standpoints. Their epistemologies are performative, not descriptive; and the effect is radical transformation. By writing their "feminine" mestizajes they stage fluid, transcultural self/worldviews that they invite their readers—whatever their cultural backgrounds—to adopt. Instead of recovering precolonial mythological systems erased by patriarchal structures, they invent what I would describe as ethical, *artificial* mythologies—*ethical*, because their new metaphors of Woman provide imaginary alternatives to contemporary western definitions of the "feminine;" and *artificial*, because the "feminine" they affirm does not—yet—exist.

Their revisionist mythmaking illustrates what Drucilla Cornell calls "ethical feminism," or what I would describe as the use of performative speech acts to disrupt the prevailing phallocentric sociosymbolic order. Significantly, Cornell's ethical feminist does not attempt to replace contemporary definitions of the "feminine" with alternate definitions that more accurately reflect the truth of women's experience. Instead, s/he speaks from "the utopian or redemptive perspective of the not yet" by using allegory and myth to *imaginatively* reconstruct the "feminine" (1993, 59). Thus, ethical feminism occurs in the subjunctive, in a liminal space between past, present, and future definitions. Or as Cornell explains, ethical feminism "explicitly recognizes the 'should be' in representations of the feminine. It emphasizes the role of the imagination, not description, in creating solidarity between women. Correspondingly, ethical feminism rests its claim for the intelligibility and coherence of 'herstory' not on what women 'are,' but on the remembrance of the 'not yet' which is recollected in both allegory and myth" (59). In other words, ethical feminism reclaims and rereads already existing stories and myths of the "feminine" but interprets them in new ways.

At this point I want to adopt Cornell's ethical feminism and apply my own "redemptive perspective" to a reading of Daly's origin myths. Despite Daly's apparent comments to the contrary, I believe that her discussions of a female Elemental Race, women's ancestral memories, or the Radiance of our own Origins "should be" read performatively, as potentially transformational metaphors. In other words, I am suggesting that these metaphoric images do not represent accurate descriptions of an authentic female identity; nor do they indicate the recovery of women's essential inner nature. Such literal interpretations are far too limiting, for they lead to restrictive definitions of the "feminine" and confine women's experiences to a predetermined set of characteristics. More importantly, if we read Daly's metaphoric language descriptively, we deny its performative effects and overlook the visionary, ethical dimensions of her work.

Like Allen, Anzaldúa, and Lorde, Daly employs metaphoric language performatively, to transform her readers. She too invents an ethical, artificial mythology and a fluid, transcultural self/worldview that she invites her readers to adopt. In her revisionary myths, representation and creation become blurred. Her celebration of women's "Female/Elemental divinity" indicates an ongoing creative process that involves what Cornell describes as the recovery of the "feminine" as an imaginative universal. According to Cornell, this recovery "feeds the power of the feminine imagination and helps to avoid the depletion of the feminine imaginary in the name of the masculine symbolic. This use of the feminine as an imaginative universal does not, and should not, pretend to simply tell the 'truth' of woman as she was, or is. This is why our mythology is self-consciously an artificial mythology; Woman is 'discovered' as an ethical standard. And as she is 'discovered,' her meaning is also created" (1991, 178).[32] As Cornell's oscillation between creation and discovery indicates, this use of the "feminine" as an imaginative universal draws on the rhetoric of authenticity yet goes beyond existing definitions to emphasize the artificial, inventive nature of these mythologies of Woman.

I want to underscore the open-ended possibilities in this use of the "feminine" as an imaginative universal. Because the "discovery" of Woman as an ethical standard occurs within mythic metaphors, it defies literal, monologic interpretation, thus making possible a proliferation of meanings, meanings that must be invented and lived out by each reader. But by phrasing her new definitions in the language of discovery, origins, and excavated pasts, Daly (like Allen, Anzaldúa, and Lorde) authorizes her words. Revisionist mythmaking plays an important role in Daly's newly authorized "discoveries," for mythic images are open to multiple interpretations. As Cornell points out, "It is the potential variability of myth that allows us to work within myth, and the significance it offers, so as to reimagine our world and by so doing, to begin to dream of a new one" (1991, 178).

Yet Daly's critics rarely recognize the "potential variability of myth" in her work. Because they view her primarily as a philosopher, they evaluate her according to conventional academic standards and overlook the creative, performative dimensions of her revisionary mythmaking. By reading Daly in dialogue with Allen, Anzaldúa, and Lorde—writers generally viewed as poets and storytellers—I have attempted to suggest another perspective for Daly's work. Like these ethnically marked writers, Daly uses language performatively, to create a reality that does not—yet—exist. She too draws on her own version of oral traditions as she attempts to inspire her readers.

In various ways and to various degrees, all four writers employ revisionist myth to invent new forms of identity and new social actors. Their use of origin stories and prepatriarchal creatrix figures does not indicate a nostalgic desire to return to some prehistorical, utopian gynecentric, Native American, Mexican Indian, or Yoruban/Fon community of women. By going "back" to previously erased conventions, they go forward—far beyond "God the Father"—rewriting the past from their present perspectives and inventing new definitions as they go. As Trinh asserts, "the return to a denied heritage allows one to start again with different re-departures, different pauses, different arrivals" (1989, 14). These "returns" are performative, not descriptive, and enable them to construct nondual epistemologies that destabilize the boundaries between writer, reader, and text. They engage in to-and-fro movements that take up yet disrupt conventional interpretations of Woman, "American Indians," "Mexican Americans," "African Americans," and the "feminine." These disruptive oscillations enable readers to go beyond conventional feminist identity politics and open up new thresholds, textual and psychic locations where transcultural identifications—feminized, mestizaje connections—can occur.

Notes

Thanks to Renae Bredin, Marilyn Frye, and Sarah Hoagland for valuable comments and suggestions. And thanks to Gloria Anzaldúa for conversations on the topics explored in this essay.

1. According to Butler, "If . . . it is a life of the body beyond the law or a recovery of the body before the law which then emerges as the normative goal of feminist theory, such a norm effectively takes the focus of feminist theory away from the concrete terms of contemporary cultural struggle" (1989, 42).

2. Throughout this essay I will capitalize "Woman" when indicating the term's metaphoric character, including both the oppressive and the potentially liberatory aspects of the term. Also, in this chapter I will put "feminine" in quotation marks in order to emphasize the provisional, speculative, and potentially transformative dimensions of the term.

3. Butler summarizes this view in *Gender Trouble* (1989), 3–6.

4. Nancy Morejón, quoted in Lionnet 1989, 15–16. As Lionnet notes, mestizaje is incompatible with conventional notions of a singular origin: "In this constant and balanced form of interaction, reciprocal relations prevent the ossification of culture and encourage systematic change and exchange. By responding to such mutations, language reinforces a phenomenon of creative instability in which no 'pure' or unitary origin can ever be posited" (16). I discuss my theory of "feminine" mestizaje at greater length in *Women Reading Women Writing* (1996).

5. According to David Murray, for example, "continuance" and "nostalgia" are often used synonymously. As he explains in his discussion of twentieth-century self-identified Native writers' attempts to synthesize precolonial images of the past with present-day conditions, the "invocation of unity is a recurrent theme in American Indian writing." He argues that although this holism could be politically motivated, generally it is not: "[I]n the existing body of American Indian writing, the ideas of wholeness and unity are more usually an expression of a nostalgia without any political cutting edge—a nostalgia for a tribal unity, and for a simplicity which fits neatly into the patterns of literary Romanticism" (1991, 88).

6. See also Daly's comment: "The past is repeatedly encountered, but it is also transmuted, since the context in which it is remembered is moving" (1973, xiv). And in *Pure Lust* she refers to "new beginnings . . . grounded in buried, ancient Origins" (1984, 265).

7. "Cosmogyny" is Allen's neologism. She explains, "For my purposes, 'cosmogyny' is more accurate [than 'cosmology']. It connotes an ordered universe arranged in harmony with gynocratic principles" (1991, xiii–xiv).

8. For a discussion of how christianized informants defeminized Native myths, see Linda Danielson's "Storyteller: *Grandmother Spider's Web*" (1988).

9. For examples of feminist celebrations of motherhood, see Elinor Gadon's *The Once and Future Goddess* (1989) and Kathryn Rabuzzi's *Motherself: A Mythic Analysis of Motherhood* (1988).

10. Athene represents a highly masculinized version of femininity, or what Daly appropriately describes as "Daddy's Girl, the mutant who serves the master's purposes. The token woman, who in reality is enchained, possessed, 'knows' that she is free. She is a useful tool of the patriarchs" (1990, 8).

11. In *Grandmothers of the Light*, Allen writes, "The basic nature of the universe of power is

magic," and she associates this "magic" with her "feminine" mestizaje: "the name given to the practice of a mage Ma (the *m*-syllable again) comes in variants. . . . All are versions of the same morpheme . . . and refer in one way or another to the Great Mother or Great Goddess of the Indo-Germanic tradition" (1991, 15). According to Allen, then, "[M]agic, as the word itself implies . . . is primarily a womanly enterprise" (24).

12. See, for example, Allen's preface to *Grandmothers of the Light*, where she explains that thought, "when exercised within the life circumstances common to women everywhere[,] can reshape (terraform) the earth" (1991, xvi).

13. According to Meaghan Morris, for example, "Daly pursues a politics of subverting isolated signs, not discourses. The 'word' is what carries, conveys and contains 'meaning' " (1988, 31). Throughout her essay on Daly, Morris argues that this politics is too restrictive to be effective. Rosi Braidotti makes a similar point in *Patterns of Dissonance* when she claims that Daly's "words modify nothing and offer absolutely no innovation in terms of the ideas of structuring the current moral and religious order. Daly simply indulges in a substitutive operation which puts women in the place of men, on earth as in heaven, thus preserving the state of things. . . . The latent dogmatism in Daly's thought, quite as much as its reactionary nature, seems . . . potentially dangerous for current feminism, insofar as it subverts the signs, not the codes" (1994, 207).

14. *Borderlands/La Frontera* (1990a), 66 and "Haciendo caras, una entrada" (1990), xvi.

15. I use the term "god/dess" to indicate the inclusionary nature of Anzaldúa's mythic figure, which encompasses what we generally consider to be "feminine" and "masculine" attributes.

16. See, for example, "*Tlilli, Tlapalli*, The Path of the Red and Black Ink" in *Borderlands/La Frontera* where Anzaldúa contrasts the Aztecs' "ethno-poetics" with western culture's "white sterility." She urges North American readers of all racial and ethnic backgrounds to reexamine our rationalist assumptions and free ourselves from "the tyranny of Western aesthetics": "Let's all stop importing Greek myths and the Western Cartesian split point of view and root ourselves in the mythological soil and soul of this continent" (1987, 68).

17. Similarly, in *Borderlands/La Frontera* Anzaldúa describes the writing process as a conversation between her "Self" and the world: "I am in dialogue between my Self and el espíritu mundo. I change myself, I change the world" (1987, 70).

18. Daly associates her writing with shape-shifting in *Gyn/Ecology*, where she describes the writing process she used in this book as "a Stunning experience of *Shape-shifting*" (1990, xviii–xix). Unlike Anzaldúa, however, Daly does not associate this shape-shifting with any culturally specific traditions.

19. For Daly's comments on goddess terminology, see *Gyn/Ecology* (1990) lxv–lxvi and *Beyond God the Father* (1973) xviii–xix.

20. As William Doty explains, because mythical symbols contain "units of information that are not bound up by the immediate contours of what presently is being experienced, . . . [they] provide concrete conveyances for (abstract) thought. Alive in a world of metaphoric and symbolic meanings, they allow experimentation and play with images, ideas, and concepts that otherwise would remain too incorporeal to be engaged" (1986, 20).

21. Anzaldúa, unlike Daly, invites men to participate in her culture-building activities. For more on this topic see my *Women Reading Women Writing* (1996).

22. See Lorde's "Open Letter to Mary Daly" (1984, 66–71); Sojourner 1982; and Bádéjó 1989.

23. See, for example, Rosi Braidotti's (1994) discussions of Gilles Deleuze.

24. While I agree with Holloway that often there are significant differences between depictions of Afrocentric and Eurocentric goddesses, I think she overstates her case.

25. As my use of the term "transgendered" suggests, the transcultural communities invented by Allen, Anzaldúa, and Lorde are not always gender specific. As I explain in *Women Reading Women Writing* (1996), all three writers use nonwestern myth to break down the binary opposition between male and female identities. This deconstructive gesture is, perhaps, one of the greatest differences

between their writings and Daly's, for Daly's more recent work focuses exclusively on women and female identity.

26. See, for example, *Gyn/Ecology*, where Daly points to Libyan, Irish, pre-Hellenic, and Hellenic versions of "the Triple Goddess" (1978, 75–76). Similarly, in *Pure Lust* she finds "Egyptian/African sources" for Mexican and European black madonnas and associates these culturally specific "images of female divinity" both with a cosmic commonality and with nature: "[T]hese glimmerings of our Archaic Elemental heritage . . . stir deep Memory, enabling Hags to ride the Metaphors of the Black Madonnas to spheres of imagination that transcend insipid caucasian cookie-cutter depictions of the Arch-Image. Having glimpsed the Arch-image as black earth, we are prepared to see her associations with other elements" (1984, 117).

27. For a concrete example of the ways Daly's universalism inhibits dialogue among women, see Morris 1988.

28. For an extensive discussion of the ways Allen, Anzaldúa, and Lorde redefine ethnicity, see my *Women Reading Women Writing* (1996).

29. Ernesto Laclau and Chatal Mouffe describe this process of articulation in *Hegemony and Socialist Strategy: Towards a Radical Democratic Politics* (1985).

30. I borrow the term "metaphoric transference" from Drucilla Cornell; she explains that "[t]he metaphors of Woman, in and through which she is performed, are enacted signifiers which, as such, act on us as genderized subjects. But this performance keeps us from 'getting to the Other' of the prediscursive 'reality' of gender or of sex. Metaphoric transference, in other words, recognizes the constitutive powers of metaphor, but only as metaphor" (1991, 100).

31. As both Cornell and Bracher point out, these shifts in self-image play a vital role in transforming social systems. Bracher, for example, insists that "any real social change must involve not just changes in laws and public policy but alterations in the ideals, desires, and jouissances of a significant number of individual subjects" (1993, 73).

32. Cornell further asserts that "[w]e re-collect the mythic figures of the past, but as we do so we reimagine them. It is the potential variability of myth that allows us to work within myth, and the significance it offers, so as to reimagine our world and by so doing, to begin to dream of a new one. In myth we do find Woman with a capital letter. These myths, as Lacan indicates, may be rooted in male fantasy, but they cannot, as he would sometimes suggest, be reduced to it" (1991, 178).

References

Allen, Paula Gunn. 1983. *The Woman Who Owned the Shadows*. San Francisco: Spinsters/Aunt Lute.

———. 1986. *The Sacred Hoop: Recovering the Feminine in American Indian Traditions*. Boston: Beacon.

———. 1991. *Grandmothers of the Light: A Medicine Woman's Sourcebook*. Boston: Beacon.

Annas, Pamela. 1982. "A Poetry of Survival: Naming and Renaming in the Poetry of Audre Lorde, Pat Parker, Sylvia Plath, and Adrienne Rich." *Colby Library Quarterly* 18:9–25.

Anzaldúa, Gloria. 1987. *Borderlands/La Frontera: The New Mestiza*. San Francisco: Spinsters/Aunt Lute.

———. 1990a. "Haciendo caras, una entrada." In *Haciendo Caras/Making Face, Making Soul: Creative and Critical Perspectives by Women of Color*, edited by Gloria Anzaldúa, xv–xxviii. San Francisco: Aunt Lute Foundation.

———. 1990b. "Metaphors in the Tradition of the Shaman." In *Conversant Essays: Contemporary Poets on Poetry*, edited by James McCorkle, 99–100. Detroit: Wayne State University Press.

———. 1991. "To(o) Queer the Writer—*Loca, escritora y chicana*." In *Inversions: Writing by Dykes, Queers, and Lesbians*, edited by Betsy Warland, 249–64. Vancouver: Press Gang.

Bádéjó, Diedre L. 1989. "The Goddess Osun as a Paradigm for African Feminist Criticism." *Sage: A Scholarly Journal on Black Women* 6:27–32.

Balibar, Etienne. 1995. "Ambiguous Universality." *differences: A Journal of Feminist Cultural Studies* 7:48–74.

Ballinger, Franchot, and Brian Swann. 1983. "A MELUS Interview: Paula Gunn Allen." *MELUS* 10: 3–25.

Bar On, Bat-Ami. 1993. "Marginality and Epistemic Privilege." In *Feminist Epistemologies*, edited by Linda Alcoff and Elizabeth Potter, 83–100. New York: Routledge.

Bauman, Richard. 1984. *Verbal Art as Performance*. Prospect Heights, Ill.: Waveland Press.

Bracher, Mark. 1993. *Lacan, Discourse, and Social Change: A Psychoanalytic Cultural Criticism*. Ithaca: Cornell University Press.

Braidotti, Rosi. 1991. *Patterns of Dissonance: A Study of Women in Contemporary Philosophy*. Translated by Elizabeth Guild. New York: Routledge.

———. 1994. *Nomadic Subjects: Embodiment and Sexual Difference in Contemporary Feminist Theory*. New York: Columbia University Press.

Butler, Judith. 1989. *Gender Trouble: Feminism and the Subversion of Identity*. New York: Routledge.

Collins, Patricia Hill. 1990. *Black Feminist Thought: Knowledge, Consciousness, and the Politics of Empowerment*. Boston: Unwin Hymen.

Cornell, Drucilla. 1991. *Beyond Accommodation: Ethical Feminism, Deconstruction, and the Law*. New York: Routledge.

———. 1993. *Transformations: Recollective Imagination and Sexual Difference*. New York: Routledge.

Daly, Mary. 1973. *Beyond God the Father: Toward a Philosophy of Women's Liberation*. Boston: Beacon.

———. 1984. *Pure Lust: Elemental Philosophy*. Boston: Beacon.

———. (1978) 1990. *Gyn/Ecology: The Metaethics of Radical Feminism*. Boston: Beacon.

Danielson, Linda L. 1988. "Storyteller: *Grandmother Spider's Web*." *Journal of the Southwest* 30:325–54.

de Lauretis, Teresa. 1987. *Technologies of Gender: Essays on Theory, Film, and Fiction*. Bloomington: Indiana University Press.

Doty, William G. 1986. *Mythography: The Study of Myths and Rituals*. Tuscaloosa: University of Alabama Press.

Gadon, Elinor W. 1989. *The Once and Future Goddess: A Symbol for Our Time*. San Francisco: Harper and Row.

Gatens, Moira. 1988. "Towards a Feminist Philosophy of the Body." In *Crossing Boundaries: Feminisms and the Critique of Knowledges*, edited by Barbara Caine, E. A. Grosz, and Marie de Lepervanche, 59–70. Sydney: Allen & Unwin.

Grosz, Elizabeth. 1993. "Bodies and Knowledges: Feminism and the Crisis of Reason." In *Feminist Epistemologies*, edited by Linda Alcoff and Elizabeth Potter, 187–215. New York: Routledge.

Hanson, Elizabeth I. 1990. *Paula Gunn Allen*. Boise State University Western Writer Series. Boise: Boise State University Press.

Haraway, Donna. 1990. "A Manifesto for Cyborgs: Science, Technology, and Socialist Feminism in the 1980s." In *Feminism/Postmodernism*, edited by Linda J. Nicholson, 190–233. New York: Routledge.

Hodge, Joanna. 1988. "Subject, Body, and the Exclusion of Women from Philosophy." In *Feminist Perspectives in Philosophy*, edited by Morwenna Griffiths and Margaret Whitford, 152–68. Bloomington: Indiana University Press.

Holloway, Karla F. C. 1992. *Moorings and Metaphors: Figures of Culture and Gender in Black Women's Literature*. New Brunswick: Rutgers University Press.

Irigaray, Luce. 1993. *Sexes and Genealogies*. Translated by Gillian C. Gill. New York: Columbia University Press.

Keating, AnaLouise. 1996. *Women Reading Women Writing: Self-Invention in Paula Gunn Allen, Gloria Anzaldúa, and Audre Lorde*. Philadelphia: Temple University Press.

Laclau, Ernesto. 1995. "Subject of Politics, Politics of the Subject." *differences: A Journal of Feminist Cultural Studies* 7:146–64.

Laclau, Ernesto, and Chantal Mouffe. 1985. *Hegemony and Socialist Strategy: Towards a Radical Democratic Politics*. London: Verso.

Lionnet, Françoise. 1989. *Autobiographical Voices: Race, Gender, Self-Portraiture*. Ithaca: Cornell University Press.

Lorde, Audre. 1978. *The Black Unicorn*. New York: Norton.

———. 1982. *Chosen Poems: Old and New*. New York: Norton.

———. 1982. *Zami: A New Spelling of My Name*. Freedom, Calif.: Crossing Press.

———. 1984. *Sister Outsider*. Freedom, Calif.: Crossing Press.

Moi, Toril. 1991. "Patriarchal Thought and the Drive for Knowledge." In *Between Feminism and Psychoanalysis*, edited by Teresa Brennan, 189–205. New York: Routledge.

Morris, Meaghan. 1988. *The Pirate's Fiancée: Feminism, Reading, Postmodernism*. London: Verso.

Mouffe, Chantal. 1988. "Radical Democracy: Modern or Postmodern?" In *Universal Abandon? The Politics of Postmodernism*, edited by Andrew Ross, 31–45. Minneapolis: University of Minnesota Press.

Murray, David. 1991. *Forked Tongues: Speech, Writing, and Representation in North American Indian Texts*. Bloomington: Indiana University Press.

Rabuzzi, Kathryn Allen. 1988. *Motherself: A Mythic Analysis of Motherhood*. Bloomington: Indiana University Press.

Sojourner, Sabrina. 1982. "From the House of Yemanja: The Goddess Heritage of Black Women." In *The Politics of Women's Spirituality: Essays on the Rise of Spiritual Power Within the Feminist Movement*, edited by Charlene Spretnak, 57–63. New York: Doubleday.

Tate, Claudia. 1983. *Black Women Writers at Work*. New York: Continuum.

Trinh T. Minh-ha. 1989. *Woman Native Other: Writing Postcoloniality and Feminism*. Bloomington: Indiana University Press.

Whitford, Margaret. 1988. "Luce Irigaray's Critique of Rationality." *Feminist Perspectives in Philosophy*, edited by Morwenna Griffiths and Margaret Whitford, 109–30. Bloomington: Indiana University Press.

14

Psychic Liberation: Feminist Practices for Transformation Among Irish Women

Geraldine Moane

Oppression, Liberation, and Psyche

Radical feminist writings on oppression and liberation highlight the political, economic, social, and cultural conditions associated with oppression and liberation and also recognize that oppression and liberation involve the psyche.[1] The psychic damage associated with oppression has often been referred to as "internalized oppression," with more specific examples including "internalized racism" and "internalized homophobia."[2] Liberation will therefore involve not just transformation of political and cultural patterns, but also transformation of the psychic damage associated with oppression. These connections are made by the feminist phrase "the personal is political."

Psychic damage can be systematically linked to the social conditions of oppression.[3] For example, the violence of oppression is associated with fear, and lack of political power can be associated with helplessness and despair. Economic dependency can foster psychological dependency and insecurity. Culture and discourse play a crucial role in maintaining oppression, often convincing the oppressed that their oppression is natural and good for them.[4] Culture and discourse are vital in control of consciousness—of imagination, identity, passions—which is a key strategy of oppression. Referring to patriarchal oppression as colonization Daly writes: "Nor does this colonization exist dimly 'outside' women's minds, securely fastened into institutions we can physically leave behind. Rather, it is also internalized, festering inside women's heads, even feminist heads."[5] Daly captures the ways in which our psyches can be manipulated in writing of "ghostly false images of ourselves which have been deeply embedded in our imaginations and which respond like unnatural reflexes to the spookers' unnatural stimuli."[6]

For Daly, oppression involves an attack on spirit and energy, a disconnection with Original Self, a foreground fixation, while liberation at the psychic level occurs through reconnecting with Original Self and journeying into the Background. At the psychic level, liberation can been seen as a journey of becoming, of undoing the "mindbindings" and "psychic numbing" to which women are subjected, and creating new consciousness. Daly sees liberation as a journey of "Exorcism and Ecstasy," a journey that involves "confronting and transcending the State of Possession"[7] and journeying into the Background, "the realm of the wild reality of women's Selves."[8] It involves the realization of Pure Lust: "*Pure Lust* Names the high humor, hope, and cosmic accord/harmony of those women who choose to escape, to follow our hearts' deepest desire and bound out of the State of Bondage, Wanderlusting and Wonderlusting with the elements, connecting with the auras of animals and plants, moving in planetary communion with the farthest stars. This Lust is in its essence astral. It is pure Passion: unadulterated, absolute, simple sheer striving for abundance of be-ing. It is unlimited, unlimiting desire/fire."[9] It is a journey of "spinning integrity"—"participating in Integrity beyond that integrity—the ever moving Dance of the Universe, the Harmony of the Spheres."[10]

Daly's overall analysis is an ontological one. The urge toward transcendence, or "participation in be-ing" or Elemental Be-ing, is a central focus of her work; this urge is blocked or destroyed by patriarchy, and its realization is a goal of liberation. The realization of Elemental Be-ing obviously requires fundamental and radical change in consciousness and social organization, which of course requires taking action. Changes in consciousness are linked to actions that are linked to social change. As Daly writes: "The foreground fathers offer dual decoys labelled 'thought' and 'action' which distract from the reality both of deep knowing and of external action. There is no authentic separation possible."[11] While Daly does not spell out explicit political goals or strategies, it is clear from her writings that activism of various kinds is seen as a natural outcome of psychic transformation. The enormous variety of activisms engaged in by radical feminists is reflected in references throughout her works to such areas as violence and pornography, poverty, racism, medical and scientific exploitation, and ecological and nuclear destruction.

Liberation at the psychic level—psychic liberation—can be seen as a journey or a developmental process, a movement (not necessarily in linear sequence) from the initial steps of raising consciousness or awareness through to taking action. In Daly's terms, it may be seen as a spiraling process. As she points out in *Outercourse: The Be-Dazzling Voyage*, each movement or moment creates momentum for the next: "One Moment leads to an Other. This is because it has consequences in the world and thus Moves a woman to take the Leap to the next Moment."[12] This quote highlights the feedback loop between psychic transformation and taking action, as each enhances the other.

The journey of liberation being discussed here obviously involves personal transformation. Too often, personal transformation has been associated with therapeutic approaches such as psychotherapy, counseling, twelve-step and other self-help programs, which have been the subject of extensive feminist critiques.[13] If personal transformation is part of liberation, then it is vital to distinguish practices that place personal transformation firmly in a political context and result in action from the practices found in therapeutic programs that often result in counterproductive self-absorption and alienation.

Daly has been scathing in her critique of psychiatry and psychotherapy, arguing that they are clearly patterned as Sado-Ritual Syndromes, and as forms of social control, keeping women "supine, objectified and degraded."[14] Daly argues that the language and methods of psychotherapy constitute a system "of creating and perpetuating false needs, of masking and maintaining depression, of focusing/draining women's energy."[15] As psychotherapy, counseling, personal development, twelve-step and other programs have proliferated, many feminists have become increasingly critical of the obsessive preoccupation with the self and with feelings that these practices engendered. They argue that too often women enter therapy for feelings such as depression, alienation, and exhaustion, which could clearly be linked to oppression, and end up focusing on their childhood and enmeshed in endless analysis of their feelings, which leave them feeling inadequate and confused. Friendships and communities are undermined as women seek support from therapists rather than from one another. The quest for the "real" or "inner" self leaves women "locked into perpetual cycles of 'self-discovery.' "[16] Indeed, Kitzinger and Perkins argue that among many American and British lesbians (those, it must be added, who are middle class), psychotherapy and personal development have become substitutes for political action. Furthermore, the discipline of psychology itself, its language and methodology, has been criticized for sexist, racist, and class bias, for perpetuating individualism, consumerism, and the myth of self fulfillment.[17]

There are thus strong reasons to be cautious in any discussion of personal or psychic transformation, yet at the same time the importance of such transformations in political and social change has been highlighted in numerous discussions of oppression and liberation.[18] I would like to suggest that key elements that distinguish psychic liberation practices from therapeutic practices are that, first, the practices are clearly grounded in a political analysis linking the personal and the political, and second, that the practices clearly result in taking action to bring about social change.[19] Therapeutic practices are characterized by a focus on internal mental states, self-absorption, and isolation; psychic liberation practices are characterized by being clearly linked to the social context, by action, theoretical analysis, and engagement. Psychic liberation is thus intrinsically linked to action; the goal of psychic liberation is to transform the psychic damage associated with oppression and create new consciousness that will facilitate taking action to bring about change.

Aims and Context of This Chapter

My aim in this chapter is to illuminate the journey of psychic liberation by exploring the connections between Daly's analysis and the liberation practices that Irish women have developed. The exploration undertaken here is based firstly on my own journey as a radical feminist, a journey in which Daly's works have played a key role. In my work I have developed a psychological analysis of oppression and liberation based on feminist analyses of women's oppression and on the experiences of colonial oppression.[20] I have been teaching in Women's Studies contexts (and in a department of psychology)[21] for many years, and I have also been an activist in the Irish women's movement in a variety of areas. Initially, reading Mary Daly's work, specifically *Gyn/Ecology*, provided the "earthquake experience" that Daly describes in *Outercourse*, as it exposed the systemic nature of patriarchy and its intentional assault on women's minds and bodies. My engagement with her work later became more personalized, especially through my reading *Pure Lust*, a reading that was itself a journey of personal transformation and that opened up many imaginative and practical possibilities. Her latest work, *Quintessence*, pushes her vision to new dimensions, providing further hope and courage for the journey of liberation.

One of my fundamental interests has been in the question of how to break out of the psychic damage associated with oppression, which later extended to an interest in understanding the transformations involved in liberation.[22] This double-edged emphasis—on oppression and on liberation—is an example of Daly's influence. In her work she urges the reader or journeyer to take a double-edged view, both acknowledging the horrors of oppression and evoking a vision of New Reality. She uses the metaphor of the labrys to refer to that which both exposes patriarchy and evokes Elemental reality. The labrys is a complex symbol or metaphor, for in an almost literal sense, it is a symbol of prepatriarchal Gynocentric (woman-centered) existence, of ancient prepatriarchal times. It also evokes images of wild amazons, of "Labrys-wielding Lusty Movers."[23] For me it is a symbol of my wish both to Re-member the earth-centered and Gynocentric existence of ancient Ireland and to dismantle patriarchy, with its relentless destruction of women's lives through enforced motherhood, violence, and poverty.

Of course I have had many Traveling Companions and for this essay I will draw on discussions with some of them around the question of how they have used Mary Daly's work in their own journeys as radical feminists. These discussions were not set up as "research interviews," but were focused on this question. One of the ways in which Daly's work has been liberating is in her advocacy of "methodicide," since, as she points out, "the Methodolatry of patriarchal disciplines kills creative thought."[24]

The simple practice of citing conversations and treating these with the same respect as written sources is an example of such methodicide.

In the course of working on my analysis of oppression and liberation I also undertook more formal research interviews and group discussions with the aim of charting women's journeys as they moved through the processes of developing awareness and taking action. These interviews and discussions will also provide material for the present exploration as they helped to uncover a number of practices that women used or found helpful in their journey and that clearly articulate with Daly's analysis. The experiences and activities of women in the Irish women's movement provide another vital source for the present exploration. Irish women have been involved in resisting oppression (both patriarchal and colonial)[25] for hundreds of years. Their activities included hunger strikes, armed resistance, and political organizing as well as tactics such as noncooperation, false compliance, secrecy, feigned ignorance, sabotage, and cultural resistance.

Psychic Liberation in an Irish Context

A central theme of Daly's may be introduced at this stage to clarify the discussion of the broader Irish context, namely the distinction between "foreground" and "Background." Daly defines the foreground as a "male-centred and mono-dimensional arena where fabrication, objectification, and alienation take place; [a] zone of fixed feelings, perception, behaviors; the elementary world: Flatland."[26] The foreground may be seen as the zone of patriarchy and other oppressions. Background refers to "the Realm of Wild Reality; the Homeland of women's Selves and of all other Others; the Time/Space where auras of plants, planets, stars, animals and all Other animate beings connect."[27] It is the realm of Elemental Reality, inhabited by Amazons, Crones, Dykes, Spinsters, Witches, and other Elemental beings.

In the Irish context, then, the foreground is, among other things, the political and economic establishment, or the status quo. It is similar to other Western societies in being male dominated, capitalist, democratic, and so on, and like other Western societies it has high levels of violence against women, of poverty and of inequality. It is distinctive particularly by virtue of its history of colonization and the related dominance of the catholic church. The colonization of Ireland by the British occurred over hundreds of years and involved systematic military campaigns, seizure of land and appropriation of economic wealth, exclusion from political power, attempted erasure of language and culture, and the production by the colonizers of an ideology that emphasized the inferiority of "the natives" and promulgated the advantages of colonization.[28] This history includes slaughter, terrorism, poverty, famine, enforced ignorance, emigration, and—hidden from official history—rape and forced pregnancies.

The Republic of Ireland gained political independence from Britain in 1921 (and is therefore considered postcolonial), while Northern Ireland continues to be under British jurisdiction, creating a partition on the island between the six counties of Northern Ireland and the twenty-six counties of the Republic of Ireland.[29] This division has rarely been transcended even by radical politics. It has exacerbated differences between protestants (who for the most part wish to retain the union with Britain) and catholics (who for the most part wish to see the island unified as a whole and separated from Britain). It has created barriers between women north and south of the border, and also between women within both jurisdictions, depending on their stance toward the status of Northern Ireland. It has resulted in thirty years of armed conflict (1968–98), which has involved a continuous British military presence in Northern Ireland. These and other legacies of colonialism have also created difficulties for alliances between Irish and British women. In the Irish context, where the population is more than 95 percent "christian" and white, the "national question" and class issues have posed the biggest challenges to alliances among women.

A legacy of colonialism in the Republic of Ireland has been the dominance of the catholic church, which has played an enormously powerful role in shaping political and cultural life in the postcolonial state. Many have argued that the catholic church gained dominance in the postcolonial state both because of its role under colonialism as a symbol of Irish resistance to colonization (which involved the imposition of the protestant religion) and because of the power vacuums that arose in the postcolonial context.[30] Examples of policies influenced by the catholic church were the exclusion of married women from public service positions until the 1970s and a ban on the sale or the provision of information about contraception until the 1980s, resulting in enforced motherhood and the virtual confinement of women to the home. Misogyny and distortions of sexuality were among the psychic legacies of the influence of the catholic church, whose power has only recently been undermined by the exposure of a series of sexual-abuse scandals involving catholic clergy. Ironically the strength of the catholic church can be related to a strong sense of spirituality and of mysticism, a point that has also been made in the Irish American context. Another legacy of colonialism is a highly male-dominated society, which emerged as Irish men stepped into the positions of power and privilege made vacant by decolonization and sought to exclude women from public life. Male domination in the foreground has been countered to some extent by a powerful women's movement, which drew strength from the history of women's involvement in resistance to colonization, as well as from the legacies of precolonial and prepatriarchal societies.[31]

The Irish context offers a rich Space for journeying into the Background, particularly through immersion in Nature and exploration of the remains of ancient prepatriarchal times.[32] Indeed it is arguable that the ferocity and determination underlying English colonization is related to the power of the Background in the Irish context, as English colonization involved the attempted destruction of the native Celtic or Gaelic society (which survived until the sixteenth century). Gaelic or Celtic society was itself transitional between prepatriarchal egalitarian woman-centered societies and the later Christian patriarchal societies. It was a warrior society, but women had considerably more political and economic power in their own right than in later patriarchal society. Woven through Irish Celtic mythology are strong goddess figures, accounts of healing, magic, and divination, of shape-shifting between humans and animals, and of a complex and varying sense of time.[33] Irish folklore up to the present also contains these themes of shape-shifting, magic, and otherwordly spirits, often contained in fairy stories. The literature and mythology of Irish Celtic society and folklore continue to permeate modern Irish society, offering keys to a different consciousness and cosmology.

Prior to this Gaelic or Celtic society was a Stone Age, or Neolithic, culture dating back to 10,000 B.C.E. and peaking around 3500 B.C.E. Irish Neolithic culture is referred to as megalithic because of the existence of enormous (mega) stone (lithic) structures. The best known of these structures is Newgrange, which is an enormous mound 114 feet high and 130 feet in diameter. This mound covers a large chamber, with three cavities, and a passageway. At winter solstice, the rays of the rising sun glide up this passageway and light the inner chamber, alighting on boulders covered with goddess symbols such as spirals and triangles. Newgrange is part of a complex of three mounds collectively referred to as Brugh na Boinne, Boinne being the generative (in the Irish language) of the river goddess Boann. All in all there are thousands of stone structures all over Ireland, which has one of the richest legacies of stone structures in Europe, many large and magnificent, and many clearly linked to a goddess or woman-centered consciousness.[34] In my work on this Archaic Time (which will be described more fully below) I am imagining an entirely different consciousness, cosmology, and social organization centered around healing, magic, and the channeling of energy, which is itself evoking the Background.[35]

The Irish context thus offers unique challenges and opportunities for liberation through the distinctive interplay between foreground and Background. Although colonization almost destroyed the native Gaelic culture, it ironically prevented the kind of economic and cultural developments that in other European countries resulted in the almost total erasure of the legacies of ancient societies. There are enormous numbers of stone structures from Neolithic times, and Irish mythology, the Irish language, and many folk customs remain accessible. Even modern Irish culture is imbued with imagination and sense of Other worlds, and much of the Irish landscape remains intact. Furthermore, the history of resistance to colonization provides strength and inspiration for the modern women's liberation movement, despite the fact that at the foreground level modern Irish society is highly male dominated. Liberation in this context then involves confronting a highly male-dominated foreground where there are many resources and opportunities for journeying into the Background. Interviews and discussion with Irish women about their journey of liberation indicated that many of them had some sense of a mystical and woman-centered past and believed in the strength of Irish women through the ages. It was part of what enabled them to acknowledge women's oppression and develop courage and strength.

Interviews and discussions also suggested that developing awareness about women's oppression was often accompanied by a sense of outrage and by a desire to join with other women in taking action to bring about change. These elements—analysis, anger, and taking action—were interconnected, but were blocked by the difficulties of developing a clear analysis posed by mystification, and by fragmentation or divisions between women. As women confronted the assaults on their psyches through demystification, they often became more aware of their sense that there could be and may have been another way of being, which they cultivated through woman-centered culture and through exploring the legacies of precolonial and prepatriarchal societies. This sense was also fostered by their involvement in women's groups and in political activism.

In Daly's terms, these processes may be described as confronting the foreground, joining the Race of Women, and journeying into the Background. Analysis and action are part of these processes, creating what I have called the cycle of liberation:[36] analysis exposes the foreground, which prompts women to join with other women and take action, which usually further exposes the foreground. As awareness and solidarity increase through joining up with other women, visions of woman-centered existence develop and are sought after, and these in turn further expose the foreground and motivate women to take action, feeding the cycle of liberation.

Confronting the Foreground

Mystification through Myth is fundamental to Daly's analysis. It is one of the means by which the workings of patriarchy are obscured. Demystification is therefore a central element in coming to awareness of and confronting patriarchal oppression. Demystification is a process of seeing through the lies and distortions of what passes as patriarchal myth. This does not involve dismissing or ignoring myths, but rather applying an active process of reversal and other decoding strategies. Daly sees myths as "something like distorting lenses through which we *can* see into the Background. . . . We can correctly perceive patriarchal myths as reversals and as pale derivatives of more ancient, more translucent myth from gynocentric civilization."[37]

In discussions and interviews with Irish women, Daly's analysis of christian, and particularly roman catholic, religious mythology was frequently cited as one of the most liberating aspects of her work. It is particularly relevant in the Irish context, given the enormously powerful role of the catholic church up until the 1990s. The 'internalized Godfather'[38] was alive and active in the psyches of many Irish women. Daly's analysis first undermined the potency of "God the Father." Her exposure of the reversal involved in attributing procreative powers to the male god, combined with her analysis of the roman catholic use of Mary, were particularly relevant in the Irish context, with its strong control of women's sexuality and also a strong Marian cult. The power of Daly's analysis is indicated by the number of women who said that it enabled them to abandon christian religion and pursue goddess- and pagan-based spiritual practices.

Demystification involves not just seeing through the distortions of myths, but also exposing the lies and deceptions that are part of everyday life, of mass media, academia, and the professions. Every production of patriarchy becomes both a vehicle through which patriarchy itself is exposed and a key to that which patriarchy tries to destroy, deny, or distort. Any area of discourse—mythology, literature, films, mass media, news items, advertising—could be analytically viewed through the lens of radical feminism.

Two strategies emerged from discussions as particularly useful. One was reversal, a simple example of which is to literally reverse a phrase or assertion. An example of reversal from the Irish context is the labeling of ancient stone structures as "tombs" or "cemeteries," when it is clear that at the least they were ritual centers and that they may easily be regarded as wombs.[39] The other strategy is naming the agent, whereby the agent that has been hidden by the use of the passive voice or by tokenism is identified. Many examples of naming the agent can be applied in the context of violence against women, where discussions focus on the victims rather than on the attackers, and where the passive voice ("she was raped") is routinely used. Another strategy is to creatively transform advertising and discourse generally to convey radical feminist messages. For example, Women's Aid, an organization working against male violence, produced an advertisement stating, "He gave her flowers and chocolates and multiple bruising." This ad provoked considerable discussion in women's groups and on radio programs.

Creative use of myth and media is therefore a tool for psychic liberation. Demystification can free psyches of "ghostly false images" and other "mindbinds." Active decoding through reversal and other strategies can expose the deceptions of patriarchal discourse and provide keys to woman-centered realities. Creative transformation of advertising and other elements of popular discourse can be used to convey radical feminist ideas. Myths that have been distorted to deny women's potency can be a springboard to spinning visions of Elemental powers. These strategies allow us to move into "different cognitive space . . . focusing upon different patterns of meaning than those explicitly expressed and accepted by the cognitive majority."[40]

The process of demystification is an ongoing one, as the journeying feminist becomes more adept at decoding patriarchal discourse and at "seeing" the mechanisms of women's oppression. Many women indicated that "Seeing" began with some "eye-opening" experience, such as a direct experience of injustice, which shatters illusions and exposes the systemic nature of injustice, violence, or inequality. For Daly it began with an early experience of transcendence at age five or six, which she describes as "a shock that awakened in me some knowledge of an Other dimension."[41] The experience of being fired by Boston College following the publication of *The Church and the Second Sex* exposed patriarchal tactics more fully, and propelled her into more radical analyses.

Once this jolt has occurred, the journeyer may be overwhelmed, an experience with which many readers of Mary Daly's books or women in women's groups or in Women's Studies classes are familiar, and which was recounted in discussions and interviews. A fundamental insight of Daly's is that it takes courage to maintain a clear sense of patriarchal oppression. Daly writes of the Courage to See as involving "the struggle to see through basic/base assumptions of sexual hierarchy in theology and in popular culture."[42] As she points out in *Beyond God the Father*, "It isn't prudent for women to see all of this. Seeing means that everything changes: the old identifications and the old securities are gone."[43] The Courage to See has to be maintained in the face of continuing efforts to mystify and of continuing assaults on mind and spirit.

While it is clear that Seeing or naming oppression requires courage, it is also the case that naming oppression itself provides courage. This was particularly evident in research interviews with women in which they were asked to discuss their experiences of developing awareness. Many of them indicated that it was a relief to have a clear analysis that in many ways confirmed what they knew to be true and that placed their personal experience in a political context. Women's studies classes and reading feminist works were particular examples of analysis that they found gave them more confidence in expressing their views, in resisting oppression, and in taking action to bring about change.

The theme of Courage is developed in *Pure Lust* and in *Quintessence*, where it is seen to be at the core of the Women's Movement. It requires Courage both to refuse the expectations of patriarchy, and to act defiantly, courage which Daly names as the "Courage to Sin."[44] Discussions with women indicated that, as with naming oppression, taking action itself creates courage. Acts of defiance such as refusing to wear particular clothing or asserting a particular feminist viewpoint were often accompanied by fear and apprehension, but their completion was associated with feelings of strength, pride, and courage. This in turn encouraged women to take further action.

Courage is further developed through connections with other women, and in turn its development encourages other women. Daly writes that Courage "calls forth courage in others."[45] An obvious example of making connections with other women is through joining a women's group or participating in a Women's Studies course. There were numerous accounts of the courage and solidarity that women gained from being part of women's groups. Reading, learning, or hearing about women's involvement in history or in political activism was another practice that emerged in interviews as encouraging (in other words, creating courage). This fostered a sense of solidarity and pride in women's activism and encouraged women to take action themselves.

The experience of anger or rage almost inevitably accompanies demystification and raising awareness. As Daly writes: "Anger is unpotted and transformed into Rage/Fury when the vast network that constitutes the context of our oppression is recognised."[46] Blocks to anger or rage are created by the patriarchal tactics of erasure of responsibility, use of the passive voice, tokenism, and blaming the victim. All of these have the effect of obscuring the cause or the object of anger, resulting in such "plastic passions" as hostility and resentment, which have no clear object.

The pattern of horizontal hostility or lateral violence, whereby anger and rage are directed toward those who are oppressed rather than towards oppressors, is another way in which anger and rage are blocked or misdirected.[47] Horizontal hostility or lateral violence contributes to creating divisions between women and supports complicity in women's oppression. Along with tokenism and other patterns, it prevents what Daly calls "Female-identified Outrage,"[48] that is, a recognition of the nature of women's oppression as women, and a sense of outrage about it. This undermining of Female-identified Outrage is furthered by the promotion of other causes as being more important than women's oppression.

Blocks to anger and rage, and lateral violence—directing anger toward one another—were recognized by women in discussions and interviews. A clear analysis again emerged as the most effective strategy to counteract these patterns. More specifically, clearly naming the agents of oppression and the direct object of anger was seen as a practice that unleashes anger and rage. The immediate object or the cause of anger was named by many women as a man with whom they had a close relationship or who was in a position of authority in relation to them, and there were obvious difficulties in directing anger to men in these positions. On the other hand, those women who did not have close contact with men sometimes found it difficult to find a target for the anger and rage that arose from recognizing their oppression. Directing anger at specific political or economic targets emerged as a common practice in this context. The vital importance of identifying the agent or object of anger was also highlighted in a pattern many women reported of directing anger against themselves, creating either confusion or depression.[49]

Even where anger and rage have been identified, they have often been presented as problems, feelings that must be contained or rationalized. In contrast, Daly focuses on the transformative power of Rage and Fury. Rage moves women to action. She defines Rage as "transformative focusing force that awakens transcendent E-motion."[50] Rage is also the passion that "unpots the potted passions and melts down the plastic ones."[51] She writes of Righteous Rage, and of the Raging Race: "Women sever our Selves from the State of Severance by the force of righteous Fury, unleashed Rage."[52] About Fury she writes, "It is Elemental breathing of those who love the Earth and her kind, who Rage against the erasure of our kind."[53] Rage thus propels women to seek Nemesis, or retribution, and also feeds other passions and virtues such as love, joy and courage. In Daly's language, it becomes a virtue, and many women experienced this view of rage as encouraging and liberating.

Joining the Race of Women

A recurring theme is that psychic liberation is not a solitary process, but one that must occur through connecting with other women, and through creating a context, a woman-centered space. One of the strategies of oppressive systems is the creation of disconnection of and the fostering of divisions between those who are oppressed, and the separating of the oppressed from one another. It is thus essential to build bonds and develop a sense of solidarity with others who are oppressed/possessed, rather than be cut off from one another and isolated from the traditions and histories of resistance. Making connections is an active process of reaching out over the barriers and divisions created by the patriarchal tactics of divide and conquer. Daly calls for Be-Friending—"overcoming the unnatural separation of women from our Selves and each Other imposed by phallocracy, weaving a context/atmosphere in which Acts/Leaps of Metamorphosis can take place."[54]

The Irish context offers an array of opportunities for women to join with other women through the enormous variety of women's groups that may or may not be explicitly part of the women's liberation movement. The contemporary women's movement emerged in the late 1960s and early 1970s, starting as a small number of radical and reformist groups, and expanding into a spectrum ranging from establishment lobbying organizations to separatist lesbian groups. Over the years the movement has grown in size and strength and has diversified in a variety of ways. This has both highlighted diversity among women and provided a challenge to acknowledge differences and to work in alliances that respect differences.[55]

Group work, and particularly the workshop format, has emerged as a widely used strategy for working with diversity and developing solidarity. Many women's groups employ a facilitator who will use feminist groupwork practices to foster respect and solidarity within the group. The workshop format is routinely used for conferences and gatherings on such issues as poverty, the national question, or violence against women. It usually consists of group discussions involving twelve to fifteen women. The discussion is facilitated by a volunteer who does not participate but whose job it is to promote discussion on a set of commonly agreed-upon questions and to ensure equality of participation, with all that that entails—listening, turn-taking, respect for each viewpoint, acknowledgement of different voices. A large gathering will break into small groups and a workshop participant takes notes and feeds the content of the workshop back to the larger gathering. Other activities include brainstorming, exercises, and drama, which facilitate the expression of different viewpoints.

The workshop format helps to bring women from diverse backgrounds together in a group context where there is an expectation of being heard and respected. Obviously this format does not prevent conflict and disagreement, but it offers an opportunity for different perspectives to be voiced and heard. Recent examples of this practice include conferences involving more than three hundred women on feminist human rights organized by the women's group of the Irish Council for Civil Liberties, on violence against women organized by Saint Michael's Resource Centre, and on Women's Studies organized in Trinity College, Dublin. Although the organizers and the topics of these conferences were quite different, they all employed a format whereby women from diverse backgrounds in terms of class, ethnicity, race, religion, sexual orientation, and disability came together for plenary sessions, drama, workshops, and entertainment.

Most of the women interviewed either joined a local women's group, that is, a women's group formed in a particular locality for the purposes of support, education, and local activism, or became part of a feminist political grouping formed for specific political purposes. Whatever the context, the women involved recognized either implicitly or explicitly the value of women-only groups for personal and political transformation. Women's groups provided support for challenging the status quo and developing a feminist analysis, offered support and solidarity, provided a base for engaging in political action, and provided a context for developing new visions and ways of being.

Joining a women's group is both a form of making connections and a form of separatism or separation, a vital part of the journey of liberation for many groups. Daly sees separating from patriarchy as a key strategy for psychic liberation. If patriarchy is a state of possession, where our psyches are assaulted by false images and symbols designed to separate us from Nature and from participation in Be-ing, what is necessary for liberation is "paring away from the Self all that is alienating and confining."[56] This may be called "psychic separatism,"[57] a separation from the numerous messages in patriarchal culture that activate the "ghostly false images" referred to above, and that block a clear view of patriarchal oppression. As Daly writes: "It is axiomatic for Amazons that all external/internalized influences, such as myths, names, ideologies, social structures, which cut off the flow of the Self's original movement should be pared away."[58]

Almost all of the women who participated in interviews and discussions practiced some form of psychic or cultural separatism. Most, for example, avoided films, music, or other cultural forms containing violence against or humiliation of women, with an explicit understanding that such cultural forms would undermine them personally. Such a practice obviously required excluding or screening out the vast majority of available cultural products, which are permeated with violent, demeaning, or otherwise damaging antiwoman messages. Most women not only screened out damaging cultural forms, but also sought out cultural expressions that were woman centered.

Separation can also be applied to institutions and individuals who engage in oppressive practices. These include religious, educational, medical, political, and other institutions, as well as individual men (and women) who enact patterns of domination. What is involved here is the creation of "New Space," which Daly refers to as "Living on the Boundary." As Daly writes in *Beyond God the Father* "The new space is located always 'on the boundary.' Its center is on the boundary of patriarchal institutions, such as churches, universities, national and international politics, families. Its center is the lives of women, whose experience of becoming changes the very meaning of center for us by putting it on the boundary of all that has been considered central."[59] As resistance, "Real boundary living is a refusal of tokenism and absorption."[60] For Daly, separatism involves not just a paring away, but a creation of room in which to Spark and Spin. It is not a solitary process, but rather a "communal process, affirming the flow of connectedness within each woman."[61] It means creating a context that can evoke Elemental powers of women through, for example, woman-identified writings, images of women's power, and creative connecting. It is the realization of woman-centered consciousness and the cultivation of a sense of Otherness, which are keys to overcoming the mindbinds of patriarchy and connecting with women's Elemental powers.

The Irish Women's Camp is an example of creating a women-only space explicitly informed by radical feminist principles. The camp is organized for a week or two each year in July to coincide with a particularly fraught time in Northern Ireland when sectarian conflict is heightened. The aim is to provide a safe space for women and children from both north and south in which radical feminist visions can be enacted. The organization of the camp is informed by such values as respect for nature and the environment and for each individual woman and child. It is run collectively, with decisions taken on a consensus basis. There are workshops and cultural events ranging from exercises in women's self-defense to drumming and cabaret performances. Each evening there is a "camp" meeting in which practical matters are dealt with and contentious issues are discussed. Since there are women from Northern Ireland, the Republic, and Britain at the camp, issues of identity and nationality arise. Class issues also arise, and workshops are frequently organized to allow discussion of these issues. Over the course of the camp the "paring away of false selves" is visible as gynergetic connections are made between women from north and south and between Irish and British women.

The Irish Women's Camp is just one example of the myriad women's groups in Ireland, north and south. It is exceptional in aiming explicitly to bring women from north and south together, although there are increasing numbers of groups and programs that aim to do this, many of them using the workshop format described above. While not all of the women's groups in Ireland are feminist, they are committed to empowering women, and many use feminist group-work methods and collective organization. Ironically, lesbians are probably most "at risk" for losing women-only spaces as the queer movement, with its disregard for oppression based on gender, encroaches.

While the emphasis in this discussion has been on women's groups and women's spaces, Daly also reminds us that solidarity and connectedness can be gained not just by bonding with other "Lusty" women, but also with foresisters, women from the past who have resisted and created, again emphasizing the importance of uncovering the past and creating a woman-centered "herstory." Daly has reclaimed a host of words to refer to these "Travelling Companions"—"Hags, Crones, Harpies, Furies, Amazons, Spinsters"[62] and many more. These form the Race of Women—"the sisterhood of Racy, Raging Women who experience Archaic memories and Tidal encounters and who participate in the Race of Elemental be-ing, bonding/bounding with our own kind."[63] The Race of Women evokes sisterhood, resistance, courage, hope, vision, what is needed for defiance and liberation. By Re-Calling the Race of Women—calling to mind or evoking the spirit of those who have gone before as well as those across the globe who are actively resisting—we encourage ourselves and one another.

Journeying into the Background

Psychic liberation so far has involved analysis that exposes the nature of patriarchal oppression along with making connections with other women and taking action. These experiences also opened up new possibilities for woman-centered existence and for new ways of being. Indeed much of feminist activism is informed by a vision of an egalitarian society free from violence and economic and sexual exploitation and in which there are opportunities for creative and cultural expression. Feminist visions have been developed in a variety of ways ranging from philosophical and political analysis to poetry and healing methods. Daly's vision is captured by the phrase "journeying into the Background." This involves the creation of new consciousness that requires sensing connections with other women, with a woman-centered past and future, with female power and energy. It involves Re-membering Original Self, "the Original core of one's be-ing that cannot be contained within the State of Possession; living spirit/matter: the psyche that participates in Be-ing."[64] This new consciousness is evoked by Daly's language of be-ing. Abundance of be-ing, Expansion of be-ing, Powers of be-ing, Brilliance of be-ing evoke the blossoming, the opening up, the surging dynamic process, the "constant unfolding, creating, communicating . . . the Radiant Realms of Meta-being."[65]

Evoking the Archimage is a specific example of a practice that can construct new consciousness. The Archimage is a reversal of the archetypical or stereotypical representations of women as impotent objects. The Archimage "is power/powers of be-ing within women and all biophilic creatures."[66] Evoking the Archimage is a process of reconnecting with memories of female potency, or a process of Re-membering: "healing the dismembered Self—the Goddess within women; Re-calling the Primordial connections/conversations among women, animals, and Other Elemental beings."[67] This is an undoing of the erasure of woman-centered traditions and mythologies, uncovering and rereading myths of ancient goddesses that often contain the most powerful and inspiring descriptions and images of female energy and power.

As already noted, the Irish context offers a wealth of mythology and other artifacts from the "Archaic Past" that provide inspiration for Re-membering. A pioneer in this area is Mary Condren, who has mined Celtic mythology for stories and metaphors of goddesses and other manifestation of female potency, and who has recently formed the Institute of Feminist Religion to run goddess-centered rituals at Celtic cross-quarter days. Celtic mythology contains numerous triple goddesses, one of which provided Ireland with its Irish name, Eire—Eire was one element of the triple goddess whose names were Eire, Fodhla, and Banba. Many place-names in Ireland can be traced to Irish names, which in turn evoke the goddess—for example the meaning of "the Paps" in Kerry may be traced to the breasts of the goddess Danu. Danu was a mother goddess in Celtic mythology.

Other mythologies and cosmologies provide numerous examples of female potency—Skadi, Scandinavian goddess of the north wind, is a skilled and powerful communicator; Pele, Polynesian fire goddess, evokes female energies of fiery liquid; Kuan Yin, Chinese earth goddess, evokes compassion and magical powers; Jemaja, African goddess of the sea, evokes love and nurturance.[68] Female power and capacities refer not just to everyday powers, but also to magical and psychic powers that have been almost totally erased from social institutions, but that are present in many Goddess mythologies from all over the world. As Daly points out, such material has been a target of erasure—the burning of books is an obvious tactic of erasure, but failure to publish, storing in inaccessible places, and discrediting in various ways are other examples.

My work on ancient or Archaic times is an example of evoking the Archimage. This work is an evocation of a new consciousness and social organization based on archaeology, mythology, astrology, feminist herstory and feminist visions, and systems of healing, magic, and psychic capacities. The aim is to evoke a consciousness connected with nature and with the cosmos—that is Elemental—and a society that is egalitarian and woman centered. The work is informed first by the legacies of prepatriarchal Irish society referred to earlier, which involve thousands of stone structures ranging from single standing stones to the huge mounds of Newgrange. These structures are decorated with artwork such as triple and double spirals, triangles, chevrons, lozenges, and wavy lines. Gimbutas and others have interpreted these as symbolizing aspects of the Great Goddess, the center of life in ancient European societies.[69] They are also aligned to the sun and the moon in extremely accurate ways, marking solar and lunar cycles such as the solstice, the harvest moon, and so on. They are located on sites near rivers or valleys or on mountaintops, sites that many believe are connected with energy lines in the earth.

When viewed through lenses such as those provided by Daly and Gimbutas, these structures can easily be seen as complex centers that were part of a cosmology and mythology based on planetary and cosmic cycles. The modern view of the human body, the earth, and the cosmos as an interconnected energy field prompts the view that the enormous resources that went into the construction of these structures reflected their role in the channeling of energy for healing and other purposes. The later Celtic mythology supports this interpretation, with its accounts of shape-shifting, of Other worlds where time is of a different dimension, of healing through the laying-on of hands and connecting with the earth's energy, and of druidic trances where psychic capacities for telepathy, augury, and healing were manifested.

While this work began as a research-based argument for a particular interpretation of the archaeological legacy of ancient Ireland, it has evolved into a work of fiction that could more effectively evoke the egalitarian, communal, woman-centered, energy-oriented cosmic consciousness that I believe was characteristic of ancient societies globally. The voice for this work is a narrator who "re-members" the life of the time. Language immediately poses a problem here, because the English language is permeated with domination-subordination, with its accompanying misogyny, racism, linearity, dualism, androcentrism, and so forth, which is totally at odds with an egalitarian consciousness. The Irish language offers one possibility for accessing such a prepatriarchal consciousness more fully. Nuala Ni Dhomhnaill, who writes poetry in the Irish language, argues that through its grammar and vocabulary the Irish language evokes a more fluid, nonlinear, less egocentric way of being.[70] For example, the verb is placed before the subject, the object of possession is placed before the possessor, and there is a continuous present tense. Ways of speaking about emotions and states of mind are quite different—for example, emotions are spoken of as being on or around the person—"there is anger on me" rather than "I am angry."

This project is an example of work that is journeying into the Background, evoking the Archimage and spinning a vision of an Other world and Other way of being. It is clearly inspired in many ways by Daly's work on mythology and language, and by her evocation of Elemental Be-ing. There are many other examples of works in the Irish context drawing on the rich resources of archaeology, mythology, history, and folklore to create woman-centered and feminist visions. These are examples of what Daly calls Spinning: "Dis-covering the lost thread of connectedness within the cosmos and repairing this thread in the process; whirling and twirling the threads of Life on the axis of Spinsters' own be-ing."[71] Spinning implies "spontaneous movement, the free creativity that springs from integrity of be-ing."[72] The various meanings of Spinning that Daly explores include whirling, streaming or spurting, extending, spiraling. Spinning can happen when the psychic blocks of patriarchy are lifted and a freewheeling flow of gynergy is released. Many women experienced this rush of energy and freethinking in women-only spaces where there is clear naming of patriarchal oppression and then a moving beyond to a "what if" in which psyches are open and exploring new women-centered possibilities.[73]

Spinning is a form of creativity or of Telic Focusing, which for Daly is essential for reconnecting with Original Self, the Self from which women are disconnected through patriarchal oppression. Daly particularly emphasizes the value of creativity for connecting with Original Self, for participation in Be-ing, for spinning integrity. In *Quintessence* she writes of "the Courage to Create—to summon out of the apparent void New Be-ing."[74] While Telic Focusing or spinning integrity are not themselves phrases used by women in interviews and discussions, many of them were familiar with the experience of being deeply focused or connected with themselves, with nature (or both), or with the Universe. Creative activities were one experience that facilitated this deep connection. Others included spending time with nature and practicing meditation or other focusing practices such as tai chi or yoga. A key element in focusing seemed to be the capacity to screen out the foreground either physically, by creating a quiet space or being in a quiet space, or psychically, through practices such as creativity or meditation that required inner focus.

Journeying into the Background in the Irish context then can involve acts of imagination drawing on the rich legacy of ancient times. These practices not only provide new visions, they also challenge the patriarchal myth that male domination is inevitable. They provide support for the intuition long held by Irish women as they view the landscape, visit ancient sites, hear the Irish language, and learn about mythology and folklore that ancient Irish society was woman and earth centered. In doing so they expose the tactics of erasure and reversal that are part of mystification. Just as seeing through the foreground opens the way to developing new visions, so journeying into the Background in connection with other women further exposes the foreground in the spiraling movement toward liberation.

Psychic Liberation and the Cycle of Liberation

In this discussion I have outlined a journey of psychic liberation that involves the interconnected processes of confronting the foreground, joining the Race of Women, and journeying into the Background. I have identified a number of elements of this journey which were elaborated based on Daly's work and on the experiences of women involved in the women's liberation movement in Ireland and have highlighted many possibilities for being an active agent in the journey of liberation. Each element that was identified as part of the journey found its counterpart in Daly's work, either because her work had been consciously used by women to further their journey, or because it provided further clarification and discussion of the path that women described.

Examples of practices described include decoding of patriarchal discourse (Demystification), developing clear analysis (Courage to See), naming the agents of oppression (Unleashing Rage), connecting with women in groups and communities (Joining the Race of Women), creating women-only spaces (Separating from the Sado-State), seeking out material from women's herstory and from goddess mythology (Evoking the Archimage), and cultivating creativity (Telic Focusing/Spinning).

Theoretical analysis and taking action are key elements linking these processes in the cycle of liberation. Liberation involves transformation of psychic and social structures, of consciousness, imagination, and culture. This process of transformation is highly complex, but taking action is obviously a fundamental part of it. Taking action is necessary for psychic liberation to transform the alienation and helplessness that oppression creates and to develop a sense of agency. It is necessary for social transformation, to change social structures and patterns, to create new structures, visions, and ways of be-ing. Both analysis and action are part of the practices described above and are fed by them in the cycle of liberation.

These connections are made by Daly in "The Great Summoning and The Great Summation": "Let us summon our Rage. Let us summon our Grief. Let us summon our Disgust. Let us summon our Elemental Powers. It is Time to Act. It is Time to Act together. It is Time to call forth Nemesis!"[75] Nemesis evokes the double focus that Daly urges, both an assault on patriarchy and the realization of female potency, and is defined as "Elemental disruption of the patriarchal balance of terror; Passionate Spinning/Spiralling of Archaic threads of Gynergy."[76] It will be recalled that Daly uses the metaphor of the labrys to refer to that which both exposes patriarchy and evokes Elemental reality. Action for liberation aims to both smash patriarchy and evoke another way of being. This evocation of another way of being aims to, among other things, encourage and inspire, counteracting the exhaustion that often accompanies taking action against patriarchal oppression.

An example of a double-edged action from the Irish context is one referred to as the "Sistership." This action was undertaken in 1992 during a campaign for reproductive rights involving a case that outraged many in Ireland. The so-called X case involved a fourteen-year-old girl who was pregnant as a result of being raped by a neighbor. When her parents attempted to take her to England for an abortion they were stopped under a provision of the Constitution that was interpreted as allowing the state to prevent travel to have an abortion (see note 30).

The Sistership action aimed to highlight the appalling situation facing women with unwanted pregnancies. It involved hundreds of women from diverse backgrounds "taking the boat" to England as an act of solidarity with women who had traveled that route to have abortions. Furthermore, the women returned with information leaflets about abortion facilities in Britain, leaflets that were illegal in the Republic at the time. During the boat journey, women participated in workshops and discussion groups in which they developed their analysis of abortion and reproductive rights. On the return journey there was partying, storytelling, singing, and other activities that could undoubtedly be described as spinning and creating gynergy. A favourite song was about Granuaile, an Irish queen who defied Elizabethan armies and operated as a pirate on the west coast of Ireland. Granuaile is one of the many strong Irish women celebrated in song and folklore. This action was highly effective both for the participants and as a political event and was part of a successful campaign to modify the constitutional article to allow travel. It was double edged in that it both confronted patriarchy, naming women's oppression, and evoked gynergy and women's power.

The Sistership was an evocative journey both for those of us who were on the boat and for those who participated through being present at the send-off or return or who watched the extensive media coverage. In the Irish context, "taking the boat" is highly symbolic, laden with memories and meanings that range from coffin ships to pirate ships. It is associated on the one hand with grief and loss, with escaping the horrors of oppression, and on the other hand with hope and courage, with freedom and imagination. Women traveled from all directions to join the Sistership, fueled by outrage, encouraged by the sisterhood and solidarity we felt for women who had traveled to England for abortions but also for the countless women through the ages who had taken sail. In the course of the journey, we raised awareness, we forged bonds, we celebrated different ways of being, we sang and read poetry. By the end of the journey the atmosphere was charged with gynergy, with joy, hope, and courage. It was, in short, a journey of liberation.

Notes

1. It would be impossible here to cite the many relevant writings by radical feminists. For a recent collection, see Bell and Klein 1996.

2. hooks 1993, Pharr 1988.

3. Elsewhere I have synthesized feminist writing on oppression by positing six mechanisms of control characteristic of systems of oppression. These mechanisms can be identified in patriarchy, colonialism, racism, and other systems of oppression. They are violence, political exclusion, economic exploitation, sexual exploitation, control of culture, and fragmentation (or divide and conquer). See Moane 1999.

4. This is particularly obvious in the colonial context, where an explicit ideology arguing for the advantages to the colonized people of being colonized is developed by the colonizing country.

5. Daly 1978, 1.

6. Daly 1978, 409.

7. Daly 1978, 340.

8. Daly 1978, 2.

9. Daly 1984, 3.

10. Daly 1998, 4.

11. Daly 1978, 6.

12. Daly 1993, 5.

13. Daly 1978, Kitzinger and Perkins 1993, Mann 1984, McLellan 1995, Ussher 1991.

14. Daly 1978, 229.

15. Daly 1978, 280.

16. Kitzinger and Perkins 1993, 107.

17. Bulhan 1985, Burman et. al. 1996, Fine 1985, Gilligan 1982, Howitt and Owusi-Bemp 1994, Wilkinson 1997.

18. Bulhan 1985, hooks 1993.

19. I have discussed this more fully in Moane 1999.

20. Moane 1999. This involved a review of selected writings by feminists, including Mary Daly, on psychological aspects of oppression and by writers on colonialism, and the development of a psychological analysis of liberation based on interviews and group discussions with women involved in the Irish women's liberation movement.

21. I obtained a Ph.D. in psychology and hold a full-time appointment in a department of psychology. Thus I have been subject to the "discipline" of psychology in a variety of ways. However, I consider the analysis in this paper to be grounded in feminist theory and analyses of women's oppression and liberation, rather than in the fields of psychology or psychotherapy, which are deeply flawed.

22. Moane 1999.

23. Daly 1984, 205.

24. Daly 1978, 23.

25. There have been different views of the relationships between patriarchy and colonialism. See Barry 1979; French 1985; Maracle 1996; Mies 1986; Mohanty, Russo, and Torres 1991; Morgan 1976; and Trask 1993. In my work I view colonialism as involving the systematic domination of one

territory by another, and I have suggested ways in which historical patterns of colonialism have interacted with and buttressed patriarchy (Moane 1999; see also Moane 1996).

26. Daly 1988, 76.

27. Daly 1988, 63.

28. These are examples of the six mechanisms of control mentioned above, in this instance as they operate in the context of the colonization of Ireland. As noted above, feminists have documented these patterns in relation to women in many different contexts.

29. It can be noted here that the island as a whole is about the size of the state of Maine in the United States, and has a population of 5 million, of which 1.5 million are in Northern Ireland and 3.5 million are in the Republic.

30. Condren 1989, Inglis 1987, Lee 1989. The ultimate expression of catholic church influence is found in an article that was inserted in the constitution in 1983 that reads: "The State acknowledges the right to life of the unborn and, with due regard to the equal right to life of the mother, guarantees in its laws to respect, and as far as practicable, by its laws to defend and vindicate that right." This article has been a battleground ever since. See Smyth 1992.

31. Coulter 1993, Moane 1996, Valiulis and O'Dowd 1997.

32. Mary Daly described her own journeying into the Background in Ireland in her book *Outercourse* (1993).

33. Condren 1989; see also Moane 1997.

34. Dame 1992, Gimbutas 1991, O'Kelly 1989.

35. Moane, unpublished manuscript.

36. Moane 1999.

37. Daly 1978, 47.

38. Daly 1978, 1.

39. Moane 1997.

40. Daly 1978, 341.

41. Daly 1993, 23.

42. Daly 1993, 136.

43. Daly 1973, 4.

44. Daly 1984, 1998.

45. Daly 1998, 88.

46. Daly 1984, 258.

47. hooks 1993, Maracle 1996, Miller 1986.

48. Daly 1984, 376.

49. It has been a classic element of psychoanalytic theory to interpret depression as anger directed towards the self. However, the dynamics of this in psychoanalytic theory are quite different from what is being discussed here. In the case of psychoanalytic theory, the solution is to engage in analysis to "discover" early experiences of anger within the family and the release or discharge of this anger in a therapeutic context. In the present context, the focus is on identifying the sources or objects of anger in the social context and the directing of anger towards these. This provides a political analysis of anger that facilitates action, while the psychoanalytic view provides a psychodynamic analysis and contains this anger in a private therapeutic context.

50. Daly 1988, 91.

51. Daly 1984, 257.

52. Daly 1984, 257.

53. Daly 1984, 5.

54. Daly 1988, 64.

55. Connolly 1996; Devaney, Mulholland, and Willoughby 1989; Smyth 1992.

56. Daly 1978, 381.

57. Joni Crone, personal communication.

58. Daly 1978, 381.
59. Daly 1973, 40.
60. Daly 1973, 55.
61. Daly 1984, 372.
62. Daly 1984, 11.
63. Daly 1988, 90.
64. Daly 1988, 95.
65. Daly 1984, 30.
66. Daly 1984, 87.
67. Daly 1988, 92.
68. Allen 1986, Condren 1989, Morgan et al. 1988, Noble 1978, Stone 1979.
69. Gimbutas 1991.
70. Ni Dhomhnaill 1989. Ni Dhomhnaill's title, "An Ghaeilge mar uirlis fheiminfeach," translates as "For Irish is the Mother tongue."
71. Daly 1988, 96.
72. Daly 1978, 389.
73. These women-only spaces include women's groups, Women's Studies classrooms, friendship circles, celebrations, and parties.
74. Daly 1998, 92.
75. Daly 1993, 410.
76. Daly 1988, 84.

References

Allen, Paula Gunn. 1986. *The Sacred Hoop: Recovering the Feminine in American Indian Traditions*. Boston: Beacon Press.

Barry, Kathleen. 1979. *Female Sexual Slavery*. New York: New York University Press.

Bell, Diane, and Renate Klein, eds. 1996. *Radically Speaking: Feminism Reclaimed*. London: Zed Books.

Bulhan, Hussein. 1985. *Frantz Fanon and the Psychology of Oppression*. New York: Plenum Press.

Burman, Erica, Pam Alldred, Catherine Bewley, Brenda Goldberg, Colleen Heenan, Deborah Marks, Jane Marshall, Karen Taylor, Robina Ullah, and Sam Warner. 1996. *Challenging Women: Psychology's Exclusion, Feminist Possibilities*. Buckingham: Open University Press.

Condren, Mary. 1989. *The Serpent and the Goddess: Women and the Church in Celtic Ireland*. San Francisco: Harper.

Connolly, Linda. 1996. "The Women's Movement in Ireland 1970–1995: A Social Movement's Analysis." *Irish Journal of Feminist Studies* 1, no. 1: 43–77.

Coulter, Carol. 1993. *The Hidden Tradition: Feminism, Women, and Nationalism*. Cork: Cork University Press.

Daly, Mary. 1973. *Beyond God the Father: Toward a Philosophy of Women's Liberation*. Boston: Beacon Press.

———. 1978. *Gyn/Ecology: The Metaethics of Radical Feminism*. Boston: Beacon Press.

———. 1984. *Pure Lust: Elemental Feminist Philosophy*. Boston: Beacon Press.

———. 1988. *Websters' First New Intergalactic Wickedary of the English Language, Conjured in Cahoots with Jane Caputi*. London: Women's Press.
———. 1993. *Outercourse: The Be-Dazzling Voyage*. San Francisco: Harper San Francisco.
———. 1998. *Quintessence: Realizing the Archaic Future, a Radical Elemental Feminist Manifesto*. Boston: Beacon Press.
Dame, Michael. 1992. *Mythic Ireland*. London: Thames and Hudson.
Devaney, Fiona, Maria Mulholland, and Judith Willoughby, eds. 1989. *Unfinished Revolution, Essays on the Irish Women's Movement*. Belfast: Maedbh.
Fine, Michelle. 1985. *Disruptive Voices: The Possibilities of Feminist Research*. Ann Arbor: University of Michigan Press.
French, Marilyn. 1985. *Beyond Power: On Women, Men, and Morals*. New York: Ballantine Books.
Gilligan, Carol. 1982. *In a Different Voice*. Cambridge: Harvard University Press.
Gimbutas, Marija. 1991. *The Civilization of the Goddess*. London: Thames and Hudson.
hooks, bell. 1993. *Sisters of the Yam: Black Women and Self-Recovery*. Boston: South End Press.
Howitt, David, and Kwame Owusi-Bemp. 1994. *The Racism of Psychology*. London: Harvester Wheatsheaf.
Inglis, Tom. 1987. *Moral Monopoly: The Catholic Church in Modern Ireland*. Dublin: Gill and Macmillan.
Kitzinger, Celia and Rachel Perkins. 1993. *Changing Our Minds: Lesbian Feminism and Psychology*. London: Onlywomen Press.
Lee, Joe. 1989. *Ireland: 1912–1985*. Cambridge: Cambridge University Press.
Mann, Bonnie. 1984. "Validation or Liberation? A Critical Look at Therapy and the Women's Movement." *Trivia* 10:41–56.
Maracle, Lee. 1996. *I Am Woman: A Native Perspective on Sociology and Feminism*. 2d ed. Vancouver: Press Gang.
McLellan, Betty. 1995. *Beyond Psychoppression*. Melbourne: Spinifex Press.
Mies, Maria. 1986. *Patriarchy and Accumulation on a World Scale: Women in the International Division of Labour*. London: Zed Press.
Miller, Jean Baker. 1986. *Toward a New Psychology of Women*. London: Penguin.
Moane, Geraldine. 1996. "Legacies of Colonialism for Irish Women: Oppressive or Empowering?" *Irish Journal of Feminist Studies* 1:100–119.
———. 1997. "A Womb Not a Tomb: Goddess Symbols and Ancient Ireland." *Canadian Woman Studies/Les Cahiers de la Femme* 17, no. 3: 7–10.
———. 1999. *Gender and Colonialism: A Psychological Analysis of Oppression and Liberation*. London: Macmillan.
———. N.d. "Re-membering Ancient Ireland." Unpublished manuscript.
Mohanty, Chandra, Ann Russo, and Lourdes Torres, eds. 1991. *Third World Women and the Politics of Feminism*. Bloomington: Indiana University Press.
Morgan, Fiona, et. al. 1988. *Daughters of the Moon Tarot*. Rio Nido, Calif.: Daughters of the Moon.
Morgan, Robin. 1976. "Women as a Colonized Group." In *Going Too Far*. New York: Norton.
Ni Dhomhnaill, Nuala. 1989. "An Ghaeilge mar uirlis fheiminfeach." In Fiona Devaney, Maria Mulholland, and Judith Willoughby, eds. *Unfinished Revolution: Essays on the Irish Women's Movement*. Belfast: Maedbh.

Noble, Vicki. 1978. *Motherpeace: A Way to the Goddess Through Myth, Art, and Tarot*. San Francisco: Harper.

O'Kelly, Michael. 1989. *Early Ireland: An Introduction to Irish Prehistory*. Cambridge: Cambridge University Press.

Pharr, Suzanne. 1988. *Homophobia: A Weapon of Sexism*. Little Rock, Ark.: Chardon Press.

Smyth, Ailbhe, ed. 1992. *The Abortion Papers, Ireland*. Dublin: Attic Press.

Stone, Merlin. 1979. *Ancient Mirrors of Womanhood*. Boston: Beacon Press.

Trask, Hunani. 1993. *From a Native Daughter: Colonialism and Sovereignty in Hawaii*. Maine: Common Courage Press.

Ussher, Jane. 1991. *Women's Madness: Misogyny or Mental Illness?* London: Harvester Wheatsheaf.

Valiulis, Maryann, and Mary O'Dowd, eds. 1997. *Women and Irish History: Essays in Honour of Margaret MacCurtain*. Dublin: Wolfhound Press.

Wilkinson, Sue. 1997. "Feminist Psychology." In *Critical Psychology: An Introduction*, ed. Dennis Fox and Isaac Prilliltensky. London: Sage.

15

Just/ice in Time: On Temporality in Mary Daly's *Quintessence*

Anne-Marie Korte

Translated by *Mischa F. C. Hoyinck*

At the brink of a new millennium, could there be a more fitting subject for Mary Daly, renowned for her "Be-Dazzling" leaps through time and space, to thematize than time? In her latest book, *Quintessence . . . Realizing the Archaic Future* (1998), Daly emphasizes time far more than in any of her earlier works. In the narrative as well as in the central concepts of this book, Daly plays with time, molds it, and explores the temporal dimension of all that exists "as far as it will go." In *Quintessence*, historical eras flash by and narrative points of view shift according to the flow and counterflow of time. Fortunately, there are enough historical references to provide the reader with some orientation. But the characters in *Quintessence* are no longer bound to one particular historical period. They "pop up" long before they were born or long after they have died, meeting each other in the Middle Ages, throughout the twentieth century, and even in the near future (from 1998 to 2048). About this last period, however, Daly discloses tantalizingly little. With a thirst for revelations about the near future, I raced through the book—but remained largely unsatisfied.

More revealing to me, however, turned out to be Daly's reflections on time. Interestingly, she bypasses "standard questions" in feminist thinking on time, abstaining from examining such well-known issues as linear versus cyclical time, objective (given) versus subjective (experienced) time or social versus biological time.[1] As I will show, the issue Daly primarily addresses is not so much how women perceive time, but rather which notions of time we must embrace to (be able to) do women justice.

In the sense that *Quintessence* relies on an incisively sketched difference between an oppressive past and a present full of hope, it reminded me of Daly's first feminist book, *The Church and the Second Sex* (1968). Clearly, and much more straightforwardly, that book also derived its narrative structure from the end of one era and the beginning of another. Its basic idea was that the world was on the brink of a new age that would bring great substantive change. Misogyny was portrayed as a thing of the past, an ancient horror about to be overcome. Depiction of the differences between past and present served to illustrate how far-reaching this transformation would be. Daly's plea for recognition and support of the impending era of "equality" and "partnership" was based on the hopeful signs of change she detected in the Roman Catholic church in the 1960s. Thirty years on, she no longer situates this qualitative difference in the present, but in the near future. Signs of hope can no longer be found in the here and now, but in the women who look back on our own time as history. Looking back from 2048 B.E. (Biophilic Era), the feminist renaissance is a historical fact and the 1990s appear to have been the dark ages of feminism.

This, I believe, is a fundamental element of Mary Daly's feminist approach to time. Expecting, or at least hoping for, changes that will manifest themselves as entirely new eras—this is a constant theme in Daly's writings. Large-scale thinking in terms of (new) ages is, in itself, a feature of modern Western consciousness of time. Daly's view of historical change, however, bears the unmistakably prophetic signs of the Judeo-Christian notion of time. Daly's great expectations are not the forthright product of a modern belief in progress. They are based on a critical assessment of the quality of present-day life, measured by norms and values that transcend the evidences of one's own time and place. Daly's point of departure is a vision of peace, justice, and beatitude on a cosmic scale—a vision that figures prominently in prophetic biblical texts. Here, cosmic vision and judgment of "one's own time" go hand in hand, demanding immediate conversion.

It is this perspective, I believe, that has informed Daly's feminist reflection on time from the very beginning. In *Beyond God the Father*, she starts urging women to adopt a critical stance toward all kinds of order that bear the stamp of patriarchy. To underscore this point, she again invokes the metaphor of the gloomy past and the radiant new era. To be caught up in patriarchal institutions is, according to Daly, "to be living in time past."[2] By contrast, women who choose not to be party to this any longer "are vividly aware of living in time present/future."[3] Daly localizes women's new awareness of time at the core of the new era: women's own time is situated at the edges of patriarchal time. "It *is* whenever we are living out of our own sense of reality, refusing to be possessed, conquered and alienated by the linear, measured-out, quantitative time of the patriarchal system. Women, in becoming who we are, are living in a qualitative, organic time that escapes the measurements of the system."[4] Daly called for a clear distinction between patriarchal time and "women's own time" or "Life-time."

At first glance, this view seems closely related to the feminist concept of "women's time" as explored by Julia Kristeva,[5] Heide Göttner-Abendroth,[6] and others. These authors have linked the way in which women perceive time to their bodily functions, to the nature of the tasks they usually perform (a day-to-day routine rather than long-term, goal-oriented projects), and to the systematic exclusion of women from language and science. Their explorations of how women experience time have generated conceptual distinctions such as linear versus cyclical time or objective (given) versus subjective (perceived) time. As part of the same debate, widely held concepts of time and historic periodization have come under fire. The criticism focuses on their failure to account for women's tasks and lifestyles. Women's cyclical, mimetic, fragmented, or interrupted perceptions of time are ignored, or even obscured.

In calling on women to distinguish between patriarchal time and women's time, however, Daly had something else in mind. She considers it a moral imperative for women to live on the edge of patriarchal institutions and to claim physical space/time for themselves. Rather than the perception of time, it is the value of time, of the quality of life realized with/in time, that is Daly's frame of reference. She disregards any link between women's perception of time and their biological functions and reproductive tasks. This is consistent with the way she has always ignored "characteristically female" physical experiences when tackling epistemological questions.

I believe that there is a very specific reason why Daly refuses to go along with these explorations of the "cyclical rhythms" of female corporeality. Cyclical notions of time have no positive appeal for her at all, as she made clear in the last chapter of *Beyond God the Father* (1973). There she stated her faith in the power of the women's movement to radically alter the history of humankind and the course of the entire universe. She argued that women's liberation will engender an unrivaled evolutionary impulse: a qualitative leap of cosmic proportions.[7] The nonbeing of women will be undone and oppression and domination in all its forms will be rooted out. Searching for terms and categories to adequately express this cosmic change, Daly reached the conclusion that most philosophical and theological representations of the future were simply inadequate for this purpose because they could not allow for a qualitative difference. They are closed systems, depicting the future as paradise regained and thereby stamping out any difference. The merging of all that exists with God, the absorption of the finite into the Infinite is seen as a return to the womb (*exitus-reditus*) rather than a move forward into a new Space/Time of "endless divergence."[8]

In my view, it is Daly's repellence of closed systems and of the *ewige Wiederkehr des Gleichen* (endless repetition of the same) that prompted her to go beyond simply criticizing patriarchal time or replacing it with women's time. Radical feminism requires disrupting and abandoning all accepted representations of time and space. With her own leap beyond the Christian and patriarchal era in 1975, Daly put her preaching into practice. The situation was too urgent to wait for all of humankind to take a qualitative leap. Daly stepped out on her own, to begin exploring and charting the new Space/Time herself.

Prophetic judgment of her own time has become a prominent feature of Daly's work. With *Quintessence* she has embraced the opportunity to deliver a feminist mission statement on the brink of the new millennium, and rightfully so. Admittedly, I would expect nothing less from this philosopher trained in theology. To write about the *eschata*, the last or ultimate things, is not only a providentially timed project but also a logical continuation of Daly's earlier works—which, as I have shown elsewhere, reinterpret the main theological issues from a radical feminist angle.[9] Eschatology, the last item on the theological agenda, deals with the final destiny of all that exists, in terms of both the universe as a whole and the fate of individual people. From a Christian perspective, the latter manifests itself as the resurrection of all individuals, including their bodily existence. This should be preceded by the Second Coming of Christ in an apocalyptic time of catastrophe, violence, and destruction, followed by a thousand-year reign of Christ. In my view, *Quintessence* provides a unique rereading of these issues.

Just like Daly's other post-Christian books, *Quintessence* criticizes its own present as an evil time, an era full of dangers and attacks on women and "all of their kind." But the call to depart from the existing era is expressed in new ways and gives rise to new reflections on the notions of time and space. Ever since *Gyn/Ecology*, Daly has characterized the detachment from the dangerous, perverted, and patriarchal present as the development of a critical distance. She illustrated this with the image of a (space) journey, a synchronous spiritual movement that allows the traveler to discover the depths and dynamic possibilities behind and beyond the reality of the present. One's inauthentic present life in the foreground directed by the fathers had to be exchanged for the authentic life of presence in the Background that women would control themselves. Daly put special emphasis on the idea that this life in the Background was "elsewhere," in other words, clearly distanced from here and now. But the metaphors used for imagining the necessary distancing, like traveling, moving, spinning, or hopping, also indicated a different temporal dimension of the Background. These metaphors suggest movements that "take their time," that have their own pace and intensity, and that make it possible to perceive and value one's own and one another's presence in other, maybe even multitemporal ways.

In *Quintessence*, these temporal dimensions of life in the Background are far more highlighted. At a future point of time, this life in the Background turns out to have been concretely realized. The new postpatriarchal age finally has arrived. Or so it seems, from the vantage point of the year 2048, on Lost and Found Continent, a special place on our own planet inhabited by a community of women who have managed to leave life-destroying patriarchy behind. We get glimpses of a multicultural group of women leading a life of paradise and extraordinary ecological awareness. The point of view in *Quintessence* alternates between 2048 and 1998, and sometimes the two perspectives blend. Mixing these two points of view also creates room to "realize" other moments in time.

Until now, Daly mainly explored shifts in historical time in the prefaces and epilogues to her writings. In *Quintessence* it has become the main focus. Temporal discontinuity is no longer primarily a way to depict the changes Daly herself in fact has experienced, such as abandoning Christianity or developing an increasingly radical feminist vision. These shifts in time are now also used to visualize substantive and much longed-for changes that have not happened yet.

In her previous books, Daly expressed qualitative changes as a detachment from the present or from the past which was once her present. To this end, she had her present-day self look back in amazement at the "prehistoric" writings of the earlier Mary Daly. This time, the present-day Daly and her work are "discovered" by a young, "future foresister," an inhabitant of the 2048 Lost and Found Continent who is surprised and upset at the situation of the 1990s, an era before her time. She is staggered by the insensitivity and ruthlessness of the people living then: why did they not recognize that they were perpetuating the wholesale destruction of life on earth? Why did the women do nothing about this? In order to answer these questions, she invokes Mary Daly, one of the few authors of the time who were studying this problem. Mary Daly appears before her in body and spirit. Together the two women reconstruct the obstacles that women faced in the horrible nineties. In those days, women were easily scared off and intimidated because of the serious sanctions against "aberrant" behavior. Women were manacled by religious fundamentalism and alternative religions. Moreover, there was a backlash against feminism itself. Many women were loath to associate with it, radical feminist literature was removed from the bookshops and pseudo-feminism, such as postmodern or French feminism, took over the universities. What is more, is it not possible that women suffered some form of slow physical numbing as a result of the large-scale poisoning of the earth?

Quintessence unfortunately does not explain how this process was stopped, although it is suggested that the earth itself ultimately and just in time revolted against its abuse. Increasing numbers of natural disasters and famines finally broke the life-destroying patriarchal hegemony. The fall of worldwide patriarchy has clear overtones of the apocalypse that precedes the Second Coming of Christ—in *Quintessence*, a Second Coming of Women, as Daly herself had prophesied in *Beyond God the Father*.[10] Yet, this apocalypse is discussed in very veiled terms—we are spared the details, to my relief and in clear contrast to the often unrestrained use of apocalyptic scenery in religious fundamentalism. It is also telling that the residents of Lost and Found Continent commemorate the plagues that visited the earth, but do not celebrate the final victory over patriarchy. They are well aware that patriarchy is tough to wipe out entirely and are wary of a possible resurgence. For that reason, they want to study the lives of their foresisters under the patriarchal order. They wish not only to mourn the injustice done to their sisters, but also to learn from the past.

In *Quintessence*, Mary Daly does not explore the perception of time in relation to women's day-to-day tasks or their physical functions. Nor does she discuss stress, or the feeling of "always being pressed for time," two experiences so characteristic of Western women's lives in the late twentieth century. When the Mary Daly character ends up in the Lost and Found Continent of the future, she is astonished by the clean air, the pure water, and the organic food, but makes no mention of a change in the pace of life. Nor does Daly comment on time as described by modern physics. Some see in Einstein's relative notion of time—that it is a function of place and movement, rather than linear and absolute—support for the feminist criticism of linear time. Despite such labels as Archaic Time or Original Time, Daly's own leaps and shifts in time do not result in a reclaiming of what other feminists characterize as "women's time," a primeval time in which birth and death, menstruation and pregnancy, sun and moon, mark the days, weeks, and years and divide them into rhythmic cycles.[11] It seems that for Daly, the importance of temporal discontinuity is that it grants distance from the present, the here and now we live in, in order to judge it. Temporal discontinuity constitutes difference, evokes and expresses the experience of a self that is not (any longer) undifferentiatedly immersed in the flow of time—a self that is capable of judgment.

To me, all of this raises the question of whether Mary Daly is interested in the phenomenon of time per se. After all, times and eras can be judged without any reflection on the concept of time as such, as the judgment might only have a bearing on the quality of life at a given time. So, must we conclude that Daly regards time merely as a given structure? Judging from the obvious passion and joy with which she employs temporal discontinuity, it seems more likely that she indeed considers time inherently significant. The shifting temporal point of view in *Quintessence* may provide the distance/difference necessary to judge the present, but it has other meanings too. The shifts in time also bring about encounters between completely different creatures, creating "elemental connections" that spark off renewal and change. In *Pure Lust*, Daly already used the term *synchronicity* (or in her own words, Syn-Crone-icities) to denote meetings at crossroads of species and souls, such as exchanges between women and cats or other sensitive beings. These encounters "convey a sense of harmony among apparently dissimilar Elemental phenomena."[12] In addition, she used the terms "Tide" or "Tidal Time" in the same sense.[13] To her, these are movements of the elements that can be experienced by those who leave patriarchal time/space and that can cause cosmic connections or "planetary communion." These connections are characterized by the crossing of boundaries. They make it possible to "pick up messages from an Other and better World."[14]

In *Quintessence*, Daly adds the temporal factor to these cross-border encounters. Flashbacks, foresight, and temporal contractions in which past, present, and future converge are quintessential moments in this type of meeting. Boundaries thought to be absolute, such as of time, place, species, or physical entity, are transgressed, while the boundaries of individual creatures are respected and remain intact. After all, Daly considers the violation of boundaries of individual creatures—or simply put, rape—the trademark of patriarchy, as is again stated in *Quintessence* where Daly displays the persistent terror of this violation, with examples ranging from the rape of women in the Bosnian civil war to biotechnological tinkering with humans and animals.

I believe that Daly assigns a positive meaning to time in the sense that she sees it as the dimension of extension and realization—a dimension women still have not claimed forcefully enough. Existing in time means more than endurance; it also means realizing volume, substance, and constancy. Time not only "makes difference," but is also the medium through which we can extend in all directions, reach, stand out, connect, be transformed, in short, become more without losing our contours and hence our concreteness as well as our limitations. While many Western theologies and philosophies regard time as a limiting factor at the level of the individual—time being directly linked to finiteness and death—Daly, at this level, seems to opt far more strongly for regarding time as the dimension of transformation and renewal.

In *Quintessence*, Daly develops promising images and concepts exploring the positive connotations of time as a facilitator of extension and realization. The epitome of this meaning of time is Quintessence, the book's guiding theme. To Daly, Quintessence denotes the completely different reality she yearns for. It is the opposite of the "soul-shrinking, stinking manmade mess that they have made of 'the globe' and everything else within reach."[15] Quintessence is a new way of expressing what Daly earlier called "Verb" and "Goddess," metaphors for "the Be-ing in which we live, love, create, and are."[16] Quintessence, she states, "is that which has drawn me on in my writing and searching. The Quest for Quintessence is the most Desperate response I know to the Call of the Wild. It means throwing one's life as far as it will go."[17]

The term Quintessence is derived from ancient Greek and Hellenistic philosophy and enables Daly to incorporate the space/time dimensions into her image of the ultimate reality in a far more explicit way than before. Quintessence is the last or highest essence, above the four elements of fire, air, water, and earth. It permeates all nature and is seen as the Spirit that gives life and vitality to the whole universe. Time and space, energy and matter, converge in this fifth or ultimate essence. It is in the context of this premodern metaphysical and mystical philosophy that Daly defines Quintessence as "the unifying Living Presence that is at the core of integrity and the Elemental connectedness of the Universe and that is the Source of our Power to Realize true Future—an Archaic Future."[18] Quintessence is "the Magnetizing Idea of the Good which is the Final Cause."[19] In sum, Quintessence enables extension and realization par excellence.

Daly's *Quintessence* makes clear that the feminist debate on time should neither be limited to the issue of how women experience time, nor left to those poststructuralist interpretations whose rejection of metaphysics inclines to foreclose any discussion of temporality related to the physical universe. Time should neither be reduced to subjective experience, nor be taken for granted—because too much is at stake. As is urged from Daly's writings, it is imperative that we also explore how time and our notions of time can realize justice.

Notes

1. See also Forman 1989b.
2. Daly 1973, 42.
3. Daly 1973, 42.

4. Daly 1973, 43.
5. Kristeva 1979, 5–19. See also Clément and Kristeva 1998.
6. Göttner-Abendroth 1989, 108–19.
7. Here, Daly's frame of reference is the cosmology developed by Pierre Teilhard de Chardin, a Roman Catholic geophysicist and philosopher, who envisaged evolution to arouse a continual improvement of the quality of the human mind.
8. Daly 1973, 193.
9. See Korte 1992, 339–41; "Deliver Us from Evil," in the present anthology.
10. Daly 1973, 95–97.
11. See, for example, Göttner-Abendroth 1989.
12. Daly 1984, 312–13.
13. Daly 1984, 290–91; Daly 1987, 231.
14. Daly 1984, 416.
15. Daly 1998, 4.
16. Daly 1998, 95.
17. Daly 1998, 4.
18. Daly 1998, 11.
19. Daly 1998, 102.

References

Briggs, Sheila. 1997. "A History of Our Own: What Would a Feminist Theology of History Look Like?" In Chopp and Davaney, 165–78.

Chopp, Rebecca S., and Sheila Greeve Davaney, eds. 1997. *Horizons in Feminist Theology: Identity, Tradition, and Norms*. Minneapolis: Fortress Press.

Clément, Catherine, and Julia Kristeva. 1998. *Le féminin et le sacré*. Paris: Stock.

Cooey, Paula M., Sharon A. Farmer, and Mary Ellen Ross, eds. 1988. *Embodied Love: Sensuality and Relationship as Feminist Values*. San Francisco: Harper and Row.

Daly, Mary. 1968. *The Church and the Second Sex*. London, Dublin and Melbourne: Geoffrey Chapman.

———. 1973. *Beyond God the Father: Toward a Philosophy of Women's Liberation*. Boston: Beacon Press.

———. 1975a. "Autobiographical Preface to the Colofon Edition," and "Feminist Postchristian Introduction." In *The Church and the Second Sex: With a New Feminist Postchristian Introduction by the Author*, 5–51. New York: Harper and Row.

———. 1975b. "The Qualitative Leap Beyond Patriarchal Religion." *Quest* 1 (Spring): 20–40.

———. 1978. *Gyn/Ecology: The Metaethics of Radical Feminism*. Boston: Beacon Press.

———. 1980. "Vorwort zur deutschen Ausgabe von Beyond God the Father." In *Jenseits von Gottvater, Sohn & Co: Aufbruch zu einer Philosophie der Frauen-befreiung*, 5–10. München: Frauenoffensive.

———. 1984. *Pure Lust: Elemental Feminist Philosophy*. Boston: Beacon Press.

———. 1985a. "New Archaic Afterwords." In *The Church and the Second Sex: With the Feminist Postchristian Introduction and New Archaic Afterwords by the Author*, xi–xxx. Boston: Beacon Press.

———. 1985b. "Original Reintroduction." In *Beyond God the Father: Toward a Philosophy of Women's Liberation, with an Original Reintroduction by the Author*, xi–xxix. Boston: Beacon Press.

———. 1987. *Websters' First New Intergalactic Wickedary of the English Language* [Conjured by Mary Daly in cahoots with Jane Caputi]. Boston: Beacon Press.

———. 1991. "New Intergalactic Introduction." In *Gyn/Ecology: The Metaethics of Radical Feminism, with a New Introduction by the Author*, xiii–xxxv. Boston: Beacon Press.

———. 1992. *Outercourse: The Be-Dazzling Voyage*. San Francisco: Harper.

———. 1998. *Quintessence . . . Realizing the Archaic Future: A Radical Elemental Feminist Manifesto*. Boston: Beacon Press.

Davaney, Sheila Greeve. 1998. "Problems with Feminist Theory: Historicity and the Search for Sure Foundations." In Cooey, Farmer, and Ross, 79–96.

Ermarth, Elizabeth Deeds. 1989. "The Solitude of Women and Social Time." In Forman 1989a, 37–46.

Forman, Frieda Johles. 1989a. "Feminizing Time: An Introduction." In Forman 1989b, 1–9.

———, ed. With Caoron Sowton. 1989b. *Taking Our Time: Feminist Perspectives on Temporality*. Oxford: Pergamon Press.

Garcia, Irma. 1989. "Femalear Explorations: Temporality in Women's Writing." In Forman 1989a, 161–82.

Göttner-Abendroth, Heide. 1989. "Urania-Time and Space of the Stars: The Matriarchal Cosmos Through the Lens of Modern Physics." In Forman 1989a, 108–19.

Korte, Anne-Marie. 1992. *Een passie voor transcendentie: Feminisme, theologie en moderniteit in het denken van Mary Daly* (A passion for transcendence: Feminism, theology, and modernity in the thinking of Mary Daly). Kampen: Kok.

Kristeva, Julia. 1979. "Le temps des femmes." 33/44: *Cahiers de Recherche de Sciences de Textes et Documents* 5 (Winter): 5–19.

Lloyd, Genevieve. 1993. *Being in Time: Selves and Narrators in Philosophy and Literature*. London: Routledge.

Maïr Verthuy. "Hélène Parmelin and the Question of Time." In Forman 1989a, 94–107.

Secondary Sources on Mary Daly: A Selected Bibliography

Hayes Hampton

Adams, Carol J. 1993. Review of *Outercourse: The Be-Dazzling Voyage*, by Mary Daly. *Women's Review of Books* 10, no. 6:1.

Allen, Christine G. 1976. "Self-Creation and Loss of Self: Mary Daly and St. Teresa of Avila." *Studies in Religion/Sciences Réligieuses* 6:67–72.

Anderson, Kristine. 1991. "The Encyclopedic Dictionary as Utopian Genre: Two Feminist Ventures." *Utopian Studies* 2:124–30.

Barr, Marleen S. 1995. "Goodnight *Gynesis*, Goodnight *Gyn/Ecology*." *Extrapolation* 36:181–83.

Batz, Jeanette. 1996. " 'Smuggle Back What's Lost,' Wild Mary Daly Tells Women." *National Catholic Reporter* (31 May): 18.

Berry, Wanda Warren. 1978. "Images of Sin and Salvation in Feminist Theology." *Anglican Theological Review* 60:25–54.

———. 1988. "Feminist Theology: The 'Verbing' of Ultimate/Intimate Reality in Mary Daly." *Ultimate Reality and Meaning* 11:212–32.

Brewer, K. 1974. "The Self as Temporalizer: Time, Space, and Salvation for Women." *Radical Religion* (Summer–Fall): 52–60.

Carr, Anne. 1982. "Is a Christian Feminist Theology Possible?" *Theological Studies* 43:279–97.

Christ, Carol. 1984. "A Work of Feminist Erraticism." Review of *Pure Lust: Elemental Feminist Philosophy*, by Mary Daly. *New Woman's Times* (December).

Culpepper, Emily Erwin. 1983. "Philosophia in a Feminist Key: Revolt of the Symbols." Ph.D. diss., Harvard University.

Contemporary Authors. New Revision Series. Detroit: Gale Research. S.v. "Daly, Mary."

D'Angelo, Mary Rose. 1986. "Remembering Her: Feminist Christian Readings of the Christian Tradition." *Toronto Journal of Theology* 2:118–26.

Dion, Michel. 1987. "Mary Daly, théologienne et philosophe féministe." *Études Théologiques et Réligieuses* 62:515–34.

———. 1991. "Pour une interprétation féministe de l'idée chrétienne de Dieu." *Laval Théologique et Philosophique* 47:169–84.

———. 1996. "La théologie /philosophie féministe de Mary Daly et le socialisme réligieux de Paul Tillich." *Studies in Religion/Sciences Réligieuses* 25:379–96.

Donovan, Josephine. 1992. *Feminist Theory: The Intellectual Traditions of American Feminism*. New York: Continuum.

Douglas, Carol Anne. 1984. Review of *Pure Lust: Elemental Feminist Philosophy*, by Mary Daly. *off our backs* (June): 20–22.

———. 1990. *Love and Politics: Radical Feminist and Lesbian Theories*. San Francisco: ism Press.

———. 1993. Review of *Outercourse: The Be-Dazzling Voyage*, by Mary Daly. *off our backs* (January): 19.

———. 1998. Review of *Quintessence: Realizing the Archaic Future*, by Mary Daly. *off our backs* (December): 14.

Dumais, Monique. 1984. "Voyage vers les sources: Quelques discours féministes sur la nature." *Révue Internationale de Sociologie de la Réligion* 13:345–52.

———. 1987. "Pour que les noces aient lieu entre Dieu et les femmes." *Studies in Religion/ Sciences Réligieuses* 16:53–64.

Dunlap, Lauren Glen. 1993. Review of *Outercourse: The Be-Dazzling Voyage*, by Mary Daly. *Belles Lettres* 8:42.

Durham, Paula Hope. 1997. "Patriarchy and Self-Hate: Mary Daly's Assessment of Patriarchal Religion Appraised and Evaluated in the Context of Karen Horney's Psychoanalytic Theory." *Journal of Feminist Studies in Religion* 13: 119–30.

Eisenstein, Hester. 1983. *Contemporary Feminist Thought*. Boston: G.K. Hall.

Everson, Susan Corey. 1984. "Bodyself: Women's Bodily Experience in Recent Feminist Theology and Literature." Ph.D. diss., University of Minnesota.

Field-Bibb, Jacqueline. 1989. "From *The Church* to *Wickedary*: The Theology and Philosophy of Mary Daly." *The Modern Churchman*, n.s., 30:35–41.

Fitts, Catherine Louise. 1990. "Reading Flannery O'Connor by the Light of Feminist Theology." Ph.D. diss., Texas Christian University.

Foss, Sonja. 1979. "Feminism Confronts Catholicism: A Study of the Use of Perspective by Incongruity." *Bulletin: Women's Studies in Communication* 3:7–15.

Frye, Marilyn. 1984. "Famous Lust Words." Review of *Pure Lust: Elemental Feminist Philosophy*, by Mary Daly. *The Women's Review of Books*, 1, no. 11:3–4.

Griffin, Cindy L. 1993. "Women as Communicators: Mary Daly's Hagography as Rhetoric." *Communication Monographs* 60:158–77.

Gudorf, Christine E. 1993. Review of *Outercourse: The Be-Dazzling Voyage*, by Mary Daly. *National Catholic Reporter* (5 February): 37.

Hampson, Daphne. 1990. *Theology and Feminism*. Signposts in Theology. Malden, Mass.: Blackwell.

Hampton, Hayes. 1996. "A Grammar of Ecstasy: Rhetorics of Feminist Spirituality." Ph.D. diss., University of South Carolina.

Harrison, Beverly Wildung. 1981. "The Power of Anger in the Work of Love." *Union Seminary Quarterly Review* 36 (Supplementary Issue): 41–57.

Hedley, Jane. 1992. "Surviving to Speak a New Language: Mary Daly and Adrienne Rich." *Hypatia* 7:40–62.

Henking, Susan E. 1993. "Rejected, Reclaimed, Renamed: Mary Daly on Psychology and Religion." *Journal of Psychology amd Theology* 21:199–207.

Heyward, Carter. 1979. "Ruether and Daly: Theologians Speaking and Sparking, Building and Burning." *Christianity and Crisis* 39:66–72.

Howell, Nancy R. 1989. "Radical Relatedness and Feminist Separatism." *Process Studies* 18:118–26.

Jaggar, Alison. 1983. *Feminist Politics and Human Nature*. Totowa, N.J.: Rowman and Allenheld.

Johnson, Fern L. 1986. "Coming to Terms with Women's Language." *Quarterly Journal of Speech* 72:318–30.

Juett, Joanne Crum. 1994. "Feminism in the Work of Mary Daly, Toni Morrison, Pauline Oliveros, and Laurie Anderson." Ph.D. diss., University of Georgia.

Keller, Catherine. 1986. *From a Broken Web: Separation, Sexism, and Self*. Boston: Beacon.

Keshgegian, Flora Angel. 1992. "To Know By Heart: Toward a Theology of Remembering for Salvation." Ph.D. diss., Boston College.

Knutsen, Mary M. 1994. "Beyond God the Father: Toward a Trinitarian Theology of the Cross." Ph.D. diss., University of Chicago.

Kraemer, Ross S. 1979. Review of *Gyn/Ecology: The Metaethics of Radical Feminism*, by Mary Daly. *Signs* 5:354–56.

Lansbury, Coral. 1988. "What Snools These Mortals Be." Review of *Websters' First New Intergalactic Wickedary of the English Language*, by Mary Daly with Jane Caputi. *New York Times Book Review*, 17 January, 9.

Lienert, Tania. 1996. "On Who Is Calling Radical Feminists 'Cultural Feminists' and Other Historical Sleights of Hand." In *Radically Speaking: Feminism Reclaimed*, edited by Diane Bell and Renate Klein, 155–68. North Melbourne, Australia: Spinifex.

Lorde, Audre. 1981. "An Open Letter to Mary Daly." In *This Bridge Called My Back: Writings by Radical Women of Color*, edited by Cherríe Moraga and Gloria Anzaldúa, 94–97. Watertown, Mass.: Persephone Press.

MacEoin, Gary. 1999. Review of *Quintessence: Realizing the Archaic Future* by Mary Daly. *National Catholic Reporter*, 5 February, 29.

McManus, Jim. 1989. "BC Students Protest Over Daly Bread." *National Catholic Reporter*, 7 April, 5.

McNeil, Helen. 1980. "Hag-ography." Review of *Gyn/Ecology: The Metaethics of Radical Feminism*, by Mary Daly. *New Statesman*, 4 April, 514–15.

Maher, Mary. 1985. Review of *Pure Lust: Elemental Feminist Philosophy*, by Mary Daly. *Women and Therapy* 4:76–78.

Meyer-Wilmes, Hedwig. 1994. "About the Schizophrenia in Women's Beings: A Rereading of Mary Daly." *Feminist Theology* (May): 67–81.

Morstad, Jill Suzanne. 1994. "Fuzzy Logic: Toward a Feminist Philosophy of Language and the Animals." Ph.D. diss., University of Nebraska.

The Nature of Woman: An Encyclopedia and Guide to the Literature. Inverness, Calif.: Edgepress. S.v. "Daly, Mary."

Olds, Linda E. 1989. "Metaphors of Hierarchy and Interrelatedness in Hildegard of Bingen and Mary Daly." *Listening* 24:54–66.

Pangerl, Susan M. 1992. "Radical Feminism and Self-Psychology in Dialogue: A Critical Evaluation of the Models of Women's Experience in the Works of Mary Daly and Heinz Kohut." Ph.D. diss., University of Chicago.

Pearce, Elizabeth Helen. 1993. "Mary Daly and Feminist Dis-Coveries." Master's thesis, University of St. Michael's College, Toronto.

Pollak, Michael. 1999. "Enforced retirement." *The New York Times*, 2 June, C27.

Poppe, Terre. 1979. Review of *Gyn/Ecology: The Metaethics of Radical Feminism*, by Mary Daly. *off our backs* (March): 20.

Porper, Rebecca. 1980. Review of *Gyn/Ecology: The Metaethics of Radical Feminism*, by Mary Daly. *Union Seminary Quarterly Review* 35:126–28.

Porterfield, Amanda. 1987. "Feminist Theology as a Revitalization Movement." *Sociological Analysis* 48:234–44.

Raphael, Melissa. 1997. "Thealogy, Redemption, and the Call of the Wild." *Feminist Theology* (May): 55–72.

Raschke, Carl. 1978. "The Death of God the Father." *Iliff Review* 35:55–64.

Ratcliffe, Krista. 1996. *Anglo-American Feminist Challenges to the Rhetorical Traditions: Virginia Woolf, Mary Daly, Adrienne Rich.* Carbondale: Southern Illinois University Press.

Raymond, Janice. 1982. "Mary Daly: A Decade of Academic Harassment and Feminist Survival." In *Handbook for Women Scholars: Strategies for Success*, edited by Mary Spencer, Monika Kehoe, and Karen Speece. San Francisco: Americas Behavioral Research Corporation.

Reiniger-Shapiro, Meredith. 1982. "Traces of Misogyny in Women's Schooling." Ed.D. diss., University of Rochester.

"The Rib Uncaged." *Time*, 19 April 1968, 70–71.

Rich, Adrienne. 1979. "That Women Be Themselves." Review of *Gyn/Ecology: The Metaethics of Radical Feminism*, by Mary Daly. *New York Times Book Review*, 4 February, 10.

Riswold, Caryn. 1997. "From a Babylonian Captivity to the Otherworld: Martin Luther and Mary Daly." *Comments in Theology and Mission* 24:50–58.

Russ, Joanna. 1979. Review of *Gyn/Ecology: The Metaethics of Radical Feminism*, by Mary Daly. *Frontiers* 4:68–70.

Santoni, Ronald E. 1974. "Paean to Women." Review of *Beyond God the Father*, by Mary Daly. *Progressive*, May, 59–60.

Schaeffer, Pamela. 1999. "Law Firm Forces Mary Daly's Hand." *National Catholic Reporter*, 5 March, 3.

Schultz, Debra. 1988. "An Antidote for Academentia." Review of *Websters' First New Intergalactic Wickedary of the English Language*, by Mary Daly with Jane Caputi. *Belles Lettres* 3:4.

"Snools Deny Daly Tenure: Hags Revolt." 1989. *off our backs* (May): 11.

Spender, Dale. 1982. *Women of Ideas and What Men Have Done to Them.* London: Routledge.

Star, Susan Leigh. 1979. "To Dwell Among Ourselves." Review of *Gyn/Ecology: The Metaethics of Radical Feminism*, by Mary Daly. *Sinister Wisdom* 8:87–98.

Sturgeon, Rebecca L. 1995. "Jeanette Winterson's Postmodernist Spirituality." Master's thesis, University of Louisville.

Sturgis, Susanna. 1979. Review of *Gyn/Ecology*, by Mary Daly. *off our backs* (March): 18–19.

———. "Priests Monitor Hag." 1979. *off our backs* (April): 11.

Suchocki, Marjorie Hewitt. 1994. "The Idea of God in Feminist Philosophy." *Hypatia* 9:57–68.

Tong, Rosemarie. 1989. *Feminist Thought: A More Comprehensive Introduction.* Boulder, Colo.: Harper-Westview.

———. *Feminine and Feminist Ethics.* 1993. Belmont, Calif.: Wadsworth.

Tulip, Marie. "Religion." 1990. In *Feminist Knowledge: Critique and Construct*, edited by Sneja Gunew, 229–68. London: Routledge.

Tyminski, Renia. 1996. "Divinity, Transcendence, and Female Subjectivity in the Works of Mary Daly." Ph.D. diss., University of Toronto.

Weaver, Mary Jo. 1985. "Daly, Daly, Sing to Mary." Review of *Pure Lust: Elemental Feminist Philosophy*, by Mary Daly. *Cross Currents* 14:111–15.

———. "Notes of a Nag-Gnostic." 1993. Review of *Outercourse: The Be-Dazzling Voyage*, by Mary Daly. *New York Times Book Review*, 24 January, 15.

Wehr, Demaris. 1984. "Fracturing the Language of Patriarchy." Review of *Pure Lust: Elemental Feminist Philosophy*, by Mary Daly. *New York Times Book Review*, 22 July, 14.

Weil, Lise. 1999. Review of *Quintessence . . . Realizing the Archaic Future* by Mary Daly. *Women's Review of Books* 16, no. 6:21.

Williams, Brooke. 1982. "Toward a Semiotic Beyond Feminism." In *Semiotics 1980*, edited by Michael Herzfeld and Margot D. Lenhart, 549–59. New York: Plenum.

Wilson, Richard Francis. 1982. "Human Liberation and Theology: An Examination of the Theology of Gustavo Gutierrez, James H. Cone, and Mary Daly." Ph.D. diss., Southern Baptist Theological Seminary.

Contributors

WANDA WARREN BERRY is professor of philosophy and religion at Colgate University in Hamilton, New York. During the sixties she was one of the first women to teach at Colgate while it was still an all-male college. She credits Daly's early writings with sparking her into becoming a feminist theologian. Now she regularly participates in the women's studies program, teaching such courses as Feminist and Womanist Religious Thought. She also teaches widely in the Department of Philosophy and Religion, specifically such courses as Religion and Psychology and Religious Existentialism. In her most recent essays, she is developing a series of feminist analyses of Søren Kierkegaard; two of these essays appear in the Re-Reading the Canon volume on Kierkegaard.

PURUSHOTTAMA BILIMORIA (Ph.D. La Trobe University) was educated in New Zealand, Australia, and India and has held fellowships at Oxford and Harvard and visiting professorships at the State University of New York; Boston; and the University of California, Santa Barbara. At the University of California, Berkeley, Purushottama held the visiting chair in India Studies and Contemporary Ethics (Fall 1995), and was visiting professor at Emory University in 1999. Areas of specialist publications and teaching include Indian philosophy and ethics; the philosophy of religion; crosscultural issues in ethics, bioethics, social thought, and culture; a major work on theories of testimony and scriptural hermeneutics. Other interests and writings extend to Hinduism; Indologism; Gandhian philosophy of moral training, art, and nationalism; emotions in East and West; and diaspora studies. He also serves as editor of the international journal *SOPHIA*, in the cross-cultural philosophy of religion, a/theology, and ethics and is associate professor at Deakin University in Australia and research fellow with the Department of Philosophy, the University of Melbourne.

DEBRA CAMPBELL is an associate professor and chair of the Department of Religious Studies at Colby College in Waterville, Maine, where she has also served as director of women's studies. She has published articles on Catholic women and modern women's religious history in *Signs*, *Commonweal*, *Crosscurrents*, and *The Christian Century*. She is working on a book on twentieth-century Catholic women's departure narratives.

MOLLY DRAGIEWICZ is a graduate student in cultural studies at George Mason University. Her research interests focus on epistemology and representations of violence against women.

MARILYN FRYE teaches philosophy and women's studies at Michigan State University and is co-owner/manager of Bare Bone Studios for Women's Art.

FRANCES GRAY teaches philosophy and studies in religion at the University of New England, Armidale, New South Wales, Australia. She studied for her bachelor's degree at Monash University. She completed her Ph.D. in 1996 at the Australian National University. Her main interests are in philosophy of religion and feminist theory in philosophy.

HAYES HAMPTON is assistant professor of English at the University of South Carolina, Sumter. In addition to having research and teaching interests in rhetoric, women's studies, and American literature, he is a writer of both linear and hypertextual fiction. He is currently at work on an article exploring the connections between Mary Daly's stylistic strategies and those of medieval Sufi writers.

SARAH LUCIA HOAGLAND is a Chicago dyke and philosopher. She is a member of the Institute of Lesbian Studies, a community-based collective in Chicago, and a member of the Escuela Popular Norteña, a school of popular education in Valdez, New Mexico. She teaches philosophy and women's studies at Northeastern Illinois University in Chicago. She wrote *Lesbian Ethics*, and co-edited the anthology *For Lesbians Only* with Julia Penelope. Her recent work includes essays in the Wittgenstein and Sartre volumes of the Re-Reading the Canon series, and a forthcoming essay titled "Resisting Rationality."

AMBER L. KATHERINE teaches philosophy, critical thinking, and women's studies at Santa Monica College. Her intention, in much of her work, is to raise awareness and encourage fruitful dialogue about the ways in which histories of oppression and liberation are present today in our individual and collective thinking and living.

ANALOUISE KEATING is an associate professor of English at Aquinas College. She is the author of *Women Reading Women Writing: Self-Invention in Paula Gunn Allen, Gloria Anzaldúa, and Audre Lorde* (Temple University Press, 1996). *Interviews/Entrevistas*, a collection of interviews with Gloria Anzaldúa, is forthcoming from Routledge. She and Anzaldúa are co-editing an anthology tentatively titled *This Bridge Called My Back: Twenty Years Later*. AnaLouise has also published essays on a variety of subjects, including queer theory, African American literature, Latina writers, multiculturalism, eighteenth- and nineteenth-century American writers, feminist theory, and pedagogy.

ANNE-MARIE KORTE is professor in women's studies in theology at the Department of Theology of the University of Utrecht and associate professor in theological women's studies at the Catholic Theological University in Utrecht, the Netherlands.

MARÍA LUGONES is a feminist philosopher and popular educator who theorizes resistance to interconnected oppressions. She teaches at Binghamton University in comparative literature and the philosophy, interpretation, and culture program, and at the Escuela Popular Norteña. Her writings include "The Discontinuous Passing of the Cachapera/Tortillera from the Barrio to the Bar to the Movement" and "Enticements and Dangers of Community and Home for a Radical Politics."

GERALDINE MOANE has been active in the Irish women's movement since 1976 in the areas of violence, reproductive rights, and lesbian issues. She teaches psychology, women's studies, and equality studies at University College, Dublin, and also in community settings. She has published on violence, women's health, lesbian issues, colonialism, ancient Ireland, and liberation psychology. She spends as much time as possible journeying into the Background and having much fun in Lesbiana.

SHEILAGH A. MOGFORD is a lecturer in the English Department and the women's studies program at the University of Northern Colorado.

RENUKA SHARMA, trained in medicine with a specialization in psychotherapeutic psychiatry, has worked in South Asia with various NGOs in the area of health provisions for women and is presently working toward establishing a mental health clinic in Bangalore. Renuka founded the South Asian Women's Studies Group in the diaspora and provides consultancy for a wide range of immigrant women's groups. Renuka has published in the areas of philosophical phenomenology, psychoanalysis and cross-cultural bioethics, and health issues for women. She edits the Naari Series in Gender, Culture, and Society. Currently a research fellow at Melbourne University, Renuka teaches gender studies at Monash University; she has also taught at Berkeley and Stony Brook. The latest works in the Naari series include *Representations of Gender, Democracy and Identity Politics in Relation to South Asia; NGO and Feminist Perspectives from South Asia;* and *The Concept of Empathy and Its Foundations in Psychoanalysis* (The Edwin Mellon Press).

LAUREL C. SCHNEIDER is an assistant professor of theology, ethics, and culture at the Chicago Theological Seminary. She received her Ph.D. from Vanderbilt University and her M.Div. from Harvard University. She is the author of *Re-Imagining the Divine: The Feminist Challenge to Monotheism* (Pilgrim, 1998) and various articles on the limitations of monotheism as a conceptual construct in feminist theology.

MARJA SUHONEN is a postgraduate student at the University of Helsinki. She is studying Mary Daly's understanding of sexual difference and ethics in relation to Simone de Beauvoir's phenomenological-existentialist thinking. In addition to her study on Daly she has published an article (in Finnish) on the (il)logic of Christian heterosexism.

Index